Educational
ASSESSMENT

DEDICATION

This book is affectionately dedicated to my wife, Jeanne. Her intellect and energy are a constant inspiration to me. Jeanne is my ultimate editor, tireless helper, and best friend.

Educational ASSESSMENT

Tests and Measurements in the Age of Accountability

ROBERT J. WRIGHT
Widener University

SAGE Publications
Los Angeles • London • New Delhi • Singapore

KH

For information:

Sage Publications, Inc.
2455 Teller Road
Thousand Oaks, California 91320
E-mail: order@sagepub.com

Sage Publications India Pvt. Ltd.
B 1/I 1 Mohan Cooperative
    Industrial Area
Mathura Road, New Delhi 110 044
India

Sage Publications Ltd.
1 Oliver's Yard
55 City Road
London EC1Y 1SP
United Kingdom

Sage Publications Asia-Pacific Pte. Ltd.
33 Pekin Street #02-01
Far East Square
Singapore 048763

Printed in the United States of America

Library of Congress Cataloging-in-Publication Data

Wright, Robert J., 1945-
Educational assessment: Tests and measurements in the age of accountability / Robert J. Wright.
    p. cm.
Includes bibliographical references and index.
ISBN 978-1-4129-4917-0 (cloth)
   1. Educational tests and measurements. 2. Educational accountability. I. Title.

LB3051.W679 2008
371.26—dc22   2007036348

This book is printed on acid-free paper.

07 08 09 10 11   10 9 8 7 6 5 4 3 2 1

Acquisitions Editor:	Diane McDaniel
Editorial Assistants:	Ashley Plummer and Leah Mori
Production Editor:	Diane S. Foster
Copy Editor:	Tony Moore
Typesetter:	C&M Digitals (P) Ltd.
Proofreader:	Theresa Kay
Indexer:	Kay M. Dusheck
Cover Designer:	Glen Vogel
Marketing Manager:	Nichole M. Angress

1/21/11

BRIEF TABLE OF CONTENTS

Preface		**xxiii**
PART I	EDUCATIONAL ASSESSMENT IN AMERICA: HISTORY, GOALS, AND APPLICATIONS	1
Chapter 1	Issues and Measurement Practices in the Schools	3
Chapter 2	History of Testing in American Education	41
PART II	THE MEANING AND QUALITY OF TEST SCORES	81
Chapter 3	The Measurement and Description of Variables	83
Chapter 4	Reliability as a Measure of Test Quality	121
Chapter 5	Validity as a Measure of Test Quality	145
PART III	TESTING OF STUDENTS BY CLASSROOM TEACHERS	163
Chapter 6	Planning and Constructing Classroom Tests	165
Chapter 7	Classroom Development and Use of Extended Answer Tests	197
Chapter 8	Item Selection and Analysis	221
Chapter 9	Performance Assessments	243
Chapter 10	Grades, Progress Reports, and Report Cards	271
PART IV	TESTING FOR STUDENT LEARNING, TALENT, APTITUDE, AND SPECIAL NEEDS	313
Chapter 11	Standardized Measures of Learning	315

Chapter 12   Testing of Aptitude and Selection   343

Chapter 13   Identification of Learning Problems   381

PART V   NO CHILD, TEACHER, OR SCHOOL LEFT BEHIND   423

Chapter 14   International, National, and Statewide Testing Programs   425

Chapter 15   Student, Family, and Teacher Factors in Test Scores   465

Chapter 16   Test Preparation for Successful Schools   495

Chapter 17   Accountability and Evaluation   531

Glossary   G-1

References   R-1

Index   I-1

About the Author   A-1

DETAILED CONTENTS

Preface   **xxiii**

PART I   EDUCATIONAL ASSESSMENT IN AMERICA:
              HISTORY, GOALS, AND APPLICATIONS   1

Chapter 1   Issues and Measurement Practices in the Schools   **3**

Issues and Themes   3
Learning Objectives   4
    Accountability, Assessment, and Testing   4
Why Do We Test?   6
    School Strategies   9
Types and Varieties of Tests   12
    Published Tests   13
    Scoring Criteria   14
    Administration   15
    Information Sources   16
Assumptions Made by Test Developers   16
Trends in Testing   17
    Early Use of Computers in Testing   17
    New Technology   18
    Online Report Cards   18
    Computerized Grading   19
    Qualitative Assessments   19
Law and Testing   20
    Legislation   20
    Miracle of Texas   21
Case Law   22
    Special Education   22
    High-Stakes Tests   23
    Advanced Program Admission   25
    Higher Education   26

      Early Case Law on Admissions   26

      Score Gap   27

      Parental Factors   29

      Affirmative Action in Admissions   31

      Court Challenges   32

   Educational Ethics and Testing   34

   Summary   36

   Discussion Questions   36

Chapter 2   History of Testing in American Education   41

   Issues and Themes   41

   Learning Objectives   42

   Scientific Measurement and Racism   42

      European Connection   42

      American Science   44

   The Next Generation   46

      Child Study Movement   46

      Readiness   47

      Mental Ability   48

      Study of the Gifted   49

      Meritocracy in America   49

   Single-Factor Models   50

      Charles Spearman   50

      Cyril Burt   51

      First IQ Tests   52

      Between Wars   55

   Multiple-Factor Models   63

      L. L. Thurstone   63

      E. L. Thorndike   63

      Raymond B. Cattell   64

      J. P. Guilford   64

      Howard Gardner   66

      Robert Sternberg   69

   Contemporary Public Schools   70

      Standardized Tests   70

   Winds of Change   71

      Nation's Report Card   71

      Lake Woebegon   71

      Test Score Gap   72

      A Nation at Risk   72

      From Minimum Competency to High Standards   72

New Goals   73

No Child   74

Summary   77

Discussion Questions   78

PART II   THE MEANING AND QUALITY OF TEST SCORES   81

Chapter 3   The Measurement and Description of Variables   83

Issues and Themes   83

Learning Objectives   84

Variables   85

Ratio Scales   85

Interval Scales   86

Ordinal Scales   86

Nominal Scales   88

Parametric vs. Nonparametric   88

Level of Precision   89

Central Tendency   90

Mean   90

Median   90

Mode   91

Normal Distribution   91

The Bell Curve   91

Skew   92

Corrections for the Data   96

Variation and Variance   96

Variance and Standard Deviation   97

Percentiles   99

Standard Scores   103

Stanine   103

Deviation IQ Scores   103

College Board Scores   104

ACT Scores   104

Computer Adaptive Graduate Admissions Testing   105

Professional Schools Admission Testing   105

Grade-Equivalent Score   106

Variation   107

Covariance   107

Correlation   108

Pearson Correlation Coefficient   108

Spearman Correlation Coefficient   110

Scatterplots   112

Prediction 113

Error of Prediction 115

Multiple Correlation 115

Summary 116

Discussion Questions 117

Chapter 4   Reliability as a Measure of Test Quality   121

Issues and Themes 121

Learning Objectives 122

Reliability 123

Test–Retest Reliability 124

Alternate Form Reliability 124

Alternate Forms Over Time 125

Internal Consistency 126

Split-Half Reliability 126

Spearman–Brown 127

Kuder–Richardson 128

Cronbach α 129

Gains and Losses 129

Standard Error of Measurement 130

Factors With an Impact on Reliability 132

Test Length and Item Difficulty 132

Guessing the Answer 132

Test Length 132

Regression Toward the Mean 133

Residual Scores 133

Reliability of Cut Scores 135

Setting Cut Scores 135

Anchor Items 137

Upward Drift 137

Reliability of Performance Tasks and Criterion Tests 139

Performance Test Items 139

Criterion-Referenced Tests 140

Coefficient Kappa 141

Summary 142

Discussion Questions 143

Chapter 5   Validity as a Measure of Test Quality   145

Issues and Themes 145

Learning Objectives 146

Validity: The Traditional Context of Validity 146

Concurrent Validity 148

Predictive Validity   148
Construct Validity   149
Content Validity   149
Contemporary View   150
　Fidelity   151
　Commonality   154
　Predictive Functions   154
　Shared Variation   155
　Appropriateness and Validity   155
Comparison Groups   157
　Validity Problems   157
　Cohort   157
　Geographic Representation   158
　Rolling or Annual Norms   158
Test Bias and Fairness   158
　Statistical Bias   159
　Score Gap   159
　Sensitivity Review   160
　Differential Item Functioning   160
Summary   160
Discussion Questions   161

PART III   TESTING OF STUDENTS BY
　　　　　　　CLASSROOM TEACHERS   163

Chapter 6   **Planning and Constructing Classroom Tests**   **165**

Issues and Themes   165
Learning Objectives   166
Testing and Teaching   166
　Testing and Instruction   167
Formative Tests   167
　Application of Formative Measures   168
　Student Response Pads   169
　Special Needs Children   170
　Learning Standards   171
　Test Preparation   171
　Parental Reports   172
Summative Evaluations   173
　Classroom Achievement Tests   173
　Classroom Test Validity   174
　Curriculum Mapping   175
　Table of Specifications   175

Cognitive Requirements   177
Cognitive Taxonomies   179
Testing Formats   180
Item Format   180
Selected Response   180
Summary   193
Discussion Questions   194

Chapter 7   **Classroom Development and Use**
             of Extended Answer Tests   **197**

Issues and Themes   197
Learning Objectives   198
Homework   198
Grading Homework   199
Parents and Homework   200
Size of Assignments   201
Impact of Homework   201
Completion or Short Answer   202
Short Answer and Mini-Essay Items   205
The Essay Test   207
Cognitive Requirements   208
Bluffing   209
Essay Test Format   210
Essay Test Security   211
Essay Grading   211
Grading With a Scoring Guide   212
Grading With Blind Reading   213
Grading and Writing Style   213
Comments   213
Assembly-Line Grading   214
Computer Grading of Essays   214
The SAT Essay Test   215
SAT II   216
Artificial Intelligence   216
Summary   217
Discussion Questions   218

Chapter 8   **Item Selection and Analysis**   **221**

Issues and Themes   221
Learning Objectives   222
Classroom Testing   222
A Priori Qualitative Assessment

and Analysis of Tests   224

Item Difficulty Index   225
   Calculation of the Difficulty Index   226
   Guessing   226
   Levels of Difficulty   226
   Diagnostic Testing   227
   Out-of-Level Testing   227
Distracter Analysis   229
Item Analysis With Constructed or Supply-Type Items   230
Discrimination   230
   Software Support   234
Computer Adaptive Testing   234
Item Response Theory (IRT)   235
   Applications of IRT   235
   Assumptions   237
   Polytomous Models   239
Summary   239
Discussion Questions   239

Chapter 9   Performance Assessments   **243**

Issues and Themes   234
Learning Objectives   244
Assessment and Instruction   245
   Timing   245
Performance-Based Assessments   246
   Other Applications   247
   Toward Perfection   248
   Development of Performance Assessments   249
   Credibility   249
   Breadth and Fairness   250
   Structure   250
Scoring   252
   Evaluation   252
   Students   252
   Holistic Assessment   252
   Analytical Assessment   254
   Reliability   257
   Validity and Generalizability   257
   Authentic-Type Performance Assessments   258
Portfolios   259

Evaluative Portfolio   260
High-Stakes Portfolio Evaluation   261
Getting Started   262
Portfolio Conferences   263
Portfolio Advantages   264
Portfolio Disadvantages   265
Portfolio Contents   265
Statewide Portfolio Assessment Programs   266
Summary   267
Discussion Questions   268

Chapter 10   Grades, Progress Reports, and Report Cards   271

Issues and Themes   271
Learning Objectives   272
Background and History   273
History   273
Purposes of Report Card Grades   276
Elementary   276
Middle School   277
High School   277
Student Grades   278
The Modified Standards-Based Approach   278
Weighted Combinations   279
Point System   279
Grading by Local Norms   280
Problems   280
Best Use   281
Magic Pencil   281
Standardized Scores   282
Standards-Based Grades   283
Report Card Comments   285
Online Report Cards   286
Report Card Ownership   287
Report Card Grades for the Gifted   287
Elementary Level   288
Middle School Level   288
Gifted Programs in High School   289
Weighted Grades   290
Grades and Students With Special Needs   290
The Case of Transfer Students   292
Grade Point Average and Class Rank   292
Honor Roll   294

Teacher–Parent Conference   295

Grade Inflation   296

   Public Schools   296

   NCAA   299

   Higher Education   299

Promotion and Graduation   301

   Strategies   307

Summary   308

Discussion Questions   309

PART IV   TESTING FOR STUDENT LEARNING,
TALENT, APTITUDE, AND SPECIAL NEEDS   313

Chapter 11 Standardized Measures of Learning   **315**

Issues and Themes   315

Learning Objectives   316

Explaining Test Scores to Parents   316

   Legal Basis   316

   Informing Parents   317

   Accomplishment Ratio   320

   Test Publishers   321

   Early History of Achievement Batteries   322

   General Characteristics of Commercial Achievement Tests   324

Major Achievement Test Batteries   325

   Metropolitan Achievement Tests, 8th ed. (MET-8, 2001)   326

   Stanford Achievement Test, 10th Ed. (SAT-10)   327

   Terra Nova (CAT-6), 2nd Ed. (TN2)   327

   Iowa Tests of Basic Skills, 2000/2005 (ITBS)   329

   Comprehensive Testing Program 4 (CTP 4)   330

State-Mandated Assessments   333

   No Child Left Behind High-Stakes Achievement Test
Problems   334

   No Child Left Behind Positive Impact   336

Summary   340

Discussion Questions   340

Chapter 12 Testing of Aptitude and Selection   **343**

Issues and Themes   343

Learning Objectives   344

Aptitude   345

Scholastic Aptitude and Intelligence   345

Training of Test Administrators   347

Level A   347
Level B   347
Level C   348
Tests of Intelligence Administered One-on-One   348
Stanford–Binet   348
Wechsler Scales   349
Woodcock–Johnson Tests   353
Kaufman Tests   353
Slosson   354
Tests of Intelligence Administered to Groups   354
Cognitive Ability Test   355
Kuhlmann–Anderson Test   355
Otis–Lennon   355
Test of Cognitive Skills   356
Group-Administered Aptitude Tests   356
Intelligence and Success   356
Accounting Aptitude Test (Psychological
Corporation, 1992)   358
Revised PSB Health Occupations Aptitude Examination
(Psychological Service Bureau, 1992)   358
Musical Aptitude Profile [1995 Revision] (Gordon, 1995)   359
Detroit Tests of Learning Aptitude, 4th Ed. (DTLA-4)   359
Differential Aptitude Test, 5th Edition (DAT-5)   360
Armed Services Vocational Aptitude Battery (ASVAB)   360
Assessment of Talented and Gifted Children   360
Talent Identification   360
Merit Scholars   365
Creativity and Its Measurement   366
Theories   366
Characteristics   367
Connectionism   368
Creative Assessment Packet   371
Assessment of Aptitude for College Study   373
First College Boards   373
Harvard Scholarships   373
Educational Testing Service   374
Recentering the SAT   374
SAT II   375
American College Testing Program (ACT)   376
Summary   378
Discussion Questions   378

Chapter 13 Identification of Learning Problems   381

    Issues and Themes   381
    Learning Objectives   383
    Incidence   384
    Informal Screening   384
      Anecdotal Records   385
    Instructional Support Team   386
      Membership   386
      Schedule   387
    Referral, Assessment, and the IEP Committee   388
      Parent Participation   388
      Membership   392
      Schedule   392
    Assessment Process   393
      School Psychologist   393
      Curriculum-Based Assessment   393
    Formal Assessments of Attention and Focus   394
      Incidence   394
      Checklists   395
    AD/HD Measurement Scales   396
      Behavior Assessment System for Children 2nd Edition
        (BASC-2)   396
      Brown ADD Scales for Children and Adolescents   397
      Conners' Rating Scales–Revised (CRS-R)   398
      Early Childhood ADD Evaluation Scale (ECADDES)   398
      Scales for Diagnosing AD/HD   399
      Diagnosis vs. Disability   400
    Assessments of Reading Problems   400
      Learning to Read   400
      Phonemic Awareness   401
      Comprehension   401
      Environmental Factors   401
      Diagnostic Tests   402
    Early Reading Tests   402
      Woodcock–Johnson   402
      Wechsler Individual Achievement Test   403
      Dynamic Indicators   404
      Test of Early Reading   404
      STAR Early Literacy   405
      Elementary School Reading Tests   406
    Assessments of Language and Speech Problems   406

Measures for the Identification of Language Problems   406

Communication Abilities Diagnostic Test   407

OWLS   407

Test of Early Language   408

Measures for the Identification of Problems Learning
Mathematics   408

Occurrence   409

Nature of the Problem   409

Key Math–Revised   409

Diagnostic Math Test   410

Individualized Educational Plan (IEP)   411

NCLB Special Education Conflict   411

Individual Educational Plan Format   414

Accommodations for Children With Disabilities   415

Testing Environment   417

Time   417

Modality   418

Summary   418

Discussion Questions   419

PART V   NO CHILD, TEACHER, OR SCHOOL LEFT BEHIND   423

Chapter 14   International, National, and Statewide
Testing Programs   425

Issues and Themes   425

Learning Objectives   426

International Comparisons   427

First International Mathematics Study   427

Second International Mathematics Study   428

Third International Mathematics and Science Study   429

Programme for International Student Assessment   429

International Adult Literacy Survey   432

Progress in International Reading Literacy Study   433

Civics Education Study   433

Status of American Education   433

Nation's Report Card   437

First National Assessment   438

NAEP   438

National Sample   439

School Assessments   442

Minimum Competency Testing   443

No Child Left Behind   445

   Requirements and Sanctions   446

   Assistance for Children   447

   Interim Outcome   449

   Concerns and Problems   451

   Public Reaction   455

   State Concerns   456

Summary   460

Discussion Questions   461

Chapter 15   Student, Family, and Teacher Factors in Test Scores   465

Issues and Themes   465

Learning Objectives   467

Students   467

   Ability   468

   English-Language Learners   468

   Motivation   469

   Work Habits   469

   Homework   470

   Peers   471

   Attendance   472

Families   472

   Parental Education   472

   Home Environment   473

   Home–School Communication   474

   Mobility   475

   Parenting   476

Teachers   478

   Impact   479

   Hiring of Effective Teachers   480

   Hiring Highly Qualified Teachers   481

   Experienced Teachers   482

   Teacher Examinations   483

   Minority Teachers   484

   Alternative Tracks   485

   National Certification   488

   Empowerment   489

Summary   490

Discussion Questions   491

Chapter 16   Test Preparation for Successful Schools   **495**

Issues and Themes   495
Learning Objectives   496
Accountability Angst   497
   Cost of Failure   498
   Popular Culture   499
   Cutting Corners and Cheating   500
Legal and Ethical Requirements   502
Marginal Ethics   502
   Parental Strategies   502
   School Strategies   505
   Merit Pay   507
   Merit Pay vs. Signing Bonus   507
   Merit Pay as a Unit Reward   508
   Merit Pay Problems   508
   Merit Pay in Play   509
Successful Schools   509
   Data Management   510
   Schedules   512
   Time on Task   512
Classroom Instruction   515
   Reading   516
   Writing   518
   Mathematics   519
   Test-Prep Curricula   522
Architecture and School Design   522
   School Buildings   522
   Class Size   523
   School Size   524
Administration   525
   Leadership and Outcomes   525
   Leadership Style   526
Summary   527
Discussion Questions   527

Chapter 17   Accountability and Evaluation   **531**

Issues and Themes   531
Learning Objectives   532
Evaluation Overview   533
   Evaluation Models   534
   Evaluation Standards   535

    Accountability and Public Opinion   535

  Systematic Program Evaluation   537

  Steps in a Systematic Evaluation   539

    Stakeholder Identification and Goal Setting   539

    Audience   541

    Objectives   541

    Management Plan   542

    Data Collection and Validity   543

    Record Keeping   548

    Collection of Data   548

    Analysis   549

    Dissemination   550

  Value-Added Evaluation   551

    Statistical Solution   553

    Value-Added Outcome   555

    Limitations of Value-Added Assessment   558

    Statewide Application of Value-Added Assessments   559

    Local Applications of Value-Added Data Management   559

    Staff Development and Value-Added Assessment   560

  Summary   560

  Discussion Questions   561

Glossary   **G-1**

References   **R-1**

Index   **I-1**

About the Author   **A-1**

PREFACE

COMMISSION AND NISUS

My goal in writing this book is to provide students with an understandable and useful interpretation of the critical information related to educational measurement. There has never been a time when it has been more important for educators to have an understanding of educational assessment and measurement. Educational accountability has taken root in our nation, and our political leaders are all looking for "scientific" documentation of our successes. It is no longer prudent or even possible for educators to ignore this national zeitgeist.

Our political leaders have decided that the high-stakes testing of public school children is the best way to provide this documentation. For that reason, educational testing now provides one unifying theme in the lives of all American educators. Today the testing industry in this country has literally become a billion-dollar business. No longer is it just the students who can "flunk" a test. In today's schools, educational measurements are all too often the driving force behind curriculum decisions, hiring practices, salary and benefit packages, and the politics of school boards. The annual release of average test scores to the news media has changed how schools operate and what goes on in the classrooms.

GAME PLAN

During the thirty years that I taught educational testing to graduate students, I was never completely comfortable with the textbooks that were available. It seemed that every year I adopted a different textbook, and every year I was never completely satisfied with my choice. It was my impression that the books were either too pedantic and designed to make students dislike this exciting field, or they were vacuous and devoid of the central core of knowledge required to develop the next generation of educational specialists and leaders.

This new book is the outcome of my quest for a readable and highly engaging textbook that does not compromise the core principles of measurement. In that regard, there are chapters covering traditional topics such as reliability, standard error of measurement, validity, classroom test construction, performance assessments, standardized achievement tests, item analysis, and the application of Item Characteristic Curves (ICC) for Differential Item Functioning (DIF).

Beyond these traditional concerns, this book is grounded in the real world of public schools and students. It is not designed for psychology or sociology courses but is targeted to meet the needs of educators and future educational leaders. This school-based focus was accomplished in several ways. As a case in point, a school focus pervades the numerous examples that describe the implications of measurement decisions on the lives of students and teachers. As another, more than 90% of the 860 references cited in this book are from either the educational literature or education-focused agencies.

Heretofore, textbooks in educational measurement have lost students in scientific discussions of the arcane and complex principles of psychometrics. Unlike what has gone before, this text provides an engaging, insightful, and highly readable introduction to the inner workings of educational measurement. Traditional topics are presented in approachable and understandable ways. This book employs an issue-oriented approach to the analysis and interpretation of complex measurement concerns, most of which are being debated in public forums today. As an example, this book examines issues such as the score gap, high-stakes tests and the dropout crisis, and the problem of grade retention versus social promotion. Intriguing real-life examples are introduced in each chapter, selected to demonstrate how the technical measurement principles actually affect those who are involved. The approach I used to write this textbook involved drawing from my public school experiences and years as a teacher–educator and then amalgamating my experiences into a narrative presentation designed to explain the science of educational measurement. This provides the text with a true school-based focus.

The grounding of this work in the real world of public education is evident from the book's emphasis on matters such as high-stakes testing. The narrative also presents the position that the justification for much that has occurred in the name of educational accountability was originally based on erroneous readings and interpretations of international academic achievement assessments. The point is also made that during the 1980s the concern for American education led inevitably to the Improving America's Schools Act (1994) and then to the No Child Left Behind Act (NCLB, 2002).

In this new book, the testing mandates of the NCLB Act are presented in their historical context. In this historical interpretation, they are seen as a continuation of European social science traditions begun during the Victorian era. This approach to measurement-based accountability as prescribed by the NCLB mandates follows a psychometric model that was first proposed in 1923 by Lewis M. Terman. Today's high-stakes assessments are an extension of the American belief in an industrial model for management, which requires an "input–output" evaluation. This approach focuses on observable outputs and products and pays little attention to the processes or the initial condition of raw materials.

Another description presented in the text elaborates on the link between the No Child Left Behind Act and the so-called miracle of Texas. Additionally, the NCLB Act is discussed in the context of the goals of the original Elementary and Secondary Education Act (1965) and that legislation's mandate for a longitudinal educational evaluation, "The Nation's Report Card" (NAEP).

The book includes a lengthy discussion of ethical and unethical approaches used to improve scores on the mandated assessments. It also addresses the relationship between factors such as the child's personological characteristics, familial structures, teacher background, instructional approaches, and the leadership style of the principal and the outcome scores on mandated assessments.

This text also addresses the needs and problems incurred by students with significant learning problems who must take the mandated assessment tests. The difficulty of reconciling special education programs with the tenants of the No Child Left Behind law are explored in depth. The steps in the identification of significant learning problems and interventions that are called for as part of the special education entitlements are also described in some detail. Related issues such as the testing of English Language Learners and the NCLB mandate for the testing of four-year-old inner-city children are also included.

Administrative concerns linked to educational assessment are not ignored. I have included a chapter on school evaluation that includes value-added assessments and longitudinal data management. The book examines the traditional approaches used to integrate both formative and summative assessments into a "systematic educational program evaluation." The chapter on evaluation also presents examples illustrating the design of an evaluation section for an application for external funding or subvention.

"Hot button" problems for school leaders such as the relationship between high-stakes testing and grade retention, the dropout problem, and even "academic red shirting" are part of this text. Also discussed are the concerns held by many high school administrators regarding "academic press" and the striving of students to be one of the "deserving ten" or even the one with the best GPA who is selected to give the valedictory speech. In this context, the text provides an examination of the grading policies associated with gifted students, AP classes, and even the report card options for children with disabilities.

Finally, the application of educational technology in testing and measurement is explored, and the future trends for the applications of educational technology are noted and discussed. A section is included describing the use of computer adaptive testing (CAT) and its potential impact on the achievement score gap with students who are part of ethnic minorities. This description includes a discussion of the problems associated with item development and test security. Other technological applications for measurement are also explored, including classroom clickers and real-time formative evaluations, on-line parent–teacher communications, and online grade books.

HELPFUL APPARATUS

I have included a number of learning aids throughout this textbook. They have been incorporated in an effort to improve the quality and depth of learning that occurs for the reader.

1. Section descriptions running a page or two lead off each conceptual segment of the book. These section descriptors provide an overview and framework for the next few chapters.

2. A page or two at the start of every chapter provides a statement of "Issues and Themes." This section provides the reader with insight into the perspective that I have taken in researching and writing the chapter.

3. The learning goals for each chapter following the Issues and Themes section are presented in a sequential list. Taken together these three elements provide the reader with a set of advanced organizers designed to provide him or her with an awareness of what is being learned and a structure for understanding how to interpret the new material.

4. Each chapter includes several sections labeled "Case in Point." Each Case in Point provides a real-life example or application of the material presented in the text. This is included as a motivational component.

5. Another motivational device in every chapter is a cartoon addressing an aspect of the chapter's narrative. These cartoons were drawn by some of America's leading cartoon humorists, including those of the *New Yorker*.

6. A total of 118 URLs are included in the chapters of the book. These Internet resources provide students with access to an expanded library of information associated with the material in the book.

7. Each chapter provides a list of discussion questions designed to initiate classroom discussions and motivate students to employ higher-order cognitive processes when considering the material herein.

8. A detailed glossary of terminology including over 600 technical terms and laws is also part of this book.

9. Over 860 references, including another 250 URLs, are included as support material for the book.

A WORD TO INSTRUCTORS

Educational tests and measurements constitute a topic that is now central to the preparation of educational leaders and specialists. It is also a germane topic for all classroom educators working in our public schools. For that reason I advocate using this book with classes that are composed of graduate and upper-division students in education and teacher preparation. Students who would gain the most from this book are first-year graduate students and sophisticated undergraduate students.

I also encourage you to review and consider the "Teaching on Point" components included on the Instructor's CD. They provide teaching and discussion ideas that are keyed to the real-world examples, known as "Case on Point" in each chapter (as mentioned above). That Instructor's CD also provides a multiple choice test (type-A format) for each chapter. I have also provided discussion questions for each chapter, which can spark classroom or seminar interactions and promote analytical and evaluative thinking.

Finally, I encourage you to contact me with your ideas and thoughts about this text. I am also open to interacting with students during one of your classes using Internet video technology or by conference call. E-mail me at widenerbob@hotmail.com to explore this further. (Include the word *textbook* as part of the subject line.)

Congratulations for electing to teach this course, and best wishes for a successful semester.

Robert J. Wright, Ph.D.
Professor, Center for Education
Widener University

A WORD TO THE STUDENT

I accept the fact that very few students who enroll in collegiate and graduate courses in educational tests and measurements do so voluntarily. Yet, the study of educational measurement can be an engaging and truly empowering experience for teachers and school leaders.

From my perspective, there are four things about any college class or graduate seminar that are central to its success. These include the students who take the course, the instructor who provides the class, the content of the discipline being studied, and the books and resources that are available to the students.

During the intersessions of my university I have heard colleagues comment on how much easier it is to be a professor when the students are away from campus. However, to be a professor is to profess to others. Students are the reason colleges exist, and students are the life force inspiring each of us who enter the lecture halls and classrooms. The only things a college instructor asks for are students who have an open mind to the discipline and who are truly willing to learn.

I took my first class in educational measurement as a graduate student in 1968. In that summer course, I was inspired by a good teacher. That experience eventually led me to earn my doctorate in educational psychology. Good teaching is always the key to success for every course.

Beyond the ability of an instructor to inspire and motivate students, the next most important component of a good learning experience is the topic itself. Educational testing and measurement is now the central focus of ongoing public policy debates and is also an ever-present concern for all public school educators. It is the "tests" that have become the bane of so many teachers and administrators. The continuing presence of mandated assessment programs in the schools is not debatable. There can be no argument that they will be with us for the foreseeable future. Having a solid foundation in the knowledge about educational measurement is therefore a matter of survival for those who earn their living in the front offices and classrooms of our schools. The topics that a course in educational tests and measurement presents are seen far beyond the lecture hall: These issues and concerns are seen throughout our popular culture, in our mass media, and even in the value of our real estate. Today it is axiomatic that no prudent educator can take the topic of educational tests and measurement lightly.

I have written this book with these concerns in mind. The text provides grounding in all of the aspects of measurement that a public school educator must have as background and goes on to provide insight into the inner workings of the state agencies involved in creating high-stakes educational measurements. I have worked to write this book in a highly readable and engaging style. By reading and studying the material herein, you will gain the ability to maximize the test outcomes for your students and be better equipped to advocate for improved approaches to the measurement of learning.

TO THE PROFESSION

A diligent and documented search has been made to assure that the copyright holders of all material included in this work have been contacted and have approved use here. Also, all cited reference materials have been checked for accuracy. The URLs listed in this book have been carefully examined for accuracy as well. If the reader finds that errors have been made in some of these efforts, please contact me at widenerbob@hotmail.com.

SUPPLEMENTAL MATERIALS

Additional ancillary materials further support and enhance the learning goals of *Educational Assessment: Tests and Measurements in the Age of Accountability.* These ancillary materials include the following:

Instructor's Resources CD

This CD offers the instructor a variety of resources that supplement the book material, including PowerPoint lecture slides, Web resources, "Teaching on Point" ideas to accompany the "Case in Point" discussions in each chapter, ideas for class discussions and projects, and sample syllabi for both quarter and semester courses. The CD also includes Brownstone's Diploma Test Bank software so that instructors can create, customize, and deliver tests. The Test Bank consists of 20 multiple choice questions, 10–15 true/false questions, 10 short answer questions, and 5 essay questions for each chapter. Answers and page references are provided for each question.

Web-Based Student Study Site

www.sagepub.com/wrightstudy

This Web-based student study site provides a variety of additional resources to enhance students' understanding of the book content and to take their learning one step further. The site includes comprehensive study materials such as chapter objectives, flash cards, and practice tests. The site also includes the following special features: Web resources, "Learning From Journal Articles," and "Considerations on Point" discussions to accompany each chapter's "Cases in Point."

ACKNOWLEDGMENTS

No project of this magnitude can be completed by one person working in isolation. This textbook would not have been possible without the encouragement, editorial assistance, intelligence and creativity, and freely given help of my wife and partner, Jeanne.

In addition I must provide a word of thanks to Ms. Molly Wolf, Education Collection Librarian at Widener University's Wolfgram Memorial Library; Gloria Floyd, my secretary; the librarians and assistants at the Bonita Springs, Florida, Library; and Drs. Richard and Ann St. John, my technology support team, critics, and friends.

Kudos are also due for the team at Sage Publications, including my editor, Dr. Diane McDaniel, whose belief in this project and support of my efforts has been invaluable. Also, I owe a special debt of gratitude to Ms. Ashley Plummer, the editorial assistant working with this manuscript. It was Ashley who coordinated this project, bringing together the many reviews and permissions that are part of this book. I also wish to express my gratitude to the many editorial reviewers who worked to make this the best possible textbook. This group of faculty reviewers includes the following:

Morris I. Beers, State University of New York College at Brockport

Tyrone Bynoe, University of the Cumberlands

Ollie Daniels, Barry University

Delisa K. Dismukes, Jacksonville State University

Holmes Finch, Ball State University

Sheryl R. Glausier, Southeastern Louisiana University

Renée N. Jefferson, The Citadel: The Military College of South Carolina

Kae Keister, Wilmington College

James Pelech, Benedictine University

Kaye Pepper, University of Mississippi

Thomas R. Scheira, Buffalo State College

Thomas J. Sheeran, Niagara University

John Shimkanin, California University of Pennsylvania

Ellen Bennett Steiner, University of Denver

John J. Venn, University of North Florida

Colleen Willard-Holt, Penn State–Harrisburg

PART I

EDUCATIONAL ASSESSMENT IN AMERICA

History, Goals, and Applications

The first section of the book provides an overview of education in the United States from kindergarten through high school graduation. It introduces the No Child Left Behind Act and discusses the law's impact on children, schools, and educators. This section provides a review of the case law that led to high school graduation examinations and made possible other educational decisions that are based on high-stakes assessments. The new age of educational accountability has also caused the canons of professional ethics for educators to be seriously challenged. Both parents and teachers are searching for ways to optimize the achievement levels of school children, and in that search ethical standards have been stretched to the limits of casuistry.

A historical context for the current testing programs is also presented in this section. This traces the idea for the "scientific" study of individual differences from the teaching of G. Stanley Hall through the first large-scale tests of military recruits during the First World War. There was an unquestioning belief in the application of the scientific method to all human dimensions and activities. The study of the human intellect was one example of where this belief in science had a dark side: the scientific racism of the eugenics movement. The same authors that created the early tests of mental ability were also seminal in the development of other large-scale assessments, including standardized achievement tests. The link between these early measurement efforts and the modern standards-based assessments is explored.

The newest trends in educational technology and the future directions for educational measurement are examined. Testing technology is now being applied by the states to meet the challenges created by the No Child Left Behind Act. It is also being used in the classroom to provide real-time information on student learning while instruction is ongoing. The application of technology to teacher–parent communication is also introduced.

Chapter 1

Issues and Measurement Practices in the Schools

We must start where men who would improve their society have always known they must begin—with an educational system restudied, reinforced, and revitalized.

—Lyndon B. Johnson
January 12, 1965

Issues and Themes

Testing is an integral part of the life story of all American children. The American public supports verifying the quality of public education through accountability. This press for educational accountability has increased both the number and importance of educational assessments in the schools. An assessment is a multidimensional method for collecting data that usually includes testing. Educational testing is normally conducted to measure the status of the child on one dimension, such as arithmetic, whereas an assessment is designed to provide multiple sources of data. A battery of tests is often the core component of the assessment. Batteries are a collection of tests that are designed to measure different parts of the curriculum—e.g., mathematics, reading, and science.

High-stakes assessments are educational measures that have significant negative consequences for failure. The No Child Left Behind Act (NCLB; P.L. 107-110, 2002) is the latest major stimulant for the use of high-stakes assessments in public education. During the past 20 years, federal court rulings have supported both the use of these high-stakes tests and the sanctions that are applied when children and schools fail to measure up. One outcome of the No Child Left Behind Act mandates is a major boon for the publishers of educational tests. Over a billion dollars are now being spent by the states to develop, administer, and score these new mandated tests. The whole face of testing is changing rapidly with the introduction of technology into the assessment process. With all of these changes, the education profession has scrambled to provide statements of ethical principles and practitioner guidelines for testing programs.

Learning Objectives

By reading and studying this chapter you should acquire the competency to

- Describe the relationship between accountability, assessment, and testing
- Explain the major reasons why children are assessed
- Describe the three assumptions made by test developers
- Discuss the relationship of formative and summative testing in the classroom
- Contrast norm-based and criterion-referenced tests
- Describe the case law related to the selection of students for admissions into advanced high school programs
- Explain how case law has affected the college admission process
- Explain how case law has affected the practice of educational testing and assessment
- Present and discuss the core ethical canons related to educational testing

Accountability, Assessment, and Testing

Accountability refers to the linkage and balance between the outcome of an enterprise and the efforts and resources used to achieve that outcome. In education, **assessment** provides an accounting of how much children learn in school and what resources are expended on achieving those learning outcomes. The need for accountability grew in this country as the cost of education grew. In the 1960s, the cost of public education was not just the largest part of each states' budget; it was actually equal to the cost of running every other state agency *combined*.

Educational accountability requires that all students be assessed to quantify what they have learned and what skills they have developed. Commercially published tests of student achievement have been around since the 1920s. The publishers of these tests have formed a cozy relationship with the schools that bought into their use for school and student **evaluation**. By the 1980s, virtually every school system could make the illogical boast that their school district was above average. A West Virginia physician (John J. Cannell, M.D.) was first to ask the question: If the average is in the middle of the data, how it is possible for everyone to be above average (Phelps, 2005)?

The 19th century saw the first efforts in the United States to determine the success of schools in meeting local and statewide goals for the education of children. The first attempt to assess a large American school system involved a test administered to the children of Boston in 1845. That testing program was organized by Massachusetts's new state school superintendent, Horace Mann (Crocker, 2003).[1] With this effort to assess educational outcomes, the students of Boston were tested for their understanding of the facts that they were learning in the new "**common schools**" of Boston. In 1864, the Board of Regents of New York initiated a statewide "preliminary test" for junior high–aged school students. This measure was used as a basis for allocating state funds to the various school systems.[2] This was supplanted by a mandated set of examinations known as the New York Regents Examinations in 1878, which assessed all high school students (New York State Education Department, 1987).[3]

The assessments of student educational progress can be accomplished using several different methods. In this text there is a chapter describing alternative approaches to assessment (Chapter 9) and another describing the use of essay tests (Chapter 7). However, the paper-and-pencil test with **multiple choice questions** is the dominate method of constructing all the state-mandated tests designed for the assessment of achievement. The advantages to this approach to assessment include the fact that these "**objective tests**" are less expensive to score and involve less effort by local school personnel to develop and administer than do alternative assessment approaches. Also, data from these tests are readily quantifiable and familiar to the policy makers and the general public. The downside of this approach to assessment is that the multiple choice questions used to build these measures tend to stress rote learning, favor students from middle-class backgrounds, and are based on a technology born under a cloud of tacit racism (see Chapter 2).

In summary, accountability in education is an inevitable requirement that is associated with spending large amounts of public tax funds. Educational accountability requires that an assessment be made of the outcome of the educational process. One method of assessment involves using paper-and-pencil tests. Typically these tests are primarily composed with multiple choice format questions. When there are several tests that make up the assessment, the term **test battery** is appropriate to describe the **measurement**.

WHY DO WE TEST?

At one level we test to protect the health and physical status of the child. This type of testing starts at the moment of birth. Typically, it is the attending obstetrician who welcomes the newborn into the world, and it is this physician who is first to formally assess the child. That medical status examination, the **Apgar**, is an observational rating scale that is administered one minute after the birth of the child and again four minutes later (see Table 1.10). From this starting point, the growing child will be assessed and measured by a pediatrician on a regular basis.

By the age of four, children enrolled in **Head Start programs** are tested to determine how well those centers are doing their jobs. This is one of the accountability functions of testing. This assessment process is then repeated in the public schools under a federal mandate beginning in third grade and extending into the high school years.

In 1965 President Lyndon Johnson's legislative package included a new act directed toward providing federal assistance to the nation's public schools. This act, the **Elementary and Secondary Education Act** (**ESEA**, 89-10, 1965) provided money to improve the educational achievement of children living in poverty. One part of this act created a method to measure the impact of the improvements being instituted throughout the schools of the country. That method resulted in the development of what is known as the Nation's Report Card (**National Assessment of Educational Progress** [**NAEP**]). Today this measure provides a picture of how well each state is doing in educating its children.

Also, we test to measure how much progress each child is making toward developing proficiency in core areas of learning. The driving issue here is also one of accountability in education. This type of testing was begun during the 1990s and became mandatory in 2002 under terms of the revised ESEA, now

Table 1.1   A Proposal of a New Method of Evaluation of the Newborn Infant

A score is given for each sign at one minute and five minutes after the birth. If there are problems with the baby, an additional score is given at 10 minutes. A score of 7–10 is considered normal, while 4–7 might require some resuscitative measures. A baby with Apgars of 3 and below requires immediate resuscitation.

	Sign	*0 Points*	*1 Point*	*2 Points*
A	Appearance (Skin Color)	Blue-gray, Pale All Over	Normal, Except for Extremities	Normal Over Entire Body
P	Pulse	Absent	Below 100 bpm	Above 100 bpm
G	Grimace (Reflex Irritability)	No Response	Grimace	Sneeze, Cough, Pulls Away
A	Activity (Muscle Tone)	Absent	Arms and Legs Flexed	Active Movement
R	Respiration	Absent	Slow, Irregular	Good, Crying

SOURCE: From "A proposal of a new method of evaluation of the newborn infant," by V. Apgar, 1953, *Current Researches in Anesthesia & Analgesia, 32*, p. 261–267. Reprinted with permission from Eric Apgar.

known as the **No Child Left Behind** (NCLB) Act. Today, all 50 states have both specified what all children are expected to learn at each grade level in the core subjects (reading, mathematics, and science) and have developed tests to measure achievement in those areas. Naturally, our schools have revamped their curriculums in an effort to stress these core subjects. This has had a negative impact on the variety of subjects and disciplines taught in the schools (Jennings & Rentner, 2006).

✱ The curriculum most public school children are exposed to has been skewed away from the arts and humanities and toward the content covered by the **mandated assessments** (Dillon, 2006; Manzo, March 2005). This has done great damage to those curriculum areas that are not tested. As a result, the curriculum followed in most schools now de-emphasizes areas such as the arts, social studies, modern language, and physical education while providing extra doses of basic skills-development drill and practice in reading, mathematics, and science.

For more
information, see
"Considerations on
Point" at
www.sagepub.com/
wrightstudy

Case in Point (1a)

A group of music educators in Florida spent three years and $90,000 developing a music test that can be used as a part of a statewide assessment (Gupta, 2005). This test is presented on a CD and is answered by students on machine-scorable multiple choice forms. This test is scheduled to be a part of the statewide assessment program in 2008. By going on the offensive and forcing their subject into the state testing system, music educators have saved a place for themselves in the school curriculum. Many other subjects such as art and physical education may find that they have less space in the curriculum as they are not part of the statewide tests.

To verify the old adage that no bad idea stays dead forever, a number of states are using these student data from the NCLB Act to award teachers with pay raises. **Merit pay** is incredibly difficult to institute fairly. There are so many differences between schools and the children who populate them that a system based on student **achievement test** scores is inherently flawed. The pressure for merit pay is an extension of the **accountability** focus of policy makers who look at schools in much the same way as they look at corporations. The dismal results from almost two centuries of trying this in Great Britain have been ignored in the United States (Wilms & Chapleau, 1999).

Those same state-mandated tests perform a second accountability function: They provide the data needed to determine if various groups of students within each school are making progress toward the goal of being proficient in the core subjects. This function of the mandated tests is linked to the NCLB requirement that all identified groups of children are proficient in the core subjects by the year 2014. Each school must show that all groups—including children receiving **special education**, Native American children, non-Hispanic Black children, Hispanic children, children with one or more disabling conditions, Anglo-White children, and children from impoverished homes—are making Adequate Yearly Progress (AYP) toward the goal of universal proficiency by 2014. The various states have each identified specific standards for student learning and have established proficiency targets for the children of each grade level. Those targets or **benchmarks** are unique to each state but must be approved by the U.S. Department of Education (U.S. Department of Education, 2007). The argument can be made that the policy of evaluating all schools exclusively on arbitrarily established standards for learning, and fixed levels of achievement, do not do justice to the diversity of communities, students, and schools. The central requirement of the NCLB legislation (viz., that all children achieve at a proficient level by 2014) is one that will result in nearly all schools failing to meet the mandate (Linn, 2007b).[4]

School Strategies

Schools have taken steps to reduce the number of children scoring below the level of proficient on these mandated assessment tests. One step involves the introduction of a published achievement test during first and second grades. This achievement testing provides the teachers with data that can identify weakness in the curriculum and spot those children who may be at risk of failure on the mandated assessment in third grade. Other steps schools can take may involve after-school and summer remediation programs or revising the school's curriculum to emphasize the elements measured by the assessment program. Yet another strategy involves the addition of supplementary instructional staff to tutor and provide individualized assistance to children identified as being at risk for failure.

Case in Point (1b)

Perhaps the best strategy that a school can take to improve test scores is to involve the teachers in reviewing the curriculum and the tasks required on the mandated test. One component of such a review relates to the learning standards that are being measured on the assessment and verifying that the school's curriculum provides all students with instruction in those areas (Kristoback & Wright, 2001). The second component is one that is frequently overlooked. This involves assuring that all the test's modalities are familiar to all students. For example, a school that teaches spelling by having children memorize spelling lists, and then tests its students by having them write down the dictation of their teacher, may do badly on a standardized spelling test. Standardized tests measure spelling achievement by having children mark all the words in a printed passage that are not spelled correctly. If children never saw this method for testing spelling achievement, they will not score well no matter how good they may be at spelling. Their low scores will not indicate what they know, only their lack of familiarity with that particular modality of testing.

For more information, see "Considerations on Point" at www.sagepub.com/wrightstudy

Testing is also done in the classroom by classroom teachers. For the most part the measures used by teachers are created by teachers or borrowed and modified by the teachers from the publisher of classroom textbooks. These teacher-made tests may be designed to check on student understanding and used in "real time" to inform the ongoing classroom instruction (see Chapter 6). In this way, testing occurs in a formative environment. A *formative test* is one used to check on the efficacy of the teaching-learning process. It can identify problems in understanding and guide the teacher in reteaching difficult topics and assisting students in achieving the instructional objective.

Alternatively, teacher-made tests may be designed to provide an "end of the instructional unit" summary of what each child has learned. This is known as the summative function of tests. **Summative testing** provides data needed to make objective judgments about the child, including assigning report card **grades**. To the extent possible, teachers should always work toward assigning grades that do not appear to be either arbitrary or capricious. For this reason, test data built from measures of the curriculum that were actually taught should be at the core of the report card grades.

Testing is also done to determine the special needs that some children may have for additional learning support and individualized education. This type of testing is part of the process of making an **entitlement decision**. An entitlement decision can provide extra assistance to a child who has fallen significantly behind his or her peers in terms of classroom achievement. The regulations of the various states provide that all children are entitled to a thorough and efficient education. An assessment is one approach that can provide the necessary data to document the need for assistance.

Finally, testing is also done to determine which children are selected to receive advanced or specialized educational opportunities. This type of testing can be as prosaic as deciding if a young child is ready to attend kindergarten or should wait for a year.

For more information, see "Considerations on Point" at www.sagepub.com/wrightstudy

Case in Point (1c)

Eighty years ago, the first tests for infants and young children were devised by Arnold L. Gesell at Yale University. It was Gesell who introduced the word *readiness* into the lexicon of educators. His research demonstrated that children have points in their development when they are mentally or physically ready to acquire a new skill or learn a new concept. Instruction before that time of readiness is futile, but once the child has reached readiness, then learning proceeds rapidly (Gesell & Thompson, 1929). Until recently, this construct was widely employed by public schools to decide which children were ready for admission into kindergarten and first grade and which should wait a year. In 2000, the use of these assessments for readiness screening was deemed unacceptable by the National Association of Early Childhood Specialists in State Departments of Education (NAECS/SDE, 2000). School readiness tests are still widely used and are even mandated in several states (Stephens, 2006).

Today, parents are more likely to hold their children back from enrolling in kindergarten (Datar, 2003; Gootman, 2006; Russell & LaCoste-Caputo, 2006). This voluntary delay in starting public education is being done more frequently in states where grade promotion from third grade is contingent on a test score.[5] Parents who do this want their children to be a year older and more mature than their peers entering school (Brock, 2006). This practice is so widespread that it has its own sobriquet: **"academic redshirting."**

About half of the states require that specialized educational programs be made available to the brightest and/or most **gifted** students in the schools. Admission into these programs typically involves cognitive tests covering dimensions such as mental ability and **creativity**. This type of cognitive testing

"Which is yours?"

Figure 1.1   "Which Is Yours?"

is also linked to college admission and certain scholarship award programs. Parents of gifted children are generally not satisfied with the NCLB testing program and the resulting curriculum modifications in the public schools. These parents see the present curriculum, with its heavy emphasis on drilling basic skills in reading, mathematics, and basic science, as not meeting the needs of their children (DeLacy, 2004; Reed, 2004; Tierney, 2004). These parents are secure in the belief that their children will pass any state assessment and want them to have an educational experience rich in complex thinking tasks, and they want an educational program that is supplemented with advanced coursework in the sciences and arts. Research has supported this parental concern. A study using **computer adaptive testing** in Idaho demonstrated that as educational resources are focused on children who have the greatest educational needs, advanced students experience minimal achievement growth. This reflects that observation that the new curriculum over-teaches concepts that the advanced students already understand and know (Clark, 2005).

To make matters worse, there is a clear and direct relationship between measures of **cognitive ability** and the outcome on statewide assessments (Burson & Wright, 2003). In other words, those children who are the most gifted in academic ability do well on the high-stakes tests while those who have less cognitive ability are less likely to score at the level of proficient.

This raises a question of what the state-mandated high-stakes tests actually measure. These assessments are supposed to be a measure of how well students have achieved the state's approved learning standards. A general criticism of the tests is that they lack cognitive richness and are not designed to elicit complex thinking (Lane, 2004). Research has documented that many of the questions included on statewide assessments are written in a way that requires less complex thinking than the state's own standards may require (Webb, 2002, 2005).

Because there is no federal mandate requiring the states to address the differential educational needs of academically gifted children, many of those programs for the academically talented or gifted have been truncated or even eliminated to provide the resources needed to help the academically less able reach the goals of the No Child Left Behind Act (Berger, 2007). This has not gone unnoticed by the parents of gifted children, who have become vocal critics of the No Child Left Behind Act (Clark, 2005; Cloud/Thornburg, 2004; DeLacy, 2004; Goode, 2002).[6]

TYPES AND VARIETIES OF TESTS

There are four sources of achievement tests administered in the public schools today: classroom tests and quizzes, published achievement tests, and the high-stakes tests required by the state education departments. In addition to these there are a myriad of other tests that are administered as part of guidance activities, by reading specialists, by **school psychologists**, and by speech and language therapists. A primary focus of this book is on achievement testing in the schools.

The four sources of achievement tests can be further organized into two groups. One group consists of tests and quizzes made by the classroom teacher. Teacher-made tests are described in some detail in Section III, Chapters 6, 7, 8, and 9. The second group consists of the published tests and assessments that are developed by private contractors and public agencies.

Published Tests

One type of school-based achievement test is published by the large conglomerated education publishing houses. Each year hundreds of millions of published tests are taken by students in the United States. This represents billions of dollars in revenue for the test publishers each year. These corporations publish numerous products and offer a range of consulting services in addition to providing educational measurements. Included among the major publishers are Pearson Assessments (www.pearsonassessments.com), Riverside Publishing (www.riverpub.com/products/index.html), CTB McGraw-Hill (www.ctb.com), and Harcourt Assessment (https://harcourtassessment.com).

A second source of published tests is the various state departments of education. Under the provisions of the No Child Left Behind Act of 2002, all states must assess their public and charter school children starting in the third grade. This assessment must involve a test based on the state's approved learning standards. Because there are consequences for schools that do not meet the Adequate Yearly Progress (AYP) mandate of the NCLB Act, these tests are referred to as **high-stakes tests**. Not only can schools and educators be excoriated over poor student performance, but in eight states grade promotion for the children is contingent on achieving good scores on these measures.

Case in Point (1d)

In addition to parents, school administrators have also begun to encourage the **grade retention** of primary grade children who are at risk for not passing the statewide assessment test in third grade. A clear example of this is the State of North Carolina, which initiated a required test, the North Carolina End of

For more information, see "Considerations on Point" at www.sagepub.com/wrightstudy

Grades Test. Since requiring that test, the number of students retained in kindergarten and first and second grades has increased twofold. Grade repetition is a major expense for the schools. It now costs North Carolina approximately $140 million a year to educate these extra children (those who were not promoted) in the primary grades.

In 22 of the 50 states there is also a mandated test for high school graduation (Olson, August 2006). In 2007, approximately 65% of all high school seniors were required to pass a state test to qualify for their diploma. For these students, the term *high-stakes* is especially poignant. With a few exceptions, like Oregon, most state education departments do not actually write or score their own tests. These tasks are outsourced to private contractors (for more detail, see Chapter 11).

The final group of published tests used in the schools is provided by the **College Board** and the **American College Tests**, the **ACT**. There is a description of these two competing admission testing programs in Chapter 12.

Scoring Criteria

One way to classify tests is by the way they are scored. A published test may be scored using an absolute standard or criterion. These tests are referred to as being **criterion referenced** and are used to demonstrate whether the student has reached a required level or standard of achievement. For example, the 50 statewide mandated assessment tests each have a required level of success that children must reach to be graded as proficient. Other examples of criterion-based tests include licensing tests such as the PRAXIS published by ETS and the Class III Pilots Written Examination administered by the Federal Aviation Administration. In each of these cases there is a required passing score expressed in terms of the number of questions answered correctly that the test taker must obtain to pass or be proficient.

A second approach to scoring published tests is to employ a norm-reference group. A **norm-referenced test** is scored by comparing the **raw scores** from a current test taker with the scores achieved in the past by a sample of subjects used to establish the expected scoring pattern for the test. This group used to set the expected pattern of scores is referred to as the "norm group." Thus, each test taker is assigned a score that has been compared to a standard established by previous test subjects. The comparison group may have been established once in the past when the test was originally published. This model is followed by the popular Terra Nova achievement test published by CTB/McGraw-Hill.

Many states have it both ways. They report the scores of individual students in terms of a criterion based on **cut scores** and also report norm-based scores to the schools. These norm-based scores can be aggregated and the average score calculated for each school. These data are then reported in the local press and published as part of a required **school report card**. This school report card is designed to make it easy for parents to see which schools in a community are doing better than others. Unfortunately, private and parochial schools are not required to use the state assessment and rarely make a public report of the results of their own testing programs.

Administration

Published tests can be administered to groups of students in classrooms or even given to hundreds at a time in large halls. Group-administered educational measurements can involve a single dimension test, such as a test of mental ability (e.g., Otis Lennon School Ability Test [OLSAT] from Harcourt Assessment), or, they can be multifaceted, covering a range of different curriculum areas (e.g., Iowa Tests of Basic Skills [ITBS] from Riverside Publishing). Tests such as the ITBS are referred to as **test batteries**. In this context, the word *battery* refers to the fact that there are two or more parts to the test, much like a musical batterie (homophone), which can be used to describe the different drums in the percussion section of a band, or an artillery battery, which describes two or more cannons able to fire projectiles together.

Tests are also administered one-on-one. These are usually diagnostic measures designed to identify specific areas in which the student is experiencing learning problems. These tests may also measure mental ability with individually administered instruments, such as the battery of mental ability tests of the Wechsler Intelligence Test for Children, third edition (WISC III), from Harcourt Assessment.

Individually administered **diagnostic tests** can be customized for the child by the psychologist who is doing the testing. An example of this is **curriculum-based assessment** (**CBA**), which involves a brief series of problems or tasks taken from the curriculum material that the child is studying. The repeated measurement over time using these brief tests, known as **curriculum probes**, provides a picture of the progress a child is making toward learning the subject area or required skill.

Information Sources

With the hundreds of different tests available to use in the schools, there is a need to find unbiased sources of information about these measures. Not all educational tests are created equal, and many commercially published assessments are rubbish. Others may be well designed but are still inappropriate for a particular school to use. The first step in selecting the optimal published test for a school's use involves identifying the goals for testing. It is an axiom of measurement, that the test must match the purpose and goals defined by the educators of the school. Once that has been decided, it is then appropriate to review all of the possible measures that could meet the identified goals for testing.

The largest collection of tests is the one maintained by the **Educational Testing Service**. That collection extends from the present time and goes back over a hundred years. All in all, there are over 25,000 published tests maintained in the ETS collection. Online test descriptions can be reviewed on the ETS Web page (http://ericae.net/testcol.htm#ETSTF then open "ETS Test Collection Page ETS"). Independent reviews and evaluations of tests are available from the Buros Institute of Mental Measurements on the campus of the University of Nebraska, Lincoln. A total of over 4,000 tests are described and reviewed in this collection. These reviews and descriptions can be found on the Buros Web page (http://buros.unl.edu/buros/jsp/search.jsp). In 2007, the fee for this service is $15 per test review.

ASSUMPTIONS MADE BY TEST DEVELOPERS

With the plethora of assessments and tests used to measure our children, few educators ever consider the basic assumptions that underlie this endeavor. The first assumption is empirical. This assumption is one implying the belief that by carefully observing small aspects of a child's behavior it is possible to make an informed conclusion about what he or she has learned or is able to do.

The second assumption is one linked to the adequacy of the coverage provided by the test. It is never possible to exhaustively assess every bit of knowledge and every skill a child has learned through instruction. Therefore, all educational tests are only a small sample of what the child knows or can do. This leads to questions of how adequate is the curriculum coverage provided by the test. Does the test evaluate only a select portion of the content being evaluated? Or does the test measure the full domain? To assure complete coverage, the test should include an array of items selected randomly from the whole domain of possible content areas designated for assessment.

This is a goal rarely achieved by professional publishers and almost never by classroom teachers. A test should be viewed as a sample of behaviors. As a sample, a test is not a perfect representation of the full domain of knowledge or skills being evaluated.

Another point is that all tests and assessments represent the performance of the child at one moment in time. The condition of the child changes on a regular basis, and therefore we should anticipate that all test and assessment scores are going to vary. These two points combine to imply that the outcome of all tests includes a component of error and that all test scores have a degree of instability. This point should always be emphasized, as our society relies on the scores from tests and other assessments to make critical personnel and **placement decisions**.

TRENDS IN TESTING

The use of tests and assessments in public education will increase in both the near and long-term future. The format of educational tests will also evolve as testing becomes more closely integrated into ongoing instruction. This instructional integration will be facilitated by the application of modern online technologies.

Early Use of Computers in Testing

Over the past 50 years, schools have made a number of attempts to integrate computers into instruction. These efforts date from the first interactive learning systems of the late 1960s. Systems such as the first generation of PLATO (Programmed Logic for Automatic Teaching Operations) and TICCIT (Time-Shared Interactive Computer Controlled Information Television) were linked to university-based mainframe computers. These learning systems required a great deal of expertise at both the university computer center and in the public school to operate. These interactive systems also required expensive hardware and were very expensive to maintain. Naturally, without federal funding this first generation of interactive instructional systems was soon considered déclassé. In part, this was also owing to the natural limitations of the technology of the era. By 1972, it was only possible for 1,000 students to log on and use the PLATO system at the same time (McNeil, 2004). Today, most schools have scores of computers with broadband Internet connections. Interactive tests and tutorials were a part of these early mainframe-supported learning systems. These first online instructional programs were the true precursors of what is happening in educational measurement today.

New Technology

The educational world was changed forever when Steve Jobs and Steve Wozniak began to market the Apple I in 1976. Through the next three decades, one generation of desktop computers followed another. In the schools these computers were usually kept under lock and key in a "computer laboratory." The computer applications typically involved word processing and the use of instructional software that was in a game format (Wright & Lesisko, 2007).

Today there is a new technology, and the children entering school are already sophisticated in its use. Schools are now scrambling to catch up with the technological skills of the offspring of the X generation. Schools are now employing online testing and assessment, including online diagnostic evaluations that are matched with individualized tutorials. In a number of school districts it is now possible for parents to communicate with teachers online and read up-to-the-moment evaluations of their child's progress.

For more information, see "Considerations on Point" at www.sagepub.com/ wrightstudy

Case in Point (1e)

In 2003, Tennessee parents became able to access the full file of school assessment data records for their children and could read the predicted likelihood of their children passing the state-mandated state assessment. These parents could even access and read a projected score for their children on the SAT and ACT examination programs.

Online Report Cards

After 100 years, the era of the quarterly report card is almost over. The online system is also eliminating the old paper grade book. Teachers can now post grades from school or home and parents can read those grades when they get home from work each day. This allows parents to see problems as they develop and take action as needed. Parent conferences will no longer hold surprises for the parents, who will be well versed as to the daily progress of their children. This form of parent–school linkage is already in large-scale use in Arizona and will soon impact all schools (Ryman, 2005).

Computerized Grading

The evaluation of student writing is now also being done by computers online. The state of California has contracted with the Educational Testing Service to provide an online essay examination as a part of that state's required high school graduation test. In 2004, 17 states administered mandated state assessment tests to students over the Internet. That number is growing and will soon include all schools in this country. But it is not only the children who are being assessed online; schools have started to use online talent tests to prescreen prospective teachers (Keller, 2004, May).

It is possible to tour this new system online and have a practice session with it by visiting the California Education Department's Web site: www.cde.ca.gov/ta/tg/sr/resources.asp.

Qualitative Assessments

The second new direction in the future of testing will see the reemergence of a more qualitative form of assessment. Standardized tests are designed so that the student is required to get the one correct **answer**. The new trend is toward a more open format of assessment. The introduction of written essays and open-ended mathematics problems on standardized assessments is a step in this direction. Perhaps a clearer picture of the future is the new statewide testing program in Nebraska. That state has attempted to meet part of the NCLB mandates by allowing school systems to employ a **portfolio** assessment system from the third through the eighth grades. This portfolio assessment serves as an optional part of the mandated statewide testing program. The Nebraska program, the School-based, Teacher-led Assessment and Reporting System (**STARS**), has been shown to provide a good measure of achievement in mathematics; however, the reading assessment has not proven to be as reliable as the typical standardized assessment test (Brookhart, 2005).

Qualitative assessment such as that used in Nebraska requires a holistic, open-ended scoring system. **Holistic scoring** implies that the evaluation is of the whole of the child's work considered in its totality and not conducted as a simple summation of the quality of the various parts. In a real sense, this process is much like selecting a Most Valuable Player (MVP) in sports. The electors do not grade individual components of each player's performance but make one overall judgment of quality. This type of assessment provides classroom teachers with information that is far more useful in planning for instruction with individual children. This reflects the fact that evaluation data gathered in this informal way can be integrated into the instructional program immediately and the results of instruction can be assessed in real time as the teaching is occurring.

LAW AND TESTING

For over 40 years the federal government has established laws mandating various testing programs. State legislatures have also been involved in establishing large-scale testing programs by writing mandated tests and test policy into state codes. Yet, there is another level where testing programs and the legal system interact. That interface occurs through the courts and what is referred to as "case law."

Legislation

The use of test data, and other school records, was first addressed by the federal government in the **Buckley Amendment**, or the Family Educational Rights and Privacy Act (20 USC S. 1232g, 1974). This law details the parent's right to inspect and offer corrections to the educational records maintained by the school. It also assures that information from those records is not released without the signed permission of the parents. The exceptions to this release rule provide for ongoing educational research, accreditation reports, school-to-school transfers, and for the local planning of the educational program for the child.

The last quarter of the 20th century saw a number of reports and reviews that were highly critical of American education. These included the **First and Second International Math Study** (**FIMS & SIMS**) and the **Third International Math and Science Study** (**TIMSS**; U.S. Department of Education, National Center for Educational Statistics, 2004), as well as the widely read report, *A Nation at Risk: The Imperative for Educational Reform* (National Commission on Excellence in Education, 1983). The media coverage and political fallout from these and other reviews of American education created an added impetus for statewide assessment programs. They also served to provide the background arguments for the **Improving America's Schools Act of 1994**. Much of the testing-based reform movement was started in 1994 under the program initiated under President Clinton known as the Improving America's Schools Act (IASA; P.L. 103-382, 1994). This act was the first to require that each state develop learning standards and monitor schools by using tests of those standards. Prior to that time, several states had taken the lead in implementing statewide testing programs. The states at the forefront of this movement in the 1970s and 1980s were Florida, New Jersey, New York, Pennsylvania, and Texas. In states like New Jersey and Texas, the business community was the force behind instituting testing-based educational reforms.

Miracle of Texas

One example of this process can be seen in the home state of President George W. Bush. Texas has been a leading state in the educational assessment movement since 1983. That year, Governor Mark White asked fellow Texan and business leader H. Ross Perot to chair a select committee of business leaders to identify ways to improve education in Texas. The Perot Commission reported ideas for a number of major revisions to public education, which were quickly passed into law and were well funded by the Texas legislature in 1984. Part of these reforms was a call for standardized achievement tests. This resulted in the publication of the Texas Educational Assessment of Minimal Skills (TEAMS) in 1985 (Haney, 2000).

This was replaced with the Texas Assessment of Academic Skills (TAAS) in 1990. The TAAS was used to document what became known as the "**miracle of Texas**" and served as the template for much of the No Child Left Behind Act of 2002 (Haney, 2000). The miracle of Texas was the name given to what was perceived to be a significant improvement in the number of children who scored at the proficient level on the TAAS. The Texas Education Department required many of the same things that are now a part of the NCLB Act. These include public reports of school scores, penalties for schools where children do poorly, and a required graduation test.

Recently there has been a reexamination of these outcomes, and much skepticism has been expressed in the educational research literature (Haney, 2000; Kellow & Willson, 2001). Criticism of this assessment, and of the reported success of the Texas model, led to the development of a new assessment, the Texas Assessment of Knowledge and Skills (TAKS), in 2003.

For more
information, see
"Considerations on
Point" at
www.sagepub.com/
wrightstudy

Case in Point (1f)

The largest city in Texas is Houston. The superintendent of Houston's schools in the 1990s was Rod Paige (later U.S. Secretary of Education 2001–2005). He reported that the assessment test scores in his district had soared and that dropouts were an issue of the past. All of this miraculous good news was attributed to the "tough love" of the new Texas reforms. When Governor Bush became president, those reforms became the core of the federal legislation known as No Child Left Behind. An investigation by the TV news show *60 Minutes* (Fager, 2004) demonstrated how students who were being given their exit interview on deciding to drop out of school were asked about their future plans, including their education plans. If the students said that they planned to "get a diploma someday" through the GED, they were not counted as being a dropout. Thus, virtually no student was classified as a school dropout.

The average school test scores were also found to be manipulated. Students who were at risk for failure were retained in a lower grade before they had to face the test. Once they repeated that grade once or twice, they were double promoted over the grade level where the test was required. The result was that Houston's high schools had bulging enrollments in grade 9 and anemic enrollments in grade 10, the grade where the high-stakes test was given.

One reason for this dubious policy was that Dr. Rod Paige only gave his high school principals one year contracts with reappointment being contingent on the school's test scores and dropout rate.

CASE LAW

Special Education

Case law has focused on three central issues related to testing. In general, the courts have followed a practical approach to determining the **appropriateness (validity)** of a test, focusing on the consequences of the measurement and the content that was included in the test (Sireci & Parker, 2007). The first of these cases involved the use of tests and assessments in placing children into special education programs. The central issue in these cases had been related to whether there was some form of measurement bias against minorities on the standardized measures. Two old cases demonstrate this issue. In a series of state and federal court cases between 1972 and 1984 referred to as *Larry P. v. Riles*, the schools of the City of San Francisco were prevented from using standard **intelligence tests** to place African American children in special education classes. This was based on the observation that all racial sub-groups within the population do not have the same profile of test scores. Also, it was argued that the professional community was not sensitive to group differences when making placement decisions. The later decisions (1984) upheld the lower court ruling and eventually enjoined all school systems in California from using any of 20 different measures of mental ability when making placement decisions for African American children.

A few years later, and a half a continent away, the case of *Parents in Action on Special Education (PASE) v. Hannon* resulted in the opposite outcome for special education testing. Here the use of standard intelligence measures was found to be without bias and was permitted for all placement decisions. The difference between the two outcomes is that in the latter case the judge read and evaluated each item on the measures to determine if he could see any obvious bias. Also, these intelligence measures were not used as the sole criteria for a special education placement but were a part of a larger, multidimensional assessment of the child.

High-Stakes Tests

Another area where case law has had an impact on testing is with high-stakes tests in the public schools. Florida was among the first states to require students to pass a graduation test before they could be awarded a high school diploma. This was challenged in 1978 when 10 African American students from Hillsborough County, Florida, who failed their competency tests, sued the state for being denied a high school diploma. The plaintiffs argued that the disproportional number of minority students who had been denied a diploma was a violation of the 14th Amendment of the U.S. Constitution (see Table 1.2).

The resolution of the case, known as *Debra P. v. Turlington*, happened in 1981. The courts ruled in favor of the state of Florida. This ruling came after the court noted the fact that Florida had aligned the test items with the curricula taught in the schools, and that all students had several opportunities to learn what was required to pass the assessment and earn a diploma. Florida awarded those students who failed the assessment a "Certificate of Completion," which allowed them to enroll in adult education through which they could work toward their diplomas.

The issue of denying a diploma to students with disabilities who cannot pass a state-mandated graduation test was resolved shortly after the Florida decision. The parents of a child with disabilities in Illinois who was denied a diploma after failing a graduation test sued and lost in the case of *Brookhart v. Illinois State Board of Education* (1983). In this case the courts expressed the opinion that a school district's desire to "ensure the value of a high school diploma" is admirable, and that the courts should avoid interfering in educational policy unless a constitutional or statutory right of the child has been clearly violated.

Table 1.2   Pass Rates on Exit Exams

Percentages of Students Passing State Exit Exams on the First Attempt						
States	*English*			*Math*	*Science*	*Social Studies*
	Reading	*ELA*	*Writing*			
Alabama	88%	86%		83%	82%	
Alaska	66%		47%	44%		
Arizona	67%		68%	31%		
California		64%		44%		
Florida	58%			72%		
Georgia		94%	92%	91%	68%	80%
Indiana		68%		65%		
Louisiana		78%		65%		
Massachusetts	82%			75%		
Minnesota		80%	91%	75%		
New Mexico	92%	82%	95%	82%	80%	79%
South Carolina	85%		86%	81%		
Tennessee				76%	95%	
Virginia	82%	82%	84%			

Percentages of Students Passing on the First Attempt by Subgroups for Three States						
Student Groups	*Indiana Math*	*Indiana English/LA*	*Minnesota Math*	*Minnesota English/LA*	*Massachusetts Math*	*Massachusetts English/LA*
All students	65%	68%	75%	80%	75%	82%
Asian	79%	72%	62%	61%	84%	79%
Black	31%	38%	33%	46%	46%	59%
Hispanic	46%	49%	43%	52%	41%	51%
White	70%	73%	80%	86%	82%	87%
Free/ reduced lunch	42%	45%	51%	59%	Not Available	Not Available
Students with disabilities	24%	19%	33%	40%	39%	46%
English language learners	33%	28%	32%	30%	42%	39%

SOURCE: From Center on Education Policy; based on information collected from state departments of education. Copyright 2002 by Center on Education Policy. Reprinted with permission.

Advanced Program Admission

Another area in which case law is guiding the use of educational tests is in the admission of students into advanced programs. The question is one of the selection of children for gifted programs. An example is that of the three selective secondary schools for the gifted in Boston. In Boston, the use of a test score to place students into these programs for the academically talented resulted in racial and ethnic disparities in enrollments. To correct the imbalance, the school admission policy was modified to include racial set-asides. Differential admissions programs for minority groups at these schools have come under court review, and the three schools have all been ordered to stop racial set-asides in their admissions (*Wessmann v. Gittens*, 1998). In 2005, it was noted that the end of the set-aside policy in Boston has resulted in a skewing of the enrollment in programs for the gifted toward White and Asian students and away from African American students (Sacchetti, 2005).

Higher Education

Most of the case law issues regarding admissions have taken place with colleges and graduate schools. Most higher education institutions have the admissions goal of creating a diverse population of undergraduate students. This tenet is established to assure that different communities and ethnicities are part of the culture of the institution. The assumption is that living in such a culture becomes an important part of the learning experiences of undergraduate students. It should also be noted that not all higher education institutions seek diversity in all dimensions of the student body. For example, almost all the students attending Bob Jones University (evangelical Protestant) and Ave Marie University (Roman Catholic) share a common campuswide doctrine and religious faith. Alverno College only accepts women, while Wabash College is an all-male institution. Historically there are a number of colleges that were originally established to educate African American students. Most of these institutions of higher education are still primarily attended by African American students.

The easiest solution for the admissions office to promote student diversity is an open-door approach. The problem occurs for those institutions that maintain a selective admissions policy while still seeking student diversity. This can be a daunting challenge.

Early Case Law on Admissions

Over the past 50 years the legal battles over enrollment in America's schools and colleges have gone through a 180-degree turn. In the 1950s and 1960s the fight led by the attorney general and the Supreme Court under Chief Justice Earl Warren was to desegregate unwilling school systems and colleges. Most of these were located in the South and in the antebellum border states. The landmark Supreme Court decision was *Brown v. Board of Education* (347 U.S. 483 [1954]). This decision did away with the concept of "separate but equal" in all matters of public accommodation, including education.[7] During the 1960s, Attorney General Robert Kennedy brought desegregation lawsuits against hundreds of school systems and the state departments of education in a dozen states.

A major shift in the zeitgeist occurred during the late 1960s, and by the 1970s many school systems and most colleges were working to remove all vestige of segregation from their student populations. During that era, colleges and professional schools began to take positive (affirmative) steps to increase minority enrollment.[8]

Score Gap

The persistence of significant differences between the average scores of different racial groups on all high-stakes and admissions tests is a vexing and longstanding problem for educators (see Table 1.3). In an earlier era this differential would have been explained as being a function of inherited differences in ability. Today, a number of observers are willing to explain the difference in

Table 1.3   Tables From ACT Scores by Gender and Ethnicity

National Average ACT Composite Score by Gender, 1994–2006													
	1994	*1995*	*1996*	*1997*	*1998*	*1999*	*2000*	*2001*	*2002*	*2003*	*2004*	*2005*	*2006*
Males	20.9	21.0	21.0	21.1	21.2	21.1	21.2	21.1	20.9	21.0	21.0	21.1	21.2
Females	20.7	20.7	20.8	20.6	20.9	20.9	20.9	20.9	20.7	20.8	20.9	20.8	21.0

National Average ACT Composite Scores by Race/Ethnicity, 5-Year Trends					
	2002	*2003*	*2004*	*2005*	*2006*
All Students	20.8	20.8	20.9	20.9	21.1
African American/Black	16.8	16.9	17.1	17.0	17.1
American Indian/Alaskan Native	18.6	18.7	18.8	18.7	18.8
Caucasian American/White	21.7	21.7	21.8	21.9	22.0
Hispanic	18.4	18.5	18.5	18.6	18.6
Asian American/Pacific Islander	21.6	21.8	21.9	22.1	22.3
Other/No Response	20.3	20.6	20.9	20.9	21.1

SOURCE: From www.act.org. Copyright © 2007. Reprinted with permission from ACT, Inc.

achievement between groups in terms of group attitudes and motivation (Thernstrom & Thernstrom, 2003) (see Table 1.4).

Confounding this problem of differential average scores on achievement tests is the fact that there is a direct, monotonic relationship between the income level of families and the admissions test scores of children in those families. Likewise, there is a direct relationship between the quality of the high school that students attend and the admissions test scores students earn. In part, this reflects the availability of a competitive academic environment in the high schools of high-scoring students (Bridgeman & Wendler,

Table 1.4   Tables From SAT Scores by Gender and Ethnicity

2006 COLLEGE-BOUND SENIORS TEST SCORES: SAT Approximately 1.47 million test takers, of whom 53% were female				
	Verbal	Math	Writing	Total
Gender				
Female	502	502	502	1506
Male	505	536	491	1532
Ethnicity				
American Indian or Alaskan Native	487	494	474	1455
Asian, Asian American, or Pacific Islanders	510	578	512	1600
African American or Black	434	429	428	1291
Mexican or Mexican American	454	465	452	1371
Puerto Rican	459	456	448	1363
Other Hispanic or Latino	458	463	450	1371
White	527	536	519	1582
Other	494	513	493	1500
No Response (5%)	487	506	482	1475

SOURCE: *2006 College-Bound Seniors.* Copyright © 2006 the College Board, www.collegeboard.com. Reproduced with permission.

2004). The complexity and rigor of high school curriculums followed by students have been shown to predict how well those students do in undergraduate college (Glickman & Babyak, 2006).

Parental Factors

Middle-class families are likely to pay the required tuition for their children to attend a test-preparation course and to hire academic and test-preparation tutors (Chiles, 1997). It is clear that family income and parent education level have a lot to do with student achievement (Joireman & Abbott, 2004) (see Table 1.5).

Table 1.5   Average SAT II Reasoning Scores by Family Income Group

Family Income	Reading	Math	Writing	Total
Less than $10,000/year	429	457	427	1313
$10,000–$20,000/year	445	465	440	1350
$20,000–$30,000/year	462	474	454	1390
$30,000–$40,000/year	478	488	470	1436
$40,000–$50,000/year	493	501	483	1477
$50,000–$60,000/year	500	509	490	1499
$60,000–$70,000/year	505	515	496	1516
$70,000–$80,000/year	511	521	502	1534
$80,000–$100,000/year	523	534	514	1571
More than $100,000/year	549	564	543	1656
No Response (35%)	Scores not reported			
ALL TEST TAKERS	503	518	497	1518

SOURCE: *2006 College-Bound Seniors*. Copyright © 2006 the College Board, www.collegeboard.com. Reproduced with permission.

These factors are linked to parental behaviors such as the enforcement of homework time and the setting of limits on television watching. Home factors are central to the academic success of all students. In a recent study of the students in several middle schools in Pennsylvania, it was found that 15% of the **variance** in success on the mandated statewide assessment was accounted for by a vector of **variables** that measure home life. These variables included parent education level, parent expectations for the child's education, hours spent reading for pleasure, the number of books and magazines at home, family **mobility**, frequency of absenteeism by the child, and the number of hours the child spent watching TV (Holbrook & Wright, 2004). Howard Gardner once quipped that we can predict with surprising accuracy whether a youngster will eventually graduate from college by only knowing his/her zip code (personal communication, Howard Gardner, April 2007).

The **score gap** on admissions tests has been examined by a number of authors, including Claude Steele. He presents evidence that there may be at least two extraneous factors in the SAT scores of African American and Latino children. One source is produced by the "**stereotype threat**" created by the test situation (Steele, 1997, 1999). Steele has demonstrated that "stereotype threat" occurs when minority students are placed in a high-stakes test situation. His research has shown that in those situations minority students feel the added stress of the stereotypical expectations held for them. The extra pressure caused by the fear of proving the stereotype correct correlates with lower performance.

The second problematic area is related to the linguistic aspects of the test items (Freedle & Kostin, 1997). Roy Freedle (2002) has identified differences in word utilization patterns between White and Black adolescents. This has the potential of producing differential test item performance (Dorans & Zeller, 2004). The unexpected and unexplained finding is that African American test takers perform better on the hardest items and less well on the easiest items. This is the opposite of what occurs with a population of middle-class White test takers. If the harder items were to be given extra weight on the test, the score gap would be reduced by a third. Also, Freedle points out the **correction for guessing** that ETS applies to all the SAT II scores disproportionately lowers the scores of minority students who make more errors on the easier items of the test.

Standard formula for the correction for guessing on a test composed of multiple choice questions that each have four answer options,

$$\text{total corrected raw score} = \frac{total\ correct - total\ wrong}{4}$$

There is also reason to believe that tests involving essay writing may also present a problem. Essay tasks that provide background information about the topic for the writing assignment tend to be easier to write than essay tasks that provide no structure or guidelines. The performance of African American adolescents is best when the essay format is the hardest (i.e., no structure).

The move toward the use of **computer adaptive testing** may prove to lead to an even wider score gap between White and Black students (see Chapter 2). This reflects the way computer adaptive systems are designed to first attempt to determine an approximate ability level for the test taker (Cheng & Chang, 2007). This is done by presenting several items of a mid-level of difficulty at the start of the test. Based on the student's performance on those items, the test taker is then presented with items assumed to match his/her ability. If Freedle's model is correct, it is possible that African American students could never be presented with the more difficult level of test items and thereby have test scores based on easier questions. The result will be low scores that are assigned to those answering easier questions.

Affirmative Action in Admissions

It was a natural step for highly selective institutions to adopt an **affirmative action** model for their admissions processes. One reason for this decision is that the pool of available minority students who have high SAT scores is very small. Research sponsored by ETS has shown that only 3.3% of African American test takers scored over 1300 on the SAT I, while 9% of Hispanic students and 39% of Anglo-White students scored at that level (Bridgeman & Wendler, 2004).

Case in Point (1g)

Admission test scores are one of only two primary predictors of college potential. The other is high school **class rank**, which is derived from the high school **grade point average** (**GPA**) of students. The importance of tests like the SAT II in the admission process is increasing because high schools have begun not reporting either a GPA or class rank (Finder, 2006). This reflects an effort by a number of suburban high schools to remove unhealthy levels of letter-grade stress on students. The movement began with private schools that were trying to provide a way for the good students who attend their highly competitive schools to be admitted into the most elite colleges (Zweigenhaft, 1993).

Those college admission officers who evaluated the entering class of 2009 reported that half or more of the applicants' transcripts did not report the class rank or the high school GPA. The result was that SAT II and ACT scores were more important in the admissions decision than ever.

For more information, see "Considerations on Point" at www.sagepub.com/wrightstudy

Affirmative action plans made it possible for both selective public schools[9] as well as institutions of higher education to set minority enrollment targets and actively work to achieve them. Such strategies took the form of simple quotas or in some cases the addition of bonus points to the admissions file of minority students.

Recently reported research into the admissions process at highly selective institutions demonstrates that several classes of students were given preference in admission.[10] The advantage given to African Americans is the equivalent of 230 extra points on the 1600-point (SAT I) scale being added to their test score. The advantage to Hispanic Americans has been worth 185 extra points (Espenshade & Chung, 2005). The advantage to Asian students has been negative, equaling a loss equivalent to 50 points.

Naturally, when higher scoring students of one racial group were rejected for admissions and lower scoring students from a minority were accepted, tension ensued. It had to be anticipated that these affirmative admissions systems would be criticized and come under legal challenge.[11]

Court Challenges

When an otherwise well-prepared non-minority student receives a letter of rejection from a college or professional school, the personal pain can be excruciating (Kinzie, 2007). The rejected student may well blame the admissions process or others who are perceived as receiving special treatment.

The first challenge to affirmative action in admissions was a case involving admission into the Medical School of the University of California at Davis. In this case, a White male applicant was rejected for admission in 1974 and sued the regents of the university on the basis of Title VI of the Civil Rights Act of 1964 and the **equal protection** clause of the 14th Amendment of the Constitution of the United States (*University of California Regents v. Bakke*, 438 U. S. 265 [1978]). The university had established a special admissions program for the economically disadvantaged and members of targeted minority groups, including African Americans, Chicanos (Mexican Americans), Asians, and Native Americans. This special admissions process used a set-aside program that guaranteed that there would be 16 seats available for the targeted groups. This approach to admissions was rejected, but a separate opinion written by Justice Powell, and affirmed by the Court, did recognize student diversity as a compelling state interest.

The second major blow to affirmative action in admissions came from a case in Texas. In that case, *Hopwood et al. v. The State of Texas* (1994), the issue before the courts involved admission into the Law School of the

University of Texas, Austin. Among the many Anglo-White students who were rejected for admission into the Law School were four who sued. The Law School had previously created a second parallel admissions process reserved for African American and Mexican American applicants. These targeted minority groups were subjected to a less selective admissions test score requirement than were Asian and Anglo-White students, including the four who brought the lawsuit. Based on their scores on the Law School Admission Test (LSAT) and undergraduate grades (GPA), the four who sued all would have been admitted if they were members of either of the targeted minority groups. At the first level, the state courts agreed with the university and its admissions system, rejecting the Hopwood petition. On appeal, the U.S. Fifth Circuit Court overturned that decision and effectively ended that affirmative admissions practice (*Hopwood et al v. University of Texas*, 861 F. Supp. 551, 578–579 [WD. Tex. 1994] 5th Circuit [1996]).

The final defining cases for affirmative action in admissions involved two of the colleges of the University of Michigan in 2003. The first, ***Gratz et al. v. Bollinger et al.***, involved admission of two undergraduates into the College of Literature, Science, and the Arts. The university used a point system to assist in the admission decision process. Admission was granted to all students who reached a total of 100 points using a system that included a **weighted combination** of test scores, GPA, and **Advanced Placement** (AP) course completion. All targeted minority group members (African American, Hispanics, and Native Americans) were automatically awarded a bonus of 20 points on their admissions files. The Supreme Court held for the plaintiffs and rejected the admissions model employed for undergraduates at the University of Michigan (*Gratz v. Bollinger* [02-516]. U.S. [2003]). The court rejected the argument that Michigan's admissions office needed a simplified point system because the number of applications was too high to give individual attention to each case.

A second case, ***Grutter v. Bollinger et al.***, at the University of Michigan has provided guidance for all admissions systems that strive to be both highly selective and also enroll a significant number of minorities. The university's law school employs a **holistic approach to admissions**, which includes LSAT scores and undergraduate GPA. It also looks at "soft variables" including enthusiasm, recommendations, the quality of the applicant's essay, life experiences, and the difficulty of the undergraduate course of study. The stated goal of this admissions system is to select motivated and able students with the best potential to contribute to the practice of law in Michigan.

Barbara Grutter had excellent grades and a high LSAT score, but she was not admitted. She argued that the admissions process was biased in favor of minority students. She won her case in the district court but had it reversed by the U.S. Sixth Circuit Court. On appeal, that decision was upheld by the

U.S. Supreme Court (*Grutter v. Bollinger et al.,* 02-241. U.S. [2003] 288 F.3d 732, affirmed). The opinion of the Supreme Court was that the admissions system of the law school met the requirements as specified in the opinion of Justice Powell from the Bakke case of 1978.[12] The justices recognized that there is a compelling reason for an agency of the state (University of Michigan) to consider the race of potential students. Thus, it is possible to include race as a variable in admissions decisions when those decisions are made following a holistic approach to student selection.[13]

The compromise implied by the Bollinger cases not withstanding, in 2007 the regents of the University of Wisconsin voted to approve a policy requiring that the race of applicants be considered as one salient factor in the admissions process. In addition, a special scholarship program available only to students who are members of one of three different ethnic minority groups was continued for undergraduate students of the university (Schmidt, 2007). When UCLA initiated a holistic system in 2006 for use in the admission of undergraduate students, that institution was able to report an increase in the proportion of African American students of approximately 40% (Schmidt, 2007).

EDUCATIONAL ETHICS AND TESTING

Professional associations hold themselves to be keepers of the best traditions and practices of their fields and assume that the general public will have confidence in their work and respect for their members. To assure this continuing regard of the public, the various professional associations publish guidelines for the ethical behavior and practice of their members. In the field of educational testing, the primary associations with an interest in the issues of educational measurement have published a single document on ethics. This document is the combined effort of the American Counseling Association (ACA), the American Educational Research Association (AERA), the American Psychological Association (APA), the American Speech–Language–Hearing Association (ASHA), the National Association of School Psychologists (NASP), the National Association of Test Directors (NATD), and the National Counsel on Measurement in Education (NCME).

The following are four principles that are drawn from that document (Joint Committee on Testing Practices, 2005).[14]

1. The first of these principles for the ethical practice of testing involves communication with those taking the test. The purpose of the test and the areas that are to be measured should be fully understood by the test taker prior to the time of the test. The use of scores from the

test should be explained and the test takers should be told how long their results will be kept on file. This communication includes providing test takers with practice on similar materials to familiarize them with the mechanics of the measure. Also, the test administrator should be aware of the need for special **accommodations** that test takers may require prior to the time of the administration of the test.

2. The second area involves confidentiality. It is necessary for the test administrator to put into place procedures that ensure that the scores from individual students are never disclosed to people not having professional need for those data. The students' parents are included in the group who should have access to the test score data.

   At another level, confidentiality involves the test itself. It is critically important that test materials be stored in a secure location and never released for review by interested others.

3. The third point is that the interpretation of the test scores should be carried out in a way consistent with the guidelines provided by the test developer and publisher. This also implies that the person interpreting the scores should be trained in the process and knowledgeable of the test and its scores. Parents and students should be informed of the scores and their interpretation in a developmentally appropriate way, using understandable language. Educators who discuss score reports with parents and students should avoid educational jargon and provide clear descriptions to the parents and students. This includes the process used by the various agencies in setting cut scores and minimal standards for success. If there is a scoring error it should be corrected immediately and that correction carried through on all of the student's records.

4. Finally, a single score on a test should never be used to determine the placement of a student. Interpretations should always be made in conjunction with other sources of information.

A last point involves the development and selection of tests. A test or assessment should never be used for a purpose for which it was not designed and has not been standardized. The test should provide a manual documenting that the measure is valid and reliable for the tasks it is designed to accomplish. Also, the measure should provide evidence that there is no consistent gender bias or ethnic or racial group bias represented in the scores. The test should provide users with detailed directions for the test administration as well as for those who score the test.

Summary

The people of this country are investing enormous amounts of their resources in the endeavor of public education. Therefore, it is not a surprise that the public has expressed a need for accountability in education. To have accountability there must be regular assessments of educational outcomes. The most common vehicle for those assessments is through the use of batteries of paper-and-pencil format achievement tests. This accountability system has been ratcheted up under the provisions of the No Child Left Behind Act of 2002. That legislation was designed to close gaps in the average levels of achievement between groups of students. This act also furthered the use of high-stakes tests in the assessment process and required that schools make adequate yearly progress toward the goal of having all students achieving at a proficient level. These assessments are established by each state and are based on specific standards that each state has established. This legal position established by case law does not conform with the ethical principles established by the learned and professional societies that have a vested interest in educational testing programs.

Educational technology is changing the format and nature of educational assessments. Increasingly, assessment tests are administered online. The same technology is improving the communication between teachers and parents and making it increasingly possible for parents to be partners in their children's education.

Legislation and case law have provided guidance in the use of educational tests and assessments. Federal legislation ushered in a new era for children with disabilities with the passage of laws including the Individuals with Disabilities Educational Act (1997) and the Individuals with Disabilities Educational Improvement Act (2004). Also, the rights of parents to control the flow of testing data were established in the Family Educational Rights and Privacy Act of 1974. The federal courts have also shaped testing policy by approving the use of high-stakes assessments in making graduation and even grade promotion decisions. These high-stakes uses of tests and assessments are permitted even if the sanctions that are imposed are felt disproportionally by one or more of the minority groups of students.

Discussion Questions

1. How does the British experience over the 18th and 19th centuries with testing school students and awarding merit pay to teachers compare with the current reforms in American education?

2. Should parents be able to hold their children out of public education for an extra year ("academic redshirting") to give them a developmental advantage over their peers? Explain your position.

3. What arguments can be made for and against retaining children in third grade who do not achieve a score of proficient (pass) on the state-mandated high-stakes tests? What do you believe should be done with low-performing children on the state tests?

4. Should the 50 states be permitted to replace the use of standardized tests composed of multiple choice questions with a more open-ended form of assessment (i.e., portfolio assessments)? Explain your position on this issue.

5. Should the business community have the ability to initiate educational reforms in the public schools? What advantages and disadvantages are there to having business leaders and entrepreneurs set goals and create priorities for educational reform?

6. What specific procedures should a state department of education take to standardize how its many school districts count the number of students who have dropped out of school?

7. In the selection of students for special programs, and in college admission, should educators take specific steps to ensure a proportional ethnic/racial mix in the student body? If you feel that diversity is an appropriate goal to work toward, how can this be achieved within current case law as adjudicated?

8. Check with your local school system and ask to see a copy of its written guidelines for the maintenance and distribution of student test data. After reviewing that policy, determine if it seems to meet the requirements under the Buckley Amendment.

Student Study Site

Educational Assessment on the Web

Log on to the Web-based student study site at www.sagepub.com/wrightstudy for additional Web sources and study resources.

NOTES

1. The first sophisticated educational testing system emerged in Great Britain. The British system reflecting a new nationalism started in 1710, just three years after the Crowns of England and Scotland were united into one United Kingdom. That testing program assessed students against national educational standards in reading, writing, and arithmetic. By the 1860s, teachers throughout Great Britain were even paid on the basis of student test scores, a system that lasted for another 30 years (Troen & Boles, 2005). The result was the truncation of the curriculum, and instruction focused on only those three core areas included on the test, the famous three R's. It also brought about the demoralization of the teaching profession and widespread cheating and corruption.

2. A number of terms are used throughout this book and have both vernacular and technical meanings. One is *evaluation*, a process of judging or making a decision based on observations and/or measurements; another is *measurement*, a method or device used to assign a numerical value to a characteristic of people or objects; *assessment* is a broad term encompassing all the methods employed to gain information about a person or object, including tests and other measures; and finally **test**, a word describing on organized task or series of tasks employed to represent and demonstrate knowledge, a skill, or a trait of an individual.

3. Many of the Regents examinations from the past 50 years can be seen at www.nysl.nysed.gov/regentsexams.htm.

4. In 2006 at total of 22,873 public and charter schools failed to make Adequate Yearly Progress (AYP; Packer, 2006).

5. The states that require a score of proficient on the state's assessment to be promoted to the next grade include Delaware, Florida, Georgia, Louisiana, North Carolina, Texas, and Wisconsin.

6. Bowing to parent pressures, several states reconsidered their lack of educationally challenging programs for gifted students (Samuels, 2007).

7. This did away with the notorious case law set by the Supreme Court in 1896 known as *Plessy v. Ferguson,* which had permitted states and local governmental units to provide "separate but equal" facilities, schools, and programs for identified racial groups. This court decision legalized the policy of American apartheid.

8. A subsequent exception was in Virginia, where the Virginia Military Institute (V.M.I.), a public college, fought against the admission of women students (*United States v. Virginia et al.,* and *Virginia et al. v. the United States,* 94-1941 & 94-2107, § 64 U.S.L.W. 4638 [1996]). In August of 1997, following the decision of the U. S. Supreme Court (7–1), V.M.I. enrolled 30 freshman women.

9. There are a number of public schools that are designated for the most talented and/or mentally gifted students in the country. Many of these "admission by testing" and highly specialized schools are located in urban centers. They include

Lowell High School, San Francisco; Boston Latin High School; Eastern Sierra Academy, Bridgeport, California; Philadelphia's Central High School; Dallas School for the Talented and Gifted; Bronx High School for the Sciences; Buffalo's (NY) Honors High School; Bloomfield Hills, Michigan's, International Academy; and Alexander W. Dreyfoos School of the Arts, West Palm Beach.

10. There is no evidence that a degree from a highly selective or elite college is related to the level of success experienced by the graduate later in life. More critical are the factors of motivation, ability, and personal desire (Easterbrook, 2004).

11. The administration of President George W. Bush was at the forefront in the fight against any consideration of race or ethnicity in admissions decisions. Critics of the administration have raised the issue of the provisions of the No Child Left Behind Act, which require performance assessments that are tabulated and reported by race when those data are never permitted for use in the admission process (Gershberg & Hamilton, 2007).

12. Allan Bakke went to the Medical School at the University of California, Davis, and eventually became a respected anesthesiologist in Minnesota.

13. Following the Grutter decision, in 2006 the American Bar Association began requiring all law schools in the United States to demonstrate concrete steps toward developing student bodies, faculties, and staffs that are racially and ethnically diverse. In 2006, Jennifer Gratz, a plaintiff in the *Gratz v. Bollinger* case, led a statewide drive in Michigan to pass Proposition 2 outlawing all forms of affirmative action in that state. The measure passed on November 7, 2006. As written, the new law prevents any consideration of ethnicity in admission to any publically supported program, school, college, or professional and/or graduate school. This law stands in opposition to the admission policies required for accreditation of various professional programs (e.g., law).

14. The ethical principles for classroom-level testing by teachers are similar to those for large-scale assessment tests. Those issues are presented in Chapters 6 and 7, which focus on the use of high-stakes measures and other standardized measurements in the schools.

Chapter 2

HISTORY OF TESTING IN AMERICAN EDUCATION

History repeats itself. That's one of the things wrong with history.

—Clarence Darrow

Issues and Themes

The American testing movement is one product of 19th-century European social science. The impetus came from the laboratories of Wilhelm Wundt at the University of Leipzig and Sir Francis Galton at University College London. Nineteenth-century Americans were pragmatic innovators, and the scientific method brought from Germany and England was readymade to support the exponentially rapid development of educational and psychological testing.

The scientific study of children in the United States began in the 1880s at Clark University under the direction of G. Stanley Hall. His students went on to become the originators of developmental assessments, intelligence measures, and norm-referenced achievement tests in the United States. The driving force behind this movement was an unquestioning belief in the primacy of genetics in producing all individual differences.

As the 20th century began, the scientific management model widely used in American industry was brought to the schools. Testing provided the new breed of educational manager with a "scientific" measuring device to classify, group, and track children.

The first serious assault on this testing ethos came in the form of a curious observation by John Cannell, who noted how all 50 states were above average on norm-referenced achievement tests. He coined the term "Lake Woebegon effect" to describe this observation. This sobriquet was borrowed from humorist Garrison Keillor's mythical hometown where "all the children are above average."

As one generation of norm-referenced measures was displaced, the states developed a new generation of minimum competency tests. These were displaced by "standards-based assessments." The driving force behind testing today is the No Child Left Behind Act (2002).

Learning Objectives

By reading and studying this chapter you should develop the competency to

- Explain the impact of the research methods developed by Wundt and Galton on American psychologists and educators.
- Describe the connection between the writings of Darwin and the belief of American psychologists in the primacy of genetics.
- Explain how the First World War brought about a new generation of mental-ability tests.
- Discuss the connection between the testing of army recruits and grouping and tracking in the schools.
- Describe how the Cold War changed the nation's views of talented and gifted students.
- List the recommendations that the National Commission on Excellence in Education made that became part of the No Child Left Behind Act.
- Describe the differences between the testing provisions of the Educate America Act and those of the No Child Left Behind Act.
- Discuss the major provisions of the No Child Left Behind Act as they relate to testing programs.

SCIENTIFIC MEASUREMENT AND RACISM

European Connection

The course of American psychology and the educational testing movement in this country was greatly influenced by two 19th-century European figures. One was Wilhelm Wundt, a professor at Leipzig University, who established the principles of detailed scientific observation and new rules for experimental research in psychology. The other was a wealthy English dilettante, Sir Francis Galton, who brought statistics to the study of individual differences.

Case in Point (2a)

The century and a half that testing has been scientifically studied and applied in Western Europe and the United States is but a drop in the bucket when compared with the elaborate testing programs of ancient China. The first large-scale testing program was a civil service examination initiated over 4,000 years ago during the Shang dynasty of ancient China. By the time of the Ming dynasty (circa C.E.1368),[1] the testing program was highly structured, tightly organized, and very sophisticated. The examinations consisted of a battery of tests including civil law, military affairs, tax and revenue accounting, agriculture, and geography. Testing was done at local test centers, and each test taker worked independently in a private booth. Those test takers scoring well went on to two more rounds of examinations, first at the provincial capital and eventually at the court of the emperor. Those testing highest were then eligible for high office in the government (Higgins & Zheng, 2002).

For more information, see "Considerations on Point" at www.sagepub.com/wrightstudy

---

Galton, a cousin of Charles Darwin, was greatly influenced by the publication of Darwin's *Origin of the Species by Means of Natural Selection* (1859). This acclaimed work turned Galton's focus to the study of the how the laws of heredity affect the development of mental ability. This approach to the study of individual differences was a major "change of sea" during the 19th century. The dominant belief during the Victorian era was that all people are endowed at birth with approximately equal abilities, and any change in circumstance through life was a function of hard work and diligent effort.

Case in Point (2b)

The belief in the inheritance of intelligence is central to one being a hereditarian. Hereditarian beliefs dominated American psychology and social science for over 100 years. The American social scientists were following a research paradigm that assumed that the model for inheritance as presented by Charles Darwin applied to mental ability.

For more information, see "Considerations on Point" at www.sagepub.com/wrightstudy

The first published research into a genetic basis for high levels of intelligence was presented by Sir Francis Galton (1869) in his text *Hereditary Genius: An Inquiry Into Its Laws and Consequences*. His research involved only men, most of whom were British. The sample consisted of justices, hereditary peers of the British Empire, military commanders, divines, graduates of Cambridge University, leading men of the arts and sciences, oarsmen, and wrestlers. The last two groups were added to provide examples of men who rely on their strength instead of intellect. Galton selected 18 oarsman and 46 prize-winning wrestlers for this comparison sample. All together his sample involved a total of 516 men, over 100 of which were British judges. The personal history of each man was reviewed by examination of biographies and dictionaries of eminent men of Great Britain. Using those data sources, Galton then divided his sample by "ability." The sample was divided into one of five levels of ability based on Galton's reading of each man's "natural gifts" and "reputation." The male ancestors of each subject were then traced, and Galton found that each genius of his era (as defined on Galton's scale of natural gifts and reputation) were the scions of previous generations of eminent men. He concluded that greatness is the product of inherited natural ability, *res ipsa loquitur.*

American Science

Galton's fame in Great Britain was matched in the United States and seen in the curriculum of the new graduate programs in this country. His theory of an inherited core, or **general factor**, to all mental abilities greatly influenced American test developers and social scientists.

Two other important players in all this were also British scholars, Charles Spearman and Karl Pearson.[2] They provided the mathematical models that were used to construct the new mental tests. They gave methods of statistical analysis to the theorists that were used to document the notion of a single core factor of inherited mental ability.

One of the most influential American psychologists of this early era was James McKeen Cattell, who left the United States to study with both Wundt and Galton (Boeree, 1999–2000). While in London, he became fascinated with the application of statistical methods to the study of individual differences. He also saw the logic of applying the "scientific use of statistics" in support of an American eugenics movement, which had its start in England by Sir Francis Galton.

On returning to America, Cattell set up the graduate program in experimental psychology at Columbia University. In 1917 he was forced to resign from that post after taking an unpopular public position opposing the use of drafted soldiers to fight in World War I. On leaving Columbia he went on to establish the Psychological Corporation, a test publisher that is still a major player in the test market.

The American Eugenics Society (AES) flourished during the first third of the 20th century. Its role was, among other things, to teach "race hygiene, race biology and the advantages and dangers of race crossing."[3] It also sought to promote as a prophylactic task for public health agencies the prevention of the mentally defective from being parents. The AES also sponsored contests that celebrated racial quality, such as "Better Baby Contests" (see Photo 2.1).

To learn more about the eugenics movement in the United States see www.eugenicsarchive.org/eugenics/list_topics.pl. [4]

Photo 2.1   Better Baby Contests Were Conducted by Eugenics Organizations to Celebrate Quality Human Genetic Examples

SOURCE: Taken by Jasper G. Ewing Sr., circa 1910. Reprinted with permission from Jasper Ewing and Sons, Inc.

The "golden age of testing" in the United States had much to do with one man, G. Stanley Hall. Like other young American scholars, Hall also studied with Wundt and read the works of Galton. Hall's primary area of interest was in the new field of child development. His theoretical framework assumed that child growth and development was genetically driven and occurred in predictable stages. This variation on the Darwinian (1877) model was passed on to his graduate students at Clark University.[5] (See www.clarku.edu/aboutclark/history.cfm.)

Hall's research in child development focused primarily on the adolescent years. He advocated for a change in American high schools away from the single focus on classical languages and a college preparatory curricula. G. Stanley Hall espoused the notion that high schools should be designed for all adolescents, not just those headed toward college.

THE NEXT GENERATION

Child Study Movement

The research framework based on a genetic model for child development became the benchmark for a generation of child psychologists from Clark University. One of these men was Arnold L. Gesell. In 1911 he began a career at Yale University, where he became the director of the Clinic of Child Development. For over 40 years he collected normative data and published the most widely read reports and texts on child development of that era. Parents and educators turned to his books for advice and benchmarks for comparison with other children. In 1928 he used these data to publish the Gesell Developmental Schedules. This instrument provided educators and pediatricians with a valuable tool to chart the growth and development of children. Its deficiency was that it was based on data collected from an all White, middle-class population. Most of the subjects in Gesell's studies were the children of the faculty and graduate students of Yale University. This was not exactly a population with a high degree of diversity, and it certainly did not represent the general population of the nation.

One area in which the Gesell Developmental Schedule had a significant impact was with child adoption. Gesell championed the use of testing to screen out of the adoption-pool children who were in some way "defective." He and his staff certified for adoption only children who were measured and found to be normal on his screening test. By 1939 the Clinic at Yale had assessed over 1,500 infants and young children who were put up for adoption (see Photo 2.2). Of these, 90% were found to be in fine fettle and ready for adoption (Herman, 2002, 2005).

Photo 2.2   Professor Gesell Interviewing a Child

SOURCE: Yale University, Harvey Cushing/John Hay Whitney Medical Library.

Readiness

An important contribution of the research of Arnold Gesell was in the area of school **readiness**. In 1929 Gesell and Thompson published research with identical twins demonstrating that learning proceeds most efficaciously when the child has reached a maturation level equal to the learning task. In other words, they were the first to use the term *readiness* and to encourage educators and parents to set learning expectations to the child's developmental level. Today the Gesell School Readiness Test is still used for kindergarten admission screening. This is done in spite of the criticism that the test norms exhibit a middle-class bias (Bradley, 1985).[6]

Mental Ability

The development of the intelligence test is the legacy of another of Hall's students, Lewis M. Terman. He must be credited for planting the term *IQ* in the American vocabulary (Leslie, 2000). In 1910, after five years as a high school principal, Terman became a member of the education faculty of Stanford University. His first order of business was to revise the Binet scales developed by Simon and Binet in Paris five years earlier. That scale by Binet and Simon was a collection of problems and tasks that were sequenced from easy to difficult. The point in the scale where a sample of children of a particular age had a hard time with the test and could not solve the problems was noted. That age, for the children who had difficulty with the test items, became the "**mental age**." This "mental age" was simply a point on the list of tasks and questions where children at one particular age faltered. The mental age was then associated with that point in the sequence of items. Later, when other children were tested with the scale, the point where they experienced failure was referred to as being their mental age.

The Americanization of that test did more than just translate it into American English. The new test, the Stanford Revision and Extension of the Binet–Simon Scale (Terman, 1916), was a major transformation of the original scale. It was changed from being a way to identify children who would need extra help in school into a core measure of a genetically determined general level of mental ability possessed by individuals. Terman's design for this measure was based on the concept that human intelligence is composed of a single general core of mental ability.

Terman's new measure of intelligence was the measurement device that the new breed of educational managers needed to track students and to establish ability groups at all grade levels. By the 1920s, children were routinely administered tests of mental ability. These data combined with teacher recommendations were used to divide students into classes of similar levels of ability—homogenous grouping. This idea of ability grouping was believed to be the most efficient method for teaching, and it persisted as the dominant approach to instruction until the 1980s. Research on the efficacy of grouping by ability has shown that its effect is minimal or small at best. Only the high-ability classes were shown to benefit from this form of grouping, and then only when the curriculum was modified to match the abilities and specialized needs of the most able learners (Kulik & Kulik, 1992).

A more insidious practice of that era involved tracking children by their measured ability levels. By this system, students were divided into several ability groups on the basis of a measure of mental ability. Those in the upper ability track were enrolled in college preparatory courses, while students in the lowest, general track were provided with a less academically challenging curriculum to follow.

Both of these practices have fallen into disuse. The National Association of School Psychologists (NASP) has published a policy endorsing heterogeneous grouping with classrooms made up of children of all ability levels (NASP, 2005).

Study of the Gifted

Academically talented children were a major focus of Terman's research at Stanford. In 1928, Terman used surveys of teachers and principals to identify "gifted" children and young adults. After testing, he identified a sample of 1,528 subjects with high IQ scores, who ranged in age between 3 and 28 (Leslie, 2000). These people and their families were studied extensively. This long-term study of the gifted, which began in 1928, was still ongoing in 2000. By then, Terman had been dead for 44 years, and the sample was down to only 200 survivors from the original sample. The sample used by Terman and the data his team collected are badly flawed but still provide a rich story of the lives of academically talented people.[7] Today, educational programs for the academically talented are one product of the research by Terman.

Meritocracy in America

Lewis Terman believed in an America run as a meritocracy, where the brightest people would be in positions of responsibility and power. At the other extreme, he like other hereditarians believed in the link between criminal behavior and mental ability. Terman assumed that "feebleminded" women were likely to become prostitutes and "feebleminded" men were likely thugs and thieves (Gould, 1996).

This belief in a ruling class of the most meritorious is not a new one for the United States. In 1813, the author of our Declaration of Independence, Thomas Jefferson, wrote in a letter to another founding father, John Adams,

The natural aristocracy I consider as the most precious gift on nature for the instruction, the trusts, and government of society. And indeed

it would have been inconsistent in creation to have formed man for the social state, and not to have provided virtue and wisdom enough to manage the concerns of the society. May we not even say that that form of government is the best which provides the most effectually for a pure selection of these natural aristoi into the offices of government?

SINGLE-FACTOR MODELS

Charles Spearman

A mathematical model demonstrating a single core factor of intelligence was first presented by Charles Spearman at University College London in

"Meritocracy worked for my grandfather, it worked for my father, and it's working for me."

Figure 2.1   "Meritocracy Worked for My Grandfather . . ."

1904 (Spearman, 1904, 1939). Spearman's work was accomplished by employing a new mathematical approach: principal component factor analysis. Spearman knew that whenever a collection of mental tests is taken by a group of subjects there will be a degree of interrelatedness among those tests. By analyzing the correlations among a large number of ability measures administered to many subjects, he found that there exists a central factor, or central axis, that can be used to link them all. This central factor is referred to as being a latent component of the data. This reflects the fact that mathematically derived factors are not usually intuitively evident. The mathematically derived central factor from mental tests was assumed by Spearman to be the principal factor (general factor, or "g") of all human intelligence. This belief in a general factor of mental ability became a common theme in the writings of British psychologists for most of the 20th century (Vernon, 1961).

This principal factor could not account for all the relationships found within the full matrix of correlations from the mental tests. This led Spearman to propose that small sub-factors of ability also existed, which he labeled specific factors (see Figure 2.2). He proposed that these specific factors were like small engines that could perform a specific task, and the general factor was the source of all mental energy for those engines.

Even with the specific factors, Spearman's model still needed to explain more complex mental skills, such as verbal ability. Therefore, in addition to the specific factors, Spearman proposed the existence of several group factors. These interrelated skills (specific factors) work in association to produce a more complex ability. An example of this is the dimension known as "mathematical reasoning." He proposed that this factor includes several specific factors, including computation ability, problem solving, and abstract reasoning. Together they add up to another more complex mental ability: mathematics reasoning.

Cyril Burt

The notion of a single central factor to intelligence made the argument that it is an inherited trait easier to support. The linkage between the general factor of mental ability and human genetics was made by Cyril Burt (1955, 1958), another professor at University College London.[8] This was done using factor analytic mathematics along with genetics-based studies of the mental ability of twins. In Burt's work, the estimation of about 70% of the variance produced by individual differences in measured levels of intelligence is inherited. From that point, it is a short step to describing all group differences in measured levels of IQ as being the product of genetic differences between ethnic and racial groups (see Table 2.1 on page 53).

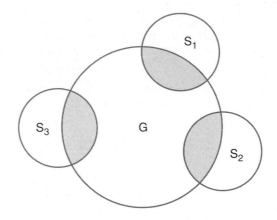

General Factor "G" and Group (Specific) Factors "S"

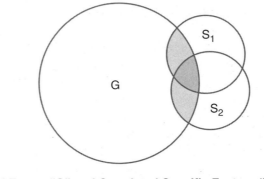

General Factor "G" and Correlated Specific Factors "S"

Figure 2.2   Spearman's Model Using Venn Diagrams

First IQ Tests

World War I provided an opportunity for another graduate of Clark to field test the idea of an American meritocracy. Henry H. Goddard worked as a member of a small select committee chaired by Harvard professor Lieutenant Colonel Robert M. Yerkes. When America entered the war in April of 1917, Robert Yerkes was the incumbent president of the American Psychological Association. He made it his task to convince the Wilson administration of the value of mental testing with all of the American troops. This led to his being given a temporary officer's commission and appointment as the chair of the Committee on the Psychological Examination of Recruits. The other members of this committee were selected by Yerkes and were all

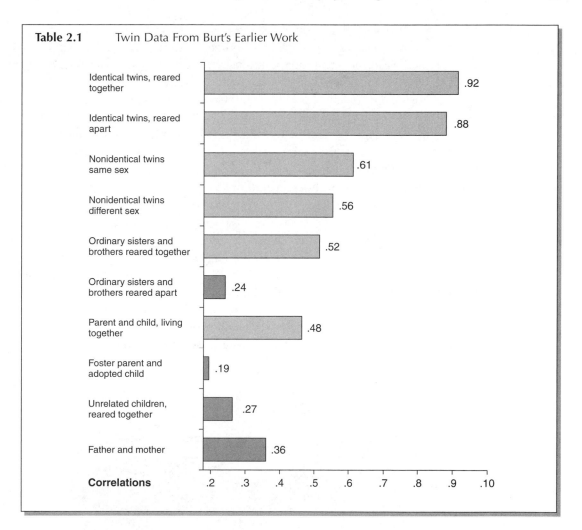

Table 2.1   Twin Data From Burt's Earlier Work

Category	Correlation
Identical twins, reared together	.92
Identical twins, reared apart	.88
Nonidentical twins same sex	.61
Nonidentical twins different sex	.56
Ordinary sisters and brothers reared together	.52
Ordinary sisters and brothers reared apart	.24
Parent and child, living together	.48
Foster parent and adopted child	.19
Unrelated children, reared together	.27
Father and mother	.36

Correlations   .2   .3   .4   .5   .6   .7   .8   .9   .10

psychologists holding strong beliefs that mental ability was a single factor that was inherited. These psychologists are therefore described as being hereditarians. Recent examples of theorists supporting this position include Richard Herrnstein and Charles Murray (1994) and Arthur Jensen (1999).

This committee then designed the first group-administered, paper-and-pencil tests of general intelligence: **Army Alpha** and **Army Beta**. The format for the test, multiple choice questions, was the idea of one of Terman's graduate students, Arthur S. Otis (Ballantyne, 2002). The Alpha was a written test requiring the subject to answer a number of orally read items, solve analogy problems, respond to vocabulary items, and solve arithmetic number series problems. When an Army recruit "failed" the test, he was retested with the "nonverbal" version, the Beta. Among other tasks, the Beta involved maze tasks, digit symbol substitution, picture completion, and geometrical construction puzzles. If he failed again, he was tested individually with the Stanford Revision of the Binet–Simon Scale. The Army tests were assumed by the authoring committee to measure the general factor of inherited intelligence (see Photo 2.3).

The test was administered to almost 2 million young men by 1919. High-scoring recruits were sent on to officer training school. Low-scoring recruits were given low-skilled jobs in the infantry battalions (see Photo 2.4). Through the military, these psychologists of Yerkes' committee were able to put their ideas of a **meritocracy** into practice.

For a critical analysis of these tests, see www.holah.karoo.net/gould study.htm.

Henry Goddard also introduced the use of measures of intelligence with the people arriving at the Ellis Island Immigration Center. Using an intelligence test, he set arbitrary standards that denied many people admission into the United States and sent thousands of immigrants back to their homelands (see Table 2.2). The research and writings of Goddard, Yerkes, and Terman were instrumental in the restrictive immigration policy passed into law in 1924, the Immigration Restriction Act (Johnson–Reed Act, 1924). This act reduced the

Photo 2.3   Handscoring Examination Alpha at Camp Lee, 1917. A distinctive feature of the group examination designed for Army use was that it could be scored by the use of objective keys.

SOURCE: Courtesy U.S. Army.

Photo 2.4   Recruits Taking an Examination at Camp Lee

SOURCE: U.S. Signal Corps #11-SC-386, in the National Archives.

number of people who could immigrate to the United States from southern Europe and barred immigration from Asian nations. When signing the act into law, President Calvin Coolidge said, "America must be kept American." The restrictions of this immigration policy weren't revised until 1952.

Between Wars

By 1920, American public schools were world leaders in the use of standardized tests. Administrators were routinely taught that the letter grades and student evaluations made by their teachers were not trustworthy.

> The mark assigned by the teacher is also dependent upon her standards as to what should be required of a class, her judgment as to the comparative importance of various points, and her conception as to the worth of various types of answers. In spite of the best of intentions the mark may be influenced somewhat by her mood at the time, and perhaps toward the boy in question. In contrast the score which a boy obtains on a modern "test" is always fair and impartial, and uninfluenced by the special factors just mentioned; the score is thoroughly objective. (Pressey & Pressey, 1923, p.15)

BOX 2.1

Instructions and Items From Examination A, Form A,

U.S. Army, 1917

TEST 1

This test was administered orally. Diagrams for the first three items follow.

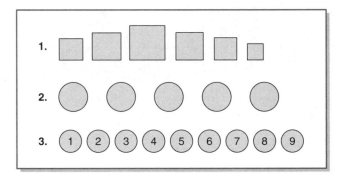

Instructions given by the examiner were:

1. "Attention! 'Attention' always means 'Pencils up!' Look at 1. When I say 'Go' (but not before), make a cross in the largest square—GO!" (Allow not over 3 seconds.)
2. "Attention! Look at 2. When I say 'Go' make a cross in the first circle and also a figure 1 in the third circle—GO!" (Allow not over 5 seconds.)
3. "Attention! Look at 3. When I say 'Go' draw a line from circle I to circle 4 that will pass *above* circle 2 and *below* circle 3—GO!" (Allow not over 5 seconds.)

TEST 2

Test 2, *Memory Span,* was also administered orally. Instructions to the examiner were as follows:
    Read the numbers (next page) in this text very distinctly at the rate of 1 digit per second, taking special care to avoid grouping or accenting. Allow not over 10 seconds for writing 4, 5, and 6 digit numbers. Allow not over 15 seconds for writing 7, 8, and 9 digit numbers. Proceed with the numbers of Form A (or B, etc.), giving the two 3-digit numbers, the two 4-digit numbers, the two 5-digit numbers, and so on through the two 9-digit numbers. Announce before each set the number of digits and the number of the set. Thus, begin by saying:
    "Attention! Look at the directions while I read them. 'This is a test to see how many figures you can remember and write down after they are spoken. In the first row of empty squares write the first set of figures you hear, as shown in the samples; in the second row write the second set you hear, and so on.'"
    "In this test I shall not say 'Go,' but you are to keep your pencils raised until after I have read the whole set of figures.

"Attention!" (Hold up the hand as an example.) "Keep pencils up until I am through reading. Three figures, first set, 1 3 5." (Drop hand. Allow not over 10 seconds.)

"Attention!" (Be sure that every pencil is up.) "Three figures, second set, 6 4 1." (Drop hand. Allow not over 10 seconds.)

"Attention! Four figures, first set, 2 8 6 1."

"Attention! Four figures, second set, 5 3 9 4."

From his booklet the examinee could read instructions as given by the examiner orally:

"This is a test to see how many figures you can remember and write down after they are spoken. In the first row of empty squares write the first set of figures you hear, as shown in the samples; in the second row write the second set you hear; and so on."

Diagrams for samples, three figures and four figures are given below.

Sample one	4 | 7 | 5
Sample two	8 | 1 | 4
Three figures: { First set	☐ ☐ ☐
Second set	☐ ☐ ☐
Four figures: { First set	☐ ☐ ☐ ☐
Second set	☐ ☐ ☐ ☐

Directions for Tests 3 through 10 were read aloud by the examiner as the examinees looked at them. The examiner then said "Ready-GO!" and, after the time allowed was over, "STOP! Turn over the page to Test 4" (or whatever the number of the next test might be).

Directions and a few items of each of these tests follow:

TEST 3

The words

MORNING THE RISES EVERY SUN

in that order don't make a sentence; but they would make a sentence if put in the right order:

THE SUN RISES EVERY MORNING

and this statement is true.

Again, the words

ANIMAL A IS THE RARE DOG

would make a sentence if put in the order:

THE DOG IS A RARE ANIMAL

but this statement is false.

(Continued)

BOX 2.1 (Continued)

Below are twenty mixed up sentences. Some of them are true and some are false. When I say "go," take these sentences one at a time. Decide what each sentence *would* say if the words were straightened out, but don't write them yourself. Then, if what it would say is true, draw a line under the word "true"; if what it would say is false, draw a line under the word "false." If you cannot be sure, guess. The two samples are already marked as they should be. Begin with No. 1 and work right down the page until time is called.

SAMPLES { morning the rises every sun _____ <u>true</u>—false
{ animal a is the rare dog _____ true—<u>false</u>

1. wood guns of made are _____ true—false 1
2. people are many candy of fond _____ true—false 2
3. war in are useful airplanes the _____ true—false 3

TEST 4

Get the answers to these examples as quickly as you can.
Use the side of this page to figure on if you need to.

SAMPLES { 1 How many are 5 men and 10 men? _____ Answer (15)
{ 2 If you walk 4 miles an hour for 3 hours,
      how far do you walk? _____ Answer (12)

1. How many are 30 men and 7 men? _____ Answer (   )
2. If you save $7 a month for 4 months,
   how much will you save? _____ Answer (   )
3. If 24 men are divided into squads of 8, how
   many squads will there be? _____ Answer (   )

TEST 5

Notice the sample sentence:
    People hear with the eyes ears nose mouth
    The correct word is <u>ears</u>, because it makes the truest sentence.
    In each of the sentences below, you have four choices for the last word.
    Only one of them is correct. In each sentence draw a line under the one of these four words that makes the truest sentence. If you cannot be sure, guess. The two samples are already marked as they should be.

SAMPLES { People hear with the eyes <u>ears</u> nose mouth
{ France is in <u>Europe</u> Asia Africa Australia

1. The snow comes in winter fall summer spring
2. The lungs are for seeing breathing digestion hearing
3. Milk comes from oxen cows trees vines

TEST 6

If the two words of a pair mean the same or nearly the same, draw a line under <u>same.</u> If they mean the opposite or nearly the opposite, draw a line under <u>opposite.</u> If you cannot be sure, guess. The two samples are already marked as they should be.

SAMPLES { good-bad   _____   same—<u>opposite</u>
          { little-small _____   <u>same</u>—opposite

1. empty-full _____   same—opposite
2. fall-rise _____   same—opposite
3. confess-admit _____   same—opposite

TEST 7

This is a test of common sense. Below are ten questions. Four answers are given to each question. You are to look at the answers carefully; then make a cross before the best answer to each question, as in the sample:

SAMPLE | Why do we use stoves? Because
       | ___they look well
       | ___they are black
       | _X_they keep us warm
       | ___they are made of iron

Here the third answer is the best one and is marked with a cross. Begin with No. 1 and keep on until time is called.

1. Why ought every man to be educated? Because
   ___ Roosevelt was educated
   ___ it makes a man more useful
   ___ it costs money
   ___ some educated people are wise

2. Why ought a grocer to own an automobile? Because
   ___ it looks pretty
   ___ it is useful in his business
   ___ it uses rubber tires
   ___ it saves railroad fare

3. Why is the telephone more useful than the telegraph? Because
   ___ it gets a quicker answer
   ___ it uses more miles of wire
   ___ it is a more recent invention
   ___ telephone wires can be put under ground

4. Why are war-ships painted gray? Because gray paint
   ___ is cheaper than any other color
   ___ is more durable than other colors
   ___ does not show dirt
   ___ makes the ships harder to see

(Continued)

BOX 2.1 (Continued)

TEST 8

In the lines below, each number is gotten in a certain way from the numbers coming before it. Study out what this way is in each line, and then write in the space left for it the number that should come next. The first two lines are already filled in as they should be.

SAMPLES	2,	4,	6,	8,	10,	<u>12</u>
	11,	12,	14,	15,	17,	<u>18</u>

	5,	6,	7,	8,	9,	____
	9,	11,	13,	15,	17,	____
	12,	10,	8,	6,	4,	____

TEST 9

SAMPLES
> sky—blue: grass—(grow, <u>green</u>, cut, dead)
> fish—swims: man—(boy, woman, <u>walks</u>, girl)
> day—night: white—(red, <u>black</u>, clear, pure)

In each of the lines below, the first two words have a certain relation.

Notice that relation and draw a line under the one word in the parenthesis that has that particular relation to the third word. Begin with No. 1 and mark as many sets as you can before time is called.

1. cradle—baby: stable—(horse, man, dog, cat)   _____   1
2. man—home: bird—(nest, fly, insect, tree)   _____   2
3. ear—hear: eye—(hair, blue, see, eyebrow)   _____   3

TEST 10

Draw a line under the largest number and also under the smallest number in every column on the page.

Begin Here

Samples

34	31	12	47	75	41	49	57	14	45
79	48	64	56	11	91	54	53	50	77
<u>87</u>	66	17	29	24	16	88	27	93	46
68	26	23	61	55	12	42	15	84	73
25	60	70	69	37	36	29	97	44	38
82	<u>98</u>	33	20	39	75	22	58	90	54
27	33	93	71	38	18	79	19	32	70
30	<u>23</u>	45	68	49	60	43	85	74	89
<u>19</u>	52	87	48	88	92	35	81	17	42
24	78	28	26	15	96	47	57	91	31

SOURCE: From "The history of psychological testing," by P. H. Du Bois, 1970, Boston: Allyn and Bacon. Originally from "Report of the committee of the National Research Council," by R. M. Yerkes, 1919, *Psychological Review, 26*(1), 83–149.

Table 2.2   Impact on Immigration of the Immigration Act of 1924 in Terms of Northern vs. Southern Europe

Immigration Statistics, 1920–1926				
		Country of Origin		
Year	Total Entering U.S.	Great Britain	Eastern Europe*	Italy
1920	430,001	38,471	3,913	95,145
1921	805,228	51,142	32,793	222,260
1922	309,556	25,153	12,244	40,319
1923	522,919	45,759	16,082	46,674
1924	706,896	59,490	13,173	56,246
1925	294,314	27,172	1,566	6,203
1926	304,488	25,528	1,596	8,253

SOURCE: Bureau of the Census.

The graduate programs in education encouraged administrators to trust the new standardized tests. This all played well into a cult of efficiency that saw American schools reconfigured. An architect of this movement was John Franklin Bobbitt, who rewrote the curricula of many large American city school districts. His goal was for social efficiency and the elimination of waste. To this end, children were grouped in elementary school according to their mental abilities and later tracked by the same tests in high school. Grand new high schools were built in urban areas, and districts were regionalized to facilitate the construction of larger suburban and rural schools. Along with these larger schools came the assumed efficiency of ability grouping.

The years from World War I through the 1960s were the golden era in testing. Schools evaluated all students on one or another standardized test each year. Mental ability, aptitude, and achievement were routinely evaluated in the schools. Once a child was labeled and placed into an ability group for instruction, he or she tended to stay in that track for the rest of his or her school career. Very little vertical movement was ever possible across these ability groups. This belief in the efficacy of the ability-grouping model persisted despite the fact that there never was any consistent research demonstrating an advantage for it. This vestige of an earlier era in education persists in a number of school systems today.

For more information, see "Considerations on Point" at www.sagepub.com/wrightstudy

Case in Point (2c)

The prominence of eugenics in American society from the 1910s through the end of the 1930s was reflected in the policies directing public school education. The eugenics movement was well endowed by the wealthiest of all Americans, including John Davidson Rockefeller, who is also responsible for the Rockefeller Foundation, the University of Chicago, and Rockefeller University (Marrs, 2001). Authors such as Lewis Terman at Stanford University and Leta Hollingsworth at Teacher's College, Columbia University, set the tone that resulted in tracking children on the basis of their measured level of general cognitive ability. This belief in tracking persisted into the 1970s and saw the "brightest" children encouraged to follow an academic or college preparatory curriculum and the "less able" students shunted into vocational and general studies tracks (Stoskepf, 1999).

This reliance on ability grouping for setting up classrooms was used as a backdoor method to keep segregation alive in a number of southern school districts after the 1954 *Brown v. Board of Education* decision by the Supreme Court (Kusimo, 1999). By using mental ability tests, schools were able to create classes of low-performing children, which were populated primarily by minority students.

A possible end of the gap in scores from tests of cognitive ability between ethnic groups was noted by Dickens and Flynn (2006). They noted a consistent trend between 1972 and 2002 (the last year for which data are available) toward smaller average group differences between Black and White children. This is part of a much larger trend noted by Flynn of ever-increasing average IQ scores among peoples throughout the world. Flynn found that each generation exhibits significantly higher average IQ scores than the proceeding generation (Flynn, 1987).

One possibility that can explain how the average level of mental ability has improved involves the complexity of our lives and jobs (Schooler, Mesfin, & Oates, 1999). Each generation, people are faced with ever-more-complex processes to master and skills to learn. Even our games today have high-tech requirements. All of this can result in improved cognition.

Another explanation has to do with diet. The growth of the human brain is supported by early nutrition, and the closing of the nutrition gap may also be related to the closing of the cognitive ability gap (Colom, Lluis-Font, & Andrés-Pueyo, 2005).

MULTIPLE-FACTOR MODELS

L. L. Thurstone

The link between a general factor of mental ability and its mathematical proof had to be challenged before a multiple-intelligence model could be accepted. This was done by an American, Louis L. Thurstone (1927, 1938, 1947). In developing a model that included seven primary factors of mental ability, Thurstone modified the basic computational algorithm for the analysis of mental ability.

Spearman's approach to this analysis involved drawing only one central factor from all variables used to measure mental ability. Spearman approached the task by mathematically maximizing the relation of each of the various measures to the latent factor that was central to all ability measures.

The innovation presented by Thurstone involved using a mathematical approach that divided the array of measures of mental ability into clusters of variables that share high degrees of commonality. He then calculated separate and distinct factors that were central to each of these clusters. Thurstone then labeled these new dimensions as factors or primary mental abilities.

Thurstone's original work identified seven "Primary Mental Abilities," including Verbal Comprehension (V), Word Fluency (W), Number (N), Spatial Visualization (S), Associative Memory (M), Perceptual Speed (P), and Reasoning (R); (Thurstone, 1947). A test of Primary Mental Abilities (PMA) was published in 1938, making it possible to see variations in the patterns of mental abilities of children. This system went far beyond the single IQ score available through the measures developed by Terman and Spearman. Using the PMA, educators could see where the child excelled and identify what dimensions were not areas of strength.[9] The PMA is now out of print, but it ushered in a number of other conceptualizations of multiple intelligences.

E. L. Thorndike

Most psychology students know Thorndike as a learning theorist and the father of connectionism; however, just after the First World War he explored the nature of mental functioning and ability (Catania, 1999). From his research at Columbia, Thorndike proposed that the human intellect functions across three broad dimensions: abstract intelligence, mechanical understanding, and social intelligence (Thorndike, Cobb, & Bergman, 1927). These factors were measured by a test he developed, the CAVD. This acronym stands for its four subtests: Completion, Arithmetic, Vocabulary, and Directions. While Thorndike's model involved several factors of mental ability, he held that these various mental abilities were the product of neurological bonds or connections that were rooted in the child's genetic potential and elaborated through experience and learning.

More about Edward L Thorndike can be found at the following two sites:

www.kdp.org

http://fates.cns.muskingum.edu/~psych/psycweb/history/thorndike.htm

Raymond B. Cattell

A colleague of Thorndike at Columbia University opened the door even wider to the role that environment plays in the elaboration of human intelligence. His model proposed that the core general factor of intelligence is made up of two parts, one a fluid, or genetically given factor (Gf), and the other a crystallized factor of ability (Gc), which is given structure by the environment and elaborated through learning (Cattell, 1963). The relationship between the two changes as the person moves through life. In early childhood they are similar, but the differential life experiences of individuals result in ever greater disparity between the two over time. Deterioration and disease in later phases of life can work to close this gap.

Recently, the original two-factor model was transformed into a multifactor theory of mental abilities, known as the Cattell–Horn–Carroll (CHC) taxonomy of human cognitive abilities (McGrew, 2003). This model starts with the two core abilities as in the original work of Cattell, Gf and Gc, and adds another 14 factors. This model of human mental ability is significant because it is now being used by several of the major test publishers as the theory on which their tests are based (e.g., Woodcock–Johnson, 3rd ed., from Riverside Publishing [Woodcock, McGrew, & Mather, 2001]). See www .iapsych.com/ chcdef.htm.

J. P. Guilford

It was during World War II that a U.S. Army Air Force psychologist, Col. J. P. Guilford, became concerned by the fact that over a third of the officer candidates in flight school were washing out. This was despite the fact that these officers were all tested before being admitted into the

BOX 2.2   Factors in the Cattell-Horn-Carroll Model of Human Cognitive Ability

- *Fluid Intelligence, Reasoning* *(Gf)* Deliberate mental operation directed to solving new problems. This includes both inductive and deductive reasoning, analysis and synthesis, problem solving, and concept formation.
- *Crystallized Intelligence, Knowledge* *(Gc)* Acquired knowledge derived from the culture with universal applicability. This involves verbal comprehension, oral production and communication, multiple language proficiency, and general information.
- *General Domain Specific Knowledge* *(Gkn)* Highly specialized knowledge acquired with practice and effort. This may be linked to a profession and involve technical information and complex skills, for example, the ability to diagnose and repair a car's transmission, the ability to communicate in Morse code or American Sign Language, or the clinical understanding of human feelings and emotions in a therapeutic context.
- *Visual Spatial Ability* *(Gv)* An ability to interpret, remember, and mentally transform visual images. This skill area involves seeing patterns, being able to interpret spatial relationships in both two and three dimensional space, and to visually construct meaning from incomplete images.
- *Auditory Processing* *(Ga)* Hearing meaningful sound and separating it from background noise, and the memory for sounds and sound patterns are part of this area. The ability to make musical judgments and discriminations are part of this area.
- *Short-Term Memory* *(Gsm)* The ability to remember immediate facts or numbers for a short period of time, or the immediate recall of detail.
- *Long-Term Memory & Retrieval* *(Glr)* The storage and consolidation of information into a long term storage system. The framework and rules that provide structure to memory are a part of this ability. Ultimately, this ability involves the retrieval and reproduction of what was stored.
- *Cognitive Processing Speed* *(Gs)* Ability to rapidly perform a basic cognitive skill that was over-learned. This includes the coding of information, data entry, and pattern recognition. The speed of reasoning and reading speed are also a part of this ability.
- *Quantitative Knowledge* *(Gq)* This area includes the stored knowledge of mathematics processes and systems. This is needed before it is possible to solve mathematics problems *(Gf)*.
- *Decision/Reaction Time* *(Gf)* The latency between presentation of simple stimuli and the threshold of reaction. This all takes place in less than a second in time.
- *Psychomotor Speed* *(Gps)* This is the ability to smoothly and rapidly move the body (parts or as a whole) rapidly and on target. Writing speed and the speed of articulation are part of this area.
- *Psychomotor Abilities* *(Gp)* Dexterity, body equilibrium and coordination are components of this ability. The ability involves the skills needed to be successful in most sports and competitions.
- *Kinesthetic Abilities* *(Gk)* Ability involves receiving and interpreting sensory information and controlling body movement based in that input.
- *Tactile Abilities* *(Gh)* Abilities in this area involve the ability to interpret information through physical touch.
- *Olfactory Ability* *(Go)* The ability to remember and identify various odors.

SOURCE: Adapted from "Cattell-Horn-Carroll Theory of Cognitive Abilities: Past, Present, and Future" by K. S. McGrew, 2003, Cattell-Horn-Carroll definition project, Institute of Applied Psychometrics. Reprinted with permission from K. S. McGrew.

flight training program and were found to have high levels of general intelligence. Guilford's research identified eight specific abilities that were needed for pilots and bombardiers to be successful, and these were not part of standard IQ tests. From this start, Guilford developed a life-long research interest in developing a structural model of the human intellect. His original flying officer selection test evolved into today's Air Force Officer Qualifying Test (AFOQT), used today as the admissions test for college students wishing to join the Air Force Reserve Officer Training program.

After the war, and while at the University of Southern California, he identified three universal dimensions for all mental abilities, operations, contents, and products (Guilford, 1988). On each of these three dimensions Guilford identified a number of subcategories that, when taken together, made it possible to identify 180 unique mental abilities, each with its own operation, product, and content (see Figure 2.3). This became widely known as the SI, or structure of intellect, model. Guilford and his colleagues held the position that intelligence was teachable. With the assumption that mental ability is teachable, Guilford and his colleagues wrote an elementary school curriculum designed to help children maximize their potential on various factors of mental ability as designated in his model (Meeker & Weile, 1971). One of the dimensions (divergent thinking) identified by Guilford's model provided the first psychological measure of creativity.

> *There is no such [thing] as intelligence; one has intelligence of this or that. One must have intelligence only for what one is doing.*
>
> —Edgar Degas

Howard Gardner

Most American educators are familiar with the multiple-intelligences (MI) model proposed by Howard Gardner (1999). This is likely because the model has an intuitive appeal for educators who see the broad array of strengths and deficiencies that school children present every day. Gardner's model does not dismiss the existence of a general factor of ability; instead, it focuses on what he describes as nine unique human intelligences. Gardner describes these intelligences as evolutionary products, created over the 200-millennia history of our human species. These evolutionary products became part of our mental schema, and they make possible our efficacious interaction with the environment.

Another reason for the popularity of the MI model is that it is optimistic and allows for continual refinement and improvement by the growing child.

Guilford's Structure of the Intellect

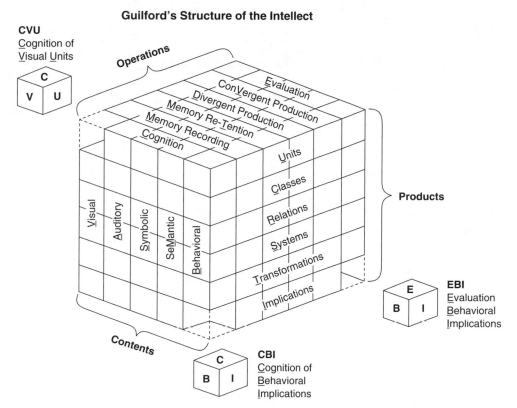

Sax, G. (1989). *Principles of educational and psychological measurement and evaluation* (3rd ed.). Belmont, CA: Wadsworth Publishing Co.

Content
- **Behavioral** – action, activities, and expressions of people
- **Figural** – sensory stimulation of receptors for color, shape, pattern, and sound
- **Semantic** – vocabulary and word meanings, verbal ideas
- **Symbolic** – letters, numbers, designs, icons, and symbols

Operations
- **Cognition** – recognition and discovery
- **Convergent production** – producing the single best solution to a problem
- **Divergent production** – producing a variety of ideas and useful solutions to problems
- **Evaluation** – judging the worth of intellectual contents

Products
- **Classes** – superordinate concepts (Children = Girls + Boys)
- **Implication** – inferring from discrete pieces of information
- **Relations** – connections and linkages between concepts
- **Systems** – an ordering and the classification of relations
- **Transformation** – altering or restructuring intellectual contents
- **Units** – individual datum, a single number, letter, or word

Figure 2.3   A Depiction of Guilford's Three-Dimensional SI Model

SOURCE: From *Principles of educational and psychological measurement and evaluation* (4th ed.), by G. Sax, 1997. Reprinted with permission of Wadsworth, a division of Thomson Learning: www.thomsonrights.com.

BOX 2.3

Howard Gardner's Multiple Intelligences

Domain of Intelligence	Related Abilities and Skills
1. Linguistic	Vocabulary readings and language skills
2. Logical-mathematical	Number and mathematics skills, logical problem solving
3. Spatial	Three dimensional thinking, perspective and painters knowledge
4. Bodily-kinesthetic	Body position and movement in space, grace and coordination
5. Musical	Musical skill and ability, appreciating, producing, creating
6. Interpersonal	Interpretation of feelings from others, interpersonal skills
7. Intrapersonal	Personal awareness and understanding
8. Naturalistic	Understanding of natural phenomena and environs

SOURCE: From *Extraordinary minds,* by Howard Gardner, 1997. Reprinted by permission of Basic Books, a member of Perseus Books.

Gardner's MI model is very different in this regard than a fixed intelligence, or g factor, model. Gardner's position is that no two children have the same pattern of intelligences over the nine domains, not even monozygotic twins.

Effort and instruction can improve any of the domains of intelligence; but, great levels of a particular intelligence require both a generous genetic contribution and appropriate environmental interactions. The MI model assumes that individuals all have unique abilities and therefore suggests that teachers should use multiple channels when teaching new concepts to children. For example, poetry or music may be appropriate vehicles for helping a struggling child learn mathematics. The goal for instruction should be to give each child the opportunity to learn in ways that are harmonious with his or her unique set of abilities.

A criticism of the MI model is that there is no way to measure it, that it stands as an unproven theory. Gardner has argued that this is a strength of MI, as the nine intelligences are not fixed and measurable but are evolving and are continually being developed. This ontological nature of the model precludes accurate measurement.

Other critics complain that Gardner has described talents, not intelligences. These talents have all been recognized by the major theorists of the past century. Also, a number of Gardner's "intelligences" are highly interrelated and are part of a common factor. This brings the debate back to whether Gardner's model simply presents us with one general factor of mental ability with several layers of specific and group factors, along with the added embellishment of a unique set of special talents. In other words, Gardner's MI model may simply be the Spearman general–specific factor model in new packaging.

Robert Sternberg

By including a number of non-scholastic "intelligences" or "talents," Gardner has opened the door to a more practical model of mental ability. This is the direction being followed by Robert Sternberg at Yale University. The three-factor model of intelligence proposed by Sternberg is reminiscent of the three-factor model first proposed 80 years ago by E. L. Thorndike. Sternberg has proposed that the question of the amount of intelligence an individual has is trivial unless that intelligence is successfully employed. However, only the individual can define what success is for him or her.

One of the three pillars of Sternberg's triarchic (three factor) model of human intelligence is "practical intelligence." This area of ability involves the contexts in which the individual acts. It expresses how well the individual relates to the external world. The growth and elaboration of intelligence was described by Sternberg as a developing expertise, linking mental ability to mental activity (Sternberg, 1999). Thus, it is an expression of the individual's ability to adapt to the circumstance and thrive in an environment. His model has no place for a race factor to group differences in ability; indeed, Sternberg has discounted the whole issue of race by describing it as a social construct (Sternberg, Grigorenko, & Kidd, 2005).

Another mental ability identified by Sternberg is "analytical intelligence." This is a factor made up of analytical and verbal skills, which is very much in line with most theories of the past 120 years. This area of ability is what is measured on most intelligence tests used in schools. The final factor of the triarchic model is "creative intelligence," which, as its name implies, is an experiential aspect of human mental ability. Creative intelligence provides direction whenever the individual responds to novel situations and stimuli. Additionally, it contains a number of aspects related to leadership and interpersonal skills. A person with high creative intelligence can see opportunity where others do not and inspire others to accept and develop these new ideas and approaches. The triarchic model has been adopted by a number of commercial enterprises as a training tool for corporate leaders and sales managers.

Unfortunately, Sternberg has not published any of his experimental measures of the triarchic abilities. Even so, the model provides a number of intriguing possibilities for adult educators and those enrolled in education leadership programs.

CONTEMPORARY PUBLIC SCHOOLS

Standardized Tests

Social upheaval in the United States during the late 1960s led to a brief period of flirtation with a more humane model of education. Yet, even in "open" schools, students were tested on a regular basis using the tried-and-true standardized tests (Wright, 1975).

Published achievement tests were developed by the major publishing houses and sold to public school systems as a way to verify their instructional programs and identify learning problems among individual children. These tests were based on the content of the major textbooks at the time. Tens of thousands of students were tested prior to the commercial publication of a new achievement test battery. Those students became the basis for comparison (norm group) for the test scoring system. These data from the original prepublication sample of test takers didn't change until a new edition of the test was published. This means that the data used to assign contemporary students with a score were composed of information that could have been collected 8 or even 10 years earlier. The dominant question format used with these achievement tests involved the use of multiple choice items.

Once a test was administered, and the test data returned to the schools, individual scores were posted on each child's permanent record. Arguing for consistency, the school systems used the same standardized test year after year. This policy facilitated year-to-year comparisons by the school districts; however, by following this course, teachers became very familiar with what was being asked of their students on the achievement tests. Also, as the tests were purchased by the school districts, they were stored in the school building for a year before they were taken out of a cupboard and used again. Thus, in most school systems these measures were available to curious educators. Average scores from these achievement tests were typically published in local newspapers. This provided a motivation for the teachers and administrators to "review the test items." This arrangement resulted in a comfortable system in which virtually every district scored above average on their standardized tests.

WINDS OF CHANGE

This cozy relationship between test publishers and educators came under scrutiny from several directions. As the states initiated mandated achievement tests, discrepancies between local scores on published achievement tests and the results on the state assessments became evident.

Nation's Report Card

A second force for change came during the administration of Lyndon Johnson. Part of President Johnson's education initiative of 1965 included a national testing program, the National Assessment of Educational Progress (NAEP, or Nation's Report Card; Elementary and Secondary Education Act, 1965). This testing program, the NAEP, broke the mold by not focusing on the achievement of individual children. Instead, it was designed to provide a national picture of our public schools and to present data on the status of American education. In 1994, the Nation's Report Card began to publish state-by-state comparisons (NAEP Authorization Act, 1993). This became a source of embarrassment for a number of low-scoring states.

Another change to the NAEP occurred during 2006–2007 when the Nation's Report Card was first used to verify the various state assessment test scores in both reading and mathematics. This modification in the use of the NAEP is one of the mandates of the No Child Left Behind Act of 2002.

Lake Woebegon

A more prosaic source of change came from a family doctor in West Virginia. This physician was surprised to read that all 55 county school districts in West Virginia were above average on nationally normed achievement tests. With a little research he found that all 50 states, and most of the nation's urban and rural school districts, also reported being "above average" on these tests. This illogical observation was named by John J. Cannell, M.D., the "Lake Woebegon effect." Humorist Garrison Keillor wrote, "The little town that time forgot. Where all the men are good looking, all the women are strong and all the children are above average" to describe his mythical hometown, Lake Woebegon, MN (Kaplan, 1992).

The national press was not amused at the possibility that the public had been misled for years by the test publishers and our school systems. The *New York Times* broke the story in February 1988, and in June of 1990 the U.S. House Oversight Committee on Testing Assessment and Evaluation held hearings on the policies of the standardized test industry (Fisk, 1988; Testing, Assessment, & Evaluation, 1990).

Test Score Gap

The great disparity between African American children and their non-minority peers on the standardized achievement tests used in the public schools was made obvious by the work of sociologist James Coleman. The Civil Rights Act of 1964 called for an analysis of the availability of equal educational opportunity by race in public educational institutions. Coleman's research involved a national sample of over 600,000 students and teachers. One outcome from his research was to focus attention on the apparent failure of inner-city public schools to provide an effective education for minority children who were living in poverty (Coleman, 1972).

A Nation at Risk

Another force for change in the test industry came like a thunderbolt in 1983 from the National Commission on Excellence in Education when it published the report "A Nation at Risk: The Imperative for Educational Reform." This commission was established by Terrell H. Bell, the secretary of education during the administration of President Reagan. It consisted of 18 members, only one of whom was a classroom teacher. There was no representation from either of the major professional associations of classroom teachers. A number of the findings of this commission foreshadowed the elements included in the No Child Left Behind Act, which became law in 2002 (P.L. 107-110). The commission's report called for rigorous examinations requiring that students demonstrate mastery of content prior to receiving a high school diploma (p. 19). Another similarity to the NCLB Act is the expressed concern with the lack of fully qualified teachers in the secondary school subjects (p. 23). And finally, the report noted that the minimum competency examinations used in 37 states at that time were lowering the standards for all children (p. 20).

From Minimum Competency to High Standards

Public schools became an increasing part of state budgets. By the 1970s, education expenditures reached 40% or more of the budget of every state. With this increase in school funding came accountability in the form of required statewide testing programs. By the middle of the 1990s, only Iowa, Nebraska, and Wyoming did not administer a statewide test.

The form that many of these mandated tests took was that of a minimum competency assessment. This system is one in which the state's educators define what minimum levels of learning are required for students to be competent in each area of achievement. This is a system that has been used for many years by the military in its training programs. It is also used in a number of professional licensing examinations covering diverse professions, including the written examinations for aircraft pilots, teacher certification, clinical psychologists, ship captains, real estate agents, and the medical boards. The minimum competency examinations developed in most states employed the tried-and-true technique of "select-type items"—mostly multiple choice questions.

It is easier to document the negative effects of **minimum competency testing** than it is to prove any advantage. This is because the minimum competency measures are so similar to all other achievement tests. Thus, any instructional effort focused on basic skills should show a change on all similar measures of those skills. The value of such findings is very limited. The fact that competency tests are highly related to other tests doesn't answer the question of whether students who are found to be competent on the test have the skills needed to actually succeed at work or in college (Marion & Sheinker, 1999).

One downside to minimum competency testing involves the increasing likelihood that marginal students will drop out of school. In addition, teachers deemphasize curricular areas not directly connected to the basic skills being tested. Logically, there is also a question raised by the very idea of instruction geared to helping all children meet a minimum level of competency.

New Goals

In 1989, increasing public concern over the state of American education was translated into political action. That year an education summit, chaired by Governor Clinton of Arkansas, was held in Williamsburg, Virginia. During this governors conference the need for educational reform was discussed and a new set of national educational goals were proposed. These became known as Goals 2000.

There were eight goals in the framework proposed at that conference. The first of the goals represented a major paradigm shift in that it proposed that all children should start school ready to learn (North Central Regional Educational Laboratory, 1993). This proposal is reminiscent of the era prior to G. Stanley Hall when all children were assumed to enter this world with roughly equal potential. Other goals included improving the high school graduation rate, the promotion of parent and community involvement in the schools, and the attainment of high levels of achievement in literacy, mathematics, modern language, social studies, and science. Concerns over school management and leadership were also addressed by the governors at this conference. These goals were incorporated into the Educate America Act (1994) and signed into law by President Clinton in March of that year.

Each state was encouraged to develop high standards for student performance and assessment systems for use in all schools. Critics have made the case that this top-down approach to the development of learning standards is not appropriate. It has been argued that standards are best developed by parents and other community members, not state bureaucracies (Richman, 2001).

During the 1990s, various professional organizations offered revised standards for student achievement in their respective disciplines. This was a first step toward a national set of learning standards. Funding for Goals 2000 ended on June 30, 2001, yet the call for higher standards continued.

To learn more about educational standards see the following:

(Math) http://standards.nctm.org/document/appendix/numb.htm

(English/Language Arts) www.ncte.org/about/over/standards/110846.htm

(Social Studies) www.socialstudies.org/standards/execsummary/

(Science) http://nap.edu/openbook/0309053269/html/1.html#pagetop

Survey research reported in 2005 demonstrated that after graduation both students who did not attend college and those who did felt that high school was too easy and they could slide by with minimal effort. Both groups reported that they would have worked harder if more were asked of them (Achieve, Inc., 2005). Two parallel findings were also reported. One was that university faculty felt incoming freshmen were poorly prepared, and the other was that employers were also unsatisfied with recent high school graduates.

No Child

A priority during the first term of the administration of President George W. Bush was a revamping of the Elementary and Secondary Education Act. The result was the **No Child Left Behind Act** of 2002, which was signed into law on January 8, 2002. The 10 titles of this act were designed to "close the achievement gap with accountability, flexibility, and choice, so that no child is left behind" (P.L. 107-110, 2002). Accountability and high standards are the hallmark of this legislation, and an emphasis on assessment testing is the vehicle that is central to documenting progress. One outcome of this has been a real boon for the test industry, where expenditures for the development of new statewide high-stakes assessments grew from $572 million in 2003 to a projected $810 million in 2008 (Olson, 2004). (See Chapter 14 for more detail.)

Three other goals of the legislation that are related to testing include closing the achievement gap between racial and ethnic groups, certifying a highly competent teaching corps, and assuring that federal funds are only spent on curricula that are supported by rigorous scientific evidence.

Regarding the first of these goals, the legislation requires that statewide test data be disaggregated and presented so that the performance of all identified groups of students can be tracked. These groups include students with disabilities, children who are English-language learners (ELL), Anglo-White students, Native American and indigenous American students (these include Hawaiian, Inuit, Planes Indians, and Polynesian children), Hispanic students, and African American students. In addition adequate yearly progress (AYP) must be evident toward the goal of having the children of all groups achieve at a proficient level on the state assessment. Thus, a major goal is having the gap in average subgroup performance closed. This is not as straightforward as it may seem. The statistical model used to determine what differences are significant across the disaggregated groups varies from state to state (Miller, 2004). Also, under the provisions of the NCLB Act, the schools and school systems can ignore any identified group if it has less than 45 members per school. This was added to the law to prevent individual children from being identified because they are in an extreme minority in their schools. This has provided a major loophole in the provisions of the law that was used by virtually all school systems. The art of hiding scores from minority and disadvantaged students was highly developed in some states, especially Wisconsin, Iowa, Connecticut, and Nebraska (Borsuk, 2006).

Despite this statistical reporting problem, it is clear that the achievement of African American children and English-language learners is below that of the both Asian and Anglo-White children (American Educational Research Association [AERA], 2004a, 2004b). This perplexing truth is evident from the first of the high-stakes tests at third grade through the mandated high school exit tests.

This achievement gap is the product of an interaction effect between the home situations of the children and the support and expectations of the schools (Barton, 2004; Ferguson, 2002). Intensive social support is one of the core elements in closing the achievement gap. Another is using the best quality of teachers with those children who are most likely to score at the lowest level. Finally, there is a need for more time to be spent on task and for the teacher contact time per child to be higher than with other groups of children who are not at-risk for failure (see Chapter 14).

All of these needs are expensive, and not all middle-class taxpayers are ready to put more resources into schools where the children who are at-risk are clustered. Indeed, most states will provide financial incentives to schools where achievement is highest and provide ways for parents to transfer children away from schools where the failure rate is high. Schools in this latter group are rarely given the extra human and fiscal resources that are needed to close the achievement gap (Cary, 2004; Education Trust–West, 2005).

The various states cannot afford to hire the teaching force that is necessary to meet the ambitious goals specified in the NCLB Act. For that reason, all 50 states have put into place "alternative channels" for reaching the teaching profession. A component of most of these programs is the use of a teacher certification test. A total of 40 states use the PRAXIS series published by ETS in the certification process. The required cut score for these tests is set by each state. Because of that flexibility, the minimum criterion score for passing the license test tends to fluctuate from state to state and from year to year within states where the market for new teachers is changing (Elliott, 1995). Alternative routes to teacher licensure are now responsible for a large portion of our teachers in rural communities, as well as the teachers working in our inner cities (see Chapter 15).

For more information on the PRAXIS test see www.ets.org/praxis/.

The use of "proven" methods for educational reform came from the federal government with the Improving America's Schools Act of 1994 (Elementary and

---

BOX 2.4   National Reading Panel's Keys to Effective Reading Instruction

The National Reading Panel working under the auspices of the Department of Health and Human Services reviewed all of the published reading research. For a published paper to be included in the analysis its authors had to have employed a rigorous scientific model. Only a small fraction of the published research met the criteria of the National Reading Panel. Of the accepted reading research the National Reading Panel identified five essential components that lead to effective instruction in reading.

- Phonemic awareness: learning to identify the sound units that make up spoken language, phonemes
- Phonics: learning to connect the phonemes to written letters and words
- Fluency: learning to read with increasing speed, becoming a good oral reader
- Vocabulary: learning new words that enrich and expand reading. Learning to translate unfamiliar words into spoken language
- Comprehension: the essence of reading, learning to attach meaning to written words through the active engagement in what being read

To read the report from the National Reading Panel see

http:/www.nichd.nih.gov/publications/nrp/report.htm

SOURCE: National Reading Panel, Institute of Child Development, U.S. government.

Secondary Education Act [ESEA]). In 1998 this theme reappeared in the Obey-Porter Act (ESEA, 1998). Title X of Obey-Porter specifies that there be "scientifically based proof" of the effectiveness of any of the funded reform programs. This call for scientific proof was carried over and expanded in the NCLB Act. Reading was the first area in which the Department of Education enforced the need for scientific evidence for curricular effectiveness.

Summary

The application of the scientific method to the study of testing, and to the measurement of children and adults, was initiated in 19th-century Western Europe. Early in the 20th century, the general population's belief in a form of social Darwinism, and the unwavering optimism of social scientists, along with their confidence in the instruments they were developing, led to an era of scientific racism. This era was characterized by the rapid development of numerous measures of mental ability and academic achievement. For the most part the authors of these measures were also leaders in the eugenics movement in the United States and helped shape public policy. The policy implications of their theoretical grounding are still felt today in public school education and the distribution of our population based on immigration.

The first dimension to be studied during the early era (19th century) of testing was human ability. A heredity-based model worked well with the single-factor theory as proposed by Charles Spearman and Sir Cyril Burt. Today the concept of multiple intelligences dominates the literature and appears in education courses at all levels.

Another product of the testing movement was the development of achievement tests. These batteries of tests were advertised as providing an unvarnished look at the strengths and weaknesses of the schools that adopted them. That ideal was easily subverted by the pressure felt by educators who knew the test scores would appear in the local newspapers. The cozy relationship between test publisher and schools ended with the publication of the observations of John J. Carroll, M. D., whimsically named the Lake Woebegon effect.

There was what appeared to be a spate of bad results reported in the press comparing our American students with those of other nations. This led first President Bill Clinton then President George W. Bush to require all states to develop learning standards and initiate a testing program to monitor progress toward achieving those learning standards. This resulted in the No Child Left Behind Act of 2002.

Discussion Questions

1. It can be argued that the AYP provisions of the No Child Left Behind Act are an attempt to address the "soft racism" implicit in the "score gap." Do you think that the NCLB Act is a positive or negative influence for poor and minority students? What evidence is there to support your position?

2. It can also be argued that the foundation for the assessment testing required by the NCLB Act has a history that can be traced to the U.S. Army recruit training centers of 1917 through 1919. Do you agree with this thesis? What evidence can you use to support that position?

3. What elements from the European revolution in social science research of the 19th century can be found in the high-stakes testing programs in the public schools of the United States today?

4. It has been argued that the last outpost of the eugenics movement in the United States is found in schools that employ ability grouping and tracking. Is that a fair characterization, or is there another position that should be taken regarding these practices? Please explain your position on this question.

5. Is there a conflict between the ethical principles for the use of tests as adopted by the professional and learned societies engaged in educational testing and the high-stakes testing requirements of the various states? Please elaborate on your position with examples.

6. What forces and school issues resulted in the "Lake Woebegon" conclusion of John J. Cannell regarding standardized achievement tests? Do you think those same forces are having an impact on the outcome of the high-stakes tests required by the NCLB Act? Please explain your answer with examples.

Student Study Site

Educational Assessment on the Web

Log on to the Web-based student study site at www.sagepub.com/wrightstudy for additional Web sources and study resources.

NOTES

1. c.e. is an abbreviation for the "Common Era" and is the scientific (i.e., non-religious) numeration for what was once referred to as *Anno Domini* or a.d. The Latin translates as "Year of our Lord." Likewise scientific literature refers to b.c.e. for Before the Common Era instead of b.c., which is an abbreviation for time before Christ.

2. British statistician Karl Pearson was also a member of the eugenics movement. In 1912 he was quoted as stating, "The right to live does not connote the right of each man to reproduce his kind. . . . As we lessen the stringency of natural selection, and more and more of the weaklings and the unfit survive, we must increase the standard, mental and physical, of parentage" (O'Connor & Robertson, 2003).

3. Modern genetic analysis of DNA structures has shown that there are minor variations in the genetic code between various identifiable populations of humans. These DNA differences have not been shown to be related to cognitive ability (Hinds, et al., 2005). Yet, even this difference is destined to disappear as the various ethnic and racial groups of this country continue to blend. Census data have shown that the mixed racial category is an increasingly popular choice on the census report form (Kasindorf & Nasser, 2001).

4. The horrific outcome of race hatred that became evident during and after World War II sealed the fate of the AES. However, this insidious concept of scientifically justified racism is alive and well in today's world. Recent examples of genocide in African nations such as Rwanda and Darfur as well as "ethnic cleansing" in the Balkans and Iraq bear testimony to the continuation of race hatred.

5. G. Stanley Hall was named the first president of Clark University in 1887. He established what was America's largest graduate program in psychology at Clark and by 1898 had personally chaired 30 of the 54 doctorates in psychology awarded anywhere in the United States.

6. The National Association for the Education of Young Children has developed a position opposed to school readiness testing. That professional society bases its argument on the point that schools need to meet the special needs of all children and that public schools cannot pick and choose which children to admit and teach. See www.naeyc.org/about/positions/pdf/PSready98.pdf.

7. The sample included only two African Americans and six Japanese. No one of Chinese or Hispanic heritage became a part of this study of the gifted.

8. Recently the veracity of research by Cyril Burt has been questioned, and the controversy still is unresolved.

9. Parts of the PMA are still used by medical professionals. Neurologists use the subtests for Spatial Visualization (V) and Perceptual Speed (P) in making differential diagnoses. The Associative Memory (M) subtest is frequently used to chart Alzheimer's patients.

PART II

THE MEANING AND QUALITY OF TEST SCORES

Not all measurements have the same levels of precision. That statement is fine because not all variables are equally precise in how they are expressed. Some variables are highly quantifiable with exact numbers, while others can only exist as named categories. For that reason, the rules for describing and summarizing data from different variables are a function of the precision of those variables.

One 18th-century mathematical tool that is integral to understanding modern test scores is the Gaussian normal distribution (aka, the "bell curve"). This probability distribution provides a format for explaining, summarizing, and comparing data between subjects and also within one subject over time. That curve is symmetric and has known parameters (limits). One way educational data frequently violate that symmetry is by having an excess of either high or low scores in a data set. This requires careful management and can limit the usefulness of the data.

When more than one variable has been measured on a group of subjects, or when one variable has been measured several times with a group of subjects, it becomes possible to statistically assess the degree of concordance between the various measures. With precise measures, this value can be expressed as an amount of correlation. When we know the concordance between two variables and we also know a person's score on one of those variables, it becomes possible to estimate how well that person would do on the other measure. This is referred to as a prediction.

Not all tests are created at an equal level of quality. One good indication for a test is if subjects earn the same or similar scores on retesting. This is an issue of reliability. Another form of reliability occurs when the measure has high internal consistency. That consistency means that all the test's items are in agreement with the test's final outcome score for each subject.

There are three approaches to documenting validity, the second aspect of test quality. Validity can be demonstrated by showing the test to have fidelity to the topic or curriculum being measured. The second approach to verifying validity is communality, a dimension related to how well the test is linked to similar measures or how accurately it can predict an outcome. There is an argument today as to whether the SAT is a good way to predict how well college freshmen will do as students. This is an issue of validity as expressed as communality. The final approach to documenting validity concerns the appropriateness of the measure being used with a group of subjects.

Chapter 3

THE MEASUREMENT AND DESCRIPTION OF VARIABLES

Statistics: The only science that enables different experts using the same figures to draw different conclusions.

—Evan Esar
American Humorist (1899–1995)

Issues and Themes

The bottom line is that variables vary. The variables used in school-based educational research have four levels of precision. Different types of arithmetic and different forms of graphic displays can be applied with each of the four. When a large amount of test data (scores) from an educational measure that was given to a general population of students are plotted along a straight line, from the lowest to the highest score, those data are likely to assume the configuration of a bell-shaped curve. We can find the center of these arrayed data by either counting to the midpoint, or by arithmetically averaging them (mean). If these scores are not distributed in a symmetric bell curve, these two points, the midpoint by count (median) and the arithmetically determined average, will not be in the same location. That condition makes it much more difficult to interpret and understand the test scores.

The spread of the scores along the straight line forming a bell curve holds the key to understanding "standardized" scores. This involves calculating the square of the amount that the typical score spreads out away from the mean (arithmetic average) of the data. This is known as variance, and it makes all standard scoring systems possible. The square root of variance provides the statistic, standard deviation, which is central in the creation of standard scores. Standard deviation can be used to convert a series of raw scores into standard scores that are based on the normal curve and easily compared with other standard scores. Standard scores are used to make it possible to compare various measures, even measures that were taken years apart. Thus, an SAT score from a student's junior year can be meaningfully compared with that student's SAT score taken during the senior year.

Covariance is the amount of common variance shared by two measures. It is reported as a coefficient of correlation and can be considered as being the extent to which the two measures are measuring the same underlying property or dimension. One application of the correlation coefficient is in the area of academic prediction. The accuracy of such predictions is linked to the size of the correlation between the predictor and criterion variables. It is possible to combine several variables into a multiple correlation (aka multiple regression, or in statistics books as ordinary least squares [OLS] regression). A multiple correlation expresses the relationship between a vector (collection) of predictor variables and one criterion variable such as academic success as a college freshman.

Learning Objectives

By reading and studying this chapter you should acquire the competency to do the following:

- Explain the four levels of measurement.
- Describe how unusual cases can affect the mean score of a data set.
- Explain the concept of variance.
- Calculate the mean and median of a data set.
- Explain the relationship of standard deviation to the Gaussian normal curve.
- Interpret various standard scores in terms of a normal distribution.
- Explain the meaning of the term *covariance*.
- Describe the similarities and differences between Pearson and Spearman correlation coefficients.

- Discuss and explain the prediction application for a correlation coefficient.
- Interpret the coefficient of determination in terms of shared variance.

VARIABLES

Not all variables are created equal; they can exist at one of four different levels of mathematical precision. Variables may be measured as continuous numbers or they may exist as a series of descriptive names. In education, as in the other social sciences, conceptual constructs all exhibit a degree of variation; thus, educational constructs are, by their very nature, variables. Variables are the central issue in all educational measurement in that they are what is being measured. Physical properties and dimensions also vary and are thereby also considered to be variables. A variable is defined as being "a symbol or word that stands for a quantity or function that may assume any or a range of values." Thus, when we measure conceptual constructs such as cognitive ability, religious affiliation, reading achievement, shyness, attention deficit disorder, and a host of other dimensions, we are measuring variables. In the physical world variables include, among others, systolic blood pressure, height, body mass index, sound intensity, gender, heart rate, vapor pressure, color, volume, Galvanic skin response, and serum oxygen level.

Ratio Scales

Some variables are measurable using a continuous mathematical scale known as a ratio scale. The ratio scale implies that the unit of measurement is a "real number" where fractions and decimals are appropriate and where a true zero point exists. These measures include most of the physical dimensions, such as volume of water needed by a school each day, the weight of the physical education teacher, the relative humidity of the air in the classrooms. When the variables are measured with continuous numbers and have a zero point, they are referred to as ratio variables. These measurements tend to be of observable dimensions and might include such variables as height, ear diameter, amount of cash in your pocket or purse, your raw scores on the Graduate Record Examination (GRE), and your serum hemoglobin count. Because these are real numbers, arithmetic procedures can be performed with them. Thus, it is possible to determine which NBA team has the tallest back-court, and it is also possible to determine if the average weight of the offensive line of the Pittsburgh Steelers is as heavy as the defensive line of the New England Patriots.

Interval Scales

A second class of measurements for variables is that which reports equal interval data. These values are created through the use of standard scores that may be drawn from a normative comparison group or even created from the data set itself. The name applied to the data reported for these variables is interval. These data have no real zero point, but the unit size of the measurement is constant. This makes it possible to do all the arithmetic processes required for statistical presentations. These variables include the Educational Testing Service (ETS) scores across the range of tests that the corporation publishes, the standard scores reported on statewide assessments, IQ scores, scores on the tests of the American College Testing program (ACT), and the standard scores reported on the state mandated high-stakes tests.

Ordinal Scales

Theoretical constructs can present more of a measurement problem. For example, "faculty rank" is a construct. The commissioned corps of officers in the Navy include ensign, lieutenant junior grade, lieutenant, lieutenant commander, commander, captain, rear admiral–lower division, rear admiral–upper division, vice admiral, and admiral of the fleet. We know they exist in an order, but they are not measurable with a mathematical system. To test this, note that if you subtract an ensign from a captain, you don't get a commander plus change. It is clear that this rank system, like many others (e.g., military rank, church hierarchy, NCAA competition level) is an ordered sequence, not a numerical system. For that reason these types of data are referred to as ordinal data.[1]

For more information, see "Considerations on Point" at www.sagepub.com/ wrightstudy

Case in Point (3a)

Ordinal scores (positions) from various scales can be compared. Consider the military, in which the Army rank of warrant officer is equivalent to the Marine Corps rank of master gunner, which is equivalent to the Navy rank of master chief. People holding one of these ranks will have a similar level of responsibility and authority to their peers in the other branches. Another example is found in academic rank. In American higher education the highest academic rank is professor, as it is in British universities. The academic ranks in American universities in descending order are professor, associate professor, assistant professor, instructor, and lecturer. The equivalent academic ranks in the traditional universities of Great Britain are professor, reader, senior lecturer, principal lecturer, and research fellow.

A commonly applied ordinal in education is grade level in school, or years of education completed. Most graduate students would be hard pressed to give a meaningful answer to the question, "How many years of schooling did you finish?" This is because this variable is an ordinal. Once again, remember our little test (a tenth grader minus a sixth grader does not equal a fourth grader). The step between being a person who drops out of school after 11th grade is only a year away from a person who is a high school graduate, but that is a very big step. It is clearly larger than the one year step between being a 10th-grade dropout and being an 11th-grade dropout.

Counting college years of education is another difficult task. Does a student who takes five years to earn a bachelor's degree have more education than a person who completes the degree in the standard four years? Does a doctoral student who takes six years to write a dissertation have five more years of college when compared to his or her peer who only took one year to write the dissertation?

Classroom teachers assign letter grades every day. Each of these grades is an ordinal datum. We know they are ordinals because they do not have a continuous numerical basis. The distance between a grade of A and a B is not the same in all classrooms, and it is not necessarily the same as the distance from the grade of D to the grade of C in the same teacher's classroom. In the pure world of mathematics, letter grades are ordinals, and it is not correct to perform most arithmetic operations on them. Yet, we ignore the rules and do what we want with grades. We create grade averages and class ranks based on those averages. We use these averages to select valedictories and award honors. We even admit students into prestigious colleges and award financial aid based in part on grade averages.

This violation of the rules of arithmetic also occurs whenever an attitude scale is used in an evaluation where it is averaged. When students evaluate their instructors using an opinion measuring instrument, there is a real compulsion on the part of administrators to average the data. Using data from a faculty evaluation by students, the ordinal score from each evaluation form on each item is added to that of all other the students and then divided by the number of responders to determine an average value on the item. As an example, the following frequently appears on teaching evaluation forms:

Overall, how well organized are the lectures that this instructor presents?

1. Always very well organized and easy to follow

2. Usually well organized, and most days they are possible to follow

3. Less well organized about half of the time and well organized otherwise

4. Typically not well organized and difficult to follow

5. Completely disorganized and impossible to follow

Clearly, when a number of these items about a teacher are averaged together, the teacher or professor being evaluated would want to have an "average" score that is low, near the value of 1. This would indicate that he or she is viewed by students as being well organized. Some administrators (probably not golfers) do not like items that have this reversed valance (low score is good). For them, it is possible to multiply each ordinal number by the value −1.0 and then add six. This reverses the valance, making the item work in a more intuitively obvious way (high score is good).

The fact that this process of using arithmetic procedures with ordinal data is so prevalent leads some researchers to refer to items such as these as Ordinal Type II. That designation implies that Ordinal II is someplace between the precision of interval and ordinal data.

Another special case is that of a dichotomy. There are variables that exist as natural dichotomies (e.g., gender) that are not ordered in some hierarchy. Thus, such variables are binary[2] making it possible to use them in mathematical analysis. The binary variables can be artificially created by dividing a ratio or ordinal data set into two parts. One way to do this is to divide the variable at the median. Then, one category would include all those above the median and the other all that are below. Another binary variable could be defined as all those who get a test item correct and the other group would be all who get it wrong.

Nominal Scales

When the data from a variable exist in categorical form, and those categories cannot be placed into a logical order, then the variable is nominal. As the word implies, these categories exist as names only; and therefore the only possible arithmetic operation is counting. An example is the initial teaching certification that an educator earns. The certificate could be elementary, secondary social studies, general science, or special education. There is no logical sequence to this list; one teacher is just as valuable as another.

Parametric vs. Nonparametric

If we were to create a nominal variable of the sequence of mathematical precision of variables it might look like the following:

R ratio

I interval

O ordinal

N nominal

The term *parametric* is often applied when describing ratio and interval data. It means that the variables can have the full range of mathematical operations performed with them. The term applied to ordinal and nominal data is *nonparametric*. While there are a large number of nonparametric procedures for data analysis that can be used with variables of all four levels of precision, the range of procedures reserved for parametric variables tends to have greater statistical power (Cohen, 1988; Siegel & Castellan, 1988).

Level of Precision

When scientific instruments are used to measure a variable, it is very possible that the resulting score or measurement will be highly precise. High precision of measurement can be seen when medicine is measured and distributed in milligrams. Such scientific measurements are normally ratio scales. It is always possible to reduce the level of precision for a variable, but the reverse is not usually possible.

Case in Point (3b)

A good stopwatch can be used to determine the exact amount of time that runners of a 5K race need to complete the run. The posted results from this are an excellent example of ratio data. Yet, the same race can be reported as places-at-finish. Here all that is reported is who came in first, second, third . . . last. By only reporting ordinal numbers, the race results were changed to a less precise measurement, an ordinal scale.

If there were no timing device available for the race, and the results were reported as places-at-finish, it would not be possible to go back and create a ratio scale.

For more information, see "Considerations on Point" at www.sagepub.com/ wrightstudy

CENTRAL TENDENCY

Mean

The vernacular meaning of the word *average* refers to what a measurement specialist would describe as the "**mean** of the data" and a statistician would describe as

$$\overline{X} = \sum_{i=1}^{n} \frac{X_i}{n}$$

In this equation, the symbol $\overline{X}$ is used to represent the arithmetic average or mean of the data.

The Greek letter sigma with the superscript n and the subscript $i = 1$ ($\sum_{i=1}^{n}$) instructs us to add all cases from 1 to n.

The symbol X_i represents the raw score of an individual or case (for each individual).

The lower case letter n represents the number of subjects or cases in the data set.

The equation can then be read as, "the mean equals the sum of all the cases divided by the number of scores in the set of data." The mean is one form of average that can be calculated for ratio and interval data. It is the arithmetic center point in the data and can be viewed as a balance point or fulcrum for the data. Obviously, it is never possible to determine the mean of most ordinal and nominal data because addition and division are arithmetic operations not available with those data.

Median

The center (average) of ordinal data can also be found. This average of ordinals is referred to as the median, and it is the case that lies in the middle of an ordered set of data. In other words, it is the halfway point in the data, with half of the cases above it and half below. Thus, the median is also the 50th percentile. It is important to note that ratio and interval data can be lowered in precision and become ordinal data for which a median can be calculated. In the following set of numbers, the median is 14: 9, 11, 15, 20, 17, 10, 14. If the data set had two values of 14, the median would still be 14. But, if the data set were 9, 11, 15, 20, 17, 10, 14, 13, the median would lie between the value of 13 and 14. The median is another way of reporting an average or center of the data. The median can be found for ordinal, ratio, and interval data. When the distributions of ratio or interval data are symmetric, and there are no unusual cases, the two statistical values, the mean and the median, are approximately the same value.

Mode

This statistic is appropriate for variables of all four levels of precision. There is no way to identify a center point among nominal data. The lack of any type of sequence in the categories prevents the determination of a central category. The mode is the category that has the greatest number of cases. For example, "it was recently reported that at an ecumenical breakfast there were more Baptists in attendance than any other denomination." This statement presents the mode (Baptists) in a data set (those at breakfast), which is measured as nominal data (denominations).The mode can also be found for ratio, interval, and ordinal data. For example, "surveys have found that most school principals have a master's degree." Here the modal category (master's degree) of a data set that is ordinal (education level) has been identified for a data set (school administrators). Modes for ratio data can take the following form: "An analysis of all the school systems of the state indicates that the largest single expense in education is the salary of the professional employees." In this case, the mode (largest expense category) is used to summarize ratio data (school district finances).

NORMAL DISTRIBUTION

The Bell Curve

Undergraduate college students want to know if their professors "grade on a curve," but few really know what they are asking (see Chapter 10). For students to understand the "curve" that is used in grading, they must be familiar with a "distribution of errors" first defined 350 years ago. In 1669, the second Lucasian Professor of the Natural Philosophy of Mathematics at Cambridge University, Isaac Newton, was recognized as Great Britain's leading scientist and mathematician. One of the mathematicians in his orbit was Abraham de Moivre, a Huguenot, who escaped from France when King Louis XIV purged all of the Protestant intellectuals from France. This Huguenot émigré was an important mathematician in his own right. De Moivre studied the properties of the binomial distribution and with the help of the calculus of Newton was able to define what is now recognized as the normal distribution in 1718 (see Figure 3.1). In the early 19th century (1809) this mathematical model was applied by Carl Friedrich Gauss to the astronomical research dealing with asteroid orbits. It is Gauss whose name is associated with the development of this powerful mathematical tool.

Today most students have never heard of either de Moivre or Gauss, and they refer to the statistical distribution not by its originator but by its shape: the "bell curve."

The curve depicts a randomly occurring continuous probability distribution. It can be used to approximate a number of different distributions in nature (Anton, Kolman, & Averbach, 1988). For example, the normal curve can approximate the distribution of the weight of the population of adults, the SAT scores (raw score form) of all high school seniors, the length of blades of grass growing wild in a meadow, and the IQ of the population of elementary school children. Central to the use of all standardized measures including high-stakes tests is the assumption that the raw scores from the population of tested children are distributed as a Gaussian normal curve (see Figure 3.2).

Skew

There are several ways that the normal symmetry of a distribution can be lost. One of these is when there is an excess of extreme scores, either too

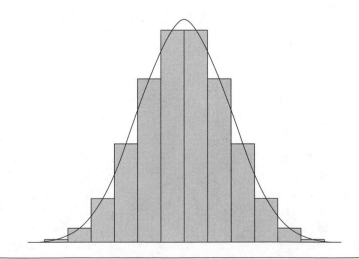

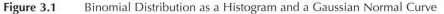

Figure 3.1   Binomial Distribution as a Histogram and a Gaussian Normal Curve

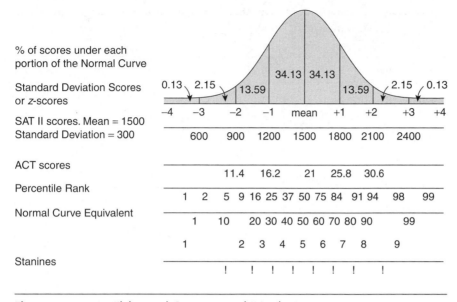

% of scores under each
portion of the Normal Curve

Standard Deviation Scores
or z-scores

SAT II scores. Mean = 1500
Standard Deviation = 300

ACT scores

Percentile Rank

Normal Curve Equivalent

Stanines

Figure 3.2   An Elaborated Gauss Normal Distribution

many high or too many low scores. The excess of unusual scores results in a separation of the mean and the median of the data. The mean always moves in the direction of the unusual scores, while the median is the middle case in the data set. A surfeit of unusually high or low scores will cause the mean to be drawn in the direction of the unusual cluster. The median tends to be much less volatile and only exhibits a very small movement when there is an unusual cluster of either high or low scores.

Test refusal[3] behavior by disgruntled adolescents is a perplexing problem for secondary school educators. One result of test refusal is the introduction of a number of extremely low scores on mandated high-stakes tests. These low scores distort the symmetry of a Gaussian normal distribution of scores.

Table 3.1 presents the scores of two classes of eighth-grade students on a pre-algebra mathematics test. Both classes have 19 students. The scores from both are the same but for three exceptions. Three adolescents in class Beta really tanked on the test. The result is that class Alpha has a median of 83 and mean score of 83.3, while class Beta also has a median of 83 but a mean of 75. This separation of the mean and median is evidence of significant skewness in the data. When the distortion is caused by unusually low scores, the skewness has a negative value, and when there is an excess of unusually high scores the skewness is referred to as positive skewness (see Figure 3.3). The mean will be greater than the median when the data have a positive skewness.

Table 3.1 Scores From Two Hypothetical Eighth-Grade Classes

Class Alpha	Class Beta
66	16
70	20
75	21
76	75
76	78
78	78
80	80
80	80
82	82
83	83
85	85
86	86
88	88
89	89
90	90
92	92
94	94
96	96
97	97

The curves depict the location of the median and means of both distributions.

In this age of accountability, educators are all too frequently evaluated on the basis of the test scores of their students. In this regard it is important to note that a few disgruntled students can introduce negative skewness into the data and thereby reduce the mean score for the entire school. In the example provided in Figure 3.3 there is a very high probability that the scores exhibit a significant level of skewness. The calculated value for the skewness of these data is (Sk $= -1.78, p > .01$).[4]

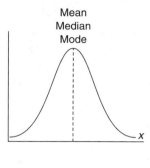

Normal Distribution

Mean
Median
Mode

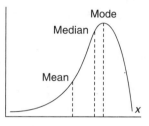

Negative Skew

Mode
Median
Mean

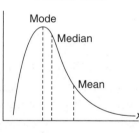

Positive Skew

Mode
Median
Mean

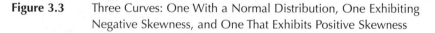

Figure 3.3   Three Curves: One With a Normal Distribution, One Exhibiting Negative Skewness, and One That Exhibits Positive Skewness

---

Case in Point (3c)

The faculty of an urban university went out on strike a few years ago. By the fourth week of the semester both sides were at a serious impasse, and both appealed to the media to support their position. At a press conference called by the public relations office of the university the press was informed that the

For more information, see "Considerations on Point" at www.sagepub.com/wrightstudy

Case in Point (3c) (Continued)

faculty was being greedy. The point was made that the average faculty member earned a salary of over $85,000 per year. And, when the benefits were added into the total package, the average faculty member received over $105,000 in annual compensation. At a local church, the representatives of the faculty union held a press conference a day later. The faculty reported that the average full-time faculty member earned just under $50,000 a year; when the benefits were added into the mix, the total compensation was only $66,500.

The fact is that both parties reported the same data and told the truth. The data on faculty pay were badly skewed. The schools of medicine, engineering, and law had faculty members that were paid at a much higher level than were their peers in the other large colleges of the university. This excess of high salaries resulted in a positive skew in the salary data. The vast majority of the faculty of the university taught in the College of Arts and Science and the Schools of Education, Nursing, and Social Work. Those faculties were paid low salaries and had a meager benefit package.

The administration of the university reported the average (mean) salary while the union reported the average (median) salary. Both were correct.

Corrections for the Data

When data are badly skewed there is good reason to investigate the reason for the cluster of very unusual scores. If it were a result of test-refusal behavior, then there is reason to remove the unusual test scores from the set. This, however, could be viewed with some skepticism by those in the greater community. A statistically sound method for correcting this type of error is known as "trimming the mean." By this technique both the bottom outlying scores and an equal number of top scores are removed from the data, and the mean is recalculated. In the case of class Beta, removing the three lowest and three highest scores and then recalculating the mean results in a trimmed mean of 83.38 while the median held constant at 83.

VARIATION AND VARIANCE

By definition, a variable will vary. Of concern to educators who review test scores is the degree of variation, or score dispersion, being exhibited by the data. To determine the amount of test score variation, one initially appealing idea involves subtracting the mean from each individual score and then summing the result: $\sum_{i=1}^{n} (X_i - \bar{X})$. The problem with this approach is that it always sums to zero. The scores that are greater than the mean will be cancelled out by those below, and the net will always be zero.

A solution to this mathematical cul-de-sac is found by multiplying the subtraction remainders by themselves. Both positive and negative values are both positive after squaring. Squaring the subtraction remainders produces a series of squared difference scores from the mean. The "average" of these squared differences is known as variance.

$$\text{variance} = \frac{\sum_{i=1}^{n} (X_i - \bar{X})^2}{n}$$

This average is found by dividing the sum of the squared difference (mean − individual score) by the number of subjects.

Variance and Standard Deviation

Variance is the "average" of the squared deviations around the mean of a data set. The value of variance is always greater than zero and has no upper limit. For most measurement applications, variance is presented in the form of standard deviation. This statistic is the square root of variance.

$$\text{standard deviation} = \sqrt{\frac{\sum_{i=1}^{n} (X_i - \bar{X})^2}{n}}$$

The statistic standard deviation is sometimes presented as the symbol s or SD, and in the case of an entire population, σ. The utility of this statistic is drawn from its relationship to the Gaussian normal curve. This relationship can be seen on Table 3.2. When data are collected from a random sample of a normal population, a distribution of those scores will approximate the normal curve. The approximate proportion of scores that will lie between the mean and one standard deviation s over the mean is a constant 34.13%. The normal distribution is symmetric, so another 34.13% of all the scores in the sample will lie between the mean and one standard deviation s below the mean. Thus, just over 68% of all scores lie between $-1s$ and $+1s$. By expanding this to almost ±2 s it is possible to account for 95% of all scores within a normal sample. That represents 47.5% above and 47.5% below the mean.

It is this consistency of the normal distribution that is the foundation of large-scale test score reports. The distribution may be of scores that are based on large numbers (e.g., SAT scores range 600 to 2,400), or small numbers (e.g., high school grade point averages range from 0.0 to 4.0), but the relationship of the standard deviation *s* to the distribution will be constant.

For more information, see "Considerations on Point" at www.sagepub.com/ wrightstudy

Case in Point (3d)

The following table is from the dissertation of Sandra Rex (2003). In this study of statewide reading test data at 11th grade, mean scores (reported as school averages) are reported for the eight standards for reading established by the Pennsylvania Department of Education. The mean on standard 1 is 1317.06, and it has a standard deviation of 89.01. That indicates that approximately 68% of the schools will fall between a high of 1406.07 (1317.06 + 89.01) and a low of 1228.05 (1317.06 − 89.01). The standard deviation of 89.01 is the square root of the variance 7923.16. On this statewide test the lowest possible standard score is 700 and the maximum score possible is 1590. The range (highest score earned − lowest score earned) is 890.

Table 3.2   Distribution of Grade 11 PSSA Reading Scaled School Scores by Standard

Descriptor	Standard 1	Standard 2	Standard 3	Standard 4	Standard 5
M	1317.06	1317.81	1309.49	1314.57	1319.98
SEM	3.67	3.72	4.45	3.63	3.93
SD	89.01	90.27	108.10	88.07	95.45
Variance	7923.16	8149.11	11684.77	7756.83	9111.39
Range	890.00	770.00	790.00	820.00	770.00
Minimum	700.00	820.00	800.00	780.00	780.00
Maximum	1590.00	1590.00	1590.00	1600.00	1550.00

SOURCE: From *Reading strategies as a predictor of student scores on the Pennsylvania System of School Assessment Reading Exam at the eleventh-grade level,* by S. L. Rex, 2003, unpublished dissertation, p. 82. Reprinted with permission from Sandra L. Rex.

The scores from any normal sample can be converted into units of standard deviation. This process makes it possible to compare one set of test scores to the scores from another test or measure. For example, if the undergraduate GPA of an applicant to graduate school is set side-by-side with the applicant's GRE score, the two seem incompatible. Both the GPA and GRE can be converted into standard deviation (standard score) format. The symbol of this standard score is z. This score, z, is a way to express any raw score in terms of its location in the distribution using units of standard deviation. If an individual score and the sample mean are exactly the same, the z-score will be 0.0. If the score is equal to one standard deviation above the mean, the z-score will be +1.0. To find any z-score, it is necessary to know the original score, sample mean, and the sample's standard deviation.

The z-score can be found as follows:

$$z = \frac{X - \overline{X}}{s} \qquad z = \frac{3.25 - 2.5}{0.5} \qquad z = 1.5$$

In this equation, the value of X is the individual score being changed into a z-score (standard score). As an example, if an applicant to graduate school has a GPA of 3.25 from a sample with a mean of $\overline{X}= 2.50$, and a standard deviation of 0.50, that student would have a z-score of +1.50. This indicates that this student had a college grade point average that was equivalent to one and a half standard deviation units above the mean.

Percentiles

The consistency of the normal curve makes it possible to interpolate z-scores into percentiles. For example, the score point in the center of the Gaussian normal curve ($z = 0.0$) is the 50th percentile. That point has half of all scores below and above it. The Gaussian normal curve starts and ends at infinity. Because of that, there can never be a zero percentile point with these transformed scores. Likewise there can never be a score equal to the 100th percentile.

Percentiles represent an ordinal transformation of data. The concept behind percentiles is that each percentile represents 1/100th of the data. The first percentile includes all those data points arranged from the lowest score to the point where 1% of the data are included. The first quartile is the 25th percentile, the point that cuts off the lowest 25% of the scores in the data set. The second quintile is the point that cuts off the lowest 40% of the scores from the data set. The median is the 50th percentile, and the seventh decile is a score that cuts off the lowest 70% of the data.

An online table for the conversion of area under the normal curve and z-scores is available at www.isixsigma.com/library/content/zdistribution.asp.

Table 3.3   Areas Under the Normal Curve and z-Scores

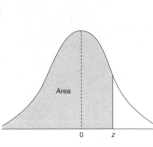

Area

0   z

(a) Area under the normal curve

z	0.00	0.01	0.02	0.03	0.04	0.05	0.06	0.07	0.08	0.09
−3.4	0.0003	0.0003	0.0003	0.0003	0.0003	0.0003	0.0003	0.0003	0.0003	0.0002
−3.3	0.0005	0.0005	0.0005	0.0004	0.0004	0.0004	0.0004	0.0004	0.0004	0.0003
−3.2	0.0007	0.0007	0.0006	0.0006	0.0006	0.0006	0.0006	0.0005	0.0005	0.0005
−3.1	0.0010	0.0009	0.0009	0.0009	0.0008	0.0008	0.0008	0.0008	0.0007	0.0007
−3.0	0.0013	0.0013	0.0013	0.0012	0.0012	0.0011	0.0011	0.0011	0.0010	0.0010
−2.9	0.0019	0.0018	0.0017	0.0017	0.0016	0.0016	0.0015	0.0015	0.0014	0.0014
−2.8	0.0026	0.0025	0.0024	0.0023	0.0023	0.0022	0.0021	0.0021	0.0020	0.0019
−2.7	0.0035	0.0034	0.0033	0.0032	0.0031	0.0030	0.0029	0.0028	0.0027	0.0026
−2.6	0.0047	0.0045	0.0044	0.0043	0.0041	0.0040	0.0039	0.0038	0.0037	0.0036
−2.5	0.0062	0.0060	0.0059	0.0057	0.0055	0.0054	0.0052	0.0051	0.0049	0.0048
−2.4	0.0082	0.0080	0.0078	0.0075	0.0073	0.0071	0.0069	0.0068	0.0066	0.0064
−2.3	0.0107	0.0104	0.0102	0.0099	0.0096	0.0094	0.0091	0.0089	0.0087	0.0084
−2.2	0.0139	0.0136	0.0132	0.0129	0.0124	0.0122	0.0119	0.0116	0.0113	0.0110
−2.1	0.0179	0.0174	0.0170	0.0166	0.0162	0.0158	0.0154	0.0150	0.0146	0.0143
−2.0	0.0228	0.0222	0.0217	0.0212	0.0207	0.0202	0.0197	0.0192	0.0188	0.0183
−1.9	0.0287	0.0281	0.0274	0.0268	0.0262	0.0256	0.0250	0.0244	0.0239	0.0233
−1.8	0.0359	0.0352	0.0344	0.0336	0.0329	0.0322	0.0314	0.0307	0.0301	0.0294
−1.7	0.0446	0.0436	0.0427	0.0418	0.0409	0.0401	0.0392	0.0384	0.0375	0.0367
−1.6	0.0548	0.0537	0.0526	0.0516	0.0505	0.0495	0.0485	0.0475	0.0465	0.0455
−1.5	0.0668	0.0655	0.0643	0.0630	0.0618	0.0606	0.0594	0.0582	0.0571	0.0559
−1.4	0.0808	0.0793	0.0778	0.0764	0.0749	0.0735	0.0722	0.0708	0.0694	0.0681
−1.3	0.0968	0.0951	0.0934	0.0918	0.0901	0.0885	0.0869	0.0853	0.0838	0.0823
−1.2	0.1151	0.1131	0.1112	0.1093	0.1075	0.1056	0.1038	0.1020	0.1003	0.0985
−1.1	0.1357	0.1335	0.1314	0.1292	0.1271	0.1251	0.1230	0.1210	0.1190	0.1170
−1.0	0.1587	0.1562	0.1539	0.1515	0.1492	0.1469	0.1446	0.1423	0.1401	0.1379
−0.9	0.1841	0.1814	0.1788	0.1762	0.1736	0.1711	0.1685	0.1660	0.1635	0.1611
−0.8	0.2119	0.2090	0.2061	0.0233	0.2005	0.1977	0.1949	0.1922	0.1894	0.1867
−0.7	0.2420	0.2389	0.2358	0.2327	0.2296	0.2266	0.2236	0.2206	0.2177	0.2148
−0.6	0.2743	0.2709	0.2676	0.2643	0.2611	0.2578	0.2546	0.2514	0.2483	0.2451
−0.5	0.3085	0.3050	0.3015	0.2981	0.2946	0.2912	0.2877	0.2843	0.2810	0.2776
−0.4	0.3446	0.3409	0.3372	0.3336	0.3300	0.3264	0.3228	0.3192	0.3156	0.3121
−0.3	0.3821	0.3783	0.3745	0.3707	0.3669	0.3632	0.3594	0.3557	0.3520	0.3483
−0.2	0.4207	0.4168	0.4129	0.4090	0.4052	0.4013	0.3974	0.3936	0.3897	0.3859
−0.1	0.4602	0.4562	0.4522	0.4483	0.4443	0.4404	0.4364	0.4325	0.4286	0.4247
−0.0	0.5000	0.4960	0.4920	0.4880	0.4840	0.4801	0.4761	0.4721	0.4681	0.4641

z	0.00	0.01	0.02	0.03	0.04	0.05	0.06	0.07	0.08	0.09
0.0	0.5000	0.5040	0.5080	0.5120	0.5160	0.5199	0.5239	0.5279	0.5319	0.5359
0.1	0.5398	0.5438	0.5478	0.5517	0.5557	0.5596	0.5636	0.5675	0.5714	0.5753
0.2	0.5793	0.5832	0.5871	0.5910	0.5948	0.5987	0.6026	0.6064	0.6103	0.6141
0.3	0.6179	0.6217	0.6255	0.6293	0.6331	0.6368	0.6406	0.6443	0.6480	0.6517
0.4	0.6554	0.6591	0.6628	0.6664	0.6700	0.6736	0.6772	0.6808	0.6844	0.6879
0.5	0.6915	0.6950	0.6985	0.7019	0.7054	0.7088	0.7123	0.7157	0.7190	0.7224
0.6	0.7257	0.7291	0.7324	0.7357	0.7389	0.7422	0.7454	0.7486	0.7517	0.7549
0.7	0.7580	0.7611	0.7642	0.7673	0.7704	0.7734	0.7764	0.7794	0.7823	0.7852
0.8	0.7881	0.7910	0.7939	0.7967	0.7995	0.8023	0.8051	0.8078	0.8106	0.8133
0.9	0.8159	0.8186	0.8212	0.8238	0.8264	0.8289	0.8315	0.8340	0.8365	0.8389
1.0	0.8413	0.8438	0.8461	0.8485	0.8508	0.8531	0.8554	0.8577	0.8599	0.8621
1.1	0.8643	0.8665	0.8686	0.8708	0.8729	0.8749	0.8770	0.8790	0.8810	0.8830
1.2	0.8849	0.8869	0.8888	0.8907	0.8925	0.8944	0.8962	0.8980	0.8997	0.9015
1.3	0.9032	0.9049	0.9066	0.9082	0.9099	0.9115	0.9131	0.9147	0.9162	0.9177
1.4	0.9192	0.9207	0.9222	0.9236	0.9251	0.9265	0.9278	0.9292	0.9306	0.9319
1.5	0.9332	0.9345	0.9357	0.9370	0.9382	0.9394	0.9406	0.9418	0.9429	0.9441
1.6	0.9452	0.9463	0.9474	0.9484	0.9495	0.9505	0.9515	0.9525	0.9535	0.9545
1.7	0.9554	0.9564	0.9573	0.9582	0.9591	0.9599	0.9608	0.9616	0.9625	0.9633
1.8	0.9641	0.9649	0.9656	0.9664	0.9671	0.9678	0.9686	0.9693	0.9699	0.9706
1.9	0.9713	0.9719	0.9726	0.9732	0.9738	0.9744	0.9750	0.9756	0.9761	0.9767
2.0	0.9772	0.9778	0.9783	0.9788	0.9793	0.9798	0.9803	0.9808	0.9812	0.9817
2.1	0.9821	0.9826	0.9830	0.9834	0.9838	0.9842	0.9846	0.9850	0.9854	0.9857
2.2	0.9861	0.9864	0.9868	0.9871	0.9875	0.9878	0.9881	0.9884	0.9887	0.9890
2.3	0.9893	0.9896	0.9898	0.9901	0.9904	0.9906	0.9909	0.9911	0.9913	0.9916
2.4	0.9918	0.9920	0.9922	0.9925	0.9927	0.9929	0.9931	0.9932	0.9934	0.9936
2.5	0.9938	0.9940	0.9941	0.9943	0.9945	0.9946	0.9948	0.9949	0.9951	0.9952
2.6	0.9953	0.9955	0.9956	0.9957	0.9959	0.9960	0.9961	0.9962	0.9963	0.9964
2.7	0.9965	0.9966	0.9967	0.9968	0.9969	0.9970	0.9971	0.9972	0.9973	0.9974
2.8	0.9974	0.9975	0.9976	0.9977	0.9977	0.9978	0.9979	0.9979	0.9980	0.9981
2.9	0.9981	0.9982	0.9982	0.9983	0.9984	0.9984	0.9985	0.9985	0.9986	0.9986
3.0	0.9987	0.9987	0.9987	0.9988	0.9988	0.9989	0.9989	0.9989	0.9990	0.9990
3.1	0.9990	0.9991	0.9991	0.9991	0.9992	0.9992	0.9992	0.9992	0.9993	0.9993
3.2	0.9993	0.9993	0.9994	0.9994	0.9994	0.9994	0.9994	0.9995	0.9995	0.9995
3.3	0.9995	0.9995	0.9995	0.9996	0.9996	0.9996	0.9996	0.9996	0.9996	0.9997
3.4	0.9997	0.9997	0.9997	0.9997	0.9997	0.9997	0.9997	0.9997	0.9997	0.9998

SOURCE: From *100 statistical tests*, G. K. Kanji, 1999, pp. 159–160. Reprinted with permission from Sage.

In Table 3.3, it can be seen that a student who has a GPA equal to a z-score of 1.50 would be in the 93rd percentile of a normally distributed set of grade point averages. Likewise, a student who has a score on the statewide assessment equal to a z-score of –0.7 (negative sign means below the mean) would be in about the 24th percentile. Tests of cognitive ability typically have a mean of 100 and a standard deviation of 15. A basic requirement of most school systems for admission into a program for the gifted is an IQ of 130. That can be changed into a z-score, knowing that the published mean of IQ tests is 100 and the standard deviation is 15:

$$z = \frac{130 - 100}{15} \quad z = 2.0$$

On a larger table it can be seen that a z-score of 2.0 can then be read as equaling about the 97.7th percentile. In other words, only a little over 2% of a normal population of school children (1 out of 50) should qualify for admission into the gifted program.

For more information, see "Considerations on Point" at www.sagepub.com/wrightstudy

Case in Point (3e)

In April of 2005, Secretary of Education Margaret Spellings clarified a rule of the No Child Left Behind Act (2002). The change now allows the public schools of some states to use an alternative assessment with those children who are in the lowest 3% of the population in terms of cognitive ability. To determine the IQ score that is equivalent to the 3rd percentile it is first necessary to find the z-score equal to that percentile. That percentile can be seen in Table 3.3 as the 47th percentile below the mean ($z = 0.0$) and equal to a z-score of about –1.88. To find the equivalent IQ:

$$IQ = [(z\text{-score}) \times s] + \text{mean}$$
$$IQ = (-1.88 \times 15) + 100$$
$$IQ = 72$$

Thus, in those states approved by Secretary Spellings, children with an IQ less than 72 can be assessed using a developmentally appropriate measure and their progress charted as annual improvement on the developmental measure. In those states that have not been approved by the secretary of education, only 1% of the student population can be tested using a developmentally appropriate measure. That is equal to a z-score of –2.33 on a test of mental ability. That z-score is equal to an IQ less than 65. When Terman published the first edition of his revisions of Binet's test, the term *moron* was ascribed to people who tested that low. It is unfortunate that those old classifications popularized by H. H. Goddard's review of Terman's new test ("moron," "imbecile," and "idiot") have been adopted into the vernacular of our everyday language (Gould, 1996). Today, those once "technical" terms from standard IQ classifications have been replaced. Now a person with an IQ less than 62 would be classified as being mildly retarded, while a student with a tested IQ of 72 is classified as exhibiting borderline mental deficiency.[5]

STANDARD SCORES

Stanine

Scores that are reported on measures that are administered on a regular basis need a presentation system that facilitates the comparison of scores from one year to another. One of the simplest of these reporting systems is that which was developed by Lt. Col. J. P. Guilford during World War II. His system involved converting raw test scores from the Army Air Force Test into *z*-scores and then reporting those *z*-scores using a nine-point scale, known now as stanine (from *stan*-dard *nine*). Each stanine covers 0.5 standard deviations (see Figure 3.4). The middle of the normal distribution was assigned the value of stanine 5. The first, and lowest, stanine covers all cases below one and three-quarters standard deviations below the mean ($z < -1.75$), while the ninth stanine covers all those scores above +1.75 standard deviations above the mean ($z > 1.75$). (See Figure 3.4.) The scores in the first and second stanines represent the lowest 10% of all scores, while those in the eighth and ninth stanines are the top 10% of all scores. Thus, all those between the third and seventh stanines represent the middle 80% of all scores.

Deviation IQ Scores

In 1949, when David Wechsler published the Wechsler Intelligence Scale for Children (WISC), he set the norms so that the mean score, $\bar{X}$, would be 100 and the standard deviation, *s*, would be 15. This system provides an ability scale by which 50% of the children from a normal population who are

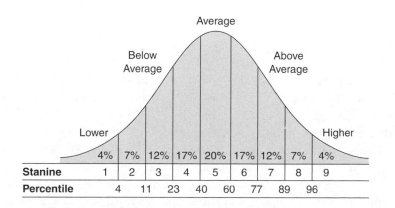

Stanine	1	2	3	4	5	6	7	8	9
	4%	7%	12%	17%	20%	17%	12%	7%	4%
Percentile		4	11	23	40	60	77	89	96

Figure 3.4   Stanines and the Normal Distribution

tested will have an IQ score below 100 and 50% above that median point of 100. A full 68% will have cognitive ability scores that fall between full-scale IQ scores of 85 and 115 ($-1.0s$ to $+1.0s$). Because these scores are linked to standard deviations under the normal curve, they are often referred to as deviation IQ scores (DIQ).

The 1916 mental ability test developed by Lewis M. Terman, the Stanford Revision of the Binet Scale, defined mental ability as the subject's mental age divided by his or her chronological age. This ratio was then multiplied by William Stern's 1912 correction (100) to create the familiar IQ score. The second edition of Terman's test in 1937 saw the introduction of a deviation IQ score that was standardized with a mean of 100 and a standard deviation of 16. The fifth edition of the Stanford Binet has a mean of 100 and a standard deviation of 15.

College Board Scores

The Educational Testing Service provides a broad spectrum of tests and assessments. The largest of these is the College Entrance Examination Board's SAT II. Originally, the SAT I was set to have a combined (Verbal and Mathematics) mean score of 1000 with a standard deviation of 200. Either half was designed to have a mean of 500 and a standard deviation of 100. That original distribution from 1941 is another classical example of the Gaussian normal curve with nearly perfect symmetry. Today, the SAT II has three parts, and the combined mean is approximately 1500, with a standard deviation of 300. Thus, a combined score of 1,200 would be about one standard deviation below the mean ($X_i = -1s$) and approximately equal to the 16th percentile. Likewise, a total score of 1800 would be about one standard deviation above average and in about the 84th percentile.

ACT Scores

Over 1 million high school seniors take the American College Testing Program (ACT) examinations each year. The composite mean on this test in 2004 was 20.9 and the standard deviation 4.8. Following the rule for normal distributions, the composite score of 25.7 ($X_i = +1.0s$) would be one standard deviation above the mean, or about the 84th percentile. An ACT composite score of 18.5 ($X_i = -0.5s$) would be approximately the 31st percentile, one-half of a standard deviation below the mean, while a score of 16.4 would be a full standard deviation below the mean and at the 16th percentile.

Computer Adaptive Graduate Admissions Testing

Graduate programs in education typically use the Graduate Record Examination (GRE) as one source of information when making an admissions decision. This examination is another product of the Educational Testing Service. This measure is different from the SAT II in that it is now administered online, and the test taker only sees one item at a time with the test items appearing in a nonrandom sequence. The test taker is first presented with items that have proven to be of an average level of difficulty. If those items are answered incorrectly, the computer asks easier items, and unless there is a dramatic recovery, the resulting score for this hapless scholar will be below the mean. If the initial few items are answered correctly, the computer will go on and present increasingly difficult items to the student. This places the more capable student in an upper bracket, where it is possible to earn a higher GRE score. This type of computerized testing is referred to as computer adaptive testing. This same model is now being implemented by state education departments in the development of online high-stakes assessments under the NCLB Act.

For both the verbal and quantitative sections of the GRE, the software attempts to determine the test taker's ceiling level. A logical consequence of this approach to online testing is that the first few questions are the most critical in determining the student's score.[6] Originally, the GRE was centered with both the verbal and quantitative sections having a mean of 500 and standard deviations of 100. These scores have drifted since the first publication of the test in its original form in 1966. The drift away from the original normative (centered) data has resulted in a lower mean verbal score, now just 470 with a standard deviation of 121, and an increased mean quantitative score of 598 with a standard deviation of 148. The distributions of both subtests are skewed with the quantitative scale skewed negatively and the verbal scale showing a small positive skew.

Professional Schools Admission Testing

All 186 American Bar Association accredited schools of law use the Law School Admission Test (LSAT) as a part of the criteria for selecting students. This admission test from the Law School Admissions Council uses an approach for reporting scores that is similar to other admissions tests.[7] Each year the LSAT consists of about 100 or so items that are converted to a standard score that falls in a range between 120 and 180. The mean is approximately 150.5 with a standard deviation of 10. As the difficulty of the test changes from edition to edition, the raw score associated with any particular LSAT standard score will be different from year to year. This is often noted by students who take the test more than one time. There is also a tendency for the distribution of scores to exhibit a slight trend toward a negative skewness.

Grade-Equivalent Score

The least useful of the various test score reporting systems is the **grade equivalent score**. This score is read as a grade level expressed in years comprising ten months (the academic year is ten months, from September to June). Therefore, a grade equivalent score of 4.5 indicates the fourth grade, fifth month. These scores are created by extrapolating from the normative scores achieved by children of different grade levels taking the same test. There are four major problems with these scores. For one, scores removed from the grade in which the child is enrolled are very unstable. A third-grade child reading below grade level by two or more years will experience enormous shifts in his or her grade level score on retesting. This is a function of both the statistically projected score used to norm the test and to the effect of the tendency for all extreme scores to move toward the center of the data set on retesting. This phenomenon is described as regression toward the mean, and it is discussed in Chapters 4 and 17. The second problem with these scores is that they are ordinal. Yet, there is a real tendency for educators to try to find the mean of a set of grade equivalent scores.

The third problem is that any grade equivalent score is a median value, a statistical fact that is not well understood by national policy makers. Grade equivalent scores are not absolute values; they simply divide children into two groups, the 50% above some measurement point named the grade equivalent level and the 50% with scores below that point. Thus, when Secretary Spellings announces that the goal of the U.S. Department of Education is to assure that all children are at or above grade level, she is expressing a statistical impossibility.

The final issue is the most problematic. Most educators, and virtually all parents, think that if children who are enrolled in the fifth grade, and are tested and reported to have a grade equivalent score on a reading test of 9.1, can read ninth-grade books. This is absolutely wrong. What those data indicate is that the child in fifth grade did as well on the fifth-grade reading test as would the average child in the ninth grade if that ninth-grader took the fifth-grade test. If the well-meaning, but misinformed, fifth-grade teacher assigned ninth-grade material to that good little reader, the child would have great difficulty and would likely be totally lost. Grade equivalent scores should be avoided if at all possible. They are not parametric, they are unstable, and almost no one seems to understand what they really indicate.

VARIATION

To understand the score reports from most large-scale testing programs it is necessary to understand the basic concepts of variance and standard deviation. The fact that scores will vary from person to person is the source of variance, and standard deviation is used to interpret test scores in terms of the normal curve. When two tests are given to a group of subjects, covariance comes into play.

Covariance

Many times the tests and measures we use in educational settings have much in common with each other. This tendency is because of the commonality or shared variance of the various tests. We can see this in the tendency for the test scores from different tests to be similar for a child. Indeed, if one of the subtests of an achievement test battery is significantly out of alignment with the other subtests, that outlying achievement area is considered to be a possible diagnostic indicator. Regarding any particular child we expect to see consistency. In other words, in general we have an expectation that measures will co-vary.

Covariance is the statistical expression of the amount of commonality shared by two different measures. When the covariance is high, the two variables tend to move together. Thus high scores on one measure presage high scores on the other measure. A hundred years ago, Charles Spearman saw this tendency and postulated the existence of a general (common) factor that runs through most cognitive tasks (see Chapter 2).

Covariance can be either positive or negative. If the value is positive, we know that if one test is high so will be the second. Likewise, a low score on one test is likely to be followed by a low score on the second. An example of this is the covariance between cognitive ability as measured by IQ and the level of achievement on a standardized test of mathematics. Here a high score on either one of the measures tends to lead to a high score on the second.

A covariance with a negative value is just the opposite. In that case, a high score on one measure is likely associated with a lower score on the second. This can be seen in the relationship between measured levels of manifest anxiety and reading comprehension. As the anxiety level increases, scores on the test of reading comprehension tend to be lower.

Covariance is expressed as

$$\mathrm{Cov} = \frac{\sum\limits_{i=1}^{n}(X_i - \overline{X}) \sum\limits_{i=1}^{n}(Y_i - \overline{Y})}{n-1}$$

If test X is a midterm examination, the deviation from the mean for an individual is the value $X_i - \overline{X}$. Likewise, the deviation of that individual's score from the mean of the final exam is $Y_i - \overline{Y}$. When the two values are multiplied together the result will be positive, if both the midterm and the final were very high or very low. However, if the midterm was very low, and our hypothetical student hit the books and did well on the final, then the covariance value will be negative. A negative midterm deviation from the mean, multiplied by a positive deviation from the mean of the final, will result in a large negative covariance value. If there is no relationship between the two measurers, the value of the covariance for a sample of students will be zero. This happens when the positive covariance scores of some students are canceled out by the negative covariance values found for others. Thus, when all of the covariance scores for the students in the sample are added together, the summation results in a zero total covariance value.

CORRELATION

Pearson Correlation Coefficient

There are no practical limits as to how large either a positive or negative covariance can become. This makes covariance very difficult to interpret. For this reason, the statistic, covariance, is rarely reported along with the other statistics used to describe data. The interpretability of covariance was made possible 120 years ago by the formulation of the Pearson Product Moment Correlation Coefficient. That correlation coefficient has a minimum value of zero and a maximum value of ± 1.0. Negative covariance is expressed as a negative correlation, and a positive covariance is shown as a positive coefficient. Karl Pearson defined the correlation coefficient as

$$r = \frac{\sum_{i=1}^{n}(X_i - \overline{X})^2(Y_i - \overline{Y})^2}{\sqrt{\left[\sum_{i=1}^{n}(X_i - \overline{X})^2 \sum_{i=1}^{n}(Y_i - \overline{Y})^2\right]}}$$

The following is a computational model that facilitates calculation of the Pearson correlation coefficient:

$$r = \frac{N\sum XY - \left(\sum X\right)\left(\sum Y\right)}{\sqrt{\left[N\sum X^2 - \left(\sum X\right)^2\right]\left[N\sum Y^2 - \left(\sum Y\right)^2\right]}}$$

In this equation, the coefficient of correlation is expressed as the letter r.

- $N\sum XY$ represents the number of subjects multiplied by the sum of all the multiplication of individual pairs of scores on both tests.
- $(\sum X)(\sum Y)$ is the sum of all scores on the first test multiplied by the sum of all scores on the second test.
- $\left[N\sum X^2 - (\sum X)^2\right]$ is the sum of all of the squared scores on the first test, multiplied by the total number of subjects, from which the sum of all the scores squared is subtracted.
- $\left[N\sum Y^2 - (\sum Y)^2\right]$ is the sum of all of the squared scores on the second test, multiplied by the total number of subjects, from which the sum of all the scores squared is subtracted.

The correlation coefficient is an easily interpreted statistic. It is an expression of the amount of variance shared by two measures. It does not show a causal relationship, only that the two measures have a common element. Thus, the fact that there is a correlation of about $r = +0.40$ between the combined SAT scores from high school and the GPA of students at the end of their freshman year of college does not imply that SAT scores caused college grades. The common element behind both may be reading ability, motivation, or perhaps the cognitive ability of the students. To correlate a set of data online see www.wessa .net/corr.wasp.

There is a quantitative measure of the amount of communality shared by the two measures. This value can be determined directly from of the correlation coefficient. When the Pearson correlation coefficient is squared, the resulting value can be read as the proportion of variance shared by the two measures. This statistic is known as the coefficient of determination (cd). Thus, the Pearson correlation of $r = +0.5$ between IQ scores from the Cognitive Ability Test and scores on a mandated statewide assessment test indicate that the shared proportion of variance is about 0.25 or 25% (Burson & Wright, 2003).

By this simple system, any correlation coefficient can be easily interpreted in terms of the amount of shared variance. A correlation of $r = 0.0$ would indicate that there is no shared variance or communality. For example, there is a negative correlation between the value of used portable classrooms and the years since they were new. If that correlation is $r = -0.6$, then the amount of shared variance between the two measures is 36% ($r^2 = -0.6 \times -0.6$). Many other factors are a part of the resale value of old portables, including extra features such as in-classroom plumbing and a bathroom, physical appearance, condition of the heating and cooling systems, and the condition of the blackboards. But 36% of the variation of prices for used portables is a function of the age of those units.

Spearman Correlation Coefficient

The computational algorithm used to calculate the Pearson correlation coefficient between two variables is one that requires that both measures are either ratio or interval. Charles Spearman devised a way to calculate the correlation coefficient if one or both variables is an ordinal. This coefficient has the same limits (0.0 to ±1.0) and is interpreted the same way as the Pearson correlation coefficient. The statistic is known as the Spearman rho, and its symbol is the Greek letter ρ, or rho.

The data presented on Table 3.4 depict a hypothetical homeroom class of 11th-grade adolescents who all plan to attend higher education after graduation. In the fall of 11th grade they all took the Preliminary SAT/NMSQT, and

"Think!"

Figure 3.5   "Think"

in the late spring they all took the American College Testing Program test (ACT). Also shown in Table 3.4 are the midyear grade point averages for the homeroom.

Table 3.4 Table Format for Data From Hypothetical High School Homeroom

Student	PSAT	GPA	ACT
Ann	60.00	3.23	23.00
Bill	45.00	2.33	20.00
Carol	50.00	2.79	21.00
Doug	55.00	3.00	27.00
Edith	40.00	3.11	17.00
Frank	60.00	3.20	23.00
Gert	70.00	3.70	28.00
Hal	35.00	1.95	15.00
Irene	65.00	1.66	24.00
Jorge	50.00	3.00	23.00
Kay	50.00	2.60	20.00
Louis	45.00	2.20	21.00
Mary	55.00	3.10	22.00
Norm	30.00	2.00	14.00
Opal	75.00	4.00	30.00
Pete	50.00	3.01	28.00
Quinne	45.00	2.05	20.00
Robert	40.00	2.46	18.00
Sue	50.00	2.98	23.00
Tom	60.00	3.61	28.00

The correlations among the three variables are presented in Table 3.5. From this matrix, it is evident that the largest Pearson correlation is between the two college admissions tests, the PSAT/NMSQT and ACT ($r = +0.87$). This indicates that amount of shared variance between them is approximately 76% $(0.87)^2$. The lowest correlation was found between GPA and the PSAT scores ($r = .65$), indicating that there is a 42% $(0.65)^2$ overlap of variance for these two measures.

Table 3.5   Correlation Matrix From Hypothetical Homeroom

	ACT	*GPA*	*PSAT*
ACT Score	1.00	.69	.87
H. S. GPA		1.00	.65
PSAT Score			1.00

Scatterplots

Correlations can be depicted by plotting scores of the two variables on a linear coordinate graph. The data shown on Figure 3.6 depict the relationship between the PSAT/NMSQT scores and the midyear GPA of students. The *x*-axis (abscissa) of the graph shows the possible range of PSAT/NMSQT scores, and the *y*-axis (ordinate) shows the range of GPA values. In this figure, each dot represents both scores for one student. As an example, student 10 has a GPA of 3.00 and a PSAT score of 50. That score point has been highlighted on the Figure 3.6.

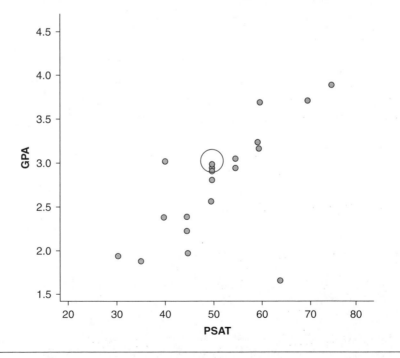

Figure 3.6   Scatterplot

Figure 3.7 depicts scatterplots for a number of other possible correlations. These depictions include both positive and negative correlations. In all cases, the correlation coefficient is expressing the amount of variance shared (commonality) by two variables measuring one group of people.

> *But my concern, given the relatively low predictability of these tests, is that there may be people who have tremendous talents, creative and practical talents, who, because they don't do well on these tests, never get the chance to show what they really could do in important jobs.*
>
> —Robert Sternberg

Prediction

One of the employments for correlational statistics is the task of predicting.[8] As an example, we know the correlational relationship between the scores earned by our hypothetical high school juniors on the PSAT/NMSQT and their midyear GPAs. With these data we have the tools in place to make an academic prediction. Starting with the correlation between the score on

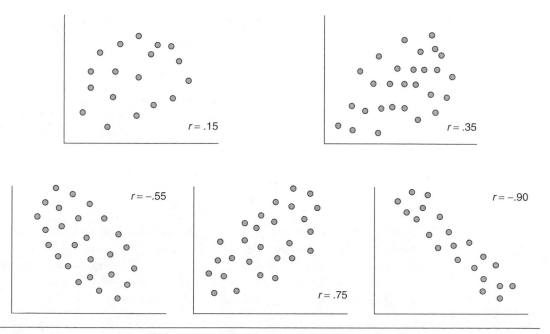

Figure 3.7   Five Scatterplots

the PSAT/NMSQT and the GPA from the previous school year ($r = 0.65$), it is possible to build a prediction equation that will estimate the GPA of next year's 11th-graders. This prediction will be based on the new PSAT/NMSQT scores earned by the next class of 11th-graders in the fall. That prediction equation is as follows:

$$\hat{Y}_i = bX_i + c \text{ Where } b \text{ is defined as } b = r\,(s_y/s_x)$$

This prediction equation is the same as the algebraic equation for a straight line. The line that is part of the prediction equation is one that is aligned through the center of the scatterplot of the two variables, PSAT/NMSQT scores and GPA. The slope function of that straight line in this equation is shown as the letter b. The name applied to this value by statisticians is "raw score regression weight" or "b weight" (Tatsuoka & Lohnes, 1988). The value $\hat{Y}_i$ is the predicted value of an individual's future 11th-grade GPA. The letter c represents a constant that is the value of the PSAT/NMSQT score equal to what would happen if a student actually had a GPA of 0.0. In statistics, that is referred to as the y-axis intercept.

To determine the slope function (b) it is necessary to know the correlation between the two measures from the previous school year (r) and the standard deviations of the two variables, last year's PSAT (s_x) and last year's GPA scores (s_y). If we assume the correlation between these two variables is $r = 0.65$, the standard deviation of the PSAT/NMSQT is 11.4, and the standard deviation of the GPAs is 0.63, it then becomes possible to put it all together and make our prediction about how well the new 11th-graders will do in terms of their GPAs.

$$b = 0.65 \times (0.63/11.4)$$

$$b = 0.034$$

This shows that the regression weight (b, also known as the slope) is 0.034. In other words, every time the PSAT score goes up one point, the GPA increases 0.034 points.

$$\hat{Y} = 0.034X_i + 1.0$$

The value of the constant can be estimated by a straight line drawn through the center of all the points on the scatterplot. It can also be found through the application of differential equations using the raw score data. By this prediction equation, a student who scores 60 on the PSAT/NMSQT in the early fall would be predicted to have a GPA equal to 3.04:

$$\hat{Y} = (0.034 \times 60) + 1.0$$

Prediction systems are employed at most large universities for the first screening of undergraduate applicants. This type of equation is typically modified by the addition of other valid predictive variables.

Error of Prediction

The accuracy of any correlational prediction is a function of the size of the correlation between the two variables. The greater the correlation, the less will be the amount of error that results when estimations are made. Error can be thought of as the difference between the GPA values we predicted and what actually occurred with our students. It is depicted as the difference between the predictions and the observed real scores ($\hat{Y}_i - Y_i$). This difference is called error of prediction, and it is also distributed as a normal curve. Therefore, we can create yet another statistic, the standard error of prediction ($s_y - \hat{Y}$). Using the standard error of prediction, it becomes possible to develop a band of confidence around any prediction that we make using correlational statistics. The larger the correlation coefficient on which this is based, the smaller will be the error of prediction. Likewise, larger correlations will result in smaller standard errors of prediction.

Multiple Correlation

The basic correlation equation can be expanded by adding other predictor (independent) variables to the correlation.[9] This makes it possible to use two or more variables to predict another (criterion) variable. Using this statistical tool, college admission systems are able to simultaneously use all three subtests of the SAT along with high school GPAs as predictors in a multiple-correlation equation.

$$\hat{Y} = b_{SAT-V} + b_{SAT-M} + b_{SAT-W} + b_{GPA} + c$$

The assignment of regression weights, *b* weights, is accomplished by an application of differential calculus known as the least squares method. For this reason, the multiple-correlation equation is frequently referred to as an ordinary least squares (OLS) regression equation (Long, 1997). This equation combines the three predictor variables with the constant (intercept) and provides the correlation between this vector (collection of variables) and the obtained college grade point average (GPA; criterion variable). In other words, the predicted value of the unknown grade point average $\hat{Y}$ can be estimated by a set of scores that have each been multiplied by a unique mathematically derived value (b weight). To that lot, a numerical constant is added, which rounds out the elements in the prediction equation.

Summary

Entities that are conceptually consistent and that have varying quantities or levels are variables. In education there are four levels of precision that may be used to describe all variables: nominal (named category, no natural sequence), ordinal (ordered sequence without equal measurement units), interval (ordered sequence based on a standardized [normal curve based] scoring system), and ratio (real numbers are used to measure these variables of physical properties and/or counted items).

Descriptive statistics are employed to make a set of data understandable. One descriptive statistic that is widely reported is the central tendency (average) of the data. The average can imply either the mean (arithmetic average) or the central score by count (median). The former use is appropriate for interval and ratio data, while the latter is appropriate for ordinal, interval, and ratio data.

Another important descriptive statistic is variance. This value can be calculated for ratio and interval data, and it describes the average squared difference between each score and the mean. The square root of variance is the descriptive statistic, standard deviation. This statistic makes possible all standardized scores. These standardized scores are the product of a conversion from a raw score into a score that is expressed as a measure based on the normal curve. Standardized scores are widely used in education to report the results of major testing programs. Among others, these include the ACT, SAT, GRE, LSAT, MCAT, PRAXIS II, mental ability measures, state-mandated high-stakes assessments, and the Armed Services Vocational Aptitude Battery.

Variations of the distribution of raw scores away from a normal curve can make the data difficult to interpret accurately. One such variation occurs when the distribution is not symmetric and has too many extreme scores on either the low- or high-score side of the distribution. This condition is referred to as skewness. Positive skewness occurs when there are too many unusually high scores and negative skewness if there are too many unusually low scores. A skewed distribution can be identified when the median and the mean of the data have separated on the plot of the distribution. In public school achievement testing, negative skewness can occur when a group of students exhibit "test refusal" behavior. These students are those who have capitulated and have decided not to make a serious attempt on the test. The surfeit of low scores that these students receive causes the school's mean score to be significantly lower than the school's median score.

Scores will distribute around the mean of a set of data. The amount of such variation around the mean is measured as variance. The square root of variance is standard deviation, the key to understanding all standard scores. Standard deviation can be used as a link between any distribution of test data and the normal distribution: the bell curve.

When two sets of scores are examined for one group of subjects, it is possible to find the amount of shared variance between them. This is covariance, and it is expressed as correlation. Correlation can show us the amount two measures have in common. Correlation can also be used to predict or estimate the score on a variable. This prediction function has many applications, including admission screening.

Discussion Questions

1. Letter grades on a report card are ordinals. Could report card grades ever report interval grades? What changes in the grading system of schools must occur if report card grades become interval values?

2. Could the negotiating team from the professional association representing the interests of teachers exploit the skewness in a school districts salary scale in their contract negotiations? How would that occur?

3. Explain how a hard-core group of "test refusing" students can affect the average score of an entire school population. How can this problem be corrected? What potential problems would an administrator face who initiated a correction for test-refusing students?

4. In American vernacular English there are a number of aphorisms that can be expressed in correlational terms. For example, "Absence makes the heart grow fonder." This can in correlation speak be expressed as, "The length of time apart is positively correlated with fondness." Select any appropriate aphorism and rewrite it in terms of a correlation.

5. It has been said that every child who grew up to become an incarcerated criminal drank orange juice as a young child. Can we conclude that there is a positive correlation between criminality and early orange juice consumption? Explain your answer.

6. What exactly is so bad about reporting the grade equivalent scores of children to their parents on the report from a published achievement measure?

Student Study Site

Educational Assessment on the Web

Log on to the Web-based student study site at www.sagepub.com/wrightstudy for additional Web sources and study resources.

NOTES

1. Ordinal data are a logically ordered series of datum points, where each datum is larger than the proceeding datum and smaller than the next datum in the sequence.

2. Binary variables can be assigned values of 0 or 1.

3. Test refusal occurs when children are not motivated to take a required test. They make random marks on the answer sheet, or they may just put their heads down and go to sleep while their classmates are taking the test.

4. There is less than 1 chance in 100 that this much skewness could be a random occurrence for a class of 19 students drawn randomly from a normal population. In other words, these data are skewed-up.

5. Another term applied to children who score in the borderline range on an IQ test is "an educateable level of mental retardation."

6. Computer adaptive testing is especially vulnerable to cheaters who memorize the first clusters of items and then pass them along to other students. This is not a small issue for ETS and others who construct these systems (Yi, Zhang, & Chang, 2006).

7. There are a number of companies providing online tutoring services for the LSAT. The following was selected as it provides a sample set of LSAT test questions: www.lsat-center.com/lsat-sample.html

8. Prediction equations are used in all areas of business (to predict trends), insurance (to set actuarial risk tables), and in higher education (to predict which students will do well academically). While ubiquitous in our world, they have rarely been employed in public schools until recently. Current data management

programs in some states, such as Tennessee and Pennsylvania, make the prediction (estimation) of a students' future success possible.

9. The term *multiple correlation*, while correct, is more commonly referred to as *multiple regression* in most introductory statistics books, and as *ordinary least squares regression* (OLS) in advanced statistics courses. The term *multiple correlation* was selected for this chapter because it is consistent with the description of correlation as developed here.

Chapter 4

Reliability as a Measure of Test Quality

Not everything that can be counted counts, and not everything that counts can be counted.

—Albert Einstein

Issues and Themes

The most important characteristic of a test is that it provides scores that are reliable (Sawilowsky, 2000). **Reliability** expresses the extent to which test scores provide consistent and dependable information.[1] Unreliable scores provide meaningless data that lack credibility. Ethical measurement practices require that measures designed to evaluate or place students have a high degree of reliability (Joint Committee on Testing Practices, 2005). Reliability is a characteristic of test scores, not of the test itself (Thompson & Vacha-Haase, 2000).

The level of reliability expresses the extent to which a test yields the same score each time the same subjects are retested. For that reason, one form of reliability is an expression of the **stability** (reproducibility) of test scores. A procedure that can be used to measure this quality of a test is the correlation between the scores from two or more administrations of the test to the same people.

Another approach to measuring the reliability of a test is as the correlation of the test's items to one another. This type of reliability is referred to as the test's internal consistency. The consistency or homogeneity of the test items is related to the test's stability of scores.

The meaning of any test score is a function of reliability, and it is usually expressed as the standard error of measurement. Standard error of measurement is a statistic that delineates the extent to which measurement errors are part of a set of test scores. Balanced against measurement error is "**true score**," the actual amount that the subject knew on the test. Any test score is composed of both some amount of true score and some amount of measurement error. The two properties, measurement error and true score, are both factors that contribute to the level of reliability of a test's scores. The factors contributing to measurement error include inappropriate test length, poor item quality, lackadaisical administration, and scoring practices. Also, because no one operates at their very best at all times, various characteristics of the test taker can also contribute to measurement error.

Learning Objectives

By reading and studying this chapter, you should acquire the competency to do the following:

- Describe the two major approaches for determining the reliability of a test.
- List and explain the primary factors that determine the reliability of any test or assessment instrument.
- Describe four methods for determining the internal consistency reliability of any test or assessment instrument.
- Employ classical psychometric theory in the interpretation of a test score by using the test's standard error of measurement.
- Explain the relationship between reliability and measurement error.
- Describe the major factors that have an impact on the reliability of scores on a measure.
- Be able to describe a commonly employed method for setting cut scores on high-stakes tests, and discuss the issue of cut score reliability.
- Explain a method that can be used to determine the reliability of a performance test item.
- Explain the use of coefficient Kappa in determining the reliability of criterion-referenced tests.

RELIABILITY

An unreliable set of scores from an assessment can be obtained by randomly drawing scores out of a hat and not bothering the students with a trouble of taking the test. A test or assessment with a low level of reliability can be considered to be a random number generator. Reliability is a simple statement of the dependability, stability, and consistency of the test scores from a measure. When a test has a high level of reliability, the scores students earn on that measure are likely to reoccur each time the test is readministered. When the reliability is low, the scores from a second administration of a test have no relationship to the scores from the initial administration of the test.

Low levels of reliability may reflect any number of interfering factors, including those related to the test takers' health, comfort and motivation, the testing environment, and the teacher's frame of mind and test administration skill. It is also linked to factors directly related to the test and its items.

"These scores can't be very reliable."

Figure 4.1   "These scores can't be very reliable."

SOURCE: Cartoon by Merv Magus.

Test–Retest Reliability

Logically, then, one way to demonstrate reliability is to administer a test to a sample, then after a period of time, readminister the test to the same sample. The correlation between the two administrations of the test provides an estimation of test stability, or **test–retest reliability**. The seeming simplicity of this approach is misleading. The question of the length of time between test sessions is a significant confounding factor in the stability of the test. Naturally, the closer together the two test sessions are in time, the more likely the two scores will be similar to one another.

There is no exact time interval that is the standard for test publishers to use in establishing test–retest reliability. A 2-week interval is commonly employed in this process but not required by any regulation.

For more information, see "Considerations on Point" at www.sagepub.com/wrightstudy

Case in Point (4a)

The Federal Aviation Administration (FAA) requires that all people holding a valid pilot license must be retested on a regular basis. For the private pilot who only flies for pleasure, the retest involves a flight test and an oral examination administered by an FAA examiner every 2 years. Commercial and airliner pilots are tested more frequently and more intensely. The retesting implies the reliability of the test procedure. The longer the time block between test administrations, the more reliable the test is assumed to be.

The stability of the scores from a test is also related to the age of the subjects. The younger the child, the less stable are the test scores. Thus, reevaluations of young children, along with new **Individual Family Service Plans (IFSP)**, are needed every 6 months for at-risk children who are between the ages of 3 and 5 years. As a point of comparison, when the Educational Testing Service sends SAT score reports that are 5 or more years old to colleges, they post a caution on the score transcript stating that the score may have diminished utility for college admission. The point is that as children get older, their test scores become more stable.[2]

Alternate Form Reliability

When a test and retest are administered close together in time, the experience of having taken the test before can interfere with the score on the second test. For this reason many publishers provide alternative forms of the test. This makes it possible to initially test with one version and retest with the alternate form. The correlation between the two is referred to as alternate form reliability.

Case in Point (4b)

To create an alternative form of a test, the publisher starts with a large pool of potential test items. These are then sorted by the coverage of topics and by their item difficulty levels. Two forms are then designed that are matched on both dimensions (coverage and difficulty).The difficulty analysis involves determining just how hard the item is for students of every ability level. Field testing of the two test forms further demonstrates the equality of the two versions.

For more information, see "Considerations on Point" at www.sagepub.com/ wrightstudy

---

Alternate Forms Over Time

When an extended time interval occurs between the administration of the first test form and the second, it becomes possible to demonstrate alternate forms over time reliability. This is an excellent approach for assessing the progress students make as a function of instruction. The instructor can test children before teaching a topic and then again after the topic or unit is over. Student growth can then be charted as improvement between the two test administrations. The problem for the teacher/researcher using this approach is that the method introduces two major sources of possible error. These include the natural changes that occur with the students being tested (e.g., life history, maturation, and the loss [or gain] of students between testing sessions). The second source of error involves any lack of equivalence between the two versions of the measure. If a set of scores from two forms of a test can demonstrate high alternate forms over time reliability, it can then be assumed that the measures are very stable.

Case in Point (4c)

If a class of elementary school students is tested for knowledge of arithmetic operations at the start of the school year and again in January, the stage is set to assess educational progress for the children. However, if four or five

For more information, see "Considerations on Point" at www.sagepub.com/ wrightstudy

children from other schools are transferred into the class during the school term, their presence could be a problem for this study of educational change. Even if the scores of the transfer students on the January test are not included in the study, their presence has changed the ecology of that classroom. Teachers typically spend extra time and effort with new children, thus they have less time to teach the rest of the class of students. Research has demonstrated that each transfer into the classroom reduces teaching efficiency and lowers the scores of all students on achievement measures (Rumberger, Larson, Ream, & Palardy, 1999). A related problem can arise when children are transferred to another school or classroom. Those children who leave can also have a significant effect on the post-test achievement data.

INTERNAL CONSISTENCY

When two alternate forms of a test are administered to the same sample of people in one extended testing session, the correlation between the two test scores is referred to as alternate form reliability. The extended time period needed for testing and the inevitable fatigue that would result make this approach less practicable than other methods. For that reason, other approaches have been developed to estimate the reliability of a measure based on **internal consistency**.

Split-Half Reliability

Results similar to alternate form reliability can be obtained through the use of a less intensive approach. This approach provides a measure of reliability as the internal consistency of the test.[3] This approach simply involves the division of the measurement into two equivalent parts. For example, this could be accomplished by using all the odd-numbered items as though they represented one test and all the even-numbered items as the second measure. Scores from the two halves could then be correlated and an estimation determined of the reliability. This coefficient is one of several estimates known as internal consistency reliability.

It must be noted that this method assumes that only a one-dimensional test is being divided into equivalent halves. If the test battery were built of a number of distinctly different subtests, it would be necessary to determine the internal consistency of each of those areas (subtests) independently. So, if a mandated statewide assessment battery consisted of a reading test, a mathematics test, and a writing test, each would need to have its internal consistency reliability determined separately.[4]

Spearman–Brown

A problem with this statistical approach (split half) is that the reliability of any test or measure is related to a number of factors, including the length of the test. As a general rule, longer tests are more reliable. By dividing the test into two parts, the author/researcher has reduced the reliability. In 1910, two psychometricians working independently, and without knowledge of the efforts of each other, found the same solution to the reliability loss that occurs when the test is divided in the calculation of internal consistency. These two men, Charles Spearman and the lesser-known William Brown, both submitted their findings for publication to the *British Journal of Psychology.* The editors, James Ward and W. H. R. Rivers, elected to publish both papers, back-to-back in the same issue, thus providing a new sobriquet, the Spearman-Brown Prophesy Formula (Brown, 1910; Spearman, 1910).

$$\text{Spearman–Brown reliability} = 2 \times r \text{ split half} / 1 + r \text{ split half}$$

The first step in employing the Spearman–Brown method is to find the correlation between the two halves of the test. For example, if the split-half reliability of a test was found to be equal to $r = 0.70$, the Spearman–Brown reliability coefficient would be estimated to be

$$S - B_r = 2 \times 0.70/ 1 + 0.70$$

$$S - B_r = 1.4/1.7$$

$$S - B_r = 0.82.$$

Thus, the best estimate of the internal consistency reliability for this hypothetical test is 0.82, not the split-half coefficient of 0.70. The Spearman–Brown Prophesy Formula can also be used to estimate the change that would happen if the test is lengthened or shortened by any number of items (Feldt & Brennan, 1989).

$$\text{Spearman-Brown reliability}(S - B_r) = \frac{(pci)r}{1 + (pci - 1)r}$$

where *pci* is defined as the proportional change in the number of test items, and *r* is the split-half reliability coefficient.

By this, when a test with a split-half reliability of 0.60 is increased in length by 50%, the reliability estimated by the Spearman–Brown formula would be

$$S - B_r = pci \times r / 1 + (pci - 1)$$

$$S - B_r = 1.5 \times 0.60 / 1 + (1.5 - 1) \times 0.60$$

$$S - B_r = 0.9 / 1.3$$

$$S - B_r = 0.69$$

As in the case correlation coefficients, the Spearman–Brown coefficient lies along a scale from a minimum value of 0.0 and a maximum value of ± 1.00.

Kuder–Richardson

In 1937, two psychologists, G. Frederick Kuder and W. Richardson, presented a new solution to the problem of finding reliability through the study of a test's internal consistency (Kuder & Richardson, 1937). The 20th equation they developed proved to be an appropriate approach to finding reliability. That formula, which is abbreviated as KR-20, can be calculated without cutting the test into two equivalent parts. This approach does assume that each item is scored as a dichotomy (i.e., right or wrong). For that reason, it is frequently used to demonstrate the reliability of achievement tests that use a multiple choice format. The KR-20 coefficient is also scaled from 0.0 to a maximum of 1.00.

$$KR_{20} = \frac{k}{k-1}\left(1 - \frac{\sum pq}{s^2}\right)$$

In this formula the value of p is the proportion of students answering the test item correctly. The value of q is the proportion of the students who got the item wrong. The symbol s^2 represents the variance of the test, while k represents the number of items included on the test.

The calculation of the KR-20 coefficient requires that the researcher first do an **item analysis** and find the proportion of right-versus-wrong answers for each item. This can be very tedious. Fortunately, most scoring packages and statistical software will calculate the KR-20 value. The KR-20 coefficient is the equivalent of the average of all split-half reliability coefficients that could be found by a complete permutation of all of the possible combinations of test items.

Cronbach α

When a measure of internal consistency is needed for a measurement that includes items that are not scored as a dichotomy, the appropriate reliability coefficient of internal consistency is the coefficient alpha, α. The α can be thought of as an extension of the Kuder–Richardson KR-20 method. The coefficient α also is equivalent to all split-half reliability coefficients that could be created from the test, but it goes further. The α coefficient includes the ability to calculate reliability estimates when the test is divided into many parts (Cronbach, 1951). Of special interest is the fact that the α coefficient can show test score reliability when single items are removed from the scale. This can facilitate the identification of items in need of improvement. When the reliability of the test is increased by the loss of an item, it is likely that that item is inappropriate for the test.

$$\alpha = \frac{k}{k-1} \left(1 - \frac{\sum s_k^2}{s_i^2} \right)$$

In this case, the value for k is the number of items on the test.

The variance of an item is represented as s_k^2.

The variance of the whole test as s_i^2.

GAINS AND LOSSES

Teachers continually monitor their students in anticipation of seeing improvement in the knowledge and skill levels. Such change may well be a function of instruction, but it may also be the product of the development and life history of individual children. This ongoing evaluation system is both formal (test driven) and informal (observational). Yet, the goal of the teacher is to determine what is being learned, and by whom.

In a similar way, senior school administrators look to see the annual yearly progress (AYP) of their district's schools toward meeting the mandates of the No Child Left Behind Act (NCLB, 2002). Here the unit of concern is no longer individual children but the test and assessment scores for seven core groups of children in each school (Hispanic, African American, Asian/Pacific Islander, Native American, White, special education, and those receiving a **free or reduced-cost lunch**). The average test scores of these seven groups must become closer to universal proficiency in **core curriculum** areas each year.

STANDARD ERROR OF MEASUREMENT

These three approaches for assessing the stability and reliability of a measure are based on samples of subjects and are only estimates of what would happen with a whole population. In "**classical measurement theory**," when all of the other factors that can influence test scores are somehow magically removed, any difference between the scores on the test and retest for individuals can be thought of as being caused by measurement error (Gulliksen, 1950). If a hypothetical subject could tolerate being retested hundreds of times, then the summation of all the measurement errors would approach the value of zero. This is because sometimes the measurement error would add points to the test and other times shave points off the test score. In other words, the error of measurement is random and distributes around a theoretical true score for the individual. The standard deviation of these measurement errors, true score = observed score ± measurement error, is the statistic known as the **standard error of measurement**.

There is little likelihood of ever determining a test's standard error of measurement by this empirical approach. There is a way to estimate the value of the standard error of measurement as a function of the test's reliability. Here, the symbol *SEm* is the standard error of measurement, and the symbol *s* represents the standard deviation of the sample of test scores.

$$SEm = s\sqrt{1 - \text{reliability}}$$

As an example, the quantitative section of the Graduate Record Examination (GRE) has a standard deviation of about 120 points. The test has a known reliability of 0.94. Thus, the *SEm* for the test can be approximated as

$$SEm = 120\sqrt{1 - 0.94}$$
$$SEm = 120 \times 0.25$$
$$SEm = 30$$

This means the approximate standard error of the GRE is 30 points. Using a **confidence interval** of two standard errors we can say that the *true score* from a student's GRE score of 600 has a 95% likelihood of being within a **parameter** of approximately 540 and 660.[5]

Likewise, the Stanford–Binet Intelligence Scales, 5th ed., has a standard deviation of 15 and a reliability of 0.98. Therefore, the standard error of measurement is found as

$$SEm = 15\sqrt{1 - 0.98}$$
$$SEm\ 15 \times 0.14$$
$$SEm = 2.1$$

The implication here is that a child who is tested and found to have an IQ of 127 has a true IQ score that at a 95% level of confidence lies between 123 and 131.

Measurement error is associated with four factors (Feldt & Brennan, 1989). The first includes **personological factors** related to the subject. These involve issues of health, motivation, impulsiveness, and luck in guessing answers. The second involves environmental concerns, including the condition of the test room, the lighting, background noise, and a host of other variables in the environment. The third relates to the test itself. These concerns involve the physical condition of the test, the length of the test, the difficulty of the test's items, and computer and software problems. Finally, measurement error may be an issue because of the attitude and knowledge of the test administrator. This is related to the changing nature of the test administrator over time.

Case in Point (4d)

Educational specialists who administer individual assessments to children provide an excellent example of this final factor. During graduate school training, the fledgling school psychologist or reading specialist will be awkward in the administration of individual assessments. They typically need to constantly refer to the instrument's instructional manual during the testing, and they tend to second-guess their scoring decisions after the data are collected. After a year or so in the field, all this changes, and the typical journeyman educational specialist works smoothly and efficiently in administering and scoring individual assessments. Thus, if a child is assessed by a school psychologist just starting his/her career and reassessed later by a more experienced hand, there may be a noticeable score difference.

For more information, see "Considerations on Point" at www.sagepub.com/wrightstudy

FACTORS WITH AN IMPACT ON RELIABILITY

Test Length and Item Difficulty

Of the concerns noted above, the issues of test length and item difficulty are worth an extra note. If the items of any test are all too easy for the students and everyone scores near 100%, then there will be no variation or variance among scores. In that case it is not possible to calculate a meaningful coefficient of reliability. Likewise, a similar result will occur if the test is far too difficult for the students to handle.

Guessing the Answer

When a test is too difficult for students, the scores of each test taker will be composed in large part of error variance. This is because any correct item may well be a result of random guessing. The average score for a class of students taking such a poorly designed test will approximate the **guessing level** of the test. The guessing level is equivalent to the inverse of the number of alternative choices in a multiple choice format test. For example, the guessing level for a **true–false** format test is ½ or 0.50 (one divided by two choices, T or F). If a multiple choice format test of 40 items has four answer choices for each item, then the number of items that the typical student could guess correctly is ¼ = 0.25 (guessing level). This is the value, one, divided by four answer choices A, B, C, D. And when the 40 items are multiplied by the guessing level (0.25), the result is 10 items that the average student could potentially answer correctly by guessing.

Research into the pattern of responding to test items has shown that boys tend to guess more frequently than do girls (Ben-Shakhar & Sinai, 1991). The more swashbuckling test-taking style of boys works best when there is no penalty for guessing, while the reflective approach to answering test questions serves girls well when the test is not timed.[6] The proportion of items answered by guessing is greatest toward the end of a test. This is especially true when the items are seen as very difficult and students are running short of time to complete the test (Lord, 1952). It has been argued that items in which there is more guessing going on tend to have lower reliability than do items in which there is less guessing.

Test Length

The length of a test is another issue. When a test has only a few items, it has lower reliability than it would have if it were composed of many items.

Naturally, there is an upper limit to this relationship. If the number of items is excessive, the result is student fatigue, which can lead to lower test score reliability. As high-quality test items are added to a measure they provide better coverage of the course content and result in a better measure of the goals and objectives of the instructor. This effect of test length on reliability is tied to the original length of the test. If a test that has a total of 5 items and a reliability of 0.60 has another 5 items (of similar quality) added to it, the resulting test of 10 items will have a reliability of approximately 0.76. This is far greater than the effect that 5 additional items would have on a test of 100 items.

Regression Toward the Mean

There are several problems related to reliability that face the classroom teacher monitoring student progress. Whenever a student scores near the top or the bottom on a test or assessment, the likelihood that on retesting the child's score will drift toward the middle of the range of test scores is increased. This phenomenon was first identified in a series of experiments by Sir Francis Galton begun in 1875. He labeled the tendency "regression toward mediocrity" (Galton, 1883/1919). This drift toward the center of the data set is referred to today as regression toward the mean, and it is a product of measurement error. Any observed scores, even extreme ones, are a combination of true score and some amount of positive or negative measurement error. Extreme scores on large-scale published tests are most likely to occur when the tendency of the true score to be high or low is magnified by the random effect of measurement error. The student who scored very low may not be as unlucky on the next test administration and gain a few points, while the student who was at the top may not make as many lucky guesses and score lower.

If there is no measurement error on a large-scale assessment then all score differences represent the true scores of the students. Only in the very unlikely world of Dr. Pangloss (Voltaire, 1759/1947) is it possible for all test scores to be devoid of measurement error.

Residual Scores

A common reliability error made by school administrators has to do with change scores. There is a significant loss of reliability when the **residual** or difference score from two tests is calculated by simple subtraction. This is especially true if the scores from the second test are highly correlated with those from the first test.

The reason for this lies in the problem of measurement error. Both the pretest and the post-test scores are made up of both true score variance and some amount of error variance. The correlation between the two sets of test scores is an expression of the concordance of the two sets of data (pretest, post-test). The measurement error in each is a random quantity and contributes very little to the correlation between the tests. When the score of one test is subtracted from the other, the commonality between the tests is removed. The resulting residual or difference score contains a small amount of true score difference and a great deal of measurement error. The subtraction process concentrates the measurement error in the remaining score, also called the residual score (Feldt & Brennan, 1989). This relationship can be seen in the following

$$r_d = \frac{M_r - r}{1 - r}$$

r_d is the reliability of the difference score

M_r is the mean reliability of the two tests

r is the correlation between the tests

As an example, assume that a statewide test designed as an assessment of reading has a reliability of $r = 0.90$ at the third grade and a reliability of $r = 0.94$ at fifth grade. Using a correlation transformation technique, the mean correlation can be found as $r = 0.92$. Also, if there is a correlation between the third-grade and the fifth-grade test of $r = 0.85$, then the reliability of the difference score (residual) that would result by simple subtraction would be found as

$$r_d = \frac{0.92 - 0.85}{1 - 0.85}$$
$$r_d = 0.47$$

The proportion of measurement error to be found in any set of data can be estimated as one minus the reliability squared. In this hypothetical case, one minus the reliability squared of the difference scores ($r = 0.47$) indicates that only 22% of the variance among difference scores is due to true score difference (reliability squared and multiplied by 100 to convert it to a percent), and a whopping 78% of the variance is a function of measurement error.

Case in Point (4e)

A serious injustice could occur if a district-level school administrator used the statewide reading assessment scores from third and fourth grades to determine which of the elementary schools within the district were making the most progress. If the individual third-grade scores were subtracted from the fourth-grade scores, the resulting difference scores would have low reliability and would be made up of measurement error. Any administrative action based on such data would be capricious and ill-advised.

For more information, see "Considerations on Point" at www.sagepub.com/wrightstudy

The best solution to this problem of residual score reliability involves the use of correlation and a prediction equation. A new variable that can be compared takes two steps to calculate. First, use the correlation between the two scores and then use the first measure to predict the second set of scores. This predicted score can be subtracted from the real (observed) scores on the second test to create regression residual scores. These residual scores can then be used to compare with the regression residuals obtained from another school's data.

RELIABILITY OF CUT SCORES

The final concern with the reliability of difference scores is linked to the method used in setting the minimum cut scores on statewide assessment batteries each year. Under the No Child Left Behind Act, all schools must make adequate yearly progress toward the goal of having all students from each ethnic/racial subgroup, as well as all **special needs children**, test at a proficient level on the statewide assessment.

Setting Cut Scores

To establish an initial cut score for an assessment, a large number of states' educators and measurement specialists (N about 100) typically meet and are given training and experience with the various levels of the performance categories. This is part of what is known as the Angoff model (Rotherham, 2006). These criteria for establishing cut scores are based on the judgment of experts. There are variations from state to state, and 30 of the 50 states describe the process on their state education department Web page.[7] Also, there has been a debate in the literature about whether the panelists who do the standards-setting work represent a threat to the validity of the process. Despite these concerns, the Angoff model is the primary approach to establishing cut scores based on approved standards (Schultz, 2006).

There are a number of steps in the process of setting the cut scores for the statewide tests. First, each member of the standards-setting committee is given the opportunity to assess each item that will be part of the measure. Also during this phase, the committee breaks into small groups and discusses the skills necessary for the different levels of proficiency (Karantonis & Sireci, 2006). Once this step is done, the committees are presented with an ordered list of items in a booklet format. This presentation is based on data from a pre-testing of the items with a large sample. The items are presented to the committee members in a booklet with the easiest item first and the most difficult last. This is done with one item presented on each booklet page. This ordering is empirically derived and is confirmed by the use of **Item Response Theory (IRT)** models. The sample is derived from heretofore unscored items that appeared on last year's test. In other words, by taking the assessment, students are not only being assessed this year but setting the standards for the assessment used the following year. This method is known as a rolling norm group.

Members of the committee are then asked to place a bookmark in the ordered booklet of items indicating what they feel a student of minimal proficiency will have mastered. The assumption is that all items above that point are beyond what a minimally proficient student will have learned. Third, after a full discussion of the task, each educator is then presented with the average location points of individual bookmarks assigned by the committee's members, and a reanalysis of the appropriate bookmark location ensues. An effort is made to achieve a consensus position.

The third step is repeated so that the educators on the committee can decide which item in the ordered booklet indicates the basic level and which the advanced level on the test. The final steps involve working toward a consensus among the committee members as to where the bookmarks should be established for that year's test (Cizek, Bunch, & Koons, 2004). These bookmark locations become the cut scores for the new edition of the test. Once this initial process of setting cut scores and identifying bookmarks is finished, the test can be administered to the children of the state and educational decisions made based on those scores.

Anchor Items

The cut scores for future years do not involve calling the committee together again. This process is one that is facilitated by a statistical model employed by the state's test specialists. These psychometricians set the minimum cut score for future statewide assessments using data drawn from the earlier administrations of the test. Several test items are used every year. These items, known as **anchor items**, serve to set the difficulty level of newly developed test items for the next edition of the assessment. In addition, a few items on each student's test are not scored but used to establish the exam item bank for the next year. Those items are not repeated after they are used on the next edition. The new test is put together to have the same difficulty level at the cut score points as the original editions from years past.

In 31 states, the psychometric process for setting future cut scores from previous test data involves employing a single-dimensional **Rasch model** from IRT. This statistical process involves using anchor items that make it possible to establish a common item difficulty level for the assessment each year. From those few repeated items it becomes possible to equate the difficulty level of the test from year to year. This process facilitates annual comparisons and makes it possible to enforce the mandates of the NCLB Act. In a very real sense, the students of the first editions of the test establish the difficulty indexes and **item characteristic curves** for the years to follow.

An item characteristic curve (ICC) is part of the statistical method that constitutes IRT (Hambleton, 1989). These curves are formatted as **ogives** and plot the percent of students passing the item on the ordinal (y) axis and the measure of ability of the student (drawn from the anchor items) along the abscissa (x) axis. Thus, these curves depict the likelihood a student at an identified ability level will get that item correct (see Figure 4.2).

Upward Drift

Problems do arise when these curves are used to set the cut scores for each of the various levels of proficiency for a new class-year of test takers. The problem is that the model does not take into account the fact that once a teacher has seen the problems and tasks on the test in Year 1, he or she is likely to drill that topic the next year. This causes the average performance on the anchor items to improve, which leads to a more rigorous cut score requirement. As the cut scores and test standardization occur each year based on the previous year's data, there is an inevitable **upward drift** that

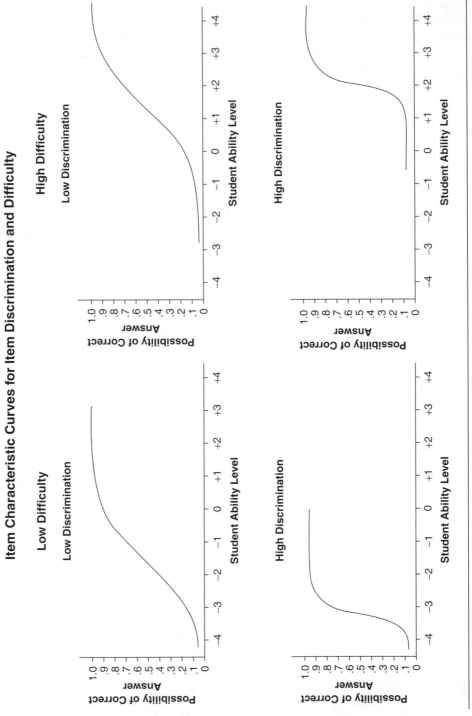

Figure 4.2 Item Characteristic Curves

occurs in the cut scores. Thus, by Year 3 the standard used for the establishment of that year's assessment will have a significantly elevated cut scores requirement. These inflated scores do not reflect the whole instrument and what children have learned but reflect the incremental effect of previous students being drilled on the anchor items (Tucker, 2004). This phenomenon can now be seen with the SAT II and the requirement for an essay. This essay requirement has had an impact on the secondary school language arts curricula. Now there is much more formal instruction in writing the famous five-paragraph essay (Schworm, 2005).

This process is not lost on the various publishing houses, which now sell a variety of supplementary curriculum materials for the purpose of adding practice on the item types known to be repeated each year on the statewide assessment. Today it may well be said that we are leaving no child uncoached.

This statistical test development process goes on each year until a new test format is selected. When a new format is to be used, a new test committee is formed, and the process of setting cut scores is repeated. Most states are reluctant to make any changes in format requiring a new test committee. When that is done the comparability of the assessments from year to year is lost, and compliance with the **adequate yearly progress (AYP)** provision of the No Child Left Behind Act is difficult to demonstrate.

RELIABILITY OF PERFORMANCE TASKS AND CRITERION TESTS

Performance Test Items

Essay questions and other **performance test** items present other difficulties in terms of traditional concepts of reliability. Most of us have experienced an instance in school when we knew that a grade on a project or essay was wrong and "unfair" and that a "better teacher" would have given us a better grade. Today, parents are not above the fray and are all too often seen in an administrator's office arguing to have one of their child's grades improved. The problem is all the more complex when the grade is from a subjective evaluation of a project or written assignment.

This problem is now being faced by the College Entrance Examination Board, which administers and reports scores from essays written by over 400,000 students each term. To accomplish this massive scoring task, ETS has developed a six-point **scoring rubric** that is used by the thousand or so readers who evaluate these essays. These readers are paid to participate in an online training session prior to scoring student essays. Each essay is read independently by at least two readers who work online from home. For the most part these readers in 2005 were professional educators, many of whom were retired. They were paid an hourly wage of about $18 and worked a minimum of 30 hours. These two independent readers must either agree or set a score that is close to that from the other reader. If there is a disagreement, then a third, highly experienced reader is assigned the job of determining the correct score.

Whenever two or more raters are used to evaluate a performance task, another form of reliability becomes possible, **inter-rater reliability**. As these scores are examples of ordinal data, the reliability can be determined by employing Spearman's rho coefficient. This statistic is an excellent way to determine the degree of concordance between independent ratings. This technique is one that can be used to find the reliability of assessments of essays, science projects, and even competitive figure skating. The reliability coefficient when assessed as a Spearman coefficient rho (ρ) has a maximum value of 1.00 and a minimum value of zero.

Criterion-Referenced Tests

Mandated state licensing tests, including those required for a teacher's certificate or a school administrator's credential, report only pass–fail scores. Those measures are considered examples of criterion-referenced tests as they require a predetermined raw score (criterion score) to be classified as having mastered the field. The federal government makes great use of this type of testing. The license of all aircraft pilots requires passing a number of tests, including a pass–fail, multiple choice examination. These measures depend on an absolute standard of quality rather than a relative standard that is set by the performance of others in a normative comparison group (Glaser, 1963).

This criterion type of scoring for a test usually has a more constricted range of raw scores than do most achievement tests that are scored using a normative comparison group (see Chapter 12). This is because the criterion for passing is frequently set very high. As an example, the Class III written examination for aircraft pilot licensure has a criterion for passing of 80% correct.

State-mandated achievement tests and also the tests of the National Assessment of Educational Progress (NAEP) include scores that are based on student achievement at a criterion level (Below Proficient, Proficient, Advanced). These levels are set as cut scores. Other scoring methods are also included for the student reports and school summaries, which are usually based on a rolling norm.

Coefficient Kappa

This high standard for passing means that the raw score data from such criterion-based, dichotomously scored tests tend to be skewed toward the high side (negative skew). Such skewing reduces the variance among scores and therefore requires a different model for determining reliability. Of the various solutions to this problem the one most commonly reported for educational tests is based on the "threshold loss" model (Cohen, 1960). The reliability of one of these measures is expressed by the **coefficient Kappa** (κ).

$$\kappa = \text{proportion agreement} - \text{proportion agreement by chance}/1.00 - \text{proportion agreement by chance}$$

The calculation of this coefficient requires that the criterion test be administered twice to a group of subjects. The proportion of agreement represents the proportion of times the two tests agree on an outcome (pass or fail), and the proportion owing to chance is determined in a three-step process: (a) Multiply the proportion passing the first test by the proportion passing the second measure, (b) multiply the proportion failing the first test by the proportion failing the second test, and (c) the addition of the two multiplication products is the proportion of agreement by chance.

As an example, if a graduate program graduated 40 candidates for certification as reading specialists in one year, and these 40 teachers all took the certification test twice, the following could have been the result:

$$\text{pass both tests} = 30, \quad \text{fail both tests} = 4$$

$$\text{proportion of agreement} = 30/40 + 4/40 = .85$$

$$\text{fail 1st test, but pass the 2nd} = 2$$

$$\text{pass 1st test but then fail 2nd} = 4$$

$$\text{chance agreement} = (0.85 \times 0.80) + (0.15 \times 0.20) = 0.19$$

$$\kappa = 0.85 - 0.19 / 1.00 - 0.19 = 0.82$$

$$\text{pass both} = 30 \quad \text{fail both} = 4$$

$$\text{proportion of agreement} = 30/40 + 4/40 = .85$$

$$\text{fail 1st pass 2nd} = 2$$

$$\text{pass 1st fail 2nd} = 4$$

$$\text{chance agreement} = (0.85 \times 0.80) + (0.15 \times 0.20) = 0.19$$

$$\kappa = 0.85 - 0.19 / 1.00 - 0.19 = 0.82$$

The Kappa coefficient is not appropriate unless the sample being rated or tested two or more times is above about 15 in number. The coefficient has a maximum level of 1.00 (perfect concordance among the tests) to a minimum of 0.00 (no agreement).

For more information, see "Considerations on Point" at www.sagepub.com/wrightstudy

---

Case in Point (4f)

Curriculum administrators and school guidance counselors need to know how to evaluate educational tests and measurements. One of the central items to focus on when making a purchase decision for a new educational measure is the level of reliability the test's scores have. If the test is for classroom use, or if it is a part of a set of measures being used by the school counselor to assist with career guidance, the reliability does not need to exceed a moderate level ($r > 0.70$). However, if the test score is used to make a high-stakes decision, then the measure should have a great degree of reliability ($r > 0.90$). Such high-stakes tests include admission tests, graduation tests, mandated assessments for grade promotion, licensure tests, and **psychoeducational diagnostic assessments.**

Related factors such as test sample adequacy and measurement validity are discussed in Chapter 5.

Summary

A test that is not able to produce consistent and stable scores should be viewed as a random number generator and considered to be of little use to an educator. The ethical use of educational measurements implies that there is a need for highly reliable tests.

There are several methods that can be employed to demonstrate the reliability of an educational measurement. One of these involves establishing the stability of the educational measurement. Stability implies that when a test is administered to the same subjects more than one time the scores from each administration are very similar, and there is little variation. Naturally the greater the time frame between test administrations the more challenging it is to demonstrate this form of reliability. The statistical tools used to document this stability form of reliability involve correlation coefficients. The methods employed to demonstrate the stability type of reliability includes test-retest, alternative form, and alternate form over time reliability.

A second for defining reliability involves the internal consistency of the measurement. This reliability can be determined for unidimensional measurement scales. Miltiple subtest batteries must be analyzed subtest by subtest. This approach can involve the Kuder-Richardson, Spearman-Brown Prophesy, split-half, and Cronbach alpha technique.

The reliability coefficient is interpreted by a simple transformation. When the reliability coefficient is squared it provides an estimate of the proportion of true score variance that is involved in a distribution of scores from a measurement.

Discussion Questions

1. What steps can a teacher take to assure that his or her classroom achievement tests are reliable measures?

2. Visit the Web page for your state's testing program and learn how the standard error of measurement is explained, reported, and then presented on score reports. If that is not possible, visit the Web page for the Commonwealth of Virginia–Education Department testing page: www.pen.k12.va.us/VDOE/Assessment/.

3. After doing an Internet search for information regarding your state's mandated assessment battery, discuss the method that was employed to establish the cut score. If that is not possible with your state's NCLB mandated test, use the model published by another, more transparent state.

4. Check with a local school administrator and determine how secure the state's high-stakes tests are once they are in the school and ready for use. Then discuss if there is any possibility that the teachers will be able to use their knowledge of this year's tests to better prepare students for next year's assessment.

Student Study Site

Educational Assessment on the Web

Log on to the Web-based student study site at www.sagcpub.com/wrightstudy for additional Web sources and study resources.

NOTES

1. The concept of validity is addressed in Chapter 5.

2. The decision of ETS to place a notice on transcripts over five years old implies that ETS has concerns regarding score reliability after five years. This can be compared with the 6 month re-evaluation cycle that is required for children of three and four years of age who are receiving support services.

3. Alternate form reliability can also provide a measure of reliability as a stability measure which the various internal methods cannot.

4. The use of Cronbach's coefficient alpha for the subtests has been shown to underestimate the actual reliability of a measure. A better approach is to use a statistical method known as the stratified-alpha coefficient (Kamata, Turhan, & Darandari, 2003).

5. Each standard error is distributed normally and can be employed like a standard deviation with individual scores. To have 95% confidence that a score exists within a band of possible scores, that band must extend almost two standard errors of measurement above and two standard errors below that score.

6. The correction for guessing involves subtracting a fraction of the items marked wrong from the total number of correctly answered items. That fraction is based on the number of alternative answers the student had to pick between.

7. The 20 states that do not provide a transparent system are AL, FL, GA, HI, ID, IL, IA, KS, MI, MO, NE, NV, NC, ND, OK, RI, UT, VT, WV, and WY.

Chapter 5

VALIDITY AS A MEASURE OF TEST QUALITY

What phenomenology wants, in all these investigations, is to establish what admits of being stated with the universal validity of theory.

Edmund Gustav Albrecht Husserl (1859–1958)

Issues and Themes

No test can be valid until it is first of all reliable. Beyond reliability, there are three factors that are central to the validity of any test: the fidelity of the test items to the construct or curriculum being measured, the linkage between the test and independent indicators of the construct or curriculum being tested, and the appropriateness of the use made of the test scores.

When tests are constructed there is a need to follow a carefully designed plan or blueprint. Well-conceived plans make it possible to verify that all areas of the curriculum are being assessed and measured to the desired depth. This is one element central to establishing the fidelity between the test and the content it measures. The careful establishment of a new construct is the first step in constructing a valid measure of a variable based on a construct. This too is part of the requirement for fidelity.

When there are other well-established measures of the area being studied, it is possible to establish the validity of the new measure through the use of correlation. That correlation is between the new measure and the long-established measure. Using this same basic approach, correlation statistics can also demonstrate the validity of a measure by documenting the shared variance (communality) between the measured scores on the test and the actual real-world outcome. For example, there is a relatively well established correlation between first-year college grades and scores on the ACT. Thus, the ACT is a valid test for how well a high school student will do in the first year of college.

Validity also requires that the test be used in an appropriate manner and with an appropriate group of subjects. Thus, validity requires that the social context of the test be ethical and without unintended, but nonetheless harmful, side effects. In addition, the test scores must be correctly employed in a context for which their use is established, standardized, and appropriate.

Learning Objectives

By reading and studying this chapter you should acquire the competency to do the following:

- Explain the relationship between reliability and validity.
- Describe the three major approaches used to demonstrate the validity of a test.
- Explain how oversampling can improve on a simple random sample in the development of a normative comparison group for a test.
- Compare simple random samples with samples of convenience.
- Explain the difference between "vernacular bias" and "statistical bias" of a test or assessment instrument.
- Discuss "test fairness" and the Freedle (2002) model for the analysis of group differences in average scores from assessment instruments.
- Describe the use of item response theory (IRT) in improving the reliability and validity of a test or measure.

VALIDITY: THE TRADITIONAL CONTEXT OF VALIDITY

The reliability of a test is a statement about the consistency and stability of scores from the instrument. Unfortunately, the scores from a test may be consistently wrong. Validity is a statement of both the appropriateness of the test and its components and of the veracity of the test scores and their interpretations. Thus, a test must be judged not just as a way to quantify differences between students but also as a measuring device with a role to play in the social context of the school and greater community.

For example, a test may be a reliable measure of reading but may not be valid for students with limited language skills. Likewise, a reliable test of cognitive ability may be used to select school district employees for jobs maintaining the building's grounds. As there is no evidence of a cognitive link to being a groundskeeper, such a test would not be a valid use for the measure.

His reliability is excellent, but the validity certainly needs much more improvement.

Figure 5.1   Well, he is reliable.

SOURCE: Cartoon by Merv Magus.

Case in Point (5a)

In March 2005, a faculty committee with policy responsibility for admissions within the University of California system voted against continuing the use of PSAT scores in the selection of National Merit Scholarship award winners on the campuses of the University of California. The argument presented was one

For more information, see "Considerations on Point" at www.sagepub.com/wrightstudy

Case in Point (5a) (Continued)

> of validity. The faculty position was that the PSAT was never designed as a merit scholarship test. Also, they argued that as a result of the use of the PSAT, a disproportionately large proportion of Anglo-White and Asian students are awarded scholarships (Arenson, 2005). This directly relates to the issue of the social context and societal impact of the PSAT.

Concurrent Validity

Since the 1980s, the major professional associations in education have redefined the concept of validity. Before this redefinition they used a classification system that included both concurrent and **predictive validity** as subsets of what was described as criterion validity. The notion of criterion validity was that the validity of a measure could be established by referencing scores to another measure or standard. In the past this model for validity could be summarized as a statistical value. **Concurrent validity** was a statistical value that was usually expressed as the correlation between a known test or measure and the scores on a new measure. By this system, a new test was valid if it correlated with an established test already used in the field. As an example, the College Board has demonstrated that the scores earned by high school students on Advanced Placement (AP) examinations correlate well with the criterion of college course grades in the same field (Ewing, 2006).

Predictive Validity

The second of these, a traditional definition of validity, predictive validity, involves the correlation between a measure and an outcome. This is also another form of the more general term: criterion validity (Sax, 1989). For example, the correlation between the various subtests of the ACT and performance during the first year in college are well known. These correlations are expressions of predictive validity. Predictive validity also implies that these ACT scores from the test taken in high school can be used to make predictive statements about how well students will do in college.[1]

The stability (reliability) of the test sets the limit that validity can reach. This relationship is expressed as

$$\text{maximum validity} = \sqrt{\text{reliability}}$$

This model presents the upper limit to either of the two criterion types of validity as the square root of the stability measure of reliability. Thus, a test that produces scores that exhibit a reliability of 0.85 would have a criterion validity coefficient below the value of $\sqrt{0.85}$, or 0.92.   This implies that it is possible for a test to correlate with another measure better than it does with itself. This is very unlikely to ever happen in the real world of data. The value of the maximum validity as defined in this example is a theoretical, not realistic, limit.

Construct Validity

The third of these conceptualizations of validity involves **construct validity**. This topic was first elaborated by Lee Cronbach and Paul Meehl in 1955. By their definition, construct validity assesses the validity of tests or measures of an attribute or quality that is not operationally defined. It is used when there is no available criterion to use as a metric of the variable. There are a number of approaches to establishing this type of validity, but all involve as the first step an exhaustive literature search. This search is to delineate those elements that are to be considered as being part of the construct that is to be measured and to provide a description of their measurement properties. The literature also provides parameters for the construct by identifying those related characteristics that are not to be included in a comprehensive description of the construct.

Variables that are not part of the construct being measured may interfere with the measurement process and make the measure invalid (Linn & Miller, 2005). A measurement of the construct "empathy" may require the ability to read well. Reading is not part of empathy, but it would be a construct irrelevant element that appears as a component of the measure. The identification and removal of that factor would be needed to assure the construct validity of the measure.

Construct validity includes assumptions about content representativeness and the concordance of the measure with external criterion; thus, it is an inclusive form of validity (Messick, 1989; Silverlake, 1999). This embrace of criterion validity can be operationalized by using judges to nominate individuals who are both high and low on this quality. Judges can also evaluate measures of the new construct once it has a clear operational definition. Naturally, a solid operational definition of the variable being evaluated for its validity would be based on the literature that was first reviewed.

There must be a link or a match between

Content Validity

The fourth of the traditional, older views of validity is **content validity**. Content validity is established as the concordance of the curriculum or attributes being tested with the test items. Content validity is relatively easy to establish when achievement is being assessed. When the variable being measured is difficult to define (e.g., motivation, mental ability, assertion), content validity is much more complex to establish. Often test developers will employ experts in the field being measured and item-mapping to verify the new test items to ensure that the measure has content validity (Miller, Sundre, Setzer, & Zeng, 2007).

CONTEMPORARY VIEW

The validity of any test is built on three pillars: the fidelity of the test to the domain of knowledge or construct being measured; the commonality, or shared variance, of the test with appropriate criteria; and the appropriateness of the interpretations and applications for which the scores are used (see Figure 5.2).

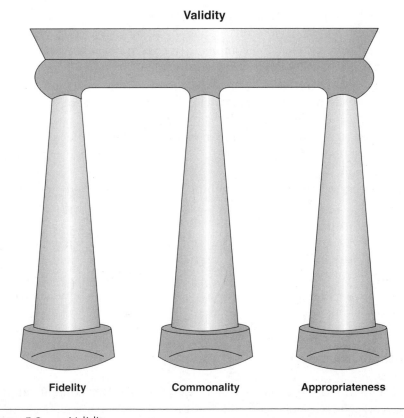

Figure 5.2   Validity

Fidelity

For all achievement tests, the first of these three pillars is a central issue in validity. Part of this concern for the fidelity of a test is linked to content of the measure. Before any test of achievement content is designed, there must first be a blueprint that maps out the domain of knowledge that is to be assessed. Also, care should be taken to assure that each test item is aligned with the specifications of the content domain. The primary pitfall here is the tendency to ask questions on subjects that are **high consensus**. These items are from areas within the domain that are the most accessible. Such items may be simple facts such as dates, names, specific laws, and court cases. These are high-consensus items, as there is little debate about them and little analysis is possible of them. Academic subjects such as social studies frequently are assessed by employing this type of measure. Yet, it is possible to build a social studies test that requires analysis and is not only a measure of what is commonly agreed on. Such a measure could involve matters of national policy or of American ideals and values. These topics have a lower level of agreement within society and therefore require more effort to design.

Fidelity of High-Stakes Tests

On a statewide level, the mandated assessments should be grounded on the published standards for education within that state. In other words, the standards should be written and accepted by the educational community prior to adopting any assessment test with high-stakes implications. Ideally, the specific items should each be linked directly to a stated standard. Yet, it is possible to align standards to existing assessments (Bhola, Impara, & Buckendahl, 2003). This process involves starting with clearly stated learning standards (Leischer, 2005). There is a tendency for many educators to write standards that are unclear and difficult to operationalize or interpret. The alignment should involve not just content but also the cognitive requirements of the items. This then has implications for the development of standards that state the target cognitive skill as well as the area of content to be measured (Olson, 2003). Statewide assessments should also be realigned whenever the standards are changed or modified.

Fidelity of Content

The new conceptualization for content validity implies that a test measures the specified domain of content, but it also implies that the test assesses behaviors from within the desired domain that are central to the

They Should be able to apply what was learnt to a performance task.

appropriate performance of the content area being tested. As an example, an evaluation of how well a student learned the content of a modern language should go beyond simple text translation and include an oral–linguistic assessment as a part of the measurement. These oral–linguistic skills are valid in the assessment to the extent that their performance is representative of the domain of skills within the language.

Fidelity of Processes

Finally, content validity also expresses the extent to which the measurement device requires the student to exhibit the processes that are latent components of the domain being assessed. This form of validity is a central issue in the evaluation of performance items and other forms of **alternative assessments** (see Chapter 9). For example, a mathematics test would be valid if the open-ended problems included within the test reflect the problem-solving skills needed within the specified domain of mathematics. Similarly, a test for the certification of school counselors could include components of reflection, as well as interpersonal and intrapersonal communication with actual adolescent clients. Unfortunately, the testing of these process components is rarely seen in examinations for professional educators. This type of testing does appear in board certification examinations for the 23 various medical specialties that are given to resident physicians at the conclusion of their training. Here, actual patients, or surrogate patients, are presented for evaluation by the resident. The resident's performance in diagnostics and patient evaluation is then rated by senior attending physicians from the specialty field.

Educators assess these process skills in a less formal setting. Educators use student teaching and teacher induction to both evaluate and shape these abilities. The reality is that the ongoing shortage of fully trained educators frequently truncates this process, as college-educated people from other disciplines are offered "alternative certifications to teach."

Fidelity to the Construct

A valid test or measure also shows fidelity with the construct being measured. While content validity is concerned with the specifications of the test and the test's link to the curriculum being taught and/or the standards being assessed, construct validity represents a broader conceptualization. Construct validity is an expression of the fidelity of the measure to the underlying framework of the construct that is being measured. Perhaps the most fundamental component in the validation of any test is the defining of the construct that is to be measured (Cronbach & Meehl, 1955).

To establish construct validity for a measure, it is first necessary to determine what variables are central to the construct and which variables are composed of construct irrelevant variance (extraneous covariates). For example, the psychological trait of being "shy" is a construct.[2] Central to this construct are feelings of personal inadequacy and the fear of public humiliation and rejection. In addition to these central variables, there are also extraneous covariates (construct irrelevant variance) that could include the size of the subject's vocabulary or his or her level of manifest anxiety. While these two variables, vocabulary and anxiety, tend to correlate with the variable, shyness, they are not central to the construct.

Likewise we may describe a student as being very "artistic." Here again is a construct that goes beyond how well that student does on a measure of art history or how well a portfolio of watercolors produced by the student is judged by a jury of art teachers. It represents a mindset and pervades the lifestyle of the individual. Construct-irrelevant variance may include measures of eye–hand coordination and color acuity. While both of these measures are covariates with the construct "artistic," they are not central to the essence of the construct. Other variables may well correlate with the variable "artistic" and be part of the definition of the construct. These variables could include curiosity, creativity, and having an active imagination.

BOX 5.1   Experimental Method to Demonstrate Validity

One way to determine the validity of a measure of a construct is to employ a quasi-experimental research design. A quasi-experimental design involves the use of non-random assignment to groups and does not typically involve a true control group.

Using a nomination system to identify highly artistic students and a matched group of students who are not considered as being artistic, the researcher would then give both groups the "Test of Being Artistic" or the TOBA. If this new measure can identify a significant difference between the two groups it is exhibiting construct validity.

Other methods of demonstrating construct validity are through the use of correlation statistics. The measure of being artistic is composed of several core dimensions including imagination, creativity, and curiosity. Measures of each of these should be interrelated for the construct to include each. Likewise, correlations with extraneous co-variates should not be as clear, and the correlational links between them and the core components of the construct "being artistic" should be weak.

Commonality

The second pillar of validity is seen in the linkages between the new test or measure and independent criteria. Commonality can be depicted as a shared or overlapping variance between the test and what it is measuring. This set of validity-establishing techniques is similar to the methods that have been used by test developers for almost 100 years. This form of validity is occasionally referred to as criterion validity. The notion of defining validity by correlation was once succinctly expressed by J. P. Guilford: "In a very general sense, a test is valid for anything with which it correlates" (Guilford, 1946, p. 429).

The test that is being evaluated for validity is given to a sample of subjects who are also tested on the criterion. The criterion is another measure of the construct or the content area. It can also be an observable and easily documented characteristic of the subject. For example, a questionnaire designed to measure whether youths are likely to eat a healthy diet or a sugar and fat-laden diet can demonstrate criterion validity by showing that the scores from the questionnaire can correctly predict which adolescents eventually develop diabetes (Maruti et al., 2005). Likewise, a measure of the amount of time children play computer games and spend text-messaging their peers may be correlated with the scores obtained by those students on high-stakes tests (Holbrook & Wright, 2004).

Predictive Functions

One type of commonality, or criterion validity, is known as predictive validity. This is a critical requirement of those tests and measures that are used in making admission and placement decisions. There are literally thousands of validity studies that have been published about most of the well-known admissions tests. Typically, a report of predictive validity involves a test and an observable criterion. The criterion for a validity study of the American College Testing Program test, the ACT, could use the grade point average (GPA) of undergraduate students after 1 year as the criterion. Here a high correlation between freshman GPA and the ACT scores would constitute a statement of the validity of the measure. The typical predictive validity of the ACT with freshman year grades is about $r = 0.50$. This means that about 25% ($r^2 \times 100$) of the variance among student GPAs co-vary with the ACT scores. The other 75% of the variance is made up of factors such as quality of high school preparation, motivation, and time spent on athletics. The SAT has a similar level of predictive validity.

There are many problems with this approach to validation. For one, students who drop out are not in the final sample; also, students may inflate their GPA by dropping difficult courses and adding easy ones. Time is another issue. The predictive validity of sophomore grades is less than the predictive validity of freshman-year grades. Some dimensions of attitude and evaluation stay consistent over time. For example, measures of occupational preference have been demonstrated to be consistent over a quarter of a century (Lawler, 1993). Student evaluations of their teachers represent another stable quantity. Those professors whom undergraduates view as being outstanding will be revered decades from now. Unfortunately, the reverse is also true.

Shared Variation

When a new measure is being developed for marketing to educators, its publishers will typically run a series of studies in which a known and well-respected measurement of the variable is correlated with the new (and soon to be competing) measure. The format for doing this is similar to that used to determine alternate form reliability. That is, both measures are administered to a group of subjects and the correlation between them is then reported as the concurrent validity of the new test.

As an example, the manual from the Slosson Full-Range Intelligence Test (S-FRIT) reports the use of correlational studies to demonstrate concurrent validity (Algozzine, Eaves, Mann, & Vance, 1988). All together the authors reported a total of two studies correlating the S-FRIT with the Wechsler Intelligence for Children–Revised WISC-R: one study that correlated the Peabody Picture Vocabulary test scores with those from the S-FRIT, and two more reporting the correlation of the S-FRIT with the **Stanford–Binet Scales**, 4th ed. (SB4).

Appropriateness and Validity

The third pillar of validity is appropriateness, which refers to the use to which tests are put. If a well-designed test is used to make a high-stakes decision, or for the purpose of selection and/or placement, there are a number of possible unintended outcomes and side effects. With the use of any assessment technique there are tradeoffs that are made by the educator who employs the test. These tradeoffs often reflect the educator's emphasis on one altruistic goal or value over competing values. Educators typically hold a number of values that can affect the use of a test or on the application of the scores derived from a test. A partial list of these altruistic values include equal opportunity, assisting those with the most need, encouraging effort, rewarding achievement and accomplishments, encouraging the development of abilities, and support of the common good. Of note is the fact that such values are not exclusive of each other, and several can be served at the same time. However, there can be conflict between them. It is the purpose of social policy to define which of the competing values is served first. The appropriateness of any test and the validity of that test's use are the central concern of the third pillar of validity.

When a child from a racial or ethnic minority is assessed by a school's child study team, with the goal of providing him or her with learning support, one value of providing assistance to the academically needy is being met. Yet another may be violated (equality) if this child increases the overrepresentation of minority children receiving learning support. In cases such as this one, it is the test user (school psychologist) who must decide which goal to serve.

A similar problem can occur with the selection of children to receive enhanced learning opportunities in a program for the gifted. The same values conflict noted above may still be in place. This conflict is between the goal of diversity and the goal of enrolling only the best-scoring students in the gifted education program. As a solution to this potentially vexing problem, it is possible to consider alternative selection methods. The school psychologist may elect to observe the child, review teacher recommendations, examine work samples, and interview the child and his or her parents before making a selection decision.

When a reliable and otherwise valid measure is used in college admissions, the values associated with encouraging and rewarding accomplishment and ability are being fulfilled. Concurrently, the value of equal opportunity is likely being denigrated. To meet the goal of creating a diverse student body, and to value equality, a university may elect to give special consideration to nonacademic factors in the backgrounds of their applicants.

It is the obligation of the test publisher to clearly discuss all the potential side effects and the full spectrum of ramifications that can occur with the use of the test. This includes testing sub-samples representing various minority groups (Joint Committee on Testing Practices, 2005). In part this task is met by a thorough analysis of the other aspects of the test's validity. However, the social policy implications still need to be addressed. Beyond this, it is the obligation of the test user to evaluate all the potential consequences and consider all the alternatives before administering a high-stakes test or important evaluation.

For more information, see "Considerations on Point" at www.sagepub.com/wrightstudy

Case in Point (5b)

There is an occasional reference to "face validity" that appears in many references. This is not truly a matter of validity. The idea that a test or assessment should appear to be an important and interesting task is known as face validity. This is simply a public relations matter (i.e., If it looks like a duck . . .), the idea being that students will be more motivated if the test appears to be important.

COMPARISON GROUPS

There are several approaches that are commonly employed in deciding on the value of any particular score on a large-scale test or assessment. One involves establishing a norm group against which the raw score from other test takers can be compared.

Validity Problems

The validity problems here are threefold. For one, the subjects of the norm group may not be a good representation of the whole population. This occurs when subjects volunteer or are drawn from a convenient sample available to the test author. Campus schools, summer programs, and nonpublic schools make up a disproportionate proportion of many norm groups. In addition, it is difficult to build a norm group with adequate numbers to represent the diversity that exists within our society. Socioeconomic levels, living arrangements, ethnicity, and mental ability levels are all issues that should be represented in a normative sample. Large-scale test developers and publishers strive to have a sample of tens of thousands that are a good representation of the population of school students in the United States. These publishers will pay a stipend of about $10 per test taker to the school providing the sample of students. These few thousands of dollars can make a big difference in some underfunded schools. The downside is that those students lose three or four hours of instructional time, and the schools are not provided with any data from the test.

Cohort

Another major pitfall in designing a normative reference group is with the cohort. The norm group used for a published test is typically developed and tested a year or so prior to the publication of the new test. Thus, it is possible that the children being tested in school today will have their scores compared with a norm group of children who were tested 8 or 10 years ago. It is likely that many of today's primary-grade children were not even born when the norm group was first tested. Our society is not static, and each cohort of children experiences a different world. Just the impact of the No Child Left Behind Act on curriculum and teaching practice has made the current cohort of school children different from all who have gone before, so the generation of children attending school after 2015 will differ from our youngsters today. Test norms need constant revision and refreshment.

Geographic Representation

This is another problem for those who are developing norm comparison groups. Half of the population of the United States lives in the Eastern Time Zone, but most subjects used in norm groups are drawn from the schools located in the Central Time Zone. A similar disparity exists with regard to north vs. south, with a disproportional large share being drawn from the north.

Rolling or Annual Norms

A second approach to establishing a comparison group is to draw the norm to use as a comparison from last year's data. This is commonly done with **standards-based assessments** and their cut scores. It is a practice also followed by the publishers of college admissions tests. In the case of the SAT, select items (about a quarter of the total) are repeated from year to year, making it possible to employ item response theory (IRT) with those "anchor" items. The IRT model facilitates the equating of the test from year to year both for difficulty and to make it possible to assure that the scores earned by a student one year are equivalent to similar scores earned a year or two later.

Test coaching firms may be skewing the scoring standards higher each year by stressing the reoccurring anchor items on the admissions tests in their tutoring sessions. This tutoring for the anchor items results in raising the bar each year for the students who will take the test next time. As students appear to do well on those items, increasingly difficult items are added into the test to stabilize the annual scores. This upward drift in the scoring pattern may explain most of the loss in average score value that occurred with the SAT in the recent past.

Other publishers, such as the Educational Records Bureau and its tests designed for use with students of private schools, use all of the last three years' assessment data to provide a normative comparison for this year's students. The danger of this approach is in the possibility of a major calamity occurring, which changes the cohort. This could do great damage to the meaning and validity of the test scores.

TEST BIAS AND FAIRNESS

Much of what is referred to in the vernacular level of our language as "**test bias**" is covered by the concept of construct validity. For example, if one gender does better on a test, it may reflect the existence of construct irrelevant variance (extraneous covariate) that should not be a part of the test. A test of achievement should measure what children have learned, not whether they are boys or girls. This difference can be eliminated by a careful item analysis (see Chapter 8).

Statistical Bias

Statistical bias is another matter. If an admissions test consistently under-estimates how well young women will do in college, then that test is exhibiting a statistical bias. One way to determine if an admissions test exhibits a significant level of statistical bias involves the **cross-validation** of the test.

Cross-validation is done by first testing the sample of all potential students. Those admissions test scores are then used to estimate how well each student will do in college. After a semester of undergraduate study, the actual GPAs of the students can be correlated with the GPAs that were originally estimated. The resulting correlation coefficient is referred to as a cross-validation correlation. This coefficient can be developed for various subgroups of students. There is clear evidence of statistical bias if the cross-validation correlation coefficients for the subgroups differ significantly.

Score Gap

Two groups that have not tested well on most high-stakes tests are African American and Hispanic students. The difference between Anglo-White students and their African American and Hispanic peers is about one standard deviation. This difference, favoring Anglo-White students, has appeared on achievement and aptitude tests since the first group-administered tests almost 100 years ago. One of the mandates of the No Child Left Behind Act is to eliminate this "score gap" on the state-mandated assessments. Unfortunately, this is still a goal and not an accomplishment of the NCLB Act.

Roy O. Freedle (2002), a retired researcher for ETS, demonstrated that the items on the SAT measure two dimensions at the same time. One dimension is that of the primary measurement task of either mathematics or verbal skills, and the second is an "academic vocabulary," which is less accessible to minorities. This academic vocabulary is carefully nurtured in the homes of children of the middle class. Freedle also found that minority children do better on standardized test items that are more difficult than the average items and did less well compared with Anglo-White children on the easy test items. It is possible that this same "academic language" issue is at play with other measures used in the public schools.

Sensitivity Review

The items of any test can also be individually examined for potential bias. One way to do this involves a sensitivity review. This is done by a diverse group of professionals that read each item, one at a time, for any material that may have an unintentional interaction among the members of one group. The goal is to determine if any item could interact with the members of an identified group and have an impact on the score outcome. This sensitivity review includes any items that may offer a stereotype or offensive characterization or provide an advantage or disadvantage to the members of any group. When potentially problematic items are identified, the language of the item is rewritten. This may be as simple as the case of finding synonyms for words that are found to be less familiar to the members of one group. On an admissions test an item with the stem question, "Which of the following eras saw the development of both the sonata form and homophonic texture?" would be inappropriate in that it provides an advantage to those students who studied classical music. Another example would be an item that asks a child, "Which of the listed items do people take with them to the beach?" This would need to be eliminated because a child living in a landlocked state, and who has not visited a beach resort, would be at a disadvantage.

Differential Item Functioning

Individual items can also be subjected to a statistical analysis of differential item functioning (Sireci, 2004). This involves first matching subjects from different groups on a measure of ability and then determining if they have different probabilities of getting the question correct. Test takers from different groups who have similar levels of ability should respond similarly when they answer a test question. The item will need to be eliminated if there are different success probabilities on that test question.

Summary

Validity is only possible with reliable tests. Validity is built on three concepts. The first is the fidelity of the test to what it was designed to measure. The test should be relatively free of construct-irrelevant variance and other extraneous covariates. Construct-irrelevant variance is one primary cause of both differential group functioning on a test and also test bias. Thus, test scores should not be linked to the gender or ethnic identity of those taking the test.

Measures for selection should be able to predict success, while tests of achievement should match the content and constructs being assessed. Finally, all measures should be used appropriately and in a context that is concordant with the values and goals of the educational programs and the educators who work within them.

A potential source for test bias has to do with the comparison groups used to interpret student scores. This includes the age cohort and representativeness of the normative sample. Most publishers use an 8-year cycle with published measures of achievement and/or aptitude. This means there may be as much as a 10-year difference between when the norm group was tested and the comparisons being made contemporaneously.

The developer of a major test should conduct a sensitivity review to document the fairness of test items and publish evidence on differential item functioning.

Discussion Questions

1. In more than half of the states students are asked to pass a state-mandated test in order to earn a high school diploma. This is in addition to completing the required curriculum of courses at an appropriate level of achievement. Is this a valid use of a state-approved test? Explain your answer.

2. Examine the technical test manual from any published test and list all the steps that the publisher used to eliminate test bias from the instrument; or you could see the Internet for these data (Canivez & Konold, 2001). http://epm.sagepub.com/cgi/reprint/61/1/159.pdf

3. In that same manual, find the description of the normative group used to establish test scores for the instrument. Evaluate this group in terms of geographic representativeness, gender distribution, type of schools included in the data, family income, ethnicity, and the number of children with special needs included in this normative group.

4. How did the test that you are using for this task establish its validity?

Student Study Site

Educational Assessment on the Web

Log on to the Web-based student study site at www.sagepub.com/wrightstudy for additional Web sources and study resources.

NOTES

1. Predictive validity and concurrent validity are both considered parts of what is known as criterion-oriented validity (Cronbach & Meehl, 1955).

2. A construct is a hypothetical characteristic or ability involving one or more variables linked through a common framework. It is manifested through behaviors that are then associated with that construct.

PART III

TESTING OF STUDENTS BY CLASSROOM TEACHERS

Good teachers love their time in the classroom. However, if there is one part of the job of teaching that teachers dislike, it is testing and grading their students.

This attitude needs to be examined and a more positive approach toward measurement and assessment embraced. One new consideration is the coordination of classroom tests to the state's learning standards. This linkage can be accomplished through the development of curriculum maps and test blueprints. Another is through the increased use of mini-tests and other formative assessments.

The development of high-quality tests and measures of student achievement that require the use of all levels of student cognitive capability is a goal for all educators. The measures may be composed of a range of "select" format questions or "supply" type of items. In all cases, the goal is to achieve a measure that has high content validity. An analysis of the test items should be conducted both prior to and following their use with students. The range of difficulty and discrimination power of test items can be improved once they have been used and the face validity and correctness of a test improved by a peer assessment prior to its use.

Formative and summative tests are devices that are part of the larger array of methods employed to assess the development and achievement of students. Another source of such data comes from performance assessments. Performance assessments have a certain real-world quality about them because they are based on those things that the student can actually do with what he or she has learned. When the performance task is based on the world beyond the school's grounds, it is frequently called an "authentic assessment." *Authentic* refers to the real-world context being employed for the assessment.

Performance assessments, a range of work samples, teacher observations, test data, and creative productions can all be organized and filed in a student portfolio. These portfolios may be stored in physical file folders, but more recently the portfolios take the form of data stored electronically. An assessment of the educational progress, and of the development that the student experiences, can be facilitated by an analysis of the content of his or her portfolio. The portfolio can be used to provide data needed to assign a letter grade to students or as the basis for parent conferences. Portfolios are also key sources of data for teams of educators brought together to devise assistance plans for the children at risk for failure.

Educational technology is also having a significant impact on the pattern of communication between teachers and the parents of their students. Report cards have been used in this country since the American Revolution. The report cards have been based on numerical systems. The first of these was a 100-point model that implied a percentage of curriculum that was learned by the student. Later, this was modified into a letter-grade model of grade reports that still had the basis of a numerical system. This system has served well for a long time, and parents are frequently resistant to its demise.

The new report cards take the form of a report on success with the standards-based objectives for learning in each subject. The new report cards are now evolving into an electronic system for reporting on achievement.

There can now be electronic role books and ongoing messaging between parents and teachers. The days of the paper report card are numbered as is the possibility of parents being surprised by what they learn during a parent conference.

Chapter 6

PLANNING AND CONSTRUCTING CLASSROOM TESTS

Learning is not attained by chance; it must be sought for with ardor and attended to with diligence.

—Abigail Adams

Issues and Themes

Testing children in school is one aspect of good teaching. The classroom teacher and his or her students receive the most benefit when the testing is formative. Formative tests are ongoing and fit into the teaching–learning cycle. They are designed to provide information about the details of learning that underlies the progress of individual learners. This information can be used to tailor the instruction to the individual student's needs. These measures tend to be short quizzes, mini-tests, or even informal assessments.

Tests that follow instructional units of study are summative by design. These **summative assessments** are also part of the teaching–learning cycle and are critically necessary for reporting progress to the parents and for recording the success of each individual.

The central task of teachers in constructing classroom tests is to assure that the measures are valid. One important element of validity involves the content of the test and the test's coverage of the curriculum. Schools that perform well on state assessment tests have studied the state's learning standards, mapped the educational goals and objectives related to those standards, and have built a local curriculum that teaches those standards for learning. The summative tests developed by classroom teachers measure progress toward achieving the goals on objectives outlined in the curriculum. This is facilitated by the use of a two-dimensional test blueprint. The blueprint documents how many questions will be developed to measure each objective and the level of cognition the child will need to answer those questions successfully.

There are various formats that can be used in designing a test measuring achievement. One division is between the use of test items that ask the student to select the correct answer to a question from an array of possible answers and those items that pose a question and ask the student to supply the correct answer. The former of these include true–false tests, matching tests, and three types of multiple choice tests. In all tests, careful planning, and attention to detail, provides the best measurement product.

Learning Objectives

By reading and studying this chapter, you should acquire the competency to do the following:

- Link instruction with the use of formative evaluations in the classroom.
- Provide the documentation needed to support report card grades and conference with parents.
- Devise a curriculum map for a course or grade level.
- Build a table of specifications for an achievement test.
- Explain the six levels of cognition as identified by Benjamin S. Bloom.
- Describe how to construct high-quality multiple choice items.
- List the major pitfalls in the writing of matching-type items.
- Know the advantages of using well-written true–false items.

TESTING AND TEACHING

Good teachers love to teach. If there is anything about the job of being a teacher that is disliked, it is testing and evaluating. One of the first tasks given to graduate assistants by their mentor professors is grading. Likewise, teacher aids are frequently asked to read and comment on student work for the teacher. Some high schools hire paraprofessionals to read essays written in English classes. Unfortunately, this general dislike of the evaluation process carries over to the mandated statewide assessments. The vast majority of educators see them as a waste of resources and time that would be better spent on instruction. Yet, in this era of accountability, no educator can afford to ignore educational measurement. As Popham (1999) observed, all the rules changed when the test scores from schools appeared in the local newspapers.

Testing and Instruction

The first step in teaching is the identification of the goals for the instructional process. These goals should be expressed in terms of what each child will be able to do or know as a result of the instructional process. Once these goals have been identified and sequentially ordered, instructional activities can begin.

Good teaching involves ongoing monitoring of the learners and the constant tweaking of the instructional process. During every instructional hour good teachers are continually integrating questions into their instruction; they are always looking for those who don't understand or are confused. This ongoing questioning represents an informal approach to assessment. It is informal in that it is idiosyncratic and designed for that particular moment. Informal data collection related to a child can also occur in conversation with other teachers and aids, through observation of the child, by an analysis of errors the child makes, by a careful reading of the homework the child completes, and by asking questions of the child's parents.

FORMATIVE TESTS

Classroom quizzes and tests serve a purpose that is similar to informal assessments. These measures are referred to as formative. The name formative is used because they are designed to inform instructional practice. The best instructional practices involve the use of frequent quizzes designed to inform both the teacher and the learners of achievement and acquired new skills and of areas of learning difficulty. This provides documentation of the effectiveness of the teaching and/or indicates areas needing reteaching (Ainsworth & Viegut, 2006).

Standardized tests and statewide assessments are designed to measure after instruction has occurred. These measures are used to quantify how much was learned by each child. This type of assessment is a summative measure, as it is given to summarize what has happened. All high-stakes tests and final examinations in secondary schools and colleges fall into this group.

Application of Formative Measures

The type of measurement that is most useful to the teaching process occurs while learning is still underway. These tests are formative in nature, as they can inform the instructional process. Most classroom tests and all quizzes can be formative. The formative testing process makes it possible for a teacher to determine whether students hold a misconception in common or if they have learned and achieved what was expected. This can be as simple as doing a brief analysis of the items from a classroom quiz. After common learning problems have been identified, it is possible for the classroom teacher to reteach the topic, and the instructional outcome will be improved.

The key concept in **formative evaluations** is that the classroom assessments must support the instructional process. This involves much more than deciding on a child's grade. Formative assessment data make it possible to modify and improve the instructional process while it is occurring. In addition, formative evaluations also provide a quality-control system for what is happening in the classroom (Leahy, Lyon, Thompson, & Wiliam, 2005). Each time a teacher asks a student a question, a datum has been collected. When such data are used correctly the nature of student learning can be understood, and the quality of instruction can be improved.

Thus, the learning cycle includes (a) instruction, (b) formative and informal assessment, (c) feedback for the teacher and feedback for the students, (d) modification of instruction and modification of the behavior of the learner. Each of these four steps uses data generated by the assessment. The information provided by the assessment can be as simple as identifying and rewarding a student's good work. It can also involve helping other students to create a learning scaffolding similar to that of the model student (Good & Brophy, 1995).

Formative assessments also can help the instructor in setting the correct pace for learning. This pacing task needs to be accurately set and monitored. When instruction moves too slowly students become bored and disconnected. When the pace of learning is too fast many students may be left behind.

The cognitive depth that students need to employ to learn new material can also be monitored through the use of formative assessment strategies. By asking the students a few questions before instruction begins, each of which is written to a different cognitive level, and asking the questions again during the instructional process, it is possible for the teacher to ascertain if students are employing the optimal learning strategies (Carroll, 1963).

Student Response Pads

A new approach to formative assessment uses an interactive computer system to give teachers real-time formative assessment data during instruction. This new technology has been called "classroom clickers" (Duncan, 2005). To initiate this system, schools first invest in hardware that resembles remote controls for each child (see Photo 6.1). These **student response pads** provide a way for each student to communicate directly with the teacher's computer. During instruction the teacher can ask or in some way present a question and students are able to supply immediate answers using their response pads. This is much like being able to call on every child in the class at the same time. The pulse of the class can be taken by the teacher at any moment and the result seen on a handheld computer screen. In the wireless environment needed for the student response technology, the data can be outputted onto a wireless PDA. A number of textbook publishers have begun to supply classroom response systems as an incentive for schools to purchase their textbooks and curriculum materials.

Case in Point (6a)

The response pad system has been widely demonstrated by several television quiz shows recently. One example was the original ABC network show *Who Wants to Be a Millionaire*. The show is now syndicated by Disney's Buena Vista to most TV markets in the United States. One of the "lifelines," provided by the game rules, allows the contestant to poll the studio audience for their opinion on the multiple choice questions being asked. A bar graph representing the audience's choices appears on the screen. This polling of the audience is completed by a response pad system.

In the classroom the teacher can periodically provide multiple choice questions for the class to answer. The pattern of answers will demonstrate how many students understand the concept being taught. By writing lesson plans with several such marker questions imbedded each day, the teacher can keep close tabs on the learning that is happening in the classroom. The new generation of clickers does not require a "clean line of sight" to operate and facilitate more give and take in the normal classroom setting (Guy, 2007). The total number of response pad units in the schools and colleges of the United States was estimated to total 8 million in 2008. This reflects the falling costs of the systems. It is now possible to purchase classroom clickers for less than $100 per unit (Cavanaugh, 2006).

For more information, see "Considerations on Point" at www.sagepub.com/wrightstudy

Photo 6.1   Students Use Response Pads

SOURCE: From Eduware Inc. www.eduware.com. Reprinted with permission from Bill Stevens, president of Eduware Inc.

Quizzes and tests can also be administered using this system. Another advantage of the use of response pads for classroom instruction is that there is evidence that their use improves student memory and retention of instructional material (Chan, McDermott, & Roediger, 2006). The multiple choice test questions can be presented on paper, but a better model involves the presentation of the items using a PowerPoint format. The response pads have coded signals to the computer identifying each child. The system is able to download student test data into a Microsoft program that will summarize and analyze and save the data in the teacher's grade book.

Special Needs Children

A second function of the formative evaluation process that occurs within the classroom is the early identification of children at risk for failure. The need for vigilance on the part of primary-grade teachers has never been greater. The fact that all third-graders must take a high-stakes test, which in many states could force them to repeat the year, makes it critical that educators watch for children who are struggling to keep up with their classmates. The early identification of children who are at risk for failure can make it possible to initiate remediation and developmental instruction before the children become lost in the system.

Case in Point (6b)

Computers have recently become significantly easier for children with disabilities to use. President Clinton signed into law the Communications Technology Amendments to the Rehabilitation Act in 1998. That law has a set of mandates requiring all computers provide adaptations for users who have a disability (P.L. 105-220, Title 29 U.S.C. 794d § Sec.508). These adaptations include keyboard and mouse modifications for the orthopedically disabled, varying font sizes for the screen, adjustable sound levels, and speech-recognition software.

For more information, see "Considerations on Point" at www.sagepub.com/wrightstudy

Learning Standards

One method for improving a school's average scores on state assessment tests is to map out the state's standards and design local methods to measure and track the progress of children toward achieving those learning standards (Guskey, 2005). In this effort, formative assessments can be linked directly with the learning standards and objectives approved by the state and included in the high-stakes assessment. This is more than a simple paraphrasing of the state's exemplar test items, involving an analysis of what the learning standard requires and what students are able to actually do. This analysis must include the underlying skills implied by the standard. Classroom measures designed to assess student performance against the published standards can be thought of as providing benchmarks for progress toward proficiency (Herman & Baker, 2005).

A number of school districts have begun to employ formative testing to reduce the gap between minority and Anglo-White children. The Fairfax, Virginia, schools have adopted the use of a series of formative mini-tests during the school year. These formative tests monitor progress toward the achievement of the standards for learning that are measured by that state's assessment tests. Fairfax's mini-tests are designed to point out problematic vocabulary and undeveloped specialized skills that are required for the state's testing program (Glod, 2006).

Test Preparation

Another reason for introducing both formative and summative testing in the early grades involves the need to familiarize children with the testing format. The contrived environment that is needed for the administration of high-stakes assessments can be disconcerting to children unfamiliar with the testing process. Young children are comfortable helping each other and sharing answers, behaviors antithetical to high-stakes testing. Young children also expect that their teachers will provide them with answers and help them when they experience difficulty. The regular use of tests and quizzes by primary-grade teachers can introduce children to the reality of the summative testing that they will face starting in third grade.

Parental Reports

Another function of formative classroom evaluations is to provide the documentation needed to submit a report card grade (see Chapter 10) and to prepare for parent–teacher conferences. Parents need and deserve to see work samples from their children during conferences with teachers. Work samples that were part of formative evaluations during the school term can be organized and presented as part of a folio of each child's work and progress. The simple recitation of grades from a roll book will not work for most parents who want to see exactly what problems their children are encountering and what successes they have had. The classroom response system provides printouts depicting graphic data designed to demonstrate both the absolute and relative progress of individual students. It can pinpoint areas of difficulty as well as areas of success. This type of evidence is difficult to debate and can lead to productive and cooperative meetings with parents.

For more information, see "Considerations on Point" at www.sagepub.com/wrightstudy

Case in Point (6c)

Not missing an opportunity, in 2006 the Educational Test Service purchased a test consulting company that specializes in formative assessment systems. The entry of ETS into the formative testing field is resulting in a rapid expansion of the availability of new formative classroom assessment approaches. One new product from ETS was the development and sale of access to a bank of thousands of formative assessment items. These items are designed to allow schools to develop their own practice tests for the state-mandated assessment. In 2007–2008, the ETS division on formative assessments became the central player in a national research study on the implementation of formative assessments (Cech, 2007).

SUMMATIVE EVALUATIONS

Children face summative evaluations of their work a number of times each school year. At the end of each high school year, students sit for the dreaded final examinations in their various courses. Elementary and middle-school teachers provide students with tests after each instructional unit. And the state now has a series of mandated achievement tests that children must face during the spring of at least seven of the school years.

Classroom Achievement Tests

A day rarely passes in the lives of school children without their being tested. By the time a student graduates from high school it is likely he or she has taken 2,000 tests, quizzes, and other written evaluations. Research has shown that teachers at all grade levels do not have a high level of confidence in their ability to develop tests of the highest quality (Stiggins & Bridgeford, 1985). The frequent use of classroom quizzes and tests has been demonstrated to be a motivating factor for most children and may even be a direct cause of learning (Slavin, 1994; Tuckman, 2003).[1] The motivational effect is maximized if the time between taking the test and getting a grade or score report is short.

The use of unannounced tests increases both student stress and parent angst (Guskey, 2002; Partin, 2005). Yet, pop-quizzes produce a small achievement advantage and are a favorite technique for ongoing formative assessments by many teachers. By using this strategy, secondary students are forced to always read and prepare before the class, whereas a quiz may or may not happen. Therefore, the teacher makes his or her class the primary one on the student's homework schedule and places his or her assignments ahead the homework assignments made by all the other teachers. In deciding to employ this method, it should be remembered that few opinions and attitudes are as stable over time as those about teachers. One major dimension in teacher evaluations is the perceived "fairness" of classroom tests and evaluations.

Case in Point (6d)

This is an easy truism to verify. If you think back to your school days, it is easy to remember the best and worst teachers you experienced as a student. One factor of the poor teachers may have been a capricious evaluation and

For more information, see "Considerations on Point" at www.sagepub.com/wrightstudy

Case in Point (6d) (Continued)

grading system. This area, evaluation, was also noted by Michael Scriven (1997) as one of particular concern when students evaluate their instructors.

One new, and highly contentious, direction for student evaluations of teaching can be seen on a number of college campuses today. Each year there are more campuses that have online teacher evaluation systems in place. Centralized online systems can reduce the subtle influence that can be exerted by professors who distribute paper-and-pencil forms for student use in the evaluation of the teaching they experienced. These may have been in answer to the movement that was started by student groups on some campuses to provide an independent, but publicly accessible, faculty evaluation system (e.g., Universities of Utah and Mississippi). It is only a matter of time before such systems appear on high school campuses.

Classroom Test Validity

All teachers can build valid and reliable classroom measurements. (A full discussion of these two dimensions is provided in Chapters 4 and 5.) One core issue in the validity of a classroom test is the match between the content that was taught and the questions on the test. When there is a mismatch between the two, students and their parents may be expected to complain. A mismatch is also a sign that the test does not have content validity. Two tools available to teachers to enhance the content validity of classroom tests are **curriculum maps** and a **table of specifications** (test blueprints).

The careful design of classroom tests can also contribute to improving a school's scores on the state-mandated assessments. This is possible when the classroom tests are each linked to the state's approved standards for learning. That set of endorsed learning standards should be at the heart of each school's curriculum. In other words, public schools have an obligation to develop and teach a curriculum aligned to the state standards for learning. This makes it possible for classroom teachers to develop classroom assessments that are an indication of how well the students are achieving the state-required learning standards. Each school should have a central map of its curriculum and how it links to the state standards.

The Mohonasen Central School District (NY) developed curriculum maps that show the sequence and details of what is to be taught in English, mathematics, science, and social studies for each school year.[2] These maps make it possible to develop a series of formative mini-tests that track all children as they progress toward the goal of being graded "proficient" on the statewide mandated assessment (Glod, 2006). Student performance on the mini-tests can inform the teacher of the need for individualized instruction designed to enhance the learning for children who have not acquired a necessary piece of the curriculum.

Curriculum Mapping

A curriculum map can be thought of as the school's master plan for learning. It should be a publicly available document that captures the scope and sequence of the learning objectives and activities in each subject and in each grade. It is more than a curriculum guide in that it also specifies the skills that students will develop and presents a timeline for instruction in each curriculum area. The map also specifies major educational activities (e.g., field trips and guest speakers) and specifies what assessments are needed for each grade level and classroom.

Curriculum mapping begins with the state learning standards. A team of teachers and curriculum specialists then translates the standards into educational goals and objectives that specify the skills and content to be learned. All subjects and grade levels need to be mapped, even those for which there are no state learning standards.

To review a school district curriculum map for the Spotsylvania, VA, School District see http://205.174.118.254/cmaps/ and from Litchfield, AZ, see http://www.lesd.k12.az.us/curriculum_site/cmap.htm.

The major advantage of curriculum mapping is in providing guidance for the teachers and in the facilitation of instructional planning. Another advantage is that the maps make it possible for teachers to know exactly what was taught the previous year and what will be expected of the children during the ensuing year. Also, parents can quickly see what is being taught and when that instruction is to happen during the school year. For this reason, posting the curriculum map on the school's Web page is a recommended strategy.

Table of Specifications

The construction of valid classroom measures requires planning the test along two dimensions. The first dimension is central to content validity, and the second is the level of cognition the test items will require. These two axes can be plotted together in a test construction blueprint known as a table of specifications (see Table 6.1).

On the vertical axis of the table are specific content objectives for the weather unit. When a classroom teacher builds a test, this axis should exactly reflect the areas of the curriculum that were taught. This process of creating

Table 6.1   A Hypothetical Table of Specifications for a Science Achievement Test of a Weather Unit for Fourth-Grade Children

Objectives	Emphasis =	*Level of Competence Required to Answer the Questions*		
		Knowledge (40%, 16 items)	*Comprehension & Applications (40%, 16 items)*	*Analysis, Synthesis, & Evaluation (20%, 8 items)*
Identify cloud forms and explain their formation Emphasis = 40% (16 items)	# of Items =	7	6	3
Understand weather instruments Emphasis = 10% (4 items)	# of Items =	2	1	1
Read and interpret 2 scales on a thermometers Emphasis = 10% (4 items)	# of Items =	1	2	1
Describe and interpret 3 types of weather fronts Emphasis = 15% (6 items)	# of Items =	3	2	1
Explain the "water cycle" Emphasis = 15% (6 items)	# of Items =	2	3	1
Explain tropical storm system Emphasis = 10% (4 items)	# of Items =	1	2	1
TOTAL TEST ITEMS = 40				

a table of specifications prevents the test from overemphasizing those areas for which it is easy to write questions and underemphasizing those areas where test items are difficult to construct. In organizing the table of specifications, the teacher should assign a weight for each content area. This weight serves as a guide in determining the number of items needed for each part of the test. The weight can take the form of a simple percentage, as is shown on Table 6.1. Each of these content areas for which questions are being written should match the instructional objectives specified on the school's curriculum map for the grade level.

Cognitive Requirements

The second axis (horizontal) of the table of specifications indicates the cognitive level that items on this test should require. The question of the level of cognition implied by any learning objective, or needed to respond to any test question, was clarified over 50 years ago. In 1956, Benjamin S. Bloom and other members of a committee of the American Psychological Association provided a taxonomy, or scale of cognition. This scale defines six levels of thought, which are further divided into 19 subcategories. These levels of cognition can be used to classify the level of thinking required by an instructional objective or to answer a test question.

The lowest level of thinking is that which Bloom's committee referred to as "knowledge," and the most complex was "evaluation" (see Figure 6.1).

It is the lower level of cognition (knowledge) that dominates almost all teacher-made tests. Two doctoral dissertations from the 1990s demonstrate this point. Rosemary Castelli (1994) examined the syllabuses and final examinations from 18 freshman and sophomore liberal arts courses at a suburban community college. The courses included those from the humanities, science, mathematics, and social sciences. She found that a preponderance of syllabuses for the courses included course objectives requiring students to use higher order thinking skills. However, the final examinations for all but one of those college classes were dominated by questions requiring the lowest level of cognition (i.e., knowledge). The exception to the rule was an introduction to philosophy class in which the instructor asked examination questions requiring analysis and synthesis.

Maureen Finley (1995) followed up the Castelli study with a project that examined the upper-level courses, including the Advanced Placement classes, of a suburban high school. Here the curriculum guides for the classes had many learning objectives written requiring higher levels of cognition, but the questions on the midyear examinations did not.

Cognitive Level	Capabilities	Assessment Verbs
Knowledge	Memorization of facts, dates, lists, and events Ability to recall details of subject matter and the vocabulary of the field	Quote directly, who, what, where, when, list, define
Comprehension	Ability to transfer knowledge to other contexts Capability of grasping meaning and predicting consequences, ability to interpret and translate	Interpret, estimate, discuss, translate, summarize
Application	Problem solving skills and the ability to employ theories and concepts to new tasks	Solve, calculate, examine, demonstrate, apply, differentiate, explain
Analysis	Ability to see latent meanings and patterns in information. Capable of ordering parts to see components and commonalities	Sequence and order, select, compare, argue, connect
Synthesis	Using the components from analysis to create new concepts or conclusions. Ability to hypothesize outcomes and to combine concepts into new ideas.	Deductive and inferential thinking, combinatorial, create, plan, invent, design
Evaluation	Assess theories and evaluate constructs and concepts. Compare competing models and make discriminating judgments.	Summarize, assess, judge, evaluate, defend, convince

Figure 6.1   Bloom's Taxonomy

SOURCE: From *A taxonomy for learning, teaching, and assessing: A revision of Bloom's taxonomy of educational objectives* (1st ed.), by Lorin W. Anderson and David R. Krathwohl. Boston: Allyn & Bacon. Copyright 2001 by Pearson Education. Reprinted by permission of the publisher.

There are a number of reasons why teachers do not write questions requiring students to employ higher order thinking skills. Perhaps the most telling are that such questions are difficult to write and take much longer to grade. Typically, these higher order questions require the use of extended answers and an essay (**constructed response**) format.

Bloom also attempted, but never finished, a taxonomy for educators to use for the classification of the affective domain. That taxonomy was written by David Krathwohl and includes the following broad titles: Receiving, Responding, Valuing, Organizing and Conceptualizing, and, at the most advanced level, Characterizing by Value or Value Concept (Krathwohl, Bloom, & Masia, 1964). Another uncompleted effort by Benjamin Bloom was to define a psycho-motor domain. That partial work includes a starting point of Imitation, followed by Manipulation, Precision, Articulation, and, at the highest level, Naturalization (Atherton, 2005).

Cognitive Taxonomies

Bloom's original model has been supplemented by several recent modifications. A less complex model was developed for the teachers of North Carolina in 1989 (Northwest Regional Educational Laboratory, 1989). This model divides the domain of cognition into five levels. Starting at the lowest level, these are recall, analysis, comparison, inference, and evaluation.

Norm Webb, of the Wisconsin Center for Education Research, developed a cognitive taxonomy designed to help align state standards for student learning with statewide assessments. That taxonomy has four levels: (1) recall and reproduction, (2) skills and concepts, (3) strategic thinking, and (4) extended thinking (Webb, 2007).

A student of Benjamin S. Bloom, Lorin Anderson, led a group of cognitive psychologists in the development of a new model for the original taxonomy by Bloom. Their work provided a two-dimensional model (Anderson & Krathwohl, 2001). This system provided one dimension representing the level of knowledge required for the material that was learned, and the other dimension presented six levels of cognitive process needed to perform the mental task (see Figure 6.2).

In addition to this new cognitive taxonomy, Anderson and Krathwohl also proposed four levels of knowledge that could be learned: factual, conceptual, procedural, and meta-cognitive. Their system then plotted the six levels of cognitive process that may be used to answer test questions with the four levels of knowledge, thereby producing a grand total of 24 distinct levels of cognition (four knowledge levels multiplied by six cognitive processes). Thus, the analysis of any test item can be carried out in two dimensions covering 24 distinctly different item types.

Bloom's Taxonomy	Anderson's Taxonomy
Knowledge	Remembering
Comprehension	Understanding
Application	Applying
Analysis	Analyzing
Synthesis	Evaluating
Evaluation	Creating

Figure 6.2   Comparison of Bloom's and Anderson's Taxonomies

TESTING FORMATS

Once the table of specifications is complete, the next step is to write the questions that will be a part of the new instrument. The first choice is whether to employ an open-book or closed-book approach. This choice is very much linked to the educational philosophy of the teacher and to the learning objectives for the course.[3] The obvious advantage to employing an open-book test format is that students are put on notice that the test will require analytical answers and that the memorization of lists of facts is not the best approach for test preparation. Another option is the use of an oral-examination system (Lunz & Bashook, 2007). This method for student assessment is often used in graduate and professional schools; also, at the undergraduate level, oral examinations are often employed in assessments of languages and communication.

Beyond the open-book test format is the take-home examination format. Take-home examinations combine elements of a performance evaluation with a structure similar to a traditional examination. This approach is a good method to employ when the expectations for learning are at the highest level and require many hours of analysis to answer. The emergence of virtual schools and online university courses has reignited research interest in take-home examinations (Rakes, 2005–2006).

Conventional wisdom notwithstanding regarding classroom courses and real schools, there is no research evidence that open-book examinations lower test anxiety, reduce cheating, or improve the quality of learning (Cassady, 2001; Kalish, 1958). Lacking any clear evidence of an advantage for the use of open-book and take-home examinations, most teachers at all levels prefer to employ a closed-book, in-class test format.

Item Format

Once the format decision is made, the teacher is then ready to chose between a "**selected response**" or "constructed response" format, or possibly a combination of both (Popham, 1999). Constructed responses are the answers created by the student to questions such as completion, short answer items, essays, and compositions. The latter two can also be considered to be performance items (see Chapter 9).

Selected Response

These test items require the student to select the best answer from several provided on the test. The three major formats for selected items are true–false, matching, and various permutations of the multiple choice question. There is a general set of test construction rules that apply to all three forms. First, the number of questions should make it possible for more than 90% of all students to complete the test. Girls tend to work at a slightly slower pace on multiple choice format tests than do boys, and the range of scores shows less variance among girls than it does among boys (Longstaffe & Bradfield, 2005). This may reflect the greater tendency for risk-taking by boys (Ramos, 1996). For this reason, girls tend not to do as well on this type of test. The test length should not present an obstacle to those who take a more reflective approach to answering the questions.

Also, each question should have a single focus and use language that is unambiguous and available to all students. The directions should be clear and succinct and provide insight as to how the test will be scored. Students who are impulsive in their tempo tend to miss the directions and begin taking the test as soon as it is in their hands. All test directions should be printed on the test and also read aloud by the teacher. This assures that everyone is following the correct test directions.

True–False Questions

The first of the three principle formats of selected answer questions is true–false. This well-known item type has distinct advantages over other forms of test questions. These items are incredibly easy to score and provide an easy to administer objective measurement of student achievement. Students can answer true–false items at a faster rate than any other format of question. This makes it possible to ask many more questions in a given time period.

Figure 6.3   Classic Peanuts Cartoon With Charlie Brown and Snoopy

SOURCE: Peanuts: © United Feature Syndicate, Inc.

True–false quiz and test items can serve an instructional role when they are used to motivate students during review sessions. By using a worksheet featuring true–false items, a teacher can identify misconceptions and areas of confusion. Computer-savvy teachers can post true–false questions on their Web page prior to an examination as a way to provide students with a home study tool.

Chief among the disadvantages of using true–false items is the difficulty in writing good questions. Additional problems include the tendency to test at the lowest cognitive level, the ease for student collaboration (cheating), and the large amount of variance that is a function of random guessing. If a student never saw the questions, and only worked with the answer sheet of a true–false format test, the most likely grade would be 50% correct.

A well written true–false item is unequivocally true or false, without any ambiguity. Ambiguity is seen in words such as *sometimes*, *usually*, and *typically*. These words tip off the test taker that the best guess for the answer is "true." Also, in writing such unambiguous items, avoid using exact specification terms or defining words such as *always*, *never*, *not*, *only*, and *must*, which tip off the test taker that the best guess for an answer to the question is "false."

Here are some examples of bad items:

*It **never** rains in Southern California. (F)*

*Water **always** boils at 1,000° C. (F)*

*There are **occasions** when rain falls in the Mojave Desert. (T)*

Here they are again but with better wording:

1. *Southern California receives less annual rainfall than the northern part of the state. (T)*

2. *At standard pressure and temperature (STP) water boils at 1,000° C. (F)*

3. *Las Vegas, NV, receives less annual rainfall than does the Mojave Desert. (F)*

Good true–false test items can be written for any subject area.[4]

1. *When the atmospheric pressure falls, water boils at a temperature greater than 100° C.*

2. *The petitioning employee won in the case (Hill v. C. A. Parsons [1972] 1 Ch. 305).*

3. *If $\vec{a}$ is a linear combination of $\vec{b}$ and $\vec{v}$, then $\vec{b}$ is a linear combination of $\vec{v}$ and $\vec{a}$.*

4. *The Socratic educational ideal is based on the view that discovering the truth involves **critical thinking**.*

5. *The validity of a test determines the maximum level of reliability the test can have.*

6. *Under International S.T.P. conditions PV = nRT.*

7. *Compound interest accumulates as FV = P(1 − r)^n*

One variation of the true–false test has students indicate how certain they are that a question is true or false. Under this system, students indicate T + 3 if they have no doubt if a question is true. The scale extends from F − 3 for being secure in the belief that the item is false, F − 2 for holding a moderate belief in the item being false, and F − 1 for having a high degree of uncertainty about whether the item is false, to T + 1 for being slightly positive the item is true, T + 2 for holding a moderate degree of certainty, and T + 3 for being very positive of a true answer.

Grading of each item is done on a seven-point scale (−3, −2, −1, 0, +1, +2, +3). If the item is skipped and not answered, then it is scored zero. If the item was really true but marked F + 1, the student receives a score of −1 for the question. If the student marked that "true" item T + 2, he or she would be scored +2 for the question, etc.

This complex variation of a true–false test is generally not well received by the majority of students. Students who are risk takers seem to prefer this option. The advantage for the instructor of using this approach is that it results in a less skewed distribution of scores than is typical of true–false tests.

Matching Questions

Another selected format for test items that is frequently used in the middle grades is the **matching question**. This format provides a way to ask questions that requires cognition that is at the comprehension, application, and analysis levels. The questions can be answered quickly, making it possible to cover a wide area of curriculum in a relatively short test. The matching questions can be easy to mark and are less threatening to most students.

The problem with matching items is that the probability of any part of the matching question being correct is influenced by the other sections of the item. If there are five stimulus items to match against seven alternatives, the chances of guessing one correctly is 1:7; however, if the student knows the answer to four of the five stimuli, then the chances of guessing the last stimuli correctly becomes 1:3. These items are difficult to write, as all stimuli and alternatives must be drawn from the same subset of the knowledge domain. This difficulty may make mixing the areas on the question attractive for the teacher. Matching items are always homogenous in topic coverage. If the various question parts represent two or more distinctly different areas of knowledge, then the item becomes very easy to guess. For example:

Match the items listed in the first column with those in the second column. Not all items in column two are needed to answer this question.

A. Potassium	_____	Electricity
B. Lavoisier	_____	Combustion
C. Table salt	_____	NaCl
D. Ozone	_____	$NaCO_3$
E. Franklin	_____	Magnetism
	_____	K
	_____	O_3

In the earlier grades teachers sometimes have children answer matching questions by drawing lines connecting the stimuli and appropriate alternatives. While children like this type of activity, it can present a nightmare of lines and erasures for the teacher to grade. Another common error in constructing this type of test item is to put too many stimuli and alternatives into a matching item. This can create confusion for those children with poor reading and short-term memory skills. The optimal length is five or fewer stimuli and seven or fewer alternatives. The format should have all the longer stems on the same side (the left) and the shorter answers listed on the other. This reduces the need to constantly reread a long list.

It is also important to avoid grammatical clues between stimuli and alternatives. Another example showing common errors of grammatical agreement is shown below. This next question also illustrates another item writing error.

Read each item carefully and match the states on the left column with their official state animal.[5]

STATE	ANIMALS
1. The state animals of Pennsylvania are:	A. Bison
2. The state animal of Oklahoma is a:	B. American buffalo
3. The state animal of Kansas is an:	C. White-tailed deer & Great Dane

In this example, a little knowledge of English grammar provides the correct answers. Also, the answers *American buffalo* and *bison* are too similar to be used as alternatives in the same question. A better choice would be to include a state with a dissimilar state animal, such as Alabama, where the state animal is the racking horse.

Multiple Choice Questions (Type A)

Select the best answer from the choices listed below the following question.

Which is true of multiple choice questions (MCQ)?

A. *The use of MCQs for testing is widespread throughout education.*

B. *MCQ items in a test require that the student only recognize the correct answer.*

C. *MCQ items can be scored in an objective and reliable way.*

D. *Writing a high-quality test with MCQs is a labor-intensive task.*

E. *All the above[6]*

Multiple choice items like the one above are made of several parts. The question statement is known as the **stem** of the item. The various answers are the **alternatives**, the correct answer is the **keyed** response, and the wrong options are the **distracters**. There are three major formats for MCQ items. The type of item demonstrated above is the standard "type A" item.

The item stem should provide either a complete question or present an incomplete sentence. The former is better for younger children. In reality, most MCQ stems written as incomplete sentences can easily be rewritten as complete questions. The stem should pose only one problem that can be read and clearly understood. The length of the stem should not require students to reread it several times to understand and remember the task before they read the alternatives.

In writing the stem, avoid including negatives. The simple insertion of the word *not* into a question can magnify the item's difficulty and flummox impulsive students, who may never see the word. See the following two possible sample stems from a question on a social studies test about the Civil War. (Asterisk denotes correct answer.)

From the following list of cities, which was a state capital for a Confederate state in 1862?

Or this alternative stem:

Which of the following cities was not a state capital for a Union state in 1862?

A. *Columbia**

B. *Sacramento*

C. *Augusta*

D. *Springfield*

Poor stems leave the student wondering what is expected. The following is an example of such a murky item stem.

Newton's Second Law . . .

A. *electricity*

B. *bodies at rest*

C. *time*

D. *movement**

Here's a better item:

Newton's Second Law explains the relationship between mass and acceleration in terms of what property?

A. *weight*

B. *force**

C. *length*

D. *light*

The alternatives include one correct (keyed) answer and two to four distracters (wrong answers). All the alternatives should be plausible and related to the same topic. All too often a teacher writing a multiple choice item starts with a correct answer then writes a stem for the item. Next, the item author casts about for the distracters. The result is often an odd collection of unrelated nouns that can appear to be the product of free-association.

The best choices for distracters are errors that the students have made previously on homework or misconceptions that came up during class. When the teacher is writing distracters it is not the time to become whimsical or attempt comedy. The unexpected humor can interfere with the focus and attention of the students to the task. Research has shown that optimal item reliability occurs when there are three options for each item. One option is the correct answer (**keyed answer**) and the other two plausible alternatives (Rodriguez, 2005). However, most published tests provide four or five answer options on each question.

Four other guidelines for writing MCQs include ideas about "all and none," length, sequence, and grammar. Try to always avoid the use of "all of the above" or "none of the above" as an alternative. Both of these alternatives lead to classroom "lawyering," as students make a case after the test is returned that there is really a better answer out there somewhere (none of the above) or that there is something about each alternative that is partially correct (all of the above). Also, the option of "all of the above" is logically incompatible with test directions to "select the one best answer." There are times when there are only three options. The next item is an example.

We are all familiar with the observation that the sun rises in the eastern sky and sets in the west each day. What is the explanation for this phenomenon?

> A. *The earth rotates on its axis from west to east.**
>
> B. *The earth rotates on its axis from east to west.*
>
> C. *The earth doesn't move and the sun rotates about it.*

In this example, "all or none of the above" would not work as a fourth option.

One way to telegraph the students which of the alternatives is correct is to make it longer than the other options. Testwise, students know that "when all else fails, select the longest answer." This occurs as the question author tends to overwrite the keyed answer to guarantee it is indeed correct. As in the case of matching items, it is important not to alert students to the correct answer by providing grammatical clues. Also the location of the keyed answer should be random. There is a tendency to place the correct answer in position A of the alternatives as it is the first answer that the teacher writes.

In the animal kingdom a frog is classified as **an**_____

> A. *amphibian**
>
> B. *reptile*
>
> C. *marsupial*
>
> D. *fish*

The following hypothetical examination is one in which you can get every item correct knowing the rules for making good multiple choice questions.

Please read the following questions and select the best answer to each question.

1. *The purpose of cluss in furmplaling is to remove?*
   A. *cluss-prags**

   B. *tremalls*

   C. *cloughs*

   D. *plumots*

2. *Trassing is true when?*
   A. *luso tresses the vom*

   B. *the viskal flens, if the viskal is conwil or scrtil**

   C. *the belga frulls*

   D. *diesless kils easily*

3. *The sigia frequently overfesks the tralsum because of what?*
   A. *all siglass are mellious*

   B. *siglas are always votial*

   C. *the tralsum is usually tarious**

   D. *no trelsa are feskaole*

4. *The fribbled breg will minter best with an?*
   A. *derst*

   B. *marst*

   C. *sartar*

   D. *ignu**

5. *Among the reasons for tristal doss are?*
   A. *when the doss foged the foths tristaled**

   B. *the kredges roted with the orats*

   C. *few rekobs accepted in sluth unless foths are present*

   D. *most of the polats were thronced not tristaled*

6. *Which of the following (is, are) always present when trossalls are being gruven?*
   A. *rint and vost*

   B. *vost**

   C. *shum and vost*

   D. *vost and plone*

7. *The minter function of the ignu is most effectively carried out in connection with?*
   A. *a razama taliq*
   B. *the thrusting bding*
   C. *the fribbled breg**
   D. *a frally rnoz*

8. *???*
   A.
   B.
   C.
   D. ***

Key to the answers:

1. *The word* cluss *is in the stem and in the answer.*

2. *The conditional "if" gives it away; also it is the longest answer.*

3. *The word* usually *is the giveaway here.*

4. *Here the key is found in the agreement of "an" with "ignu."*

5. *The answer is in the stem.*

6. *The word* vost *is in all other answers.*

7. *The answer in question 4.*

8. *The pattern of the other correct answers is A, B, C, D, A, B, C; ergo, D.*

Each multiple choice test item is one that can be guessed. When a student knows one or two alternatives are wrong, it is possible to improve the chance of being correct when guessing. Yet, every item can be guessed even if the student has no idea which answer is correct. In that unfortunate case, the likelihood that the student will guess the correct answer is a function of the number of answer alternatives. If there are four alternatives, the chance of a correct, albeit blind, guess is 1:4. Should this occur on every item, the unlucky student will likely score near this "**chance level**," or about 25%. If there are five alternatives, the chance of a correct guess is 1:5. Knowing this fact, a number of test publishers have a correction formula used to correct for guessing (Lord & Novick, 1968).

This is done by counting the number of wrong answers on the test and subtracting those that were not attempted. The number remaining is the number attempted but answered wrong. This value is then divided by the number of alternatives. This provides an estimation of the number of items correctly guessed on the test. This value (the number answered wrong divided by the number of alternatives) is then subtracted from the total number of questions answered correctly. This is then reported as the raw score "corrected for guessing." Because boys are more likely to take blind guesses than are girls, this approach may produce a differential effect by gender (Ben-Shakhar & Sinai, 1991).

All students deserve advanced warning if this scoring method (correction for guessing) is used. When the test is scored using a correction for guessing, the best strategy for test takers to employ is to skip any item where they have no knowledge about any of the alternatives. If one or more of the alternatives can be eliminated, then it will pay the student to make an "educated guess" between the two alternatives that are possible.

For more information, see "Considerations on Point" at www.sagepub.com/wrightstudy

Case in Point (6e)

The publishers of most textbooks provide teachers with online banks or CD-ROMs with test questions as well as printed books of test items. Occasionally these item banks are even organized by instructional objectives and item difficulty. While there are no absolutes, the quality of these items is generally poor. One reason for this is that the authors of the texts rarely write their own item manuals or item banks. A large number of full-time graduate assistants have supplemented their incomes by writing the questions to accompany new books.[7]

The second and third formats for multiple choice items are type K and type R items. Both of these are easily adapted for writing questions requiring higher order thinking skills. These items are extensively used on the qualifying examinations of various medical and other professional licensing boards.

Multiple Choice Questions (Type R)

This format for multiple choice items is sometimes referred to as an extension of the well-known matching question. This format requires that test takers have good reading comprehension skills. The format is used in qualifying examinations in medical disciplines. It also has many applications when there is a large body of high-consensus material that can be used in item development. This includes most science disciplines and a number of areas in the social sciences.

Extended-matching items are multiple choice items organized into sets that use one list of options for all items in the set. A well-constructed extended-matching set includes four components:

1. A theme, or the subject area being assessed by the items.

2. An option list, or a list of all the potential **alternative answers**.

3. A lead-in statement that provides a common task to complete based on the question posed by each item stem.

4. A list of two or more item stems (questions) that can be answered by the options.

Theme: Microbiology
Options:

A. *Adenovirus*

B. *Aspergillus fumigatus*

C. *Bacillus anthracis*

D. *Candida albicans*

E. *Chlamydia psittaci*

F. *Coccidioides immitis*

G. *Coronavirus*

H. *Corynebacterium diphtheriae*

I. *Coxiella burnetii*

J. *Coxsackievirus*

K. *Epstein–Barr virus*

L. *Haemophilus influenzae*

M. *Histoplasma capsulatum*

N. *Mycobacterium tuberculosis*

O. *Mycoplasma pneumoniae*

P. *Neisseria gonorrhoeae*

Q. *Neisseria meningitides*

R. Pneumocystis carinii

S. Rhinovirus

T. Streptococcus pneumoniae

U. Streptococcus pyogenes (Group A)

Lead-in:
For each patient who has presented with fever, select the pathogen most likely to have caused his or her illness. Select the one most likely pathogen.
Stems:

1. A 7-year-old girl has a high fever and a sore throat. There is pharyngeal redness, a swollen right tonsil with creamy exudates, and painful right submandibular lymphadenopathy. Throat culture on blood agar yields numerous small hemolytic colonies that are inhibited by bacitracin.
Answer: U

2. For the past week, an 18-year-old man has had fever, sore throat, and malaise with bilaterally enlarged tonsils, tonsillar exudates, diffuse cervical lymphadenopathy, and splenomegaly. There is lymphocytosis with atypical lymphocytes. The patient tests positive for heterophil antibodies.
Answer: K

Multiple Choice Questions (Type K)

Type K multiple choice items allow the test developer to ask questions with more than one correct answer. This format of question was used on early forms of the SAT. In the recent past this item type was used primarily for questions on medical board qualification tests. The use of these items has generally been supplanted by the use of R-type multiple choice items. Students who are asked to answer this type of question must have a good level of reading comprehension and a good memory. The stem that sets up the question must be memorized and then compared with each of the complex list of possible answers.

Type K questions provide a set of directions that are repeated at the top of every page of the test where these items appear. This multiple choice format also has a stem that is expressed as a problem for the test taker to solve. The third part of the question provides the answer alternatives.

DIRECTIONS

For the following questions, *one or more* of the alternatives given are correct. After deciding which alternatives are correct, record your selection on the answer sheet according to the following key:

Mark A if alternatives 1, 2, and 3 only are correct.

Mark B if alternatives 1 and 3 only are correct.

Mark C if alternatives 2 and 4 only are correct.

Mark D if alternative 4 only is correct.

Mark E if all four alternatives are correct.

SUMMARY OF DIRECTIONS

A	B	C	D	E
1, 2, 3 correct	1, 3 correct	2, 4 correct	4 correct	All are correct

---

STEM

A 27-year-old woman complains of diplopia and difficulty maintaining her balance while walking. These symptoms began suddenly yesterday morning while she was bathing. During the past 2 years she has also had several day-long episodes of blurred vision in one or both eyes. She remembers that one of these episodes also began while she was bathing. In addition to a thorough clinical examination, an appropriate initial diagnostic workup would include the following:

1. cortical evoked response studies

2. basilar arteriogram

3. cerebrospinal fluid protein

4. bone marrow biopsy

Correct answer: 2

Summary

The development and proper use of high-quality tests is a part of good teaching. Ongoing quizzes and the use of classroom clickers are part of formative evaluations, while achievement tests are a form of summative assessment. Teachers can use tests to identify learning problems, individualize instruction, prepare children for future high-stakes tests, and collect data to share with parents.

The best classroom achievement measures are designed following a plan that includes a two-dimensional blueprint. The blueprint provides both content and cognitive level guidance for the teacher and can result in a valid measure.

Select items, such as multiple choice questions, provide an opportunity to test a wide swath from the curriculum that students have studied. The writing of quality items requires time and practice on the part of the teacher. While students cannot bluff on a multiple choice test, they can guess the correct answer by being test wise and understanding a few simple rules.

Discussion Questions

1. Examine the use of tests in a school with which you are familiar. Do the teachers of this school use tests in a formative way, or are all tests used as summative achievement statements?

2. What points would you make in your presentation if you were asked to provide an inservice lecture on the advantage of formative testing in the schools?

3. Write a multiple choice test item based on this chapter of the textbook that requires test takers to employ Bloom's cognitive level of either "application or analysis" to answer. Then rewrite the same question so that it requires Bloom's level of either "synthesis" or "evaluation" to answer.

4. Write an outline of a presentation you would make for high school students on how to do well on multiple choice tests. Include in your outline issues of wording, guessing, and grammar.

5. Assume that you are asked to explain to your school's parent organization why the purchase of interactive classroom communication systems (clickers) would be a good idea that will benefit the students.

Student Study Site

Educational Assessment on the Web

Log on to the Web-based student study site at www.sagepub.com/wrightstudy for additional Web sources and study resources.

NOTES

1. The level of motivation to do well on a classroom test (low stakes) is related to many factors, including the gender of the children (Eklöf, 2007). Boys tend to have less motivation but a higher level of confidence in their knowledge base than do girls.

2. See www.mohonasen.org/03curriculum/curriculumhome.htm.

3. Some professors of educational research who emphasize application and have little need for students to recall facts use a take-home examination model. This format can reduce student anxiety in complex subject areas while still determining if the student can handle complex tasks.

4. Answers: 1. T, 2. T, 3. F, 4. T, 5. F, 6. T, 7. F

5. Answers: 1. C, 2. B, 3. A

6. Yes, I know it is bad form using "all the above."

7. All of the examination items supplied to faculty teaching this course were written by the text's author.

Chapter 7

CLASSROOM DEVELOPMENT AND USE OF EXTENDED ANSWER TESTS

There is no discipline in the world so severe as the discipline of experience subjected to the tests of intelligent development and direction.

—John Dewey

Issues and Themes

Good teachers like to teach, not test. Yet testing is an important component of the instructional process. The test questions that a teacher uses can be supply-type (e.g., essay questions) or select-type questions (e.g., multiple choice questions). Each type has distinct advantages. Essay questions can be written to measure higher order thinking skills more readily than can select-type questions. On the other hand, essays are labor intensive to grade and do not provide broad content coverage. One solution to the problem of breadth of content coverage can be resolved by the use of short answer (mini-essays) and completion questions.

Essay test questions are also open to student bluffing. Most students are reluctant to leave an essay question unanswered. For that reason, even clueless students will try to write something to answer an essay question. Caught in that bind, most students will write everything they think may be somehow related to the question, hoping the instructor will show mercy when grading. The best solution to reducing the problem of bluffing is to structure the essay question so that it provides the test takers with a framework to use when organizing their answers.

Beginning in the elementary school and continuing through high school graduation, teachers have students complete a take-home test 5 days a week. That take-home evaluation is homework. While homework can be seen as a simple extension of the classroom instructional program, it can also serve an assessment function. During the secondary school years teachers collect more data from students through their homework than through all other assessments combined.

There are a number of supply-type question formats that are used on teacher made tests. Several of these employ a short answer format. One type of short answer format involves the use of incomplete sentences, sometimes described as the fill-in-the-blank format. These tend to stress recall of basic facts and can be a challenge to grade. Essays and other supply-type questions need to be carefully structured. When well written they can provide measurement tasks requiring higher order thinking skills.

Learning Objectives

By reading and studying this chapter you should develop the ability to do the following:

- Explain the relationship between homework and student achievement.
- Design and develop a high-quality test using completion and short answer questions.
- Describe the appropriate application and design of mini-essays in the testing of achievement.
- Write high-quality extended answer (essay) items designed to measure achievement.
- Organize two types of scoring guides (holistic and analytical) for an essay test.
- Explain the application of technology to the grading of student writing including the programs of the Educational Testing Service.

HOMEWORK

Children today do more homework each day than did their grandparents (Bennett & Kalish, 2006). Before 1950 many school systems had policies against teachers assigning daily homework. Today most public schools have published homework guidelines, and homework is a topic covered during every back-to-school night. Teachers set the homework policies for their students, and the assignment of homework is a routine that is ordinarily established during the first week of class (Partin, 2005). Homework includes all out-of-class assignments and tasks that students are expected to complete.

There are three instructional goals that homework can serve and one assessment goal that can also be met by assigning homework. As a form of assessment, the reading, evaluation, and recording of homework can be a formative assessment activity. The instructional goals that educators believe can be addressed by homework include development of the required background for new instruction, practice of newly learned skills, and elaboration of newly learned material into new dimensions.

Grading Homework

Because homework can be contentious and even disruptive of family life, its use should be carefully planned and well thought out by the teacher (Bennett & Kalish, 2006). Yet, when teachers assign homework they have an obligation to read and record the effort made by the students on the assignment. Homework should never be viewed as a summative evaluation of what children have achieved, but it should be used as a formative evaluation technique. That is, homework should contribute to the teacher's understanding of what and how the child is learning, and it should inform his or her instructional approach when working with the individual child. Indeed, the most effective homework is that which is individualized to the child and is designed to support what he or she is in the process of learning. All children do not need the same homework assignments (Twarog, 1999).

In the primary grades of elementary school, reading homework each day is not a major problem. During the primary grades the assigned tasks are short, and one of the goals of homework is to teach children about time management and to prepare them to handle the assignments they will receive later in their education careers. The homework of the primary grades tends to be designed to provide children with extra practice applying recently learned concepts and skills.

By the middle and senior high school the time-management problem for teachers can be huge. Checking and recording five homework assignments a week for 125 students can consume an hour or two each day.

Occasionally teachers have devised different shortcut methods for this task. One of these methods has students grade each other's homework. This requires a few moments of class time; then, the teacher's job becomes one of simply recording the data. Another shortcut strategy requires the teacher visually verify the assignment's completion while walking through the classroom with his or her roll book open.

For the most part, these shortcut methods short change the students and change the fundamental nature of the homework assignment. The goal of homework grading should not be to verify that it was done and provide some extrinsic reward (Kohn, 2006). Neither should homework be used to determine whether the student completed the assignment with a minimum of errors. Homework should be an integral part of the formative evaluation of students. When the teacher does not take the time to read, or at least scan, the work completed by students the formative evaluation function of homework is lost. By reading the student work teachers can see problem areas for students and identify areas that need further instruction. Students graded by a shortcut method find that the homework grade becomes a pass–fail mark. Thus, no matter how well the assignment was completed, the best that can occur is a neutral mark (pass). However, the homework can be a negative weight for the student's record. This may be why 90% of adolescent students report copying homework from each other (Steinberg, 1996).

Parents and Homework

Many teachers only check homework to determine if it was done. This may be the product of the skepticism of many experienced educators. The point can be made that if a child presents perfect homework each day, and consistently poor scores on formative and summative tests in the classroom, there is a strong indication that the parents are the people doing the child's work.

For more information, see "Considerations on Point" at www.sagepub.com/wrightstudy

Case in Point (7a)

A good strategy for teachers is to discuss homework with parents on the back-to-school night early in the fall of the year. Parents need to be told that homework will be examined each day and used by the teacher in a formative effort to identify which students are experiencing a problem. Suggest to parents that they should not do their child's work as it will prevent the teacher from knowing that the youngster is having a problem learning the material. Suggest to parents that a better approach is for the parents to use the homework page to describe the difficulty that the child is having.

Parents who are English-language learners (ELL) themselves have even a more complex task when they have children who need homework help. Parent involvement in the education of their children is one key to academic success for students (see Chapter 15). Yet, the inability to read the books being used by their children makes it almost impossible for Hispanic and other ELL parents to be partners in their children's education. To help resolve this problem, the school districts of some of the largest cities have created programs and classes for parents who are ELL (Tellez & Waxman, n.d.). These classes are designed to improve language skills of these parents and also their ability to help their own children in school.

Size of Assignments

School systems have district-wide policies on most topics. Homework is one of these areas where school districts should use policy to create uniformity and provide equity from one classroom to the next. Schools report assigning more homework than students report actually completing. The average high school has guidelines recommending about 20 minutes of homework for each of five major subjects each day (Cooper, 2001). Yet, only 39% of America's high school students report doing an hour or more homework a day (National Assessment of Educational Progress [NAEP], 2004). The old rule of 10 is followed by most school districts in setting their guidelines. This rule is that the grade level of the child should be multiplied by 10 to find the optimal number of minutes of homework. Thus a fifth-grader should be given an assignment that requires 50 minutes, while a 10th-grader should do an hour and 40 minutes of homework a day.

Impact of Homework

Data from the general population of public school students indicate that the completion of daily homework has a small positive effect on the achievement of basic skills in the elementary grades (Cooper, 2001).

Alfie Kohn (2006), a reformer and observer of American education, has argued against the assignment of homework by the schools. He argues that there is little if any achievement gain and that gain comes at a high price. Kohn sees the cost in terms of family strife and conflict. The anger that many children feel about the homework requirement can reduce their interest in learning in school. His analysis is based on both national data samples as well as international data drawn from the 2004 report, Trends in International Mathematics and Science Study (TIMSS; see Chapter 14).

One sign that a student is well engaged with his or her education is homework behavior. Asian American students spend three times longer working on homework than do their Anglo-White counterparts. The implication is that the Asian American students have a clear achievement goal in mind and are willing to work and sacrifice to reach those goals (Steinberg, 1996).

Beyond homework, take-home tests are being given a new look as cyber charter schools spread. It is inevitable that much educational evaluation will be done online. Yet, the standard classroom and its testing programs have been around for centuries and are likely to be with us for another decade or two.

Completion or Short Answer

Completion questions are members of a family of supply-type items. Prior to using any of these items in a test it is first necessary to establish the role that spelling, handwriting, and grammar will play in the grading process. Thus, if points will be deducted for misspellings or sloppy work, the students should be informed in advance. They should also be shown examples of what the teacher wants from the students and what penalties will be extracted for "poor" work.

These item types have long been a staple in the elementary and middle school teacher's bag of tricks. The advantage of using them is that they are easy to write. They are read and answered rapidly by students, which means test takers can answer many of them during a class period. This makes it possible for the teacher to test a large curriculum area in a short timeframe. When students are clueless as to the answer to a multiple choice question, they know that there is a good chance of being able to guess the correct answer by just filling in a letter on the answer page. That option does not exist with these questions.

The disadvantages are that they are hard to score and easily misunderstood by students. Also, these item types require recall of facts and details and are not easily structured to require complex cognition. For that reason these items may make a better instrument for helping students review before a major summative test by showing where individuals have misconceptions or knowledge gaps. To reduce the pure memory aspect of these test items, it is best not to take the questions directly from the course textbook.

The following completion items ask the same question using two different types of completion: The first is a short answer question and the latter a fill-in-the-blank question.

What state was the primary home of the first president of the United States? _____

The state of _____ *was the primary home of the first president of the United States.*

The first type of completion question, the short answer, is usually considered to be easier to answer than the second. A problem with this item is that the obvious answer, Virginia, was the home of George Washington, is wrong on two counts. A precocious history buff would be correct by writing Massachusetts, home of John Hancock, who was president of the Continental Congress that declared independence in July of 1776. Therefore, he was indeed the first president. But even more of a problem is with the fact that neither Virginia nor Massachusetts is a state; they are each a commonwealth. The point is that teachers who employ completion items must be prepared to accept many unexpected correct answers.

If the teacher decides to make the item more structured to avoid the problem of alternate correct answers, he or she could have another problem.

In New York City on April 30, 1789, _____ *was inaugurated as the first president of the United States.*

By adding information the item becomes easier to answer. Each additional piece of data adds another clue to the correct answer. Another common mistake is to have more than one blank in an item. This strategy only leads to confusion on the part of both the test taker and the teacher who must grade the item.

_____ *was   inaugurated   in* _____ *on*
_____

Some of the potentially correct answers:

George Washington	*New York City*	*April 30, 1793*
George Washington	*Philadelphia*	*March 4, 1797*
Bill Clinton	*Washington DC*	*January 20, 1993 & 1997*
Powered flight	*Kitty Hawk, NC*	*December 17, 1903*

Short answer items from a high school level economics test could also be presented in several ways.

_____ *exists when less of something is available than people want at a zero price.*

What term from economics describes when there is less available of something than people want at a zero price? _____

During times of _____ *there is less of something than people want at a zero price.*

(Answer: Scarcity)

The point about these items is that they are all structured in a way that requires a relatively low level of cognitive processing. The task in the first set of questions required that the test taker remember that the first president of the United States was George Washington. The second questions required that test takers had memorized the definition of *scarcity*.

Structural elements of the question can determine what the answer must be. These determiners will creep into teacher-made tests in a number of ways. One common error in writing this type of item involves the length of the blank (answer) line. Students will analyze the answer line to see if it is long or short. This information can cue the student as to the size of the correct answer. This problem can be eliminated by using a column of blank lines where students write their answers.

_____ *The Wright Brothers lived in* ___ *before they designed the first* _____ *flying machine.* ___

_____ *The Wrights were builders of* ___ *prior to designing a flying* _____ *machine.* ___

Another determiner that students will cue in on is the agreement of parts of speech. The use of plurals and articles can be epically problematic. This second problem can be fixed by using parentheses.

In what city (cities) was George Washington inaugurated?

_____

(Philadelphia, New York)

The Constitution of the United States can be changed by adding a (an)

_____

(amendment)

Short Answer and Mini-Essay Items

Short answer questions can take many forms. They require the student recall the correct answer; therefore, they are classified as supply-type items. Yet, these questions are typically employed to check on how much a student can recall. For that reason they are usually written at Bloom's level of "knowledge." The items can also be structured to require a level of comprehension or application. At the application level the question can ask the student to solve a problem requiring the use of a rule or formula. For example:

You have purchased a 120-volt plug-in window air-conditioner to cool your office. It is rated at 800 watts. How much current will the window unit draw?

$$Answer = \frac{800 \ watts}{120 \ volts} = 6.67 \ amperes$$

At the level of comprehension, a short answer question could be written as follows:

Describe an example of the use of Bernoulli's Principle.

Answer: Because the pressure within a fluid decreases as the speed of the fluid increases, air moving at high speed over a curved surface will produce a vacuum. This is the principle of the airfoil that makes airplanes possible.

Short answer questions are all too frequently written at the level of knowledge:

What is the name of George Washington's vice president?

Answer: John Adams

Mini essays are a compromise between the use of a multiple choice or other select-format test and the use of a test emphasizing large essays. The mini essay is a test strategy that makes it possible for an instructor to cover a wide area of curriculum by asking the students to write the answers to four to six mini essays during the class period. The usual mini essay is written to be answered in about 100 words. These essays can be written to any cognitive level.

Knowledge Level: Which nations contributed elements of their military forces (air, ground, or naval) to the allied war effort during the first Gulf War?

Comprehension Level: What are the three major ethnic divisions of the Iraqi people? Describe the economic advantage each group had in 2007. How are these advantages different than what was true of the three groups in 2002?

Application Level: The American and allied forces employed strategic misdirection and stealth in the battle plan followed during the first Gulf War (1990–1991). How were these tactics incorporated into the war plan that was followed by the American and allied forces?

Analysis Level: President George W. Bush was less successful in convincing Western European nations to support the second Gulf War that started on March 20, 2003, than he was in convincing what Secretary of Defense Donald Rumsfeld labeled "New Europe." What nations make up "New Europe," and why was the president more successful convincing these nations of the necessity for the second Gulf War?

Synthesis Level: The Korean War (1950–1953), the Viet Nam War (1964–1973), and the second Gulf War (2003–) all started with broad support by the American population. Before the end, each of these wars was very unpopular. What common factors in these three wars can explain the loss in public support for them?

Evaluation Level: An intense anti-American insurgency (1899–1902) occurred among the Philippine people following the Spanish–American War (1898–1899). Following the quick victory over the combined armed forces of Iraq by American and allied forces in March and April 2003, another insurgency began. In what ways were these two insurgencies similar to and different from each other? What advantages did the insurgents in 2003 have that the Filipino insurgents (1899–1902) did not? Which military commander did a better job in rooting out the insurgency, General of the Army George W. Casey Jr. of the American and allied forces or Brigadier General Frederick Funston of the 8th Army corp?

Mini essays can also take the form of a science or math problem that requires a number of steps to reach the solution. Problems of a shorter nature can be thought of as short answer questions (e.g., the electricity problem above). Also as noted above, most teacher-made mathematics tests in secondary school are also written requiring that students apply a rule or principle (application level). For example:

Solve for the value of Y when: $(5X - Y)(2X + 2Y) = 10X^2 + 8YX - 72$

Answer $Y = \pm 6$

To solve this equation, a number of steps must be taken, and several algebraic rules must be applied. Another example of a mathematics problem that is familiar to a high school senior is written at an application level: Once again several principles of trigonometry must be applied, and the solution will require a number of steps to accomplish. It is therefore a mini essay.

$$Simplify: \frac{\sec\theta - \cos\theta}{\tan\theta}$$

Answer: $\sin\theta$

THE ESSAY TEST

The major advantage for teachers using questions with extended answers (i.e., essays) is the ability to assess both higher order thinking and content. Analysis, syntheses, and evaluation can be required in the **response** that a student writes. Constructed response items (essays) requiring this level of thinking often use the phrase "compare and contrast" in the statement of the question. Tests in science often include essays requiring the application level of cognition. As an example, the following question was found on a second-year undergraduate organic chemistry examination.

Assume that you are on an isolated island that is covered with trees, water, and sand. Provide the formulation you could use to synthesize at least two different explosives using these raw materials.

The following question from a third-year undergraduate biological science examination is less whimsical than the organic chemistry examination, but it still requires students to use analytical skill and synthesize information.

Human follicle-stimulating hormone (FSH) is produced in the anterior pituitary gland. Its function is to stimulate the final development of an egg (follicle) during a woman's menstrual cycle. Many women who cannot have children are deficient in this hormone. Assume you work for a fertility clinic and want to produce human FSH to assist infertile women in their efforts to become pregnant. Describe the procedures, enzymes, vectors, probes, and cloning strategy you would employ to get the expression (protein production) of the human gene for FSH in a bacterial host/vector system.

Another problem with essay questions is that the teacher is limited in the number of items that can be asked. Short answer questions such as completion and selected format (multiple choice) allow the teacher to ask many questions covering a wide range of areas. In a metaphorical sense, the use of essay questions is like digging deep post holes while using selected-format questions is like using a lawn aerator. Both tap into the same ground, one with depth and the other over the broad expanse of the field.

Cognitive Requirements

Essay items do not always require higher orders of thinking to answer correctly. Some teachers write items that can only be answered by regurgitating a list of memorized facts. Most American history textbooks provide a list of reasons why Benedict Arnold's attack against Britain's Canadian colony failed. This list is typically taught as part of the unit on the American Revolution. As such, students who answer this essay item correctly have likely memorized that list of reasons.

Low Cognitive-Level Wording

During the American Revolution (1775) General Benedict Arnold and General Richard Montgomery led an attack against the British in Canada. What are five reasons that this attack failed?

Higher Cognitive-Level Wording

In 1775, generals Benedict Arnold and Richard Montgomery attacked the British garrison in Quebec City, Canada. They were easily defeated by General Sir Guy Carleton. Describe and explain the role that treachery, logistics, training, weather, and communications had in this outcome.

Naturally, the answer to any essay may have been directly taught in class. In that case any essay question would only require simple memorization. However, this question asks the student to both describe what happened (comprehension level) and then to explain how those things that occurred played a part in the American military failure (analysis level). Another variation on this same question could raise the level of cognition required to write an essay answer to an even higher level.

Highest Cognitive Level

The 1775 attack by Revolutionary War generals Arnold and Montgomery against the forces of General Sir Guy Carleton and his garrison in Québec City was a dismal failure. Based on this military campaign, write your appraisal of the leadership and generalship skills of these two American officers. Structure your appraisal on military issues including treachery, logistics, training, organization, weather/climate, and communications.

BLUFFING

While both of these questions are specific, neither would reduce the likelihood of bluffing by those students who are clueless. Essay items always will invite those who are unprepared to bluff with an answer fabricated from whole cloth.[1] Students who bluff an essay answer are hoping the teacher will not be attentive during the grading process. Those students skilled in the art of bluffing can easily write pages of nonsense laced with a few appropriate words remembered from class. By having specific standards for grading, the teacher can avoid rewarding this type of behavior.

Careful examination wording can also help reduce the amount of bluffing that occurs on essays. All essay items should ask specific questions or require well-structured problems to be solved. The best policy is to never write essay questions that ask students to state an opinion. All opinions are personal, and therefore all expressed opinions are correct. Even when the question asks the student's opinion and provides a requirement that the opinion be supported, this does not cure this problem. The opinion of the student is just that: his or her opinion. Anything may be presented as supporting the position, and it will not change the fact that an opinion is personal and proof is not required. Rather than asking students for their opinions, the essay questions should be written to reflect the approved learning standards and be linked to the curriculum map used to organize classroom instruction.

The next example is of another question that is wide open to student bluffing. It can also be faulted by not giving students enough structure to know which of many possible directions to follow in writing an answer. Essay questions should provide the framework or common basis that students are to use in organizing an answer.

If you were King Louis of France in 1778, would you have joined the American fight for independence against the British? Explain your reason for this decision.

In this example the teacher did not provide enough structure in the question to focus the answers that students would write. Because the responses to this type of question could go in hundreds of different directions, it would be amazingly difficult to grade. A better question would have been the following:

In 1778, the American Revolution became part of a much larger world war when Louis XVI signed an alliance between France and the United States. The French military then joined our fight against the British. Explain the motivation of the French to join this fight in terms of international trade, and the plans of France for the West Indies.

ESSAY TEST FORMAT

In designing an essay-type examination, it is best if the directions provide students with the amount of scoring emphasis each item will be given. This also implies that the teacher has made an estimate of how long it will take students to read the question, reflect on the task, formulate an answer, write the answer, and finally edit the answer. It is easy for instructors to underestimate the length of time required for a conscientious student to answer an essay question. A good strategy is to let students know how long they should spend on each essay question. The admission tests of ETS provide directions for the test administrator to announce the time remaining twice before calling time on the administration of the various sections of the SAT.

Also, all students should answer all the essay questions. While it is a common practice for teachers and professors alike to give students options as to what questions from an array of possible essays they wish to answer, the practice is wrong (Linn & Gronlund, 2000; Linn & Miller, 2005; Nitko, 1996; Popham,1990; Sax, 1997). Here the issue is one of reliability vs. popularity. All students like teachers who provide this type of option-based test. Popularity notwithstanding, to create a reliable measuring system it is necessary for all students to be evaluated by the same measuring instrument. That does not occur if each student can pick which questions they wish to answer. This same point, that all students should answer the same essay questions, can be argued from the point of view that requires a high-quality assessment be specified on a clear and exacting test blueprint (Millman & Greene, 1989).

Essay Test Security

Secondary school teachers and some undergraduate faculty who teach several sections of the same subject need to be mindful of test security. Essay items that are on the examination of a morning class will be all over the school after lunch. What once was a problem is now a major issue. Text messaging makes it possible for students to send questions and answers to other students in the same and other classes in real time. One solution is to require all cell phones be turned off. Another is to have a number of essays available and give different class sections different tests. Naturally, this means that two tables of specification must be developed, one for each test form, and the two forms of the test cannot be graded together. However, this can reduce the potential for collusion-threatening test security.

Case in Point (7b)

In 1951, a highly successful Army football team at West Point was rocked by a cheating scandal. The participants in this cheating would memorize test questions and then pass them on to other students who were scheduled to take the examination later. The result was the dismissal of 90 cadets from the United States Military Academy at West Point for cheating and breaches of the honor code (Blackwell, 1996).

For more information, see "Considerations on Point" at www.sagepub.com/wrightstudy

---

ESSAY GRADING

The evaluation of essay examinations can be very tedious. Teachers should take breaks periodically as they grade a stack of essay examinations. One sign of the fatigue factor in essay grading is the tendency for those papers that are graded first to have lower grades than those examinations graded toward the end of the set. This phenomenon is well understood by performance athletes. For example, championship figure skaters never want to be the first to appear in a competition.

The time requirement is clearly one downside for using essay examinations. Secondary-school students are taught in English class to write five-paragraph essays as a normal part of the typical preparation program for mandated high-stakes tests. If a teacher assigns two essays on a test, and has five classes of 25 students each, then that teacher could conceivably be faced with the task of reading 1,250 handwritten paragraphs of student writing. Not only is that grading task going to take a lot of time, but there is a real danger that the tests may not be graded in a reliable manner.

Teachers should be aware that essay items give an advantage to students who are good writers and to those who can organize their thoughts logically and quickly. These abilities are not just learned skills but also involve a cognitive style not evident in all students (Bridgeman, 1980). Related to this is a differential effect by student gender. Boys tend to outperform girls on **select-type questions** (multiple choice), and girls do better on essay questions (DeMars, 2000).

Grading With a Scoring Guide

An important tool to have on hand when grading essay examinations is a **scoring guide** for each item. This scoring guide is similar to a rubric and should be written at the time that the item is written. Teachers should never read essay examinations without knowing exactly what they expected students to have written. If the essay is to be scored analytically, this scoring guide may take the form of an outline listing what is expected and the number of points or scoring emphasis that is assigned for each point listed on the guide.

For more information, see "Considerations on Point" at www.sagepub.com/ wrightstudy

Case in Point (7c)

One technique used by a few tired, overworked teachers to avoid the task of developing a scoring guide or rubric for grading the answers to an essay test involves relying on previously good student's work. To score the essays, these fainéant instructors locate the answer written by their best two or three students and then use those answers as the model for grading all other students.

This provides a reliable approach to scoring and is less susceptible to student bluffing. The test can also be scored holistically. In this case, the teacher should first develop a five- or six-point scale for grading the answers.

These points can correspond to letter grades for the essay. Once the point scale has been selected, the next step involves providing the benchmark examples for each of the point values on the scoring guide.

Grading With Blind Reading

It is usually not possible for teachers to read tests blindly without knowing which student wrote which test. Yet, every effort should be made to prevent the **halo effect**. There is a real tendency for our expectations of students to color our evaluations of their work. Those students who did well in the past are expected to continue, while those who have had low test scores in the past are anticipated to continue that way in the future. Perhaps the best approach to anonymity is to have students take the essay examination using the classroom computers. This would also eliminate the interfering effect of handwriting and improve the spelling of the student authors.

Grading and Writing Style

Teachers need to decide in advance if the grammar, spelling, and handwriting are to be counted as part of the scoring of the examination. This issue has initiated numerous debates among educators enrolled in testing courses, and no consensus is ever likely. Yet, measurement validity assumes that a science test is a measure of the achievement of science content, not English syntax. Whichever approach the teacher decides to use, students need to know in advance how the test will be graded. Even when teachers try to ignore problems in the mechanics of writing, bad writing may still influence student grades. It has been shown that when teachers use constructed response items for tests of mathematics, reading, social studies, and science, the scores on them are not significantly influenced by spelling, handwriting, and syntax. However, while not significant, there are slight positive advantages in terms of course grades in these curriculum areas for students who write well on essay tests. This is not the case with tests of language arts and writing, where writing mechanics is what the class is all about. Not unexpectedly, good writing is well rewarded by language arts teachers (Schafer, Gagné, & Lissitz, 2005).

Comments

When grading a student's essay, the classroom teacher should provide written comments identifying both the strength and weakness of each answer. When an essay examination is made up of several essays, the teacher should read them "across students." That means that the first essay on every paper should be read prior to reading the second answer. Each question should be read in turn, and a final compilation and grade should be marked on each paper after all the essays have been evaluated.

Assembly-Line Grading

On the campuses of several large state universities, grading **assembly lines** have been established. By these systems, freshman students enrolled in a first-year writing course submit all drafts of writing assignments over the campus computer server. Those papers are then sent to the computers of graduate assistants who can work at home and grade and comment on the undergraduate student writing. As an example, Texas Tech University employs 60 graduate students to help teach freshman composition, each of whom has a weekly quota of online grading to complete (Wasley, 2006). The key to reliable scores for essays is the training received by those evaluating student writing. The best approach to this training has been shown to occur in a workshop format (Kanada, Kreiman, & Nichols, 2007).

Computer Grading of Essays

There are now a number of software packages that can be used to grade student writing. This software was first designed with the English teacher in mind and was able to read, evaluate, and provide diagnostic comments on student compositions (Gilbert, 2005). The Educational Testing Service (ETS) expanded the capability of essay-reading software with the development of a computerized essay scoring system for the Graduate Management Admissions Test (GMAT). ETS is also marketing an online **computer grading** system to educators called Criterion, which includes an online essay-reading and scoring system known as e-Rater. In 2005, there were half a million school students and another 400,000 graduate school applicants who had essays scored by this system. Research has shown that human scoring provides scores that are significantly lower on written essay examinations than is true of computer-based scoring systems (Wang, Young, Brooks, & Jiao, 2007).

A growing number of colleges use computerized scoring as part of a program to improve student writing. The University of Phoenix has a system that reads and comments on a million student essays a year. A new software package for grading written assignments for a number of subject areas was developed under a grant from the National Science Foundation. That program also checks the student work for possible plagiarism. This software, SAGrader, became available for purchase in 2006. Information about this system is available at www.sagrader.com. Another vendor that offers an essay grading system is Pearson Knowledge Technologies. That system uses a mathematical algorithm to determine the level of essay-writing quality. Unlike other approaches that employ **artificial intelligence** that has been informed by the course instructor, this method employs a complex matrix solution (Williams, 2006).

While the advantages are obvious, the downside of this system for grading lies in the removal of the teacher from the process. It also changes the rules for how student writing is taught. For example, students who sprinkle big words throughout their essays are given better scores than those who do not. Likewise, varying the sentence structure by using longer complex sentences combined with shorter declarative sentences improves the score. Another high-scoring strategy is to repeat the terms and phrases used in the stimulus **prompt** of the essay. Research has also shown that repeating paragraphs over and over while varying the wording of the first sentence by simply changing the word order can also earn a high score. All of these strategies make it possible to trick essay-reading software (Powers, Burstein, Chodorow, Fowles, & Kukich, 2001).[2] Also, it is still not possible for a computer to evaluate creative production or to understand and correctly grade new phrases, jokes, poetry, or even a pun.

THE SAT ESSAY TEST

The College Entrance Examination Board tests were initiated in 1901 by the admissions officers of a dozen colleges who formed the first Board. That examination program used essay-type items and was initially administered to 8,000 high school and preparatory school seniors. Many of the questions from that first examination would be classified as performance items today. Tasks such as translating paragraphs and writing essays required much effort and time on the part of those taking the test and an enormous investment of time by those grading the tests. In 1926, Carl Brigham, the admissions dean at Princeton University, developed the **Scholastic Aptitude Test**, which was designed using items similar to the World War I Army Alpha and Beta intelligence tests. Dean Brigham had worked as an Army examiner during World War I and saw the multiple choice format of the Army tests as an efficient admissions assessment system. To review a few items from the first College Board Examination, see www.pbs.org/wgbh/pages/frontline/shows/sats/where/1901.html.

SAT II

In 2005, the test was changed again, and an essay test, Critical Writing, was reintroduced.[3] By doing away with the old section on vocabulary and analogies and creating a new test of critical reading, the old SAT had a whole new structure. The mathematics section added more advanced questions from the curriculum of algebra II and geometry. The new essay test is not computer scored but is read online by professional teachers from across the United States. To qualify as a reader, an educator must have taught a high school or collegiate class requiring writing and must hold at least a bachelor's degree.

Research by the College Board has shown that there are common elements that are exhibited in essay tests that have high scores: a length in excess of 330 words, which covers at least two pages; the use of a five-paragraph format; and the use of the first-person voice (Kobrin, Deng, & Shaw, 2007).

For more information, see "Considerations on Point" at www.sagepub.com/ wrightstudy

---

Case in Point (7d)

Before the new SAT II was introduced, ETS supported several studies on its potential impact on test takers. A concern of the test developers was the likelihood of mental and/or physical fatigue on the part of test takers. One study sponsored by the College Entrance Examination Board demonstrated that while mental fatigue is possible with the greater length of the new test, it would not alter test-taker performance (Liu, Allspach, Feigenbaum, Oh, & Burton, 2004; Wang, 2007). After a year of experience with the new SAT II there was clear evidence of a small but nonetheless noticeable decline in scores (Pope, 2006). This pattern was seen again in 2007. It is likely that the SAT II will be modified again by 2009.

Artificial Intelligence

New essay-grading software is written using a sophisticated form of artificial intelligence known as **latent semantic analysis** (Miller, 2003). To use this software, teachers must first teach the computer what makes a good essay answer and what makes a bad one. This is done by feeding the database examples of both. To give the computer the ability to evaluate the content of student essays, the instructor must also provide the computer with an example of a stellar answer with all the correct content and connections made. This high-quality answer may even be copied from the textbook. All of

Figure 7.1   *Zits*, by Jerry Scott and Jim Borgman. Published on May 9, 2006

SOURCE: © Zits Partnership. King Features Syndicate.

the various permutations and wording variations that can be a part of a correct answer must also be present in the material submitted to "teach the computer." With this background in place the computer is ready to read student essays and provide scores for content, style, and mechanics. When programmed with the grading standards of the teacher, the system can even recommend an overall letter grade. To learn more about this grading system and to have an interactive experience see http://lsa.colorado.edu.

The time required to write out a sterling answer for the essay item and to provide all the combinations of wording for a correct answer can involve several hours of work. The time required to read and evaluate a few dozen essays is eclipsed by the time required to "teach the computer" to do the evaluation job. Clearly this approach to grading is best used with large classes of students.

It is now also possible to link computerized grading systems with automated tutoring systems. This makes it possible to have the computer both grade the student work and also remediate and reteach the topic as needed.

Summary

Most public school teachers prefer not to use take-home examinations with their students; yet, they collect more grades from assigned homework than from any other source. Homework has several important roles in education, one of which is as part of a system of formative assessments. For that reason it is necessary for teachers to take the time to grade homework daily.

The construction of in-class tests using short answers is a tried-and-true method for student assessment. These questions, if structured well, can be used to assess thinking skills at the application and understanding level as described by Bloom's Taxonomy (see Chapter 6). When teachers employ longer questions such as short (one paragraph) essays, it becomes possible to tap into the student's ability to use even more advanced levels of thinking. Full-scale essay questions requiring three to five paragraphs to answer can tap into all levels of the cognitive spectrum.

Reliable grading of all supply-type questions requires that the teacher have a solid knowledge base of the topic being measured. This makes it possible to recognize unexpected but otherwise correct answers. Longer responses for essay questions require the teacher to have constructed a scoring guide. This guide takes the form of either an analytical or **holistic rubric**.

One annoying student behavior on all supply-type items is the tendency for the uninformed to attempt to bluff. The use of scoring guides is one method for reducing that tendency.

Technology is making inroads into the essay-grading business. Major universities as well as corporations such as the Educational Testing Service now provide teachers and faculty with automated grading methods.

Discussion Questions

1. Describe the instructional implications and typical achievement outcomes of assigning daily homework. How much homework should an elementary school teacher assign each day? What types of homework assignments work best for secondary-school students? How should a teacher count homework when assigning report card grades?

2. Using the information contained in Chapters 4 and 5 of this textbook, write five or six completion questions that are designed to assess achievement of the material in those chapters.

3. Take the following two poorly conceived essay questions and edit them into high-quality items.

   First objective being tested: *Students will be able to describe the history, responsibilities, and function of each of the cabinet departments of the federal government.*

   First poor question: *Discuss in some detail the U.S. Department of Homeland Security.*

Second objective being tested: *Candidates for administrator certification will be able to describe the history of the Elementary and Secondary Education Act of 1965 as amended through 2007–2008. Candidates for certification will be able to describe the current elements of the No Child Left Behind Act as they relate to public and charter schools and describe how they are implemented in practice and policy.*

Second poor question: *Are the changes mandated for public and charter schools by the No Child Left Behind Act improving education in America?*

4. Create an analytical grading guide (rubric) for the evaluation of one of the two improved questions from Question 3 above.

Student Study Site

Educational Assessment on the Web

Log on to the Web-based student study site at www.sagepub.com/ wrightstudy for additional Web sources and study resources.

NOTES

1. The old student aphorism is relevant here: "If you can't dazzle them with your brilliance, then baffle them with your blarney."

2. Caution is urged for those thinking of using these methods. Remember that research and development is an ongoing activity at places like ETS.

3. To learn more about the Critical Writing Test, or to apply to become a reader, see http://www.flexiblescoring-SAT.pearson.com.

Chapter 8

ITEM SELECTION AND ANALYSIS

Statistician: A man who believes figures don't lie, but admits that under analysis some of them don't stand up either.

—Evan Esar

Issues and Themes

Teachers spend many hours developing classroom tests. These efforts notwithstanding, no test is ever perfect. By reusing their short answer and multiple choice test items, teachers can save time and continually improve the quality of these classroom measures. Test items should be analyzed for their strengths and weaknesses and then tweaked or discarded as necessary. The analysis should occur both before the test is administered and after it has been administered and scored.

A test should be informally reviewed prior to its administration. After the test has been administered and scored, a thorough review or item analysis should be done. The postmortem on the test involves the use of several statistics. One of these statistical tools is the **item difficulty index**. Another involves the discriminating power of the item. This discrimination index is closely linked to the reliability of the test. Major testing corporations employ item response theory (IRT) to maximize the discrimination power of the items on achievement tests. It is also employed in computer adaptive testing (CAT), an interactive, online form of measurement. Item characteristic curves (ICC), which are central to IRT, can be used to empirically examine test items for bias.

Learning Objectives

By reading and studying this chapter you should acquire the competency to do the following:

- Edit and proofread newly developed examinations.
- Determine the difficulty level of the items on a multiple choice examination.
- Discuss the relationship between guessing and the difficulty level of a test item.
- Explain the link between item discrimination and test reliability.
- Calculate the difficulty level of the items from a multiple choice test.
- Use biserial correlation to determine the discrimination level of any multiple choice question.
- Determine the difficulty index and discrimination level for any essay test item.
- Discuss computer adaptive testing.
- Present three applications for item response theory (IRT).

CLASSROOM TESTING

Testing is a major part of most school days for both teachers and students. With the current emphasis on mandated standardized tests, it is easy to overlook the fact that testing and student evaluation is a normal and ongoing activity that is a regular part of the instructional process. A national survey of teachers from the 4th, 6th, and 10th grades found that elementary school teachers spend about 10% of the time allotted to instruction testing their children, while secondary-school teachers spend about 13% of the time available on testing (Dorr-Bremme & Herman, 1986). It is very likely that the time spent testing and grading has increased over the last two decades. The nature of the typical teacher's day was analyzed by the National Educational Association in 2001. They found that the median teacher spent 12 hours a week grading and planning at home and another 10 hours a week working extra hours in the school (National Education Association, 2003). More recently, the teachers of the state of Hawaii were found to work an average of 48 extra hours a week on grading and preparation activities. This means that teachers in our 49th state work an average of 15.5 hours each school day (Creamer, 2007).

The tests and quizzes designed and administered in classrooms vary greatly in quality. The effort to improve individual questions after they are used is known as item analysis. This analysis process implies that the teacher must keep his/her test questions from year to year and cannot release them to students. The item analysis process, with its focus on individual items, differs from a study of test reliability and validity in which the focus is on the entire measure. Yet, the item analysis process can improve the reliability of the next edition of a classroom test.

The use of item analysis before a test is administered helps assure that the test is a reliable and valid measure. The application of an analytical study of item quality after the test has been administered makes it possible to build a bank of high-quality test items for use during future years. This post hoc–type of assessment does not assure validity, but it is related to test reliability. An item analysis after the test has been administered also permits the teacher to remove errant questions that adversely affect the quality of the classroom measure this year. Thus, more equitable grading is possible because the test will become a better measurement instrument.

Figure 8.1   "So Far, All We're Learning Is How to Take a Math Test . . ."

SOURCE: Cartoon by Robert Englehart. Reprinted with permission from Robert Englehart.

A PRIORI QUALITATIVE ASSESSMENT AND ANALYSIS OF TESTS

First-year teachers, as well as experienced teachers working in a new grade level or teaching a new subject area, face a significant task creating all new classroom tests. An excellent policy for teachers is to conduct two reviews of newly developed tests before they are used with students. The first editorial review should come a few hours after a draft of the test has been written. Editing is likely to identify typographical errors, content errors, and errors of construction. It is never a good policy to go from the computer to the printer without reading a "hard copy," and the best time to do this is after a little time has passed. Having "fresh eyes" makes it so much easier to spot errors and confusing wording. Careful editing before giving a test makes it easier, and often less embarrassing for the teacher. Students enjoy catching their teacher making mistakes. The time to edit the test is not when it has been returned to the students and a classroom review has started.

State departments of education are not immune from these editing problems. Texas, one of the states that release their mandated achievement tests, received critical review of their new TASK science test (Guernsey, 2005). Question number 13 on the fifth-grade test asked the following:

Which two planets are closest to Earth?

A. Mercury and Saturn

B. Mars and Jupiter

C. Mercury and Venus

D. Venus and Mars*

Later a physicist noted that the orbital positions of the various planets indicate that for much of the year the nearest two planets to Earth are Mercury and Mars, not the keyed answer, Venus and Mars (Texas Assessment of Skills and Knowledge, 2003–2004). To see a full copy of this and the other released state assessment tests from Texas, visit http://www.tea.state.tx.us/ student.assessment/resources/online/2003/grade5/science.htm.

The second review for a new test should involve one or more other teachers. If possible, enlist help from others who have content knowledge of the field covered by the test. New teachers can turn to their mentors for this type of assistance. The editing of new tests could even be formalized by the school administrator responsible for the mentoring assignments. Others can simply ask the indulgence of their faculty peers in this review process.

This qualitative reading of the test can identify obvious errors in wording, confusing question stems, typos, and poor distracters. The review by colleagues will also identify errors of content and fact. Even assuming that the test is designed around a well-conceived table of specifications (see Chapter 6), the review should also verify that the content being tested is representative of the curriculum and that it stresses what was actually taught.

This qualitative review should also check for possible unusual language or vocabulary that may not be familiar or even accessible to all children in the class. Words that reflect one cultural viewpoint or that are drawn from the vernacular of one ethnic group should be avoided. This is not a time for the teacher to attempt to pose as being "cool." For example, coastal communities have many children who are familiar with boating, but the introduction of nautical terms such *starboard*, *windward tack*, and *gunnels* is to be avoided. These are words that are not a regular part of the lexicon of those children who do not have boats or boating experience.

ITEM DIFFICULTY INDEX

Perhaps the easiest task in an item analysis is the determination of the level of difficulty of the test's items. For most tests each item should have been correctly answered by a little over half of the class. Occasionally everyone in the class knows the right answer. This unlikely outcome can be explained several ways. The students may have learned the information on their own or from a previous teacher, or they may have brought the new knowledge from home, where it was taught. An unusual high level of success may also be a reflection of excellent teaching. Finally, it may simply imply that the test question was poorly conceived and easily guessed.

When the scores on a classroom test are low, some teachers are quick to blame their students for "not trying." In point of fact, there are at least three reasons why a test item may produce low scores. The first two have to do with instruction and focus on the related issues of the motivation level of the students and the ability of the teacher to get a point across. The third reason has to do with the construction of the test item.

To determine the difficulty of a selected-response-type test item, the teacher should count of the number of students who actually got the item wrong as well as the total number of students who took the test. If the item appeared near the end of the test, a count should also be made of the students who did not get a chance to answer that question. If more than 5% of the students did not have enough time to reach that item, then the test was too long or there was not enough time allotted to the task. In either case, item analysis for such a question could result in erroneous findings.

Calculation of the Difficulty Index

Mathematically, the item difficulty index is defined as the proportion of test takers who got the item correct on the test.

difficulty index (p) = total who answered correctly/total taking the test

For example, if a class of 25 students takes a test and 15 get the item correct, the difficulty index is 0.60 (p = 15/25). If everyone gets the item correct, the difficulty index would be 1.00. The lower the decimal value of the difficulty index, the fewer the number of students who gave the correct answer. An item having a .90 (high difficulty) index is one that 90% of the students are getting correct. This does not mean that the item is too easy. The index of .90 or more could indicate that the students were well taught. Likewise, items with low difficulty levels (p < .30) may be a signal that many children didn't understand the concept that was being tested. It may also have something to do with the item's characteristics.

Guessing

There is another critical factor that plays a role in the difficulty index of an item. That factor is guessing. The more difficult the item is, the greater the likelihood that students will guess an answer to the question. The likelihood of guessing the correct answer for a multiple choice question is a function of the number of answer alternatives that make up the item. If there are four alternatives the chance of guessing correctly is 1:4 or 25%. For that reason it is likely that a multiple choice item with a low difficulty index (p < 0.30) has a higher proportion of those answering correctly by guessing than does an "easy" item with a high difficulty index (Lord, 1952).

Levels of Difficulty

The optimum difficulty index for any item is dependent on the teacher's grading philosophy and his or her goal for testing. If the goal of the test is to maximize the differences seen between students, the optimal difficulty index is 0.50. When this is corrected for guessing, the following holds true for the optimum difficulty level:

Item type	Optimum difficulty
True–false	*0.75.*
MCQ 3 alternatives	*0.67*
MCQ 4 alternatives	*0.625*
MCQ 5 alternatives	*0.60*
Essay test	*0.50*

If a well-constructed test designed with items of this difficulty level is administered to a population of students, the scores from those students should distribute as a Gaussian normal curve. That distribution will have a mean score equal to the average difficulty level of the test items. This can pose a problem for those educators who assign grades according to a rigid scale. Such scales are often adopted by schools and require teachers to give students who score in the 60%–69% range a grade of D. In other words, on a test designed to have the optimum difficulty level, well over half of all students will fail or be given a grade of D. For that reason, teachers usually design test items to have difficulty indexes over 0.70.

Diagnostic Testing

When the average difficulty index is high ($p > 0.70$), the data are skewed negatively with most scores clustered on the high side and the unusual (low) scores spread out over the wide area of the distribution. This type of distribution is useful in identifying those students who are experiencing difficulty in learning the material (see Figure 8.2).

This model is employed in what is known as **diagnostic testing**. The goal of diagnostic testing is the identification of learning problems experienced by a child. Diagnostic tests are made up of fairly easy test items that cover the core skill areas of a subject, such as mathematics or reading. Most children will score very high on these measures; however, children with learning problems will be easily identified by their pattern of lower scores.

Out-of-Level Testing

The opposite case, in which all the test items are difficult, is the model for **out-of-level testing**. Out-of-level testing is used to select the very best of the

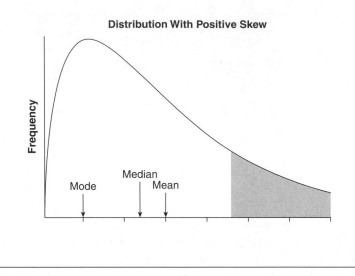

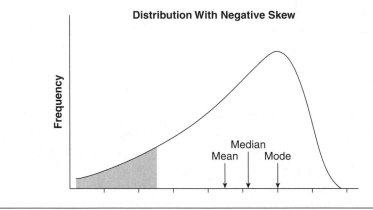

Figure 8.2   Skewed Distributions Illustrating the Two Variations

top students for special programs. Examples of this are the many programs for gifted children that are held on college campuses during the summers. One of the first of these was established at Johns Hopkins University under the leadership of Julian Stanley (Keiger, 2000). To enter the summer program at Johns Hopkins, seventh-grade students first had to be assessed using the standardized tests required by their schools. Admission into the Hopkins program required that they achieve a minimum score equal to the 97th percentile. Next, these children had to take the SAT I and score above the national average (Score > 1000). This second level of testing using the SAT I is an example of out-of-level testing. The use of out-of-level testing provides a method to identify and separate exceptionally bright children from those with superior academic ability (i.e., the best of the best). The standardized achievement tests used in the schools cannot demonstrate the differences that exist among children who are at the very highest levels of ability. This is why Julian Stanley used a test designed for high school graduates, the SAT I.

Case in Point

When a test is being designed for selection purposes, the optimal level of item difficulty can be estimated as the ratio of the number of applicants to the number that will be selected or admitted. Suppose that a highly select residential summer program on a university campus is designed for advanced high school science students. If funding limits participation to only 40 students, but 200 students are nominated by their high schools, the university may decide to select the 40 that will be admitted on the basis of a test. That admission test should have an average item difficulty level equal to the **selection ratio**. This selection ratio can be calculated as the 40 admissions/200 applications or 0.20. Thus, a test should be designed to have an average difficulty level of about 0.20. This test would seem to be very difficult for most of the applicants. The average score would be only 20%, plus a bit more for the guessing factor. The distribution of scores would show a positive skew, and the best students would be evident at the upper end of the distribution.

For more information, see "Considerations on Point" at www.sagepub.com/wrightstudy

DISTRACTER ANALYSIS

When a multiple choice item is unexpectedly found to have a low difficulty index ($p < 0.30$), the next step for the teacher is to examine the item's distracters. By compiling the total number of students who select each of the distracters, the teacher can readily see if one choice is drawing most of the students. Also, if one of the distracters is so off base that few or no students select it, it should be either discarded or rewritten on a future examination. Note the following example:

All answer choices	*Number who selected choice out of 50 test takers*
Choice A	*2*
Choice B	*26*
Choice C	*7*
*Choice D**	*15*

This test item had 15 students select the correct answer. This results in a difficulty index of 0.30 (p = 15 / 50). Choice A is selected by only 2 of the 50 students, indicating that it may be too obviously wrong. Choice C is working well, while choice B has drawn far too many students. This choice should be examined to determine what has caused this choice to be the most commonly selected distracter. Also, the teacher should consider reteaching the topic and explaining why the answer choice was wrong. For the next edition of the test, alternative choices (distracters) A and B need to be rewritten.

ITEM ANALYSIS WITH CONSTRUCTED OR SUPPLY-TYPE ITEMS

Constructed items including essay questions can also be subjected to a post hoc item analysis. It does not matter whether the essay is scored analytically or holistically. The difficulty level is defined as the ratio of the average score for the class on that essay question divided by the maximum possible score on the essay.

p = mean score on the essay/maximum possible score

By this formula, an essay that had a mean score of 16.5 and a maximum score value of 20 would have a difficulty index of 0.825. A holistically scored test with a six-point rubric and a mean score of 3.3 would have a difficulty index of 0.55.

DISCRIMINATION

The second major dimension in the analysis of any item is the extent to which success on the item corresponds to success on the whole test. One approach to determining the **discrimination level** of an item is to find the **point–biserial correlation** between individual student scores on the item and the student's scores on the whole test. The first step involves the item that is being analyzed to be scored as either right or wrong (scored as 1 or 0). Point–biserial correlation is then used to correlate the item scores with the scores of the whole test. Point–biserial correlation is a special case of the Pearson Product Moment Correlation, in which one variable is binary (right vs. wrong), and the other is continuous (total raw score on the test). The following is the formula for determining the point–biserial correlation:[1]

$$r_{pb} = \frac{\overline{X}_1 - \overline{X}_0 \sqrt{p(1-p)}}{S_X}$$

In this equation, the symbol $\bar{X}_1$ is the mean raw score on the test of all the students who got the item correct. The symbol $\bar{X}_0$ is used to represent the mean raw score on the test of all the students who got this item wrong. The value S_x is the standard deviation of the raw scores. The letter p is used to express the proportion of students who got the answer to the test item correct.

There is an online location where point–biserial correlations can be calculated from raw data: http://faculty.vassar.edu/lowry/vscor.html. Most hand-held calculators will calculate Pearson correlation coefficients, which can also be used for this item analysis task. Like most correlation coefficients, the point–biserial coefficient has a minimum value of 0.0 and a maximum value of ±1.0. A negative point–biserial correlation means that the students who did well on the test missed that item, while those students who did poorly on the test got the item right. The item with a negative point–biserial correlation is clearly doing something wrong and should be rewritten.

A variation on the use of correlation statistics to determine **item discrimination** involves the use of the reliability statistic, **Cronbach's coefficient α** (see Chapter 4). This system involves determining the internal consistency of the test using the alpha coefficient, then recalculating the same coefficient after removing the item under review. The item needs to be rewritten if the overall internal consistency (reliability) of the test is improved when it is gone. When an item is removed from the test and the coefficient alpha for the total remaining items stays consistent, or possibly falls slightly, then that item can be considered to be an appropriate part of the overall measure.

In 1939, Truman Kelly identified a way to estimate the discrimination value for any test item. His technique is rarely employed today, as computer solutions are readily available for multiple choice tests. This technique was designed for use with very large samples of subjects. However, by bending Kelly's rules, it is possible to "guesstimate" what the discrimination level is without using computer software. This process begins by scoring the responses of all students to all the items on the test. Once all the tests have a total score and have been graded by the teacher it is possible to determine the discrimination level of each item that used a selected response format. Next, the top 27% and bottom 27% of the students should be identified. These two groups are the criteria against which each item is evaluated for its ability to discriminate between them. In other words, the task is to determine the extent to which each question is in agreement with the group membership.

Working with only 54% of the available data (27% + 27%) each item is reviewed to see how many students in the top group and how many students from the bottom group got it correct. Perfect discrimination would occur if all the top students got the item correct and all students in the low group got it wrong.

Example: *In a class of 37 students the high scoring group (27%) equals 10 students and the low group would be 10 (27%). The actual calculation occurs as follows:*

$$D_{is} = \frac{NUG - NLG}{total\big/2}$$

NUG = Number in the upper group who got item right

NLG = Number in the lower group who got item right

$total\big/2$ = Half of the total number in the upper and lower groups together

If one item from that test had eight students in the upper group get the item correct and only four students from the lower group got it correct, then the calculation of the item's discrimination level would look like this:

$$D_{is} = \frac{8 - 4}{10 + 10\big/2}$$

$$D_{is} = \frac{4}{10} = +0.4$$

As another example: *A teacher found that in a combined class of 56 students that one question had 14 in the upper group of 15 that had the item correct and only 3 in the low group of 15 had it right. What is that item's discrimination?*
    Answer:

$$D_{is} = \frac{14 - 3}{15 + 15\big/2} = {}^{11}\!/_{15} = +0.73$$

A third example: *The instructor of a large class found that one item on a test given to her class of 148 students had a problem. There are 40 students in both the upper (27%) and lower scoring groups. This item was found to have only 10 students in the upper group get it correct, while 25 in the lower group got it correct. What is the discrimination of this item?*
    Answer:

$$D_{is} = \frac{10 - 25}{40 + 40\big/2} = -{}^{15}\!/_{40} = -0.375$$

The negative discrimination value indicates that this item is difficult for the best-scoring students to get correct and easy for low-scoring students.

This item should be subjected to further analysis and either rewritten of removed from the test.

To interpret item discrimination scores, the rule of thumb is that items with discrimination levels of $+0.30$ and above are reasonably good questions. All others should be subjected to another level of review and tweaked or rewritten before being used again.

Truman Kelly's approach to determining item discrimination levels can also be applied to essay questions. The first requirement for using Kelly's (1939) approach is that all students must have written answers to the same set of essay questions. No optional item selection by students can have occurred. After the essay test is graded the teacher must identify the 27% of the class with the highest total test scores as well as the 27% with the lowest scores. The next step is to find the mean score for both subgroups on the essay that is being analyzed. The last thing needed for Kelly's analysis is the total range of possible scores on that essay. This is found by subtracting the lowest score on the item in question from the best score anyone achieved on the item. If the item was scored using a six-point rubric, the range would be five (range $= 6 - 1$). Then the discrimination level (D_{is}) for the essay item is found as

$$D_{is} = \frac{upper\ group(\overline{X}_U) - lower\ group(\overline{X}_L)}{Range}$$

Discrimination scores obtained using the upper group minus the lower group divided by the score range are interpreted in much the same way as are point–biserial correlation coefficients. That is, an essay test item with a negative discrimination level is one that penalizes students who scored well on the total test. Students who did not score well on the total test were able to write high-scoring answers to that essay question. Clearly, such essay questions must be rewritten or removed from the test item pool.

As an example, an English teacher included an essay test question on an examination given to three sections of students totaling 74 kids. Those test scores were found to have a scoring range from 0 to 30. The teacher also found the median of the top-20-scoring (27% of 74) students was 30, while the median score in the lowest 20 students was 10. To find the **essay item discrimination level**, he or she made the following calculations:

$$D_{is} = \frac{upper\ group(\overline{X}_U) - lower\ group(\overline{X}_L)}{Range}$$
$$Dis = \frac{30 - 10}{30}$$
$$D_{is} = 20/30$$
$$D_{is} = 0.67$$

The resulting discrimination index of 0.67 indicates that the essay task is an appropriate measurement component of the test.

Tests in which the overall discrimination level is high provide the best possible evidence for assigning student grades and making other important educational decisions. Both the shape of the distribution and the difficulty level of the test items have an impact on the overall discrimination level of the test. When the test scores are normally distributed, the overall discrimination level of the test is optimized. When the distribution of scores is skewed, the maximum discrimination occurs where the scores are widely spread. Most educators design tests that are negatively skewed. The result of this is that the high-end scores are bunched up at the top of the distribution. This makes it difficult to differentiate between levels of performance among the better students. However, the negative skew to classroom tests makes it easier to differentiate among the low scores.

The discrimination level of a test is also impacted by the difficulty level of the test items (Kelly, 1947). When items on a test are easy (high difficulty index) students will score at the high end of the distribution. Thus, the distribution of test scores will be negatively skewed. The maximum discrimination level occurs when the average difficulty index for the test is 0.50 (again, see Figure 8.2 on page 228).

Software Support

The Statistical Package for the Social Sciences, SPSS has been widely available on the campuses of this country for the past 35 years. It provides an easy solution to the problem of conducting an item analysis with student test data (SPSS, 1998). The system employs a basic "drag and drop" approach to data entry and has great flexibility for student use.

A more universal system for conducting item analysis is through the use of Microsoft's Excel spreadsheet program (Elvin, 2003). Excel facilitates direct data entry and the calculation of item difficulty levels and item discrimination indices and even facilitates the analysis of the distractor quality from multiple choice questions.

A free software solution to item analysis is provided by a member of the faculty of James Madison University. This software can accommodate both binomial format (right vs. wrong) and **polytomous** items, such as those on a **Likert type of scale**[2] (Meyer, 2006).

COMPUTER ADAPTIVE TESTING

The various methods of item analysis described in this chapter are appropriate for classroom use. Large-scale testing (see Chapter 11) employs another method of determining the difficulty level of test items. This method is also well suited for online testing programs. Online measurement programs involve computer adaptive testing models that require detailed information as to the difficulty of individual items (Hambleton, 2004). The days of the paper-and-pencil achievement test are clearly numbered. Computer adaptive testing now provides online assessments for graduate and professional school admission and is used in 17 states to administer mandated high-stakes assessments in the schools. This approach to testing is highly efficient and reduces the lag time for getting feedback into the hands of teachers and school administrators. It also reduces the length of time that is needed for test administration.

Computer adaptive testing employs software that can estimate the ability and background knowledge of each test taker. This estimation is then used to guide the selection of test items from a computerized item bank. Test items are then presented to the examinees in an interactive format. Each time the student answers a question, the computer decides his or her ability level and presents another question written at the optimum difficulty level. Once the software has decided if a particular learning standard has been measured for the examinee, it moves on to select test items from another learning standard. On a standard paper-and-pencil test, every student must answer every question; whereas with computer adaptive testing, items that the computer determines are superfluous are skipped. This provides for optimal efficiency and minimizes the amount of time each student must spend being tested. Thus, in a room full of students taking an online test, it can be assumed that beyond the opening questions, all of the students are seeing different tests.

ITEM RESPONSE THEORY (IRT)

For computer adaptive testing to work it is necessary to first have a pool of available items that has been analyzed and coded as to how students of many different ability levels perform on them. An item difficulty index score does not provide enough information about the item to make this possible. The difficulty level only shows how the average examinee performs on the item. The difficulty index does not show how students of various levels of ability will perform when answering that question. In 1960, Danish measurement specialist George Rasch addressed this problem and presented a new model for item analysis. This technique has the general name, item response theory (IRT), and one form of IRT is named the Rasch model for item response theory, after its originator (IRT)[3] (Rasch, 1960/1980).

Applications of IRT

By using IRT it is possible for test makers to know the likelihood that any individual student will get a particular item right. This facilitates the individualization of testing for any number of measurement applications. Using IRT, a computer can build and administer a measurement that has been closely matched to the student on a trait. The trait is assumed to be ability in the area being measured. This ability trait is a complex conglomeration of elements such as motivation, knowledge, reading ability, and cognitive capacity. It is indeed a latent, not intuitively evident, capability that is linked to test performance.

Another common application of the Rasch model for IRT is for the development of alternate forms of paper-and-pencil tests. The IRT method can match items on both versions of a test for difficulty and balance the two versions for different types of students. This equating of two versions involves matching items along the full spectrum of student ability levels. Thus, high ability students will perform as well on the items of one version as they will on the alternative form. Likewise, the same will hold for average and low-ability students.

The Rasch IRT technique is also applied to the task of analyzing test items for bias. This analysis is known as testing for **differential item functioning (DIF)**. Using the Rasch model it is possible to determine if an item functions differently for different groups (e.g., gender, ethnicity, SES—the socioeconomic level) of students. Bias can be easily seen by examining the item characteristic curves (ICC) from various groups of students.

The relationship of item performance and the underlying ability of the examinees can be graphed as an item characteristic curve. These curves are presented as ogives,[4] which are cumulative frequency curves. The abscissa of an item characteristic curve presents the various levels of examinee ability. These are expressed in standardized units above and below the mean, which is coded as zero. The ordinate depicts the cumulative number of examinees who chose the right answer on the item. An ogive differs from Gaussian normal curve by the fact that it shows the cumulative number of examinees passing the item.[5] The ICC curve can be thought of as a probability distribution for an item depicting the likelihood that examinees of different abilities will answer it correctly (see Figure 8.3).

The discrimination level can be seen on the ogive as an acute change in the slope of the curve. The point of inflection along the abscissa (where the slope of the curve changes) denotes the item's difficulty level. If the inflection occurs at a point below the mean on the ability axis (abscissa), the item is easy and has a relatively high difficulty index. When the inflection occurs at a point well above the mean on the ability axis, the item is difficult and would have a low difficulty index score.

Out-of-level testing is facilitated when the test is composed of items that have high discrimination values and medium difficulty (Lord & Novick, 1968). Likewise, tests designed with relatively easy items (high difficulty indices) and medium discrimination levels are best for diagnostic decisions.

The examples shown below demonstrate the use of item characteristic curves in determining whether items exhibit gender bias (see Figure 8.4). It is

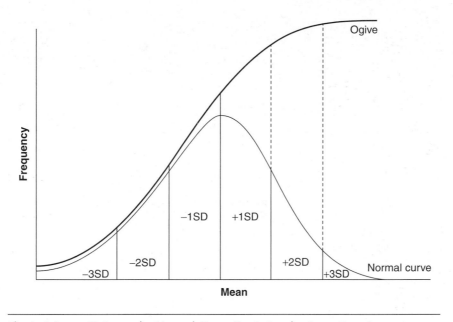

Figure 8.3 Ogive and a Normal Curve Depicting the Same Data Set

important that all published tests demonstrate that different subgroups of examinees are measured equitably. This requirement for equity is critical with high-stakes measures and for those tests used for admissions decisions. As well as being seen on ICC graphs, the difference between groups on the slope and shape of these curves can be statistically tested to determine if the difference between two groups' curves is grater than a chance variation (Cole & Moss, 1989).

Assumptions

The Rasch model requires that the performance of the examinees on the test items being analyzed is a function of a single ability or trait. Also, the model assumes that when the ability level increases so does the probability that test takers will answer the question correctly. The third requirement of the Rasch model is that it is only employed to analyze data from selected-response-format questions such as multiple choice items. In other words, the items must be scored as either right or wrong. Finally, an item analysis employing the Rasch model should be based on a large number of subjects representing a normal distribution in terms of ability (Hambleton, 2000).

The basic IRT model developed by Rasch is a two dimensional system that includes item difficulty and one dimension of the ability of examinees.

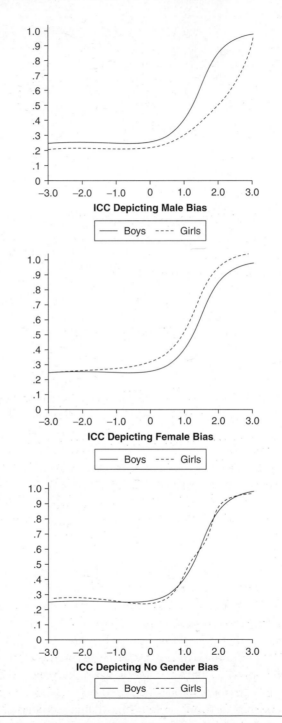

Figure 8.4   Figures Depicting Three ICCs: One Favoring Boys, One Favoring Girls, and One Favoring Neither

This two dimensional IRT model is an elegant solution to item analysis. However, it does have limitations.

Polytomous Models

This basic Rasch model for IRT has been expanded to include a number of other factors or dimensions into the analysis. These polytomous IRT models now make it possible to employ IRT analysis with a wide range of psychological scales and opinion questionnaires. These attitude and opinion scales are not scored like achievement tests in which items are either right or wrong (+1 or 0). Likert-type items are scored as ordinals that cover a five- or seven-point range (Murphy & Likert, 1938). Each of the opinion points on a Likert scale can be entered as a dimension in the expanded IRT model.

Summary

Students deserve to be assessed with well-conceived, high-quality tests and other measures. One way to improve upon the quality of classroom measures is to continually strive to improve the items that make up the quizzes and tests. Tests should be reviewed prior to being used with students for content and editorial detail. Following the administration of a test, it should be subjected to an item analysis. Each question of a classroom test can be examined for both item difficulty and item discrimination. It is not just the short answer items but also the constructed response (essay) questions that can be analyzed for difficulty and discrimination. Additionally, the questions of a multiple choice format examination should be subjected to a study of its distracters.

To construct optimally balanced tests, large-scale published tests including statewide assessments employ statistical models that are based on item response theory. These methods make it possible to assure that each item is free of bias while being highly discriminating. This quality is critically important when the test is administered through computer adaptive testing.

Discussion Questions

1. Just how difficult should a teacher-made test be for students? Do current school policies interfere in the process of designing tests of optimal difficulty?

2. Should students of different ability levels be given tests written to their different levels of ability (e.g., more difficult items for students in gifted classes and easier items for those in special support programs)?

3. How would you explain a negative index of discrimination on a test item to a teacher who wrote the test being analyzed?

4. Assume that you do a detailed item analysis after giving a multiple choice test to a class of students. If two or three items have negative levels of discrimination, should you remove those questions from the test before returning it to the students? Remember that the low-scoring students will have chosen the correct answer.

5. Is the emerging system of computer adaptive testing with high-stakes tests fair for all test takers? Explain and elaborate on your answer.

6. Using data from a teacher-made test in your school, conduct an item analysis calculating the difficulty level and discrimination index for each test item. If you are not a school employee, use the data set provided on the student Web page for this chapter.

Student Study Site

Educational Assessment on the Web

Log on to the Web-based student study site at www.sagepub.com/ wrightstudy for additional Web sources and study resources.

NOTES

1. The formula for the Pearson coefficient is also appropriate for correlating binary and continuous variables.

2. In 1932, social scientist Rensis Likert first employed a semantic survey scale to measure political attitudes. This new scale used items composed by presenting (a) a political statement, which was followed by (b) an ordinal array of levels of agreement with the statement, ranging from complete agreement to complete disagreement. Today such scales are used to measure a myriad of different opinions.

3. The IRT model is also known for the person who first identified this method, George Rasch, and the technique is referred to as a Rasch model for item analysis.

4. This word is pronounced o-jives.

5. Just as the shape of the Gauss normal distribution provides its name, the "bell curve," so does the cumulative normal distribution take its name from its shape. The statistical application of the word *ogive* refers to a part of all Gothic church architecture. Ogives are the intersecting transverse ribs of the arches that support the great vaulted ceilings. They have a characteristically "lazy S" shape that looks like the cumulative normal curve.

Chapter 9

PERFORMANCE ASSESSMENTS

At college age, you can tell who is best at taking tests and going to school, but you can't tell who the best people are. That worries the hell out of me.

—Barnaby C. Keeney (1955–1966)

President, Brown University

Issues and Themes

The best assessments are those that inform instruction. If the information from an assessment does not reach the teacher in a timely manner, then it cannot have an effect on the teaching and learning process. All too often scores from state-mandated assessments are not returned to the school until long after the school year is over.

Many generations of elementary school teachers have collected and maintained portfolios of student work. By assessing student work using rubrics and maintaining a collection of the student's work products, it is possible to trace educational growth and chart student development. The ongoing evaluation of student progress through the use of alternative assessments stored in portfolios makes it possible to link assessment directly to classroom teaching (Burke, 2005).

Alternative assessments include an array of different data sources. Among these are creative and expository writings of children, reading logs, samples of mathematics problem solving, and projects completed for other curriculum areas.

Alternative assessments maintained in the classroom provide information that parents can understand and that children can accept as truly their own. They also provide an important source of diagnostic information for a child study team.

During the 1980s and 1990s a number of states experimented with alternative assessment models for their assessment programs. For the most part, these were supplanted by standards-based, multiple choice examinations following the passage of the No Child Left Behind Act. Only the states of Nebraska (grades 3–8) and Rhode Island and New Hampshire (high school) have put into place a locally developed system of tests and portfolio assessments that is used to meet the requirements of the NCLB Act with children below the ninth grade.

Learning Objectives

By reading and studying this chapter you should develop the ability to do the following:

- Provide reasons why state-mandated assessment tests are typically administered during the spring of the school year.
- Describe how alternative assessments can interact with the teaching–learning activities in the classroom.
- List the considerations that should be addressed by educators prior to using a performance assessment.
- Describe several possible performance assessment activities appropriate for use in a public school.
- Describe how the grading of a performance assessment can be made reliable.
- List the advantages and potential problems involved when a portfolio assessment system is used.
- Describe how performance assessments can be validated.
- Explain how a teacher can establish a reliable system for portfolio assessment.
- Explain how the STARS works in Nebraska's public schools.

When the cook tastes the soup, that's formative assessment; when the customer tastes the soup, that's summative assessment.

—Grant Wiggins, 1998

ASSESSMENT AND INSTRUCTION

As specified by the requirements of the No Child Left Behind Act, our public schools have contracted with their communities to provide evidence that the schools are providing quality learning experiences for all children. The U.S. Department of Education provides the states latitude to specify learning standards and design statewide assessment systems. What 47 states have chosen to use to meet the obligation of the NCLB Act is a summative examination administered annually in the spring of the school year.[1] The logic of this choice is evident. If the assessment is given in the fall, there would be too little time to recover the "summer loss," which occurs universally but most intensely among the children of poverty. If given in the winter, there is a high likelihood that weather could play havoc with the test schedule. The spring is when our schools administer mandated assessments.

Timing

The choice of the spring has its downside. For one, as the tests are not given until 7 months into the school year, results for individual children and the overall evaluation of the schools are often not reported until the end of the academic year or even over the summer months when school is out of session. An example of this occurred in New York City, where the scores from the state's assessments were not returned for 8 months in 2006. This only added to confusion with grade promotion decisions for city children. For that reason, with the exception of those children who "fail a grade," the mandated NCLB assessments have little direct impact on the cohort of children who are actually tested. Curriculum revisions that may be initiated after the test results are known will not affect those students whose scores prompted the action.

Case in Point (9a)

One high school principal expressed her frustration with not being sent the results of the state-mandated assessment test until late in the summer when the school was out of session. The state in which her school is located mandates that students achieve a passing score on this test as a requirement for graduation. Two developmental classes designed to better prepare students for the test were in the high school schedule for the fall term; however, as the students did

For more information, see "Considerations on Point" at www.sagepub.com/wrightstudy

Case in Point (9a) (Continued)

> not know their scores on the state test when time came to set the class schedules for the next year, no one signed up for them. Then in August, families and students had to be contacted, and high school schedules were then modified for the students who did not achieve at a proficient level. This required hundreds of hours of work by counselors and administrators in late August.

A second issue associated with spring testing is that it provides 6 months or more for schools to make the primary focus of each school day improving test scores. What is lost is conceptual understanding and curriculum breadth. Lorrie Shepard argues for moving the assessments to the middle of the instructional year to have time to actually integrate information from the tests into ongoing instruction (Shepard, 2000).

Assessment should be an ongoing and natural part in the instruction of children (McTighe & O'Connor, 2005). Data from an ongoing assessment program are needed to support the decisions made during the teaching–learning process every day. These instructional decisions are not limited to once a year, when the results of an assessment are mailed from the state capital (Stiggins, 2004). For testing to have a positive influence on the instructional practice at the classroom level, there must be a program of ongoing formative assessments.

PERFORMANCE-BASED ASSESSMENTS

Every assessment of students requires a type of performance from those being evaluated. Performance measures and performance assessments are very different from most classroom measures, and with the exception of essay writing, all standardized achievement tests as well. Performance assessments measure both the skills and knowledge acquired by students and also assess the application of judgment and insight on the part of the students. Performance assessments require students to demonstrate critical-thinking and complex problem-solving skills. Teachers employing a performance assessment model are as concerned with process as they are with outcome. Even mathematics and science topics can be assessed using a performance assessment. In mathematics, the teacher looks for the analytic skill the student demonstrates in reaching an answer. For this reason, partial credit is often awarded when science and mathematics teachers embrace this approach to assessment (Millman & Green, 1989). This product-oriented evaluation is one that both students and their parents can more easily understand than the **decontextualized** score on a traditional achievement examination.

Teachers have used performance evaluations since the advent of the comprehensive high school. Some secondary school subjects have always used performance as the central focus of assessment. These courses include subjects such as family and consumer sciences, industrial arts, art, music, and physical education. This is not to say that a music appreciation class would never employ a multiple choice examination. Some parts of all secondary school subjects are most effectively evaluated using selected response (multiple choice) format examinations. Many aspects of the arts as well as many music courses can only be evaluated using performance assessments. For example, teachers of pottery will grade student work by judging the quality of the art they actually produce.

Other Applications

The application of the principles of performance assessment to the assessment of other subject areas is not a new direction for educators. The assessment of the quality of student writing (performance) is once again nothing new to teachers of English. These teachers have never hesitated to grade student writing. Nor is performance assessment a stranger to science teachers who grade laboratory reports and judge student work displayed at science fairs.

A new dimension in performance assessment is the linking of these measures to the state learning standards. This linkage makes it possible to evaluate the performance task against the learning standards by measuring the qualitative level of student performance (Ainsworth & Viegut, 2006). The qualitative levels are presented on an elaborated ordinal scale known as a **rubric**. Each rubric provides benchmarks for the various levels of student performance. Benchmarks are the examples describing the different levels of quality for each level of performance. Differential grading using a rubric is based on the level of quality exhibited by the student's performance. These ordinal levels can also assume a traditional letter grade or can be presented as standards-based proficiency levels. The great advantage in performance assessments is that they demonstrate something the child can actually do.

Case in Point (9b)

Performance assessments are an integral part of the world of international athletic competition. The governing boards of numerous sports have established scoring rubrics and benchmarks for their competitions.

For more information, see "Considerations on Point" at www.sagepub.com/ wrightstudy

Toward Perfection

Performance assessment may also imply that further refinement and improvement of the student's work is possible. Essays can be rewritten, student written reports can be upgraded with more research of the topic, and better art can be produced with the enhanced use of materials. The analytical grading of the performances of students provides them with the guidance needed to make changes and better approximate the highest benchmark.

The real-world nature of performance assessments implies that they are authentic and relate to something beyond the classroom. For that reason, these assessments are seen by employers as methods of documenting the skills that are needed in the world of work (DiMartino & Castaneda, 2007).

In the case of Olympic diving, performance assessments measure skills that have been learned and that are subject to improvement by direct instruction (see Photo 9.1). The instruction may be formal school-based

Photo 9.1   Once every 4 years this performance scoring system is applied to many of the Olympic competitions. For example, a ten point scale of performance is used to evaluate Olympic diving competitions.

SOURCE: Photograph taken by Mike Hirai. Reprinted with permission from Kimiko Hirai Soldati.

learning or may have occurred through the student's interaction with others in the environment. Tutors, coaches, parents, and even peers often teach children the necessary skills that facilitate improvement in their performance in many fields (e.g., salesmanship, sports, music, and the art of teaching). This desire to create a great athlete is one impetus behind the decision of some parents to homeschool their children. This educational approach makes it possible for the parents to devote untold hours to the refinement of their child's prowess.

Performance assessment can provide a clear demonstration of a child's ability to meet the standards for competition or for learning. Naturally, these assessments are best used to evaluate clearly observable achievement. In the core secondary subjects, these would include areas of achievement that are product oriented. These include bench skills in science, writing and rhetoric skills in English, conversational skill in modern language, report development and research skills in social studies, and problem solving in mathematics.

Development of Performance Assessments

Before employing a performance assessment, the teacher should have precise learning standards available that have been approved and fully adopted. Each of the major learning standards is normally broken into a number of sub-standards or goals around which instruction and assessment should be designed. Linking the performance assessment with the learning standards facilitates the design of assessments that both measure achievement and are germane to the school's curriculum. What teachers need to do is avoid being viewed as a creative odd duck who cares less about the required curriculum and more about completing complex projects with the students. Such activities may be enjoyable to all involved but will result in poor performance on the mandated high-stakes assessments. The compilation of successful performances by a student should document that he or she has progressed and achieved the primary learning standards.

Credibility

The flexibility of time schedules makes it possible for elementary-level teachers to employ performance assessments for many areas of the curriculum. The learning standards and goals assessed by the performance assessment may well include all of the domains of the curriculum, including the cognitive and metacognitive, psychomotor, and affective.

Each time a teacher decides to use this assessment technique, he or she should consider whether the assessment is worth the time invested in the task. As the elementary school year provides up to only 1,000 hours for all classroom instruction, and secondary schools provide a maximum of only 150 hours for each major subject per year, this decision regarding the credibility of the assessment task is important. In other words, teachers should be prepared to prove and document that the performance task produced learning that justified the instructional time spent on the activity.

Breadth and Fairness

Secondly, the teacher must verify that the performance assessment will involve several aspects of the curriculum. Performance assessments should be broader in scope than a standard classroom test. Part of this decision to employ a performance assessment should also involve consideration of the fairness of the project or task. Do some children have a significant advantage over others in the performance task? This can be especially evident with projects started in school and finished at home. But, fairness can also involve children's reading levels, access to computers, and facility with the English language. The task should be authentic and based on the use of real-world skills. This means that the performance assessment task isn't just another academic exercise completed without a realistic context and basis.

Structure

When the task is presented to the class, a scaffolding or framework should be provided for the students. This may take the form of a suggested outline to follow or a list of key words. The framework could also provide a list of readily available resources and materials that children can use to create their performance or project. The teacher could provide a checklist of components that should be included in the completed project. This inclusion of scaffolding along with the performance task can provide a more equal playing field for all the students in the class.

Each performance task should provide students with clear and precise directions, timelines, and expectations. The directions provided to the students should detail the role of the teacher as a resource and explain his or her role in the formative assessment of the project while it is under development. The expectations expressed in the directions should provide clear insight into how the project will be evaluated and reveal the final grading process to the children.

BOX 9.1   Examples of Performance Assessments in Education

There are a number of tried-and-true performance assessments that have been adapted to most subjects and grade levels. Some of these are as follows:

- Write in-depth research papers on topics pertaining to influential persons and significant movements (e.g., in what way did the union movement of the 19th century change the nature of the middle class in America?).
- Research background information and write a faux newspaper article.
- Research the background of a local story and write a TV script for the issue or topic.
- Select an illustration or photograph and write about its meaning and the story behind it.
- Write a book review or a review of a TV show selected by the teacher (e.g., *Animal Planet* on the Discovery Channel).
- Write a comparison paper (e.g., U.S. government and the Canadian government, or angiosperm and gymnosperm, or 16th-century Italian architecture and 21st-century American architecture).
- Put together a videotape of a news report on some aspect of the school or community.
- Write a comparison of two points of view on the same topic expressed by two different authors (e.g., articles from the progressive magazine the *Nation* with a story on the same topic from the conservative *National Review*).
- Evaluate the claims made in an advertisement.
- Write the biography of a person you know (grandparent, uncle, local pastor, neighbor, etc.).
- Use a computer and timetables to plan a trip around the world using these four transportation modes: bus, rail, cruise ships, and airlines. Research the lowest fares for each leg of the trip.

These represent only a small sample of the ideas that teachers have used as vehicles for a performance assessment. Other ideas can be found at the following URLs:

Multiple subjects and grade levels:

http://intranet.cps.k12.il.us/
http://mdk12.org/mspp/mspap/look/index.html
www.doe.state.de.us/AAB/DSTP_items.html
www.mark-ed.com/assessment/AssesStuPerform.htm

For geography:

www.coe.ilstu.edu/IGA?interact/assess/5-8.htm
http://education.umn.edu/CAREI/Reports/Rpractice/Fall2000/avery.html

For science:

www.sasked.gov.sk.ca/docs/elemsci/ideass.html
www.usoe.k12.ut.us/curr/science/Perform/PAST5.htm

For mathematics:

www.nottingham.ac.uk/education/MARS/tasks/
http://arlingtonschools.org/Curriculum/Assessment/mathassess.html

SCORING

Before embarking on a performance assessment model, teachers need to remember that a number of subject areas do not lend themselves to the use of performance assessments. These are subjects and sections of the curriculum in which students are expected to commit to memory a number of facts and chunks of core knowledge. These include the symbols for the elements on the periodic table of chemical elements, the vocabulary of a modern language, the spelling of words in English, and the multiplication table. The most efficient way to assess these areas is through the use of selected-item type or a short answer achievement test.

Evaluation

The evaluation of the product of a performance assessment can be accomplished by employing either a holistic or an analytical scoring system. The critical component in any performance evaluation is the assessment rubric. The rubric is a guide that presents both acceptable and unacceptable levels of performance on the assessment task. It should also provide several ordinal levels between the highest **level of proficiency** and the total failure to meet the assessment requirements. Each of the various levels should be operationalized by providing examples (benchmarks) of performance at that level along with carefully written descriptions of the performance expectation for that level. Rubrics are best developed by a team of teachers. By working cooperatively, it becomes likely that the scoring system will be reliable and relatively objective.

Students

Once developed, the scoring rubric and benchmarks should be given to the students. This is best done along with a detailed discussion of expectations and the relationship of the rubric to the final evaluation. The performance should help children to develop the ability to reflect upon their work and develop a critical eye for their own efforts. By providing and explaining how the product will be evaluated, the students have the opportunity to reflect on their efforts and self-correct along the road to completion.

Holistic Assessment

This is an approach to evaluation that provides one ordinal score for the whole performance. It is the sum total of all that was done and thereby lacks a great deal of specificity. This method does not provide much, if any, developmental help, nor does it provide guidance to the student. The great advantage of using a holistic or "big picture" assessment system is that it is time efficient and less labor intensive. The ETS written examinations, including those in the SAT II, are typically scored using a six-point holistic scoring system. This keeps the cost of assessment down, as the average assessor using a holistic scoring method can read and evaluate 10 to 20 student essays in an hour. As assessors are paid less than $20 per hour, this keeps the reader cost per essay to less than $2 per student's paper. The ETS scoring system also provides extensive (10–15 hours) training in the scoring method and the use of their rubrics. It also has quality control that works to maintain a high degree of inner-rater reliability (scoring consistency) with each essay being read at least twice by different readers. To see an example of this type of scoring system, visit www.csupomona.edu/~uwc/non_protect/student/CSU-EPTScoringGuide.htm.

BOX 9.2 Development of Scoring Rubrics

Scoring rubrics are a descriptive way to evaluate student work and assign an ordinal level or value to that work (Moskal, 2000). For a teacher to develop a scoring rubric it is first essential that he or she have a precise and easily demonstrable notion or picture of what the optimal production by a student looks like. The qualities of the work that make it optimal or of the "highest quality" will make up the elements that become part of the best score on the rubric.

The teacher developing a scoring rubric must also decide on the number of distinct categories that can be reliably identified and clearly defined for student work that is at less than an optimal level. There is no hard-and-fast rule as to how many categories can be identified to evaluate student work. With holistic scoring rubrics, something between four and six ordinal levels is most common. Too many scoring categories make it difficult to render reliable evaluative judgments between adjacent levels, while too few categories make all student work seem too similar. The various levels should each reflect specific performance characteristics of the student work. The categories should each provide an example or benchmark for what that qualitative level of work by the student would include or how it will appear. Each level can then be assigned an ordinal number or an ordinal descriptor. Ordinal descriptors can include titles such as the following:

1. Does not meet minimum standard, minimum standard met, minimum standard exceeded, standard greatly exceeded

2. Incoherent and confused, needs more developmental effort, good work, excellent work

3. Beginner or novice, apprentice, journeyman, master craftsman

4. Significantly below proficiency, below proficiency, proficient, highly proficient, exemplar for others

Analytical Assessment

The analytical approach to the evaluation of student performances requires a different type of rubric. In this case, the assessor examines a number of different aspects of the student product being assessed. Each element on the rubric is elaborated with a series of ordinal score levels. Each of those levels is defined by both examples and carefully crafted explanations. Using this multifaceted rubric, it is possible to make an independent assessment of the various dimensions of the performance task. This is similar to the Olympic scoring system now employed for evaluating and judging downhill skiing. In the world of the classroom, this type of assessment provides the student with a series of feedback points about the various dimensions of the project. Thus, students can be informed of the strengths as well as the weaknesses evident in their work. The disadvantage of this system is that it requires more time than does a one-shot holistic scoring of the performance task. An example for the development of both holistic and **analytical rubric**s can be reviewed at the following two locations:

www.basd.net/technology/STEEP/Assessment/Connections/rubrics.htm

www.relearning.org/resources/PDF/rubric_sampler.pdf

BOX 9.3   Example of Holistic and Analytical Rubrics for a Writing Assessment in Middle School

Holistic Rubric

The evaluator reads the student's essay and decides which of the five levels best describes the level of writing that was submitted by the student.

Level 5 (Excellent)	Student provides solid evidence and support for his or her position. Conclusions are well founded on evidence. All points in the question are addressed. The writing is clear, succinct, and focused.
Level 4 (Very good)	An adequate amount of information is provided in support of the arguments presented by the student. Writing is generally well organized and clear. The points in the question are all addressed.
Level 3 (Good)	The student presents an answer to most of the points made in the question. The writing is understandable but not tightly organized. Conclusions are presented but not clearly supported.
Level 2 (Below expectations)	The student answers some of the points presented in the question. The arguments are disjointed and lack a clear focus. The writing is confusing and hard to follow.

Level 1 (Poor)	The student does not answer the questions. The student does not provide evidence nor does the student state a conclusion. The writing is garbled and cannot be followed.

Analytical Rubric

The teacher reads the student's essay then evaluates the writing on three separate dimensions. These include how well the student follows the conventions of writing in English, ideas and conclusions that the student proposes and the support he or she provides for each, and the student's ability to organize and provide a focus to the writing. Each of these is analyzed separately and then weighted and averaged to find an overall evaluation level.

English Conventions

Level 5	Paragraph structure is well conceived. There are no errors of spelling, syntax, capitalization, and grammar. Sentence complexity is appropriate for the grade level.
Level 4	Most of the paragraphs are well conceived. Words appropriate to the grade level spelling list are spelled correctly. Very few errors in spelling of words from the grade level list. Grammar and most syntax are correct.
Level 3	A few of the paragraphs are not well organized. There are several errors of grammar, syntax, and usage. The sentence structure is for the most part correct.
Level 2	Paragraph form is used with many errors. Sentence structure is marginal. There are errors of usage, capitalization, syntax, and grammar in each paragraph.
Level 1	Structural errors abound. No attempt is made to follow conventions of English grammar. There is no recognizable paragraph form. Errors are so common as to distract the reader.

Ideas and Conclusions

Level 5	Student uses data and examples to propose answers to the questions posed. Conclusions are made and supported with data and examples. Writing is clear and on task as to what is presented in the assignment.
Level 4	Student presents conclusions, most of which are supported by data and examples. The questions are answered and the writing is mostly on task.
Level 3	The writing generally attempts to answer the questions in the assignment. Conclusions are not always clearly aligned with examples or data. The link between points is not always well established.
Level 2	The writing lacks a clear goal. The student attempts to answer questions but is muddled in reasoning. A lack of clarity is evident throughout.
Level 1	The questions posed in the assignment are not answered. The writing is a confused and rambling collection of scattered and disconnected thoughts.

Focus

Level 5	The student's writing is focused and on target. The writing is inviting to the reader and the sequence of points leads the reader to the conclusion made by the student. The student's work is easy to follow and a pleasure to read.

(Continued)

BOX 9.3 (Continued)

Level 4   The writing is generally well directed. Few leaps of logic are made and the sequence of points is reasonable. There is a good sense of flow and direction.

Level 3   The writing is generally well sequenced. There are a number of gaps and leaps in logic, but the reader can follow the arguments being made by the student.

Level 2   The writing lacks a reasonable structure. The arguments seem disconnected and do not lead the reader to a conclusion that answers the assigned task.

Level 1   There is no discernable structure to the arguments or ideas developed by the student author. There is only a jumble of thoughts and unsupported notions.

A performance assessment carried out by using an analytical scoring system can be easily converted into a letter grade. This requires that the various scoring dimensions be weighted as to their relative importance to the project. For example, a performance task requiring students to write a newspaper article about an environmental issue in the community could weigh the dimension of the "quality of scientific evidence" presented by the student as being three times more critical to the overall evaluation than the dimension "format." These, along with dimensions such as "use of examples" and "clarity of writing," could make up the other elements on the analytical rubric used to evaluate students. If each dimension is scored on a six-point scale, the total number of possible points would be 36. Quality of scientific evidence would be scored from 3 to a maximum of 18. The other three dimensions (format, use of examples, and clarity) would each score on scales from 1 to 6.

Before letter grades can be assigned, it is necessary to determine the minimum passing grade. This may be a score of 2 on a six-point rubric for each of the four areas. This assumes that a score of 1 on the rubric indicates that student has developed no skill and has not experienced any development on that dimension of the assessment. If this is the case, the minimum passing score (equal to a letter grade of D) is 12. This is two times the weight of 3 for "quality of scientific evidence," plus 2 more points for each of the other three dimensions being evaluated. If a decision is made to assign the letter grade of A to students who score above the level of five on the rubric, then a minimum A is a total rubric score of 31 (one more than five times the weighted levels). Having these anchor positions established, letter grades can then be assigned by using a scale similar to the following: A ≥ 30, B ≥ 25 and ≤ 29, C ≥ 12 and ≤ 24, and D ≤ 11. Naturally, the conversion of rubric points to letter grades must be carefully introduced and explained to students well in advance of implementation. The conversion system selected by a teacher should be one that can be justified and defended and consistently employed with all other performance assessments.

Reliability

One reason for the use of rubrics in scoring student performance tasks is to provide a reliable assessment strategy. The reliability of the approach can be greatly enhanced by having more than one reader independently read and assess the same student products. There is a tendency for "**rater drift**" to occur when a person reads and evaluates a number of performance assessments. Rater drift results in higher scores to the projects being evaluated toward the end of a long group. This may reflect fatigue and boredom on the part of the evaluator. Multiple raters should exhibit a high degree of agreement in the scores they assign. If there is a difference of more than a point or two, the teachers scoring the student work should stop the assessment and work together with the rubric to improve their consistency. By tweaking the rubric they may be able to improve their agreement and better understand the differentiation between assessment levels. It is also possible to use an ordinal correlation technique (e.g., Spearman's Rank Order Correlation Coefficient) to establish the inter-rater reliability coefficient. This coefficient is best calculated when the raters are employing an analytical rubric. The inter-rater correlation coefficient should be fairly high ($\rho_s > 0.80$) to ensure that the assessments are being reliably evaluated.[2]

Validity and Generalizability

The validity of performance-based tests and alternative types of assessments is built more on the question of process validity than is true of most selection format examinations (See Chapter 5). In electing to employ performance questions in a test the teacher is providing data that facilitate the examination of the cognitive processes employed by the learners (Millman & Greene, 1989). These processes should be clearly described beforehand on the table of specifications for the test. This type of specification makes it possible for the teacher to provide students with reliable feedback.

Some of the traditional notions of validity can also be applied to the analyses of performance assessment tasks. One approach for determining concurrent validity is through the correlation of the performance score with the score from a standard (normative) measure of achievement. While this is possible, it is rarely done in practice. More typically, performance tests are subjected to validity screenings in the areas of content and construct validity. This type of validation study can be carried out by the use of a focus group of experts in the discipline. These consultants can include others with teaching and curriculum backgrounds in the discipline (Millman & Greene, 1989).

A related validity consideration is the generalizability of the performance assessment. When a teacher creates a classroom test for any particular subject, a broad range of test items can be employed to provide a wide view of the student's achievement. This is not the case with performance assessments. During a 45-minute class, middle-school students can complete a 40-item multiple choice test. Such a test can demonstrate student achievement in a topic such as weather. Yet in the same class period a teacher would be able to show students a photograph of a hurricane taken from space and explain a research report he or she wants completed on how hurricanes develop, move, and eventually die. That assignment could take several class periods to research and complete. When the performance task on hurricanes is finished, an important question arises. Specifically, does the grade earned on a report about hurricanes provide adequate evidence that the student understands other aspects of the weather? This is the issue of generalizability (Popham, 1999). For the performance assessments involving hurricanes to provide evidence that students understand other aspects of weather, those assessments would need to have included information about air masses, evaporation, cooling and convection, cloud formation, weather fronts, atmospheric pressure, and the mechanisms of precipitation. To have this type of assessment product, the performance task would need to provide students with complex scaffolding and highly detailed directions.

The validation of alternative assessments that are used to measure the achievement progress of children with severe cognitive impairments is an often overlooked task of state education departments. Most states provide a special assessment program employing alternative approaches to monitor and chart educational development and progress for these children. Yet, little has been done to provide detailed analyses of the validity of those systems (Marion & Pellegrino, 2006).

Authentic-Type Performance Assessments

While not exactly the same, performance measures can also be classified as **authentic assessments** if the assessment task is one drawn from the real world beyond the school. Performance testing requires students to construct an answer in response to a prompt, question, or problem. If the task is structured to model the real world, it can be defined as an authentic assessment. These activities include tasks such as researching and writing a newspaper story, estimating the volume of dirt to be moved to dig the foundation and well for a new community swimming pool, or the cost of the additional electrical power to operate a new football stadium lighting system. Each of these problems and tasks requires that the student research the field, apply analysis, and write a final report. Thus, they meet the curriculum requirements of the school and also provide students with the ability to see the real-world application of what is being learned in school.

The traditional type of classroom test consists of a series of questions that are decontextualized, marked as being right or wrong, and presented in a single summary score or grade. Authentic performance measures use real-world situations that require the student to demonstrate that he or she can actually do something utilitarian.

The authentic performance assessment is based on interesting and engaging tasks that bear a reasonable resemblance to the adult world (Meyer, 1992). While the authentic assessment is designed around real-world requirements, it can never be totally "authentic." There is always an element of contrivance about the task and its grading (Fortier, 1993). These authentic projects require time for the teacher and child to plan, and more time for the child to carry out. Time is also needed to judge, evaluate, and revise the work. The final evaluation should also mimic the evaluation system used in the real world beyond the school.

Case in Point (9c)

A common sight at vacation resorts is the hotel-sponsored scuba class. Before the new divers go out on a scuba expedition in open water, the class is given an authentic assessment on the skills of safe scuba diving. However, a scuba-diving test in a resort swimming pool is not exactly the same as scuba diving in the open ocean. The result of this disconnect is the accidental death and injury of several vacationers each year.

For more information, see "Considerations on Point" at www.sagepub.com/wrightstudy

---

PORTFOLIOS

When a teacher elects to employ alternative assessments, portfolios are likely to be a central feature in the grading and evaluation of students. The general perception notwithstanding, portfolios are much more than a manila folder stuffed with a random assortment of mementos and memos about a student. A portfolio should be purposeful compendium of data sources documenting the growth of a student's skills and knowledge over time in an area. It should chart the evolution of what the child can do and describe the work habits that the student is incorporating into his or her school life (Collins & Dana, 1993). Portfolios provide students with the opportunity to see a picture of themselves and to contribute to and help shape that portrait.

Evaluative Portfolio

The use of a portfolio implies that the teacher has a clear plan for how it is to be used. Each portfolio provides the bridge between the teacher's instructional efforts and the child's educational attainment. That linkage means that one application of portfolios is evaluative. The portfolio can be organized to collect and organize data about the student's achievement in one or more curriculum areas; but, if it is to be holistically graded, it should represent only one dimension of the curriculum. Most student portfolios are evaluated by using an analytical rubric over several linked areas within the

"How do you like my portfolio?"

Figure 9.1   Refrigerator Magnet–Based Student Portfolio

SOURCE: Cartoon by Merv Magus.

curriculum being assessed. As is true with performance evaluations, a well-conceived rubric employed by well-trained evaluators can result in highly reliable evaluations (Gadbury-Amyot, Kim, Palm, Noble, & Overman, 2003). The goal of using the portfolio's documents and other artifacts to make an assessment of the child's learning supersedes any individual marks that may have been placed on the elements that make up the portfolio.

High-Stakes Portfolio Evaluation

An example of the use of portfolios for a high-stakes assessment can be seen in Rhode Island, where high school seniors can present evidence for their eligibility for a high school diploma by presenting a portfolio of their work (Archer, 2005). Heretofore portfolio assessments have been seen as being too unreliable for use as an assessment tool. An analysis by Mark Reckase (1995) estimated that portfolio assessments can achieve a reliability level of approximately 0.80.[3] When portfolios are assessed by well-trained evaluators, the scoring reliability is enhanced. The training programs for portfolio evaluators should include practice with the benchmarks and a number of practice evaluations. The process normally requires about 2 full days.

Second, high reliability requires that the portfolio be evaluated, element by element, using analytical assessment techniques. This precludes the use of a **holistic assessment** of the entire portfolio. Such assessments are too idiosyncratic to the classroom teacher and tend to produce reliability levels in the 0.35 range. The final grade for the portfolio is determined from the summation of all the elements contained within and can have reliability between 0.75 and 0.85 (Reckase, 1995). One-dimensional subjects such as elementary and middle-school mathematics have been demonstrated to provide reliable portfolio assessment scores on a statewide assessment in Nebraska (Brookhart, 2005). Nebraska has resisted the push by the U.S. Education Department to force the use of the typical multiple choice test to measure the state's learning standards (Borja, 2007). That state encourages the various districts to develop local assessment approaches that may include the use of portfolios. These assessments have been demonstrated to improve classroom practice and overall school morale (Roschewski, Isernhagen, & Dappen, 2006).

A portfolio that will be used to evaluate a student should contain elements (documents and artifacts) that are each linked to the approved standards for learning and identified on the school's curriculum map. In other words, a graded portfolio should be grounded in the instructional goals and objectives of the school and linked to the state's standards for learning

(Doherty, 2004). An assessment of a student's portfolio assumes that there is a unifying dimension to the portfolio.

Getting Started

When queried, each member of a school's faculty is likely to have a different idea of what should be included in student portfolios. The need for meeting time to develop a consensus decision is a first step in the process of changing the culture of a school from one that relies on selected item tests to one that uses performance assessments and portfolios to evaluate students. When the decision to use an alternate assessment system has been made, there must also be an agreement on a list of the minimum elements to be placed into each child's portfolio. Naturally, such an agreement among the faculty will provide room for flexibility. It is very likely that many teachers will wish to add to the student portfolios extra materials that are especially meaningful and that are beyond the minimum standard established for the school.

A question that should be addressed before initiating a portfolio assessment program is whether the work that is collected should be "typical products" or "best products." To maximize the reliability of an evaluation of the portfolio, the work should represent the best products of the child. Portfolios can be maintained for the entire year while still being segmented to permit evaluations at several points (report card periods) in the school year.

The students' "best products" at the end of the year should be qualitatively different from the best products at the start of the year. This growth pattern is another topic for the faculty to discuss. The issue for a faculty decision involves the development of a policy for report card grading and the role of improvement in that grade.

Another question that must be discussed by the faculty is what materials in the child's portfolio should be retained and sent on to the teacher in the next grade level? Most school faculties elect to retain only a minimal amount of material from year to year, which serves as a baseline for the new grade level.

An important element that must be agreed upon is the role that students play in selecting items to include in the portfolios. This role is likely to change between the primary (K–3) grades and the intermediate grades (grades 4 to 6). Also, students should review their portfolios periodically during the year and write their reflections on its contents. This reflective narrative can provide the child's own take on his or her learning. The task of reflecting on one's own work, and including these musings in the portfolio, is central to the idea of a **process portfolio**. This self-reflective information could be invaluable to the teacher and also provide the child with the opportunity to develop the ability to self-assess. In terms of student "ownership" and educational development, the best approach is to have students involved from the beginning of the process.

BOX 9.4   Student directions for a Language Arts Portfolio in 6th Grade

A portfolio is an organized collection of your best work in 6th-grade English. It should include all the areas we learn about in class and should show how you improved your skills during the year.

1. It will be used as part of your report card grade. It will equal some fraction of that grade.

2. Your parents will be able to see the portfolio when they come to school to meet with me. The portfolio cannot be taken out of the classroom.

3. I will keep all the portfolios in my cabinet and let you use yours once or twice a week. I am always interested in helping you with your portfolio.

4. The portfolio is your showcase, where you can display all the things you have learned and all the new skills you have developed. Everything in your portfolio should be dated so that it is possible to see change during the year. It may contain the following:

   - Reviews of books you have read
   - Letters you have written
   - Sample of a humorous story you have written
   - Grammar notebook
   - Vocabulary-builder notebook
   - Examples of how you edit and improve your writing drafts
   - Writing journal
   - Your evaluation and thoughts on each item
   - Special items of your selection

By bringing together all the child's best work examples, the collection becomes a **showcase portfolio**. Among other things, the showcase portfolio provides a superb vehicle to facilitate parent conferences.

Portfolio Conferences

Most elementary schools and many middle schools schedule parent conferences near the time of the first report card (first quarter). Other conferences can occur at the request of either the parent or teacher at any other time during the year. Also, high school teachers typically see parents by appointment.

All of these conferences are typically held in the afternoon and evenings to facilitate parent attendance. The regular elementary conference is scheduled to last about 20 minutes. The typical classroom with 24 students can take 10 or 12 hours for the teacher. This time is usually not compensated and is donated by the faculty in the name of parent communication.

Teachers should spend some time in preparation for these conferences. This includes a review of all of the student's records and the student's portfolio. A good idea is to make a short list of questions to ask and issues to discuss with the parents during the short time that the conference will run. A proactive strategy is to schedule parents to arrive 15 minutes prior to when they will meet with the teacher. During that time they should be given access to their child's portfolio. It is best if a teacher's aid or student teacher be available to monitor the parents until it is time for them to meet with their child's teacher.

The portfolio of the child's work will demonstrate to the parents any observations by the classroom teacher and his or her insights into their child's learning. The portfolio can also be used to help parents know how they can play a part in supporting their child's learning. The best thing about the portfolio is the implied optimism that it represents. Parents can see the progress their child is making. At the close of the school year, those elements from the portfolio that are not maintained for the next teacher can be given to the parents. This can provide parents with artifacts that may be trivial to the school but precious to them.

Portfolio Advantages

The decision to employ a schoolwide program of portfolio assessment provides several immediate advantages. For one, it brings the assessment of students directly into the instructional process. It also provides an opportunity for teachers to see clear evidence of the effectiveness of their efforts.

A study of the impact on mathematics instruction caused by the introduction of a portfolio assessment system found that teachers do change their instructional approach. When students' work is evaluated through portfolios, mathematics teachers spend more time teaching about the applications for mathematics and showing the natural patterns of mathematics (Koretz, Stecher, Klein, & McCaffrey, 1994). When a school adopts a portfolio assessment system, there is a classroom trend toward the increased use of cooperative learning in the classrooms.

Portfolios also provide students with the ability to see their progress and define for themselves those areas that can be improved. Improved student attitude was one of the unexpected outcomes of the implementation of a statewide portfolio assessment system in Vermont (Koretz et al., 1994). Portfolio assessment systems also provide information that parents truly appreciate. They can trace their child's development and skill acquisition by seeing tangible evidence of that development.

Portfolio Disadvantages

There are a number of problems that a portfolio assessment system introduces into schools. For one, a great amount of time is needed to inservice teachers as to how to set up a portfolio system, how to evaluate children on the basis of that system, and in deciding what will be included in the portfolios.

There is no doubt that the use of a portfolio system requires a faculty with a great deal of self-discipline and a dedication to orderliness. The physical task of file maintenance can be a burden to an already overworked teaching staff. Unless there is careful monitoring by the school administrator, the files may disintegrate into an amorphous clump of quizzes and worksheets completed by the students. Many of the storage and maintenance problems can be eliminated by the establishment of a digital storage system (Niguidula, 2005). Each document can be scanned into a classroom computer and maintained in digital storage. By this system, parents can be given a CD-ROM copy of the child's portfolio at any time. Once again, this digitized portfolio also takes considerable self-discipline and careful attention to the portfolios on a daily basis.

When portfolios are used as the basis for assigning a report card grade, another problem will need to be addressed. The evidence to date is that portfolio systems typically have marginal levels of reliability (Reckase, 1995).

Portfolio Contents

The content of a student's portfolio should be one-dimensional. By limiting the content to a single area of the curriculum, the portfolio can be evaluated with a high degree of reliability. Much like an achievement test, portfolios that cover a range of topics and different areas of the curriculum lack the consistency required for reliability. When there is a need to bring together the learning products from other curriculum areas, a second portfolio should be established. For example, a single file for a curriculum area such as language arts may be too diverse and require two or more portfolios (e.g., writing should be a separate file).

Another question is the role of the student in the collection of learning products for the portfolio. Educational measurement authors have argued both sides of the issue. However, the consensus now is that students should consult with the teacher in the selection of material for inclusion in the portfolio (Burke, 2005).

BOX 9.5   Portfolio Items

The types of items that may be collected in a portfolio include products such as the following:

Audio tapes of the child's reading

Samples of narrative writing

Samples of poetry and other creative writing

Science laboratory reports

Science projects

Mathematics projects

Mathematics and arithmetic problem solutions

Social studies reports

Book reviews

A showcase portfolio (not for use in evaluation) for a child can contain attestations about the child, which may include the following:

Newspaper or other media stories mentioning the child

Prizes won by the student

Awards presented to the child

Letters of commendation regarding the child

Statewide Portfolio Assessment Programs

During the 1990s, a number of states tooled up to establish portfolio assessment programs. These states included California, New Jersey, Maine, and Pennsylvania. In addition, two states actually went ahead and initiated portfolio assessments. These states were Vermont and Tennessee. After the passage of the No Child Left Behind legislation in 2002, all of these programs and initiatives were terminated and replaced by standardized achievement tests. Today, a handful of states, including Vermont, Maine, and Massachusetts, assess a small number of children with profound disabilities using an alternative portfolio assessment system.

When the NCLB Act became the law of the land, one state, Nebraska, took a different course to compliance. Nebraska developed a statewide assessment system that let local school districts develop their own vehicles for school and student assessment. This unconventional system was approved by the U.S. Department of Education in 2004 (Simon, 2004). Nebraska's system, the School-based, Teacher-led Assessment and Reporting System (STARS), is the only truly locally administered accountability system. Nebraska's Department of Education has developed a series of learning standards for the children of the state and identified five commercially available norm-based assessment tests that can be used as a part of the assessment system that each school system must put into place. The local districts of Nebraska also have the power to develop their own learning standards (Rural School and Community Trust, 2007). The approved tests have been analyzed and each found to cover about a third of the standards set by the state. The local districts are responsible for establishing their own assessment plans to "**wrap around**" the commercial test and provide a full assessment of the standards.

These wraparound assessments can involve a locally developed curriculum assessment, but they usually involve a locally developed portfolio assessment system. The Nebraska assessment model makes assessment an ongoing part of the teaching–learning process in each classroom. Parents, teachers, and local politicians are all very pleased with the STARS model (Christensen, 2001).

The detractors have criticized Nebraska's STARS as not permitting school-district-to-school-district comparisons. Concern has also been expressed over reliability of the portfolios. In part, that was addressed in research by Susan Brookhart (2005), who found that the inter-rater reliability of the mathematics portfolios was reasonable high, but that the reading portfolios are not yet being scored in a consistent manner.

Summary

For evaluations of student progress to have any meaning they must be timely. Large-scale test batteries and statewide assessments are rarely returned to the classroom teacher when they could be of use with those students currently enrolled. Classroom teachers rely on locally developed classroom assessments and performance samples of student work to evaluate student learning, plan instruction, and individualize the learning experiences for children.

Performance assessments are at the heart of much of what teachers know about their students. This form of assessment occurs as a regular part of each school day and can include student writing, problem solving, projects, and various creative products. The careful development of rubrics and benchmarks can assure the reliability of scoring and assuage the concerns of students regarding the teacher's grading standards. The scoring rubrics can be either holistic or analytical in nature.

The organization and analysis of the range of student work, including performance assessments, can be managed through the use of portfolios. The portfolio system can also serve as the central feature in both the ongoing formative evaluation of children as well as in parent–teacher conferences and in developing a report card grade. One state, Nebraska, has adopted the use of portfolios to meet the mandate for assessments under the No Child Left Behind Act.

Discussion Questions

1. What percentage of the combined report card grades of elementary and middle-school students should be determined by an assessment of the student's portfolio in a subject area?

2. Are all of the "major" curriculum areas (subjects) of the typical high school appropriate for using a portfolio evaluation system? What areas of a high school curriculum are the best fits for portfolio assessments? Which areas are least well suited for portfolio assessments? Explain your reasoning.

3. What can teachers do to assure that portfolio assessments are reliable and valid measures?

4. Which separate subject areas should be subject to portfolio assessment in the elementary schools?

5. When preparing for a parent conference, are there items that should be removed from the child's portfolio? What would you not show to the parents?

6. Design a performance assessment task that could be employed in your school. Discuss this assessment in terms of the amount of support that the students will require to complete it. Create a holistic rubric with benchmarks that can be used for its evaluation.

Student Study Site

Educational Assessment on the Web

Log on to the Web-based student study site at www.sagepub.com/wrightstudy for additional Web sources and study resources.

NOTES

1. The exceptions are Nebraska in grades 3 through 8 and at the high school level in Rhode Island and New Hampshire. All three programs combine portfolio and performance assessments as a part of the assessment of a student's level of proficiency (DiMartino, 2007).

2. See Chapter 3 for a description of the Spearman Correlation Coefficient rho.

3. See Chapter 4 for a full description of the meaning and calculation of reliability coefficients.

Chapter 10

GRADES, PROGRESS REPORTS, AND REPORT CARDS

The roots of education are bitter, but the fruit is sweet.

—Aristotle

Issues and Themes

Grading and the periodic issuing of report cards are central features in the communication between teachers, students, and parents. The use of a 100-point scale for each subject area has given way to the use of letter grades. These letter grades are derived in ways that are often idiosyncratic to the teacher. The approach most teachers use in marking student work involves a "modified standards-based approach." This approach is also employed in combining marks into a final report card grade.

A second approach to determining report card grades involves the use of a total point system. By this system the teacher becomes the teller, keeping the records of how many points each student earns. Cut scores are established for the total accumulation of points, and grades are awarded on the basis of total points (Marzano, 2000).

When teachers have large sections or a number of classes each day that are all learning the same material, it becomes possible to use a standard score model for grading. A fourth approach to report cards and grades is a product of the new era of accountability. The use of the traditional letter grades for report cards in the elementary school is giving way to report cards that are based on learning standards. Grades on this new version of the report card are often designed to look like scores on state assessment tests. Recently schools have begun to use online report cards. This is just one component in forging teacher–parent communication through computer networking.

Report card grades for students in honors-level courses frequently receive a boost through grade weighting, which results in potentially higher grade point averages. Special education students enrolled in regular education classes are typically graded following the same standard as the other children in the class (Mehring, 1995). The only exceptions occur when a different grading model is specified on an Individual Educational Plan.

The use of high-stakes tests has changed the grade promotion system from one that was teacher centered to one that is measurement centered (see Table 10.1 on page 278). The provisions of the NCLB Act provide for several support programs when children fail. A cottage industry has sprung up that provides tutoring support for children at risk for grade retention and failure.

Learning Objectives

By reading and studying this chapter you should develop the ability to do the following:

- Trace the history of "letter grading" in the schools of the United States.
- Describe the policy of grade weighting in tabulating a student's GPA.
- Explain the use of standards-based grades on report cards by the schools.
- Describe two methods for designing a modified standards-based grading system.
- Describe the self-fulfilling prophesy for failure that can result from high-stakes testing programs.
- Describe the new online report card systems.
- Be knowledgeable of the elements of a successful parent–teacher conference.
- Describe the nature of grade inflation in schools and colleges of the United States.
- Explain the extent of the problem of grade retention as a function of high-stakes testing.

BACKGROUND AND HISTORY

The teacher's role in marking student work and grade reporting is multifaceted and complex. Teachers should consider their marks and the comments reported on student tests and projects as a way of communicating with both the student and his or her parents. The primary goal of this communication is to address the perceived quality and depth of learning that has occurred. However, grades and scores are also viewed as motivational tools and even as methods for rewarding and punishing students for their efforts (Brookhart, 1994, 2004). However, one core assumption about grades should always be that they are unbiased and intellectually honest statements.

The meaning of the composite grade that is recorded on a report card is even murkier. This grade represents many pieces of student work that have been weighted and combined into a single statement. The weighting of the various achievement measures, and the addition of outside factors such as classroom behavior, make report cards a truly idiosyncratic product. It is not uncommon for a student who receives a grade of C to ask his or her teacher what would be necessary to get a B, only to be told to "work harder." This provides the child with virtually no guidance and reflects how report card grades have an almost ephemeral nature (Clarridge & Whitaker, 1997). At best, these grades can be viewed as a rather crude summary that tells nothing of the efforts and difficulties that the student experienced in learning the material. It does not demonstrate strengths, nor does it elaborate on the child's areas of weakness (Brookhart, 1991).

History

In 1778, just 2 years after the American Revolution and 6 years before the ratification of the Constitution, Yale University introduced the first report card for its students. Achievement was reported using a four-point ordinal scale that ranged from the best grade of *Optimi* (very good) to the lowest grade of *Pejores* (very bad). In between these two anchor points were the grades of *Second Optimi* (less than good) and *Inferiores* (further down) (Buchanan, 2002). Harvard soon followed with a grading system based on a 100-point ordinal scale. One reason for the development of a scale for grades was the establishment of the first **honor society**, which required a method to demonstrate academic excellence.[1]

The ongoing informal contact between parents and teachers of the small public schools of the 18th and early 19th centuries made formal reporting unnecessary. Private academies were the dominant secondary schools of the

19th century. The grading system used in these academies was modeled after that employed by the leading colleges of the era. The great expansion in public secondary schools did not occur until late in the century.

The first elementary school that was divided into grade levels opened in Boston in 1848. This was followed by hundreds of other graded elementary schools in the larger cities. These elementary schools began issuing report cards, sometimes referred to as progress reports, before the Civil War. By the late 19th century, America still had the majority of its population living in rural communities and small towns. Transportation and communication limitations led to the growth of small ungraded schools that were frequently constructed with only one or two classrooms. Some of these "one room" schoolhouses are still employed today in rural New England.

Secondary education assumed the standard 4-year design (grades 9–12) following the recommendations of the **Committee on Secondary School Studies**, more popularly known as the "Committee of Ten," in 1892–1893. This committee appointed by the National Education Association was led by Charles William Eliot, president of Harvard University. It established a minimum core curriculum of 24 classes, including nine curriculum areas[2] (Ornstein & Levine, 1989). In 1906, the newly chartered Carnegie Commission recommended that these core courses be taught over time blocks of not less than 120 clock hours per year (Clabaugh & Rozycki, 1990). To enforce the 120-hour policy, the Carnegie Commission required that colleges that participated in the Carnegie's new faculty retirement program, Teachers Insurance and Annuity Association, require all of the secondary schools sending students to their institutions use the standard 120-hour course unit. This gave birth to the 180-day school year and the 45-minute high school teaching period.[3] The term "**Carnegie Unit**" then entered the lexicon of American education for this standard unit of instruction (Shedd, 2003).

At the opening of the 20th century the use of report cards as the primary way to communicate progress to parents was well established. Typically, grades were reported for each of a number of academic and attitudinal areas. Most schools reported grades as a number that was scaled from 0 to 100. This system was designed to show parents what proportion of the material taught was mastered by the student. The grade was then, and continues to be, a compilation of any number of formal and informal measures. The attitudinal areas reported to parents on the report card included dimensions such as "deportment, citizenship, cooperation, and work habits." These were purely the subjective opinion of the classroom teacher. It is easy to visualize a parent trying to determine what a grade of 75 in deportment was all about.

By the First World War, teachers who had difficulty justifying the implied precision of a 100-point scale began rounding their report card grades to the nearest unit of 5 or 10. This truncation of the 100-point scale led to the use of letter grades. Before the start of World War II, the use of a scale of letters ranging from A to E or F supplanted the use of other reporting scales, including the longstanding 100-point system. Even though the 100-point system is out of favor as a report card reporting method, it is still employed in the schools. To this day, the majority of teachers employ 100-point scoring systems on many classroom projects and tests.

By the 1950s, most school systems had experimented with other approaches to assigning report card grades (see Photo 10.1). These included the use of three-point scales such as "Satisfactory (S), Needs Improvement (I), and Unsatisfactory (U)," and "pass–fail." For the most part, both teachers and parents did not like these methods. It was not long before the use of the addendums "plus and minus" soon became a part of the new grading systems. This created an odd-looking collection of combinations (e.g., Pass plus or Satisfactory minus).

The late 1970s saw most school systems return to the use of the traditional letter grade. By the late 1990s, 91% of the high schools in America used a five-point (A to F) letter scale for reporting grades (New Jersey School Boards Association, 2003).

This return to letter grades has been challenged again by the high-stakes tests of the No Child Left Behind Act (PL 107-110, 2002). That law does not

Photo 10.1   Education in Shelby County, Iowa (1941)

SOURCE: U.S. National Archives and Records Administration.

prescribe a specific report card system, but it has reinforced the use of standards-based testing in the core skills. Since 2002, the majority of school districts have redesigned their report cards to better inform parents of the progress children are making toward meeting the required learning standards. Along with new report cards have come revised methods for grading. These "new grades" are reminiscent of the reforms of 50 years ago. The elementary schools of Albuquerque, NM, use report cards that provide grades of "Advanced, Proficient, Nearing Proficient, and Emerging." The Palm Beach School System, FL, began using a three-point scale for grades in 2006. These include (1) far below grade level, (2) less than 1 year below grade level, and (3) at or above grade level. As was the case 50 years ago, there is considerable parent resistance to these new approaches to grading (Guskey, 2002; Reid, 2006; Sacchetti, 2004).

The assigning of grades by teachers is an idiosyncratic act. Even though school systems try to achieve a degree of homogeneity in the grading process, there is a point where the judgment of the teacher comes into play (Marzano, 2000). This is especially true when the student is marginal and the choice is between two possible letter grades. It is at such a time that the teacher is likely to take student effort or ability into account in deciding on a grade (Brookhart, 1991).

PURPOSES OF REPORT CARD GRADES

Elementary

The purpose of report card grades changes with the age of the child. At the primary grade levels (kindergarten through grade 2) most school systems' report cards are a way to inform parents of the developmental and educational milestones the child has accomplished. Only 15% of kindergartens use letter grades on report cards (New Jersey School Boards Association, 2003). Primary grade reporting systems and report cards typically are standards based and provide a method for parents to learn how well the young child is achieving the primary-grade skills. These primary report cards are typically designed to report on the learning standards as approved by the local school district.

By third grade the nature of the report card usually changes to provide a summative statement about the achievement of the child in each of the various curriculum areas. However, the report card grade is not a clean reflection of just the child's achievement. Throughout the elementary school years, teachers infuse other factors into the grades they report for their students

(Hopkins, 1998). These factors include issues such as class participation, behavior, organization skills, punctuality, neatness, and attitude. **Non-content factors** become more prominent components of the grade when the child is at a marginal position between two possible letter grades.

Also by third grade, children achieve the cognitive development required to understand how report cards are all about them. It also becomes apparent to children in third grade that some of their peers are winners and others are losers in the "game of school." It is at this point that the grading process begins to affect the self-esteem and motivation levels of all children. Third grade is also a critical year as it is the first time children must take a mandated statewide assessment test. This first exposure to high-stakes tests results in a failure rate (Below Proficient) much higher for minority children than for Anglo-White children. It is also higher for children who come from impoverished home environments. The combination of poor grades, failing assessment test scores, and low self-esteem interact with the instructional process and lead to self-fulfilling prophecies of failure for children who are as young as eight years of age.

Middle School

A cross-disciplinary team of different subject area teachers each contribute to the report card of middle-school students. These teachers often meet as a team and discuss the children for which the team is responsible.[4] Yet, each course grade isn't a team decision. Subject grades reflect the perception of the individual subject teachers who are on the team. Like all teachers, middle-school faculties also tend to bring non-achievement elements into the grading process. The benefit of a team approach is that it makes it possible for teachers to discuss grading philosophies. Also, the team can facilitate efforts to individualize remediation efforts for children at risk for failure.

High School

Report card grades in high school are the product of individual teachers and reflect the perspective of these content specialists. There is little coordination between teachers at this level. For that reason, it usually becomes the task of the guidance counseling staff to keep track of children at risk for academic problems. The counselors can meet with the various teachers and initiate coordinated efforts for remediation. There are a number of philosophical differences between secondary school teachers in terms of what goes into any report card grade. This division can occur whether or not there is a stated policy or published school guideline for report card grades.

Teacher autonomy not withstanding, school administrators can open the file and change any student's grade. This principle was established in Texas when a football player had the school principal order a teacher to change a report card grade to keep the student eligible to play (Brookhart, 2004). In Gwinnett County, Georgia, a high school science teacher was fired as being insubordinate for not changing an athlete's grade on the orders of the school's principal (Dodd & Morris, 2005).

One such division occurs between those who believe that only the content of the subject area should be part of any grade and those who feel writing skills, effort, and other non-content issues should be a part of all grades. One icon of education, Jaime Escalante, whose AP calculus class inspired the movie *Stand and Deliver*, said "if the kid put in a lot of hard work, I had to recognize that" (Mathews, 1988, 2005). This difference in grading philosophy also influences report card grades. Thus, in one high school department it is possible that every teacher uses a somewhat different set of criteria for assigning report card grades.

STUDENT GRADES

Most experienced teachers have a clear idea of what constitutes excellent work by students. They also have a clear notion of what is needed for students to pass the course. What is less clear is the distinction between the other ordinals on the grading scale (i.e., D, C, B). This lack of clarity becomes more acute when plus and minus grades are added to the five basic letter grades. With this addition teachers must decide between any of 12 possible grades to put onto report cards. To make these decisions, most educators of the upper elementary, middle, and senior high school employ either a **modified standards-based approach** or a total point system. Two other grading systems are also available: **grading by local norms** (curving) and standards-based grading.

The Modified Standards-Based Approach

This is a method of grading by which the teacher starts with a grading scale that is fixed and divided into ordinal marks, which are presented as letters. A common example of this is one where the grade of A is set equal to 95% and the grade A– requires 90%. The grade of B has a minimum of 85% and a grade of B– needs 80%. Likewise a C requires 75%, and 65% is the minimum for a D. While the scale is fixed, what isn't clear is the answer to the question, "percent of what?" School board policy often sets these percent values for the various letter grades, yet there is no way to know exactly what the percent is based on. Some teachers add and then average their test scores and then use this simple average percent as the foundation of the course grade. Yet there is no way to know if the test scores that were averaged were good representations of the required curriculum. All classroom tests are designed by the teacher and reflect the teacher's take on what is important for students to learn (Frary, Cross, & Weber, 1993).

Weighted Combinations

In addition to deciding what areas of the curriculum to test, the classroom teacher also decides how to combine marks and test grades to produce a report card grade. This combination could include oral presentations, papers, homework, quizzes, projects, and tests. It may also take into account all the elements collected in the student's portfolio of work. The teacher can appraise the student's development over time by reviewing his or her portfolio of work. This evaluation of progress is highly subjective. Nonetheless, progress is frequently weighted into the report card grade, especially for children in the lower grades and children with special needs.

Point System

A variation on the modified standards-based approach for grading is the point system. This approach to classroom record keeping and student grading is a favorite of the majority of secondary-school teachers (Stiggins, Frisbie, & Griswold, 1989). By this system everything (e.g., homework, tests, reports, projects, quizzes) that goes on in the classroom is assigned a point value. The teacher becomes a teller keeping track of every point earned by the students. These teachers are never without their roll books in which all the points are tabulated. This approach to grading can be thought of as a stimulus–response reward system in which the rewards consist of small points and check marks in a roll book. Under this system, academically talented students tend to track their point totals and evaluate their every move on a cost-vs.-benefit basis. Teachers can bribe students to do extra projects by offering "extra credit points." These extra credit points work to lower the reliability of the system because all students are not being evaluated using the same metric.

Under the point system, teachers assign report card grades on the basis of some arbitrary point total system. Thus, an A may require that the student has earned 1,000 or more points over the marking period, while a C student needs to have accrued a total of at least 725 points.

The chief advantage of the point system and the modified standards-based approach to grading is in the seeming objectivity of these approaches. Even though both methods are fraught with the subjective decisions and opinions of the classroom teacher, they both appear to be objective. Thus, these two approaches tend to be easier to defend when challenged by students and/or parents.

Grading by Local Norms

When a teacher has a large number of students learning the same material, it becomes possible to employ a **norm-based scoring system** for assigning grades (see Table 10.1). The vernacular for this method is "curving." This term describes how the assumption of a Gaussian normal curve underlies the technique. A troubling side effect of this approach is that top achieving children will be in keen competition for the few grades of A that are available. In 2007, a student sued his college when the professor used a curved grading system and awarded the course grade of C to a student who had a class average of 84.5 ("Watch for Curves," 2007). The course averages for the students had a significant negative skewness. The top achieving students will watch each other to see if anyone is breaking away from the peloton and threatening the status quo.

Problems

Teachers employing this approach decide in advance how many students will be given each letter grade. The students are arranged in order

Table 10.1   Example of the Basic Grading by Local Norm Model for a Class of 25 Students

A Priori Decision ×	Total No. of Students =	No. of Grades
A = 16%	25	4
B = 24%	25	6
C = 32%	25	8
D = 16%	25	4
F = 12%	25	3

by their total achievement, and grades are then attached and recorded. The ordering by achievement can be done by using either a total point system or by a modified-standards approach. There are many problems with this approach.

Perhaps the most serious problem with this model is that individual grades are totally dependent on the other students in the class. In the example, four students will be given the grade of A no matter how well the class does as a whole. Thus, a bright and well-motivated student would do better in a class where the others were neither. Such students may not achieve an honors grade, A, in a class where there were a number of other excellent students. Likewise, a student with modest skills and motivation could earn a grade of A in a class where he or she was better than the others.

Best Use

The best application of this grading practice is with large heterogeneous classes. By having more than 60 students who represent heterogeneously distributed skills and abilities, it is possible to assign grades that follow an assumed normal distribution. Yet, even if this distribution problem is achieved, the local norm grading method is still limited. It does not provide for the case where all students learn well and deserve good grades, nor does it provide for the opposite condition. The major advantage to this approach is that test scores no longer need to be clustered at the upper end of the distribution (negative skew). When there is a percent basis to grading, the distribution must be skewed to provide for an average score near the 75% or 80% level. Any lower average would result in an inordinate number of students who would have failed. Thus, the average item difficulty level on tests and quizzes can be closer to the ideal of 0.50 or 0.60.

Magic Pencil

A variation of this method known as the "**magic pencil**" involves creating a **histogram** of all the students in terms of either average score or total points. Once the histogram is established, the teacher uses a "seat of the pants" approach to draw lines through the distribution to define the various letter grades. The obvious advantage or disadvantage to this approach to grading is that it is easier for the teacher to manipulate than any of the other approaches to grade reporting.

Standardized Scores

Another model of this local norm grading system that can be used to assign report card grades involves turning every test and other measure into a standard deviation score (z-score) (see Figure 10.1). This step of converting

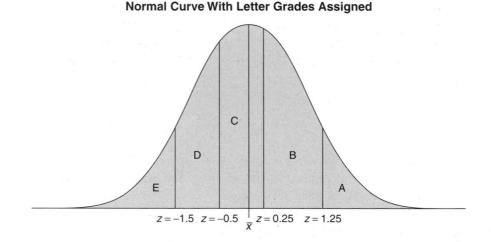

Normal Curve With Letter Grades Assigned

$z = -1.5$ $z = -0.5$ $\overline{x}$ $z = 0.25$ $z = 1.25$

Figure 10.1a   Normal Curve With the Letter Grades Assigned

A = average z-score ≥ 1.25

B = average z-score ≥ 0.25

C = average z-score ≥ –0.50

D = average z-score ≥ –1.50

F = average z-score ≤ –1.51

Student (z-score test 1 × weight 1) + (z-score test 2 × weight 2)
    +(z-score Quiz 1 × weight q1) = average Z = grade

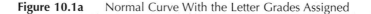

Abe	(0.76 × 1.0)	+	(0.59 × 1.0)	+	(1.2 × 0.5)	=	0.74	B
Betty	(1.20 × 1.0)	+	(2.00 × 1.0)	+	(1.0 × 0.5)	=	1.48	A
Craig	(−0.60 × 1.0)	+	(−0.80 × 1.0)	+	(0.74 × 0.5)	=	−0.41	C

Figure 10.1b   Combination of z-Scores and Assigning of Grades

raw scores to standard deviation scores is why the term ***standardized score*** is applied to this method. When this has been done, the teacher then multiplies each by the appropriate weighting factor. Finally, the weighted z-scores are added for each student. The weighting factors are selected by the teacher and represent the relative importance of each test, quiz, paper, and all other marked student assignments that are a part of the combined grade. The combined letter grade then can be assigned based on a fixed scale of average z-scores that the teacher set in advance.

There are several problems with this approach, including the assumption of a normal distribution and the fact that all students cannot be given high grades if a whole class does well.

Standards-Based Grades

It is evident that there is little about grading and report cards that is really new. The grading models that have been used for the past 225 years in this country are still widely employed today. Yet, there is a new direction for educational grading and report cards. Following the efforts of the Clinton administration to move American education to a standards-based curriculum, and the subsequent passage of the No Child Left Behind Act in 2002, a standards-based approach to grading is now emerging. Standards are the statements of what each child should know or be able to do at a particular point in time. The simple premise behind these new report cards is that if the high-stakes decisions made affecting the child are based on state-approved learning standards, the report cards should also reflect the progress of the child toward achieving those standards. For the most part, school districts are introducing these new report cards for the elementary grades first. There is evidence that the amount that children learn as reflected through standardized test scores is enhanced by the switch to a standards-based grading system (Clymer & Wiliam, 2006/2007).

Standards-based report cards present the child's progress using scales indicating the performance level of the child on each standard. A number of new computerized reporting systems also provide parents with a diagnostic statement for children who are below the basic level on the standard. Typically, school districts report grades on a four-point performance scale such as the following:

Advanced: The student demonstrates in-depth understanding of the extended concept or skill. The knowledge or skill can be applied with skill and precision.

Proficient: The student exhibits a clear understanding and is knowledgeable of the basic concept. The child can apply the concept or skill with accuracy.

Basic: Student has developing understanding of the basic skill or concept. Performance of the skill, or application of the concept, is not consistent in quality or accuracy.

Below Basic: The student does not understand the concept and cannot demonstrate the application of the concept or skill even with support and guidance.

Five-point systems are also being employed by school districts that wish to be able to demonstrate the progress of the slowest of their students. The added category "Far Below Basic" provides a benchmark that can be surpassed, thereby demonstrating the low-achieving child's progress.

Occasionally the new report card will provide a list of benchmarks for children to achieve during the school year. The benchmarks are sequential and reachable targets. This type of computerized report card describes activities that parents can do to assist their children in reaching new benchmarks and improved proficiency levels. Along with a report of the benchmarks and performance levels for the various standards, the new report cards can also provide a copy of the rubric used in assigning the performance levels. The rubric is a statement of the specific applications and characteristics used by the teacher in identifying the child's performance level. A compilation of rubrics has been organized by the Chicago School District. This can be seen at http://intranet.cps.k12.il.us/ Assessments?Ideas_and_Rubrics?Rubric_Bank/ rubric_bank.html.

In moving toward a standards-based report card, many schools have done away with letter grades for subject areas such as language arts and arithmetic. Not unexpectedly, parents have criticized the complexity of the new standards report cards and school systems often report both the performance levels on standards as well as composite subject area grades. In 2003, the schools of New York City tried a new 12-page, standards-based report card that covered assessments for 145 standards. The complexity of the document befuddled parents and angered teachers, who not only had to complete it but also had to explain it to parents. This report card did not last a year and was replaced in 2004 (New York United Federation of Teachers, 2004). An example of a commercially available standards-based report card using a four-point system can be seen at the following: www.gradebook.com.

This example incorporates a traditional letter grade for the subject along with the standards-based report card. The following five-point reporting system from the schools of Travis, California, does not include a traditional letter grade, just the standards and a place for teacher comments: www.travisusd.k12.ca.us/travisusd/tusd/Administration/Departments/ Educational_Services/SBPR/index.asp.

One of the concerns of parents with the new standards-based report cards is the lack of a method of calculating grade point averages, tabulating class rank, and offering membership in honor societies. This issue has been resolved by schools that use an average proficiency level as the way to determine relative achievement. One model involves assigning every standards-based grade with an ordinal number. That involves assigning all of the highly proficient evaluations the student received with a value of 4 and all proficient grades the value of 3, etc. Then it is possible to treat the numbers as level II ordinals and average them. (For a review of ordinal data, see Chapter 3.) Once averaged it is possible to assign "honor values" to the mean grades.

Mean Performance Level	*Honor Level*
4.00	Highest honors
3.50–3.99	High honor
3.00–3.49	Honor

REPORT CARD COMMENTS

Report cards have greater reliability and are less subjective when they are based on the single factor of achievement. Other nonacademic factors about the classroom performance of the child that are of concern for both teachers and parents can be included in the comment section. Writing comments on report cards is a labor-intensive job that most educators dislike. Yet, these comments are important links in the chain of communication between the home and the school. As the report card is a permanent record for the child, these comments must be carefully crafted and well written.

Space is limited on the report card comment area; therefore, the comments need to be pithy, accurate, and succinct. This implies that the comments are specific and address an identifiable issue. Filling in the comment section can be a time to provide the child with kudos and present a positive image of him or her. Such positive comments may contain words such as *efficient*, *thorough*, *committed*, *caring*, and *insightful*. Likewise, the comment section can provide parents with insight into problems the child is experiencing. Comments such as the following can direct parents to these areas needing attention: *has difficulty with . . .*, *must be reminded to . . .*, *has failed to master . . .*, and *continues to struggle with . . . .* There are no

absolutes in education; for that reason, the use of words and phrases implying an absolute should be avoided in the comment section. Such words and
phrases include *can't*, *will not*, *is unable to*, *inevitably*, and *always*. There is
an increasing number of school systems that have moved to using an
approved list of comments that teachers can select from for the report cards.
These are typically part of a computerized report card system. Internet locations offering hundreds of comments are also available to be used by teachers
in writing report cards. The following are examples:

www.teachersnetwork.org/ntol/howto/align/reportsam/

www.teachnet.com/how-to/endofyear/personalcomments061400.html

www.teachervision.fen.com/page/6964.html

ONLINE REPORT CARDS

The standard written report card will soon be viewed as a quaint technique
of a bygone era. There is a move today to use an online approach to parental
communication. Web-based systems can now facilitate the continual communication between the homes of students and the classroom. By this system,
parents are able to communicate with teachers during online office hours,
and teachers are in daily contact with the parents of children who need extra
help. Teachers post daily homework assignments, which makes it possible for
parents to check student assignments. Attendance is posted daily, making it
impossible for a child to play hooky without being caught. Through these systems, parents can track the daily progress of their children.

There are problems with the system that are related to system security
and to having the entire school community wired and online. When an online
reporting and communication system is implemented, it is critical that no
family be left behind. To achieve that goal, parents must be computer literate
and check the system every day. Inservice education for parents and help in
the parents' acquisition of home computers must be addressed by school
systems moving in this direction. To see this model for an online reporting
system, visit Web pages such as the following:

www.engrade.com/

www.thinkwave.com/

www.mygradebook.com/

www.ahisd.net/gradespeedparent.htm

www.apple.com/education/powerschool/

The online reporting system is well suited for the new standards-based report cards. Information can be provided by the teacher on a regular basis about benchmarks and student progress toward achieving them. The software to implement this reporting and communicating system is very costly, but the model is growing in use.

Report Card Ownership

With all report cards and progress reports, the parents are the owners of the student record. It is the parents who have full responsibility for the minor children in their families. During the senior year, an exception occurs when the high school student has his or her 18th birthday (Family Educational Rights and Privacy Act, 1974). That age makes the teenager an adult, and the young adult owns his or her records. The parents no longer have a right to see the academic record of the 18-year-old student without written permission from the student. Public high schools need to develop release forms to distribute to children on their 18th birthdays. A model for this can be seen on the following Web pages: www.middlebury .edu/NR/rdonlyres/25C9F706-E363-4E4B-B8D8-D2F8179A7233/0/gradere portauthorization.pdf

www.registrar.emory.edu/changeof info/parentreport.htm

REPORT CARD GRADES FOR THE GIFTED

The assigning of grades for students enrolled in programs for the gifted is a thorny problem for school administrators. One of the problems is that the No Child Left Behind Act has drained much from the resources that once had supported programs for the academically talented and gifted. There is no federal law that mandates that school districts protect the rights of gifted children. That is a matter left to the states. The Jacob K. Javits Gifted and Talented Students Act has now become Title V, Part D, of the NCLB Act. This title provides grants for demonstration and research in gifted education. There are 29 states that have embraced programs for the gifted, of which only 4 provide funding and guidelines for their operation within the state's school systems.

Gifted education has always been suspect in this country. All too often it is seen as elitist and somehow un-American. Taxpayers have difficulty with the idea of spending more to educate students who have more to start with than do others. Yet, most adults have no problem having the schools offer competitive programs for elite athletes and talented young musicians. In 2005, a coalition of parent groups in suburban Montgomery County, Maryland, began a campaign to end the identification of gifted students and the termination of all special programs for gifted children (Aratani, 2005). The primary point made by this group was that programs for the gifted were not equitable and should be open to all students. Other critics have argued that persistent personality problems are experienced by academically gifted students who attend highly selective schools (Marsh, Trautwein, Lüdtke, & Baumert, 2007).

Elementary Level

The rationale for programs for gifted children is based on the observation that our most talented students are languishing in classrooms that offer hours of repetitious drill for mandated tests but little or no intellectual stimulation for students who are thirsting for greater cognitive challenges. Oddly, the dropout rate for gifted children is not far behind that of the general population of students (National Association for Gifted Children, 2005; Renzulli & Park, 2002).

A number of suburban school systems provide specialized programs for the gifted that may involve specialized small-group instruction within the regular classroom. In large cities there are entire schools designated for academically gifted students.

Gifted education offerings at the elementary level are usually "**pull out**" programs. These provide gifted children with a few hours each week of small-group instruction outside of their regular classroom. During the 1980s, most school systems did away with ability grouping at the elementary and middle-school levels. Today that trend may be reversing. More homogenous classrooms make it easier to offer remedial programs and instruction to small classes of at-risk children as well as intellectually enriched programs for the gifted.

Middle School Level

Gifted students can quickly come to feel that they have been victimized when they are assigned extra work while receiving no recognition or reward for the additional expectations. This need for recognition and reinforcement can be provided by the elementary school through awards assemblies and special notations on the report cards. At the middle-school level students can be grouped together and follow an "**honors track**." Those in the honors track should be recognized and perhaps receive special certificates at the eighth grade graduation assembly. Also, their transcripts and report cards could indicate that they participated in a program for gifted students. School policy for these students should recommend that gifted students receive relatively high report card grades. The negative skew to the distribution of report card grades reflects that the top of the distribution of students has been clustered together. Students in this honors section who are in the middle of the range of their gifted peers in terms of achievement are achieving more than the students in the other homogenously grouped classrooms. If a child is unable to be successful in the program, he or she should be counseled and tutored. If that is not successful, and only as a last possible resort, a change of placement should be considered.

Gifted Programs in High School

During 9th and 10th grades students can elect honors classes, and in thousands of high schools, juniors and seniors can elect Advanced Placement (AP) classes and/or International Baccalaureate (IB) classes. Only one in six students enrolled in an AP class is in 10th grade. In 2004, there were a total of 14,900 high schools that offered one or more of the 37 different AP classes to over one and a half million American students (College Board, 2005). In 2006–2007, the College Board began a national audit to document the level of academic requirements for AP courses (Dessoff, 2007).

Both the IB and the AP programs provide the possibility of college credit for a successful performance in the advanced courses.[5] These advanced classes have more requirements and use college-level textbooks. There is ample evidence that the AP classes require more of students and have more exacting standards (Popielarski, 1998). Research evidence has been provided proving that, when tested, students who complete AP classes and achieve a score of 3 or more on the five-point ordinal scale have a significantly greater likelihood of entering college and finishing a bachelor's degree within 5 years than do students who do not take AP classes (Dougherty, Mellor, & Shuling, 2006; Klein, 2007). It is an unfortunate fact that African American and Hispanic high school students are underrepresented in advanced placement programs.[6] Minority students are enrolled in AP courses at a rate that is proportionally less than half what would be expected based on the number of minority students in high school (Dillon, 2007-a; Wasley, 2007). In contrast, Asian American students are twice as likely to take Advanced Placement courses as their numbers would predict (Maxwell, 2007).

Weighted Grades

Most school systems give extra weight to the grades earned in these advanced courses than is true for regular high school classes (see Table 10.2). Thus, students enrolled in these advanced courses can give their grade point an upward push.

Table 10.2   Data From the Report Card of a Hypothetical Student

Course	Credit	Grade	Bonus	Grade Points
Intro. Calculus (AP)	1	A(4)	1	4+1 = 5
English (Honors)	1	B(3)	0.5	3+0.5 = 3.5
German (Honors)	1	A(4)	1	4+1.0 = 5.0
Economics (AP)	1	A(4)	1	4+1.0 = 5.0
Physics (Honors)	1	B(3)	0.5	3+ .05 = 3.5
Health	0.5	A(4)	0.0	4/2 = 2
Phys. Ed.	0.5	B(3)	0.0	3/2 = 1.5
Band	0.2	A(4)	0.0	4/5 = .8
Total	**6.2**			**26.3**
GPA 26.3/6.2 = 4.24				

The differential weighting for honors and advanced placement courses makes it possible for students to earn high school GPAs that exceed the logical limit of 4.00. The following is another example from the Dover–Sherborn High School (MA).

GRADES AND STUDENTS WITH SPECIAL NEEDS

The number of high school students taking AP classes has increased dramatically over the past few years. This may reflect the more competitive nature of college admissions, or possibly the drive for students to be in the top decile of their high schools' graduating class (Davis, 2004). The push to be

BOX 10.1

Dover-Sherborn HS Student Handbook—Dover, MA

To Drop a Class: After fifty percent (50%) of a course's class meetings have passed, (for full year courses, this includes the mid-year exam), a student cannot withdraw from a course without resulting in a failing grade of (F). The result of this action will appear on a student's permanent record/transcript as a failure (F) for this course.

Calculating a Grade Point Average

Cumulative Grade Point Averages are calculated at the end of a student's fifth, sixth, and seventh semesters of high school. The GPA is calculated by using the grading code below and assigning the correct weight to each letter grade in the following academic subjects taken at Dover-Sherborn High School that meet six or more times in our eight day cycle: English, mathematics, science, world language and social studies. (Virtual High School courses are not included in GPA calculations.) After determining the weights for each course, a sum is calculated. This sum is then divided by the number of counted courses completed. *Please note:*

- The weight for a one semester course is half the weight of a full year course.
- If a course is repeated then both final grades count in the GPA.
- In calculations for the five and seven semester GPA, first semester grades are used and are weighted as one-half of the other full year calculations.
- GPAs are not calculated for any student transferring to Dover-Sherborn after first semester of Grade 11. Additionally, courses taken by students participating in elected alternative programs will not be included in a Dover-Sherborn GPA.

Dover-Sherborn does not provide any rank-in-class distinctions.

Grading System

Dover-Sherborn does not compute class rank for its students due to the school's small class size and its competitive, academic environment.

Grade	Numeric Equivalent	AP	Honors	CP
A	93–100	5.00	4.80	4.00
A–	90–92	4.58	4.40	3.67
B+	87–89	4.17	4.00	3.33
B	83–86	3.75	3.60	3.00
B–	80–82	3.33	3.20	2.67
C+	77–79	2.92	2.80	2.33
C	73–76	2.50	2.40	2.00
C–	70–72	2.08	2.00	1.67
D	65–69	1.25	1.20	1.00
F	Below 65	0	0	0

Honor Roll

Dover-Sherborn High School publishes an Honor Roll every term. To attain honor roll, a student must earn grades of B- or above in <u>all</u> subjects.

SOURCE: From *Dover–Sherborn High School Student Handbook,* p. 11. Reprinted with permission from Dover–Sherborn High School.

among the top students is often inspired by the goal of qualifying for scholarship money and guaranteed admission into the flagship universities of state systems such as Massachusetts, Florida, and Texas.

As noted above, advanced classes are frequently given a boost in their credit weighting to reflect the difficulty of the required academic work. A parallel question relates to grades for students with disabilities. Students who have a cognitive impairment are mainstreamed into regular education programs and are typically graded on the same basis as students having no disabilities. One exception to this policy may involve the Individual Educational Plan that was written for the student when he or she was assessed. In middle school and elementary school, the Individual Educational Plans have been known to specify the minimum grade that a teacher may give to a child with special needs. These limits are often in place to bolster that child's self-esteem and academic confidence.

Another exception to this policy is in the case of developmental classes that are designed for some students with disabilities.[7] With these classes it is possible to assign a slightly lighter weight to the course grade. This policy is in place in some school systems to "protect the integrity" of the grades earned by students enrolled in the regular college preparatory curriculum. The adoption of such an approach implies the school has an absolute standard for learning and can make distinctions between the various course levels.

THE CASE OF TRANSFER STUDENTS

A quandary for many school administrators and guidance staff involves the calculation of grade point averages for transfer students. A student who has moved into a new high school in the junior year may have a long transcript of courses and grades from the previous school. It is the responsibility of the guidance counselors to interpret those classes on the transcript and decide on an appropriate placement for the new student (see Table 10.3). Often that includes the calculation of credits and determining a GPA (Ayers, 2005). When students are from other countries the complexity of that task is magnified greatly. Not all schools use the same grade units or standards.

GRADE POINT AVERAGE AND CLASS RANK

The longstanding high school tradition of using grade point averages to select the valedictorian and salutatorian of the graduating class may be coming to an end. The problem is the extreme level of competition that has

Table 10.3 What's an A?

Counselors throughout the area use different strategies to weigh grades and transcripts from various countries. Counselors at Creekview High School in the Carrollton–Farmers Branch Independent School District use an International Grading Scale that includes the following examples:

	A	*B*	*C*	*D*	*E*
India	75 and higher	74–60	45–59	33–44	1–32
Japan	5	4	3	2	1
Mexico	9–10	8	7	6	1–5
Ecuador	18–20	16–17	13–15	10–12	9 and below
Hong Kong	80–100	70–79	60–69	50–59	0–49

SOURCE: Used with permission from Carrollton–Farmers Branch Independent School District, Carrollton, Texas.
Online at http://www.dallasnews.com/sharedcontent/dws/dn/education/stories/121405dncco foreigngrades.121a1297.html

occurred at many suburban senior high schools. Accounts of the bitter rivalries and lawsuits that have become commonplace are behind this move (Romanowski, 2004; "Summa Cum Lawsuit," 2004; Talbot, 2005). Additionally, there is also a move to eliminate the grade point average–based class rank. The stress on students who are working to assure themselves a position in the elite top 10% of the high school class is leading to a decision to eliminate rank altogether (Lizama, 2004; Moore, 2004). While this strategy may reduce a measure of angst from members of high school senior classes, it will also give cause for college admissions officers to focus more on tests such as the SAT and give less consideration to the applicants' transcripts of grades (Finder, 2006; Zirkel, 2004). To provide academic honors at graduation, some schools have gone to the college strategy of providing grade-point-based recognition. This could take the following form:

Summa Cum Laude	GPA ≥ 3.85
Magna Cum Laude	GPA = 3.70 to 3.84
Cum Laude	GPA = 3.50 to 3.69
Honors	GPA = 3.25 to 3.49

Honor Roll

The diffidence felt by many school leaders about the grind experienced by students in their quest for an ever higher GPA notwithstanding, virtually all public schools maintain some form of an **honor roll**. This list of fledgling scholars is inevitably published in the local paper, on school bulletin boards, and on Web pages. Parents are presented with braggadocio bumper stickers proclaiming the academic prowess of their children. Internet entrepreneurs have even begun to offer national honor rolls. These offer parents a line of products that they can purchase once their child is listed. Other companies offer school products that educators can award to honor roll students, including engraved pencils and medallions.

High school students in states that use class rank in the decision to admit students into the flagship state universities experience extreme pressure over grades. Highly competitive high schools will have students that experience the greatest amount of angst over grades. In Texas, 75% of the students

For more information, see "Considerations on Point" at www.sagepub.com/wrightstudy

---

Case in Point (10a)

Admission test scores are one of only two primary predictors of college potential. The other is high school class rank, which is derived from the GPA of students. The importance of tests like the SAT II in the admission process is increasing because high schools have begun not reporting either a GPA or class rank (Finder, 2006). This reflects an effort by a number of suburban high schools to remove unhealthy levels of letter-grade stress on students. The movement began with highly selective private schools that were trying to provide a way for the good students who attend their keenly competitive schools to be admitted into the most elite colleges. In the highly competitive environment of prestigious preparatory schools, those students who would likely be above most students in a public school can appear to be mediocre when compared to their schoolmates. This appearance is possible because most students attending the prestigious preparatory schools are admitted on the basis of high test scores and previous grades.

In 2005, the college admission officers who evaluated the students who became the class of 2009 reported that half or more of the applicants' transcripts did not provide the class rank or the high school GPA. The result was that SAT II and ACT scores were more important in the admissions decision than ever. In some states such as Texas, it is not possible to eliminate high school class-rank information because it is linked to state mandates for college admission policy.

admitted to the University of Texas were from the top 10% of their high school's graduating class. Much strategic planning goes into course selection by sophomores and juniors as they try to be included in the "most deserving 10" at the time of high school graduation.

TEACHER–PARENT CONFERENCE

Parent conferences are a regular part of the academic year's schedule for almost all elementary schools. Middle schools and high schools usually schedule evenings when parents are invited to meet teachers. Today, many of these communication functions are being facilitated through the use of e-mail.

The 20- to 30-minute parent conference is likely to be a part of the elementary school program for many years to come. Even though these meetings take a great amount of time and can become very tedious for the teacher, they are important. Teachers need to spend time preparing for these meetings. Also, teachers can only see two or three parents in an hour. The whole process can add the equivalent of 2 or 3 more days of uncompensated work to the teacher's schedule. Much of this time must come in the evenings and on weekends. However, parents need to meet and get to know the teacher who is responsible for their elementary-age child. Parents want to feel that the teacher really knows and cares for their youngster. This is all the more reason for careful preparation by the teacher prior to the conference.

Preparation for the conference by the teacher should include a review of all the files and information sources about the child. If the conference is scheduled early in the school year, this preparation may involve a review of last year's work. A précis should be written on a card where it can be quickly reviewed between parent conferences. The information should be drawn from the following:

1. The child's teacher last year

2. The school nurse

3. The child's health file

4. The guidance counselor

5. Attendance records

6. The child's portfolio

7. Standardized test scores

8. Lunchroom and recess playground aids

9. All teacher-made test results

In addition to these, the teacher should make a brief description of important "talking points" that he or she wishes to remember to discuss with the parent.

During the conference the first priority is to put the parent(s) at ease and prevent any feelings of confrontation. This may be achieved by encouraging the parents to discuss their observations and raise any questions they may have. Teachers should be positive when describing the child's work habits, social interactions, and academic gains. The conference is an excellent time to remind the parents to keep the lines of communication between home and school open.

GRADE INFLATION

Over the past three decades there has been an upward shift in the average grades awarded in both public schools and in colleges (see Table 10.4). One reason for this **grade inflation** in the schools is linked to the desire of teachers to motivate and encourage students of marginal ability (Birk, 2005). Grade inflation in higher education most likely began about 1970 when the war in Vietnam saw undergraduate male students with low GPAs drafted out of college and sent in harm's way. Most college faculty members generally opposed the war and were reluctant to lose marginal students in the maelstrom.

Public Schools

Secondary-school research by the Higher Education Research Institute has documented that the number of students reporting an A average in high school increased from 17.6% in 1968 to 44.1% in 2001 (Engle, 2002). David Woodruff and Robert Ziomek (2004) of the ACT have documented the amount of high school grade inflation and corrected it for the concomitant increase in scores on the ACT.

They conclude that between the years 1991 and 2003 the mean GPA improved 0.25 as based on a 4.00 scale. In part this reflects the greater number of students enrolling in advanced and AP courses, which are weighted higher on grade reports than are regular academic classes. Further analysis of the ACT data estimated the high school grade inflation level over that 13-year period resulted in a 12.5% increase in high school grade averages (ACT, 2004). This was underscored by a 2005 report from the National Assessment of Educational Progress (NAEP) that described how the average

Table 10.4   Average Grades for All 23 Courses Used in Computing HS Overall GPA for All 13 Years

Year / Course	1991–2003	1991	1992	1993	1994	1995	1996	1997	1998	1999	2000	2001	2002	2003
English 9	0.23	3.05	3.06	3.09	3.12	3.16	3.19	3.21	3.24	3.25	3.26	3.27	3.27	3.28
English 10	0.23	3.02	3.05	3.07	3.10	3.14	3.17	3.19	3.22	3.22	3.23	3.24	3.25	3.25
English 11	0.26	2.98	3.01	3.04	3.08	3.11	3.13	3.14	3.18	3.18	3.20	3.21	3.22	3.24
English 12	0.30	3.02	3.05	3.08	3.13	3.15	3.17	3.19	3.24	3.25	3.27	3.29	3.31	3.32
Speech	0.25	3.32	3.35	3.36	3.39	3.42	3.44	3.45	3.48	3.50	3.53	3.55	3.56	3.57
Algebra 1	0.26	2.91	2.93	2.96	2.99	3.02	3.05	3.08	3.13	3.13	3.15	3.16	3.16	3.17
Algebra 2	0.22	2.88	2.90	2.93	2.96	2.98	3.01	3.02	3.06	3.07	3.07	3.08	3.09	3.10
Geometry	0.26	2.82	2.84	2.86	2.89	2.93	2.96	2.98	3.03	3.04	3.05	3.06	3.07	3.08
Trigonometry	0.21	3.10	3.12	3.15	3.17	3.20	3.22	3.23	3.26	3.27	3.27	3.28	3.03	3.31
Calculus	0.09	3.39	3.39	3.41	3.44	3.44	3.44	3.45	3.45	3.45	3.45	3.46	3.46	3.48
Advanced Math	0.15	3.18	3.19	3.22	3.24	3.25	3.26	3.27	3.31	3.30	3.31	3.32	3.32	3.33
Computer Sci.	0.23	3.36	3.39	3.42	3.45	3.49	3.51	3.52	3.55	3.56	3.57	3.58	3.59	3.59
General Sci.	0.25	3.10	3.12	3.14	3.18	3.21	3.24	3.27	3.31	3.32	3.34	3.34	3.35	3.35
Biology	0.24	2.98	3.00	3.03	3.06	3.10	3.12	3.14	3.18	3.20	3.20	3.21	3.22	3.22
Chemistry	0.25	2.87	2.90	2.92	2.95	2.97	3.00	3.02	3.06	3.06	3.07	3.09	3.10	3.12
Physics	0.19	3.11	3.13	3.16	3.19	3.20	3.23	3.23	3.26	3.26	3.26	3.27	3.29	3.30
US History	0.27	3.09	3.12	3.15	3.19	3.22	3.25	3.27	3.31	3.31	3.33	3.34	3.35	3.36
World History	0.26	3.10	3.12	3.15	3.18	3.22	3.24	3.27	3.31	3.32	3.33	3.34	3.35	3.36
Other History	0.26	3.21	3.23	3.25	3.29	3.32	3.36	3.38	3.42	3.44	3.45	3.46	3.47	3.47
US Government	0.24	3.12	3.14	3.17	3.20	3.23	3.25	3.28	3.32	3.32	3.34	3.35	3.36	3.36
Economics	0.24	3.12	3.14	3.16	3.19	3.22	3.23	3.26	3.31	3.32	3.33	3.35	3.36	3.36
Geography	0.25	3.23	3.25	3.28	3.31	3.34	3.37	3.39	3.44	3.44	3.46	3.47	3.47	3.48
Psychology	0.29	3.17	3.20	3.22	3.26	3.29	3.31	3.34	3.38	3.40	3.41	3.43	3.45	3.46

SOURCE: From "High School Grade Inflation From 1991 to 2003," by D. J. Woodruff and R. J. Ziomek, 2004, Iowa City, IA: ACT. Copyright 2004 by ACT, Inc. Reprinted with permission.

high school grade point average had climbed to 3.00 while there was no sub-sequent improvement in NAEP scores (National Center for Educational Statistics, 2007). There is no sign that schools are concerned with grade infla-tion and have only initiated methods to cover up the problem (Zirkel, 2007). Instead, some schools have simply stopped reporting student class rank and changed the basis used for reporting student GPAs.[8]

While the average report card grades are improving for secondary school students, a gender gap is developing in the distribution of those grades. In a series of studies with middle school children, girls were found to have slightly lower scores on measures of mental ability, but significantly better average grades. One possible reason proffered by the researchers is that girls exhibit more "self-control" (Duckworth & Seligman, 2006). They see self-control to be a central value for teachers and one factor in both learning and the atti-tude of teachers toward students.

The fact that letter grades often represent more than just achievement, and are used to encourage marginal students, is postulated to be one factor in causing this trend. Lisa Birk (2005) noted that the amount of grade inflation is most acute in schools enrolling primarily children from impoverished homes.

Figure 10.2   Academic Pressure

SOURCE: Zits Partnership. King Features Syndicate.

Children in these schools who receive a report card grade of A in language arts have reading and writing skills similar to children enrolled in affluent schools who received a grade of C. This phenomenon of greater grade inflation in schools with the lowest overall achievement levels on standardized tests was also noted by Donald Thomas and William Bainbridge (1997). Their data were collected by conducting a series of "school effectiveness audits." They describe the problem as academic fraud. They posit that by having low standards and high grades for children of poverty, the schools are passing on a false message of accomplishment and skills to the parents and children. President G. W. Bush (2003) has described the holding of low-achievement standards for children from impoverished homes as a type of "soft bigotry."

A statewide audit of the high schools of Arkansas has identified a clear trend in that state toward grade inflation. In the Arkansas study, ACT scores were used as the yardstick against which high school grades were evaluated. The study found no significant improvement in the ACT scores over the years, but a clear trend was identified indicating the Arkansas high schools gave better grades to their students. This research found that the smaller rural high schools in Arkansas had the greatest tendency to award inflated grades (Vasluski, McKenzie, & Mulvenon, 2005). This trend for higher grades in rural high schools may reflect the close and supportive culture typical of small town high schools.

NCAA

Grade inflation in the murky world of unregulated private high schools was recently addressed by the National Collegiate Athletic Association (NCAA). The recruitment rules for colleges who compete at the highest level are stringent regarding the courses and grades that recruited high school athletes have on their transcripts. When some students had too few credits or a low GPA that would have precluded their playing college sports, coaches and others would have them attend private high schools and/or cyber-schools where "watered down" courses led to high grades and a repaired transcript. The new rules mandated by the NCAA will not let a college count grades and courses from unregulated "diploma mill" high schools (Wolverton, 2006).

Higher Education

This grade inflationary era has also been evident for American colleges, where over the past 35 years there has been a consistent monotonic trend toward higher grades. This tendency has added about 0.15 to the grade point average of college students each decade. The modern era of grade inflation in higher education dates from the war in Vietnam and is going strong today.

Grade inflation is greater in private colleges and universities but evident for all sectors of higher education (Rojstaczer, 2003). Stuart Rojstaczer believes that the inflation in grades in higher education is a reflection of the

Figure 10.3   Monotonic vs. Gin-n-Tonic

SOURCE: Cartoon by John Glick. From www.aaai.org/AITopics/assets/Page%20Art/ tonictoon.gif. Reprinted with permission from the AAAI Press.

new consumer culture among college students. College administrators in institutions that are tuition driven, and in marginal financial condition, must hold onto every student. It can cost a college upward of $5,000 to recruit and place an undergraduate student in a freshman class. That new student's tuition income is very precious for many colleges. This consumerism is also seen in the trend toward students and parents haggling with financial aid officers for a discounted tuition rate. Parents and students doing comparison shopping among second- and third-tier colleges is now a commonplace occurrence.

Grade inflation is the logical byproduct of this consumerism. Benedict College (SC) was recently censured by the American Association of University Professors (Smallwood, 2005). This was done because the college fired faculty who did not consider the students' "effort" in tabulating course grades. In part this was a statement by the AAUP regarding grade inflation. The problem of grade inflation is not just one experienced by small tuition-driven colleges. Over 90% of the students who graduate from Harvard do so at an honors level. In commenting on this, Alfie Kohn (2002) suggests that grade inflation is not a new problem, citing a Harvard committee report from 1894: "Grades A and B are sometimes given too readily—Grade A for work of no very high merit, and grade B for work not far above mediocrity."

Kohn goes on to suggest that colleges consider doing away with grades altogether and concentrate on the development of earnest young scholars who are intrinsically motivated (see Figure 10.4).

At Princeton University, the faculty, reacting to the perceived rampant grade inflation, voted to limit the number of A grades that a professor can give in any course to 35% of the total enrolled (Eshel, 2004). Within a year there was evidence that the number of A grades awarded to Princeton's undergraduates fell by about 25% (Aronauer, 2005).

Needless to say, this change has students very concerned. Princeton's students fear that the change will reduce the eye appeal of their undergraduate transcripts when they apply for admission to graduate and professional schools. The admission committees of graduate and professional schools are under pressure to bring into their programs students with high undergraduate grades. The graduate programs are also rated by national publications, and the admission of students with GPAs below 3.00 could hurt their public image and standing (Arenson, 2004).

PROMOTION AND GRADUATION

Prior to 2002, the decision of whether to promote a child to the next grade was one made by educators (see Table 10.5). If the child was to be retained in the same grade for another year, the child's parents would normally also be involved in the decision process. Being "left back" was always a traumatic occurrence in the life of a child. By the time students reach their senior year

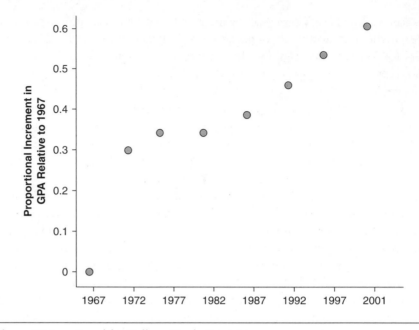

Figure 10.4   Trend for College Grade Point Averages

SOURCE: Adapted from gradeinflation.com by Professor Stewart Rojstaczer, Duke University.

Table 10.5   Maryland Graduation Test Outcomes

Percent of Students in Maryland Passing the Maryland High School Assessment (HAS), 2005							
Subject	*American Indian*	*Asian*	*African American*	*White*	*Hispanic*	*Disabled*	*Free/Reduced Lunch*	*Total*
English2	51.7	74.5	38.8	70.9	45.8	15.8	35.3	57.3
Biology	57.6	76.9	38.7	71.6	43.3	18.9	35.3	57.6
Government	61.4	82.1	46.8	76.0	56.6	25.2	45.5	66.4
Algebra	47.2	79.9	30.0	71.2	41.9	16.3	33.7	71.2

SOURCE: *2006 Maryland Report Card*, by the Maryland Department of Education, 2006. Annapolis: Author.

in high school, one in five will have been retained in grade at least one time (Massachusetts Department of Education, 2005).

In the recent past, being the one who did not move on with his or her peers opened the child up to personal embarrassment and ridicule.[9] Being retained in a grade greatly increases the likelihood that the child will eventually drop out of high school. Being retained twice is tantamount to a guarantee that the child will never graduate from high school (Jimerson, 2001a, 2001b).

That all changed with the No Child Left Behind Act of 2002. In eight states and many large urban school systems, the decision to retain a child in a grade is now determined by the score on a mandated test. The use of promotion tests has led to a significant increase in the number of retained children in those states where tests are the deciding factor (Georgia Association of School Psychologists, 2003). Nationally the failure rate on these high-stakes tests is running about 15% of the student population; however, it is much higher in inner cities and in schools enrolling many ethnic and minority students (Sunderman, Kim, & Orfield, 2005). With this large cohort of children being retained, the stigma associated with "flunking a grade" in school has been reduced. For example, in 2005, Texas schools held 40,000 children back in fifth grade. This was done on the basis of a test score. The retention of so many children in grade could add a significant cost to the operation of any school district. North Carolina found the cost of grade retention based on test scores to be $140 million during the first year. This may eventually prove to be a zero-sum game. This is because the students who are retained in grade are likely to drop out of school before the 12th grade. One unfortunate fact is that three out of four children retained in grade are members of minority groups. In those states where there is a requirement that children pass the state assessment test in eighth grade to be promoted into high school, there is a significant increase in the number of children who drop out of school before the 11th grade (Reardon & Galindo, 2002). All too often these children are members of an ethnic minority. Richard Stiggins observed that our obsession with high-stakes testing is causing major segments of our student population to be left behind because the mandated measures are causing many kids to give up in hopelessness (Stiggins, 2002).

In 2005–2006, 8,000 children in Florida (one of the first states to mandate promotion tests) spent a third year as third graders. In an attempt to prevent a buildup in the number of children stuck in third grade, Florida began to put repeating third-grade children into fourth grade halfway through the school year. Each school district was given permission to decide how to determine if a retained child was able to move on to fourth grade. Yet, many of these children

For more information, see "Considerations on Point" at www.sagepub.com/ wrightstudy

still could not be promoted at midyear because they were unable to pass the local assessment test. All too often these retained children are English-language learners who cannot read and understand the tests, which for them are written in a foreign language. In 2005, one county school system in Florida gave 750 repeating third graders early promotion into fourth grade only to find that 84% of them failed the mandated fourth-grade examination (Harrison, 2005).

Case in Point (10b)

A statistical analysis of the grade retention problem in Florida has shown that one outcome has been a slight improvement in the average Florida Comprehensive Achievement Test scores after third grade. This "apparent" improvement happens in schools where there is a high failure rate. This has nothing to do with improved instruction but is caused by the state's policy of taking low scoring and English-language learning children out of the pool of fourth-grade children and making them recycle through third grade. This results in an artificial improvement in the achievement scores of the fourth grade class. The average state test scores for the subsequent grades also benefit from this policy of retaining third graders (Haney, 2006). However, the price that must be paid for this is what occurs in the third grade, where average scores are falling.

In 2005, Texas faced a similar crisis when 40,000 children were retained in the fifth grade. When a large portion of these children failed the state test again they were held back another year. By the time children who are retained two times in a grade reach middle school they are well into their adolescent development and possibly are even postpubescent. These twice-retained children will be old enough to have a driver's license while they are still in middle school and be of voting age as a high school sophomore. It is possible that these twice-retained children could run for election to the school board from their high school homerooms.

Another related problem is that of high school graduation (see Table 10.6). In 2006, there were 22 states that required high school students to pass a mandated examination before they graduate with a diploma. The goal of such tests is to provide an assurance to the public that graduates have acquired the necessary skills to function in society. The problem with these testing programs is that they are associated with an increase in the number of dropouts and lower SAT scores among those who do graduate (Marchant & Paulson, 2005). The failure

Table 10.6   Summary of the 12 Points of a Plan to Reduce Dropouts as Proposed by the National Education Association

1. Students may not leave school until they have a diploma or are 21 years old.

2. Create graduation schools (day, evening, weekends) for older students who dropped out.

3. Improve school climate and environments. Better safety, flexible schedules, and small learning communities.

4. Provide alternative options by partnerships with community colleges and career academies.

5. Expansion of workforce readiness and career education programs.

6. Universal preschool and full-day kindergarten programs.

7. Involve children, families, and schools in a working relationship to support learning.

8. Careful use of multiple sources of data to monitor and evaluate each learner.

9. Organize and analyze data from assessments with identifiable groups of learners, and report those findings using established protocols.

10. Develop community involvement and volunteerism programs, and provide time for teachers to meet with parents.

11. Design and offer relevant inservice professional development efforts that focus on the needs of the diverse population of each school's community.

12. Make dropout prevention a priority for federal research and program funding.

SOURCE: "Inside the Law: Cheating on NCLB Tests? Maybe," by A. Pascopella, 2007a, *District Administration*, *43*(1), p. 20.

rates on these graduation tests have also been high. In some school districts where there is a large minority population or where there are many families living in poverty, the proportion failing often exceeds 50% (see Table 10.7). In 2004, two states, Arizona and California, had to postpone their plans to require that students first pass a mandated graduation test (Accountability Division, 2004). In California this decision reflected the fact that 20% of the seniors set to graduate would not have earned a diploma. California reinstated the testing requirement in 2005–2006 and found that only 64% of the seniors earned a diploma that year, a drop of 9% over the previous 5 years (Rogers, Holme, & Silver, 2005).

Table 10.7   Pass Rate for First-Time Test Takers

Percentage of Students Passing an Exit Exam on the First Try for All Students and by Subgroups										
Student subgroups	AK math 2002	AK reading	FL[1] math 2002	FL[1] reading	GA math 2002	GA ELA	IN math 2002	IN ELA	LA math 2002	LA reading
All	64%	70%	73%	59%	91%	95%	68%	68%	62%	76%
White	74%	82%	85%	73%	94%	95%	73%	74%	80%	89%
Black	35%	54%	47%	32%	77%	90%	35%	38%	43%	61%
Hispanic	53%	64%	64%	45%	82%	80%	49%	49%	62%	74%
Asian	56%	59%	87%	67%	95%	87%	84%	73%	83%	78%
ESL	28%	26%	39%	8%	68%	46%	35%	24%	51%	46%
Free or reduced-price lunch	42%	42%	57%	38%	NA	NA	47%	48%	48%	63%
Students with disabilities	24%	28%	37%	24%	50%	68%	27%	20%	17%	21%

Student subgroups	MN math 2003	MN reading	NV[2] math 2002	NV[2] reading	NM math 2002	NM reading	SC math 2002	SC reading	WA math 2002	WA ELA
All	72%	81%	36%	71%	79%	87%	81%	82%	37%	59%
White	78%	87%	45%	82%	92%	97%	90%	90%	42%	65%
Black	33%	49%	16%	54%	73%	88%	66%	70%	13%	36%
Hispanic	43%	55%	17%	52%	77%	87%	73%	72%	14%	35%
Asian	61%	62%	43%	73%	91%	90%	91%	85%	45%	62%
ESL	34%	35%	7%	20%	63%	76%	NA	NA	9%	13%
Free or reduced-price lunch	49%	60%	22%	56%	NA	NA	67%	67%	19%	39%
Students with disabilities	30%	42%	6%	23%	NA	NA	55%	50%	4%	13%

SOURCE: From *State High School Exit Exams Put to the Test*, by K. Gayler, N. Chudowsky, N. Kober, and M. Hamilton, 1999, Washington, D.C., Center on Educational Policy. Copyright 2003 by the Center on Education Policy. Reprinted with permission.

[1] Florida's figures include a small proportion of retained 10th graders, which may affect pass rates. In addition, Florida's figures are for ESLs with less than one year of services in English as a second or other language.

[2] Nevada's figures for students with disabilities are only for students with Individualized Education Programs under the Individuals with Disabilities Education Act and do not include students with disabilities who are served under Section 504 of the Rehabilitation Act.

In Arizona the situation was direr. In that state, only a third of the seniors who were set to graduate with a diploma were qualified by the state's test to do so. In an attempt to have more Arizona seniors qualify for a diploma, the legislature passed a law that would award extra credit to some students on the Arizona assessment test. The extra credit could be used toward earning a diploma. These extra points went to students who maintained a high grade point average in the required core courses. Unfortunately, few of the 23,500 students who could not pass the test in 2005 had high school course grades high enough to help them earn the coveted high school diploma. This failure rate has added fuel to the complaints of educational critics who point out that the typical graduation test only requires that students score a little over the 50% mark on academic material that is more appropriate in the eighth grade than in a high school (Saunders, 2007).

To date, the remediation efforts designed to help students pass the mandated exit examinations have not been very effective (Gewertz, 2007). Those programs held after school or on weekends have not been well attended. The most promising programs are proactive and held during the school day. Longitudinal research in two urban school systems where high school graduation requires students pass an exit examination has shown that major curricula modifications have resulted from the testing mandate. The change resulted in a major increase in subject coverage of topics included on the test and the dilution of untested topics (Zabala & Minnici, 2007). There are many hidden costs that school systems must pay when an exit examination program is employed at the high school level. These include the cost of curriculum materials, teacher inservice education, and after-school or weekend programs. Indiana estimated that it spent an average of $551 for every student who needed extra help to pass the state's high school exit examination (Gayler & Kober, 2004). If the child is enrolled in special education, that cost goes up another $100.

The graduation of students with disabilities from high schools in states requiring a graduation test is another problem area. A total of 22 states require students with disabilities to complete a graduation test prior to being awarded a diploma. Of these, 21 hold students with disabilities to the same standard that must be met by non-disabled students (Johnson & Thurlow, 2003; Johnson, Thurlow, Cosio, & Bremer, 2005).[10] One outcome of this requirement is that in many states very few students with disabilities earn a diploma.

Strategies

There is evidence that school administrators are increasing the number of children retained before the third grade. This is being done to reduce the number of children who will not pass the mandated high-stakes test in third grade. One motivation for this move to retain children who are at risk for failure in the first and second grades is tied to public relations. Broadcast media and local newspapers publish a summary of the number of failures at each grade and in each school. Parents are also becoming attuned to this issue, and a number have taken the proactive step of waiting to start their children in public school until they are a year or so older than their peers. This extra year, a year of academic redshirting, can make a big difference in terms of the normal development of cognitive and physical skills.

One strategy being adopted by parents of children who fail the state assessment in third grade is transferring their children to a parochial or private school, or possibly home-schooling the children. States do not require high-stakes tests of students enrolled in parochial and private schools. Fewer than half of the states have testing requirements for home-schooled children, and those that do often leave it up to the parent to select and administer the examination that is to be used. To learn about home-schooling and the testing standards for the various states, see www.nhen.org/leginfo/state_list.asp.

Summary

The process of reporting to parents on student progress is now undergoing an ontogenesis urged on by the tsunami of technological developments now underway. What once was a simple written report carried home several times a year by nervous children is now in the process of evolving into a system of real-time, ongoing communication between parents and educators.

Irrespective of the format, the grades awarded by teachers are summative statements made on the basis of classroom performance. There are a number of models employed by teachers when deciding on a grade for any child. These may include standards-based, normative, and modified standards-based grading systems. The data that go into these decisions are also varied and may be point based or weighted statistical compellations of various measures and marked projects. Report cards also provide an opportunity for teachers to write comments to the parents. These comments may become part of the child's permanent record and must be carefully crafted by the teacher.

The calculation of grade averages and publication of class rank lists are educational activities now becoming déclassé. This has resulted in many high schools eliminating the tradition of having a valedictory presentation at graduation. Related to this change is a well-documented trend toward students being awarded ever higher grades. Grade inflation was so rampant at some Ivy League colleges that the faculty senates have revised the acceptable grading policy.

Another special problem for awarding grades in public schools is related to children at either end of the normal distribution. Teachers of children with special needs as well as children enrolled in programs for the gifted need to take special care when crafting report cards and transcripts. One controversial approach to grading these special children is to differentially weight the classes they complete. This happens more often in high school, when extra quality points for Advanced Placement classes are awarded to high-ability students and less quality points are awarded for developmental or basic skills classes.

Discussion Questions

1. Is there a truly intellectually honest way to award letter grades on school projects, tests, and report cards? Discuss the various options a teacher may use in grading, and include in the discussion the strengths and weaknesses of each.

2. Parents like to see the type of report card grades with which they are familiar. As students themselves, parents saw letter grades summarizing the amount of learning in each subject area on a written form several times a year. How can that desire be reconciled with the modern standards-based report card systems?

3. Should students in honors and AP classes be awarded extra points on their grade averages for having taken more challenging course work? Should students in developmental classes be awarded less than the standard level of credit toward their grade point averages for having taken less demanding courses?

4. Should elementary, middle, and high schools publish honor rolls through the local media?

5. Should schools continue the policy of awarding a valedictorian at the high school graduation?

6. How could a school district address the problem of grade inflation without jeopardizing their high school graduates who are applying to competitive colleges?

Student Study Site

Educational Assessment on the Web

Log on to the Web-based student study site at www.sagepub.com/ wrightstudy for additional Web sources and study resources.

NOTES

1. Phi Beta Kappa was established on the campus of the College of William and Mary in 1776 and was soon followed by chapters at Yale (1780) and Harvard (1781).

2. These included Latin, Greek, English, Modern Languages, Mathematics, Physical sciences, Biology, History, Government & Economics, and Geography.

3. The 180-day year reflects our rural past and the need for farm labor during the productive months of the summer. Children were expected to assist with farm operations during the 10-week summer break. A third of the population lived on farms in 1890. See http://fisher.lib.virginia.edu/collections/stats/histcensus for more details of the era.

4. While not all adolescents are taught in a cross-disciplinary middle school, that model is the most commonly employed approach to adolescent education (Manning, 2000).

5. In 2007 students who were admitted into the state universities of Texas were awarded a legislatively mandated minimum of 24 semester hours of undergraduate credit if they had completed all the requirements for an International Baccalaureate Diploma while they were in high school (Hellon, 2007).

6. There are several reasons for the lower enrollment of minority students in AP classes. One is systemic and caused by the lack of funding for teachers and program materials for advanced placement in urban schools. Another is related to the daunting developmental process that minority students face in creating a "racial identity" that can support their academic development (Noguera, 2003).

7. Courses designed for students with disabilities must not be identifiable as special education on transcripts. The content of the curriculum, however, may be used to title the class (e.g., basic math skills instead of remedial math).

8. A handful of school systems have begun to use a 6.00 GPA system, in which an A in an AP class is equal to 6.00 points and the same grade in a regular class is awarded a point value of 4.00. This alteration muddies the waters when a college official is looking over the transcripts of applicants. This is different than changing a course's weight. That system is more common and is discussed in the chapter.

9. Children who were enrolled in special education and learning support programs were free from the specter of "flunking the grade."

10. The attorney general of Arizona opined that schools are not required under the testing laws of Arizona to hold special education students to the requirement of passing the high school exit examination to earn a high school diploma (Goddard, 2005).

PART IV

TESTING FOR STUDENT LEARNING, TALENT, APTITUDE, AND SPECIAL NEEDS

S ince the 1920s, America's students have been subjected to paper-and-pencil tests covering a number of dimensions related to school success and progress. This "golden age" of educational testing in the United States was built upon the empirical foundation of measurement science that came into its own during the First World War. By the 1920s, schools were testing children to determine their mental aptitude and their achievement. Learning problems were screened by examining patterns of discrepancies between the two measures.

Achievement tests were at first a sideline for the publishing houses that produced and sold textbooks to the schools. The linkage between the curriculum laid out in the textbooks and the tests that measured the achievement of that curriculum resulted in a natural symbiosis that served the publishers and schools well for over 50 years. Critical reviews of the achievement of American students, and misinterpretations of the differences between school outcomes in this country compared to that from other countries, were a source of pressure for reform.

Educational reforms came with standards-based evaluations and pressure to bring all children up to a level of proficiency in the basic skills. This caused a rapid expansion of the testing industry and the development of 50 statewide standards-based assessment systems.

The cognitive abilities of children have been tested in the schools since the 1920s. These tests have been subsumed into the testing programs offered by the major publishers and are administered to children along with achievement tests.

Other aptitude tests are also used extensively in the schools. The National Merit Scholar program and college admission tests provide examples that are clearly measures of ability. These tests have long histories and have evolved over the years. Originally, two very different philosophies structured the major admissions tests, the SAT and the ACT. These two have moved closer to each other during the last two decades.

One longstanding use of testing in the schools has been to identify students who have truly impressive abilities and talents. The ability to measure creative potential is one outcome in the effort to refine aptitude measures during the Second World War.

More critically, testing plays a central role in the identification of students with disabilities and special needs. Assessment data are used to inform those educational specialists that design and organize curriculum modifications and learning programs for students with one or more disabling conditions.

Chapter 11

STANDARDIZED MEASURES OF LEARNING

Anyone can confirm how little the grading that results from examinations corresponds to the final useful work of people in life.

—Jean Piaget

Issues and Themes

One obligation all educators have as defined by federal law is to be able and willing to explain student test score reports to parents. This must be done without using confusing jargon or being pejorative. One of the items that an educator must be prepared to explain is the score report from published achievement tests including the mandated statewide assessment program. One result of the No Child Left Behind Act (2002) has been a rapid expansion in the use of published tests of achievement.

Achievement testing was a product of the large publishing houses that developed, printed, and sold the textbooks that were used in the schools in the 1920s. The result was a natural symbiosis that proved to be financially successful. School administrators were also in this cozy relationship. They were able to assure parents that real learning was occurring while assuring classroom teachers that everything on the test was in the textbooks used in the classroom. The comfortable relationship ended in 1994 when the Improving America's Schools Act required that all states develop learning standards for all grades and testing programs for those learning standards and educational goals. The No Child Left Behind Act put real teeth into the 1994 law. The results from the NCLB Act have been mixed. A new intensity has now been directed toward teaching reading and mathematics, and schools have worked to improve teacher quality and close the gap between the achievement levels of children from diverse backgrounds.

Learning Objectives

By reading and studying this chapter a student will be able to do the following:

- Explain a student's score report from a commercially published achievement test to parents.
- Discuss the use of scores from a test of mental ability in relationship to scores from an achievement test battery.
- Discuss the major differences between the five principle achievement test batteries.
- Describe the relationship between the mandated state assessment systems and the commercial publishers of the major achievement tests.
- Explain a score report from a state's high-stakes testing program to parents.
- Explain a school's summary report from the state's high-stakes testing program to an audience of parents.

EXPLAINING TEST SCORES TO PARENTS

Legal Basis

Most of us have had the experience of watching a well-written medically based television drama. On those shows the writers pride themselves in using correct medical/procedural terms and acronyms that are exact duplicates of what would be heard and seen in a large urban medical center. In watching this type of entertainment, it is easy to feel both impressed by the ability of the actors to deliver such complex arcane lines, while also feeling totally "at sea" with what is being depicted. Not knowing the language is a major disadvantage for those trying to make sense of what is being portrayed.

Parents attempting to ascertain what educators have learned by testing their child can face a similar challenge. This problem is addressed in part by the Family Educational Rights and Privacy Act (1974). The provisions of that law require that school personnel make available to a parent the full school record, including the testing data related to their child, within 45 days of the parent's request. Parents can also request to see all test and evaluation scoring rubrics used to obtain their child's score.[1] Also, parents have a right to have these data explained to them at an appropriate level for understanding, and that presentation should be in the parent's native language, if so requested.

Classroom teachers, guidance counselors, and school administrators should all be familiar with the details of the published tests used by their schools. Specialized tests for specific diagnostic purposes are beyond the expectation of what classroom educators should be able to explain to parents. Those measures should be explained by the school psychologist or reading specialist.

There are two major types of tests that classroom teachers should understand and be ready to explain to parents. One is the published achievement test selected by the school district as the basic test battery to be used in the schools. The second is the state's high-stakes measure. This latter test is most important in the schools of the eight states (Delaware, Florida, Georgia, Louisiana, Maryland, Mississippi, North Carolina, South Carolina, and Texas) where grade level promotion is contingent on achieving a minimum cut score on the mandated assessment battery.

Informing Parents

Parents should be given accurate information explaining exactly what the school's achievement testing program has learned about their child. This information should be presented in language that the parents will understand. This should include the following:

- The name and edition of the test battery that was used as the principal assessment vehicle and the amount of time that was spent in practice prior to the test and in test administration.
- Any special accommodations that may have been made to meet a need or condition of the child.

- A listing and explanation of each of the subtests included as part of the test battery. Parents can see released or sample items from the test that represent the various subtests of the battery.
- A description of the linkage between the various subtests included in the test battery and the state's standards for learning. Show the parents the state standards and provide several examples of how the test battery is aligned with the requirements of the state.
- Clear and simplified explanation for all scores that the test battery provides:

1. *Raw scores and total possible raw score.* Parents need to know how to interpret how well their child did on the test in terms of the total number of questions that were right and the total number of questions in the test.

2. *Reliability.* It is vital that parents learn that a test score is not an absolute number, like the child's height. Test scores are volatile and can change from day to day. Parents should know that the stability of this test has been studied, and scores on this test tend to be best described as one of the following: highly stable with little movement (e.g., up to 3 points one way or another is likely [In this example the point shift is estimated from the size of one standard error of the tests—i.e., SEm = 3.0.]); relatively stable, with movement of 4 to 6 points in either direction possible; less stable, with possible movement greater than 6 points.

3. *National percentile.* Parents should be told about the norm reference group to which their child is compared. They need to be informed that the national percentile shows how their child's score compared to the norm reference group.

4. *Local percentile.* Many tests offer a percentile score that shows how well a child performed on the test in comparison to the other children of the school district. Some parents can also be shown how discrepancies between the national and local percentiles can be seen as a way to evaluate the school. If the child's local percentile is higher than his or her national percentile, the implication is that the local students did not (as a group) do as well as the national normative group. The opposite case is also possible, where higher national percentile scores and lower local percentiles imply a school that is more competitive than the national normative group.

5. *Standard scores and stanines*. Parents should be introduced to the fact that student scores on most measures cluster near the average score, and only a small proportion fall in the extremes. The result is that when the scores of everyone are charted, the result is a curved graph that looks like a bell. They need to know that standard scores are a method of identifying where a score falls on the bell-shaped distribution pattern. Also, parents can be shown how the stanines fit onto the pattern of the bell-shaped curve of scores (remember, a low score has a stanine score between 1 and 3, while those scores between 4 and 6 are in the average range, and high scores are 7 through 9).

6. *Normal curve equivalent (NCE)*. NCE scores should be explained to parents as being a score system based on the bell-shaped distribution of scores. This link to the shape of the population distribution is seen in the fact that each cluster of 10 NCE points covers an area equal to one stanine. Yet, in some ways NCE scores are similar to percentiles. Parents should learn that the highest NCE is 99 and the lowest 1, and that the mean of all NCE scores is 50.

7. *Predicted score*. Most test batteries provide a test of mental ability. This makes it possible for the test publisher to estimate how well an individual child should perform on each part of the achievement battery. Score reports often overlay these estimates with a graphic depiction of the student's achievement on the various subtests of the battery. From the 1920s to the 1960s student reports sent to parents contained a combined statistic representing both achievement and mental ability. That statistic was the accomplishment ratio.

8. *Scores based on the criteria of a predetermined cut score (e.g., Advanced, Proficient, Below Proficient, Far Below Proficient)*. When these scores are provided by the publisher, they have been derived by the work of a nationally representative sample of educators. The process of setting the cut scores that divide the different categorical levels of achievement is the product of this panel. While these scores are the consensus opinion of educators, they are still arbitrary points.

9. *Grade equivalent scores*. Parents need to know that these scores are very unstable. The only meaningful interpretations that can be used with these scores are (a) below grade level, (b) on grade

level, (c) above grade level. Beyond that, parents can be told that the grade equivalent score their child received on a test shows the average grade level of a hypothetical student who took the same test and had the same number of items correct. They must be dis-abused of the notion that the grade equivalent score shows the grade level their child is able to handle.

- The schedule for other tests to be administered in the near future (e.g., college admission, state-mandated high-stakes test).
- Ideas and exercises to do at home with the child that the parents may wish to consider.
- Ask the parents for any and all ideas they may have that can be tried by the teacher to improve the child's achievement outcome.

Accomplishment Ratio

Commercially published achievement tests have been used by our public schools since the 1920s. These early measurement devices encouraged the schools to calculate an "accomplishment ratio" for everyone who took the tests. This was determined as the ratio of a student's "educational age" (EA) to his or her "mental age" (MA). This linked the mental age, as determined by one of the first generation of IQ tests, with the new achievement tests. The educational age in the formula is equal to the age of a group of children whose median educational achievement is the same as a particular child's level of achievement:

$$\text{accomplishment ratio(AR)} = \frac{EA}{MA}.$$

By this method, a child with an AR score above 1.0 would be described today as an overachiever because he or she is doing more than would be expected of a person with that mental ability. Likewise, an AR score below 1.0 indicates an underachieving student (Engle, 1945).

This same anachronistic model is repeated in modern commercial achievement batteries. For example, CTB/McGraw-Hill publishes the widely used Terra Nova and also the Primary Test of Cognitive Skills (PTCS). The publisher encourages the use of both measures as methods of screening children for learning problems or special abilities. Likewise, Riverside Publishing is the publishing house for the Iowa Tests of Basic Skills (ITBS) and also the Cogitative Ability Tests (CogAT). That company offers users of both measures not only achievement test scores but also the predicted

"My counselor says I'm underachieving, but I just think he expects too much."

Figure 11.1 "My Counselor Says I'm Underachieving . . ."

SOURCE: Cartoon by Merv Magus.

achievement score based on the result of the CogAT. Differences between the actual achievement and the predicted achievement can be interpreted to indicate a possible learning problem. The Comprehensive Testing Program 4 from the Educational Records Bureau measures both the ability to reason and academic achievement. "Comparisons of scores in these areas can be made to determine if the student's skills are at levels consistent with their potential" (Malcolm & Schafer, 2005).

The basic system is relatively easy to understand and to explain to others. If a child has a mental ability equal to a NCE score of around 50 (stanine = 5), then that child should score in the fifth stanine on each of the tests in the achievement battery. Any major departure (e.g., Stanine 1–3 or 7–9) from this pattern is an anomaly and deserves further study and follow-up.

Test Publishers

In the United States there are four major publishers of achievement tests, which control over 90% of the market. Three of the test publishers are commercial companies that publish a range of educational products, and one is a not-for-profit company established by the private schools of this country to develop and score achievement and admissions tests for private schools:

- CTB/McGraw Hill of Monterey California, publisher of (a) Terra Nova II, (b) Terra Nova–Comprehensive Test of Basic Skills (CTBS), (c) California Achievement Tests, 6th ed. (CAT 6)
- Harcourt Assessment of San Antonio, Texas, publisher of the Metropolitan Achievement Test, 8th ed., and the Stanford Achievement Test Battery, 10th ed. (2003)
- Riverside Publishing of Itasca, Illinois, publisher of the Iowa Tests of Basic Skills
- Educational Records Bureau of New York City, publisher of the Comprehensive Testing Program, 4th ed. (CTP 4), and the Independent School Entrance Examination (ISEE). This test publisher is centered in a not-for-profit corporation established by a 1,500-member independent schools and academies

Early History of Achievement Batteries

The word *achievement* entered the lexicon of English circa 1650, and it was used in American vernacular English in an agricultural context until the modern era of testing (circa 1910). For example, before World War I a farmer might have discussed certain achievements in animal husbandry or described the achieved yield in terms of corn production following a new crop rotation (Ballantyne, 2002). The psychometric sciences (sciences of mental measurement) developed parallel to, and frequently in cooperation with, the growth of scientific agriculture. The crossover of the meaning of the word *achievement* is not surprising.

When the World Book Company moved to Chicago and Yonkers, New York, in 1916 from Manila City in the Philippines, it added mental tests to its publication list. An early senior author and editor for World Book was Arthur S. Otis, an architect of the Army tests of World War I and a former doctoral student of Lewis M. Terman. It was not long before the World Book Company began to publish a large line of mental ability tests. One of the first of these was a version of the Army Beta that Arthur Otis authored. Today, the progeny of that test is the Otis–Lennon School Ability Test (OLSAT).

In 1923, World Book also published the first group-administered, norm-referenced battery of achievement tests, the Stanford Achievement Test. This achievement battery was viewed by its authors as being perfect for doing discrepancy studies between the intelligence test and achievement test scores of children. This type of discrepancy analysis produced misleading statistics called the accomplishment ratio, which was reported to parents and recorded in the cumulative record of school children.

In 1932, the World Book Company began to publish another achievement test, the Metropolitan Achievement Tests. The Metropolitan was originally normed using a sample of students who were more representative of urban centers of this country when compared with those used to standardize the Stanford Achievement Tests.

Case in Point (11a)

The following story was told to Tom Fitzgibbon, former president of Harcourt Brace Jovanovich:

Sometime during 1923, in Yonkers, NY, Cap Anson, president of World Book, was visited by a professor from the West Coast. This person declared that American education needed and deserved a way to gauge the success of its teaching efforts and that one of the ways to do this was by using an "achievement test." When President Anson asked, "What's an achievement test?" his visitor reached into his travel bag and pulled out several "mechanicals." (In the old days, a "mechanical" was called a "plate," which was the leaden template for a page of text copy.) These mechanicals were ready to print, and all the visitor needed was a publisher to get them to the school market. Needless to say, carrying several of these things from the West Coast by hand on a train was . . . hard physical work. In any event, the visitor indicated that he and his colleagues at Stanford University hoped that World Book, being a preeminent school textbook publisher, would see the connection between teaching something and finding out whether students were learning from their classroom experiences. Anson, who had never been involved in anything like this before, was intrigued because he and World Book had mounted a joint enterprise with Arthur Otis to publish a peacetime version of the World War I Beta intelligence test. The effort had been a successful publishing venture, so Anson was inclined to pay attention.

His visitor, of course, was Lewis Terman, who was acting as spokesperson for the rest of the authorial team. In any event, World Book introduced the series of questions we now call a "standardized achievement test."

As for the Metropolitan Achievement Test, it was a child of several large city research directors who felt they needed something a little different from the Stanford Achievement Test. It appears that they thought they needed their own instrument owing to the makeup of their school populations and the need to compare across the large city school districts. These directors met frequently

For more information, see "Considerations on Point" at www.sagepub.com/wrightstudy

throughout the year and wanted to be able to hone in on what differentiated one district from another in the sense of pupil population, curricular emphasis, and desired instructional outcomes. Then, as today, large school districts view themselves as different from smaller ones.

It's interesting to me to compare today's large-scale achievement in-house test construction to yesterday's authorial team approach. Then, the team was an amalgam of the test-making professionalism, curriculum know-how, and publishing teamwork. When these people felt strongly about the test they were creating and had faith in their publisher, a wonderfully creative world opened. That was the kind of climate in which the Stanford and Metropolitan Achievement Tests thrived.

This early link between the publishers of the textbooks used in the public schools and the development achievement tests is one that made business sense. By adopting a textbook series from one of these publishers, a school district could be assured that the tests that were used to evaluate student learning would align with what was being taught. Administrators of large school systems also knew that they could exert pressure on the test developers through the textbook division of the publishing house. This resulted in the formation of a cozy relationship that lasted until the 1970s.

General Characteristics of Commercial Achievement Tests

With the exception of the Comprehensive Testing Program, all of the major achievement batteries are similar to one another. Each of the batteries is composed of a series of content-based tests of specific subjects. The content tested on those tests is drawn from two major sources: One source is the approved learning standards of the various states, and the other is the textbooks that are widely adopted by the schools and the curricula used to teach in the classrooms. With the exception of the Comprehensive Test Program, 4th ed. (CTP-4), these publishers provide at least two alternative forms, one in English and another in Spanish. The addition of Spanish-language versions has opened the international educational test market to these publishers.

Structurally, the achievement batteries provide detailed directions for the administration of the test. This includes the exact words for the teacher to say at each step in the testing activity. Along with exact directions, the tests also provide exact time constraints for the test administration. They also provide exceptions to their own rules. These exceptions are a list of accommodations that can be made for students with disabilities.

Because of all this detail and the complexity of the directions for the test administrator, it is suggested that teachers and others charged with test administration read the test's manual with care and practice the directions prior to the day of test administration. Just as it is true of good teaching, reliable test administration requires a well-prepared teacher/test administrator.

MAJOR ACHIEVEMENT TEST BATTERIES

For the most part, these tests are used with elementary-aged school children.

By the high school years, the curriculum choices made by students reduce the ability of test developers to achieve a consensus on test content. The use of achievement tests in the first and second grades has increased since the passage of the No Child Left Behind Act of 2002. This early testing is done in preparation for the mandated high-stakes test in third grade. Likewise, the sale of these achievement batteries for use with children between the third and eighth grade has declined reflecting the mandates of the NCLB Act. The NCLB Act has not proven to be a major loss for the test publishers as they have been able to sell their measurement expertise to the states. In 2006–2007, the test publishers made $500 million on the 45 million state-mandated NCLB tests that they wrote, published, distributed, scored, and reported (Jehlen, 2007).

Another similarity between these measures is their use of large representative groups of children to establish the scoring criteria for the current students taking the test. The Terra Nova was standardized with a sample of test takers of over 73,000, while the Iowa Test of Basic Skills used 250,000 students, and the Metropolitan Achievement Test used a sample of 80,000 students in kindergarten through 12th grade in 151 school districts.

The fact that so many students are part of the standardizing group for these tests reflects the fact that schools and school systems are paid to participate. This payment is compensation for the loss of 4 hours of the school day for hundreds of children and their teachers. The local press in St. Petersburg, Florida, reported that a neighborhood middle school provided 900 students to help standardize the Iowa Test of Basic Skills. For this cooperation, the school was given an honorarium of $9,000, or about $10 per child (Solochek, 2006). While the total sum seems impressive, the instructional time that was lost was worth far more.

The Comprehensive Testing Program IV employs two different normative groups. One is a national sample of about 38,000 students selected to be a representative sample of students in grades 1 through 11. The second is a rolling norm consisting of the combined data from the last 3 years of testing with students in superior suburban public schools and independent and preparatory schools. The following is a list of the major achievement test batteries that are used in the public schools.

Metropolitan Achievement Tests, 8th ed. (MET-8, 2001)

The MET-8 is a descendant of the original Metropolitan Test published by the World Book Co. in 1932. The eighth edition of the MAT is published by Harcourt Assessment, the successor of the World Book Co. It has 13 different test levels (kindergarten to grade 11) covering a wide range of curriculum areas including reading vocabulary, reading comprehension, open-ended reading, mathematics concepts, arithmetic problem solving, science, and social studies. By the middle-school years, the subtests each provide about 50 minutes for students to complete.

The various items for the test are screened by using a large sample of subjects. Each item is examined using a statistical model to determine whether it is biased toward or against any one identified group of subjects. Items that have been shown to exhibit a statistically defined bias are removed or rewritten.

For more information, see "Considerations on Point" at www.sagepub.com/ wrightstudy

Case in Point (11b)

One of the statistical tools that can be used to identify item bias involves the Mantel–Haenszel Test of Differential Item Functioning. This is done by examining two groups of subjects (e.g., male, female) and estimating how well members of each group will do on each item being studied for possible differential item functioning. This estimation is made based on a reference score drawn from another cognitive measure. Members of both groups who should score equally (as shown on the other reference measure) are identified, and the odds that they will get the test item being studied correct are calculated by the use of the Mantel–Haenszel statistical procedure. These odds are compared as a ratio, and the average size of this ratio identifies items that exhibit item bias and that function in a differential way (Stoneberg, 2004).

The test provides score reports that are both norm based and also are presented as a basic four-point competency scale (Advanced, Proficient, Basic, Below Basic). The test is highly reliable, exhibiting very high levels of internal consistency at the upper grades and good reliability for the MAT subtests under the third-grade level (see Table 11.1).

Much like the Stanford Achievement Test, 10th ed., the MAT provides a method of comparison between scores on the Otis–Lennon School Ability Test, 8th ed., and student scores on the various MAT subtests. This provides a method of determining if the student is achieving at a level to be expected of a person of a particular level of ability.

Stanford Achievement Test, 10th Ed. (SAT-10)

The SAT-10 is the latest edition of the first battery of achievement tests developed to provide a national point of comparison for school students. This edition of the battery was published in 2003 and is appropriate for use with children between kindergarten and the 12th grade. Over the various grades there are a total of 17 different subtests that make up the test battery. Some of these are only used with the primary level tests (e.g., Sounds and Letters) while others are combined scores (Total Mathematics). The SAT-10 used 170,000 subjects in its development and the establishment of its test battery items and another 250,000 to establish the norm group. Beyond the primary grades the SAT-10 is a highly reliable measure with a median subtest reliability (consistency) coefficient (Kuder–Richardson$_{20}$) of approximately 0.90. Alternate form reliability with the combined scales such as total mathematics and total reading were also reliable (Kuder–Richardson$_{20}$ $\cong$ 0.90).

An important distinction of this test is that it provides recommended time parameters for test administration but is essentially an untimed measure. The suggested time limits are provided to assist in scheduling and planning. This step by the authors and editors at Harcourt was taken to reduce problems in providing appropriate accommodations for students with disabilities; and it was also done to better match the direction of the various states in providing high-stakes tests that are untimed and evaluated against achievement criteria (Case, 2004). Parallel to the use of the SAT-10 is the Otis–Lennon School Ability Test, 8th ed. (OLSAT-8), which is used to establish whether student scores on the SAT-10 are at an expected level for a student at a particular ability level.

Terra Nova (CAT-6), 2nd Ed. (TN2)

The Terra Nova 2nd edition (TN2) is a new edition of what was once known as the California Achievement Test (CAT-6). The second edition of the Terra Nova was published in 2002 by CTB/McGraw-Hill. It was developed and

Table 11.1 A Student Report Form From the Metropolitan Achievement Test, 8th Ed.

METROPOLITAN 8

Metropolitan Achievement Tests Eighth Edition

Elizabeth A. Tomlinson Student Report

with Otis-Lennon School Ability Test®, Seventh Edition

TEACHER: Smith - 0000000000
SCHOOL: Lakeside elementary - 0000000000
DISTRICT: Newton - 0000000000
GRADE: 04
TEST DATE: 04/00
METROPOLITAN LEVEL: Elementary 2
2000 NORMS: Spring   National
OLSAT LEVEL/FORM: E/4   OTHER INFO: 0000
National
COPY 00
PROCESS NO. 00000000-00000000-0000-08139-9

Below is your students Intervention Information.

A

Tests and Totals	Number of Items	Raw Score	Scaled Score	National PR-S	AAC Range	National Grade Percentile Bands
Total Reading	80	57	616	53-5	LOW	
Reading Vocabulary	50	19	606	48-5	LOW	
Reading Comprehension	50	38	621	55-5	LOW	
Total Mathematics	70	48	620	74-6	MIDDLE	
Concepts & Prob. Solving	40	26	609	60-6	MIDDLE	
Computation	30	22	626	76-6	MIDDLE	
Language	48	31	612	54-5	LOW	
Spelling	30	17	620	61-6	MIDDLE	
Science	35	26	625	61-6	MIDDLE	
Social Studies	35	23	621	59-5	MIDDLE	
Research Skills	43	29	624	62-6	MIDDLE	
Thinking Skills	141	97	614	60-6	LOW	
Basic battery	228	153	NA	61-6	LOW	
Complete Battery	298	202	NA	57-5	LOW	

OTIS-Lennon School Ability Test®	Number of Items	Raw Score	Scaled Score	National PR-S	Age NCE	Scaled Score	National Grade Percentile Bands
Total	72	41	105	63-6	57.0	613	
Verbal	36	19	103	58-5	54.3	607	
Nonverbal	36	22	107	67-6	59.3	619	

B

Content Clusters	RS/ NP/ NA	Below Avg	Avg	Above Avg
Reading Vocabulary	19/ 30/ 29			✓✓✓
Synonyms	8/ 12/ 12			
Antonyms	6/ 8/ 8			
Multiple Meaning	5/ 10/ 9		✓	
Reading Comprehension	38/ 50/ 49			✓✓✓
Initial Understanding	16/ 20/ 20			✓✓✓
Interpretation	12/ 16/ 16			✓✓✓
Reflective Thinking	10/ 14/ 13			✓✓✓
Thinking Skills	22/ 30/ 29			✓✓✓
Creative	11/ 17/ 16			
Informational	13/ 17/ 17			✓
Functional	14/ 16/ 16			✓
Concepts and Problem Solving	28/ 40/ 40			✓✓✓
Number & Operation	10/ 14/ 14			
Patterns & Relationships	2/ 4/ 4			
Geometry & Spatial Sense	2/ 3/ 3		✓	
Measurement	4/ 5/ 5			
Data & Probability	2/ 5/ 5			
Problem Solving Skills	6/ 9/ 9			✓
Research Skills	4/ 6/ 6			✓✓✓
Thinking Skills	19/ 27/ 27			✓✓✓

Content Clusters	RS/ NP/ NA	Below Avg	Avg	Above Avg
Reading Vocabulary	22/ 30/ 30			✓✓
Multiplication & Division Facts	5/ 7/ 7		✓	
Addition/Subtraction w/Whole Nos.	7/ 8/ 8			✓✓
Multiplication & Division w/Whole Nos	6/ 7/ 7			✓✓
Addition & Subtraction w/Decimals	2/ 4/ 4		✓	
Addition & Subtraction w/Fractions	2/ 4/ 4			✓
Computation Applications	9/ 15/ 15		✓	
Computing Skills	13/ 15/ 15			✓✓✓
Thinking Skills	11/ 15/ 15			✓✓✓
Language	31/ 48/ 48			✓✓✓
Prewriting	10/ 14/ 14			✓✓✓
Composing	10/ 17/ 17			✓✓✓
Editing	11/ 17/ 17			✓✓✓
Research Skills	10/ 14/ 14			✓✓✓
Thinking Skills	20/ 31/ 31			✓✓✓
Spelling	17/ 30/ 30			✓✓
Homophones	4/ 6/ 6			✓✓✓
Phonetic Principles	8/ 12/ 12			✓✓✓
Structural Principles	3/ 9/ 9	✓		
No Mistake	2/ 3/ 3			✓

Content Clusters	RS/ NP/ NA	Below Avg	Avg	Above Avg
Science	26/ 35/ 35			✓✓
Life Science	13/ 15/ 15			✓✓
Physical Science	6/ 10/ 10			✓✓
Earth/Space Science	7/ 10/ 10			✓✓
Science Process Skills	18/ 25/ 25			✓✓
Research Skills	7/ 10/ 10			✓✓
Thinking Skills	15/ 21/ 21			✓✓
Social Studies	23/ 35/ 33			✓✓
Geography	7/ 8/ 8			✓✓
History	5/ 7/ 7			✓✓
Political Science	3/ 7/ 7			
Economics	3/ 7/ 6		✓	
Culture	5/ 6/ 6			✓✓
Research Skills	8/ 13/ 13			✓✓
Thinking Skills	10/ 17/ 15			✓✓
Research Skills	29/ 43/ 43			✓
Thinking Skills	87/141/138			✓

SOURCE: Metropolitan Achievement Tests, 8th Edition. Copyright © 2000 by Harcourt, Inc. Reproduced with permission.

normed on a sample of 280,000 students enrolled in over 1,300 public and private schools during 1999–2000. During the norming process a test of mental ability, the InView, was also standardized. It was developed to replace the Test of Cognitive Skills that was part of the first edition of the Terra Nova. This mental ability measure makes it possible for the TN2 to provide an ability–achievement comparison. The TN2 provides a series of different test batteries covering kindergarten to the 12 grade. At the high school level the administration of the full scale of 20 subtests would require over 6 hours dedicated to the administration of tests. The teacher's manual provides a detailed content analysis of each of the subtests. This information makes it simple for teachers to determine if the test matches the classroom curriculums and provides "talking points" to use with parents of the test takers.

The TN2 was constructed to resemble standard classroom materials and workbooks. The test developers felt this would make the Terra Nova 2 seem to be less of a threat (Cizek, Johnson, & Mazzie, 2005).

The TN2 has unusually high levels of internal consistency at every grade level and on every subtest ($r \cong 0.95$). Bias analysis was conducted for all permutations of ethnicity and gender using DIF equations.

Iowa Tests of Basic Skills, 2000/2005 (ITBS)

The ITBS was first published almost 80 years ago. It is the direct descendant of the University of Iowa and Prof. E. F. Lindquist. During the 1920s he ran a summer contest for Iowa's children that rewarded academic skills. In 1935 he published the Iowa Every-Pupil Testing Program. Lindquist worked with the old-line publishing house of Houghton-Mifflin to develop the Iowa Test of Basic Skills. A corporate reorganization in 1979 saw the resurrection of an earlier Houghton-Mifflin trademark and the establishment of the Riverside Publishing Co. as the test publishing arm of the book publisher.

The other notable product of Professor Lindquist's oeuvre was the American College Testing (ACT) program. Like the ACT, the ITBS is an in-depth measure of academic learning. The test is available at levels 5 through 14. These levels correspond to the approximate age that is appropriate for the test takers. The basic skills that the test designers focused on measuring are central to all learning and include inference and analysis, comparison, classification, and interpretation. These higher-order thinking skills are measured by building questions using curriculum areas such as reading, mathematics concepts and estimation, mathematics problem solving and data management, social studies, and science. It also measures five areas of language arts.

The ITBS has good levels of reliability in the middle and upper elementary school grades (r ≅ 0.90) and moderate levels among kindergartners and first-graders (r ≅ 0.80). Content validity was established through an analysis of textbooks and curricula. The ITBS also accounts for the recommendations of professional associations and learned societies in organizing the blueprint for the ITBS. The full battery administration of the ITBS requires over 5 hours of test time and like the other achievement batteries should be broken up and administered over several days.

One advantage of the ITBS is that it provides several normative comparison groups from which a school can select. It offers norms for a national sample of public schools, a norm group for schools located in impoverished communities, and a set of norms for Catholic schools.

The ITBS is matched by a secondary-school examination. That test, the Iowa Test of Educational Development (ITED), is designed for grades 9 through 11. Like the other major published achievement tests, the ITBS and the ITED publish an accompanying cognitive ability test, the Cog AT.

Comprehensive Testing Program 4 (CTP 4)

The CTP 4 (Baldwin & Wylie, 2004) is the smallest and most unusual of the major national achievement testing programs. This test is published by the Educational Records Bureau, a testing and school admissions company created by 1,584 member independent schools and highly competitive suburban public schools. Technical assistance is provided by the Educational Testing Service.

The CPT 4 measures what is described as key areas of school achievement, including listening, reading, vocabulary, writing, and mathematics. The test describes itself as serving the need for measurement in those schools that set the highest standards for learning (see Table 11.2).

The test reports internal consistency reliability in the range of 0.78. It was standardized in 2002 on a national sample of just under 38,000 students in public and private schools (Fouratt & Owen, 2004). The score reports can be based on any one of three possible normative comparison groups. One is the national sample of public and private schools involving 66 independent schools and 417 public schools. A school administrator can elect to base the scores reported for the children and classrooms of his or her school on this national sample, on a sample of highly competitive suburban schools, or to the sample of students from independent schools. If one of the latter two is selected, it will be based on a compilation of scores from all students in the category over the past 3 years (rolling norms). The national norms are based on data collected in 2000.

Table 11.2   Two Graphs of Student Profiles With Annotations on the CTP 4 Sample Forms

Administrator's Summary

- Part of Basic Scoring Package (one version, e.g., district, school, class)
- Additional versions may be ordered separately (e.g., district, school, class)
- One page for each test administered

> **Upper**
> boxes compare local scale score and local norms at selected percentiles (90, 75, 50, 25, 10) with all three populations: national, suburban, independent

> **Graph**
> helps you visualize performance of this group against normal distribution for all three populations

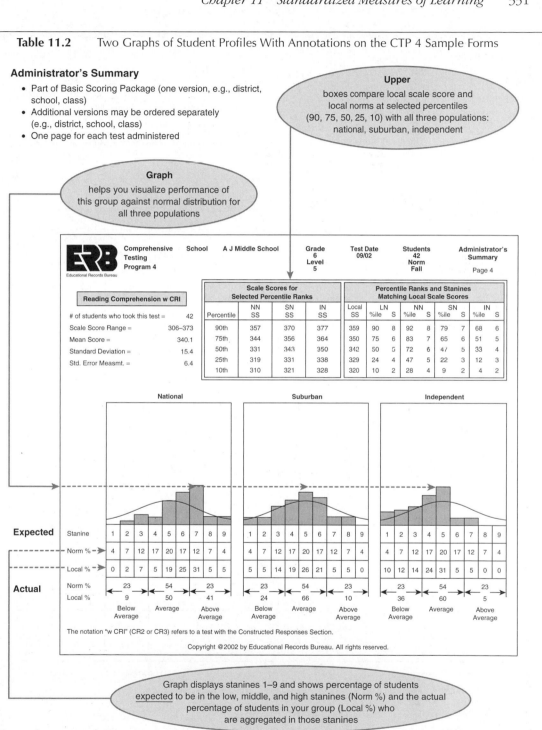

The notation "w CRI" (CR2 or CR3) refers to a test with the Constructed Responses Section.

> Graph displays stanines 1–9 and shows percentage of students <u>expected</u> to be in the low, middle, and high stanines (Norm %) and the actual percentage of students in your group (Local %) who are aggregated in those stanines

(Continued)

(Continued)

Individual Instructional Summary (IIS)

- Individual report for each student
- Easy to share with parents
- Valuable for parent conferences
- Helpful supplement to item Analysis

Since each student's results are reported separately on individual reports, the IIS provides a second, more specific level of information to share with parents. It provides information about performance on items in tests and categories that is not available on the parent reports.

Although it permits review of the percentages of items answered correctly by test and category, the IIS does not include item-by-item responses and so is not a substitute for the item Analysis.

Percent correct information and comparisons also require at least six items in any category.

(oval callout) Norms the school chooses on OSS

ERB Educational Records Bureau

Comprehensive Testing Program 4

School: Broadway Middle School
Grade: 7   **Level:** 6
Student: Wysniewski, Debra

Individual Instructional Summary
Test Date: In 1701
No. of students Tested: 29
Norm: Fall

Multiple Choice Tests and Subscore Categories	Students Tested	Number of Questions				Average Percent Correct			
		Presented	Attempted	Correct	Student %	School %	Sub. Pub. %	Ind. %
Verbal Reasoning**	28	45	45	40	89	78	68	81
Vocabulary	28	35	35	23	66	69	61	73
Word Meaning	28	13	13	8	62	72	63	75
Precision	28	9	9	6	67	67	61	71
Application	28	13	13	9	69	69	59	73
Reading Comprehension w CR3	28	37	37	30	81	78	68	78
Explicit Information	28	14	14	12	86	77	68	81
Inference	28	14	14	12	86	85	76	85
Analysis	28	9	9	6	67	69	60	68
Writing Mechanics	28	45	45	35	78	67	59	71
Spelling	28	10	10	7	70	57	50	67
Capitalization	28	8	8	6	75	75	62	75
Punctuation	28	11	11	7	64	67	63	70
Usage	28	16	16	15	94	70	60	72
Writing Concepts & Skills***	28	50	50	43	86	74	66	76
Organization	28	14	14	11	79	75	68	78
Purpose, Audience, Focus	28	10	10	8	80	71	62	72
Supporting Details	28	14	14	13	93	66	64	74
Style and Craft	28	12	12	11	92	83	70	80
Quantitative Reasoning**	28	50	50	24	48	47	44	56
Mathematics 1&2 w CR3	29	84	84	52	62	58	52	62
Numbers and Number Relationship	29	14	14	9	64	67	57	65
Numbers and Number Theory	29	14	14	8	57	50	48	59
Geometry and Spatial Sense	29	12	12	8	67	48	50	60
Measurement	29	12	12	8	67	61	49	58
Statistics	29	10	10	7	70	65	54	64
Probability	29	9	9	3	33	54	56	66
Pre-Algebra	29	13	13	9	69	60	56	62
Conceptual Understanding	29	27	27	18	67	55	52	60
Procedural Knowledge	29	28	28	18	64	58	50	62
Problem Solving	29	29	29	16	55	61	54	64

Constructed Response Questions	Students Tested	Number of Points				Average Percent of Points Earned			
		Possible on Questions Presented	Possible on Questions Attempted	Earned	Student %	School %	Sub. Pub. %	Ind. %
Reading Comprehension (4 Question) Reading for understanding	28	8	8	7	88	54	49	60
Mathematics (8 Questions) Communication	29	16	16	9	56	48	40	52

Suburban Public and Independent data are estimates based on a small combined group of Suburban Public and Independent schools for preliminary reporting
-Test not taken.
—Percentages are not computed when the number of questions presented or possible points is less than 6.
Questions are counted twice for content and Process Categories.

(oval callout) Summary of constructed response questions if taken as part of CTP 4

2006–2007 Educational Records Bureau **Catalog**

SOURCE: From Educational Records Bureau Testing Programs and Services 2006–2007 Catalog, pp. 21 and 24. Reprinted with permission from Educational Records Bureau.

Another characteristic that sets the CTP 4 apart from the others is its inclusion of constructed response items. The CTP 4 offers an optional section that provides students with a pair of readings on a topic. After reading them, the students are asked to write a position based on the two readings. This provides a measure of the student's ability to compare and contrast implicit and explicit information provided from different perspectives. It also assesses the student's ability to evaluate those data and communicate a position that is on the point. A similar format is employed in the Auditory Comprehension subtest of the CTP 4. Constructed response sections are also included in the various subtests on mathematics.

STATE-MANDATED ASSESSMENTS

In 2008, the No Child Left Behind Act was near the midpoint toward its ambitious target date of 2014 for having all American children competent in the basic skill areas (No Child Left Behind Act, 2002). The first presidential administration to require that every state establish a testing program for all children in all school districts was that of Bill Clinton, with his Improving America's Schools Act (P.L. 103-382, 1994). The No Child Left Behind Act went further and required that all children become proficient on an approved, state-administered high-stakes test. The high-stakes standards tests are essentially achievement tests that use the approved standards for learning from a state in the blueprint for the test's design. While the states have the responsibility of writing learning standards, the federal government has veto power over them. The U.S. Department of Education also has final say as to whether the various states have selected or contracted for the development of measures appropriate for the assessment of student learning (viz., the approved standards).

During the 1980s, a number of states constructed their own assessments for use as a standard achievement measure. States including New York, Pennsylvania, New Jersey, and Florida had such programs. Today, only Oregon and Kansas construct examinations for the children of their states. The pressure of the new mandates of both the Improving America's Schools Act and the No Child Left Behind Act has made it impossible for understaffed state education departments to go it alone. A second force that has made it impossible for the various state education departments to write, standardize, benchmark, publish, distribute, and score a series of new examinations covering grades 3 through 8 and 11, with appropriate standards-based coverage over four subject (reading, mathematics, writing, science) areas each year, is the public clamor to see the actual tests. Organizations such as Fair Test in Massachusetts have pressured a number of states into releasing the actual test items after they are used. This means that each of the 28 annual high-stakes tests must be reinvented every year.

Another mandate of the No Child Left Behind Act is that each public and charter school in the nation must demonstrate that it is making adequate yearly progress (AYP) toward the goal of having all children proficient.[2] Specifically, the act requires that each subgroup identified by the law (special education, English-language learners, Hispanic, African American, White, Native American, Asian American, and those from impoverished homes) show significant average group progress over the previous year toward the goal of universal proficiency (see Table 11.3).

No Child Left Behind
High-Stakes Achievement Test Problems

This application of achievement tests in the evaluation of an entire school has been questioned (Kane & Staiger, 2002; Linn & Haug, 2002). The major concern is that the core student cohort at any grade level may not be the same as the cohort the next year. The point is also made that the effect of this type of cohort volatility is more likely in smaller schools. Volatility can occur as a result of any number of environmental reasons. Possible causes of student test score volatility could include such random factors as the year of a major terrorist attack, the year the high school basketball team wins the state championship, the year of a major disruptive storm (e.g., a major hurricane), a flu pandemic, or a flood. This volatility can affect a small rural school in a positive way one year and in a negative direction the next year. This can produce a chaotic pattern of growth on the mandated statewide tests. Thus, a school may be awarded kudos in the press one year and be the object of derision the next.

Walter Way (2006), a researcher for the Educational Testing Service, has reviewed the potential for the AYP analyses being performed by the 50 states on data from their schools. He determined that these analyses may be based on flawed, volatile achievement test data and problematic for school accountability. Yet, there is evidence that when schools take the restructuring seriously, and initiate a major reformation of the curriculum and programs, significant improvement on the statewide assessment test is possible (Scott, 2007). Part of this restructuring movement has been the appearance of a new consultation specialization: "turnaround specialists." These educational leaders are hired to come into a school and provide guidance as to how to change the school's way of doing business.

Another problem in understanding the extent of the impact of the No Child Left Behind Act is that most states are measuring with rubber rulers.

Table 11.3   Report Card: State of Tennessee, Part III, Adequate Yearly Progress

Report Card 2004

State of Tennessee
Statewide Report Card 2004
Governor: Phil Bredesen
Commissioner: Lana Seivers

Part III: Adequate Yearly Progress (AYP)

+ Met Federal Benchmark
× Did not meet Federal Benchmark
<45 Fewer than 45 members, does not have to report

Elementary/Middle	All	White	Hispanic	African American	Native American	Asian	Econ Disadv	Students w/ Disabilities	Limited English Proficient
Math									
% Tested	+	+	+	+	+	+	+	+	+
% Proficient/Adv	+	+	+	×	+	+	+	×	×
Reading, Language Arts, Reading									
% Tested	+	+	+	+	+	+	+	+	+
% Proficient/Adv	+	+	+	+	+	+	+	+	×
Attendance Rate	+								
Met AYP?	×								

High School	All	White	Hispanic	African American	Native American	Asian	Econ Disadv	Students w/ Disabilities	Limited English Proficient
Math									
% Tested	+	+	+	+	+	+	+	+	+
% Proficient/Adv	+	+	+	×	+	+	+	×	+
Reading, Language Arts, Reading									
% Tested	+	+	+	+	+	+	+	+	+
% Proficient/Adv	+	+	+	×	+	+	×	×	×
Attendance Rate	+								
Met AYP?	×								

SOURCE: From Tennessee Department of Education's Web page. Reprinted with permission from State of Tennessee Department of Education.

NCLB mandated that all children will be "proficient" but lets the states determine what proficient means. Thus, if a child attending school in Massachusetts (high-standards state) is found to have achievement scores that are below proficient, a move by the family to Texas or Florida (low-standards states) could result in the child becoming proficient without any academic effort (Jehlen, 2007).

Many of the states set their standards for student achievement under policies established in response to the Improving America's Schools Act of 1994. When those standards were put into place there was no consequence for failure. For that reason the passage of the NCLB Act in 2002, a high-stakes testing requirement with teeth, came as a shock to a number of states. The political reality is that no state's political leaders could endure the prospect of having almost every school in the state labeled as being a failure (Owens & Sunderman, 2006). For those states such as Colorado that once had standards for student achievement that had the highest expectations, the cut scores had to be changed (Way, 2006). The result is that achievement that was once described as being "below proficient" is now "proficient."

No Child Left Behind Positive Impact

One change that the No Child Left Behind Act brought is that there is much more achievement testing going on in the schools than before the law. In 2000, only 19 states had mandated statewide achievement testing programs (Jennings & Rentner, 2006). In 2007–2008 every state has established a testing program.[3] This growth in the testing business has put a great deal of strain on the states and local school systems. A survey of the states by the Center on Educational Policy concluded that 72% of the states lack sufficient staff to deal with the mandates of the No Child Left Behind Act (Jennings & Rentner, 2006). Individual states find that the mandates of the NCLB Act have been underfunded, resulting in significant gaps in state budgets. Wisconsin had a shortfall of $14.5 million in 2006–2007 (Fair Test, 2007).

Few of the various states actually build their own assessment system. For the most part it is the old-line test publishers who "assist" the states and develop, print, distribute, score, and report the results of these mandated achievement tests. This situation can be seen in Figure 11.2.

From this table it can be seen that new standards-based assessments for the states are business as usual for many of the achievement test publishers. In addition to the major corporations a number of new test consulting companies have won contracts with the states. It is easy to quip that the NCLB Act has left no testing company behind.

Other outcomes of the NCLB Act are that more instructional time is being spent on reading and mathematics. This is especially true of inner-city

State	NCLB Test(s) [Primary]	Primary Contractor
Alabama	Alabama Reading & Mathematics Test (ARMT)	Harcourt
Alaska	Standards Based Assessment	Data Recognition Co.
Arizona	Arizona Instrument to Measure Standards (AIMS)	CTB/McGraw Hill
Arkansas	Benchmark Exam (Language, Math)	Questar, T.A.S.A.
California	Standardized Testing and Reporting (STAR)	Educational Testing Service (ETS)
Colorado	Colorado Student Assessment Program (CSAP)	CTB/McGraw Hill
Connecticut	Connecticut Mastery Test (CMT)	Measurement Inc.
Delaware	Delaware Student Testing Program (DSTP)	Harcourt
Florida	Florida Comprehensive Assessment Test (FCAT)	CTB/McGraw Hill
Georgia	Criterion Referenced Competency Test (CRCT)	CTB/McGraw Hill
Hawaii	Hawaii State Assessment	AIR—Am. Institute for Research
Idaho	Idaho Standards Achievement Test (ISAT)	Data Recognition Co.
Illinois	Illinois Standards Achievement Test (SAT)	Pearson & Harcourt Assessment CTB/McGraw Hill
Indiana	Indiana Statewide Testing for Educ. Progress (ISTEP)	No Single Test
Iowa	ITB—used by most, no one required test	No Single Test
Kansas	Kansas Assessment Program (KAP)	U. of KS Ctr. For Educ Testing & Eval.
Kentucky	Kentucky Core Content Test (KCCT)	Measured Progress
Louisiana	Louisiana Educ. Assessment Program (LEAP)	Data Recognition Co.
Maine	Maine Educational Assessment (MEA)	Measured Progress
Maryland	Maryland School Assessment (MSA)	Harcourt
Massachusetts	Mass. Comprehensive Assessment System (MCAS)	Measured Progress
Michigan	Michiagan Educational Assessment Program (MEAP)	Pearson
Minnesota	Minnesota Comprehensive Assessment II (MCAII)	Pearson
Mississippi	Mississippi Curriculum Test (MCTII)	Pearson
Missouri	Missouri Assessment Program (MAP)	CTB/McGraw Hill
Montana	Montana Comprehensive Assessment System (MontCAS)	Measured Progress
Nebraska	School Based Teacher Led Assessment Reporting System	Local System of Exam. & Portfolios

Figure 11.2 Table of States and Their Tests and Consultants

State	NCLB Test(s) [Primary]	Primary Contractor
Nevada	NV Proficiency Exam. Program (Gr. 3, 5, 8) & ITBS (Gr. 4, 7, 10)	Measured Progress
New Hampshire	New England Common Assessment Program (NECAP)	Measured Progress
New Jersey	New Jersey Assessment of Skills & Knowledge (NJASK)	Riverside
New Mexico	New Mexico Standards Based Assessment (NMSA)	Harcourt
New York	New York State Testing Program (NYSTP)	CTB/McGraw Hill
North Carolina	End of Grade Test (EOG)	N.C. State University
North Dakota	North Dakota State Assessment (NDSA)	CTB/McGraw Hill
Ohio	Reading, Mathematics & Writing Achievement (MAR)	AIR—Am. Institute for Research
Oklahoma	Oklahoma Core Curriculum Tests (OCCT)	Data Recognition Co.
Oregon	Technology Enhanced Student Assessment (TESA)	Oregon State Dept. of Educ.
Pennsylvania	Pennsylvania System of School Assessment (PSSA)	Data Recognition Co.
Rhode Island	New England Common Assessment Program (NECAP)	Measured Progress
South Carolina	Palmetto Achievement Challenge Tests (PACT)	AIR—Am. Institute for Research
South Dakota	Dakota State Test of Educational Progress (Dakota STEP)	Harcourt
Tennessee	Tennessee Comprehensive Assessment Program (TCAP)	Pearson
Texas	Texas Assessment of Knowledge and Skills (TAKS)	Pearson
Utah	Iowa Test of Basic Skills (ITBS)	Riverside
Vermont	New England Common Assessments Program (NECAP)	Measured Progress
Virginia	Standards of Learning Assessments (SOL)	Pearson
Washington	Washington Assessment of Student Learning (WASL)	Pearson
West Virginia	West Virginia Educational Standards Test (West Test)	CTB/McGraw Hill
Wisconsin	Wisconsin Knowledge and Concepts Exam (WKCE)	CTB/McGraw Hill
Wyoming	Proficiency Assessment of Wyoming Students (PAWS)	Harcourt

Figure 11.2 (Continued)

schools; however, the time shift is a zero-sum game. That means that if more time is being spent on reading and mathematics, some curriculum area must lose time. The big loss in instructional time and curriculum emphasis is being absorbed by the social studies. All other curriculum areas are also losing emphasis, but the biggest loser is the social studies.

Other positive outcomes include the fact that schools are spending more time and effort on improving the learning of children with special needs and those who are English-language learners. There is a credible effort being made by all school systems to close the achievement gap between different ethnic groups of children. Also, more attention is being paid to the need to build testing programs that are appropriate for English-language learners (Spellings, 2000).

Case in Point (11c)

The age of the child who is learning a second language is a critical factor in the emerging literacy in the second language. Typically all children who are placed in an environment where they cannot communicate with either teachers or other students will refrain from speaking; these children are listening and attempting to create the new language from what they see and hear going on around them. Younger children will spend a longer period of time being mute than will their adolescent siblings. Yet, preadolescent children will have less difficulty in developing fluency in the new language. This is because of the greater plasticity of their developing neurology. The language centers in the brain lose that flexibility with adolescence and learning a second language becomes more difficult.

Of special concern are those children who have a learning disability and who are also English-language learners. These children are likely not to be diagnosed and provided a special education program until they have had several frustrating years in school.

For more information, see "Considerations on Point" at www.sagepub.com/wrightstudy

---

Another positive outcome of the NCLB programs relates to staffing. More attention is now being paid to the training and qualifications of teachers and teacher aids than ever before. This focus on credentials is a direct response to one of the mandates of the NCLB Act. Historically, the most motivated teachers have ended up teaching in the high-performing suburban schools. Rural and inner city schools have had less well prepared and less experienced teachers. Pressure is now on state education departments to improve the quality of all teaching faculty, especially those of the inner city and the most isolated rural communities (Peske & Haycock, 2006).

One provision of the NCLB Act that has not yet proven to be a success is the opportunity provided to the parents of students enrolled in schools that have consistently failed to meet the AYP requirements to transfer their child to another school in the district. In 2006, only 2% of the eligible students were transferred (Jennings & Rentner, 2006).

Summary

One outcome of the new measurement sciences of the 1920s was large-scale achievement test batteries. These were developed to provide a measurement of the material covered in the curriculum being offered in the textbooks of the major publishing houses of the day. Beginning with those first publications, and continuing today, these achievement test batteries measure each child's mental ability along with his or her achievement and encourage educators to analyze any discrepancy between the two.

Parents have been granted the right to know the results of all of these test scores. This was established by federal law in 1974. For that reason it is critical that educators understand all of the various elements that appear on the student score report.

Test publishers and school administrators had a comfortable relationship throughout the 50 years following the appearance of the Stanford Achievement Test in 1923. Criticism of American education resulted in the development of state-approved standards for learning and achievement. Following the passage of the Improving American Education Act in1994 there was an earnest effort by most states to identify and approve educational standards and the appropriate measures for those standards. The pressure was turned up in 2002 with the passage of the No Child Left Behind Act. This law brought many ambitious plans for improving the educational system in this country. Important goals such as closing the achievement gap between different ethnic and social economic groups were mandated by the law. A required annual testing program involving achievement assessments that begin in the third grade is a centerpiece of this legislated program.

Discussion Questions

1. Using an achievement test score report from a regional school system, list all the elements of the score report that parents will need to have

explained. Then provide an explanation for them that is appropriate for the typical child's parent.

2. Using the Internet, examine a copy of a score report from the state's high-stakes testing program. Identify each element on that report, and provide an explanation for its meaning that would be appropriate for an average child's parent.

3. Consider a school or district with which you are familiar. Which of the several major achievement tests described in the chapter would be most appropriate to use in that school? Why?

Student Study Site

Educational Assessment on the Web

Log on to the Web-based student study site at www.sagepub.com/wrightstudy for additional Web sources and study resources.

NOTES

1. The rubric open to parental review is "the established criteria including rules, principles, and illustrations, used in scoring responses to individual items and clusters of items" (Joint Committee on Testing Practices, 2005).

2. Charter schools were mandates of the Improving America's Schools Act of 1994. Research into their effectiveness has not shown charter schools to produce any achievement advantage for students. Public schools have a better record of student achievement when compared to both charter and nonpublic parochial schools (Lubienski & Lubienski, 2006).

3. Three states—Maine, Nebraska, and Iowa—have statewide testing programs that allow the local school systems to select from several options.

Chapter 12

TESTING OF APTITUDE AND SELECTION

Talent wins games, but teamwork and intelligence wins championships.

—Michael Jordan

Issues and Themes

One of the links between this chapter on aptitude and its measurement and the previous chapter on achievement testing is the correlation between the two areas of study. The two dimensions are positively correlated with Pearson correlation coefficients in the range of $r = 0.50$. This relationship has made it possible to use discrepancies between aptitude and achievement as diagnostic indicators.

There are many dimensions that are part of aptitude. Cognitive ability, or intelligence, is a good indicator of scholastic aptitude. The theories of mental abilities vary from those steeped in the tradition of genetics to those of inherited core of capability. Other models stress the various factors or dimensions that are part of human intellect. One of the multifactor models of ability (Guilford) can account for creativity and differentiate it from other aspects of intelligence. More recent writings by Sternberg have also focused on human creativity and have integrated it into an overall model for intellect.

Mental ability is a wide construct that relates to how well a child will do in school. It has little relation to how well that child will do years later in the adult world. To provide a more precise view of a person's aptitude for learning a particular craft or skill, highly focused aptitude measures have been developed and marketed. These instruments are not easy to produce owing to the problem of precisely describing a well-conceived construct for measurement. More success has been had in developing aptitude measures that cover a range of skill areas. These can then be aligned with the student's potential for success in different technologies and or vocations. One of the most successful testing programs is now 40 years old and is used to place military recruits into the various specialty schools for the armed services of this country.

Learning Objectives

By reading and studying this chapter you can acquire the competency to do the following:

- Explain the relationship between achievement and aptitude.
- Describe the similarities and differences between measures of aptitude and achievement.
- Explain with examples the difference between single-factor and multi-factor theories of mental ability.
- Present the evidence used by those holding a hereditarian belief as to the cause of group differences in tested levels of mental ability.
- Present evidence used by those who believe that group differences on mental ability tests are primarily a function of the environment and learning.
- Describe the eight-factor theory of human intelligences as developed by Howard Gardner.
- Describe the factors included in Sternberg's triarchic model of human intelligence.
- Discuss the relationship between mental ability and creativity.
- Describe how creativity may be measured, and discuss several measuring devices for this domain.
- Contrast the testing for specific aptitudes with the measurement of cognitive ability.

Many difficulties which nature throws in our way may be smoothed away by the exercise of intelligence.

—Titus Livius

APTITUDE

The word *aptitude* refers to the ability of a person to learn a new cognitive area or acquire a new skill. The central word in that definition is *ability*. In terms of an individual's aptitude, his or her ability has two components. One of these is what some psychologists refer to as "fluid" ability (i.e., intelligence). This is the neurophysiologic capacity of the individual to learn new things. The second component of aptitude is a "crystallized" form of ability that represents what the individual has already learned and is available to facilitate further new learning.

The crystallized abilities are those that the child has acquired from the world around him or her. It includes what was learned during all conscious hours, including while watching countless hours of television, attending preschool, playing with peers, on family vacations, attending Sunday school, and being read to by a parent. Once in school, crystallized ability (i.e., intelligence) grows exponentially as the child encounters a wide range of adults, curriculums, and peers of diverse backgrounds.

Crystallized abilities are the crossover point between achievement and aptitude. They provide a foundation for further learning while expanding with all new learning. In some ways, tests such as the Stanford Achievement Test, 10th ed.; Metropolitan Achievement Test, 8th ed.; and the Terra Nova II, Comprehensive Test Program, 4th ed., represent measures of these crystallized abilities. Yet, because so much learning occurs beyond the classroom, crystallized abilities include more than just the topics measured on standardized achievement tests.

There are as many forms of aptitude as there are areas of specialization. A child can have an aptitude for painting or for algebra, for music composition or for NASCAR driving, for gardening or for human relations. Also, any person can have a great degree of aptitude in several areas and modest levels of aptitude in others. Most of these specialized fields would have little correlation with scores from those areas measured by a standard achievement test battery.

SCHOLASTIC APTITUDE AND INTELLIGENCE

Possibly the most studied aptitude is that for school learning: scholastic aptitude. Scholastic aptitude is built of those skills needed to succeed in school, including previous learnings and cognitive skills. This dimension of aptitude is partially measured by the Iowa Tests of Basic Skills. That test measures cognitive processing abilities as well as the curriculum that was learned.

The ability to learn in school was the primary focus of the early researchers into the nature of human intelligence. The first practical measure of the ability of a child to learn in school was provided by Binet and Simon in 1904 (see Chapter 2). The Americanization of their efforts to establish a method for the identification of children needing learning support resulted in an American intelligence test. This test was built on the assumption that intelligence is an inherited unitary dimension (general factor).

The first edition of Terman's Stanford Revision of the Binet Scale determined the mental age of the subject who was tested. Each item on the test was ranked by difficulty and then age graded, or normed (see Chapter 2). This was done empirically by testing many children and young adults of different ages and identifying which items were difficult for the various age groups. Once this standard was established, subjects being tested were challenged with ever more difficult items until they reached their ceiling level. The ceiling level is that point where the child can no longer solve the problems or perform the required tasks. It can then be assumed that the child cannot answer any questions that are ranked in difficulty above that ceiling level.

From this process it is possible to determine the mental age of the subject. The mental age is the normed age that is equal to the child's ceiling level. If the mental age (MA) is equal to the child's chronological age (CA), the child is of average mental ability. When the MA is greater than the CA, the child is brighter than the average for his or her age. Naturally, a CA that is greater than the child's MA indicates that the child has less than average mental ability when compared to others the same age. William Stern, a German psychologist, noticed that gap between MA and CA increases as the child matures, but that the ratio between them remains constant. This ratio when multiplied by 100 became the value of IQ (Stern, 1928).

Starting with the 1937 edition of the Stanford–Binet Scales, the test used normative comparison groups and reported **IQ scores** based on the normal curve. To remain consistent with the original 1916 edition, the mean was set at 100 and the standard deviation was set at 16. Even though not part of the calculation of the intelligence score, the test continued to publish a transformation formula for determining the child's MA. Some habits are hard to break.

In 2003, the new fifth edition of the Stanford–Binet Intelligence Scales was published. This new version changed the theoretical base of the test. It is now a measure that is established to gauge intelligence as defined by the Cattell–Horn–Carroll model (Roid, 2003).

When we assume the normal curve is the distribution of mental ability, half of all people will have IQ levels below 100 and half will be above that point. Only a little over 2% can have IQ scores over 132 or under 68.

Only a tiny percentage of people will have an IQ below 50. Those people with an IQ below 50 will need to be cared for by others and will never live independently. Children with IQ scores between 50 and 70 will need special education on a full-time basis and will eventually be employable in a sheltered work environment. Children with IQ scores between 70 and 85 can be mainstreamed into regular classes but will need learning support. Those with IQ scores between 85 and 115 are in the average range and represent more than two-thirds of all children. Most education programs for the gifted require a minimum IQ score that is two standard deviations above the mean (130 or 132 depending on the test used).

TRAINING OF TEST ADMINISTRATORS

Administering, scoring, and interpreting intelligence tests require that the test administrator be well trained for the task. There are three levels of training qualification that most publishers require of test users. This three-level classification of users system was a part of the first ethical statement published by the American Psychological Association in 1950. Even though it has been long since superseded by other statements on qualifications and ethics by that organization, the original three-level model persists today.

Level A

This level of qualification only requires that the individual have an ethical need to use these measures. No specialized education in testing and assessment is required at this level. This level of qualification includes most classroom teachers. The types of measures appropriate at this level include statewide assessments and other standardized tests given de rigueur in the school.

Level B

To be qualified to use B-level tests and assessments the user must have earned a master's in education or psychology and have advanced training in measurement, including measurement statistics, reliability, and validity. Those with advanced education in child development and early childhood assessment may also qualify at level B without a master's degree. Members of professional organizations requiring their members to be well qualified in test administration and interpretation can also qualify at level B. These organizations include the American Counseling Association, the International Reading Association, and the American Speech–Language–Hearing Association. Level B includes most group-administered tests of intelligence, measures of occupational preferences, attention deficit disorder scales, and preschool readiness measures.

Level C

To be qualified to use C-level measures, the individual must be highly educated and have had advanced training in educational and psychological measurements. Typically these people hold a doctorate in educational or school psychology or a have a Ph.D. in a clinical field in psychology. They hold advanced licensure from a state agency and are members of professional associations such as the American Psychological Association or the National Association of School Psychologists. These professional associations require adherence to an ethical canon related to education and training of those using C-level tests. These measures include most individually administered tests of intelligence and personality.

TESTS OF INTELLIGENCE ADMINISTERED ONE-ON-ONE

There are five individually administered intelligence tests that are widely used in public schools. Three of the five assume that the user is qualified at level C. Two tests, the Slosson Full-Range Intelligence Test (S-FRIT) and the Kaufman Brief Intelligence Test, 2nd ed. (KBIT-2), assume users are qualified at level B.

Stanford–Binet

The first of these level-C tests is the fifth edition of the Stanford–Binet Intelligence Scales (SB5). This test requires about an hour or so for a well-trained school psychologist to administer, plus time to enter the raw scores into a database and print out a report. If the psychologist elects to hand score the test instead of employing a computer-generated report and summary, another hour of time will be needed.

The SB5 is constructed as a measure of the human intellect as defined by the Cattell–Horn–Carroll (CHC) model of mental ability. The SB5 measures and provides scores for five of the factors of the CHC model, including **Fluid Intelligence** (Gf), Crystallized Knowledge (Ge), Quantitative Knowledge (Gq), Visual Processing (Gv), and Short-Term Memory (Gsm). The SB5 was normed on a representative sample of over 4,500 people and can provide intelligence scores for people between the ages of 2 and 85 years. The instrument is highly reliable (median factor reliability = .86, full scale IQ score reliability = .98). Because of the long history of this test, and the care and effort that the publisher put into the development of the new edition, the SB5 is the "gold standard" for intelligence tests.

Wechsler Scales

The Stanford–Binet Scales have the longest history, but the Wechsler Scales are the most widely used intelligence tests in the schools. David Wechsler emigrated from Romania as a child and after graduate study at Columbia became one of the young psychologists at Camp Logan, Texas, testing drafted army recruits in 1917. From this experience Wechsler saw a flaw with both the Army Alpha and the Stanford Revision of the Binet Scales. David Wechsler believed that those tests were both too limited by the single-factor approach used by Terman to measure an ability as complex as human intelligence.

After the war he received advanced training with Charles Spearman and Karl Pearson at University College London and served as corporate secretary for the Psychological Corporation. In 1933 he was appointed clinical professor at New York University's Medical College and senior psychologist at Bellevue Hospital in New York City. In 1939 he published a two-factor clinical intelligence test, the Wechsler–Bellevue scale. In 1949 he developed the **Wechsler Intelligence Scale for Children (WISC)**. This intelligence test used 11 subtests to measure ability along two major factors, Verbal IQ and Performance IQ. This model was repeated with the development of the fourth edition of the test, the WISC-IV, published in 2003. The new edition provides a single full-scale score and four index scores (factor scores): Verbal Comprehension Index (VCI), Perceptual Reasoning Index (PRI), Working Memory Index (WMI), and Processing Speed Index (PSI).

Full Scale IQ Score

VCI	PRI	WMI	PSI
(5 subtests)	(4 subtests)	(3 subtests)	(3 subtests)
Similarities	Block Design	Digit Span	Coding
Vocabulary	Picture Concepts	Letter-number Sequencing	Symbol Search
Comprehension	Matrix Reasoning	Arithmetic*	Cancellation
Information*	Picture Completion*	Word Reasoning*	

(*Supplemental subtests)

This test is one that is only administered by those with level-C training and can be used with children between the ages of 6 and 16. The test is well standardized and provides normative scales that can be used with both special education populations and with children without disabilities. School psychologists use the pattern of scores on the four indexes as well as observations of how the child performed the specific tasks on the subtests in forming diagnostic statements about the child's level of functioning and cognitive status (Sattler & Dumont, 2004). For example, major discrepancies (D >19) between scores on the language-based verbal scale (VCI) and the visual motor items of the performance index (PRI) are considered a significant diagnostic indicator.

The cognition of younger children (30 months to 7 years) can be assessed by the Wechsler Preschool and Primary Scales of Intelligence, third edition (WPPSI-III). There are two variations of this test, one for children between the ages of 30 months and 47 months of age, and one for children between the ages of 4 years and 7 years, 3 months. Test administrators must have level-C training and will need about an hour to administer and score the tests. Like the other IQ tests in the Wechsler line, the scoring and report writing can be facilitated by using a software program. The test was standardized on a national sample of 1,700 young children and has excellent reliability.

The **Wechsler Preschool and Primary Scales of Intelligence** is one of many individually administered measures designed and standardized to be used with young children. These measures all have inherent administration problems that are related to the normal behaviors of 3- and 4-year-old children.

Case in Point (12a)

There are many reasons why young children are difficult to test. First, young children have short attention spans and are easily distracted by elements in the environment. Long assessment protocols must be broken into several short testing sessions and may require several days to complete. Additionally, preschool children are more active and need to be physically involved in the measurement tasks. Because young children have limited expressive language, they are more likely to gesture or point than they are to verbally express answers. Most young children are shy and may be reluctant to work with an unfamiliar adult. It is not unusual for the child to need to be in visual or even physical contact with a parent during the evaluation. For that reason it is necessary for the evaluator to spend time prior to testing in a concerted effort to develop a working rapport with the young child and his or her caregiver. Also, young children need constant reinforcement for their work. Preschoolers have less emotional strength and may cry when faced with a difficult task. To avoid the possible intimidation that a visit to an office may provide, the child should be assessed in his or her home whenever possible.

For more information, see "Considerations on Point" at www.sagepub.com/wrightstudy

---

The test is designed to hold the attention of young children but provides for the possibility of taking breaks as needed. There are four possible scores that can be reported for younger children: (a) Verbal IQ (VIQ), which combines subtests of Information and Receptive Vocabulary; (b) Performance IQ (PIQ), which includes subtests of Block Design and Object Assembly; (c) General Language Composite, which is a combination of the subtests for Picture Naming and Receptive Vocabulary; and (d) a Full-Scale IQ (FSIQ). Children between the ages of 4 and 7 years have a VIQ score based on the same subtests as their younger peers with the addition of a Verbal Reasoning subtest. The performance score (PIQ) is based on subtests of Block Design, Matrix Reasoning, and Picture Concepts. A third score is the scale for Performance Speed Quotient (PSQ), which involves subtests for Coding and Symbol Search. The full-scale score (FSIQ) is a composite of these three factors: VIQ, PIQ, and the Coding subtest.

BOX 12.1   Core Subjects of the Wechsler Preschool and Primary Scale of Intelligence, Third Edition (WPPSI–III)

Core tests for children 30 to 47 months of age

- **Receptive Vocabulary:** Child is shown a series of 4 picture arrays and asked to point to the one the examiner names aloud
- **Block Design:** Child uses colored blocks to reproduce models of block arrangements
- **Information:** Child answers general knowledge questions verbally or by pointing to correct picture in an array
- **Object Assembly:** Child is asked to put puzzles together (timed test)

Core tests for children 48 to 85 months of age

- **Block Design & Information are the same tests from above with different starting points**
- **Matrix Reasoning:** Child is shown incomplete matrices and asked to pick the missing part from an array of 4 or 5 alternatives
- **Vocabulary:** Child provides verbal definitions to words spoken by the examiner
- **Picture Concepts:** Child selects one picture from two or three separate arrays that go together by sharing a common characteristic
- **Word Reasoning:** Given a series of clues, the child is asked to identify a common concept
- **Coding:** Child is asked to copy a series of symbols that are paired with simple shapes
- **Symbol Search:** Alternative to Coding. Child must find target symbol from an array of other symbols

Optional subtests for 48- to 85-month-old children

- **Receptive Vocabulary & Object Assembly are optional for 48-month-old children**
- **Comprehension:** Child is asked questions about social situations
- **Picture Completion:** Child must identify important missing part in pictures
- **Similarities:** Child must identify the shared characteristic when presented with two concepts in the form of an incomplete sentence
- **Picture Naming:** Child is asked to verbally name the objects shown in a picture book

---

SOURCE: Wechsler Preschool and Primary Scale of Intelligence, 3rd edition. Copyright 2002 by Harcourt Assessment, Inc. Reproduced with permission. All rights reserved.

The problem with this test is that the normative scales move in increments of 2 or 3 months. Testing children at an age equal to the end of an age band will make them appear brighter than if they were tested at an age near the start of an age band.

Woodcock–Johnson Tests

Another measure of mental ability used in the schools that is designed following the Cattell–Horn–Carroll model of human intelligence is the Woodcock–Johnson Tests of Cognitive Abilities, third edition (WJ III). As in the case of the Stanford–Binet, 5th ed., the WJ III can provide an assessment score for subjects between the ages of 2 and 90 years. The norms are based on a sample of almost 9,000 American and Canadian children and adults. In addition to the cognitive battery, the Woodcock–Johnson III provides a parallel, individually administered, achievement test, which makes psychoeducational diagnostic assessment very convenient for the school psychologist.

The WJ III provides the test administrator with the option of using a standard battery of 10 cognitive subtests or an extended battery of 20 subtests. The primary score report provides a highly reliable General Intellectual Ability (GAI) score based on a weighted summation of the subtests. In addition, the test provides three cognitive performance cluster scores (factor scores): Verbal Ability, Thinking Ability, and Cognitive Efficiency. Added to these three are another 10 cluster scores representing more specific cognitive dimensions. These include Comprehension–Knowledge, Long-Term Retrieval, Visual–Spatial Thinking, Auditory Processing, Fluid Reasoning, Processing Speed, Short-Term Memory, Phonemic Awareness, Working Memory, and Cognitive Fluency. Diagnostic decisions are possible from an analysis of the pattern of relative strengths and weakness shown on these cluster scores (Cizek, 2003).

Kaufman Tests

Perhaps the most user-friendly of all the individually administered tests of intelligence is the Kaufman Brief Intelligence Test, 2nd ed. (KBIT-2). This test can be administered by educational specialists such as guidance counselors or well-trained reading specialists. It is related to a more extensive measure, the Kaufman Adolescent and Adult Intelligence Test (KAIT). The KBIT-2 requires about a half an hour to administer and can provide intelligence scores for children as young as 4 years and adults as old as 90 (Miller, 1995). The normative sample included just over 2,000 children and adults. The test is best used as a screening measure for children and should not be considered as a substitute for one of the three tests described above (SB5, WISC IV, WJ III). Reliability of the scores from this test is high (rel. = .94) and the median standard error of the scores is relatively low (SE = 4). The test provides the user with three scores: vocabulary (verbal) subtest and matrix (nonverbal) subtest and a composite IQ score.

Slosson

Another test that provides a quick estimate of general cognitive ability is the Slosson Full-Range Intelligence Test (S-FRIT). This measure takes about an hour to administer and score and provides an overall, or full-range, IQ score and an estimate of the "g" factor (BgI) in intelligence. Five additional subtest scores are generated by the test: Verbal Index, Abstract Index, Quantitative Index, Memory Index, and a composite Performance Index. The test can be administered by users qualified at level B. It was normed on a population of 1,500 and designed for use with children as young as 5 and as old as 21 (Algozzine, Eaves, Mann, & Vance, 1988). The upper limit of 21 may not be realistic for highly verbal undergraduate students for whom a ceiling level often cannot be found. The test has reasonable levels of reliability but lacks a solid grounding in cognitive theory.

TESTS OF INTELLIGENCE ADMINISTERED TO GROUPS

During the 20th century, public schools routinely used group-administered IQ tests. The data from these tests were used to group and track children by mental ability. Most classrooms today are heterogeneous in terms of the ability of children. This has resulted in many fewer children being tested for IQ each year using a group test. Today, group-administered tests of mental ability are usually given along with standardized achievement tests. This paring makes it possible for the test publisher to provide a score report that not only provides achievement scores but also shows what achievement level was predicted by the IQ test. Discrepancies between the predicted level of achievement and the actual level from the test can be used to indicate problem areas for the child. Those who score lower in achievement than predicted are referred to as "underachievers," while those who do better than predicted are "overachievers." Once a child who has discrepant "Achievement to Aptitude" scores has been identified, the next step would normally involve the use of an individually administered test, such as the Wechsler Scale.

There are four group-administered IQ tests commonly used in the schools. Each of these tests has high internal consistency reliabilities and versions designed for the various grade levels from the primary grades through high school. While the composite scores exhibit high internal consistency reliability, their subtests tend to have more modest reliabilities in the 0.6 to 0.8 range. For this reason, caution must be exercised when interpreting the meaning of the subtest scores. Also of note is the fact that the most recent edition of each of these tests avoids describing itself as an IQ test. They are all designed to measure a general factor of ability related to success in school. The normative group for each of the tests is extensive, involving tens of thousands of subjects. All four of these tests can be scored by hand or by optical scanning.

Cognitive Ability Test

The first of these is the Cognitive Abilities Test, Form 5 (CogAT). This measure provides a composite score and three subtest scores: Verbal, Quantitative, and Nonverbal. The composite score is described as being a measure of general ability, or overall reasoning skill. The edition of the test designed for the upper grades is given over three 1-hour sessions. This test was developed to be paired with the Terra Nova achievement test. It can be used to determine if the scores a student earns on the various subtests of the Terra Nova battery are within a range that should be anticipated at the child's particular level of cognitive aptitude.

In 1999–2000, Riverside Publishing developed and restandardized a cognitive measure for use with the Terra Nova II achievement test. This new cognitive ability (scholastic aptitude) test is the InView. This measure provides five reasoning subtests: three verbal and two measures of quantitative reasoning. There are six levels to the test, covering the 1st through the 12th grades.

Kuhlmann–Anderson Test

The first edition of the Kuhlmann–Anderson Tests (KA) was published in 1927. The most recent edition was published in 1982. To keep the test fresh, a new normative group was established in 1997. This test provides scores that purport to represent the child's level of cognitive skill. The scores include a Cognitive Skill Quotient CSQ, along with Verbal and Nonverbal scores. The administration of this test requires about an hour and a quarter.

Otis–Lennon

Arthur S. Otis, a student of Lewis Terman, attended the meeting at the Vineland Training School in 1917 when the development of the first group-administered measure of mental ability, the Army Alpha, was developed (1918; see Chapter 2 for more on this history). His 1920 doctoral thesis was on the topic of multiple choice questions in the "absolute" measure of mental ability (Otis, 1925). The Beta form of the Army tests from 1917 were published as the first edition of this test in 1923 by World Book.

Out of this long history came the revised Otis–Lennon School Ability Test, 8th ed. (OLSAT 8). The eighth edition of this test was published in 2002. It has seven levels that cover grades kindergarten through the high school years. The OLSAT-8 requires an hour and a quarter to administer below the 4th grade and an hour to administer from the 4th to the 12th grade. It measures abstract thinking and reasoning ability. These are seen as components of "school ability." The test presents students with an array of 21 different item types, and scores that are derived from this test represent five clusters: Verbal Comprehension, Verbal Reasoning, Pictorial Reasoning, Figural Reasoning, and Quantitative Reasoning. The first two are used to create a composite score, Verbal, and the last three to produce Nonverbal. These two cluster scores are combined to provide the School Ability Index (SAI). How that differs from other measures of mental ability is not clear (DeStefano, 2001).

Test of Cognitive Skills

There are four subtests to the Test of Cognitive Skills, 2nd ed. (TCS/2). These include one scale of Verbal Reasoning, two of Nonverbal skills (Sequences and Analogies), and one of Memory. A composite Nonverbal scale is also reported with the scores of the TCS/2. The overall score from this measure is the Cognitive Skills Index (CSI). With the nonverbal subtests, this measure makes an effort to avoid using test items that are clearly linked to things that children learn in school. For this reason, the test may have a clearer link to innate ability than the other group-administered measures. The test requires about an hour to administer.

There is no such [thing] as intelligence; one has intelligence of this or that. One must have intelligence only for what one is doing.

—Edgar Degas

GROUP-ADMINISTERED APTITUDE TESTS

Intelligence and Success

A point worth noting is that IQ is an efficient method of measuring scholastic aptitude but little else. In the world of adulthood, success in a career has less to do with IQ and much more to do with a type of practical aptitudes that makes possible the facile acquisition of **tacit knowledge** (Sternberg, Wagner, Williams, & Horvath, 1995). Tacit knowledge is action oriented and purposeful; it is what makes it possible for the individual to be successful in a chosen enterprise or activity. The standard measures of IQ do not measure practical intelligence.

BOX 12.2   Sample Items Similar to Those of the TCS/2

The TCS/2 is composed of four tests, which include the following:[1]

- **Sequences:** Test 1 measures the ability to comprehend a rule or principle in a series of figures, letters, or numbers.

    Which of the following four figures does not belong with the others?

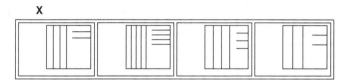

- **Analogies:** Test 2 measures the ability to discern various literal and symbolic relationships.

    Which word best completes the relationship?

    Listen is to Hear as Seek is to (A. Locate, B. Retrieve, C. Find, D. See)

- **Memory:** Test 3 measures the ability to recall previously presented pictorial materials or nonsense words.

Read the following short list of nonsense words and then cover them. Write as many from memory as you can.

ASI	NGI	NGF	ISH	SOU	NDE	DLI	KEA	BUS	KER

- **Verbal Reasoning:** Test 4 measures the ability to reason deductively, analyze categorical attributes, and discern relationships and patterns.

Three cars are parked next to each other. A sports coupe is to the right of a SUV and to the left of a sedan. If the sports coupe and the sedan change places, then which of the following is true?

- A. The SUV and the sports coupe are next to each other.
- *B. The sedan is parked between the SUV and the sports coupe.
- C. The SUV is immediately left of the sports coupe.
- D. The SUV is in the middle.

---

[1]Test items given above are similar to items of the TCS/2

For that reason, a number of tests of specific aptitude have been published. Some of these aptitude tests are very specific, defining a skill area and measuring the ability of individuals to acquire those skills. One problem with measures of a highly specialized dimension of aptitude is the difficulty in establishing the core construct that provides exacting parameters of the area being assessed. Without a clearly defined construct, it is almost impossible to demonstrate that the measure is either reliable or valid. The following is an example of this problem.

Accounting Aptitude Test
(Psychological Corporation, 1992)

This measure describes itself as being able to assess the aptitude of test takers for accounting careers. It consists of 60 multiple choice questions written to measure the test taker's communication, quantitative, and problem-solving skills. While purporting to measure a very specified area of aptitude, there is little evidence to support its claim to be a valid and reliable measure of this dimension (Carlson, 1998).

Another problem with highly specific **aptitude measures** is the tendency to combine far too many dimensions into a single measure. This may occur when the construct for the aptitude is not focused and sharply defined. An example of this issue is the following test.

Revised PSB Health Occupations Aptitude
Examination (Psychological Service Bureau, 1992)

This test purports to be a measure of a student's (a) abilities, (b) skills, (c) knowledge, and (d) attitudes. This measure provides scores in eight areas, including four measures of aptitude: Verbal Aptitude, Numerical Aptitude, Nonverbal Aptitude, and Total Aptitude. Also scores are provided of Reading Comprehension, Information in the Natural Sciences, and a Vocational Adjustment Index. The last score for vocational adjustment is an undefined construct measured by presenting the test taker with 90 statements and asking if the subject agrees with each of them. There are eight attitudes that this section was designed to measure, such as "Attitude Toward Authority."

While all very interesting, there is no theoretical model provided by the team of authors to explain how these questions and opinion items fit together and define aptitude for the health professions (Bergstrom, 1998).

Overall, the test is reliable, with coefficients well up in the 0.90s. So, whatever is being measured is stable and consistent.

Specific areas of aptitude can be measured by instruments that do not fall into this trap of not developing a well-focused and clearly defined construct. An example of that is found in the following test.

Musical Aptitude Profile [1995 Revision] (Gordon, 1995)

This well-known measure is a battery of seven aptitude measures. This complex test combines paper-and-pencil questions with information presented as sounds on an accompanying CD. The test provides two measures of Tonal Imagery (Melody and Harmony), two of Rhythm Imagery (Tempo and Meter), and Musical Sensitivity is measured by the final three (Phrasing, Balance, and Style). The test's reliability is marginal, with most coefficients falling around 0.80. Its validity comes from the consensus of musicians that the seven areas that are measured are at the core of music aptitude.

Other aptitude tests are more generalized. These tests are typically employed as part of a vocational guidance program. The pattern of high and low scores a student earns on these subtests is then used to match him or her to the profile that is required for various fields or occupations.

Detroit Tests of Learning Aptitude, 4th Ed. (DTLA-4)

This test is designed for use with children between the ages of 6 and 18 (Hammill, 1998). The battery provides 10 measurements: Word Opposites, Design Sequence, Sentence Imitation, Reversed Letters, Story Construction, Design Reproduction, Basic Information, Symbolic Relations, Word Sequences, and Story Sequences. From these 10 subtests the author has organized 16 composite scores, which are an amalgam of several subtests. These include titles such as Performance Scale and an Action-Enhanced Scale. In reality there are only 14 unique combinations that are provided by this test. Two are redundant (Smith, 2001). The Detroit Tests are an elaborated test of mental ability. The various measures in the battery can play a role in cognitive research and could also be used in the selection and placement of children in a special program. To do the latter task would require that much data be collected and local standards established before the DTLA-4 is used in selection.

Differential Aptitude Test, 5th Edition (DAT-5)

This aptitude test is designed to use with adolescent-aged children (Bennett, Seashore, & Wesman, 1992). One form is written for the 7th through 9th grades and a second version for students between the 10th and 12th grades. This aptitude battery measures Verbal, Numerical, and Abstract Reasoning; Perceptual Speed and Accuracy; Mechanical Reasoning; Space Relations; Spelling; and Language Usage. There is also a total Scholastic Aptitude score. This test has found use as a measure that can assist in the guidance of adolescent children who are making vocational and educational choices. It is also employed as a measure for placing students into career academies and technology education programs.

Armed Services Vocational Aptitude Battery (ASVAB)

More young people take the ASVAB each year than any other aptitude test (U.S. Military Entrance Processing Command, 1968, 1992). It is administered online (CAT-ASVAB) and also at locations such as high schools and National Guard auditoriums (MET-ASVAB). There is also an ASVAB that has been designed for integration into a career guidance program.

The military is the largest educational institution in the country. The armed services offer thousands of training programs, many involving high technology and complex equipment. These programs range from Diesel-Powered Field Generator Maintenance and Repair to Optical Telemetry and Instrument Landing System Technical Supervisor. Military recruits are allowed to select areas for training and are assigned to the programs on the basis of test score profiles from the ASVAB. The battery includes subtests of General Science (GS), Arithmetic Reasoning (AR), Word Knowledge (WK), Paragraph Content (PC), Mathematics Knowledge (MK), Electronics Infusion (EI), Auto and Shop Information (AS), Mechanical Comprehension (MC), and Assembling Objects (AO).

ASSESSMENT OF TALENTED AND GIFTED CHILDREN

Talent Identification

Shortly after World War II the United States was locked in a cold war with the Soviet Union. One outcome of this was a national sense of crisis and urgency. This was reflected in the federal budget, which provided a great

BOX 12.3   Armed Services Vocational Aptitude Battery

Subtests

Subtests	Minutes	Questions	Description
General Science	11	25	Measures knowledge of physical and biological sciences
Arithmetic Reasoning	36	30	Measures ability to solve arithmetic word problems
Word Knowledge	11	35	Measures ability to select the correct meaning of words presented in context, and identify synonyms
Paragraph Comprehension	13	15	Measures ability to obtain information from written material
Auto and Shop Information	11	25	Measures knowledge of automobiles, tools, and shop terminology and practices
Mathematics Knowledge	24	25	Measures knowledge of high school mathematics principles
Mechanical Comprehension	19	25	Measures knowledge of mechanical and physical principles, and ability to visualize how illustrated objects work
Electronics Information	9	20	Tests knowledge of electricity and electronics

Sample Items

1. Which of the following organisms contain chlorophyll?
    A. Viruses
    B. Fungi
    C. Bacteria
    D. Blue-green algae

2. Kangaroos are best classified as
    A. carnivores.
    B. primates.
    C. marsupials.
    D. ungulates.

3. Bryophytes
    A. make seeds.
    B. are nonvascular.
    C. produce wood.
    D. have roots.

(Continued)

BOX 12.3 (Continued)

4. The best synonym for **endeavor** is
   A. exertion.
   B. recovery.
   C. extremity.
   D. preparation.

5. The best synonym for **confirm** is
   A. verify.
   B. stand up to.
   C. imprison.
   D. baptize.

6. By 1700, two colleges had been founded in the colonies: Harvard, and William and Mary. Other cultural activities before 1700 were limited. The few writings of the colonists, mostly historical narratives, journals, sermons, and some poetry, were printed in England.

   The colonists' attempts at creative writing

   A. were printed in New England.
   B. included novels and spy stories.
   C. were sometimes written by priests or ministers.
   D. were mostly written in colleges.

7. Ralph walks from his home to the bank, which is two miles, from the bank to the pizza parlor, which is one mile, and then from the pizza parlor back home, which is two miles. What is the total length of Ralph's trip?
   A. 2 miles
   B. 3 miles
   C. 4 miles
   D. 5 miles

8. A soccer team has 11 players and 33 oranges. How many oranges will each player receive?
   A. 3
   B. 2
   C. 4
   D. 1

9. John can run six miles per hour and Bill can run four miles per hour. If they run in opposite directions for two hours, then how far apart will they be?
   A. 20 miles
   B. 10 miles
   C. 12 miles
   D. 8 miles

10. Sam had $10 and bought lunch for $4.99. How much did he have left?
    A. 5
    B. 4.99
    C. 5.99
    D. 5.01

Full practice test available from www.military.com/Millitary/ASVAB/AsvabTest?test_type=long

SOURCE: United States Military.

increase in the funding for programs in science education through the subventions of the National Science Foundation (NSF). These NSF grants went to schools and colleges for science equipment purchases, major curricular revisions, and for increased statewide testing programs. During the 1990s and into the era of the No Child Left Behind legislation, school programs for gifted children have waned. By 2007, pressure by parent groups was starting to reverse this trend (Samuels, 2007). Parental concern is that schools faced with limited resources and a mandate to bring every child to a minimum level of proficiency are not teaching higher-order thinking skills and are leaving academically gifted children behind (Goodkin & Gold, 2007). The research consensus is that gifted children learn the most when educated together in advanced classes (McClure, 2007).

The proportion of African American and Hispanic children who are enrolled in public school programs for the gifted is far lower than what should be expected in terms of population demographic statistics. This fact is true even when the test score gap is taken in account as part of the analysis. This anomaly reflects the fact that schools that enroll many minority students are not as well funded and cannot afford to support gifted education programs compared to the schools that enroll a mostly White student body (Lee & Fox, 2007).

One theme of the era was the need to identify our best and brightest students and provide them with improved access to advanced programs and support for their college educations. International pressure created by the "space race" made the identification of our most talented young people a priority. This focus on our brightest and most creative students was reminiscent of the concept of an academic meritocracy as envisioned by Lewis M. Terman. During the cold war era it was seen as a patriotic endeavor designed to keep America strong.

Case in Point (12b)

The first large-scale study of gifted children was initiated by Lewis M. Terman at Stanford University in1921, with a study of almost 1,500 California children with measured IQ scores of 140 or more. This longitudinal study lasted for the ensuing 80 years and provides a treasure trove of data on the lives of White, middle-class children as they grew, matured, and aged.

Terman's sample children were 11 years old when his landmark study began. As a group, they were well adjusted, happy, and otherwise quite normal.

For more information, see "Considerations on Point" at www.sagepub.com/wrightstudy

Case in Point (12b) (Continued)

The public schools of San Francisco and Los Angeles provided the sample in 1921. The children were all nominated by their teachers and were tested by one of Terman's evaluators. Once identified, these children began referring to themselves as the "Termites." This type of humor is another characteristic of the group. For the most part, they all possessed a well-developed and healthy sense of self-concept, which could often be seen through their humor.

Most of them were born in 1910 and lived through two world wars, the cold war, and many lived to see the liberation of Europe from communism. For the most part they had greater longevity than their peers and achieved more success in life during their adult years than did others. An unusually high total of 46% of the male sample became professionals with graduate-level degrees, and another 41% were managers and business executives. The girls in the sample as adult women were clearly ahead of their time. These women become leaders in a number of fields, including education (Shurkin, 1992). As adults the sample was productive and successful, but none of the 1,528 produced what would be considered a work of great genius. Thus, while many were physicians, professors, and lawyers, none were a Mozart or Newton.

Today, the researchers at the University of California, Riverside, are still collecting data from the sample to study the processes of successful aging. In an effort to study the pattern and causes of death among these people, death certificates are also being collected and analyzed.

In 1960, two parallel testing programs were initiated on the national level. One of these 1960 studies, Project Talent, involved the testing of over 400,000 secondary-school students. This large-scale testing effort was established to inventory the amount and the quality of academic talent coming up through our schools. The researchers were also interested in identifying the source of academic motivation among American students (Flanagan et al., 1962). From this sample of 400,000, a follow-up survey study of a random selection of 1,000 boys and girls from each class between 1960 and 1963 was conducted. This study lasted for 11 years after those students graduated high school. To date, there have been over 300 educational research reports, books, and dissertations based on analyses of these data.

For more information, see "Considerations on Point" at www.sagepub.com/wrightstudy

Case in Point (12c)

A leader in the search for the most talented of America's youth was Julian Stanley (1918–2005) of Johns Hopkins University. Professor Stanley pioneered the development of gifted programs and developed specialized programs that were offered on the Hopkins campus during the summers for extremely gifted adolescents. These students were identified by nomination and then by scoring well on the SAT I during their middle-school years. The use of the SAT with seventh-grade children seems a bit of a stretch, but many of his children did exceptionally well on this admission test, which is normally reserved for students 4 or 5 years older. Admission into the seventh-grade summer program required that students score over 1100 on the SAT I. After Dr. Stanley's death, the Center for Talented Youth at Hopkins renamed the project the Julian C. Stanley Study of Exceptional Talent. Today, over 200,000 young people around the world are participating in programs for those with exceptional talent. Most of these programs are conducted on the campus of well-known universities. The application process for the program at Johns Hopkins is available online at www.jhu.edu/gifted/.

Merit Scholars

The second effort to identify and encourage America's most talented youth is the **Merit Scholars** Program. The National Merit Scholarship Corporation began in 1954 as a way for businesses to contribute to the education of America's most gifted youth. The first Scholar Qualifying Test was administered in 1955 to more than 58,000 high school seniors. This test was developed by ETS for use by various scholarship-granting organizations. In 1958, the organization contracted Science Research Associates to build the National Merit Scholarship Qualifying Test (NMSQT). In 1971, the NMSQT was combined with the Preliminary Scholastic Aptitude Test (PSAT), another publication of ETS (Gloria Davis, of the National Merit Scholarship Corporation, personal communication, February 3, 2005).

Today, over 1 million students in the 9th through the 12th grades are tested as a part of this program. Of these, the 50,000 who have the highest combined scores (critical reading plus math plus writing skills) will qualify for recognition by the National Merit Scholars Program. Most American colleges boast the number of such students who attend their undergraduate schools. Of these students, only 8,500 will be selected to receive a one-time grant of $2,500 from the foundation. A number will also receive corporate-sponsored scholarships. In addition, a number of universities have set up sponsored scholarship for these young scholars. These finalists are selected on the basis of test scores, school grades, recommendations, and documented accomplishments (National Merit Scholarship Program, 2004).

The reliance on test scores and the disproportionate number of awards that go to high-scoring White and Asian males has prompted concern with the fairness of the NMSQT program. During the summer of 2005, the University of California system dropped its connection with the NMSQT program, citing these group differences as the reason for their decision.

Creativity and Its Measurement

In each generation there is only a handful of people who redefine or set a new standard for our arts or sciences. These are the people who can break the molds and patterns of the past and produce new ideas and create new systems that the rest of us enjoy and use.

The early identification and nurturing of creative children is not a recent idea. Twenty-six centuries ago, precocious children in ancient China were brought to Beijing to the court of the emperor, where they were raised and educated. During the European renaissance, and extending until the 19th century, gifted boys were apprenticed to master craftsmen where they used their talents and honed their skills. Perhaps the first written observations on creativity are found in the writings of the 18th-century clergyman William Duff, who in a 1767 text on the nature of genius wrote, "Genius is characterized by a copious and plastic, as well as a vivid and extensive, imagination, by which means it is equally qualified to invent and create, or to conceive and describe in the most lively manner the objects it contemplates . . ." (Duff, 1767, p. 48). Highly talented young musicians were toured and displayed in the courts of baroque-era monarchs as though they were some new species. The point that Duff did not understand is that the two dimensions of human intellect, mental ability and creativity, are not the same.

In the 19th century, Galton systematically studied those who were eminent, and at the start of the 20th century, Terman researched the lives of those with high IQs. It wasn't until the 1950s that psychologists began formal psychometric research into the nature of those who are highly creative.

Theories

Multiple-factor theorists including Guilford, Gardner, and Sternberg have all addressed the question of creativity, and all have theorized that it is a part of the intellect. Yet, this is one product of human intelligence that does not correlate well with IQ. A correlation scatterplot of the relationship between intelligence and creativity is best described as being pear shaped. The term used to describe this type of correlation between these two variables is **heteroscedastic**. At low levels of IQ, the correlation between IQ and creativity is high, and at high IQ levels (IQ >120) the correlation between IQ and creativity disappears. This disparity between the two dimensions at the upper level of mental ability explains why the highly intelligent children who participated in Lewis M. Terman's longitudinal study were academically successful, but none ever exhibited an extraordinary level of creativity (see Figure 12.1).

Characteristics

We know that highly creative children tend to be brighter than average. Other characteristics of these children are that they are open-minded, curious, humorous, highly original, risk takers, independent, and attracted by complexity (Colangelo & Davis, 1997). Unhappily, they may also be rebellious, forgetful, tactless, argumentative, egocentric, and lacking in social grace.

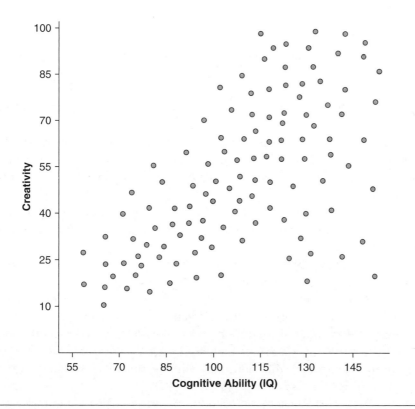

Figure 12.1   Scatter plot for the Correlation Between Cognitive Ability and Creativity $r \cong .25$

In a classic study of intelligence and creativity, Wallach and Kogan (1965) divided school-age children into four groups and found that elementary school teachers had the most difficulty when faced with children who were both high in intelligence and very creative and enjoyed teaching children who were highly intelligent but low in creativity. Guilford (1975) observed that creative children ask many challenging questions and their work is frequently off the beaten track. Parents of highly creative children have often complained that the schools are too structured and stifle the creative spirit of their children. E. Paul Torrance and his colleagues proposed a set of teaching strategies to encourage and nurture the creative ability of all school children (Torrance, Goff, & Satterfield, 1998; Torrance & Myers, 1970). One primary tenet of Torrance's approach to teaching is to do away with the evaluation of creative products from children. His approach is one of accepting and encouraging creative productions and withholding critical evaluations.

Connectionism

There are a number of conceptualizations of creativity that are linked to a measurement model. One theory is based on a connectionist view of creative ability. This approach assumes that the more neural connections a person has, the greater will be the range of responses available when faced with novel stimuli. An early test for this model was developed by Sarnoff A. Mednick (1962). This test provides questions that are simply composed of three words that appear to be unrelated. The creative person is assumed to be able to find one word that provides a common connection to the three stimulus words.

To take another version of a test of creativity built on a connectionist model, see http://enchantedmind.com/html/creativity/iq_tests/creativity_test.html.

Joy P. Guilford (1988) constructed a model of the human intellect, structure of the intellect (SI), that included a dimension of intellectual operation he named "divergent production." When this dimension is divided into six different types of products and five different contents, the result is a total of 30 distinct factors of the intellect that are related to creative thinking. Guilford assumed that creative thinking involved being able to see beyond the obvious, providing the individual with the ability to invent numerous solutions or responses to stimuli (Mayer, 1999).

This type of thinking is contrasted to **convergent production**, in which the mental tasks involve finding one correct answer. Most assessments in school involve convergent production. This distinction between the two

---

BOX 12.4   Remote Associates Test–Type Questions

1.	blue	cake	sharp	*cheese*
2.	ball	rabbit	athlete's	*foot*
3.	tiger	doll	news	*paper*
4.	spelling	busy	line	*bee*
5.	luck	liquor	wood	*hard*
6.	biscuit	deep	foam	*sea*
7.	fortune	chocolate	jar	*cookie*
8.	ink	neck	herring	*red*
9.	chair	note	dive	*high*
10.	quick	spoon	coin	*silver*

---

dimensions, divergent and convergent production, may explain why highly creative individuals don't test at high levels on standardized measures. To demonstrate and elaborate these factors, Guilford created a number of different measures that assessed the ability of the subject to break the usual frame and see alternative solutions to various problems.

A variation of these "thinking out of the box" tasks has been used by arithmetic teachers for many years. These tasks require the child to think of various permutations of the elements of a word problem. For example, here are several "pouring water" problems:

Given an empty jug with a capacity of 21 pints, another vessel with a capacity of 127 pints, and a third jar with a capacity of 3 pints, you are requested to obtain a total of exactly 100 pints of water.

In this problem the student must see that by filling the 127-pint vessel there would be 27 excess pints of water. By removing 21 pints from the large vessel using the 21 pint jug, there would be only 106 pints left in the vessel. Next, by using the 3-pint jar (two times) the final excess 6 pints can be removed. This would leave 100 pints in the large vessel.

Torrance Tests

These factors of divergent production first identified by Guilford were the basis of a test of creative thinking by E. Paul Torrance. The factors central

BOX 12.5   Items From the "Match Problems Test"

In this test you will see drawings of headless matches laid out in patterns. You are to remove some of the matches so that the ones left form new patterns.

Look at this example:

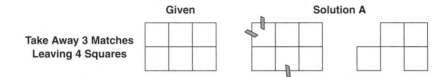

Take Away 3 Matches
Leaving 4 Squares

Your instructions for each item appear at the left. The drawing under "Given" presents the pattern of squares with which you start. To indicate a solution, mark through the matches you want removed. In the example, the solution marked would look like the pattern at the extreme right if the matches were actually removed. Note that only complete squares are left.

The attempt below is <u>not</u> an acceptable solution.

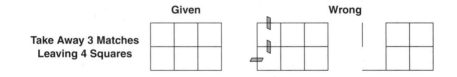

Take Away 3 Matches
Leaving 4 Squares

This attempt is wrong because it leaves two matches that are <u>not</u> parts of the required four squares. You must remove matches so that exactly the required number of complete squares remain, with no matches left over.

Now Try the Next Two

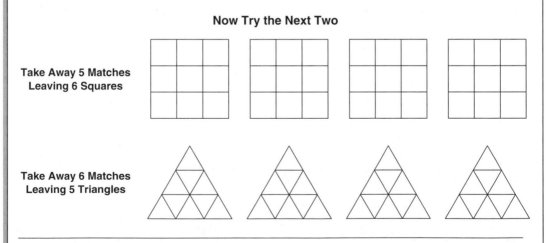

Take Away 5 Matches
Leaving 6 Squares

Take Away 6 Matches
Leaving 5 Triangles

SOURCE: From *Match Problems Test,* by R. M. Berger and J. P. Guilford, 1963, Beverly Hills, CA: Sheridan. Reprinted with permission from Raymond M. Berger.

to this test include "fluency," the number of original and useful ideas that a person can develop; "flexibility," the number of categories or different approaches that the new ideas represent; "originality," which expresses whether the productive new ideas are highly original, or even unique vs. quotidian and pedestrian; and "elaboration," which describes a degree of detail and completeness to the creative ideas and products. The Torrance tests provide measures of both "figural" and "verbal" levels of creativity (Torrance, 1966). These tests are reasonably reliable and have demonstrated good levels of concurrent validity (Treffinger, 1985).

Creative Assessment Packet

Similar to the Torrance Tests, the Creativity Assessment Packet (CAP) provides scores in the four dimensions of divergent thinking, reported as Fluency, Flexibility, Originality, Elaboration, and a fifth score purported to measure the originality of picture titles created by the test taker (Williams, 1986). It also reports scores on a Test of Divergent Feeling, including scores for Curiosity,

---

BOX 12.6   Torrance Tests of Creativity

Scoring Model

Verbal Tests

- Fluency: Ability to produce a large number of ideas expressed with words
- Originality: Ability to produce ideas that are not ordinary, banal, or already established
- Flexibility: Ability to produce a wide array of ideas, shifting context and approach as they arise

Figural Tests

- Fluency: Ability to produce many relevant responses to stimuli problem
- Originality: Unusualness of responses based on statistical norms. Thinking "out of the box" is given credit
- Abstractness of Titles: Ability to synthesize and organize thinking to capture the essence of the product
- Elaboration: Ability to express creative imagination through the exposition of detail
- Resistances to Picture Closure: Ability to resist the temptation of leaping to an immediate conclusion; keeping the task open long enough to make a creative mental leap in the service of producing a new product

SOURCE: Adapted from *Torrance Tests of Creativity*, by E. P. Torrance, 1966, 2000, Bensenville, IL: Scholastic Testing Services. See also Torrance, Safter, & Ball, 1992.

BOX 12.7   Two Forms of the Torrance Tests: Picture Completion and Product Improvement

Verbal

We are all familiar with 2-liter plastic bottles used to contain the many varieties of soda. What are some other uses for these plastic bottles? Do not limit your thinking to common uses, but try to find unusual uses for the bottles.

Highly Creative Answers

- Put straps on two and use them as floaters
- Fill with sand and use for weight training
- Cut the bottom and use as a funnel
- Punch holes and jam sticks in it and use as a bird feeder
- Tie a weight to it on a long rope and use as a marker float for a boat
- Freeze water in it and use it to cool a picnic ice chest

Low Creative Answers

- Use as a flower vase
- Use to store water
- Cut the top and fill with potting soil and plant a flower
- Cut the top and store pencils and pens in it

Figural

Complete the partial drawing shown below. Try to think of a picture that others will not draw. Then make up a clever title for your drawing.

Complete This Drawing   High Creative   Low Creative

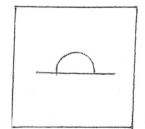  

 Title

SOURCE: Adapted from *Torrance Tests of Creativity*, by E. P. Torrance, 1966, 2000, Bensenville, IL: Scholastic Testing Services.

Imagination, Complexity, and Risk Taking. The two scales and a parent–teacher questionnaire have been sharply criticized as lacking a clear theoretical perspective and having low reliability (Damarin, 1985; Rosen, 1985).

ASSESSMENT OF APTITUDE FOR COLLEGE STUDY

First College Boards

The idea of a selective admissions procedure for higher education, based in part on aptitude test scores, is a product of the 20th century. The College Entrance Examination Board tests were initiated in 1901 by the admissions officers of a dozen colleges who formed the first Board. That examination program used essay-type items and was initially administered to 8,000 high school and preparatory school seniors.

To see a few items from the first College Board Examination, see www.pbs.org/wgbh/pages/frontline/shows/sats/where/1901.html.

Many of the questions from that first examination would be classified as performance items today. Tasks such as translating paragraphs and writing essays required much effort and time on the part of those taking the test and an enormous investment of time by those grading the tests. In 1926, Carl Brigham, the admissions dean at Princeton University, developed the Scholastic Aptitude Test, which was designed using items similar to the World War I Army Alpha and Beta intelligence tests. Dean Brigham had worked as an Army examiner during World War I and saw the multiple choice format of the Army tests as an efficient admissions assessment system.

Over the years there were over 20 different standardized scoring systems used with the SAT. The establishment of the SAT I and the centering (norming) of the test in 1941 led to the familiar score-reporting model still used today. All the SAT tests administered prior to 1941 were normed on only that year's applicant pool. The applicants of 1941 established a base against which all subsequent students over the decades were compared.

Harvard Scholarships

In 1933, the new president of Harvard University, James Bryant Conant, had his admissions dean, Henry Chauncey, develop a national scholarship program for Harvard. To do this, Chauncey selected the SAT as the required measure for all applying for the **Harvard scholarships**. This scholarship program made Harvard a national university and provided an educational opportunity for young men throughout the United States.[1] At the same time, Reynold Johnson, a laid-off science teacher, invented a machine that could read lead pencil marks on a page and sold the system to IBM (Lemann, 1999).[2] Testing using the new IBM system became greatly refined during World War II. This was done by the U.S. military, who selected the College Board as the agency to test hundreds of thousands of White male American high school seniors. The Army and Navy were looking for the best and the brightest young White men for officer candidacy education, which was being conducted on campuses throughout the nation. This test, the Army–Navy Qualifying Test, became the true precursor of the modern SAT I.[3]

Educational Testing Service

The labor-intensive task of grading essay examinations was dropped from all tests of the College Entrance Examination Board in 1941. After the war (1948), a new corporation was chartered, the Educational Testing Service (ETS), with Henry Chauncey as its first president and James Bryant Conant as its first board chairman.

In 1941, the results from the multiple choice items that a sample of 10,000 students answered became the standard and norm reference for the SAT.[4] This centering process set the mean of each half of the SAT (verbal, math) at 500 and gave it a standard deviation of 100. The inappropriateness of that norm became more evident over the years. The original sample was made up of mostly upper-middle-class and middle-class male students who were planning to attend elite East Coast colleges.

Recentering the SAT

By 1990, the combined mean of the SAT had drifted to about 900 instead of the original 1000. Education critics blamed the slide on teachers and American schools (Berliner & Biddle, 1995). Yet, during the 49 years between when the test was first centered (1941) and 1990, the population of test takers changed dramatically (see Table 12.1). Many more students from minority groups and students from impoverished homes began taking the SAT. Naturally, there was a decline in the aggraded score over the years. Yet, when the scores from the SAT are presented by class rank, they have been steady over the past few decades.[5] In 1990, the SAT I was **recentered** and a new normative comparison group established (Dorans, 2002).

Table 12.1   Percentage of Students Taking the SAT, by Class Rank

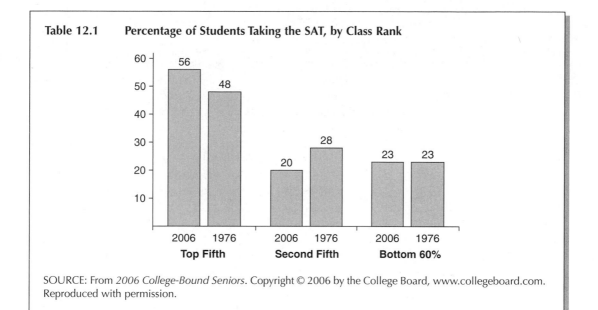

SAT II

In 2005, the test was changed again, doing away with the old section on vocabulary and analogies and creating a new test of critical reading. The mathematics section added more advanced questions from the curriculum of algebra II and geometry. An essay test, critical writing, was also added. This performance-type essay test is read online by professional teachers from across the United States. To learn more about this system, see, www.flexible scoring-SAT.pearson.com.

The new test has three scores, each of which has a mean of 500 and standard deviations of 100. Thus, the aggregated mean of the SAT II is 1500 and the standard deviation is 300. The new three-part examination requires 3¾ hours to complete. This is longer when breaks are counted into the test.[6] Despite these differences, the new SAT II has very similar measurement properties to the SAT I (Oh & Sathy, 2007).

Robert Sternberg, dean of the School of Arts and Sciences at Tufts University, has expressed concern that admissions based primarily on scores from the SAT II do not identify students with practical thinking skills who are able to apply knowledge and demonstrate wisdom (Sternberg, 2007).

For more
information, see
"Considerations on
Point" at
www.sagepub.com/
wrightstudy

Case in Point (12d)

Before the new SAT II was introduced ETS supported several studies on its potential impact on test takers. A concern of the test developers was the likelihood of mental and/or physical fatigue on the part of test takers. One study sponsored by the College Entrance Examination Board demonstrated that while mental fatigue is possible with the greater length of the new test, it would not alter test-taker performance (Liu, Allspach, Feigenbaum, Oh, & Burton, 2004). After a year of experience with the new SAT II there was clear evidence of a small but nonetheless noticeable decline in scores (Pope, 2006). It is likely that the SAT II will be modified again after 2008 if this trend persists.

American College Testing Program (ACT)

During the 1930s, one of the people that Chauncey attempted to hire for the College Boards was E. F. Lindquist, a professor at the University of Iowa. Lindquist elected to stay at Iowa, where he developed the Iowa Every-Pupil Testing Program, which later evolved into the Iowa Tests of Basic Skills (ITBS). In 1959, he was a cofounder of the American College Testing Program (ACT), the largest competitor in the college admissions testing market for ETS.

Lindquist held a very different point of view about admissions tests. He felt that tests should not be employed to skim the cream off the top of a distribution of college applicants; rather, he believed that tests should help students plan and prepare for college (Popham, 2006). He did not have a vision of admissions testing producing meritocracies on the nation's campuses; his test was designed to serve a guidance function.

The ACT tests are curriculum-based measures of the skills and knowledge base needed by college students across four academic areas: English, mathematics, reading, and science reasoning (ACT, 1997). The ACT is taken by about as many students each year as the SAT and is the dominant college admissions test in 28 states (Midwest and South). In 2005, the ACT added an optional writing test. This brings the two measures, ACT and SAT, closer together in terms of structure than ever before. That observation not withstanding, there is still a philosophical divide between them. The structure of the ACT as a measure of academic skills has led to its adoption by several state departments of education as the required high school exit examination.

Six states have begun to use the ACT as a mandated graduation test. This use of college admission tests has been criticized as potentially limiting the standard high school curricula and thereby working against the level of preparation that students have for college (Cohen, 2007).

Figure 12.2   Daily Schedule of Kindergarten

SOURCE: The New Yorker Collection. Copyright 1998 by Barbara Smaller. From cartoonbank.com. All rights reserved.

Case in Point (12e)

Guidance counselors in high schools in the Northeast, upper Midwest, and on the West Coast have often suggested that students take the ACT along with the SAT II. This reflects a belief by guidance counselors that the normative comparison used by the SAT is more competitive than the norm group used by the ACT. This opinion is based on the higher average scores on the NAEP from states in the Northeast, upper Midwest, and West Coast and lower scores in the southern, southwestern, and central midwestern states. Most colleges accept either test in the admissions decision process, and students can elect to have their best-looking test score forwarded to the college admission office.

For more information, see "Considerations on Point" at www.sagepub.com/wrightstudy

Summary

The ability of a person to acquire a new skill or learn something new is facilitated by having an aptitude for that area. One of the most researched of all aptitudes is that related to learning in school: scholastic aptitude. A generalized form of scholastic aptitude is what is measured by most tests of cognitive ability. From the time the first achievement test was published by World Book, and continuing to today, educators have looked at any clear differences between achievement scores and the measured level of aptitude as being a diagnostic indicator.

Measures of intelligence are useful in estimating achievement outcomes; therefore, by definition, intelligence tests are measures of scholastic aptitude. These measures have little relationship with success in the adult world beyond school.

The largest measurement efforts to determine the ability of young people to learn new subjects and topics are the SAT II and the ACT. These two examinations are taken by over 2 million students a year. The SAT II started life as a pure scholastic aptitude measure, while the ACT has been more of an achievement test. Yet, as both are correlated with academic success, both are classifiable as measures of learning aptitude in college.

To measure aptitude in areas beyond the classroom, single-dimensional measures of aptitude can be constructed. These one-dimensional tests are published for a wide range of skill areas and professions. One problem encountered in the construction of these aptitude measures is the vague definition of the construct being measured.

It is also possible to construct aptitude tests that provide general information on several areas of aptitude, which when viewed in combination with each other can be used to assist in vocational guidance and placement. One of these aptitude batteries is used by the U.S. military to test all new recruits.

The measurement of talent and ability has also been addressed through the development of national surveys and tests. Another dimension of talent that has seen tests developed for its identification is creativity.

Discussion Questions

1. The discrepancy between aptitude (or intelligence) and measured achievement has been studied since the 1920s. The focus of educators is on those students with achievement levels below what their

aptitude would indicate (underachievers). Statistically, there are an equal number of students who achieve above their aptitude level (overachievers). What are the implications for curriculum developers for these two groups?

2. Regarding the two groups described in Question 1, in what way could these two groups affect the results of a school's scores on the state's high-stakes tests?

3. E. F. Lindquist was a major force behind the ITBS and also the ACT program. How are these two measures different from their competitors? Is there a common thread that connects these two products of Lindquist's work?

4. Assume that the mandated statewide assessments are measures of achievement in select subject areas. Consider the fact that aptitude is highly related to the achievement scores of all students. What are the implications of these two points in terms of a logical and appropriate testing policy? Consider the policy of grade retention based on achievement test scores: How does that policy affect children with lower levels of cognitive ability?

5. What is the relationship between creativity and other areas of aptitude?

6. Design several "pouring water" tasks that can be used to help students to "think outside the box."

7. Of all the various theories of human intelligence, which one provides the best explanation for differences in adult productivity? Explain why you chose that model.

Student Study Site

Educational Assessment on the Web

Log on to the Web-based student study site at www.sagepub.com/ wrightstudy for additional Web sources and study resources.

NOTES

1. Harvard became a coeducational institution in 1943 when some undergraduate women from Radcliff College were allowed to attend classes at Harvard College.

2. Johnson went on to become an employee of IBM. Later he was the inventor of the magnetic disk drive and videotape. President Reagan presented him with the Medal of Technology in 1986.

3. The U.S. military was a segregated organization until an executive order of President Harry S. Truman (Executive order No. 9981) was issued in 1948.

4. The name SAT once stood for "Scholastic Aptitude Test." That moniker was changed to Scholastic Assessment Test in 1990. The redundancy of an "assessment test" resulted in another change in 1994, when the name was reduced to just the former acronym, SAT. In the spring of 2005, the test changed again and added a section on critical writing, becoming the SAT II Reasoning Test.

5. Over the years the SAT has been demonstrated to be a valid instrument that is appropriate for making college admissions decisions for all populations of high school students, even linguistic minorities (Zwick & Schlemer, 2004).

6. The SAT II has nine parts, three of which are multiple choice questions of critical reading. Three other sections are subtests measuring mathematics and two parts measure writing. The ninth section consists of items that are being standardized for use on a future edition of the SAT II (Wang, 2007). Research by ETS has demonstrated that the 3.75 hours that the test actually requires does not have an impact on test scores. This finding is problematic in that the SAT II average scores fell in 2006–2007.

Chapter 13

IDENTIFICATION OF LEARNING PROBLEMS

It was once said that the moral test of government is how that government treats those who are in . . . the shadows of life, the sick, the needy and the handicapped.

—Hubert H. Humphrey

Issues and Themes

There never was a time when so many children with disabilities were attending public schools as there is now. One out of every 12 children and youth between the ages of 5 and 20 has been diagnosed with a serious mental or **physical disability**. Clearly, the schools have an important role to play in the identification and education of these children.

During the 1970s, the federal government assumed a proactive stance regarding the education of children with disabilities. This position was fostered by the outcome of federal court challenges initiated by parents and advocates for students with disabilities. The first federal legislation to address the needs of children with disabilities was section 504 of the Rehabilitation Act of 1973. The second major piece of legislation was the Education for All Handicapped Children Act of 1975. This law became known by its *Federal*

Register number, P.L. 94-142. Provisions of the law were strengthened and it was reauthorized in 1986 as P.L. 99-457. The No Child Left Behind Act of 2002 has proven to be a challenge to those benignant policies expressed in the laws of the 1970s. Beyond the classroom, and throughout all aspects of American life, the rights of people with disabilities are protected by the Americans With Disabilities Act of 1990.

Classroom teachers are often first to notice the disabling conditions affecting children (Barkley, 1998). In about 10% of the cases, pediatricians, parents, and/or preschool teachers are the first to note the child's possible special needs. However, 90% of the time it is the classroom teacher who is first to identify a learning problem. The **referral** process provides steps and procedures that schools follow in identifying and implementing programs to meet the special needs of children with disabilities.

The first intervention after the initial screening by the classroom teacher usually involves an **Instructional Support Team (IST)**.[1] If the recommendations of this committee prove to be ineffective, the next step for the child may involve a psychoeducational diagnostic assessment. This large-scale assessment is carried out by a multiple-disciplinary team. Once identified as having a significant educational or physical disability, the IDEIA guarantees the child a thorough and efficient education. This education must follow an educational program designed to meet the individual needs of the identified child. The Individualized Educational Program (IEP) is developed and periodically monitored in consultation with the child's parents (Kamphaus & Frick, 2002).

Once a child has been identified as needing special educational services, and the IEP has been initiated, annual testing becomes an ongoing requirement. This provides continuous monitoring and evaluation of the child's progress and educational development. There is some question about the efficacy of special education programs, but this is the best alternative open to educators working in this age of accountability (Kaznowski, 2004; Shaw & Gouwens, 2002).

There are several thorny issues raised by the NCLB Act involving the use of high-stakes tests in grade promotion/retention, report card grades, and as part of graduation requirements for special needs children. All too frequently these contentious problems become matters of litigation. Researcher David Berliner has written, "We note in passing that only people who have no contact with children could write legislation demanding that every child reach a high level of proficiency in three subjects, thereby denying that individual differences exist" (Berliner & Nichols, 2007, p. 48).

Of all the special education issues, perhaps the largest is that of attention and focus. It is not possible for a child to learn without focusing on the task of learning and attending to the educational process. Unfortunately, 9% of elementary school children have significant difficulty doing this. These children are usually diagnosed as having **attention-deficit/hyperactivity disorder (AD/HD)**. There is no direct physiological measure for this disorder, and the primary diagnostic tools are observational checklists.

Beyond attention and focus there are a number of specific curriculum areas where children may experience significant learning problems or have identifiable learning disabilities. Diagnostic tests for reading, language, and mathematics disabilities have been developed and published for use in the schools.

Another method of leveling the playing field of the classroom is to provide all children who have one or more disabilities with certain accommodations on tests and other forms of classroom assessments. Most states have provided for accommodations to meet the needs of students with disabilities on the statewide mandated assessments.

Learning Objectives

By reading and studying this chapter you should acquire the ability to do the following:

- Describe the size of the population of special needs students attending public schools in the United States, and suggest several reasons for the continuing growth in the percentage of children in need of special education services.
- Describe what elements teachers should collect as part of an informal evaluation of a child who may be "at risk."
- Record anecdotal observations of children in an educational setting.
- Describe appropriate accommodations that should be made to "even the playing field" for children with disabilities during a test or examination.
- Explain the operation of an Instructional Support Team.
- List who should participate on a multidisciplinary team.
- Describe the elements that should be included in an Individual Educational Program.
- Discuss the process of conducting a curriculum-based assessment.
- Describe the major diagnostic indicators of attention-deficit/hyperactivity disorder.
- List and describe several tests that can be used in the identification of AD/HD.
- Describe the prevalence of reading disorders among elementary school children.
- Differentiate between standardized achievement tests and diagnostic tests.

INCIDENCE

The number of children receiving services for special education in the United States has never been greater, nor has it ever represented a larger proportion of the population of students enrolled in the schools. In 2003 there were 5,728,000 children enrolled in special education programs. This represents about 8% of the school-age population. Over 90% of these students were not identified until they began to attend public school. (To see the state-by-state breakdown of children with disabling conditions, go to www.ed.gov/about/reports/annual/osep/2003/index.html.)   The critical point is that primary-grade teachers have a central role to play in the early identification of those children who will need special assistance. The necessity for teachers to be vigilant for, and have sensitivity to, the signs that a child may need special support cannot be overstated.

Early intervention programs for preschool children who are at risk for disabilities were part of the original Individuals With Disabilities Education Act (1986). That Act focused on the families of young children who were most at risk and provided direct service to the child and his or her family (Scarborough et al., 2004). Follow-up research has shown that early intervention with preschool-aged children with special needs can reduce the long-term supplemental educational costs for assisting them later in their educational careers (Wybranski, 1996). It is not just the teacher of young children who must be cognizant of special education instructional methods; all teachers teach children with special needs every day (Alvarado, 2006; Gaetano, 2006).

INFORMAL SCREENING

Teachers have a major advantage over parents regarding the early identification of children who may need learning support. The simple fact that teachers see a large number of children each year provides them with a basis for comparison unavailable to parents. The familiarity teachers have with so many children facilitates a primary-grade educator's ability to recognize a child who is at risk for a significant learning problem. In addition to the teacher, the elementary school guidance counselor is also part of the early-identification process. In the best of circumstances, each fall the counselor should observe the youngest students both in and outside of the classroom. The role of the counselor is also to consult with the primary-grade teachers about the beginning students and their progress.

As a normal part of the educational process, primary-grade teachers should create portfolios containing work samples for each child. These materials will help with parent conferences and also provide the core elements needed in the process of identifying learning problems (see Chapter 9). The portfolio should contain samples of writing, audio tapes of the child's oral reading, art work, standardized test scores, as well as the **anecdotal observations** made by the teacher.

Anecdotal Records

Whenever a particularly telling incident occurs for a child who is at risk, the teacher should jot down a brief note to serve as a reminder, and at the first free moment write the details of the anecdotal incident. These anecdotal reports should be dated and provide a timeline and location for the occurrence. The incident should be described in a factual, straightforward way. The anecdote should not contain any value statements or judgments by the teacher. It should only list the people involved (actors) and the specifics of what they did and said. An **anecdotal record** can be described as an ongoing temporal record of an occurrence or incident. Box 13.1 is an example from a teacher's anecdotal observation of a second-grade child during recess.

BOX 13.1   Sample Anecdotal Observation

Subject: Richard P. (RP)
Location: School Playground
Start time: 10:05 am
Date: Wednesday, November 1, 2006

10:05 RP runs from the mid-hall door onto playground

10:07 RP is the first to find the 12 in. rubber ball and he takes it into his custody

10:08 RP begins bouncing the ball and running and dribbling it

10:10 Three other boys approach RP and ask to use the ball for a game

10:11 RP raises his voice and refuses to stop bouncing the ball alone

10:12 Ms. Padula, recess aid, stands between RP and the group of other boys, now 7 in number

10:13 Ms. Padula expresses to RP that "the ball is there for all to enjoy and use during recess"

10:13 RP throws the ball into the face of the largest of the boys in the group

10:14 Ms. Padula shouts for RP to follow her back into the school

10:14 RP runs away and tries to exit the school yard

10:16 RP is quickly overtaken by Mr. Blackburn, the teacher of record for the recess period

10:19 RP seated on the bench in the school principal's outer office, he appears to be crying

---

NOTE: Created from hypothetical data.

The anecdotal record should be free of any suppositions, guesses, or judgments about the child or the occurrence. This may be followed by a separate page where the teacher is free to provide his or her thoughts about what happened and why. For example, as November 1 is the day after Halloween, there may be a link between behavior and an alteration in RP's eating habits. It is also possible that the group of boys had teased him on the bus while on the way to school that morning. But, as these things were not directly observed, they are not part of the anecdotal record.

INSTRUCTIONAL SUPPORT TEAM

After the teacher and guidance counselor have conferred and reviewed what is known about a child who may have a learning problem, the next step is to meet with the child's parents. The purpose of such a meeting is to share information and determine if there is a strategy that the classroom teacher could use that would be supported at home by the parents. Only after this step has been taken, and the intervention efforts have been shown not to provide enough help for the child, would the teacher and counselor make a referral for intervention by an Instructional Support Team (IST). This step must also include the school's principal, as he or she will be directly involved in the process, and the child's parents, who are integral to the process.

Membership

The IST should include the classroom teacher, other senior teachers, a guidance counselor, educational specialists who work with children in that school (e.g., reading, art, music, and physical education teachers and the school librarian), a school nurse, and the principal or assistant principal of the building. This committee should meet as soon as a referral is received. This committee may address the educational problems the child is experiencing even though the problems are not severe enough to require special education. Parents should be part of the IST process and attend the meeting of the IST. All communications with the child's home must be in the language that the parents can understand. This can be a significant challenge, because over 50 different primary languages are common among those attending public schools in the United States (Salvia, Ysseldyke, & Bolt, 2007). The careful application of this process can meet the requirements of **section 504** of the Rehabilitation Act of 1973 (P.L. 93-112).[2]

First order of business for the instructional support team is the task of reviewing the problem and all the information that the classroom teacher has brought together in the referral process. As the plan is discussed and tentatively developed to help the child, the parents should be involved and meet regularly with the IST. They should serve as members pro tempore during all meetings. This level of parent involvement serves the function of enlisting them into the effort. Parental participation also serves to provide the IST with an invaluable source of information about the child when he or she is not in school. Each year children spend 15% of their time in school while the rest of their time is under the protection and control of their parents. Educators must always remember that parents can feel outnumbered and outgunned by the process. It is easy for parents to become defensive and angry during the committee meetings. For that reason, schools should initiate training for the staff involved with the IST committee that is focused on communication and consensus building (O'Donovan, 2007).

The outcome of the IST meeting should be a written instructional support program for the child. This instructional support program is a guide for the teacher as well as a set of educational activities that the parent should do with the child at home.

Schedule

The IST should meet on a regular basis to review the progress of the child and discuss ideas and educational strategies with the classroom teacher. These ongoing IST meetings also provide a forum in which the teacher can express his or her frustration if the efforts are not working. It is usual that toward the end of the school year a final IST meeting is held that also includes the child's parents. If possible, the teacher(s) who will work with the child in the next grade should also be present. At this final meeting the child's progress for the year may be summarized and ideas for the parents and child to work on over the summer presented and discussed. Also, tentative plans for the next year could be outlined.

When the new school year begins in the fall, it is the responsibility of the new teacher to carry out the ideas and plans spelled out in the child's instructional support plan, and enunciated again at the end of the year conference.

REFERRAL, ASSESSMENT, AND THE IEP COMMITTEE

When the intervention program is found not to have had the desired effect, a second more formal referral should be made. The referral organizes and presents all of the initial IST materials along with the instructional support plan, the interim IST reports, and any new assessment scores from tests administered since the initial referral. This effort may be coordinated by the guidance counselor or the lead teacher on the IST.

Parent Participation

Before any diagnostic testing can be done, the school must have written approval from the child's parents. This whole process may require an initial home visit by a school social worker. A number of states including Pennsylvania provide specialized certification and licenses for school social workers. The parents should be brought up-to-date with the child's progress and provided with the reasons for a new round of assessments. The entire process along with a statement of the child's rights should be thoroughly explained. This explanation should be made using nontechnical, clear language. If the parents do not speak English, this meeting and all subsequent conferences should include an interpreter. Also during a home visit the parents should be requested to attend the meeting of the Individual Educational Program (IEP) committee.

For more information, see "Considerations on Point" at www.sagepub.com/wrightstudy

Case in Point (13a)

Significant disabilities such as sensory loss or severe neurological problems are normally identified and well known by the child's family long before the youngster enters school. Mild or marginal mental retardation, attention-deficit/hyperactivity disorder, and other less obvious disabilities are frequently not identified until the child is in school. For this reason it is often the educators who must work with the parents as they come to an understanding of the nature of their child's disability.

Many times parents grieve over what they feel is a loss of their child's potential for a good life. This process of reaching acceptance takes time. To prepare for meeting with parents, educators should collect reading material about the child's condition and brochures and other literature from advocacy groups. After the parent is introduced to the nature of the child's condition, these materials will provide a bridge to help open conversations about planning a course of action to help their child with disabilities. The school should encourage the formation of advocacy groups for the parents of children with disabilities and provide such groups with meeting space and other support. The pupil services department of every school system should develop programs that could be presented to these advocacy groups. Programs could include topics such as the following:

1. Introducing your friends and family to the problems associated with your child

2. Helping neighbors work with their children to better understand your child's disability

3. Educating others on the difference between the normal, occasional misbehavior of your child and the behaviors that may be a function of his or her condition

4. Learning to advocate for your child:
    *   In regard to the thoughtless language of others . . . (e.g., "your retarded kid")
    *   In regard to the planning for your child's future
    *   For inclusion in age-appropriate activities beyond school
    *   With educators and in the development of educational (and testing) plans for your child

5. Learning to accept and channel the compassion that others will want to show for you and your child

6. Learning the support and opportunities guaranteed by legislation such as the Americans With Disabilities Act of 1990

An important resource for teachers who are not trained in special education and for the parents of children with special needs is available at www.ncld.org/content/view/978.

This important Web page was established by the National Center for Learning Disabilities in 2006 and provides state-by-state information on the rights of children with disabilities. It also provides important information about the resources available to help the families of children with special needs.

Box 13.2   Referral Form for a Multidisciplinary Team

SPECIAL STUDENT SERVICES REFERRAL FORM

Date of Referral _____

Student _____ Birthdate _____ Sex _____ Grade _____

School _____ Homeroom Teacher _____

Parents' Name _____

Address _____

_____

Phone #: Home: _____ Work: _____

Interventions Tried Prior to Referral

_____

_____

Referring Person's Signature _____

❖ What best describes child's social reactions?
  ❑ Adequate group involvement
  ❑ Few friends
  ❑ No group involvement
  ❑ Belligerent

❖ What best describes how child responds to constructive criticism?
  ❑ Evaluates realistically
  ❑ Hurt, discouraged
  ❑ Rejects, becomes hostile

❖ What best describes how others react to child?
  ❑ Actively accept him/her
  ❑ Protect him/her
  ❑ Tolerate him/her
  ❑ Ignore him/her
  ❑ Reject him/her

❖ What best describes child's attitudes toward rules and authority?
  ❑ Acceptance
  ❑ Overly conscientious
  ❑ Mild resistance
  ❑ Blames others
  ❑ Hostile resistance

❖ What best describes child's self-control and emotional expression?
  ❑ Realistic expression of emotions
  ❑ Little emotional response
  ❑ Impulsive and unpredictable
  ❑ Physical and/or verbal aggression

❖ What best describes child's independence while working?
  ❑ Works well independently
  ❑ Subtle resistance to help
  ❑ Excessive reliance on others
  ❑ Refuses to accept help

❖ What best describes child's attention span?
  ❑ Average
  ❑ Long
  ❑ Short

❖ What best describes child's oral comprehension?
  ❑ Quick understanding
  ❑ Average
  ❑ Slow to understand

❖ What best describes child's ability to follow directions?
- ❑ Follow appropriately
- ❑ Needs continued explanation
- ❑ Ignores directions

❖ What best describes child's verbal expression?
- ❑ Clear expression of ideas
- ❑ Poor expression of ideas
- ❑ Cannot express ideas

Current Achievement (Estimate if data unavailable)

	Grade Level	Performance Level
Reading	_____	_____
Language Arts	_____	_____
Mathematics	_____	_____

Records Review

Hearing Screening: Date: _____ Results: _____

Vision Screening: Date: _____ Results: _____

Other Relevant Health Information: _____

_____

Preschool Experience: Yes __ No __ N/A __ (If yes, attach any relevant documents)

Days Absent Last Year: _____ Days Absent Current Year: _____ Grades Repeated: _____

Currently receiving (Mark all that apply.):

- ❑ Title I
- ❑ Speech
- ❑ OT/PT
- ❑ Language

- ❑ Individual Guidance
- ❑ Other (explain) _____

The following records are attached (*required for all referrals; + as applicable):

- ❑ *Cumulative Records
- ❑ *Discipline Records

- ❑ +State Assessment Test Scores
- ❑ +Competency Scores

Parents' and/or student's native language or other primary mode of communication if other than English (specify): _____

State reason you believe this child has a disability (impairment and a need for special education) such as academic and non-academic performance and medical information; any special programs, services, interventions used to address this student's needs and the results of those interventions, etc.

_____

_____

Membership

The multidisciplinary team and its parallel Individual Educational Program (IEP) committee normally include the school psychologist, a special education teacher, a school nurse, the school social worker, the school's principal or assistant principal, a guidance counselor who is familiar with the child, educational specialists, and specialized therapists as needed (e.g., physical therapy, occupational therapy, a speech specialist and/or hearing specialist, and a teacher certified for the visually impaired), and the child's parents (for more on the IEP, see below). On occasion these meetings may also include a pediatric psychiatrist, neurologist, ophthalmologist, or physiatrist.

Schedule

The best practice is to have two meetings; the first is of the multidisciplinary team. Frequently the time pressures on school make scheduling difficult. The first committee meeting is a time when the plan for the child's assessment is discussed and responsibilities for testing assigned. During the first meeting of the multidisciplinary team, it is normal to discuss the child's strengths and solicit and discuss the parents' ideas for their child's education. It is also a time to discuss the child's performance on standardized tests and state-mandated assessments. During the first meeting the school psychologist (or another testing expert) normally makes a presentation of test data to the parents. The parents need to have accurate but understandable information to make an informed decision. The instruments that will be used in the full psychoeducational diagnostic assessment should also be carefully explained to the parents during that first meeting. A written record should be maintained of all phases and steps in the process, including the written request to the parents to attend the meetings, all recommendations, major observations, and the final documentation and IEP.

At the second meeting, multidisciplinary team members can morph into an IEP committee. Before an IEP can be written, the multidisciplinary team must decide if the child is eligible for special education services. If the committee determines that the child has a significant impairment that makes learning excessively difficult, then he or she exceeds the threshold for being entitled to special services.

Once a special education entitlement decision has been made, the IEP committee writes the child's educational plan using the data and recommendations brought together by the multidisciplinary team. Once again the parents should attend the IEP meeting. During this second meeting, the IEP for the child is finalized and discussed and possibly modified. A signed copy is given to the parents and another is kept in the school's records. No special educational services can be provided to the child if the parents have objections to any part of the IEP.

ASSESSMENT PROCESS

School Psychologist

Following the initial meeting of the interdisciplinary team, the task of evaluating the child to diagnose his or her specific areas of difficulty can begin. The role of the school psychologist is often central in this process. The school psychologist will coordinate a psychoeducational assessment, which may include assessments by other professionals such as the reading teacher, the school nurse, and the school social worker. The psychoeducational diagnostic assessment is likely to include an individually administered test of cognitive ability and several individually administered clinical tests of perception, personality, and learning style. The assessment may also include the clinical observations by the school psychologist of the child interacting with peers and when he or she is at free play.

Curriculum-Based Assessment

One important part of most assessment protocols involves **curriculum-based measurements (CBM)**. Curriculum-based measurements are conducted to identify problematic areas from the curriculum that is taught to the child. This specialized form of measurement is accomplished by noting the child's actual capability to perform the tasks that are seminal to the learning of any particular component of the curriculum. Once the child's capabilities are identified, the need for remediation can be established by an examination of the discrepancy between the child's performance levels to those of his or her peers. These measurements are carried out by using a series of curriculum probes (Burns, MacQuarrie, & Campbell, 1998). Each probe requires only a few minutes to complete and involves actual material used in the classroom. A probe might involve an assessment of the number of words the child can read in a minute or a brief test of the child's ability to solve multiplication problems involving two columns of numbers. CBM identifies the exact skills that need to be improved through remediation, thereby providing the precise data needed to develop an IEP. When the curriculum-based measurements are combined with more traditional measurements, including dimensions such as achievement on normative measures and cognitive/intellectual ability test scores, the process is referred to as a curriculum-based assessment (CBA) (Lichtenstein, 2002). The combination of these measures with the personality and other noncognitive measures make up the psychoeducational diagnostic assessment.

In addition to the curriculum measurements that the school psychologist may employ, the school's educational specialists may use published instruments to make assessments of possible learning problems in specific curriculum areas. Examples of measurements of reading, language, and mathematics are included later in this chapter.

FORMAL ASSESSMENTS OF ATTENTION AND FOCUS

Children who cannot attend to the tasks involved with learning and who lack the ability to focus on classroom instruction will experience great difficulty in school. This disability was named by the American Psychiatric Association (APA) as attention-deficit/hyperactivity disorder (AD/HD), predominantly inattentive type (APA, 1994).

Incidence

Even though only 8% of school children receive special education, over 9% of all children have AD/HD. One implication of this imbalance is that more work needs to be done to identify AD/HD children in the primary grades. Only 20% of those children who are identified with AD/HD are girls. Thus, it is likely that 12% of all boys have this disorder (Committee on Quality Improvement [CQI], 2000). The diagnosis of AD/HD is often found to be associated (comorbid) with anxiety, conduct disorder, and/or severe oppositional behavior (CQI). Attention-deficit/hyperactivity disorder is also found among many children with problems in language and speech development as well as those who have difficulty learning to read. There is no definitive medical or psychological test to determine AD/HD (APA, 1994). There is, however, evidence for a genetic component to the problem (Chang, 2005). For that reason, the best method for identification of a child with attention deficit disorder (ADD) or AD/HD is by observation and the use of observational checklists.

There is a new research paradigm that is exploring a possibly distinctive neurological morphology among children with AD/HD (Chang, 2005). Research into the brain's architecture has been ongoing for years. For example, the importance of the right parietal lobe of the brain in learning logic and mathematics, and the left hemisphere in learning to read, are well established (Joseph, 2000). More recently, studies involving magnetic resonance imagery (MRI) of the human brain are expanding on this understanding of neurofunctions.

Brain research conducted on a human who is responding to environmental conditions and stimuli is in the earliest stage. These small-scale studies are tentative and incomplete in 2007, but they hold promise for the future (Plessen et al., 2006; Shaw et al., 2006).[3]

Another promising direction in research into understanding AD/HD is in the area of diet. There is proof that food additives have a negative impact on susceptible children, making it difficult for them to focus on learning and possibly increasing the child's activity level (Stevenson, et al. 2007). These findings have resulted in Great Britain's health service issuing a warning to parents to limit their child's intake of the food preservative sodium benzoate and a range of artificial food colorings.

All of the checklists used in the identification AD/HD include items to be answered by the parents. The combination of both school (teacher and counselor) and home (parents) observations makes a diagnosis by the school psychologist possible. The fact that having a child who exhibits the behaviors associated with AD/HD changes parenting behavior is well documented and needs to be considered in developing the IEP (Lin, 2001). A clinical interview of the parent by either the school's social worker or psychologist can provide the data to make this possible.

Parent education through seminars or support groups can go a long way toward overcoming the child's difficulty. Another factor to keep in mind when working with the parents of an AD/HD child is the very real possibility that one or both parents may also exhibit AD/HD behaviors. This means they may be forgetful with tasks and disorganized with complex paperwork.

Checklists

There are several checklists that are used to organize the observations of children thought to have ADD or AD/HD. The diagnostic guidelines provided in the APA's *Diagnostic and Statistical Manual, 4th ed. (DSM-IV)*, provide the basis for most of these checklists. The American Psychiatric Association suggests that a child may be diagnosed with AD/HD if he or she persistently exhibits an array of these behaviors at particular times in both school and home settings:

1. Inattention
    a. Fails to follow through and complete tasks
    b. Is easily distracted by the environment and others in it
    c. Finds it hard to concentrate on schoolwork or sustain attention
    d. Does not listen when spoken to
    e. Is forgetful and tends to lose items (homework, lunch, books, etc.)

2. Hyperactivity
   a. Will climb and roam
   b. Constantly shifting from one task to another
   c. Talks excessively
   d. Is constantly on the go as if driven by a motor
   e. Is restless and cannot remain seated for a long period
   f. Does not play well with others (has few friends)

3. Impulsivity
   a. Acts without thinking or planning
   b. Frequently calls out in class
   c. Frequently interrupts others and butts into conversations
   d. Cannot wait before taking a turn

4. Early Onset

There should have been an early onset of the disorder, with the symptoms occurring before the age of 7, and the symptoms must have persisted for more than 6 months.

Jolene Huston, of the Agriculture Extension Service of the Montana State University, wrote a resource for parents and others who are learning to live with AD/HD in their families. This monograph can be seen here: www.montana.edu/wwwpb/pubs/mt200304.html.

AD/HD MEASUREMENT SCALES

There are over two dozen observational scales that have been published for the identification of attention-deficit/hyperactivity disorder (AD/HD). Five observational scales that are commonly used to gather data about children experiencing learning problems related to attention deficit are reviewed here. These same five scales are also widely used in research and are frequently cited in the educational psychology literature.

Behavior Assessment System for Children, 2nd Edition (BASC-2)

The BASC-2 can be described as a multidimensional approach to the assessment of a range of childhood disorders including attention deficit–hyperactivity. It was published in 2004 by American Guidance Service, a division of Pearson Education, and is used with children between ages 2 and 21

(Reynolds & Kamphaus, 2004).The system includes teacher, parent, and self-report personality questionnaires. It also has a formal student observation system and a form for collecting the child's developmental history. When analyzed as a whole, the instrument assesses the possibility of impairment in the child's "**executive function**" related to attention deficit.[4]

The BASC-2 was well normed and corrected for gender differences on all items. It has good internal consistency and test–retest reliability with Cronbach α' cocfficicnts in the 0.90 range. The BASC-2 system exhibits good overall concurrent validity but exhibits a modest level of predictive validity for AD/HD children.

Each part of the BASC-2 takes about 30 minutes to complete. An analysis of the various data sources can be done using software available from the publisher. An enhanced clinical diagnostic software package—BASC-2, Assist Plus—is also available for school psychologists and clinicians. The BASC-2 requires that the professional interpreting the instrument be educated to what was once described as level B.[5] (For information about these qualification levels see Chapter 12.) There is also a version of the BASC-2 that was published in Spanish. A validation study of the Spanish version in Puerto Rico raised questions about the construct validity and test–retest reliability of the parent questionnaire (Perez & Ines, 2004).

To review a sample parent report, see www.agsnet.com/Group.asp?nGroupInfoID=a30000.

Brown ADD Scales for Children and Adolescents

This scale, commonly referred to as the Brown ADD Scales for Children, was published by the Harcourt Assessment Division of the Psychological Corporation in 2001 (Brown, 2001). The Brown ADD Scales for Children includes a teacher questionnaire, parent questionnaire, and a semi-structured clinical interview. To administer to questionnaire it is necessary to have been trained at a B level.[6]

The scale exhibits a high degree of concurrent validity with other measures of attention deficit and good test–retest reliability. It was normed for use with a population between the ages of 3 and 12 years, and it provides comparative and diagnostic tables up to age 18. Unfortunately, the sampling process used by Brown opened the measure to criticism as having a potentially biased normative base (Jennings, 2003).

The Brown ADD Scales for Children requires about 20 minutes for the classroom teacher or the child's parent to complete. The instrument presents multidimensional data along six subscales that are aligned with the diagnostic criteria used in the *DSM-IV*. The test manual presents a wealth of information that can be used in developing an IEP. There are three questionnaires that make up the instrument, one each for the teacher, parents, and the child to complete.

Conners' Rating Scales-Revised (CRS-R)

The Conners' Rating Scales were designed and normed to be used with a population of children between the ages of 3 and 17 years by Multi-Health Systems Inc. of Canada (Conners, 1997/2000). They are distributed in the United States by Pearson Education. The CRS-R provides a global index score as well as scores that align with the *DSM-IV* AD/HD classification. The scoring and interpretation of the CRS-R is limited to those educators who have a B level of training in measurement.

There are seven other subscale scores that are a part of the CRS-R, including Oppositional, Cognitive Inattention and Problems, Hyperactivity, Anxious–Shy, Perfectionism, Social Problems, and Psychosomatic. The CRS-R has versions (forms) that are both long and short. These two lengths of forms are available for both the parent and teacher editions of the measure. Starting at age 12 there is also a self-report adolescent scale. This additional questionnaire adds subscales of problems with Anger Control, Conduct, Emotions, and Family Relations.

Minor gender differences are built into the instrument. The CRS-R was standardized on a large sample of students from Canada and the United States that was weighted to provide a good representation to the 1990 U.S. census. The Conners' Rating Scales-Revised exhibit impressive levels of internal consistency and test–retest reliability. Unfortunately, reliability studies of the subscales found that the three that are aligned with the diagnosis of AD/HD (Hyperactivity, Cognitive Problems, and Anxiety–Shy) have alpha levels below 0.50 (Hess, 2001).

Early Childhood ADD Evaluation Scale (ECADDES)

The Early Childhood Attention-Deficit Disorder Evaluation Scale is appropriate for children between the ages of 2 and 6 years. ECADDES was designed by Stephen McCarney and Nancy Johnson (1995) to align with the diagnostic characteristics listed in the *Diagnostic and Statistical Manual, 4th ed*. The ECADDES is published by Hawthorne Educational Services. Two observational checklists make up this instrument, one for use in the school and the other for use in the child's home. Data from the observations in the two settings are used to derive scores on two subscales, Inattentive and Hyperactive–Impulsive. The observational checklists take less than half an hour to be completed by the preschool teacher and the parent.

The ECADDES was standardized on a sample of almost 2,900 children. The sample was not nationally representative, with an underrepresentation of children from ethnic minority groups and an overrepresentation of children from rural settings in the upper Midwest (Cohen, 2001; Keller, 2001). The upper age limit of the ECADDES is 78 months, which is 6 months younger than the *DSM-IV* specifies as the lowest age (7 years) a diagnosis of AD/HD can be made (APA, 1994). The questionnaires can be completed by preschool caregivers and parents, but a B level of training is needed to interpret those scores. To learn more about the ECADDES and see a copy of the instrument, see www.hes-inc.com/hes.cgi/02250.html.

The school checklist exhibits good test–retest reliability ($r > 0.90$) and the home instrument more modest levels of demonstrated reliability ($r > 0.70$). A problem area is validity. The authors make a case for the instrument having "face validity" as judged by a panel of experts. Also they point out that the instrument can confirm that children who have been diagnosed as exhibiting behaviors similar to AD/HD score in the appropriate levels for AD/HD.

As the ECADDES has sampling problems and poorly defined validity, and because it is designed to be used prior to a child being ready for a special education intervention, it is to be viewed only as a preliminary screening device.

Scales for Diagnosing AD/HD

Gail Ryser and Kathleen McConnell (2002) developed an instrument that can identify children and adolescents (ages 5 through 18 years) who exhibit AD/HD behaviors. This instrument, published by Pro-Ed, has two forms: school and home. The questionnaires are completed with teachers and parents and are scored by a B-level test administrator. The 39 Likert-scale questions on the two forms yield three subscale scores that align with *DSM-IV* criteria (viz., inattentiveness, hyperactivity, and impulsivity).

The normative group included a representative sample of 3,448 children between 5 and 19 years of age. The two Likert scales (school and home) have very substantial internal consistency ($\alpha > 0.90$) and the test–retest reliability is even greater. Also, there is good interterm reliability ($r > 0.90$). The validity of the measurement of the three subscale scores was well established by factor analysis (Law, 2001).

This measure is a good way to screen for AD/HD, and it is also an appropriate device to use to monitor students who have an IEP for attention-deficit/hyperactivity disorder.

Diagnosis vs. Disability

Once a child has been diagnosed with an attention-deficit/hyperactivity disorder, he or she is not automatically eligible for special education. To qualify for special education services a child must meet the guidelines of the Individuals With Disabilities Educational Improvement Act (IDEIA; 2004) Section 301, parts a and b. This requires that the child persists in exhibiting a significant gap between achievement and his or her ability after a period of scientifically appropriate instructional interventions have been attempted. In other words, the old **discrepancy** idea (described in Chapter 11) is alive and well and living in the rules laid out in the IDEIA passed into law in July of 2005.

ASSESSMENTS OF READING PROBLEMS

Reading is a core skill needed by every child. The third grade, with its high-stakes reading test, can be a nightmare for those who have fallen behind in the development of this skill. For that reason it is critical that primary-grade teachers monitor the burgeoning reading skills exhibited by their students. More referrals are made for reading problems than for any other area of the curriculum (Lyon, 1998). Only 5% of children learn to read without any formal instruction, and another 35% have little difficulty learning to read in school. Another 40% of our children learn to read with considerable effort, and 20% find learning to read the most difficult task they have ever faced. Severe cases of reading disability occur in about 4% of all children and can even involve mirror-image reading (APA, 1994).[7]

Learning to Read

The task of learning to read involves having the child learn to recognize the 26 letters of the alphabet and the 40 sounds that they can represent. Next, the child must learn that the spoken language is made up of these same sounds (phonemes) and that the printed letters are representations of those sounds. Once this is obtained, the child must learn to connect phonemes into words, recognize those words, and attach meaning to them. Taken together, these steps make up the decoding process of reading. It takes the average child somewhere between 4 and 14 separate exposures to a written word before being able to quickly and easily decode it into what it represents (Lyon, 1998). Disabled readers may require 20 or more experiences with the word before being able to decode it. The amount of experience the child has had with the word in the environment relates to the numbers of exposures needed. Children who had a broader range of experiences and who had many opportunities to see and hear words read to them (parental reading) can be expected to learn to read with less difficulty.

Phonemic Awareness

It is evident that the first step in the difficult task of becoming a reader of the English language is connecting sounds with the letters of the alphabet. This process is known as **phonemic awareness**. The foundation for phonemic awareness is set long before the child enters school. A simple screening test of the child's phonemic awareness given early in kindergarten can identify those children who are at risk for having a problem learning to read. Once identified, those children need to be given direct and efficient instruction in this vital prereading skill.

Comprehension

The need for this decoding process to increase in speed is the child's next task. Comprehension is built on the rapid decoding and processing of written words. Slow decoding makes it impossible for the developing reader to understand and derive meaning from what has been read. By fourth grade some children who have had reading test scores that indicate a level of proficiency through the third grade can begin to have reading problems as comprehension becomes the new task (Leach, Scarborough, & Rescorla, 2003).

Environmental Factors

The fact that a child experiences difficulty in learning to read does not mean that there is a neurological or psychological problem. Most children who are at risk for having difficulty in learning to read are those who have had little exposure to reading materials and few literacy experiences prior to kindergarten. Children who were surrounded with numerous children's books, and who had caregivers that played rhyming games, read out loud, talked, and worked to expand the child's vocabulary, are the ones who are most likely to learn to read without difficulty. The National Reading Panel (Armbruster, Lehr, & Osborn, 2003) published a list of those parental linguistic interactions that facilitate a child's learning to read. These include talking and listening, reading children's books out loud, learning and talking about books, learning to recognize the letters of the alphabet, and demonstrating the letter–sound link.

Diagnostic Tests

The IDEIA provided a new requirement that children with disabilities be identified early. For that reason, kindergarten and first-grade children are often the focus of identification efforts. One method being employed in this effort for early identification is known as Response to Intervention (RTI) (James, 2004).

Diagnostic tests are made up of items that measure a specific skill needed to successfully learn. Students without a reading disability score relatively high on these tests. However, the full range of children is used in the normative group. This results in a distribution of scores characterized by a significant negative skewness. The skew in the data makes it possible to identify and see differences between students who are struggling to learn to read. Their scores are spread out on the long tail of the skewed data. The skew makes it possible for the instrument to be more sensitive to small differences among low-scoring children.

Data from a diagnostic test can be used to inform the IEP writing process. Reassessment with the same instrument can also be used to track improvement over the baseline established during the initial diagnostic testing.

EARLY READING TESTS

There are a number of reading tests that are a part of larger batteries of achievement tests. An example of such a test is the third edition of the Woodcock–Johnson Tests of Achievement.

Woodcock–Johnson

While much more than just a reading test, the third edition of the Woodcock–Johnson battery does provide an excellent measure of reading.

The person using and interpreting this test is required to be highly qualified at the C level and have specific training in the use of this test.[8] The Diagnostic Reading Battery (WJ III, DRB) is part of a separate achievement test—the Woodcock–Johnson III Tests of Achievement (WJ III, ACH). These measures are appropriate for all children and adolescents over the age of 2 years (Woodcock, McGrew, & Mather, 2001). The reading related subtests include (a) Letter–Word Identification, (b) Reading Fluency, (c) Passage Comprehension, (d) Story Recall, (e) Story Recall Delayed, (f) Oral Language, (g) Reading Vocabulary, (h) Oral Comprehension, (i) Sound Awareness, (j) Reading Comprehension, (k) Oral Expression, (l) Phoneme–Grapheme Knowledge, and (m) Verbal Comprehension.

The total set of all achievement tests requires almost 2 hours for administering. Each of the various subtests requires a minimum of about 5 minutes to complete, making it possible to obtain just a reading score in a little over an hour (Cizek, 2003). Computerized scoring and profiling is available from the publisher, Riverside Publishers. It is well standardized, highly reliable, and has been shown to be a valid measure of learning problems in reading (Semrud-Clickeman, 2003).

Wechsler Individual Achievement Test

Another individually administered achievement battery that can be used to measure early reading is the Wechsler Individual Achievement Test, 2nd ed. (WIAT-II). Once again, this battery provides an example of what an individualized reading test can measure; however, it is not a "one-trick pony." This test provides measures for four areas of reading, two of mathematics, a test of listening comprehension, one of oral expression, and a test of written expression. This achievement battery is appropriate for the assessment of children as young as 4 years of age. It is also a test that requires the examiner be trained in its use and have a level-C background. The test for younger children requires less than an hour to administer. The early reading tests are designed to assess phonological awareness and involve items measuring the ability to name the letters of the alphabet, identify and generate rhyming words, identify the beginning and ending sounds of words, and the matching of sounds with letters and letter blends (Psychological Corporation, 2001).

The WIAT-II is constructed to align with the recommendations of the National Reading Panel (2000) and was standardized using a stratified random sample that was balanced for ethnicity, SES, gender, and geography. It has good reliability and a solid validation (Doll, 2003).

Dynamic Indicators

There are also more than a dozen tests of early reading that can be used with preschool, kindergarten, and elementary school populations. One of these is the **Dynamic Indicators of Basic Literacy Skills**, 6th ed. (DIBELS). This measure is designed for use with children between kindergarten and third grade (Good et al., 2002/2003). It is an inexpensive, individually administered brief screening and monitoring test of children's developing reading skills. The measure should be administered by a person with a B level of training and requires about 20 minutes per child. Scoring is complex, but an online option is available.

The University of Oregon provides a Web page where it is possible to learn much more about this test: http://dibels.uoregon.edu/.

The DIBELS subtests measure Initial Sound Fluency, Letter Naming Fluency, Phoneme Segmentation Fluency, Nonsense Word Fluency, Oral Reading Fluency, and Word Use Fluency. In addition, comprehension is assessed through a measure of Oral Retelling Fluency. One of the remarkable findings in the literature about this test is the high levels of reliability exhibited by the parts of the battery. High reliability scores on a test for young children are not easy to achieve. Most of the reliabilities for this measure are in the 0.90 range (Brunsman, 2005; Shanahan, 2005).

The DIBELS is a good match for monitoring children as they approach the high-stakes reading test in third grade, and it provides a method for checking the mastery of the critical early reading skills. This test is also widely employed by primary-grade teachers as a method to track children who are in the process of developing their reading skills.

However, a lack of specificity about the norming sample data makes this instrument one that should not be used for the specific identification of disabled readers. It is best employed as a classroom measure that monitors the progress early readers are making (Brunsman, 2005; Shanahan, 2005).

Test of Early Reading

The Test of Early Reading Ability, 3rd Edition (TERA-3), is an easy to administer early reading test designed for children between the ages of 3½ and third grade. It was published by Pro-Ed in 2001 (Reid, Hersko, & Hamill, 1981/2001). This is another individually administered test requiring a half-hour of testing time per child. While the test may be given to the child by a teacher's aid, the examiner who scores and interprets the test data should have a B level of educational background.

This measure provides four scores: a measure of the child's understanding of the alphabet, the understanding of the conventions of print, and the ability to derive meaning from the printed word. The fourth and final score is a total reading quotient (deFur, 2003). The test does not provide a measure of phonemic awareness and is not well aligned with the most recent recommendations of the National Reading Panel (Armbruster, Lehr, & Osborn, 2003). The norming sample was small but representative of the diversity of the early school population. TERA-3 is a reliable and valid instrument with a quarter-century history.

STAR Early Literacy

A new direction in testing is represented by the STAR Early Literacy test. This is a criterion referenced, computer-adaptive measure written and published by Renaissance Learning in 2001. Once the software license has been purchased, children as young as 3 years of age, and as old as 9, can be given regular reading literacy assessments. These assessments can require as little as 10 minutes to administer. The score areas from the STAR Early Literacy tests include Graphophonemic Knowledge, General Readiness, Phonemic Awareness, **Phonics**, Comprehension, Structural Analysis, and Vocabulary. A major advantage to this testing system is that groups of children can take the assessment at the same time. The license agreement is sold in units of 40. The system also makes it easier for the classroom teacher to track and monitor the developing level of reading skills in a classroom of children.

To see a sample of the STAR Early Literacy test, visit www.renlearn .com/starearlyliteracy/screens.htm.

The STAR software includes 2,400 items from which only 25 are required to test an individual child. This measurement is a good example of computer-adapted testing. The system remembers each child and creates a test at the child's last reading level. All items have been well standardized and balanced for difficulty through an application of item response theory (Graham, 2003). The testing system uses a large and representative sample of subjects to balance and equate items.

The STAR Early Literacy tests have demonstrated good reliability and superior validity. The test may provide a positive advantage to those students who have had more extensive computer experiences at home. Yet, it does provide each child with a baseline at the start of the school year and through regular retesting can track individual progress toward the learning goals of the grade level.

Elementary School Reading Tests

There are more than 80 different reading tests published in English available for use in the elementary grades. Among these are several group-administered diagnostic reading tests that dominate the school market. One of these is the Stanford Diagnostic Reading Test, 4th ed. (SDRT-4). This measure is published by Harcourt Assessments. Another is the California Diagnostic Reading Test (CDRT), published by CTB, McGraw-Hill. A group-administered reading test commonly used in the schools is the Grey Oral Reading Test, 4th ed. (GORT-4).

The first Gates–MacGinitie reading test was published in 1928 and the fourth edition in 2003 by Riverside Publishing. The new Gates–MacGinitie offers an optional computerized scoring system, the Lexile Framework, which presents a customized list of 15 books selected to match the reading level of the child.

ASSESSMENTS OF LANGUAGE AND SPEECH PROBLEMS

Central to being able to communicate is the ability to decode and understand the meaning of the sounds of speech. This is referred to as the receptive task of language. Aligned with this ability are the two parts of verbal speech: articulation and expression. The last area of expressive language to develop is that of writing. Developmental problems in the child's ability to communicate can occur singly with one of these dimensions or in combination. There is also a high degree of comorbidity for expressive and **receptive language** problems with other disabling conditions, including AD/HD.

Measures for the Identification of Language Problems

The first step in determining if a child has a developmental problem in the acquisition of those receptive and expressive language skills appropriate for his or her age involves a pediatric evaluation along with an audiologist's assessment. Hearing is primary among these potential physiological problems. Possible medical problems can include neurological disorders and nutritional questions. Once these physical issues have been accounted for, language testing to establish a baseline and writing of an IEP can proceed. Ongoing testing can be used to support the special education intervention by monitoring progress toward the goals of the IEP.

Communication Abilities Diagnostic Test

One of these measures of language, published in 1990 by Riverside Publishing, is appropriate for use with children between the ages of 3 and 10. This test, the Communication Abilities Diagnostic Test (CoADT), is administered to the child in a one-to-one format by the assessor. The testing process requires 45 minutes to administer, and an equal amount of time is needed for the setup prior to testing and the scoring afterward (Johnson & Johnson, 1990). This measure represents an innovative approach to language sampling. It is not a test per se, but a structured method of sampling the child's language. It uses a storytelling technique and also an engaging board game that the examiner plays with the child. A verbatim transcript of what the child says must be kept and analyzed after testing. The complexity of this evaluation makes it essential that the examiner be educated at the B level.

From an analysis of the transcript of the child's language it is possible to measure a Total Language Score and also subtest scores of Structure, Grammar, Meaning, Pragmatics, and Comprehension. Composite scores for Semantics, Syntax, and Language Expression are also available to the examiner. The test provides a norm-based scoring system that makes it possible to determine a point of comparison. It also provides criterion scoring, which facilitates goal setting when an IEP is written (Haynes & Shapiro, 1995).

The CoADT was developed with a statistically balanced sample that is a good representation of the general population. The test is reliable and demonstrates a reasonable level of predictive validity. It does have a problem with inter-rater reliability, especially with the Grammar scale.

OWLS

A battery of language tests has been written by Elizabeth Carrow-Woolfolk, including the Oral and Written Language Scales Listening Comprehension and Oral Expression (OWLS-L; 1995) and the Oral and Written Scales Written Expression (OWLS-W; 1996). These measures require that the administrator has been educated to the B level. Both the OWLS-L and the OWLS-W are published by American Guidance Services.

The OWLS-L and its companion test, the OWLS-W, were standardized as one instrument but later separated as two different tests. The OWLS-L provides an Oral Composite score along with two subscales: Listening Comprehension and Oral Expression. The Listening Comprehension subscale presents the child with an array of line drawings and requires the child identify objects and activities on the pictures in response to the examiner's questions (Graham & Malcolm, 2001). The oral expression test uses line drawings as stimuli and asks the child to discuss aspects of what is depicted in the drawing. The scoring of the OWLS-L provides an item analysis that facilitates the study of the pattern of errors that the child made. The test is reliable and is built upon a solid theoretical foundation. It can be used as part of an evaluation and to write an IEP.

The writing test, OWLS-W, is easily administered and can be given to small groups of students. The difficult task is scoring the measure (Carpenter & Malcolm, 2001). Each writing task has its own set of directions and scoring rubrics. The measure involves having the child write sentences dictated by the examiner. The OWLS-W also has children write several short story endings and complete an expository writing task. The measure provides scores of Writing Conventions, Linguistics, and Content. The OWLS-W is reasonably reliable and exhibits both good content validity and predictive validity. The two measures, OWLS-L and OWLS-W, would be best used together in a language assessment.

Test of Early Language

The third edition of the Test of Early Language Development (TELD-3), which is published by Pro-Ed, requires only a C level of formal training (Hresko, Reid, & Hammill, 1999). This qualification level may reflect the simplified manual that accompanies the TELD-3. This publication provides excellent background and directions for the use of this instrument. The instrument requires about 40 minutes to administer and a similar timeframe to score. This individually administered instrument can be used to determine a Spoken Language Quotient and also provides subscale scores for Receptive and Expressive Language.

The TELD-3 is a highly reliable measure that has good concurrent and predictive validity (Morreale & Suen, 2001). It can be used in the process of identification of a language disability and add critical data to the child's IEP. The baseline data obtained during the use of the instrument for diagnosis can become the starting point for ongoing tracking of the child's communication development.

MEASURES FOR THE IDENTIFICATION OF PROBLEMS LEARNING MATHEMATICS

Children of all ability levels can have difficulty in learning mathematics. Being unable to understand a concept that others have mastered is frustrating for any child. Early grade difficulty with arithmetic, and the associated feelings of frustration and loss of a sense of self-efficacy, are the reasons many otherwise bright and motivated children avoid mathematics.

Occurrence

For the most part, mathematics learning problems occur in association with other learning problems. Usually, mathematics disability is paired with a reading disability. The incidence of occurrence of mathematics learning disabilities in association with other learning disabilities is about 6% among the population of elementary children (Fuchs & Fuchs, 2002). The incidence of a mathematics learning disability occurring alone is much smaller, equaling about 1% of the school-age population (APA, 1994).

Nature of the Problem

Children enter school with wide disparities in their developmental readiness for learning mathematics. To learn the basic arithmetic operations, it is essential that the child conceptualize a number as an immutable entity. Most children have acquired this concept by first grade, but as many as a third of all children will require a year or two more before they recognize that the number 10 is made up of 10 distinct and unvarying single units (Piaget, 1930,1952/1964). The presence of a high-stakes test in third grade makes it absolutely essential that all children acquire a true understanding of the base 10 system of numeration by the end of first grade. All arithmetical processes require this as a foundation.

There are a number of published tests that can quantify the development of mathematical knowledge in kindergarten and the primary grades. Scores on these measures can be used to write an IEP and also serve to establish a baseline for charting the child's growth in mathematical understanding. One of these measures is group administered and requires a C level of knowledge of testing. The other is the Key Math–Revised, an individually administered assessment that requires the user be qualified at the B level.

Key Math–Revised

American Guidance Services published the Key Math–Revised: A Diagnostic Inventory of Essential Mathematics in 1998 (Connolly, 1998). The test provides a total score based on the combination of three subscales: Basic

Concepts, Operations, and Applications. Each of the subscales is made up of several test areas.[9] Depending on the age and ability of the child, the Key Math–Revised may require up to an hour to complete. It is an appropriate diagnostic measure that can be used with children from kindergarten through middle school.

The content of the test has been criticized as being dated with an overemphasis on computational skill (Kingsbury & Wollack, 2001). The measure is easy to administer and the scoring system is not difficult to follow. It does provide valid and reliable diagnostic data that can be used in the development of IEPs.

American Guidance Service was acquired by Pearson Assessments in 2006, and in 2007, a new online edition of the Key Math Test was published. This version provides a very wide measurement range, preschool through age 21. As with the Key Math–Revised, the third edition (KMT III) presents subscale scores for Basic Concepts, Operations, and Applications. The test requires 45 minutes with young children and over an hour for adolescents and youths.

Diagnostic Math Test

The group-administered test of arithmetic skills is the Stanford Diagnostic Mathematics Test, 4th ed. (SDMT-4; Harcourt Brace Educational Measurement, 1996). This test has six versions and covers all the grade levels from first through high school graduation (grade 13). The SDMT-4 provides a total score and two subtest scores: Computation, and Concepts and Applications. There are up to 17 skill areas measured by the upper grade-level test. It takes over an hour to administer the SDMT-4 in the lower grades and over an hour and a half in the upper grades.

The SDMT-4 was normed on a large sample of the population (N = 27,000), and the various scales are reported to have very high reliabilities. The test reports are both norm based and criterion based, providing a useful set of scores. The publisher provides excellent software that assists in report writing (Lehmann, Nagy, & Poteat, 1998).

The content of the SDMT-4 was based on the standards published by the National Council of Teachers of Mathematics. As those standards were revised after the SDMT-4 was published, the validity of the test is suspect. A number of the items seem to be a bit dated. For example, a money question uses a drawing of coins that includes a 50-cent piece. Except for coin collectors, that coin has just about vanished and would not be familiar to children today.

INDIVIDUALIZED EDUCATIONAL PLAN (IEP)

The requirement for each child with a special need to have an Individualized Educational Plan is prescribed in federal legislation known as the Individuals With Disabilities Educational Improvement Act of 2004 (IDEIA; P.L. 108-446, 2004). This is the successor to the original Education for all Handicapped Children Act (P.L. 94-142, 1975) and its later versions, including IDEA (1997). One change in the focus of educational policy that was brought about by the NCLB legislation is in the way children who need special education are viewed. Heretofore, the focus of federal law and policy has been to provide access for special needs children to all aspects of the educational programs. Since the NCLB law, the focus became the learning outcomes. This changes the goal for providing assistance from providing access to working to ensure that all special education children achieve a level of academic proficiency.

NCLB Special Education Conflict

This law was written in an attempt to align special education with the provisions of the No Child Left Behind Act (U.S. Department of Education, 2005). The crux of the problem between IDEIA and NCLB is with the provisions of the NCLB Act that required that 99% of all students take the same state-mandated assessment test. In other words, the children who received special education services were required to be tested with the state's mandated NCLB test using a test form appropriate for a child of his or her age (not developmental level). Beginning in 2006, a modification made it possible for a larger group to avoid the grade-appropriate NCLB test. Yet, even with this concession, only 3% of the children can now be tested with an instrument that is developmentally more appropriate.

It has been argued that the NCLB Act is antithetical to the whole concept of special education. If all children who are currently classified as being in need of special educational services are required to be proficient by 2014, special education as we know it will disappear. This is a logical consequence of the fact that a proficient child is not one who can be classified as needing special services (Wasta, 2006). Likewise, we expect that all children, even those that we identify through our diagnostic systems and evaluation methods as having special learning needs, will somehow magically be on-grade-level (Hehir, 2007). The fact that this is a statistical impossibility was noted in Chapter 3.

There is evidence that the NCLB law has had a positive impact for some students with disabilities. Specifically students who are deaf or hard of hearing have found that public schools have increased the resources that are used on their behalf. It also appears that the amount of effort and attention that students with "low incidence disabilities" are receiving is being increased as schools work to meet the proficiency mandates of the NCLB Act (Cawthon, 2007).

High school graduation based on a required test score in 21 of the 22 states with that requirement poses a related problem for special education students. Passing a high-stakes test in high school may not be something children with cognitive deficiencies can be reasonably expected to be able to do. In 2006, California required all students to pass a graduation test to get their high school diploma. The result of this mandate for testing was an increase in the high school dropout rate, which went from 24% to 36% that year. The dropout rate is one reason why the state put off requiring students with disabilities from meeting the testing requirement until the spring of 2008 (Williams, 2007).

Massachusetts is one state that provides an alternative route for special education students to achieve a high school diploma. In 2004, 2,000 high school students attempted to earn their diploma using the Massachusetts portfolio assessment system. Of that number, only 47 (2.35%) of the special education students passed and were awarded their diploma (Schworm, 2004).

This leaves little opportunity to provide alternative assessments for students with disabilities. For those children functioning well below grade level, this provision leads to frustration and parent opposition. Likewise, the slow progress of students with disabilities toward reaching the tested level of "Proficient" is likely to introduce a negative skew to a school's data. The result is that a handful of special education students may make a school unable to reach the annual yearly progress goals set by the state. Should this occur, the whole school receives a grade of "Needs Improvement." When a school does not reach the mandated annual progress goal, the community only hears that the school "failed." All too often this designation leads to the public sanctioning of the school and its educators (Phillips, 2005).

In addition to the pressure that this possibility places on special educators and children, in eight states special education students must also face another very high hurdle. In these states special education students are required to pass the mandated NCLB test to be promoted to the next grade. The NCLB Act requires that almost all children with disabilities test at a proficient level, the same requirement that non-disabled children must meet.

In 2005, increasing opposition to this lack of flexibility for students with disabilities led U.S. Secretary of Education Spellings to allow states to petition the Education Department for permission to provide alternative assessments to 3% of the student population (Aspey & Colby, 2005). During the 2004–2005 school year, Texas was in open revolt with the NCLB mandates and used alternative assessments for 9% of their students. In 2005–2006, Texas reduced this to 5% and was in compliance with the 3% rule in 2007.

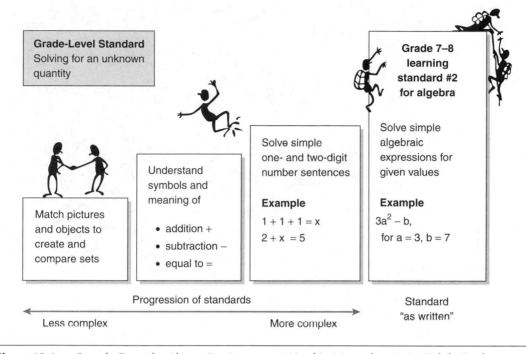

Figure 13.1   Sample From the Alternative Assessment Used in Massachusetts in Eighth-Grade
Mathematics

SOURCE: Massachusettts Department of Education.

The pressure on schools can be great. Not only must a school have the average score of all children reach an annual benchmark for adequate yearly progress, but so must every one of the **disaggregated subgroups** within the school. Schools have become adept at exploiting privacy rules within the NCLB regulations. These regulations require the public reporting data from the seven subgroups of the student population only after the size of that subgroup exceeds 45 students. Many of the classifications overlap and a child can conceivably be simultaneously classified in as many as five groups. Those seven groups include English-language learners, those receiving a free or reduced-cost lunch, special needs, Hispanic, African American, Native American, and Anglo-White. By carefully managing the classification of every child, the likelihood of a school failing to achieve adequate yearly progress can be greatly reduced.[10]

Another strategy involves the manipulation of the child's Individual Educational Plan to provide a year of private special education outside of the public school. By spending school district funds, it then becomes possible for

Figure 13.2   Left Hanging

SOURCE: Cartoon by Merv Magus.

the district to move a few students out of the database of the school during a high-stakes testing year. Another approach is to help the parents home-school their child.

Individual Educational Plan Format

While the law (IDEIA, 2004) requires an individualized education plan for all children with disabilities, it does not prescribe a particular format for the plan. Most local school systems have developed their own formats for writing IEPs. Additionally, purveyors of educational software have developed computerized techniques for writing these plans. One advantage of the computerized IEP is that it provides documents of a similar quality in all the schools and for all the special students of a school system (Margolis & Free, 2001). Examples of such software can be reviewed at the following Web sites:

www.tera-sys-inc.com/tsim.asp

www.iepware.com/IEPSD.html

The IEP must include the following items:

1. The child's current educational performance level across all areas of the curriculum and a description of how the disability affects the child's involvement and progress in school.

2. A list of annual goals that can reasonably be expected to be accomplished in the school year.

3. Description of how progress toward the annual goals will be measured and how the child's parents will be kept apprised of that progress.

4. Description of special education and related services that will be provided to the child, including any modifications and program supports the child will receive.

5. A description of the extent to which the child with a disability will participate in regular classroom activities with non-disabled peers.

6. A list of the modifications or accommodations needed for the child to take the mandated standardized tests.

7. A start date when the special education and related services will be provided to the child and the frequency and duration of these activities and support services.

8. Provision for the transition of the child into life after school. (This component must be in place before the child reaches the age of 14.)

9. Provision for counseling about the rights that the child will accrue upon reaching the age of 18. (This must be done at least one year prior to the child's 18th birthday.)

NOTE: For more information about the elements of an IEP, see www.ed.gov/parents/needs/speced/iepguide/index.html

ACCOMMODATIONS FOR CHILDREN WITH DISABILITIES

A bedrock foundation belief of the American people is that all people should be treated equally and fairly. Thus, we wrote this requirement for equal protection into the U.S. Constitution, Amendment 14, Section 1:

> No State shall make or enforce any law which shall abridge the privileges or immunities of citizens of the United States; nor shall any State deprive

any person of life, liberty, or property, without due process of law; nor deny any person within its jurisdiction to the equal protection of the laws. Ratified July 9, 1868.

This "equal protection" provision has been used as the foundation for legal arguments to provide students with disabilities with the right to an appropriate education. Providing a public school education for all children with disabilities is a recent innovation. Before World War II public schools usually referred children with disabilities to outside agencies, state hospitals, and private training homes. When Congress passed, and President Ford signed, the Education for all Handicapped Children Act in 1975, a new era for the education of students with disabilities began.

The inclusion of children with disabilities in all aspects of public school life has been one result of this legislation. Special education students now participate in regular classroom testing as well as large-scale state assessments with their non-disabled peers. This is accomplished by providing the students with special needs a "level playing field." This is done by providing certain accommodations for special education students. The goal of such accommodations is to assure that we are not evaluating what the child's disabilities prevent him or her from doing but rather measuring what has been accomplished.

One fear of special educators is that the children with the most significant reading disabilities are being left behind by the testing provisions of the NCLB Act. The point can be made that for these children who struggle to extract meaning from the written page, one morpheme at a time, and who see each paragraph as an enemy to be subdued through one-on-one combat, there are no accommodations that will somehow put them on a par with their peers who are facile readers (Meek, 2006). The state-mandated tests are all dense with reading material and require that children are able to read for understanding and meaning, or risk being forever "Below Proficient." This testing mandate can be viewed as being especially concerning for the parents of children with severe reading disabilities. Recent research has demonstrated that reading disabilities are brought about by disruptions in the normal neural processing of the posterior section (left occipitotemporal region) of the developing cortex of some children (Shaywitz et al., 2002; Shaywitz & Shaywitz, 2005, 2007). Severe reading disabilities are biological phenomena that are marginally tractable. Improvement of the neurological functions related to reading requires an organized effort by well-educated reading teachers, which begins with the child in his or her early years.

Each state has set out its own set of guidelines for providing testing accommodations during statewide assessments. A state-by-state listing of these accommodations can be found at a Web page from the University of Minnesota: http://education.umn.edu/NCEO/TopicAreas/Accommodations/AccomFAQ.htm.

In a similar way, all school systems should have an approved set of policies in place for accommodating the needs of special education students on classroom tests and examinations. A backlash of opinion against these accommodations has been reported. Students who see their peers given extra time on classroom tests and even on the SAT II have spoken out against what is perceived as a lack in equitable treatment (Green, 2007).

One accommodation that must be addressed occurs in the schools of the states that require children to pass a high-stakes test to be promoted to the next grade. In these states, children with disabilities may be retained simply on the basis of having low test scores. Yet, low test scores provide one of the reasons the children were determined by the IST (Instructional Support Team) process to be entitled to special educational services to begin with. Once a child is measured on a high-stakes test as being proficient, he or she is no longer eligible for special services. It is clear that this issue needs further clarification, and the development of a transparent model for accountability with children that have special needs (Gaffney & Zaimi, 2003).

Testing Environment

When a child is unable to attend and concentrate on the testing task, it may be necessary to have that child tested alone using a study carrel. Naturally, someone will need to administer the test to the child. This could be done by a counselor, student teacher, or even a library aid. In addition to AD/HD diagnosed children, others who may need to be tested in a separate area are those with **pervasive developmental disabilities** (e.g., Asperger's disorder), those who may be disruptive for others (e.g., Tourette's disorder), and those who may need close supervision (e.g., Oppositional Defiant Disorder).

Time

Ten or more percent of the children in school may have a specific learning disability. By far the most common among these is in reading. These children may need to be accommodated by having extra time for reading passages and answering comprehension questions. A total of 37 of the 50 states permit children with learning disabilities to have unlimited time to complete statewide assessment tests. Other accommodations that may facilitate testing for children with difficulty attending and focusing on tasks include having the child assessed in a low-distraction environment. This accommodation is an approved strategy in 41 of the 50 states (Thurlow & Bolt, 2001). When combined, these two accommodations would make it possible to provide a quiet location away from distractions and unlimited time constraints for children with attention-deficit/hyperactivity disorder.

Modality

Not all children can read or otherwise use the test material. One way this inability occurs is when children with visual impairments can't see to read the test material. Thirty-eight of the states provide a Braille version of the state's test, while 40 states offer a large-print edition for children with low vision.

Those with severe musculoskeletal spasticity or who have paresis (e.g., cerebral palsy) will need to have the test verbally administered and answered. Children with the inability to write or make small answer-sheet marks with a pencil are accommodated in 43 states by having an adult read the questions and mark the answers that the child gives. These proctors can also take dictation on performance (constructed response) questions.

Children with a hearing disability may need to have headphones to facilitate hearing test directions, while deaf children will require the test directions be signed to them. Signing is a labor-intensive activity. One sign language interpreter may not be enough for a long test.

Thirty-six states require that children who are English-language learners be provided with a qualified translator to assist in the administration and recording of the answers for the test (Thurlow & Bolt, 2001).

The decision to provide accommodations for the child with a disability during tests is something that is normally addressed during meetings of the instructional support team and addressed by the Individual Educational Plan. The goal of all accommodations is not to give the child an advantage but to make it possible for the special-needs child to fully participate and experience a level playing field.

Summary

Each decade the proportion of children diagnosed with a serious special learning need increases. Today, 1 American child in 12 has a serious disabling condition that makes learning difficult without specialized assistance. This represents almost 6 million children. Beginning in the 1970s, the federal government has worked to provide a level playing field for students with disabilities. These efforts have become more complex since the passage of the No Child Left Behind Act of 2002. The central issue is the level of test children with special needs will be required to take. Before 2002, local schools used developmentally appropriate measures to assess and chart the educational growth and development of children with disabilities. Under the rules of the No Child Left Behind Act, only a tiny fraction of the special education population can be measured following that model. The Act requires that 99% of all students demonstrate proficiency on an age-appropriate measure, not a developmentally appropriate one.

One step in the process of helping a child who experiences learning problems in school involves a meeting of parents, teachers, and others with a role to play to identify ways to assist the child. These Instructional Support Teams can provide a framework for assistance that may be all the child requires to catch up with his or her peers. If there is a greater need, the decision can be made to initiate a full psychoeducational diagnostic assessment by a multidisciplinary team. This team, with the participation of the parents, can make an entitlement decision to provide the child with special education services. The first step in that process is the development of an Individual Educational Plan for the child.

Data that become part of this process may include informal and anecdotal observations by the homeroom teacher and others in the school community of the child. The data on the child may also involve the administration of highly specialized measures of achievement and learning. These can take the form of published instruments as well as by a school psychologist probing an individual child's specific areas of curriculum weakness and strength.

Discussion Questions

1. What are some likely reasons why the number of children having disabilities in school today is greater in both absolute and relative terms than has been true of the previous cohorts of students?

2. Starting with the first informal observation by the teacher of a student's possible learning problem, list all the personnel and the amount of time each is likely to spend working on the child's behalf before the IEP is written and instituted. Then use the figure of $75[11] per hour as the cost of these faculty and specialists (including overhead) and estimate how

much it actually costs to reach an entitlement decision and start a program of special education assistance for one child. You may substitute the actual local average per hour cost if $75 is not appropriate.

3. What are the applicable federal laws that define the educational services for children with disabilities? What legal conflict exists with regard to how children with disabilities are measured and educated?

4. This week purchase a newspaper or magazine written in a language you do not know. Spend a half hour "reading" it. Now, what accommodations will you need before you can take a test on the contents of that publication?

5. What is the role of the child's parents on an IEP committee? If possible, ask a school counselor or administrator what the school's policy is regarding a child's IEP when the two parents disagree with each other about the best approach to follow with the education of their special needs child.

Student Study Site

Educational Assessment on the Web

Log on to the Web-based student study site at www.sagepub.com/wrightstudy for additional Web sources and study resources.

NOTES

1. These teams are known by many names: Student Assistance Teams, Learning Support Teams, Educational Resource Committees, etc.

2. Section 504 provides equal access to education (and all other activities) to children with disabilities. This legislation requires classroom accommodations to meet the needs created by any mental or physical disability. For example, if a child has a partial hearing loss, the accommodation may involve providing amplifiers for the teacher's voice.

3. The spectrum of autism-related problems has been reported to be a new epidemic with numbers approaching 1 in 160 school-age children. These may prove to be exaggerated and an artifact of several other factors. The U.S. Department of Education did not classify autism as a special education entitlement classification until 1992. Also, today there are more sources for help and support for families with children with autism than ever before (Wallis, 2007).

4. The "executive function" is a cognitive construct describing a mental system that controls and manages other mental processes. The abilities to plan ahead and concentrate are directed by the executive function.

5. The user holds a master's degree in psychology, education, social work, or similar field and has completed graduate-level coursework in testing and educational measurement.

6. For a review of the meaning of these qualification levels see Chapter 12.

7. Mirror image reading was formerly known as dyslexia or streptosymbola.

8. The Woodcock–Johnson III provides a test battery of cognitive abilities (see Chapter 12) that is constructed on the framework of the Cattell–Horn–Carroll theory of cognitive ability.

9. Basic concepts: numeration, rational numbers, geometry. Operations: addition, subtraction, division, mental computation. Applications: measurement, time and money, estimation, interpreting data, problem solving.

10. There is an urban legend about a school district that quietly purchased a new home for a family that had four children with profound neurologically based cognitive disabilities. The educational costs and specialized transportation needs for these children was in excess of $45,000 per year for each child. The new home the original school district purchased was located in another school system. The biennial cost of specialized private education for these seriously impaired children was more than the cost of the new house.

11. This is based on an average annual salary of about $72,000 per year for a team composed of school psychologists, school administrators, nurses, counselors, physical therapists, social workers, and reading specialists. Overhead is assumed to be about 50% of the base pay and includes health programs, Social Security, retirement, and local taxes and tariffs paid by the schools. Once a child has an IEP and is receiving services, the average cost of his or her education is approximately 1.5 times that of the student's peers who are not disabled.

PART V

No Child, Teacher, or School Left Behind

There has not been a federal law with a greater impact on American education than the No Child Left Behind Act since the initial Elementary and Secondary Act of 1965. This law, with its goal of eliminating the source of the "soft racism" of low expectations, was long overdue. Since it passed Congress and was signed by President Bush in 2002, all public and charter schools are under the gun to improve the achievement of all students and to close the achievement gap between ethnic groups.

The justification for the era of educational reforms that started in the 1980s and that continues today was based on international educational achievement comparisons. These comparisons were purported to demonstrate how poorly American schools were doing. In reality, there was much that was right about our schools then, and there is now, too.

Each year, school-aged children spend only 15% of their time in school. Much of what a child knows and can do is a function of the child's home: Involved parents tend to raise children who do well in school.

In school, the major factor in achievement is the quality of the classroom teacher. The certification of a "highly qualified" teacher is not always the same thing as a "highly effective" teacher. One of the problems our society needs to resolve is the fact that the most effective teachers and school leaders tend to gravitate to the best schools where the students already have many resources and consistently exhibit high levels of achievement. All too often the teachers with the least experience and marginal credentials find their way into schools enrolling the neediest students, who do not test well.

It is also clear that there are certain characteristics of school leaders who are successful in creating a climate that is conducive to student learning. Leadership, adequate resources, and quality instruction make a core of school-based factors that have a lot to do with student achievement. In addition to these critical factors, certain instructional strategies have also been shown through thorough analysis—large-scale statewide testing—to be effective in optimizing student achievement scores.

The ability to lead an evaluation of schools and educational programs is a basic skill of all line administrators and curriculum leaders. There are certain basic steps in the evaluation process that can be applied to a number of educational venues and evaluation tasks.

A new model of educational evaluation has emerged since the 1980s. Heretofore, teachers could point to any number of alternative explanations for poor levels of achievement by students. The new approach to evaluation is one that permits an evaluator to separate these factors and see the effect of each. This has made it possible to actually determine the individual impact on the achievement level of children of each teacher involved with his or her education. This approach is known as "value-added assessment."

Chapter 14

INTERNATIONAL, NATIONAL, AND STATEWIDE TESTING PROGRAMS

I n the politicized education environment of the new century, educators can no longer abstain from and hope that large-scale testing will go away. Popham (1999) observed that the rules for educators all changed when newspapers began to report test data and even rank schools based on the achievement outcome of students. Today, even the value of suburban homes is dependant in part on the ranking of a community's schools.

Issues and Themes

Large-scale testing first appeared in the schools of the United States during the 1840s. By the 1870s some school systems required eighth graders to pass a 2-day-long test to attend public high schools. At first this was a uniquely American phenomenon. By the First World War standardized testing became a regular part of the educational programs of Western Europe as well as in the industrialized nations of Asia. Today there are a number of achievement tests and survey questionnaires regularly administered as a part of international comparisons.

The education reform movement of the 1960s brought new efforts and money to the task of improving schools. The lead in this was taken by the federal government. The hallmark of this endeavor was the passage of the

Elementary and Secondary Education Act of 1965. Along with these funds came the need for accountability. The National Assessment of Educational Progress (NAEP) was the result of this call for accountability.

The use of standardized assessment tests for international comparisons is relatively recent, with the first of these happening only 40 years ago. Misinterpretations and over-reading of these data fueled the critics of American teachers and schools (Ravitch, 1995). One indirect outcome of the international comparisons was the passage of reform legislation, beginning with the Improving America's Schools Act of 1994. This was followed 8 years later with the No Child Left Behind Act of 2002.

This 2002 law requires the establishment of statewide standards-based assessment testing in each grade between third and eighth. One more test was mandated for the high school years. By the middle of the first decade of the 21st century, some progress had been made toward the goal of having all children test at a proficient level. The NCLB Act and the high-stakes testing program that it spawned have many critics. The focus of much of the criticism is on problems with curriculum narrowing and the time and effort needed to prepare children for the mandated tests. Additional concern is with the problem that testing has created for children with limited proficiency in English and those children with significant cognitive disabilities.

Learning Objectives

By reading and studying this chapter you should acquire the ability to do the following:

- Describe the outcome of the First and Second International Math Study for 4th, 8th, and 12th grade students from the United States.
- Describe the construction, administration, and American outcome of the TIMSS.
- Discuss the sampling problems inherent with international testing programs.
- Describe and discuss the outcome for students from American schools on the PIRLS.
- Describe the development of the measure and the outcome of the PISA for children of the United States.
- Discuss the evolution of the international educational comparisons from FIMS to the TIMSS.
- Explain the relationship between the "War on Poverty" and the "Nation's Report Card."

- Describe the various tests that make up the National Assessment of Educational Progress.
- Describe the participation requirements for the NAEP.
- Explain the role of international testing programs on the development of the standards-based testing programs in the United States.
- Review evidence for and against the testing mandates of the No Child Left Behind Act.

INTERNATIONAL COMPARISONS

Since the late 1950s, American education policy makers have had an interest in how our students compare with the students from other industrial nations (Viadero, 2006). This new interest in comparison data can be traced to concern over the scientific advances happening in the Soviet Union during the 1950s.

First International Mathematics Study

Data from the international comparisons first became available in the 1960s. From that first report onward, education reformers have used international data to criticize our teachers and the curriculums that are used in our schools. One goal of these critical reformers is a complete restructuring of American educational practice and educational policy.

> *International comparisons of student achievement completed a decade ago reveal that on 19 academic tests American students were never first or second and, in comparison with other industrialized nations, were last seven times.*[1]
>
> (National Commission on Excellence in Education, 1983, p. 8)

One of the first of the international comparison studies was begun in 1964 by the International Association for the Evaluation of Educational Achievement (IEA). This initial international assessment was a comparison of achievement in mathematics across samples of eighth and graduating high school students from 10 nations.[2] This first study, the First International Mathematics Study (FIMS), found that American eighth graders were only better than the children of one nation, Sweden, and our seniors placed dead last.

This international research was criticized for a number of reasons, including the likelihood of **sampling inadequacy** or error and the fact that

American seniors are notoriously unmotivated for taking a test that won't have any impact on their lives (Lederman, 2006). American children have another disadvantage in that all measurement questions on the test were expressed in metric units, a system unfamiliar to most Americans.

Second International Mathematics Study

The Second International Mathematics Study (SIMS) was conducted over a 13-year period between 1976 and 1989. This test measured achievement along five dimensions of mathematics and found that the eighth-graders of the United States were at about the 50th percentile among the 18 nations and 20 school systems in the sample.[3] The 12th-graders were found to be in the lower third of the international comparison group. These two reports along with two associated studies, the First and Second International Science Studies (FISS & SISS), provided ammunition for the critics of American education (Bennett, 1992; Chubb & Moe, 1992; Evers & Walberg, 2004; Finn, 1991; Ravitch, 2000). Calls for reform went so far as to propose the disbanding of all public schools and school systems. A number of these reformers felt that once all school administrators were dismissed, the schools would be reopened as private companies owned and operated by the teachers. Governments would pay the new corporate schools through vouchers that families could spend at any school (Vedder, 2000).

These critics failed to take into account the flaws in the research design and the sampling inadequacies of these comparative studies. In the United States, children who are just learning English as a second language, and children in special education, are included in standardized testing programs.[4] This is not the case elsewhere. Another sampling error involves the fact that virtually all American children attend comprehensive high schools. This also isn't the case in all industrialized countries, where attending an academic high school requires the adolescent students applying for admission have high assessment test scores (Berliner & Biddle, 1995). The reality is that many of the states within the United States have school systems that compare very well with the top tier of nations in the international studies. Those states that invest less in the education of their children tend to skew our national average downward. An analysis by David C. Berliner (1997) has suggested that the removal of five states (Louisiana, Alabama, Florida, Georgia, and Mississippi) would raise the United States into the upper quartile of nations. Berliner (2004) also posited that the American public schools are providing an exceptionally high quality of education for the middle-class communities where support for education and interest in schools are high.

Third International Mathematics and Science Study

Results from a new parallel set of science and mathematics achievement surveys were published starting in 1995 and continued to be reported into the 21st century. These new international comparisons were originally known as the Third International Mathematics and Science Study (TIMSS).

The 2003 edition of TIMSS was renamed the Trends in International Mathematics and Science Study and was administered to a sample of the fourth- and eighth-grade children of 67 nations. The test was designed by a committee using items submitted from the various nations participating in the study. Committees representing the education departments of the various governments were then contacted to review the items selected for inclusion. All items were field tested in the various participating nations and a final screening was done based on item performance. All together there were over 300 items in both assessments. For this reason, a system of **matrix sampling** similar to that used with the NAEP was employed. A number of items from earlier assessments were also included in the 2003 edition of TIMSS. These were included to allow the researchers to identify trends over time in the national data sets.

In addition to achievement test items, TIMSS 2003 also administered background questionnaires covering attitudes toward mathematics and science, home background, academic self-concept, and out-of-classroom activities. Educators and administrators answered questionnaire items about the schools and curriculum. The American children did relatively well on this international assessment. Both the fourth-grade and eighth-grade samples were above the median in both math and science.

To learn more about the TIMSS, see http://timss.bc.edu/timss2003i/technicalD.html.

Programme for International Student Assessment

In addition to TIMSS, another international comparison was released in 2005—the results of the **Programme for International Student Assessment (PISA)**. These tests are sponsored by the Organization for Economic Co-operation and Development (2006) and are administered to 10th-grade students every 3 years. The data reported in 2005 were from the 2003 edition of those tests. The next round of testing occurred in 2006 but will not be reported until 2008. These tests are concerned with the literacy related to problem solving in mathematics and science. In addition to other areas, the PISA assessment also provides a measure of reading skill. In the

BOX 14.1   Five Items From the 2003 Edition of the TIMSS Grade 8 Test

A person sorted some animals into the two groups listed on the table. Which characteristic of animals was used for the sorting?

A. Legs

B. Eyes

C. Nervous system

D. Skin

Group 1	Group 2
Humans	Snakes
Dogs	Worms
Flies	Fish

A tiny light bulb is held 20 centimeters to the left of a square card, which is in turn held 20 centimeters to the left of a poster board, as shown. The shadow of the card on the poster board has a side of 10 centimeters.

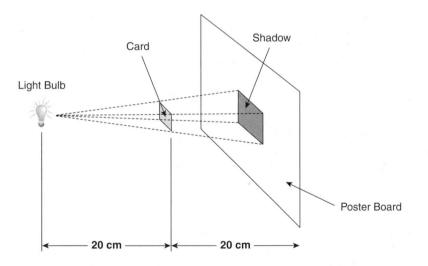

If the poster board is moved 40 cm further to the right so that it is 80 cm from the light, what will be the new size of the card's shadow on the poster board?

A. 5 cm

B. 10 cm

C. 15 cm

D. 20 cm

Joe had three test scores of 78, 76, and 74, while Mary had scores of 72, 82, and 74. How did Joe's average (mean) score compare with Mary's average (mean) score?

A. Joe's was 1 point higher.

B. Joe's was 1 point lower.

C. Both averages were the same.*

D. Joe's was 2 points higher.

E. Joe's was 2 points lower.

In square *EFGH,* which of these is FALSE?

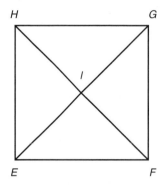

A. $\triangle EIF$ and $\triangle EIH$ are congruent.*

B. $\triangle GHI$ and $\triangle GHF$ are congruent.

C. $\triangle EFH$ and $\triangle EGH$ are congruent.

D. $\triangle EIF$ and $\triangle GIH$ are congruent.

The objects on the scale make it balance exactly. On the left pan there is a 1kg weight (mass) and half a brick. On the right pan there is one brick.

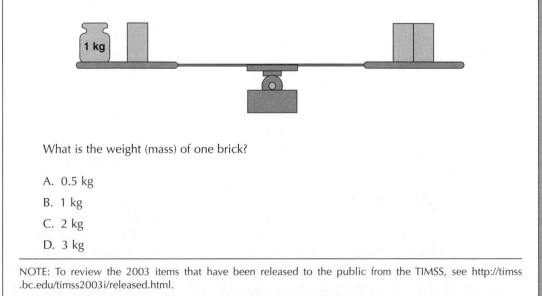

What is the weight (mass) of one brick?

A. 0.5 kg

B. 1 kg

C. 2 kg

D. 3 kg

NOTE: To review the 2003 items that have been released to the public from the TIMSS, see http://timss.bc.edu/timss2003i/released.html.

BOX 14.2   Material From the TIMSS Technical Manual, Listing All Subtests

Mathematics Content Domain		Science Content Domain	
Grade 8	Number	Grade 8	Life Science
	Algebra		Chemistry
	Measurement		Physics
	Geometry		Earth Science
	Data		Environmental Science
Grade 4	Number	Grade 4**	Life Science
	Patterns and Relationship*		Physical Science
	Measurements		Earth Science
	Geometry		
	Data		

Cognitive Domain	Cognitive Domain
Knowing Facts and Procedures	Factual Knowledge
Using Concepts	Conceptual Understanding
Solving Routine Problems	Reasoning and Analysis
Reasoning	

SOURCE: From TIMSS 2003 Technical Report, by M. Martin, I. V. S. Mullis, and S. J. Chrostowski (Eds.), 2004, p. 9. Copyright 2003 by the International Study Center. Reprinted with permission.

*At fourth grade, the algebra content domain is called patterns and relationships.
**At the fourth grade, there are only three content areas in science, namely life science, physical science, and earth science.

---

mathematics test, the American adolescents scored 13th out of 30 nations. Interestingly, the students from the United States had the best overall self-concept of their ability to do mathematics. In reading, the Americans were 23rd out of 40 nations tested, and in science 19th out of 40.

To learn more about the PISA assessments and see the outcomes and sample items, see www.pisa.oecd.org.

International Adult Literacy Survey

An assessment of adult literacy was conducted on an international basis, and the results were presented in 1998. This testing program was sponsored by the National Institute for Literacy of the U.S. Department of Education. The test, the International Adult Literacy Survey (**IALS**), involved adults between the ages of 16 and 65 from 22 nations. The American sample scored at a level 3 on a five-level rubric, placing that sample in 10th place out of the 17 "wealthy" nations surveyed.

Data from this study are available at www.nifl.gov/nifl/facts/IALS.html.

Progress in International Reading Literacy Study

Finally, an international comparative study of the reading ability of third-grade children in 35 countries was carried out under the aegis of the International Association for the Evaluation of Educational Achievement. This test, the Progress in International Reading Literacy Study (PIRLS), found third-graders from the United States to be reading at a level significantly above the international average. This ranking held up to various permutations of the method employed to establish scores on the measure (Gonzales & Kennedy, 2007).

More information about the test and the outcome from the international comparison can be reviewed at http://timss.bc.edu/pirls2001i/PIRLS2001_Pubs_IR.html.

Civics Education Study

Students from the United States outperformed students from most of the world on an international test of civics. The Civics Education Study was also sponsored by the IEA and compared 14-year-old children from 28 nations on several measures of citizenship and civics. The U.S. ninth-graders scored significantly above the international average, and the students from no other country scored significantly better (Baldi et al., 2001).

Status of American Education

It is clear that the situation in American education is not as dire as the Cassandras of the 1980s had purported. The diversity of national secondary education programs makes it incredibly difficult to make any international comparisons. However, at the elementary school level, comparisons are not as difficult to make. This reflects the fact that almost all children attend primary schools and take the same basic core of courses. Not all elementary school children are enrolled in school at the same age. There are differences between the average age of children in fourth grade, ranging from 9 years

BOX 14.3   A Sample Set of Reading Questions From PIRLS

Nights of the Pufflings by Bruce McMillan

Every year, black and white birds with orange bills visit the Icelandic island of Heimaey. These birds are called puffins. They are known as "clowns of the sea" because of their bright bills and clumsy movements. Puffins are awkward fliers during takeoff because they have chunky bodies and short wings.

Halla lives on the island of Heimaey. She searches the sky every day. As she watches from high on a cliff overlooking the seas, she spots the first puffin of the season. She whispers to herself "Lundi," which means "puffin" in Icelandic.

Soon the sky is speckled with them – puffins, puffins everywhere. They are returning from their winter at sea, returning to Halla's island and the nearby uninhabited islands to lay eggs and raise puffin chicks. These "clowns of the sea" return to the same burrows year after year. It's the only time they come ashore.

Halla and her friends climb over the cliffs to watch the birds. They see pairs tap-tap-tap their beaks together. Each pair they see will soon tend an egg deep inside the cliffs. When the puffin eggs have hatched, the parents will bring fish home to feed the chicks. Each chick will grow into a young puffling. The night of the pufflings will come when each puffling takes its first flight. Although the nights of the pufflings are still long weeks away, Halla thinks about getting some cardboard boxes ready.

All summer long the adult puffins fish and tend to their chicks. By August, flowers blanket the burrows. With the flowers in full bloom, Halla knows that the wait for the nights of the pufflings is over.

The hidden chicks have grown into young pufflings. Now it's time for Halla and her friends to get out their boxes and torches for the nights of the pufflings. Starting tonight, and for the next two weeks, the pufflings will be leaving for their winter at sea.

In the darkness of the night, the pufflings leave their burrows for their first flight. It's a short, wing-flapping trip from the high cliffs. Most of the birds splash-land safely in the sea below. But some get confused by the village lights – perhaps they think the lights are moonbeams reflecting on the water. Hundreds of the pufflings crash-land in the village every night. Unable to take off from the flat ground, they run around and try to hide.

Halla and her friends will spend each night searching for stranded pufflings that haven't made it to the water. But the village cats and dogs will be searching, too. Even if the cats and dogs don't get them, the pufflings might get run over by cars or trucks. The children must find the stray pufflings first. By ten o'clock the streets of Heimaey are alive with roaming children.

Halla and her friends race to rescue the pufflings. Armed with torches, they wander through the village, searching dark places. Halla spots a puffling. She races after it, grabs it, and puts it safely in a cardboard box. For two weeks all the children of Heimaey sleep late in the day so they can stay out at night. They rescue thousands of pufflings.

Every night Halla and her friends take the rescued pufflings home. The next day, with the boxes full of pufflings, Halla and her friends go down to the beach. It's time to set the pufflings free. Halla releases one first. She holds it up so that it will get used to flapping its wings. Then, holding the puffling snuggly in her hands, she swings it up in the air and launches it over the water beyond the surf. The puffling flutters just a short distance before splash-landing safely.

Day after day Halla's pufflings paddle away, until the nights of the pufflings are over for the year. As she watches the last of the pufflings and adult puffins leave for their winter at sea, Halla bids them farewell until next spring. She wishes them a safe journey as she calls out, "Goodbye, goodbye."

1. According to the article, which of these is a danger faced by the pufflings?
    A. drowning while landing in the sea
    B. getting lost in the burrows
    C. not having enough fish from their parents
    D. being run over by cars and trucks*

2. Why do the puffins come to the island?
    A. to be rescued
    B. to look for food
    C. to lay eggs
    D. to learn to fly

3. Write two different feelings Halla might have after she has set the pufflings free. Explain why she might have each feeling.
    1. _____
    2. _____

    Sample Answer:
    1. she might be happy that she helped a puffling in need and
    2. sad that the night of the pufflings are over because they are fun

4. Would you like to go and rescue pufflings with Halla and her friends? Use what you have read to help you explain.

    Sample Answer:
    Yes I would like to because it sounds like an adventure going to find pufflings in the middle of the night.

The Progress in International Literacy Study (PIRLS). (2003). *Night of the Pufflings* [sample item]. Washington, DC: National Center for Educational Statistics

SOURCE: From *Nights of the Pufflings*, by Bruce McMillan, 1995. Copyright © 1995 by Bruce McMillan. Adapted and reprinted by permission of Mifflin Company. All rights reserved.

and 8 months (Scotland) to 10 years 4 months (Latvia; Viadero, 2006). These age differences represent one source for the average national achievement differences. Yet, there are significant sampling differences. In the United States we test our special education students, whereas many others do not. Also, our pluralistic society does not exclude from public school education minority students or those who were foreign born.[5] In the United States, even undocumented immigrant students participate in all aspects of public school education, including testing.

"Big deal, an A in math. That would be a D in any other country."

Figure 14.1   "Big Deal, an A in Math . . ."

SOURCE: The New Yorker Collection. Copyright © 1998 by Mike Twohy. From cartoonbank
.com. All rights reserved.

At the secondary level the American experience of the comprehensive
high school attended by all adolescent students is not the international norm.
In most countries the academic high schools are reserved for those children
who have the best academic potential and who are most likely to go on to
higher education. The 12-year limit on American education is another factor
that makes international comparisons of the senior class misleading. The clear
advantage is with the students of those countries where students have
13 years of public education (Berliner & Biddle, 1995; Boe & Shin, 2005).

A review of the research comparing the achievement of American and
Chinese students in mathematics noted that Chinese children have better
concepts of numbers than American children even before they ever attend
school. This finding is not rooted in educational programs but in the nature
of Mandarin versus the English language. The Chinese language, like the language of Korea and Japan, makes the conceptualization of mathematics less
difficult for Asian children to obtain (Wang & Lin, 2005).

In most recent tests the samples of children from the United States are
performing at or above the international median. This is a good outcome in
view of the differences that exist between the samples from the different

countries. In the area of citizenship education, American children are better prepared than are the children of most other nations. A new international evaluation of civic and citizenship understanding and achievement was initiated in 2006 under the aegis of the International Association for the Evaluation of Educational Achievement. Data from these studies will be released in 2009.

Case in Point (14a)

Howard Gardner (2005), in writing about international comparisons in achievement, has described the enterprise as a fool's errand. His point is that the education leaders of too many countries see the goal of their educational offerings to achieve the best international scores on those multiple choice tests. This focus is too narrow and can lead to the perils of dishonesty and **teaching to the test**. In 2006, an analysis of a significant improvement in mathematics test scores for the eighth-grade children of the nation of Lithuania demonstrated that it was the product of a new set of mathematics standards and textbooks patterned to follow the TIMSS instructional goals and standards (Viadero, 2006). Gardner proposes that the nations should first decide what type of graduates they wish to have. He believes that it is essential for education leaders to consider what they want their students to be able to do. Gardner poses several dimensions of cognition not measured on the international tests, including creative thinking, ethical thinking, the ability to synthesize, and a disciplined mind. None of these goals is now tested and compared, and it is not likely that their measurement will ever be done with a multiple choice test.

For more information, see "Considerations on Point" at www.sagepub.com/wrightstudy

---

NATION'S REPORT CARD

Thomas Jefferson said that no nation can be both ignorant and free. Today no nation can be both ignorant and great.

—President Lyndon Johnson,
State on the Union, January 4, 1965

During the 1960s, the nation entered a progressive era for the development of educational programs. In 1965 the federal government became an active partner with local schools and state education departments. These partnerships resulted in a number of new initiatives designed to assist in the education of children from impoverished backgrounds while also providing the incentive and resources needed for school improvement. What enabled all of this activity was the Elementary and Secondary Education Act (ESEA) signed into law by President Johnson on April 11, 1965 (ESEA, P.L. 89-10, 1965).[6] This act, along with a spate of other significant social policy legislation, was a central feature in the establishment of what President Johnson described as his vision for a "**Great Society**." ESEA was also a central point on the frontline in what he described as the "**War on Poverty**" (Johnson, 1966). The Elementary and Secondary Education Act was built on the bedrock belief that the education of disadvantaged children could be improved if schools had the wherewithal to purchase instructional resources and develop innovative instructional programs.

First National Assessment

Every state department of education and some 94% of the local school districts were eligible to receive money under the original five sections or titles of this act. To determine the effectiveness of these innovative efforts, the act also provided for the establishment of a national testing program. The original national testing effort was developed by Education Commissioner Frederick R. Keppel and was funded by the Carnegie Corporation. ESEA became the force that made the National Assessment of Educational Progress (NAEP) possible. The original plans called for performance-based tests, but those plans were soon scrapped for the more pragmatic idea of an achievement test using multiple choice items. This new test soon was known by its sobriquet: the Nation's Report Card.

NAEP

The National Assessment of Educational Progress (NAEP) is the only nationally representative test that has been given continually for 40 years. This has provided a stream of data that has been used to spot trends and see the impact of new policy and procedures. Changes to the reading component of the NAEP initiated in 2008 breaks this long continuity in the data on student achievement. From its beginning in 1969, and up until 1990, the measure was only used to see the nation's educational progress as a whole. (In 1981, the NAEP became a biennial test.) In 1990, the U.S. Congress changed that mandate, and the NAEP began reporting scores that were disaggregated by the individual states. Naturally, this led to a state-by-state ranking system. This state-by-state list was not complete until 2003, when all states were required to participate in the NAEP program.

To review the state-by-state report, see http://nces.ed.gov/nationsreport card/states/ or to see a presentation including other markers of the status of education in the various states, see www.asbj.com/evs/05/state.html.

National Sample

Today, a stratified random sample of children in grades 4, 8, and 12 are tested in reading, mathematics, writing, and science during each odd-numbered year. No more than 90 **randomly selected** children from any grade level in a randomly selected school are actually tested. However, the test sample must never exclude special education students or those with limited English language proficiency.[7] Every fourth test cycle, a smaller sample also take civics and history examinations. Twelfth-graders take an additional test of economics. The reading and mathematics test is given with every biennial testing cycle, and the science and writing tests are given every other biennial cycle. The social studies areas are only tested every 8 to 10 years.

When a school district is selected to be a part of the random sample that makes up the NAEP, it must comply with the request or lose funding from federal sources. The fourth- and eighth-grade classrooms that the National Center for Educational Statistics designates as being needed for the NAEP sample must comply with the request. Participation by 12th-grade classes is the voluntary choice of the school's administration. President George W. Bush has attempted to have the participation of the randomly selected 12th-grade classes also made mandatory (Cavanagh & Robelen, 2004). Once a class is selected not all the children in the room will take the same test. The areas of achievement to be measured have been broken down into between 8 and 12 blocks of questions per grade level. During the actual test administration, each child is given only two blocks of questions to answer. Each block requires about 25 minutes to complete. Scoring is done on a group average basis. Data are aggregated across children to produce a picture of the achievement level for the whole sample. This method is referred to as "matrix sampling." It is the use of this sampling method that makes it impossible to report meaningful results for any individual child.

For more general information about the NAEP, see http://nces.ed.gov/nationsreportcard/parents/faq.asp#ques9.

There is a significant difference between what most states consider proficient and what is considered a proficient score on the NAEP. It is considerably harder for students to score at the "proficient" or at the "above proficient" level on the NAEP than it is on all but one of the mandated state assessment tests (Saulny, 2005, January). This discrepancy can be seen in states such as Texas, where the state's education department reported that

85% of the fourth-graders were proficient in reading and 87% were proficient in mathematics. Yet, the NAEP reported that only 27% of the children of Texas were proficient in reading and 33% in math (see Figure 14.1).

There are many possible reasons for this discrepancy. For one, it is clear that the NAEP and the various measures designed under the NCLB Act were developed to meet entirely different measurement goals (Carlson, 2007). The most compelling is that the two measures serve two different purposes. The NAEP is a national measure of longitudinal trends in school achievement. It has been well designed to have great stability over the years and to demonstrate only major shifts in American education. The state assessment tests were designed to identify and quantify the impact of educational reform at the local and state levels. For the most part, these tests were developed to be sensitive measures of the impact of instructional processes (Popham, 2005). These arguments notwithstanding, a number of state legislatures are considering revising statewide tests to be a close match to the National Assessment of Educational Progress (Pellegrino, 2007).

All state standards for learning must be approved by the U.S. Department of Education, and the measures of those standards must also be approved by the federal government. The discrepancy is a product of something other than the standards.

A core reason for the discrepancy is that each state sets its own cut scores for the state assessment test. The process can be influenced by any number of pragmatic and political concerns. For example, those states with minimum proficiency scores for grade promotion could face a significant challenge if more than two-thirds of the student population were retained each school year. Even in the face of these discrepancies there is a trend among the states to lower the standard used to define a proficient level of achievement on the state test. One impetus for this downward drift is the problem created by special education children who can neither pass the state-mandated assessments nor earn a high school diploma (Bowler, 2004; Rado & Dell'Angela, 2005).

One important component influencing the NAEP scores of each state is the teachability of the children of that state. In 2004, Jay Greene and Greg Forster of the Manhattan Institute developed an index of teachability. This index combines measures of poverty and social dysfunction into a single score. This was then used to rank the various states in terms of the average level of teachability of the children of each state. In other research, this teachability index was then correlated with the percentage of children measured as proficient on the NAEP in each state at fourth and eighth grades (Wright, 2006). This analysis demonstrated that the two are highly correlated, with teachability accounting for 45% of the variance in state-by-state scores.

The link between performance of American children on the international tests and on the National Assessment of Educational Progress has been

Table 14.1   Percent of Students Measured as Being "Proficient" or Better on the 8th Grade NAEP and on State Mandated Assessments

State	NAEP-8th-Reading	NAEP-8th-Math	State-8th-Reading	State-8th-Math	State	NAEP-8th-Reading	NAEP-8th-Math	State-8th-Reading	State-8th-Math
Alabama	22	16	58	25	Montana	37	35	70	69
Alaska	27	30	68	64	Nebraska	35	32	77	72
Arizona	25	21	55	21	Nevada	21	20	40	50*
Arkansas	27	19	42	23	New Hampshire	40	35	76	79*
California	22	22	30	30	New Jersey	37	33	74	57
Colorado	36	34	86	68	New Mexico	20	15	45	46
Connecticut	37	35	77	77	New York	35	32	45	51
Delaware	31	26	70	47	North Carolina	29	32	86	82
Florida	27	23	49	56	North Dakota	38	36	69	44
Georgia	26	22	81	67	Ohio	34	30	87	71
Hawaii	22	17	39	17	Oklahoma	30	20	79	73
Idaho	32	28	73	52	Oregon	33	32	60	59
Illinois	35	29	64	53	Pennsylvania	32	30	63	51
Indiana	33	31	64	66	Rhode Island	30	24	41	34
Iowa	36	33	69	72	South Carolina	24	26	20	19
Kansas	35	34	71	60	South Dakota	39	35	78	56
Kentucky	34	24	57	31	Tennessee	26	21	80	79
Louisiana	22	17	53	51	Texas	26	25	86	72
Maine	37	29	45	17	Utah	32	31	68	61
Maryland	31	30	60	40	Vermont	39	35	36	48
Massachusetts	43	38	65	37	Virginia	36	31	70	75
Michigan	32	28	61	52	Washington	33	32	48	37
Minnesota	37	44	76	75*	West Virginia	25	20	80	69
Mississippi	21	12	57	48	Wisconsin	37	35	84	76
Missouri	34	28	32	14	Wyoming	34	32	39	35

SOURCE: From "No Small Change: Targeting Money Toward Student Performance," by R. A. Skinner, 2005, *Quality Counts, 2005: State of the States, 24*(17), pp. 77–78 and 80. Copyright © 2005 by *Education Week.* Reprinted with permission.

*No state test available at grade eight. Data from fourth grade was substituted.

explored. This was done by statistically projecting the American NAEP standards and cut scores onto the TIMSS scale. When this is done, the overall mathematics and science achievement of our children can be ranked above the scores of two-thirds of the other participating nations (Phillips, 2007).

SCHOOL ASSESSMENTS

The schools ain't what they used to be and never was.

—Will Rogers

Systematic assessment testing in the schools can be traced back to the common school era and Horace Mann. Common schools were so named because they were established by local governments, were nonsectarian, and served all children (Clabaugh & Rozycki, 1990). Mann, secretary of the Massachusetts School Board from 1837 to 1848, is known for his groundbreaking efforts to open the schools for the education of both girls and boys.[8] He also worked to have women enter the teaching profession and was instrumental in upgrading the educational requirements for all teachers (Ritchie, 2004). During the 19th century, women were assumed to be less intelligent than men (Gould, 1996). This quaint male prejudice may explain why the infusion of women into the profession led to complaints about educational quality (see Photo 14.1).

Photo 14.1   Lincoln School, Circa 1900

SOURCE: Wichita-Sedgwick County Historical Museum.

In 1845, Horace Mann initiated an achievement test that was taken by 7,000 of what were assumed to be the brightest students enrolled in the public schools of Boston. The assessment was created by Mann from classroom textbooks, and the items stressed application of what was covered in those texts (Crocker, 2003). From this assessment Mann found that the schools were teaching facts and making students memorize information without any understanding of what they were learning. He noted that students could name the embargo on British and French shipping as a cause of the War of 1812 but had no idea what an embargo was. This was a major concern for Mann, who recognized the importance of students having the ability to do what we describe today as critical thinking (Rothstein & Jacobsen, 2006).

By the 1870s, common schools for children in the first through the eighth grades were established throughout New England and the other northern states (Clabaugh & Rozycki, 1990).[9] Compulsory school attendance laws soon followed. High schools were developed slowly during the 19th century and often required that students pass an application test to be admitted.

Minimum Competency Testing

Various states began assessment programs prior to the "era of accountability" that followed the publication of *A Nation at Risk: The Imperative for Educational Reform* (National Commission on Excellence in Education, 1983). For the most part the states initiated minimum competency testing to track new educational initiatives and/or to respond to educational critics.

Case in Point (14b)

A case in point is Pennsylvania, where 2,000 school districts were reorganized into 500 districts.[10] The 1963 legislation that resulted in this reorganization was accompanied by much contentious debate. To answer critics, the legislation also established a statewide achievement test, which was first designed in 1965. The focus of that test was not on individual students but on school and district outcomes.

For more information, see "Considerations on Point" at www.sagepub.com/ wrightstudy

Florida (1974) and New Jersey (1975) initiated competency tests in response to criticism from the business communities of those states. Florida was the first state to require students to pass a literacy test to graduate from high school with a diploma. When Florida prevailed in a legal action brought

BOX 14.4   Salina, Kansas, 1895: Test Items From Grade 8 Graduation Test

8th Grade Final Exam for 1895

Grammar:

1. Give nine rules for the use of Capital Letters.

2. Name the Parts of Speech and define those that have no modifications.

3. Define Verse, Stanza, and Paragraph.

Arithmetic:

1. A wagon box is 2ft. deep, 10ft. long, and 3ft. wide. How many bushels of wheat will it hold?

2. District No. 33 has a valuation of $35,000. What is the necessary levy to carry on a school seven months at $50 per month, and have $104 for incidentals?

3. Find bank discount on $300 for 90 days (no grace) at 10 percent.

U.S. History:

1. Relate the causes and results of the Revolutionary War.

2. Show the territorial growth of the United States.

3. Who were the following: Morse, Whitney, Fulton, Bell, Lincoln, Penn, and Howe?

Orthography:

1. What is meant by the following: alphabet, phonetic orthography, etymology, syllabication?

2. What are the following, and give examples of each: trigraph, sub vocals, diphthong, cognate letters, linguals?

3. Use the following correctly in sentences: cite, site, sight, fane, fain, feign, vane, vain, vein, raze, raise, rays.

Geography:

1. Name and describe the following: Monrovia, Odessa, Denver, Manitoba, Hecla, Aspinwall and Orinoco.

2. Name all the republics of Europe and give capital of each.

3. Why is the Atlantic Coast colder than the Pacific in the same latitude?

These are selected questions that appeared in the eighth grade final exam from 1895 from Salina, Kansas. It was taken from the original document on file at the Smoky Valley Genealogical Society and Library in Salina, Kansas, and reprinted by the *Salina Journal*.

SOURCE: Reprinted with permission from Mary E. Lass.

NOTE: Other questions from one of those original tests can be reviewed at the following location: www.webenglishteacher.com/text/1895test.txt.

on behalf of minority students who were denied diplomas more frequently than Anglo-White children, other states, including New Jersey, were empowered to put similar graduation requirements in place.[11] The era of minimum competency testing was short lived, ending when the various states adopted educational standards and devised all new standards-based evaluation systems. This move to standards-based assessments was reinforced by the passage of the Improving America's School Act. President Clinton was a force behind this initiative, and he signed the legislation into law in 1994.

NO CHILD LEFT BEHIND

Believing we can improve schooling with more tests is like believing you can make yourself grow by measuring your height.

—Robert Schaeffer

A centerpiece of the administration of President George W. Bush was the reauthorization of the ESEA in 2002. That legislation (P.L. 107-110, 2002) was named the No Child Left Behind Act, and it redirected the efforts of educators and schools toward improving the achievement levels of all children, including minority and special needs students. Central to the law is the mandate for annual testing in mathematics and reading between third and eighth grade and once again in high school. A science test was added in 2007. Curriculum specialists in other subject areas have complained that by not testing their fields the schools are empowered to reduce the resources invested in subjects such as the social studies and modern languages (Rabb, 2005). Even the business community has expressed concern with the narrowness of the dimensions of the curriculum that are tested (Boyd, 2007).The focus of the NCLB testing on just three subject areas has been described as being antithetical to the goals for education expressed in the writing of the country's founding fathers (Rothstein & Jacobsen, 2006).

These new tests were required to employ a standards-based model. Under this system, each state had to link its new measurements to learning standards that were first approved by the U.S. Department of Education. While no state was required to use the statewide assessment to make grade-level promotion decisions for children, eight states have done so. The target grade for the high-stakes-driven promotion decision is grade 3. This grade level was chosen as it is the last grade in which children are taught to read. It is assumed that by fourth grade children read independently to learn other subjects. The states where high-stakes tests are part of the promotion decision process are Delaware, Florida, Georgia, Louisiana, Maryland, Mississippi, North Carolina, South Carolina, and Texas. In addition, high school graduation tests are now required in over 20 states.[12]

There are two classes of students who are not subjected to these statewide tests: students attending parochial and private schools and home-schooled children. In about half of the states, those students who are home-schooled are totally exempt from taking any mandatory assessments. The lack of oversight and accountability has provided a point of criticism for those states that provide parents with vouchers for parochial and private school tuition.

Requirements and Sanctions

Scores from the state tests must be reported for each child, providing the school and parents with individualized diagnostic information. Average scores must be reported for all minority groups, as well as for special education children. Each of these group averages must show annual progress toward reaching the goal of 100% of the student population being proficient by the year 2014. Failure of a school to meet a goal of adequate yearly progress will result in the school being listed as "needing improvement." Three consecutive years on this list can cost the school students, who can transfer to schools that are performing better on the assessment, and the school must offer private tutoring to the low-performing children. Very few parents exercise the option of transferring their children. One reason for this is that there are few options for parents of the inner city but other low-performing schools (National Education Association, 2004). For another, the parents must provide their own transportation to the new school. Evidence regarding the impact of tutoring for low-scoring children is not encouraging. The results of intensive tutoring in reading and mathematics with low-performing students is negligible (Viadero, 2007). After 4 years on the list the school may see the faculty and administration replaced. The state department of education may permanently close schools with lengthy histories of not passing.[13]

For more information, see "Considerations on Point" at www.sagepub.com/wrightstudy

Case in Point (14c)

In 2002, the public schools of the City of Philadelphia were taken over by the Commonwealth's Department of Education. Pennsylvania created a quasi-experimental study when it set out to reform the district's schools. Some of the schools (a total of 16) were provided intensive teacher inservice education and extra funding and no further intervention; a second group of schools was given over to private management; a final group was restructured by Philadelphia's educational leadership. After 4 years, the schools restructured by Philadelphia's educators were found to be performing significantly better on the state's assessment (Gill, Zimmer, Christman, & Blanc, 2007).

The great proportion of schools threatened with NCLB sanctions are populated with children from impoverished families. In California, schools with mean achievement scores in the lowest 10% of the state also have enrollments with 94% of the children coming from impoverished homes. Those schools having scores in the highest 10% have enrollments that include only 7% from families of poverty (Wells, 2001).

Case in Point (14d)

The pressure to get all students to take the mandated state examinations has resulted in several unusual steps by school administrators.

In March 2006, a local newspaper reported that a fourth-grade elementary school child who had been suspended from school (for bringing a starter's pistol into school) and was awaiting transfer to a "disciplinary school" was brought back to complete the state examination. After 5 hours of testing, he was sent home to await transfer (James, 2006).

In another case a boy who was hospitalized following a bicycle accident in which he crushed three vertebrae in his neck and lost the use of his right (dominate side) arm was made to take the 10th-grade state assessment test in his hospital. The boy in question was most concerned with the timed essay portion of the examination. This part of the test he wrote in longhand using his left hand (DeGregory, 2005).

For more information, see "Considerations on Point" at www.sagepub.com/wrightstudy

---

Other provisions of the NCLB Act in 2002 required that all teachers and instructional aids in the school be **highly qualified**, that every school district must publish a school-by-school report card, and that each state is mandated to assemble statewide data and conduct a statewide self-assessment.

In 2006, the U.S. Department of Education reported that 24,470 public schools failed to meet that mandated requirements of NCLB. This represents a full 27% of all public schools. There is some question about these data, as some states have made unusual progress in only 1 year (Basken, 2006).[14]

Assistance for Children

The NCLB Act provides funds for tutoring children who have tested "below proficient." Fortunately, if a school is found to "need improvement" for 3 years it can gain supplemental funding from Title I of the NCLB Act for more individual tutors. For example, during the school year 2005–2006, the Chicago School District budgeted $50 million for tutoring services for 41,000 children who tested below proficient. These services were provided by

28 different vendors. Naturally, when such a large ad hoc effort is initiated there are problems, not the least of which are the supervision of the tutors and the evaluation of their effectiveness (Grossman, 2005). For example, the schools of Michigan were criticized by the U.S. Department of Education in 2005 for only providing tutoring services to 11,000 of the 103,000 eligible students and not doing any analysis of the effectiveness of the services the fortunate 11,000 received. An Education Department report released by Secretary Spellings in April of 2006 chastised the low performing public schools that never make the effort to inform the parents of at-risk and failing children about the tutoring option. She pointed out that of 4,000,000 eligible children in 2006 only 17% participated in the free tutoring program (Spellings, 2006a).

For more information, see "Considerations on Point" at www.sagepub.com/wrightstudy

Case in Point (14e)

Secretary Spellings was even more concerned with another provision of the NCLB Act providing for the right of children who attend low-performing schools to transfer to other schools. In these schools, less than 1% of the eligible children took advantage of this possibility. A likely reason for this is the languid pace of public schools during the summer months when the scores from the mandated statewide tests are reported. Children and families may not be easy to reach when the scores from the state's testing program are published. Another possible reason is the inertia produced when children have established themselves in a school and have made their place in a clique of friends.

The decision as to who gets the maximum effort and the lion's share of the school's resources is made locally. School administrators can initiate programs within their schools that are designed to provide developmental help and support to students who failed to reach the level of academic proficiency required by the state. In selecting which children will get how much help, some administrators have been known to conduct an academic triage. This describes an unethical process of identifying **bubble children**—that is, children who are on the cusp of reaching the level of proficient—and providing them with a large share of the school's resources (de Vise, 2007). Those children judged to be beyond the school's ability to help are provided with the equivalent of a palliative level of support. In other words, children are divided into three groups: those who are safe, those who can be helped with extra effort, and those who are beyond the resources of the school to ever help. It is the systematic incentives and sanctions built into the NCLB Act that induce educators to adopt this inequitable and amoral approach to resource allocation (Booher-Jennings, 2005).

Tutoring can happen away from school at a corporate center, church, or even in the child's home. Each eligible child (one scoring below proficient in a school that did not reach the required level of adequate yearly progress) is provided with a stipend of up to $2,500 for a program of tutoring. The tutoring company decides how many sessions are needed, what those sessions will include, and how much each will cost. Urban providers are charging about $40 per hour for semiprivate tutoring sessions. In many communities the schools provide a list of eligible children, and the tutoring companies advertise their wares to the parents of those children. It is likely that this tutoring business will grow to over $2 billion a year during the 2007–2008 school year.

A large number of the providers of these tutoring services are evangelical and other faith-based programs (Rees, 2003). Perhaps it is for that reason that the supervision of the tutors, and the oversight of the service providers, are tasks assigned under NCLB to the states rather than to local school systems. The local school districts are prevented by the language of the NCLB Act from participating in these management activities.

One new direction in the provision of tutors for American students is the outsourcing of the service. A number of tutoring companies in India have contractual relationships with American providers for online tutoring support (Reeves, 2005). This is a rapidly growing segment of the market made possible because of the Internet. Tutors in India report to work before 4:30 a.m. local time and are paid about 7,000 Indian rupees per month ($160). Their companies have offices in the United States that make all the contacts and set up the computer links in the homes of the children needing tutoring. The typical fee for these services ($20/hour) is less than half of what is typically charged in this country for private tutoring (Paulson, 2005; Shankar, 2005).

Interim Outcome

It can be claimed that after 6 years of the NCLB Act, the outcome of all these testing programs is marginally positive (Hoff & Manzo, 2007; Snipes, Williams, Horwitz, Soga, & Casserly, 2007). There was measurable improvement in the average achievement levels of most school systems, and the achievement gap between the races has closed slightly between 2002 and 2004 (Cronin, Kingsbury, McCall, & Bowe, 2005). During these first 2 years, progress made toward reducing the achievement gap was also evident in the schools of America's largest cities (Casserly, 2004). Additionally, most of the large city school systems were able to demonstrate improving test scores across the grade levels. Yet, despite these small advances, most agree that a social restructuring may be necessary to eliminate the achievement gap (Gardner, 2007). Additionally, the early gains have slowed down and at the high school level may have actually reversed during the 2 years between 2004 and 2006 (Hoff & Manzo, 2007).

The gains that have been made to date (2007) are small when projected out to the year 2014. The slope of the curve for improvement is too shallow to meet the ultimate goal of the NCLB Act (Cronin et al., 2005). Achievement gains made to this point have been demonstrated on statewide assessments but have not been evident on the National Assessment of Educational Progress scores. The actual gains a school makes any year may be explained by the volatility of school cohort group scores and have nothing to do with instructional modifications (Hill & DePascale, 2003). Another problem in making a definitive statement about student outcomes and the mandates of the NCLB law is the fact that there have not been any controlled studies. This requirement for control groups and scientific proof is a hallmark of the NCLB legislation, but there has been no such research effort initiated at either the state or national levels (Hoff, 2007).

Also, the rate of improvement of the achievement scores is slowing. The early gains may well have been a reflection of all the direct instruction that was done on the standards. Hours of drill and numerous practice tests have been a major reason for the improvements, but there may well be an upper limit to what these efforts can achieve (Lee, 2006). During his presidential address to the American Educational Research Association in 2003, Professor Robert Linn reported on linear projections of the amount of time it will take to reach the 100% proficient goal of the NCLB Act. His calculations were that the elementary school goal could be reached by the year 2060 and the high school goal by the school year 2169–2170. At the present rate of change, 99% of the public schools in California will be labeled "needing improvement" by the year 2014.

One positive outcome of the mandates of the No Child Left Behind Act has been to call school administrators and educational policy makers to the tasks of meeting the academic needs of all children (Kroeze, 2007). It has also brought the attention of the education community to the use of assessment data in the evaluation of programs and schools.

In 2005–2006, the impact of the NCLB Act was apparent in all schools. One of the largest growth industries that year was testing. Billions of dollars are now being spent each year by state departments of education to develop, administer, and score millions of these new tests. There are about a dozen test publishers, but only three dominate the market, accounting for about 75% of all sales (Olson, 2004).[15]

Case in Point (14f)

Various professional associations have taken positions opposed to the large-scale testing of preschool children with high-stakes assessments (**National Association for the Education of Young Children**, 1987, 2004). Their position is that testing should be developmentally appropriate and beneficial for the child's education. This position notwithstanding, the NCLB Act mandated the testing of all 4-year-old children enrolled in Head Start programs. This testing began in 2004 using a collection of parts from various childhood tests and several sections developed by the U.S. Department of Education. Box 14.5 shows several pages from this individually administered test for 4-year-old children.

For more information, see "Considerations on Point" at www.sagepub.com/wrightstudy

Concerns and Problems

One concern with the new standards-based tests that the states have developed for the NCLB Act is that they do not require higher-order thinking and problem-solving skills (Lane, 2004). The tests that are currently being developed and used stress lower-order skills and basic knowledge. This makes it easier for the test developers to design multiple choice measures, but it shortchanges the curriculum (Posner, 2004). This type of testing also encourages the "drill and fill" test preparation activities so common in the schools today. It has been argued that the NCLB assessments are not allowing the schools to teach children those lessons and provide those skills that correlate to living a purposeful life (Sadker & Zittleman, 2004).[16] The impact on the curriculum is most severe in schools where many children are performing at a low level. In these schools, which once had a rich and varied curriculum, the joy of learning is now a distant memory. The curriculum has been supplanted by hours of drill and repeated practice tests focused on the basic skills being tested by the state-mandated assessment (Dillon, 2006).

Music educators in Florida have taken a novel approach to achieving relevancy in this era of high-stakes assessments. Using their own funds and a small grant from the state they developed a music test that is to become part of the state-mandated assessment program in 2008 (Gupta, 2005).

Audrey L. Amrein and David Berliner (2002) at the University of Arizona have challenged the premise that high-stakes testing increases student learning. Through the analysis of a number of data sources in those states where

BOX 14.5   National Testing of 4-Year-Old Children Was Initiated Under NCLB

Example of NRS Letter Naming Instructions and Task

Here are some letters of the alphabet.

GESTURE WITH A CIRCULAR MOTION AT LETTERS AND SAY:

Point to all the letters that you know and tell me the name of each one. Go slowly and show me which letter you're naming.

INDICATE ONLY CORRECTLY NAMED LETTERS ON ANSWER SHEET.

WHEN CHILD STOPS NAMING LETTERS, SAY:

Look carefully at all of them. Do you know any more?

KEEP ASKING UNTIL CHILD DOESN'T KNOW ANY MORE.

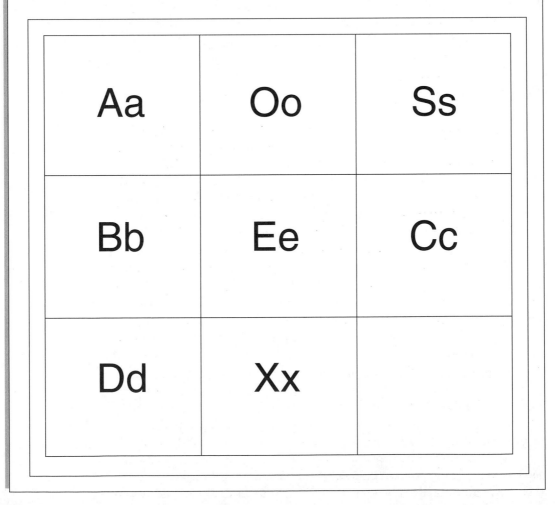

**Example of Type of Vocabulary Instructions and
Task Used in the NRS**

Say: point to mowing.

Training Plate D

(Continued)

BOX 14.5 (Continued)

Example of NRS Early Math Skills Instructions and Task

Run your finger across the item and say:

If you gave a friend one of these books, how many books would you have left?

Correct: Two (Books)

An Assessor and Head Start Student Demonstrate the NRS Assessment.

From: Government Accountability Office, Document GAO-05-343 Head Start, Highlights.

SOURCE: From "Full National Implementation of the Head Start National Reporting System on Child Outcomes, Office of Management and Budget Clearance Package Supporting Statement and Data Collection Instruments," by the U.S. Dept. of Health and Human Services, Administration for Children and Families, Administration on Children, Youth, and Families, June 23, 2003.

high stakes were attached to statewide tests, the authors found no support for a link between testing and achievement gains. The claims of positive outcomes from the NCLB testing program were recently challenged by NAEP research by members of the Berliner group at Arizona (Nichols, Glass, & Berliner, 2005). They report that the high-stakes tests are negatively correlated with the likelihood that children will complete 12th grade and that the pressure and stress generated by the test are correlated with repeating a grade and with dropping out of school.

In the 42 states that do not require elementary school children to pass the statewide assessment test to be promoted, there may be a "**standards gap**." This gap develops among school districts. The gap opens up when the schools where children have traditionally tested well adopt advanced standards for student learning, and schools where children have usually tested low adopt low-level standards. In a detailed 4-year case study, researchers found that one school system had lowered its standards the equivalent of one full school year below the published standards for the state. This was all done in the name of educational reform (Sandholtz, Ogawa, & Scribner, 2004). To justify this to the state education department, the learning standards for the school system were elaborated into three levels: Minimum, Essential, and Accelerated. The academic ability of students was used to select which of the three levels of standards the child was working toward. Most instruction was conducted to the lowest level of the test, the "Minimum" level.

Critics of the testing mandate of the No Child Left Behind Act have argued for more consideration of the differences that exist between children. They make the point that only a psychometric miracle would make it possible for all children of each state to reach the same high level of academic proficiency on a series of standardized tests (Rothstein, Jacobsen, & Wilder, 2006).

Public Reaction

Criticism from the research community notwithstanding, the NCLB Act has been shown to be popular with a broad section of the American population. Data from nine public hearings and nonscientific sampling have shown that the public is overwhelmingly in favor of the goals of the NCLB Act. There are, however, misgivings about the narrowing of the curriculum (Saulny, 2005), and students dislike the low-level cognitive tasks involved and the hours of drill and repetition that dominate the post-NCLB curriculum (Public Education Network, 2005).

In 2006, the National Council of Churches published a strongly worded condemnation of the key testing tenants of the No Child Left Behind law

(Brown & Resseger, 2005). The 10 points of this condemnation are focused on those children who are being inappropriately tested (English-language learners, special education students), the inappropriate distribution of resources, and the misinterpretation of test scores for students, schools, and teachers. The article can be found at www.ncccusa.org/news/060407 nochild.html.

State Concerns

State departments of education are not so sanguine about aspects of the NCLB Act, either. At least 20 different states have registered formal complaints and/or legal action against the provisions of the NCLB Act (Darling-Hammond, 2004). One reason for this antipathy toward the mandates of the NCLB Act by the states relates to the way that this law has moved the locus of educational decision making from the states to the U.S. Department of Education (Sizer, 2004). The tension between the states and the U.S. Department of Education is centered on three problematic areas of the law. The first of these is the standard for adequate yearly progress. Under the law, each school must move toward the goal of having all children from seven identified ethnic, ability, and income groups reach the level of proficient. For this goal to be achieved, the application of the Gaussian norman curve must no longer apply to the distribution of cognitive ability.

The state tests are not based on a normal distribution but on a predetermined set of standards. Yet, scores on the statewide achievement tests are highly correlated with mental ability. This means that until the states design a test that is independent of ability there will always be children who earn low scores. Alternatively, the states can lower the bar so that all who take the mandated tests will be proficient. There are great variations between the states as to what is considered proficient. Some states have very low expectations for their students (e.g., Colorado, Mississippi, North Carolina, and Tennessee) while others set very high standards (e.g., Wyoming and Massachusetts; Lewin, 2007; Rahman, 2007).

In addition to the problem with cognitive ability, there is also an issue with children who have learning disabilities. The NCLB Act does provide the states with permission to provide standard accommodations for special needs children, but they must all be tested at their correct grade level (Thurlow, Lazarus, Thompson, & Robey, 2002). If a state applies to the U.S. Department of Education (USDOE), their schools may be given permission to test as many as 3% of the children (those with the most serious cognitive impairments) with a developmentally appropriate test. These special needs children will be tested on ensuing years with similar tests, and annual improvements will be charted. Without that approval from USDOE, the schools may only test 1% of their student population with a developmentally appropriate measure.

These alternatives to the standard high-stakes tests must also be approved by the USDOE. Each state has created alternatives to high-stakes tests that are developmentally appropriate for children with low-incidence neurological and/or profound cognitive impairments. These tests focus on the skills and abilities that the child may have, like the ability to button a shirt or the recognition of basic colors. The alternative measures are often structured as an individualized measure featuring performance tasks designed to determine the child's English, mathematics, and language arts skill level. The scores on such measures are usually determined by a highly qualified special education teacher or a school psychologist. Scores are usually posed as ordinals that include (4) responds independently, (3) responds with minor assistance, (2) responds only with continuous assistance, (1) is unresponsive. Thus, the child is measured in terms of the level of independence in the performance of each task (Yell, Drasgow, & Lowrey, 2003).

Pressure for this came from several sources, including parents who wrote Internet blogs about how their children who were blind, deaf, and profoundly retarded were required to complete a multiple choice test. The second source was educational observers and critics, who have ridiculed the practice of testing with inappropriate tests children who cannot hold a pencil or read any word (Winerip, 2003).

One of the seven categories of students that are required to demonstrate adequate yearly progress toward the goal of universal proficiency are the students with special needs. With most of these children being tested with age appropriate, not developmentally appropriate measures, it is easy for this category of students to fail to make this "adequate yearly progress." Having a population of special needs children in a school building may therefore result in the school being rated as "needing improvement."

This designation can hurt a school's reputation in the local media, but it also releases Title I funds, which can be used to help the identified students. The problem of teaching and assessing children with specific learning disabilities and attention deficit/hyperactivity disorder is one that is not going away anytime soon. These learning problems have been part of humankind for all of recorded history. It is unlikely that 100% or even 97% of the students with disabilities will ever be able to reach the required proficiency level in achievement. In 2004, 85% of the special education students in Maryland failed to reach a level of proficiency on that state's mathematics test, and 73% failed the reading test. The NCLB Act was interpreted to make it possible for states to test only 1% of their populations of students with an alternative test for special education. Thus, 99% of the student population must take the state's standardized assessment. The 1% who are not in this pool take a developmentally appropriate test. In simplistic IQ terms, this 1% subgroup is equivalent to an IQ score equal to or less than 67.

Beyond students with cognitive impairments and those with learning disabilities are many more who exhibit severe pervasive developmental disorders such as Asperger's syndrome, autism, childhood disintegrative disorder, Tourette's disorder, Rett's disorder, and various degenerative neurological disorders. Virtually all of these children are educated in regular education classrooms. By requiring children with disabilities to take the same statewide assessment as their non-disabled peers, the schools enrolling many children with disabilities may never be able to get off the "needs improvement" list.

In addition to the special education issue is a related problem of the disproportional impact of the law on children of different socioeconomic backgrounds. Children of color, and the children living in poverty, are those who are most likely not to score well on high-stakes tests. This impact is evident in graduation rates, where we see as many as 40% of minority students leaving high school without earning a diploma (Hall, 2005). It is these children who are left behind by the NCLB tests. In 2003, 50% of the children who scored below proficient on Ohio's assessment came from families with an income below $20,000 per year. However, 80% of the children from families with incomes over $30,000 per year passed the test (Sadker & Zittleman, 2004).

Those children who have limited English proficiency may be tested in their native language. However, only a handful of states now have made the commitment to write and standardize their assessment tests in other modern languages.[17] This is a major problem in that 40% of the school-age population of the United States will be native Spanish speakers by the year 2030 (Edmonston, Lee, & Passel, 2001). It is also likely that the translation of a high-stakes test causes a loss in measurement validity and requires expensive standardization studies at every grade level and in every language (Abedi, Hofstetter, & Lord, 2004).

Most states require any child who has resided in the United States for the past 12 months to take the mandated test in English, even though English is an especially difficult and complex language to master. On average, a child who is born into a home where no one speaks English and who is immersed in an English-speaking school environment can achieve fluency at the **Basic Interpersonal Communication Skill (BICS) level** in 2 years (Roseberry-McKibbin & Brice, 2005). However, this same child will not achieve a fluency in English permitting context-reduced academic language known as **Cognitive Academic Language Proficiency (CALP)** for another 3 to 5 years (total of 5 to 7 years of immersion).

Related to this is the problem that most children who are native Spanish speakers tend to attend the same neighborhood schools. A study of the schools of California found that a natural segregation has developed, with most students who are ELL attending schools where the dominate student population is made up of native Spanish speakers (Rumberger, Gándara, & Merino, 2006). Frequently, the neighborhood school is located in a community where the local culture assumes a distinctively Hispanic flavor. In such a school environment, the process of learning to communicate and be assessed using the English language will take longer than if the child is immersed into an all-English-language school environment.

Case in Point (14g)

The fact that non-native English speakers may not have achieved the Cognitive Academic Language Proficiency level of fluency is one reason why the Florida Department of Education will not permit local school districts to employ scores from the mandated state test (Florida Comprehensive Achievement Test, FCAT) as a way to place children into **magnet schools**. The goal of the magnet schools is to provide increased student diversity within the secondary schools of the local districts. The reason for this decision to bar the use of the FCAT scores by the Florida Department of Education is that the mandated state assessment may be inappropriate for non-native speakers of English (ELL students). Yet, the same children must take that test, and if they are not found to be proficient, they can be denied promotion to the next grade. This grade repetition is done on the basis of the FCAT, a measure that the state's education department also believes may well be inappropriate for ELL students.

For more information, see "Considerations on Point" at www.sagepub.com wrightstudy

---

These problems have led several states into open revolt over the requirements of the NCLB Act. In Utah, legislation was passed in 2005 requiring the state's education department to provide first priority to meeting state goals and to spend as little money on meeting federal mandates as possible. Other states, including Virginia, attempted to base the adequate yearly progress of children with disabilities on the actual instructional level of the children instead of their grade level (Glod, 2007). This request was denied by Secretary Spellings in 2005.

Many small schools have found a loophole in the NCLB requirements for reporting the **disaggregated scores** of children in minority groups. When there are fewer than 45 children enrolled in a tested grade from an identified minority group their test scores are not required to be reported separately. In 2004–2005, this resulted in 2 million students not having their scores counted (Dizon, Feller, & Bass, 2006).

The second major area of contention between the NCLB Act and the various states has to do with funding. Connecticut has estimated that testing children annually is costing the state an additional $41 million in administrative and testing expenses. It was also estimated that millions more are needed by the local school districts to meet the mandates. For that reason, the Connecticut attorney general filed a federal lawsuit requesting the promised full funding (U.S. District Court, District of Connecticut, 2006).[18] It has been estimated that the $410 million spent under NCLB for testing in 2006 should be increased to $860 million to adequately pay for the mandated tests as proscribed by the NCLB law (Toch, 2006). Secretary Spellings suggested that Connecticut use a less expensive multiple choice format test in place of the labor intensive and very expensive performance examination now employed. By 2007, the amount of litigation over the NCLB requirements and funding levels involved school districts from Michigan, Vermont, and Texas and the departments of education for Delaware, Connecticut, and Wisconsin.

The third area of contention is that this law is a usurpation of state prerogatives and rights. By imposing this series of programs onto the state education departments, the U.S. Department of Education has become the ultimate manager of all local public schools. Most states had accountability systems in place prior to the passage of NCLB in 2002 and resent being forced to conform to a nationally approved model. States like Minnesota, New York, and Pennsylvania had long histories of accountability assessments prior to what many view as the imposition of the new requirements.

Summary

International comparisons of student development and achievement are relatively recent phenomena. Historically, the outcome of these comparisons became available at a time when the critics of American education were in the ascendancy, and the data from these assessments became the source of much of their ammunition. The reaction to the critical reports generated during this era resulted in our present age of accountability. The fact is that American education never was as bad as the critics posited, and many schools are functioning at what could be described as a world-class level.

The War on Poverty and the First Elementary and Secondary Education Act (1965) brought with them a new accountability model, which became known as the Nation's Report Card. This test has provided an important stream of data about the state of American education for over 40 years. From these data we know that some states appear to be doing a much better job educating their children than other states. Generally, the schools of the states in the "Old South" and from the lower Midwest score lower than do the schools of the northern Midwest and the schools of the states along the two coasts (Institute for Education Sciences, 2006).

Large-scale assessment tests are not a new phenomenon. The current era of standards-based assessments in the schools began during the Clinton administration. That program was folded into the No Child Left Behind Act of 2002, a centerpiece of the administration of President George W. Bush. This act has the goal of ending the "soft racism" of poor achievement in the low-performing schools in which many minority students are enrolled. Its ambitious goal is to have all American children academically proficient by the year 2014.[19] Critics have pointed out that the goal is unreachable and the mandate for the testing programs is underfunded. Other critics have pointed to the narrowing of the curriculum and the lack of spontaneity in the classroom as a sign of the times under this legislation. A still-unresolved problem involves the requirements that are being set for children who have significant cognitive and physiological impairments.

Discussion Questions

1. How would you set about the task of establishing a sample of subjects that represent high school students from two different nations, with two different cultures that are balanced and equivalent?

2. Do students who use metric measurements in all aspects of their lives have an advantage over students from the United States on international tests of science? Is there a way to equalize any advantage held by others?

3. Have the international education comparison studies entered the realm of American politics? Provide examples for your position.

4. Why do the scores of the NAEP (Nation's Report Card) differ so much from the scores on the state-mandated assessments?

5. What is the main goal behind the No Child Left Behind Act of 2002? Is that goal attainable? Provide evidence for your answer.

6. Should the regulations of the No Child Left Behind Act be modified in some way for children with significant disabilities? Elaborate on your answer.

Student Study Site

Educational Assessment on the Web

Log on to the Web-based student study site at www.sagepub.com/wrightstudy for additional Web sources and study resources.

NOTES

1. Unfortunately, the National Commission on Excellence in Education never identified the tests or the samples that were tested. They did not even reveal which industrialized countries took part in the comparisons.

2. Some industrialized nations require 13 years of public education. In the FIMS and SIMS studies, 12th graders from the United States were compared with 13th graders from those other countries.

3. England and Scotland were reported separately as were French and Flemish children in Belgium.

4. In 2005 there were 11 states that met the NCLB testing requirement in the child's native language. The IEA makes no such accommodations in the international studies.

5. Most, not all, nations in Europe have integrated long-term immigrant children into their educational programs (Eurydice, 2004). Yet, most immigrant children are taught in schools that are populated by other immigrant children (Organization for Economic Co-operation and Development, 2006). Those children of families who lack documentation are taught in centers for undocumented aliens.

6. The chief architect of the act was Francis Keppel, the former Dean of the Harvard Graduate School of Education. Dean Keppel was summoned to Washington by President John F. Kennedy in 1960 to serve as Commissioner of Education.

7. The only children who are exempt from the NAEP because they are in special education or as being Limited English Proficient (**LEP**) must have also been excluded from taking the NCLB test given in that school. Thus, only the most cognitively disabled and non-English speakers are excluded from the sample.

8. Horace Mann resigned from the school board in 1848 to become a member of the U.S. House of Representatives. He was first appointed to replace and

complete the term of John Quincy Adams. In Congress he was a staunch abolitionist. He ended his career as the founding president of Antioch College

9. States from the old Confederacy were slow to develop public schools and pass compulsory education laws.

10. There is also one nonoperational district that is based in a town established as a religious community with its own private academy.

11. *Debra P. v. Turlington* (1981) established that students must be given years of advanced notice of a new high-stakes test and that the test must have curriculum fidelity (content validity). When the schools of a state have met those requirements, the children of all ethnic groups can be denied a diploma if they fail to pass a state-mandated test.

12. In 2007, the Florida court of appeals held that teachers cannot be fired for "deficient professional performance" unless a school board can demonstrate that the teacher is linked to low scores on the state's assessment test (*Sherrod v. Palm Beach County School Board*).

13. While the states have draconian powers over the schools, most have used a light touch with their troubled schools (Olson, 2006b).

14. Oklahoma went from having 25% of its schools fail in 2004–2005 to having only 3% in 2005–2006.

15. CTR/McGraw-Hill, Harcourt Assessment, and Pearson Educational Measurement.

16. One state, Connecticut, has implemented a required high school test that correlates well to the SAT II and is a significant predictor of success in college (Coelen & Berger, 2006). This test requires students to read short stories and good literature and then answer complex questions about the passages and short stories, and write essay answers to the stimulus questions. This is clearly not the usual test model selected by most states.

17. Good examples are New York State, where a high school student who is not a native speaker of English may elect to take the required New York Regents Examination in English, Spanish, Chinese, Russian, Haitian-Creole, and Korean, and Ohio, where the state hires translators for all needed languages, including Spanish, Somali, Mandarin Chinese, Arabic, and Russian.

    Under the NCLB Act, all states must test every child with an approved achievement test starting in the third grade. Even though every child is tested, and usually in English, the states are permitted to exclude those children who have been in the United States fewer than 3 years in the calculation of whether the school meets the adequate yearly progress (AYP) requirement.

18. Coincidentally, 6 weeks after Connecticut filed this action, in April of 2006, the U.S. Department of Education challenged the certification status of 13,000 (30%) of Connecticut's teachers (Frahm, 2006a).

19. Perhaps "almost all" is a better description. Up to 3% of the population of children with severe mental deficiencies is measured using a developmentally focused assessment.

Chapter 15

STUDENT, FAMILY, AND TEACHER FACTORS IN TEST SCORES

All who have meditated on the art of governing have been convinced that the fate of empires depends on the education of youth.

—Aristotle

Issues and Themes

Children live their lives as part of a family, members of a community, and as students in school. Including kindergarten, the total amount of time children spend in classrooms before their 18th birthday is about 12,500 hours or 8% of their lives. To understand what drives assessment test scores it is necessary to examine the factors of the child's home and community that correlate with educational outcomes.

The first child-centered factor having a powerful impact on assessment scores is cognitive ability. This link is so well established that a diagnostic indicator of a possible learning disability is a discrepancy between a child's IQ and his or her achievement test score. Another important determinant of the assessment test outcome is the amount of time a child spends on computer games and television watching. Significant negative correlations between achievement and these two pastimes have been well established. A third child factor is the amount of time he or she spends doing homework and reading independently. Finally, the issue of school attendance has been shown to be highly correlated with scores on mandated assessment tests.

Parenting factors linked to student success include the level and quality of communication between the school and the child's parents. The child's birth order and the number of siblings living at home with the child are other factors related to achievement test outcomes. Also, the mobility versus the stability of the family within the community is linked to scores on the mandated assessments.

Teacher factors in the achievement success of students are linked to teacher preparation and motivation. There is a conflict between the goal of educational reformers who campaign to fill classrooms with nontraditionally educated and certified teachers and the requirement of the NCLB Act for all teachers to be "highly qualified." For some subject areas (e.g., career and technical) staffing is a critical problem. Research has demonstrated that the students of fully certified teachers who have a major in their teaching discipline tend to have higher scores on achievement tests than do students in the classrooms of teachers with less education. Schools that serve impoverished communities where many children are at risk for failure have difficulty recruiting and retaining teachers. Those schools tend to employ many inexperienced and uncertified teachers.

States offer a number of alternate routes to becoming a certified teacher. A new set of rules under the NCLB Act (HOUSSE) has been put in place for those teachers with inappropriate credentials now working in schools. Teachers for the inner cities and rural communities are being provided from a Department of Defense program known as **Troops to Teachers**. Also, a private foundation is providing about 2,000 teachers each year to those difficult-to-staff schools. These Teach for America teachers are recruited from the ranks of the liberal arts graduates of prestigious colleges and universities.

An outcome of the reform movement of the 1980s was a move toward a standards-based national teacher certificate. The National Board for Professional Teaching Standards (NBPTS, 1988) certifies thousands of experienced classroom teachers each year.[1] Research on the link between teacher certification and student outcomes has not shown a clear pattern with NBPTS certified teachers. The student outcome data have been less than positive regarding the classrooms staffed with teachers from various alternative certification programs. When these alternative certificate holders are assigned to inner-city schools there is a high dropout rate.

Learning Objectives

By reading and studying this chapter you should acquire the competency to do the following:

- Describe the relationship between cognitive ability and scores on high-stakes assessments.
- Explain the special problems faced by LEP or English-language learner (ELL) students on state-mandated assessments.
- Elaborate on the relationship between assessment test scores and the amount of time children spend watching television and playing computer games.
- Describe the role that time spent on homework plays on assessment test score outcomes.
- Explain the link between attendance and assessment outcomes.
- Describe the home environment of highly successful students and contrast that with the home environment of students who do not score well on high-stakes tests.
- Explain the role of parent–school communication on the achievement level of children.
- Describe the impact of frequent moving from one community to another on school achievement.
- Discuss the various alternative certification programs for the initial licensing of teachers.
- Describe the relationship between teacher certification and achievement outcomes for teachers holding various certifications.
- Describe the factors within schools that are related to good teacher motivation and high levels of student achievement.

STUDENTS

Personally, I'm always ready to learn, although I do not always like being taught.

—Winston Churchill

There are a number of central factors that are related to how well a child does on a high-stakes achievement test. Some of these factors are traits of the child and not readily mutable. Two of these include the child's ability and his or her primary language.

Other factors are psychological states that can be changed by environmental manipulation. They include the child's selection of peers, his or her scholastic motivation, attendance, homework completion, and work habits. Each of these, and potentially others as well, contribute to the totality that is the child and how he or she functions as a student.

In serving writs I made such a name

That an articled clerk I soon became;

I wore clean collars and a brand-new suit

For the Pass Examination at the institute,

And that Pass Examination did so well for me,

That now I am the Ruler of the Queens Navee!

SOURCE: From *H. M. S. Pinafore*, by Gilbert & Sullivan (1878).

Ability

Cognitive ability is a central factor in how well a child will do on a high-stakes test. This relationship between scores on tests of mental ability and academic success is large enough ($r \cong 0.70$) to account for half of the score variance on an eighth-grade high-stakes test and 30% of the variance among fifth graders ($r \cong 0.55$). Thus, IQ is the single most critical factor in the outcome of state-mandated assessments (Bluebello, 2003; Burson & Wright, 2003).

This relationship between mental ability and achievement test outcome has been well established in the literature. It is so strong that any discrepancy between a child's score on a cognitive ability test and his or her achievement scores can be used as an indicator of a learning disability (Evans, 1990; Ross, 1992). Thus, when a school's population of children has a normal distribution of mental ability there will be a predictable number that score low on any test of achievement. The average tested levels of mental ability in a number of isolated rural schools, as well as some urban schools, are below the average of the national norms ($\bar{X}_{12} < 100$). This implies that there will always be some schools that have a larger than average number of children who do not score well on mandated assessments.

English-Language Learners

Reading and language skills of a child are central factors in his or her measured level of performance on any high-stakes test. Children for whom

English is not the first language tend to have lower assessment scores in reading. This is also reflected in the scores on mandated assessment tests.

To review the data from different ethnic groups on the NAEP, see http://nces.ed.gov/programs/coe/2006/section2/indicator14.asp.

The testing rules under the NCLB Act provide for the Limited English Proficient child to have a 1-year waiver from testing in English and reading but no waiver with the science and math tests of state-assessment programs.[2] The assessment problem posed by language-minority children is a growing one. The fastest growing segment of the minority population and the largest minority group are children of Hispanic heritage (Cohn & Bahrampour, 2006). By 2007, eight states had developed assessment systems appropriate for the measurement of children with limited English language proficiency. As there was a question as to the validity of these measures, they were ordered to terminate all such efforts by the U.S. Department of Education during the winter of 2007 (Zehr, 2007b). A special concern is with English-language learners who also have a significant learning problem. Their communication problems in English may mask their deeper learning disabilities (Zehr, 2007a).

Motivation

Another child-centered factor is motivation/desire. Children who enjoy reading tend to read well. This may be another iterative relationship with good reading ability leading to the enjoyment of reading, which leads to even better reading skills, etc. At eighth grade, only 10% of all children describe reading as a favorite activity, while 25% report they do not like to read. Those in the former group have significantly better reading scores than do those in the latter group. Those children who like to read have much higher assessment test scores than do those who do not enjoy reading (National Assessment of Educational Progress [NAEP], 2004).

Work Habits

Children spend more time watching television and playing computer games than they spend in school. As children get older there is a shift with computer games taking over many of the hours formerly lost to television viewing. Correlational research has demonstrated a direct, negative, linear relationship between the amount of time children spend playing computer games and/or watching television and their state assessment test scores (Holbrook & Wright, 2004; NAEP, 2004).

Research from New Zealand has documented that the amount of time children spend watching television prior to reaching school age has a significant negative effect on later educational attainment. This New Zealand finding was true for all levels of mental ability (Hancox, Milne, & Poulton, 2005). In the same vein, Dina Borzekowski and Thomas Robinson (2005) found that third-grade children who have a television in their bedroom have significantly lower mathematics achievement test scores than a matched group of children who do not. This study also reported that the language arts scores of children who lived in homes with a home computer were better than those children who did not have a home computer.

There are reasons, however, that parents are advised not to place a home computer in the child's bedroom. Even beyond the possibility of inappropriate contacts being made through the Internet are problems of computer gaming addiction. The incremental complexity of online computer game formats serves as a reward for children. This cognitive reward makes gaming very compelling, and children can spend inordinate amounts of time learning new game skills and increasing the level and complexity of play. This devotion to gaming may cause a loss of sleep, inattention, and various problems in school including lower achievement and poor test scores.

There is an online support group for the parents of computer-gaming-addicted children. This group is Mothers Against Videogame Addiction and Violence: www.mavav.org.

There is also evidence that students who participate in the extracurricular programs and the education-related clubs and activities of their schools will have better levels of academic achievement and higher test scores than their unengaged peers (Noble, Davenport, & Sawyer, 2001). Also, better work habits and achievement were found among children who exhibited a sense of their own ability to influence and control events. This factor involves being able to accept one's self as the source of successes and failures and a belief in one's own self-efficacy (Zimmerman, 1989).

Homework

Another factor linked to success on assessment tests is the amount of time a child spends doing homework (Huntsinger, 1999). In a metaanalysis of effective teaching strategies, Robert Marzano and his colleagues found that of 21 teaching strategies examined, the regular assignment and grading of homework was one of the most effective (Marzano, Pickering, & Pollock, 2001). This relationship between homework and assessment test scores can be seen with the outcome of the NAEP. Middle-school students who report that they do not complete their assigned homework have NAEP achievement test scores significantly below the level of students who do an hour or more of homework a day. Likewise, those middle-school children who have parents that enforce homework rules have better assessment scores (NAEP, 2004). Parents that enforce a study hall hour 6 days a week where the child has a quiet place to read and work will have higher scoring children. The parents of high-performing students also carefully check the work the child does (Maeroff, 1992).

The importance of doing regular homework increases with the grade level. In middle and senior high schools, homework and academic success are highly correlated (Cooper, 2003). There is also a "homework gap" between the complexity and amount of homework assigned to children attending middle-class suburban schools and what is assigned to the children attending schools in poor neighborhoods (Smith, 2004).

Peers

Two other factors in a child's achievement are attendance and the attitude of his or her friends. Children who report that their friends ridicule others who try hard and do well in school have lower achievement than children who do not have such friends. The influence of the choice of friends has been shown to play an important part in general academic achievement (Buoye, 2004). Peer group control over child behaviors can be seen as early as kindergarten. Current research with a population of elementary school children has shown that extreme exclusion by the peer group leads the target child to withdraw from school-related activities, stop participating in

Figure 15.1   "It Seems Wrong for You to Have Six Hours of Homework Every Night . . ."

SOURCE: © Zits Partnership. King Features Syndicate.

the class, and to achieve low achievement test scores (Buhs, Ladd, & Herald, 2006).

Adolescent friendship cliques are closed systems that monitor each member and provide both rewards for behavior that meet the group norms and expectations and punishments for any violation of the code of the group. When children are friendly with others who are academically motivated they work to maintain good grades to stay in good standing with the group.

Attendance

School attendance is a central factor in achievement test scores. Reading achievement scores from a state assessment as well as the NAEP verify that poor attendance in elementary, middle, and secondary schools is linked to assessment scores that are significantly lower than average (Currie, 1994; NAEP, 2004). Statewide data from New Jersey have shown that about 4% of the variance in the average test scores from a school are linked to the attendance of the children enrolled there (Camilli & Monfils, 2004).

FAMILIES

The mother's heart is the child's schoolroom.

—Henry Ward Beecher

The importance of the role of parents in setting the tone and establishing a climate that nurtures and supports the child's academic development cannot be overstated. Laurence Steinberg (1996) has argued that the goal of every parent should be to develop children that are truly engaged in their educations and schools. All the healthy behaviors of academically successful children occur when the child's parents are engaged with his or her education. There are several parenting philosophies that relate to this outcome with children. In addition, there are a number of parental characteristics that correlate with the academic success of children. These correlates include parental education, family mobility, and the ecology of the home.

Parental Education

The great majority of non-school factors correlated to children's achievement test scores are controlled by their families. Foremost among these are the education levels of the child's parents. Consistent increments occur in the assessment test scores of children as a function of increasing levels of parental education (Joireman & Abbott, 2004; NAEP, 2004). One of the best predictors of how well the children of entire school districts will do on a statewide assessment is the average level of education of the parents of the community (Noble, Roberts, & Sawyer, 2006; Zackon, 1999). Of equal importance for the child's academic success are the goals that the parent(s) have for his or her education. The children of parents who express the goal of eventually seeing their child graduate from college achieve high scores on the NAEP.

Home Environment

Along with parental education is the role of reading at home. Parents who value reading and who have at least 25 books and several newspapers and magazine subscriptions have children who perform better on state assessments (Levitt & Dubner, 2005). The relationship between these two variables has been shown to account for more than 20% of the variance in assessment test scores. It is not just the existence of reading materials in the home, but rather a sign that the parents value reading and read for their own needs and enjoyment. Parental role models can be powerful influences on the growing child.

One of the most telling factors in the test-score gap between children from middle-class families and the children from impoverished families is the child's vocabulary (Hart & Risley, 1995). Longitudinal research has demonstrated that by the age of 3, children born into middle-class families have vocabularies that are twice as large as the vocabularies of children born into impoverished homes. This difference is reflected in early cognitive ability test scores and carries over to school age. This vocabulary difference is caused by the amount and complexity of the language used by the young child's parents on a day-to-day basis (Hart & Risley, 1999).

Children living in a nuclear family that includes both a father and mother have better achievement than children who live in single-parent families (Dawson, 1991). A longitudinal study of elementary school children in Canada found significantly better achievement with the children of two-parent families compared with children living with one parent (Adams & Ryan, 2000). This finding was more intense for families that were less wealthy. One outcome of divorce is often the impoverishment of the single parent living with children. By the time young people are high school seniors the effect of living in a single-parent family is even more pronounced. High school students from intact families have far better school attendance and thereby better grades and achievement than do the children of divorce

(Ham, 2003). It also seems that the impact on children and youth of living in a single-parent family is greater on girls than it is on boys.

Home–School Communication

The communication between parents and children about schoolwork is also an important factor in student test scores. Dysfunctional families that have poor lines of communication between parent(s) and children have youngsters with more school problems and lower levels of achievement and test scores. NAEP scores are significantly higher for children that report discussing school with a parent every day. Scores from children that said that they "hardly ever discuss school" with their parents had NAEP achievement scores below the national average.

When parents are involved with their child's school, the child will have better grades and higher achievement test scores. Involvement includes belonging to the parents association, volunteering to assist on field trips and outings, and having regular meetings with the child's teacher. Survey data demonstrate that only 56% of all parents attend teacher conferences and only 40% review their child's homework (Markow & Martin, 2005). A statistical analysis of **longitudinal data** by economist Steven Levitt confirms the role of parent involvement in the success of children in school (Levitt & Dubner, 2005). Education critic Chester Finn once averred, "What's most important for all parents is to share responsibility with the schools for how well their children learn" (Finn, 1991, p. 271). This parent involvement effect is a consistent one that works no matter how wealthy or poor a family may be. In addition, those parents who are engaged with the education of their children are far more likely to have children who graduate and go on to higher education (Elias & Schwab, 2004).

For more information, see "Considerations on Point" at www.sagepub.com/wrightstudy

Case in Point (15a)

In some schools the parents are too involved and must be restrained from interfering with the instructional process. This is one product of the **millennial generation** of middle-class parents. These young parents have earned the sobriquet "helicopter parents" because they hover over their children overseeing every detail in the lives of their sons and daughters. These parents will swoop into school at the slightest sign of a problem, they will berate teachers who don't give a high grade to their child, and will fax, phone, and e-mail their complaints to any and all administrators. Their children are the most protected, programmed generation of youngsters ever (Strauss, 2006). These parents even follow their children to college and have been known to call professors to express their concerns over what is happening in the college lecture hall.

Historically, the most famous of the hovering parents may have been Mrs. Arthur McArthur. When her son was accepted as a student at West Point she rented an apartment near campus to oversee his well-being for herself. Her son, Douglas, graduated and went on to become Army Chief of Staff and five-star General of the Army and Commander of the South West Pacific Theater during World War II.

One way a school can support healthy parental involvement is to establish a computer server that makes it possible to share school news with parents. Such systems also facilitate e-mail interaction between teachers and parents and can be used to post all homework assignments for parents to see. Naturally, this system requires that all parents have a computer and the knowledge of how to use it. This may require an investment on the part of the school system in parent education and computers for the homes of those in need.

Mobility

The impact of moving from residence to residence is another factor that plays a role in poor school performance (Kaase & Dulaney, 2005; NAEP, 2004). Children of families that have moved three or more times over a 2-year period have had much lower achievement test scores when compared to children who had never moved over the same time period. Socioeconomic status may play a role in the achievement impact on children of moving. Wealthy parents move because they *can*; for them it is strategic and usually well planned. This is not always so for poor families, who often move because they *must*. Therefore, the moves made by children of poverty may be far more traumatic than those of children with parents who move to improve their lives. A California study found that as many as half of the high school transfers did not involve the family moving. Factors such as custody and parent rights, violence and gang activity, and other problems of socialization are involved in the decision of a teenager to request a change of high schools (Rumberger, Larson, Ream, & Palardy, 1999). Another type of moving occurs when parents who live in impoverished communities with notoriously poor schools smuggle their children into the better suburban schools beyond their communities. This occurs frequently in the suburban school systems border-ing large cities and is a clear sign of both the devotion of parents to their children and the desperation they feel toward their home school systems (Dillon, 2007a). The findings from California are that 75% of all students make an unscheduled change of schools during their 12-year school career. When these transfers and relocations occur, there is a clear negative impact on the academic outcome for the children involved. Each time a child and his or her family moved to a new neighborhood and school, there was a signifi-cant reduction in the likelihood that the child would eventually graduate from high school (Rumberger et al.).

One group of children who move frequently and suffer little harm are the children of military personnel. The support network of other military families is one reason these children seem to thrive even though their families rarely stay at one duty assignment for more than 2 years.

There are about a million children who live in the families of migrant farm workers. Every year hundreds of thousands of families move several times following the harvest and planting cycles of farming communities throughout the United States (Méndez, 2005). Until very recently these children were indeed the ones left behind. Educational records were never complete, they often had minimal English language skills, and schools were unprepared to meet their needs. This problem was partially addressed in the NCLB legislation. Migrant children are now one of the subgroups that schools are required to track to assure continuing educational progress. In 2006, computer systems for tracking these children from community to commu-nity existed only within various states.

While the number of times the family moves does play a role in the aca-demic achievement of children, the neighborhood does not. When other fac-tors are controlled, Lisa Sanbonmatsu and her colleagues found that families that move from depressed communities to better neighborhoods do not see an improvement in the achievement levels of their children (Sanbonmatsu, Kling, Duncan, & Brooks-Gunn, 2005). Clearly, other factors are playing a sig-nificant role in achievement outcomes.

Parenting

Parents are constantly in communication with their children. Some com-munication is obvious and direct, but much of the communication is more subtle. As an example, a negative attitude about school may be subtly expressed when a family decides to take a child out of school to go on a family vacation. Or, a positive attitude can be subtly expressed when a parent takes a day to take his or her child to a science museum. It is through these

BOX 15.1   Parental Involvement Report Card Sample Questions

The following questions were taken from the Parental Involvement Report Card, an online parent education activity from Project Appleseed. The full questionnaire and scoring system is found at www.projectapple seed.org/reportcard.html

How Well Do You Support Your Child's Learning?

1. Have you identified a regular time and place in your home for your child to do homework?
2. Do you monitor your child's television viewing habits?
3. Do you ensure that your child has excellent attendance at school?
4. Have you discussed with your child the importance of a good education?
5. Did you attend Open House or Back-To-School Night at your child's school?
6. Do you support and reinforce the school's discipline plan?
7. Do you support your child's learning by providing nutritious meals and adequate time for sleep?
8. Do you read to your young child: If your child is older, do you encourage reading by paying attention to what your child reads as well as how often he/she reads?
9. Do you hold your child responsible for completing all assignments on time and to the best of his/her ability?
10. Are you knowledgeable about what information and skills your child should master at his/her major subject areas?
11. Were you a class parent, telephone tree coordinator, or a volunteer who provided parents with needed information?
12. Were you a part of parent patrols or other activities to increase the safety and operation of your child's school and programs?
13. Have you attended at least one PTA, PTO, or other support group meeting this year?
14. Have you worked on school-based management committees, district level councils and /or committees on issues concerning your school?
15. Have you attended at least one school program? (Examples are an awards assembly, a play, an athletic event, or a school party.)
16. Are you a model of "good sportsmanship" when attending school and community events?
17. Do you insist that your child exhibit good sportsmanship at all times?
18. Have you read the student code of conduct and/or discipline policy?
19. Do you regularly read the school newsletter?
20. Do you make yourself available for conferences requested by your child's teacher?
21. Have you had at least one parent-teacher conference with the teacher(s) of your child?
22. Are you familiar with the grading scale used on your child's report card?

SOURCE: From Parental Involvement Report Card. Reprinted with permission from Parents Advocating Challenging Education.

ongoing communications that the child develops a sense of self and grows into a self-directed learner. It is through this flow of communication that the child's values are defined and become part of his or her core.

The communication that all children need is one of acceptance with unquestioning, freely given, and never withheld love. Children also want and need to know that their parents have expectations and goals for them. Children need parents who provide reasonable limitations as well as set appropriate expectations. Successful parenting involves praising and supporting children while providing guidance. Parents need a feeling of their own consistency in what they are about. Children also need that consistency and clear expectations for personal behavior that parents provide.

Parents must also be able to provide incremental autonomy as the child matures. This provides the child with the opportunity to evolve as an individual. This can be done by the parents through small acts such as asking the child's opinion. Larger questions of autonomy are always going to occur as the child matures and the small ones set the tone and provide practice in the give and take that growing up involves.

TEACHERS

Who dares to teach must never cease to learn.

—John Cotton Dana (1856–1929)
Influential Librarian and Museum Director

Teaching is now and always has been a labor-intensive task. However, while teaching is important, it is not the major factor in the achievement outcomes for school children. Most teachers tend to function in about the same range of effectiveness. It is only the extreme cases that stand out, those who are horrible teachers, and those who are the outstanding exemplars of the profession.

The goal of all school administers should be to develop a faculty that is highly effective. The first step in that process involves recruiting teachers who are enthusiastic, well educated, and motivated to make a difference in the lives of children. The second is to create an environment that celebrates effective teaching and in which the faculty are nurtured and guided toward achieving their professional best. It should also be noted that the path that a teacher has followed to become licensed for the profession has little to do with how effective he or she is as a teacher (Futernick, 2007; Garnaut, 2007).

Impact

The most important decision a school administrator makes is the selection of a new teacher. It can be assumed that a newly hired teacher will eventually become protected by the state's tenure policy and may eventually teach in that school for 30 or 40 years. Highly effective teachers will contribute to the school and community for many years, while ineffective teachers will enervate the school community for years to come.

The overall effectiveness of the classroom teacher accounts for somewhere between 4% and 18% of the variance in student performance on state-mandated assessment tests (Resnick, 2004). This impact is greater for low-achieving students and lower for bright, high-achieving students. A good strategy for school systems to follow is to assign the most effective teachers to the classrooms with large numbers of children at risk for failure. This idea was recently put forward by Governor Mark Warner of Virginia. His proposal was presented through the National Partnership for Teaching in At-Risk Schools (2005).

This effect of teacher quality is a cumulative value. When a child is taught by ineffective teachers for several consecutive years, the impact on assessment scores can be devastating. This effect is most pronounced for children of marginal ability and achievement. The achievement impact on bright and otherwise successful children who are taught by ineffective teachers is minimal. Likewise, all students who are fortunate enough to be in the classrooms of highly effective teachers will have significantly improved test scores. Once again, this effect is most pronounced with the marginal students (Babu & Mendro, 2003). The effect of high-quality instruction with the teaching and learning of mathematics at the elementary and middle school level is stunning (Sanders & Rivers, 1996). This impact is additive, so after 3 or 4 years of consistently good or consistently ineffective teaching, there are large achievement differences. The measurable effect on achievement test scores for at-risk children taught by good teachers has been documented in all grades beginning with first grade (Hamre & Pianta, 2005). A major worry for educational leaders is that the best teachers may be the ones who find the current emphasis on the repetitive drilling of children with basic skills to be stultifying and lead them into early retirement (Winerip, 2004).

A first step in the improvement of achievement scores on the mandated assessments is related to having classrooms staffed by effective teachers. The State of Louisiana initiated an effort in 2001 to improve the qualifications of the state's teachers. Three years after this initiative, better assessment test scores and higher scores on the ACT are attributed to the program (Picard,

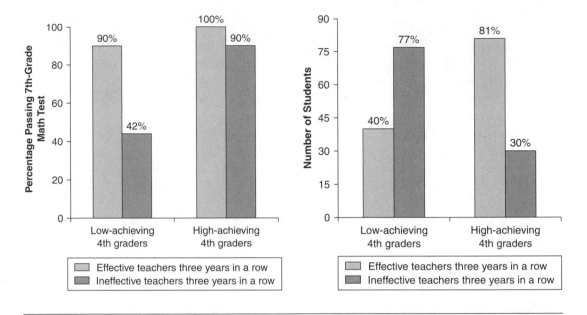

Figure 15.2   Achievement Impact of Effective Teachers and the High Likelihood of Low-Achieving Students of Getting an Ineffective Teacher

SOURCE: From "Teacher Accountability: HLM-Based Teacher Effectiveness Indices in the Investigation of Teacher Effects in a State Assessment Program," by S. Babu and R. Mendro, paper presented at the AERA annual meeting, 2003. Copyright 2003 by Babu and Mendro.

2004). While teacher background is related to effectiveness in the classroom, scores on teacher assessment tests are not. A study of North Carolina teachers found that children's test scores are unrelated to how well their teachers tested on the National Teacher's Examination, Praxis Test (Goldhaber, 2006).

Hiring of Effective Teachers

The recruitment and retention of highly effective teachers is not an easy task. The hiring problem is made all the more difficult because the initial salary of teachers is only two-thirds of what is paid to those entering other professional fields (National Education Association, 2007). Recruiting teachers for less desirable teaching positions (the schools of impoverished inner-city communities and those of isolated rural communities) is an Augean task. For this reason, inner-city and rural schools use many teachers who are less qualified and inexperienced (Lankford, Loeb, & Wyckoff, 2002). The attrition rate for these new teachers in urban and isolated rural schools is appalling, approaching a third in the first year. Teachers who leave the profession usually do not leave because the pay is dismal but because of the appalling conditions they find in their schools and the lack of support they are given (Bhatt, 2005). New teachers are frequently hazed by getting the largest classes with the most difficult students. All too often new teachers enter classrooms that are devoid of instructional materials and where books are in desperate condition if they are available at all.

It is actually surprising that two-thirds of the new teachers will return to their assignments for a second year. One result of this pattern of high attrition is that teachers working in low-performing schools that are located in high-poverty communities are twice as likely to be in their first 3 years of employment. This is not the case for their counterparts in suburban schools (Cortese & von Zastrow, 2006). This produces a distinct experience gap between the schools of our wealthy suburban communities, staffed by a coterie of confident old-timers, and the schools of our urban centers, staffed by a clutch of overstressed beginning teachers (Thiers, 2005). This gap between experienced and novice teachers is a contributing factor in the different levels of student achievement. Experienced teachers have students who score higher than do beginners (Goldhaber, 2006). Building principals in such schools start every year with a brand new staff. For these administrators there is a natural feeling of frustration in starting over from scratch every September and attempting anew to build a cohesive school community.

Hiring Highly Qualified Teachers

Highly qualified teachers have appropriate collegiate educations and are fully certified by a state education department to teach the subjects and the grade levels of their assignments (Darling-Hammond, 2000). The correlational evidence is weak between the two issues—teacher education and student achievement. The problem is that there is no clear proof that highly qualified teachers are also highly effective teachers (Kane, Rockoff, & Staiger, 2006). This point was demonstrated in a study of the classrooms of hundreds of "highly qualified" teachers in 20 different states. In that study, the teachers of first, third, and fifth grades all had met the state credentialing standards, but they did little quality teaching, keeping students occupied with busy work at their seats most of the day. Their classrooms provided a minimum of emotional support for the students, and the primary goal of all activities was scoring well on a state test (Jacobson, 2007; Pianta, 2007).

For more information, see "Considerations on Point" at www.sagepub.com/wrightstudy

Case in Point (15b)

This lack of a definitive link between holding a standard teaching certificate appropriate to the teaching assignment along with the amount of graduate education teachers completed, with student achievement outcomes, may well be an artifact of the usual research design used in studies of these two variables. In most studies, the education level of all certified personnel in a school is averaged and used as a correlational variable and mean student test scores for the school as the second variable. Those teacher education data are contaminated by the presence of counselors, specialists, and administrators. Those educators usually have more graduate education than classroom teachers but are not teachers per se. Their presence in the data attenuates the correlational relationship. More educational specialists (e.g., reading Title I teachers) are found in schools where there are more low-achieving children. The net result can be the incorrect finding that a better educated staff is related to lower student achievement levels.

Experienced Teachers

The correlational evidence notwithstanding, inexperienced teachers who are the least well qualified are routinely given assignments with children who are at the greatest risk for failure (Laczko-Kerr & Berliner, 2002). Thus, the children of the poor who live in inner cities are taught by teachers that would not be hired to work in suburban middle-class schools (Sunderman & Kim, 2005). One reason for this involves complex work rules negotiated by urban teacher's unions. These rules give senior teachers first choice of vacant positions within the school system.[3] Thus, urban school systems do not know until late in the summer exactly which vacancies are open for the new school year. By the time they start hiring new teachers the candidate pool has been picked clean by the suburban school systems. One study in Connecticut found the wealthy suburban schools were three times more likely to hire a new teacher with a year of experience and a master's degree than is true of the schools in the urban center (Frahm, 2006b). Young teachers tend to move from school districts where they feel that they have less control over their teaching to schools where they perceive they have more control over instruction (Marvel, Lyter, Peltola, Strizek, & Morton, 2007). Young teachers rarely report moving to new schools just for a pay raise. Thus, suburban schools with less bureaucracy than urban highly centralized school systems are able to recruit faculty out of the big city schools.

Seven of every 10 African American children attend a school where half or more of the students receive a free or reduced-cost lunch. In other words, the vast majority of African American children attend schools where the poverty level is the highest. By the same account, only one in six Anglo-White students attends such schools. This is a critical observation in that research from Texas has shown that the quality of education as measured by student achievement is linked to the both the amount of experience the teachers have and to the proportion of minority students enrolled in the schools (Hanushek & Rivkin, 2006).

California research has shown that high schools with the lowest proportion of fully certified teachers on staff also have the highest student failure rate on the required California graduation examination (Rogers, Holme, & Silver, 2005). A statewide study of the schools of New Jersey found that the proportion of minority children and the proportion of the impoverished students were most highly correlated with the mean test scores from that school (Camilli & Monfils, 2004). The result is a cycle where poverty breeds low average test scores for a school, which makes hiring good teachers difficult, and which in turn makes test scores even lower.

Recognizing this problem, U.S. Secretary of Education Spellings required all school systems to submit plans to the Department of Education by July 7, 2006, explaining how they would work to assure that the children of all schools experience an equal proportion of highly experienced and effective teachers. No state was able to fully comply with this reporting requirement. Nine states were admonished for not even making a good faith effort in that direction (Vu, 2006).[4]

The achievement test score advantage for children who are taught by highly effective and fully certified teachers has been documented. The effect can be as large as 18% on a norm-based, standardized measure of achievement. This partially explains the gap between the academic achievement of children from middle-class communities and those from impoverished inner-city backgrounds. There are no effective social policies in place that will end the disparity in financial resources between the two groups. Therefore, schools that enroll many children from poor neighborhoods and impoverished communities have a special responsibility to their students. Schools that provide the children from the poorest families with an annual succession of highly qualified and effective teachers will narrow the achievement gap.

Teacher Examinations

Another quality indicator for new teachers is their scores on a certification test such as the National Teacher's Examination and/or the Praxis II.[5] Teacher certification examinations are mandated by the various states and territories of the United States. Each state sets its own cut scores, which reflect both a state education department's belief in the importance of teachers' backgrounds and education (upward pressure) and the pragmatics of a diffi-cult market for recruiting new faculty (downward pressure on the cut scores). A statewide study of upper elementary school teachers in North Carolina found that there is a small but significant effect of teacher scores on student achievement in mathematics (Goldhaber, 2006). This is especially interesting in view of the fact that mathematics after third grade is less subject to parental influences than are other subject (e.g., reading and language arts).

The problem experienced by researchers attempting to find a link between teacher test scores and the achievement outcome for the students of those teachers is one of linkage. There is no obvious tie between effective teacher behaviors in a classroom and the scores on a test of basic skills like the PRAXIS I. A better measure would be an assessment of the teacher's knowledge of the subject area (Berliner, 2005).

Minority Teachers

During an era of both high-stakes accountability and teacher shortages, finding and hiring qualified minority teachers has become virtually impossi-ble. The layers of state-mandated competency exams that university-educated teachers must face have become a gatekeeper, turning away many who could become bilingual teachers (Flores & Clark, 2005). For the most part, African American college students have turned away from majoring in education and are preparing to enter other less troubled and better compen-sated fields (Bennett, McWhorter, & Kukendall, 2006). This trend is a trou-bling one for a number of reasons. One of which is that there is evidence from large scale research in Tennessee that the race of a teacher can make a difference in the amount that students learn in school. African American students have higher levels of achievement when taught by a teacher who shares an African American heritage (Dee, 2004). Likewise, Anglo-White students learn more and have better assessment scores when taught by teachers who are Anglo-White.

For more information, see "Considerations on Point" at www.sagepub.com/wrightstudy

Case in Point (15c)

The history of African American teachers in our schools is one that is not very pleasant to relate. Throughout the southern states, segregation by race in the schools was the law prior to 1954. The majority of the schools set up for minor-ity children were poorly supplied, crowded, in disrepair, and bereft of the basic amenities (e.g., indoor plumbing, school busses, and central heating). There was a good supply of African American teachers, mostly because education was one of the few jobs open to college-educated minority women. The school systems in the South maintained two separate salary schedules, paying African American teachers on average only 60% of what an Anglo-White teacher with the same background was paid.

The integration of the schools happened slowly, and minority teachers were rarely put in a position of teaching Anglo-White children. When Black administrators were moved into the central administration, they rarely had any true decision-making authority, serving instead as "window dressing" (Torres, Santos, Peck, & Cortes, 2004).

Following desegregation, schools in both the North and South hired as few African American teachers as possible. In New York City, the number of classroom teachers increased by 142,000 between 1960 and 1972. During that same time the number of minority teachers increased by only 407. During the 1960s, a number of southern districts continued to pay minority teachers less than their White counterparts by basing pay in part on scores earned on "teacher tests." During desegregation, the schools attended by minority students were usually closed, and those students were sent to what had been the school for Anglo-White children. This cost thousands of minority educators and administrators their jobs.

In view of this history, it is not surprising that so few African American college students have an interest in becoming teachers. Overall, the interest in a career in teaching by minority college undergraduates fell from almost 20% to about 9% in 1995 (American Association of Colleges for Teacher Education, 1999). Today, that proportion is even lower, as talented African American students are wooed by careers in business and technology. Also, these students have no interest in taking a required high-stakes license examination such as the Praxis series.

Today, the few African American teachers who enter the profession each year are normally employed to work in schools that are populated by children from impoverished backgrounds. The average first-year African American teacher works in a school where 60% or more of the students live in impoverished homes. The vast majority of new teachers each year are White, and almost all of them teach children who are from the middle class. One outcome of the initial teaching assignments is the fact that the African American teachers are more likely than their White counterparts to consider leaving the profession or changing jobs and moving to another school system (Frankenberg, 2006).

Alternative Tracks

The lack of certified teachers for many of the available teaching positions has led the states to initiate **alternative** tracks or routes for people to become teachers. The District of Columbia and 46 states have each created alternative routes for college-educated people to earn a fast-track teacher certificate. These programs have been shown to provide a positive developmental experience for both the mentor teachers who work with the fledgling classroom teachers, or protégées, and the protégées themselves (Stevens, 1993). The best of these fast-track programs are field based and involve university oversight, a teacher mentor, and part-time graduate coursework (Johnson, Birkeland, & Peske, 2005). Mentoring teachers can be an expensive process for the schools if it is done well. Experienced teachers do not need the extra work of mentoring new protégées. This work may include teaching principles of syntax, mathematics, and social science to the protégée teachers. It can also involve personal and career counseling, direction in instructional practice, and student behavior management (Steadman & Simmons, 2007). Mentoring teachers need to be granted released time to do these tasks, and that requires the schools to budget the money for substitute teachers.

Fast-track alternative approaches make it possible to increase the number of available teachers without expanding the schools and departments of education on the campuses of state universities. It also provides an alternative for many ethnic minorities to become teachers.

The state-mandated testing program for undergraduates working toward degrees in education took hold at the same time as the number of minority students studying to become teachers declined precipitously. The first state to initiate an alternative certification program was New Jersey in 1984. It was followed by Texas and then California, two states that had significant shortages of teachers (Feistritzer, 1999). Today, alternative teacher certification programs are being offered by states, large city school systems, service units of the state departments of education, and community colleges. All in all, there were 485 such programs in 2006, certifying about 50,000 new teachers that year (Honawar, 2007a).

There is belief among policymakers that by opening the teaching profession and making it easier for experienced adults working in other fields to become certified teachers, the problem of school staffing will disappear. This has not been the finding of research into the question of impact of alternative teacher certification. Alternative certification programs have not attracted large numbers of new teachers for the difficult-to-staff inner-city and rural schools and have not provided sufficient numbers of new teachers in the critically needed teaching disciplines of mathematics and science or in the area of special education (Cohen-Vogel & Smith, 2007).

One provision of the NCLB Act requires that all teachers must be highly qualified. Failure to reach this goal can earn schools and school systems sanctions. Many experienced teachers are not highly qualified (certified) to teach the subjects or grade levels to which they have been assigned. This is a major problem for many middle schools, where certified elementary teachers have taught secondary subjects to seventh- and eighth-grade children for years. To recruit teachers of science and mathematics for these jobs is nearly impossible. For that reason, the states were granted flexibility under the U.S. Department of Education NCLB rules to create an alternative path for experienced teachers to earn the appropriate certificates. These rules, known as **Highly Objective Uniform State Standard of Evaluation (HOUSSE)**, can involve as little as a few hours of local inservice education and/or a graduate course or two (Keller, 2004-b). Many states have adopted HOUSSE rules that involve little or no subject matter expertise and have given extra credit toward a new certification to teachers who have served on curriculum committees or who have assisted with school functions. Recent research into the relationship between the teacher's background of content knowledge and the middle and high school mathematics achievement outcome of students has demonstrated a significant link (Harris & Sass, 2007).

Another fast track for teacher certification that added many new teachers to the inner cities and to rural communities is the Troops to Teacher (TTT) program. This began as a way to employ returning military personnel after the first Gulf War. It was proposed by President Clinton in 1993 and passed into law by Congress in 1994. Under this program, each state sets standards for former military personnel who desire a civilian job in education. The **DANTES** (Defense Activity for Non-Traditional Education Support) **program** awards credit to the former soldiers on the basis of military training and experience. In 2007, a total of 9,500 former members of the armed services had become classroom teachers through this program.[6] About a quarter of those who elect the TTT program end up working in the inner-city schools, while another 40% go on to teaching jobs in rural communities. Thus, this program has become an important source of teachers for schools that have the most difficult time finding qualified teachers.

A fast track for teacher certification is provided to a small sample of the graduates of liberal arts programs from highly selective colleges and universities. This is the Teach for America (TFA) program. The goal of the TFA program is to place well-educated and highly intelligent young teachers into inner-city classrooms. These young graduates attend 5 weeks of summer classes in preparation for having their own classroom in the fall. When they volunteer they contract to work for 2 years in the rural or inner-city school to which they are assigned.

More information about the **Teach for America program** can be seen at www.TeachforAmerica.org.

Since the TFA program's beginning in 1989, thousands of the liberal arts graduates from the Ivy League and other highly competitive colleges have become teachers. In 2007 there were 19,000 college graduates who applied for one of the 3,000 TFA openings (Lipka, 2007). Research has generally shown that the classrooms of TFA teachers produce marginally better levels of student achievement in mathematics than do other novice teachers (Decker, Mayer, & Glazerman, 2004). There is little difference in reading achievement between those who entered the profession through Teach for America and those who were traditional graduates of schools of education (Decker, Mayer, & Glazerman; Raymond & Fletcher, 2002).

In 2005, Linda Darling-Hammond and her colleagues at Stanford University published data from the Houston Independent School District that showed that the Teach for America instructors were less effective than the graduates of regular teacher certification programs (Darling-Hammond, Holtzman, Gatlin, & Heilig, 2005). She also reported that they had an 85% dropout rate after 3 years. Darling-Hammond et al. concluded that the Teach for America teachers are about as effective as other uncertified teachers.[7] The Teach for America dropout rate compares unfavorably to the normal 46% dropout rate among all teachers after 5 years. In another study, Darling-Hammond's (2005) research from the schools of Houston, Texas, demonstrated that fully certified and well-experienced teachers are more effective than under-certified teachers.

National Certification

The education reform movement of the 1980s saw the publication of the Carnegie Task Force on Teaching as a Profession report, *A Nation Prepared: Teachers for the 21st Century* (1986). This task force was created by the Carnegie Forum on Education and the Economy in answer to the publication of *A Nation at Risk: The Imperative of Educational Reform* (National Commission on Excellence in Education, 1983). One outcome of this was the establishment of a National Board for Professional Teaching Standards (NBPTS) in 1987. By 1991, this group was publishing teaching standards and had begun to certify classroom teachers who could meet them. The evaluation process for the national teacher certification was taken over by the Educational Testing Service in 1996 (Harman, 2001). The National Board reported that by the end of the 2007–2008 school year the number of nationally certified teachers totaled about 2% of the profession. One major motivation for a teacher to make a commitment to the certification process is the pay incentives offered by many school systems and state departments of education. During the 2007–2008 school year the cost of the application process was $2,500. The pass rate for first attempts to gain certification have a 60% failure rate (Keller, 2007).

Information about the NBPTS and **national certification** can be reviewed at www.nbpts.org.

Research has not been able to document any effect on student achievement outcomes as a function of a teacher having achieved "national certification." A large-scale study of over 30,000 teachers in North Carolina was unable to demonstrate that better student achievement occurs in the classrooms of nationally certified teachers (Goldhaber & Anthony, 2004). In addition, a "**value-added** assessment"[8] of the effectiveness of teachers in several North Carolina school systems was unable to detect any achievement advantage for the students in classrooms staffed by NBPTS certified teachers compared with other experienced teachers (Sanders, Ashton, & Wright, 2005). This finding was verification of an earlier study of using the value-added model of assessing teacher effectiveness in Tennessee (Sanders & Horn, 1998; Sanders, Saxton, & Horn, 1997).

In 2007–2008, the State of South Carolina cut its funding for teacher bonus payments, which had been made to those classroom teachers who held National Board certification (Honawar, 2007b). This was done as Governor Mark Sanford felt that there were no differences between the achievement outcomes for children taught by NBPTS certified teachers and other classroom teachers. Finally, student achievement data from the NAEP demonstrate that children in the classrooms of teachers that report they "know nothing about the national certification" score slightly better than do children in the classrooms of National Board for Professional Teaching Standards certified teachers. The National Board has offered evidence that while there is no achievement advantage for children taught by National Board certified teachers, there are distinctive differences in the teaching methodologies employed by National Board certified and non-certified teachers (Colby & Smith, 2007).

Empowerment

Good schools where student achievement is at an optimal level, and where effective teaching is ongoing, have teachers who have taken personal responsibility for student learning (Logerfo, 2006). These teachers are of the belief that their efforts can make a difference in the lives of children. They see their schools as having few disciplinary problems, and they don't feel burdened with excessive paperwork. Teachers who feel that they work as part of a cooperative team of educators, and who believe they are valued for their efforts, tend to have students with better assessment test scores (Wheelan & Kesselring, 2005). These successful teachers also see themselves as well supplied and equipped for teaching and also have students who score better on achievement tests (NAEP, 2004). A survey of over 40,000 educators in North Carolina has revealed that teachers need to feel empowered in their jobs. This factor relates directly to job satisfaction and retention and indirectly to student achievement (Easley, 2003).

For more information, see "Considerations on Point" at www.sagepub.com/ wrightstudy

Case in Point (15c)

The teachers in many school systems are expected to supply their own class-rooms from their household budgets. This has lead to the unseemly sight of teachers taking handouts from community members in order to have enough money to put chalk on the board and paper in the hands of students. It is not surprising that this seems to occur more frequently in schools that have the largest number of children from impoverished homes. Also not surprisingly, these same schools tend to have consistently lower mean scores on high-stakes tests (Goodnough, 2002; Rosenberg, 2005).

The theme of empowerment was also present in research from the teachers in Kentucky (Kelly & Finnigan, 2003). Their research found that schools with improved student performance had teachers who felt the improvement goals set for their schools were fair and that their voices were heard in the decision-making processes.

Summary

The cognitive tasks that are a part of all mandated high-stakes tests are highly correlated to the mental ability of children. This trait paired with the child's language skill in English make up two core factors involved with success on high-stakes tests.

In addition to these "givens," there are a number of factors related to the child's status that also have a role to play in the outcome of achievement test scores.

Academically successful children are often found in two-parent families where homework is monitored and school is regularly discussed. These parents are well educated themselves and have high educational expecta-tions for their children (Holbrook, 2003). They read and have books in the home and they watch less TV than other adults. Parents of academically successful children ensure that their youngsters are well rested and alert for school each day (Fallone, Acebo, Seifer, & Carskadon, 2005). These parents are not afraid to let their child know that he or she is loved, but they do not attempt to be their child's peer. These parents are consistent and open to listen and communicate with their child. They are active participants in their child's life and have an active interest in the child's education.

These parents have computers in their homes, and they monitor what their children do with them. The combination of these parent variables accounts for about 30% ($R^2 = 0.296$) of the variance in state-mandated achievement test scores (Holbrook & Wright, 2004). These parental behaviors, when combined with the mental ability of the children, account for 60% or more of the variance in assessment test scores. This is not to downplay the role of the schools, but clearly the role of the instructional program is but one of many elements that contribute to the achievement outcomes for any child.

Teachers who are well experienced and educated tend to be more effective than their less-experienced peers. The achievement outcomes of children seem to have less to do with the teacher's path followed toward earning a teaching credential than with a teacher's experience. Teachers who work in schools located in impoverished communities tend to be less well educated and have less teaching experience than is true of suburban teachers. These same urban schools also face a greater teacher turnover than their suburban neighbors.

There is an effort in some states to encourage teachers to earn national certification from the National Board for Professional Teaching Standards, although the teachers who complete this process have not been found to facilitate student achievement at a level any different than their classroom peers without that national credential.

Discussion Questions

1. Plan, in outline form, an inservice program for the parents of a middle school that is located in a blue-collar community. Assume that there will be two class meetings, each with 2-hour-long sessions given a week apart. The theme is helping your child do well on mandated tests. Show the topics you would include and provide ideas of how to impart these ideas to the parents' group.

2. Assume the role of a personnel director for a small urban school system that enrolls a population of students who are mostly ethnic minorities, many of whom come from impoverished homes. What

policies and procedures would you request of your school board to meet the district's need for new faculty?

3. One of the largest administrative expenses faced by school systems is the cost of recruiting new teachers. If you were helping a school system shape personnel policies that would reduce teacher turnover, what are the key elements of the plan that you would recommend?

4. If a guidance counselor begins a group counseling program for seventh-grade students who do not test well on the state-mandated assessment, what topics should he or she schedule for the first few meetings?

5. Explain the distinction between highly qualified and highly effective teachers. Can a teacher be both?

Student Study Site

Educational Assessment on the Web

Log on to the Web-based student study site at www.sagepub.com/wrightstudy for additional Web sources and study resources.

NOTES

1. The minimum requirement to apply for NBPTS certification is a regular state teaching certificate and 3 years of full-time classroom experience.

2. School districts are permitted not to count ELL students who have lived in the United States for fewer than 3 years in the determination of their Adequate Yearly Progress (AYP).

3. The state of California passed a law in 2006 that broke the seniority rules in that state (SB 1209 and SB 1655).

4. The states that were criticized for not making a good faith effort were Alaska, Delaware, Idaho, Iowa, Minnesota, Montana, Nebraska, North Carolina, and Washington.

5. In 1973, James Popham proposed the development of a performance test for teachers involving an assessment of their actual teaching. This idea would be similar to the practical assessments that physicians in residency education must take. Unfortunately, that idea was never developed (Gronlund, 1974).

6. DANTES is a worldwide program that offers U.S. military personnel educational training and programs. It also provides a method (test based) for transcripting military training and education into college course credit.

7. This may be misleading, as the Teach for America candidates sign contracts promising to teach for only 2 years. For many, this 2-year break from what is normally expected of them may be a normal step in the development of an adult identity (Erikson, 1968).

8. This approach to evaluation examines the change that occurs in student achievement during the school year. More on this approach is presented in Chapter 17.

Chapter 16

TEST PREPARATION FOR SUCCESSFUL SCHOOLS

Before anything else, preparation is the key to success.

—Alexander Graham Bell

Issues and Themes

The level of success in life achieved by children, the careers of educators, and even the value and stability of entire communities is now linked to high-stakes tests required in our schools. Under the provisions of NCLB, each school within a district (except parochial and private) must publish a report card reporting among other things the disaggregated scores on mandated statewide assessment tests. There can be community-wide feelings of angst and disappointment when local schools fail to meet required adequate yearly progress goals. Avoiding the need to inure the inevitable reforms and structural changes that would be brought by the community is a powerful source of motivation for administrators. The stress of this pressure is felt by every teacher in every classroom. Under these circumstances, it is inevitable that cheating the system will occasionally occur. Such cheating violates the laws of most states as well as the ethical canons of the professional associations.

The stress is even more palatable for the students who feel they are at jeopardy for disappointing their parents and losing face within the community of other children. This pressure on children even extends to state policy. Michigan now awards high school graduates a $2,500 college scholarship if they pass the state assessment tests. This is not a small issue for many working-class families.

The influence of the high-stakes tests in the lives of children is now part of our popular culture and is elaborated in children's books and dramatically presented by the feature filmmakers of Hollywood. As our society as a whole is in favor of school and student accountability, there is no doubt that this pressure on our children will be with us for the foreseeable future.

Both parents and schools have used early (kindergarten and first grade) retention to give children a developmental advantage when they enter third grade. A number of other marginally ethical practices have been employed by educators to improve the scores of children on high-stakes tests. Some of these involve peer pressure, and others amount to little more than bribes for improved work.

A number of strategies exist for improving the assessment scores of students that are both effective and ethical. These involve the administrative leadership style, teacher inservice education, and the school's staffing and scheduling practices. Within the classrooms there are also specific instructional strategies that are effective in improving scores on the mandated assessments.

The length of the school year and the length of the school day have been examined for their influence on achievement outcomes. While little has come from these efforts, related studies of class size and school plant architecture have been shown to correlate to assessment test scores. Also, there are a number of ways that the organization and administration of the assessment tests can relate to the outcome.

These approaches to testing and test preparation may soon be the concerns of a different era as we move toward a totally wired school where all testing and remediation is facilitated online. Each year the number of states using an online method for student assessment is increasing, and by the final year of the original goals of the NCLB Act (2014), these methods will be universal.

Learning Objectives

By reading and studying this chapter you should acquire the ability to do the following:

- Explain the sources of stress on educators that are part of the high-stakes testing movement.

- Provide examples from children's literature and the popular culture of the stressful impact of high-stakes testing on children.
- List test preparation activities that are not legal and/or ethical.
- Discuss the question of staffing and teacher assignment to the outcome of high-stakes tests.
- Explain how the leadership style of a school administrator can play a role in the assessment test scores of students.
- Design a community outreach program for a school that could work to improve assessment test scores.
- Describe pre-reading and reading strategies that have been found to relate to higher scores on mandated assessment tests of reading.
- Outline strategies that can be employed to improve the writing scores of students.
- Provide strategies that can be used to improve the mathematics test scores for elementary and middle-school students.
- Explain the distinction between "teaching to the test" and "teaching for the test."
- Describe the research on the relationship between the length of the school day and school year on assessment test scores.
- Discuss the link between leadership style, school climate, and achievement outcomes.
- Describe the research consensus on the relationship between class size and student achievement.

ACCOUNTABILITY ANGST

The mind that is anxious about the future is miserable.

—Santana

One goal of the NCLB Act is to provide an open and transparent accountability system for all public schools. This involves the publication of "report cards" for every school building, school district, and state education department. At the school building level this process includes reports of the number of children at each level of proficiency on each of the required tests. It also requires that these scores be disaggregated for each minority and other identified group of children. Other items such as the number of "highly qualified teachers" who are employed to work in the school, and the student attendance and dropout rates, are also included.

Cost of Failure

From 2002 to 2005 it was necessary for adequate yearly progress to be shown by each group of students in each grade level toward meeting the ultimate goal of every student being proficient in every tested subject by 2014. In 2005, that was changed by U.S. Department of Education Secretary Margaret Spellings so that progress could be made on the basis of some grade levels, not all grade levels. That policy shift may have been in answer to the many middle-class suburban schools that found they missed meeting the AYP goals and were labeled as "needing improvement" (Tracey, Sunderman, & Orfield, 2005). The label is almost always presented to the public by local media as "failing." The general public has no way to discern anything from such headlines beyond the fact that their expensive and heretofore highly regarded suburban school system is a failure. In 2006, there were a total of 1,750 schools that had a 5-year history of failing to meet the AYP standard and were in the process of being reorganized or closed (Feller, 2006). That same year 26% of all schools, a total of 22,873, failed to meet the AYP target.

The tweaking of the rules by the Department of Education notwithstanding, respected school administrators have had their reputations sullied by media reports of the systemic failure of local schools. Entire communities can feel the impact when the scores on the mandated testing program are reported in the local press. Kurt Landgraf (2005), president of ETS, has cautioned against reading too much into assessment test scores. His caution has been ignored by the media. It had to be expected that real estate agents would follow the reports of test scores, knowing that families with young children shop for homes where the school system has a good reputation (Lloyd, 2005; Van Moorlehem, 1998). Today, even divorce lawyers have found the scores of interest when they negotiate for the custody of children.

These reports, and the inevitable public response, have put significant strain on the whole enterprise of public education. Pressure on school leaders is imparted to the teaching staff, who can find themselves surrounded by nervous children worried about the high-stakes tests, and building principals anxious for their school to score well on the next state-issued report card. As an increasing number of states move to using "value added" assessments with their annual tests, individual teachers who are less effective than their peers will become easier to identify. The future portends only more assessments and an ever-increasing emphasis on measurable outcomes.

At the personal level, children can also feel the stress that high-stakes assessments have on their lives. In 2007, approximately 100,000 nine-year-old children failed third grade and were not promoted to the fourth grade with their peers because of low test scores. In the 27 states where high school graduation is contingent on passing an exit assessment, 30% to 40% of the senior class who are non-White minorities and about half of that number of the White students will fail and not earn a standard high school diploma.

Even those high school students who have good grades and who score well on the state tests still face college admissions. College admission looms as a major source of concern until the "fat" letter full of admission material arrives in the April mail.

Case in Point (16a)

The perception of an admission crisis is expanded out of proportion in the hallways and lunchrooms of high schools when students begin to receive the dreaded "thin letter" of the wait list. School counselors often unknowingly add to the stress and feeling of urgency by posting letters of acceptance on the bulletin boards of high schools. There once was a time, not so long ago, when the goal of going to college was to get an education. What few guidance counselors or parents know is that there are only about 50 colleges in the United States that send out more letters of rejection than they do letters of acceptance (Steinberg, 2002). Some parents have been described as deeply engaged in the study of the details of college catalogues, attempting to ferret out the subtle differences between the top-ranked private liberal arts colleges in the Northeast (Cohen, 2006). Often these parents experience more concern about college admissions than do their children. Yet, the pressure is real, and teenagers are expected to stand out and somehow appear to be stellar candidates for the college admissions office. To this end, families have been known to move to communities with less competitive high schools, making it possible for the student to have a better GPA and higher class rank. Adolescents have been known to volunteer to work with community groups and agencies, not out of a sense of duty or altruism but to make their college applications look better (Matthews, 2005).

For more information, see "Considerations on Point" at www.sagepub.com/wrightstudy

Popular Culture

Popular culture has also picked up on the stress that results from mandated assessments and high-stakes tests. Children's literature has begun to play on this theme with fictional books such as Judy Finchler's (2000) *Testing Miss Malarkey*; Pansie Hart Flood's (2004) *It's Test Day, Tiger Turcotte*; Edward Bloor's (2004) *Story Time*; Andrew Clements's (2004) *The Report Card*; and Nancy Lieberman's (2004) *Admissions*. Even the fifth book of the wildly popular children's series by J. K. Rowlings (2003), *Harry Potter and the Order of the Phoenix,* finds the hero, Harry Potter, under stress to achieve a passing score on the "Ordinary Wizarding Levels Examination (OWLs)."

Hollywood has not missed this trend either. These movies are designed for an adolescent market and have common themes (viz., that youngsters must face the evil forces of the testing and assessment; then, only through their cleverness, can adolescents rise above these impediments and become successful). This is the theme of *How I Got Into College,* released in 1989 by Twentieth Century Fox (Shamberg, Cantillon, & Holland, 1989). In *Stand and Deliver,* the 1988 release from Warner, a class of inner-city students is accused of cheating on an AP examination and are subjected to a grueling retest by factotums of the ETS Company (Law & Mendez, 1988). In 2004, Paramount Pictures released *The Perfect Score,* which tells the story of a cabal of high school seniors who conspire to steal the answers to the SAT (Birnbaum & Robbins, 2004). Disney released *Recess: School's Out*, a story of a radical educational reformer who wants to cancel recess to have time to have students work on better test scores (Suzuki, Swuz, & Sheetz 2001). In 2005, Hart Sharp Video released the film *Admissions,* a fictional account of a high school graduate flubbing in her college admission's efforts (Vait & Painter, 2005). In 2002, Columbia Pictures released the film *Stealing Harvard*, the story of an uncle who turns to crime to pay the tuition to Harvard for his niece (Grazer & McCulloch, 2003). Also in 2002, Paramount released the film *Orange County*, a comedy about the admission of a surfer into Stanford University (Rudin & Gale, 2002). A romantic comedy about admissions into Princeton, *Cinderella Story*, tells the story of the life of a young woman applying for admissions into an Ivy League college (Rachmil & Rosman, 2004).

During the summer of 2005, the NBC network ran a 6-week series using a "reality TV" format that focused on college admissions. This series, *The Scholar,* had 10 high school seniors compete for financial aid to attend the colleges of their choice.

Cutting Corners and Cheating

In light of the amount of pressure on students and educators, it is not surprising that corners have been cut and incidences of cheating have occasionally been reported (Burney, 2006). Even entire states have been described as "gaming the system" (Pascopella, 2007a). While unusual, these incidences are widespread, involving an estimated 1% of the educators in our schools (Donsky, 2005). It is difficult to know how common this type of fraud is, because teachers usually do not talk to outsiders about what their colleagues are doing.

The type of cheating that occurs most often involves extra time for slower students and letting faster students work ahead on the test, answering questions in sections before they should. Other inappropriate strategies have involved having aids posted on the walls of the classroom (e.g., multiplication tables, vocabulary words). More scandalous problems have involved changing the answers of students once the test has been completed, teaching the specifics of what is on the test, and helping students while the test is in progress.

These problems seem to erupt every spring during testing season and have the potential to erode public confidence in the integrity of educational reforms under the NCLB Act. The reality is that in most states no one is even looking for unusual patterns of scores and cheating. One company, Caveon Test Security, has established a niche for itself by using statistical models to analyze school scores and even student answer sheets to detect possible cheating. Starting in 2005, the schools of Texas, Ohio, and North Carolina had their scores scrutinized by consultants. The states of Nevada, Louisiana, and Mississippi have hired in-house staff to perform such reviews (Patrick & Eichel, 2006). Meanwhile, Pennsylvania, South Carolina, and Illinois include in the test developer's contract the requirement of test reviews.

Caveon found that there were 699 Texas schools that could be identified as having unusual and hard to explain shifts in student scores from one year to the next. However, the most common way that these schools were identified was by an analysis of answer sheets, which found that too many students made the same errors and got the same items correct (Benton, 2006). Many of these anomalies occurred with the schools of Houston, where a number of administrators were subsequently demoted and teachers reprimanded or fired (Hacker & Parks, 2005). The full audit of all of Texas's schools in 2006 indicated a high probability that 1 school in 11 reported fraudulent scores on the statewide assessment.

James Popham (2006) suggested that cheating by teachers occurs because the state-mandated assessments are both correlated to the socio-economic status of the test takers and are instructionally insensitive. Thus, no matter how much effort a teacher puts into instruction and how hard he or she tries, the telling factor in student outcomes is predicated on how wealthy the test takers' families are.

Information about one company specializing in test security can be viewed at www.caveon.com/press6-3-05.htm.

Because most states provide a window of time when the schools can administer state assessments, teachers from one school have been known to e-mail or call friends in other buildings and provide a "heads-up" as to what the test contains. Parents have also been known to call relatives with children attending other schools to pass on test information, such as writing prompts and any other items their children may remember about the test.

LEGAL AND ETHICAL REQUIREMENTS

For the past 30 years, committees of the professional associations and learned societies of education have developed and published guidelines for ethical use of tests and assessments (Impara, 1996). The most recent edition of the *Code of Fair Testing Practices in Education* provides the following two relevant statements for educators administering high-stakes assessments: "Follow established procedures for administering tests in a standardized manner" and "Protect the security of test materials, including respecting copyrights and eliminating opportunities for test takers to obtain scores by fraudulent means" (Joint Committee on Testing Practice, 2005, p. 26). What this statement of ethical practice does not provide is any method of enforcement.

The introduction of high-stakes testing programs by the states changed all this by introducing an era of statute-enforced testing procedures. Now unethical testing practices are also illegal. Statutes of the various states now provide specific investigative steps and penalties for a breech of ethics. These penalties can involve forfeiture of a teaching and/or administrative license or even more serious criminal penalties. To accompany the new high-stakes assessments, the states have written prescriptive testing ethics codes and standards for practice.

MARGINAL ETHICS

While many of the methods noted above are clearly unethical and deserving serious sanctions, many other methods to influence test scores of children are questionable, but legal.

Parental Strategies

Parents have been known to transfer their child to a parochial or private school at the end of second grade. Those schools are not required to use a high-stakes test with students. After a year or two the child is quietly transferred back into public education. This strategy is not successful in states where there are tests for promotion at several grade levels. Parents can also opt to home-school a child for a year or two to avoid the jeopardy of the high-stakes test in third grade. Another parent strategy that is occurring with

BOX 16.1   "Testing Code of Ethics," as Adopted in West Virginia

WEST VIRGINIA DEPARTMENT OF EDUCATION

126CSR14

TITLE 126

LEGISLATIVE RULE

SERIES 14

WEST VIRGINIA MEASURES OF ACADEMIC PROGRESS (2340)

§126-14-8. Investigation of Security Violation.

8.1. Any written complaint and/or oral report alleging a violation of West Virginia Measures of Academic Progress testing security or copyright infringement shall be reported immediately to the county superintendent of the county (or organization) in which the violation(s) occurred. The county superintendent shall immediately contact the West Virginia Department of Education who will advise the county about the procedures to follow regarding any investigation.

8.2. All complaints will be investigated whether reported by a named individual or anonymously to insure test security for all students and reliability of school results.

8.3. An investigation must occur in a timely and efficient manner and shall be:

8.3.1. jointly conducted by the designated staff of west Virginia Department of Education and the county superintendent (or the designated staff) of the county in which the alleged violation occurred, or

8.3.2. at the request of the county superintendent, conducted by the staff of West Virginia Department of Education, solely.

8.4. The investigation must, at a minimum, consist of personal interviews with the reporter, if known; the individual(s) against whom the allegation(s) is/are filed; and any other individual who may have knowledge of the alleged incident.

8.4.1. The investigation may also consist of any other methods and review of the circumstances deemed pertinent by the investigators within the bounds of the law.

8.4.2. The investigating team must take immediate steps to protect the rights of the complainant, students, teachers, administrators and other personnel including the individual(s) against whom the allegation(s) is/are filed pending the completion of an investigation of testing security or copyright violations.

(Continued)

BOX 16.1 (Continued)

8.5. Upon completion of the investigation, written findings and recommendations based on all the facts and surrounding circumstances must be submitted immediately to the Office of the State Superintendent of Schools with a copy to the county superintendent and shall include:

8.5.1. a determination of whether any action or incident constitutes a violation of testing security procedures or copyright infringement as follows:

a. testing security procedures or copyright infringement was not breached, or

b. testing security procedures or copyright infringement breach could not be determined, or

c. testing security procedures or copyright infringement was breached and include recommendations for

  A. invalidating the test scores of students/classes/school/county,

  B. retesting of students with the equivalent form of the test with the county assuming the cost of both purchasing and scoring the equivalent form, if testing window has not closed,

  C. re-aggregating the test data for valid test results for students and school,

  D. using the equivalent form in the next year's administration.

8.5.2. Any taped conversation from the investigation shall be transcribed and a copy shall be forwarded to the county superintendent upon written request following the submission of the recommendations above.

8.6. Upon receipt of the written findings and recommendations of the investigation team, the county superintendent shall take any appropriate employment action and so advise the State Superintendent of Schools, in writing, setting forth any recommendations as follows:

8.6.1. no action was taken by the county board,

8.6.2. punitive action was taken by the county board,

a. suspension by county board,

b. termination by county board, or

c. other.

8.6.3. action against teaching license taken by State Superintendent of Schools.

8.7. Upon review of the investigation team's written findings/recommendations, the State Superintendent of schools shall take appropriate action against those found to have violated test security procedures or copyright violations.

SOURCE: WV Dept. of Education 126CSR14, Title 126 Legislative Rule, Series 14, WV Measures of Academic Progress (2340) §126-14.8. Investigation of Security Violation.

greater frequency involves holding the child an extra year in a private kinder-garten before enrolling him or her in first grade in a public school. It is likely that the school systems will see the grade level cohorts being a bit older than in the past, as this and similar methods are used more frequently.

Private tutoring and coaching for the tests have had an upsurge in pop-ularity. Private schools that coach for the exam have become commonplace. Some of these private test cram centers have even taken the name of their Japanese counterparts, *jukus*.[1]

School Strategies

Some school administrators have taken a similar approach to improving the average test scores of students. By selecting slower children for grade retention while they are in first or second grade, it is possible to give them an extra year to catch up before they face the high-stakes test in third grade. This strategy can be initiated by parents who wish to give their child the advantage of an extra developmental year over their peers. The professional associa-tions oppose grade retention for this purpose, making it a sketchy approach for a school to adopt (National Association of School Psychologists, 2003).

Another marginal school-based strategy for raising school scores on the state test was uncovered by an economist, David Figlio (2003). He found that during the times during the year when the high-stakes tests are given, and during the days set aside for make-up testing, there is a differential pattern of punishment administered by school disciplinarians. Figlio found that low-performing students who are caught violating a school rule during the testing period are significantly more likely to be punished with an extended out-of-school suspension than are others. Also, he found that students who perform well on tests who are caught in violation of a school rule during the time when the mandated tests are occurring are given less harsh punishments and usu-ally are included among those taking the assessments. This process only occurs during the years when the high-stakes tests are administered.

While it is not ethical to teach children how to answer the items on the high-stakes test they will face, an alternative strategy involving teaching old (released) test items is becoming commonplace.[2] Several states (California, Florida, Maryland, Massachusetts, Ohio, Texas, and Virginia) release some or all of their high-stakes tests a year after they have been used. An ethical ques-tion arises when these old tests are included as part of the curriculum. The direct instruction of last year's high-stakes test is clearly "teaching to the test" and not teaching the knowledge base and cognitive skills that make up the state's learning standards. This process circumvents the whole purpose of the high-stakes test, which is to assess the extent to which children have learned those skills and areas of knowledge specified in the standards. Instead, the mandated high-stakes assessment becomes a measure of how well children can remember items and test-gaming strategies.

Rewards have always been used by parents and educators to encourage children to do their best work. Recently, schools have employed a number of different rewards to motivate children to perform better on mandated assessment tests. These have included tickets to concerts, admission to professional sporting events, and free meals at local restaurants (Belluck, 2006; Knight, 2005; Lou, 2007; Pakkala, 2006; Woods, 2007). Occasionally school administrators have even used foundation funding to present savings bonds to students who show improvement on the assessments. The principal of an upper-middle-class high school that had a severe parking shortage devised a novel motivational reward. The highly coveted and very limited student parking permits were awarded on the basis of scores on the state assessment test. One school in Florida ran a cram course on nine Saturdays to get at-risk children ready for the state's mandated test. They awarded perfect attendance at the Saturday juku with a new iPod (Crouse, 2006). Other Florida high schools have provided limousine rides and prom tickets to juniors who do well on the mandated high school examinations (Bailey, 2007). Another Florida high school used various fundraisers to raise $5,000, which was used to purchase 100 MP3 players for all the juniors that did well on the state mandated examination, while an elementary school that was given a grant of $2,000 to buy school supplies used the money to buy 400 five-dollar gift cards at a local store. These were used as rewards for the children for good test scores (Ehrlich, 2007). A high school raised $18,500 to buy a new Scion car that was given as a raffle prize. The raffle was only open to those scoring at the proficient level (or above) on the state's examination.[3] The principal of an elementary school and several devoutly religious members of his faculty returned to school the night before the high-stakes tests started and blessed with holy oils the desks where children would sit to take the test the next morning (Wood, 2007).

For more information, see "Considerations on Point" at www.sagepub.com/wrightstudy

Case in Point (16b)

Perhaps the most unusual of these reward programs for children occurred in Florida. In some of the elementary schools of the City of Gainesville, the third grade students who performed best on the state assessment, the FCAT, got to stand in a chamber filled with swirling money and grab as many handfuls of $1 and $5 bills as they could in 15 seconds. This unusual project was cosponsored by a local bank.

Merit Pay

It was not until the 1960s that the traditional unequal pay scales of school systems were replaced by a single pay scale for all teachers employed in a district (Johnson, 2000). Early pay systems favored high school teachers at the expense of elementary school teachers.[4] That single pay scale is now being questioned. Critics feel that highly effective teachers should receive extra compensation above and beyond the common pay scale, in the form of merit pay or a bonus.

In some regards, the merit pay offered by a number of school systems to their teachers is similar to reward programs noted above for students. That is to say, merit pay is believed to be a way to reinforce quality teaching and thereby improve the education of all children. Additionally, it is believed that merit pay will help recruit and retain high-quality teachers. The argument that proponents of merit pay make is that the present system of having one standard pay scale for all teachers only encourages mediocrity and discourages the best and most motivated educators. Opponents of merit pay point out that merit awards are summative statements that are made only after a teacher demonstrates meritorious teaching. The concern is that merit pay provides neither a formative evaluation nor developmental steps designed to improve those teachers who are not at that meritorious level. A second concern is that teacher incentives do not address the central problems of education. It can be argued that teachers have not been withholding their best efforts, waiting for the day when they get bonus pay for better instructional efforts (Hershberg & Lea-Kruger, 2007). If classroom teachers are to be paid for performance, they should be given far more control over the instructional environment then they have today.

Merit Pay vs. Signing Bonus

A second argument that merit proponents make is that teachers of some subject areas are very difficult to find. Teachers of science, mathematics, modern language, and special education will be more likely to work in a system that offers a salary incentive based only on their disciplines. In big league sports this is referred to as a signing bonus. Critics of merit pay point out that such salary incentives amount to so little money as to be trivial to experienced teachers and would not compare favorably with the pay packages offered in the private sector to recent science and mathematics graduates.[5] Yet, there is a danger of any number of perverse effects when the incentives are substantial (Firestone, Monfils, Schorr, Hicks, & Martinez, 2004).

A number of names have been used with the concept of merit pay for teachers, including pay for performance and incentive pay. There are four ways merit pay can be awarded to a teacher. These can fit into a 2-by-2 matrix:

AWARDED TO WHOLE SCHOOL	AWARDED TO INDIVIDUAL
One-time bonuses	One-time bonus
Permanent salary increases	Permanent salary increase

Merit Pay as a Unit Reward

When the decision is made to award a whole school, there is still the question as to whether all the teaching staff will have an equal share or whether the principal will be empowered to decide who on the staff is to be given an award and how much that will be. Most school administrators do not wish to be the person who must determine merit levels and provide justifications for the decision on each teacher's merit. Elementary school administrators fear that the merit pay decision will destroy the within-grade level cohesion and morale. High school principals with a professional staff of 200 certified teachers and specialists see the job as a bureaucratic nightmare of paperwork. Most teachers do not want administrators making the merit award decision, fearing awards would go to "obsequious boot lickers" (Lieberman, 2000). They are concerned that all creativity within the classroom and all constructive criticism of the policies within a school would be stifled. These concerns notwithstanding, there is evidence that teachers have begun to have more positive opinions of the practice of awarding merit pay based on test scores (Dillon, 2007b).

Merit Pay Problems

Another concern that most teachers have is that merit pay will be predicated on the scores of mandated assessments. This type of an evaluation may also include a value-added assessment based on one of the various regression models now available. In either case, the fear is that a low-achieving class one year could affect a teacher's livelihood. Another concern has been expressed by those teachers who are not directly engaged in classroom instruction, such as librarians, media specialists, art and music teachers, and reading specialists. Other teachers in grades where there is no test (e.g., kindergarten and first grade) are also concerned with the evaluation system. Their efforts will not appear on the assessment test scores. At the secondary level, 10 or more teachers are involved in the education of any one student in a year's time. The problem for high school administrators is to unravel how effective each of these educators is and make an appropriate award to them for their efforts.

Merit Pay in Play

The school systems of several large cities (e.g., Cincinnati) have working models for merit pay in place. When state departments of education require merit pay for all school personnel, local school boards often must foot the bill.[6] In Florida, a statewide merit pay plan has been in place and generally ignored since 1998, and Colorado began a performance pay plan in 2006. In 2006–2007, the State of Texas initiated a $250 million program of merit pay incentives (Hacker & Stutz, 2006). The first year is a pilot year, and 2007–2008 merit pay plans are being initiated in over 1,000 schools serving mostly low-income children. The awards are in the form of one-time bonuses that range between $3,000 and $10,000. With the mean teacher salary in Texas (2006–2007) at $42,000 a bonus of $10,000 represents a before-tax boost of 23.8%. It is generally hoped that this plan will lure better teachers into the schools of impoverished communities. The first round of awards went to 7,900 teachers in the city of Houston. Almost all of these merit awards were given to teachers of science and mathematics and averaged $1,850.[7] The awarding of these merit bonuses produced a loud chorus of complaints from the community who felt that the selection criteria were wrong (Tonn, 2007).

To date there is no definitive empirical evidence that most large-scale merit pay plans have been effective in bringing about educational improvement (Firestone, Monfils, Hayes, et al., 2004; Jacobson, 2006). However, research based on 1992 data has indicated that there may be a small positive effect associated with merit pay in school applications (Viadero, 2007, January). This contrary finding may be a statistical artifact, but it does indicate that incentive programs seem to work best in schools populated by children of poverty. It needs to be emphasized that when surveyed, effective teachers report that their pay is not the most critical issue in the decision to remain employed by the school system. Teachers want a work environment that is replete with educational materials, where they are respected by their administrators and have good relationships with colleagues and students (Laitsch, 2007; Organization for Economic Co-operation and Development, 2005).

SUCCESSFUL SCHOOLS

There are a number of ethical and legal activities that educators can do to improve student scores on the mandated assessment tests. Some of these involve leadership and school building climate, others are instructional in nature. A third approach to improving student outcomes involves data management.

A number of the steps that can be taken to improve the proportion of students who are "proficient" on the mandated assessments have nothing to do with students or their instruction. The state departments of education can change the rules and make more schools and children seem to be successful. One example of this is lowering the bar, or cut scores, that defines what is necessary to be proficient. Another is to change the rules related to student enrollment. In 2006–2007, the State of Illinois redefined which students' scores from the state's test would be counted in determining a school's adequate yearly progress (AYP) level. To have a student's score counted in the determination of a school's AYP level, he or she had to be enrolled from October 1 until the Illinois test was given in the spring. The new rule moved the start date back to May 1 the year before the Illinois test is given (Illinois Association of Directors of Title I, 2006). This resulted in the removal of 283,000 students from consideration in determining the AYP levels. As a result, many children from transient families and low-income communities were excluded from consideration, and over 50 schools that would otherwise not have done well were suddenly found to have met their AYP target.

Data Management

School administrators are well educated in the arts of curriculum design, educational leadership, and the science of budgeting. However, all too often they are poorly prepared in statistics and data management. This poor level of knowledge about statistical analysis of test score data is exacerbated by the timing of the availability of test data.

Often educators do not receive student data reports from the annual assessment tests until it is too late in the new school year to initiate remedial efforts. Rather than wait for the state education department's data center to mail the student and school reports, it is possible to identify children at risk for failure early. The statistical information that is in the office of any school can provide an important tool for the early identification of students who will be at risk of failing.

Within the student files are three important data sources, including the most recent available assessment test or achievement test scores, school attendance for the past year, and the scores on cognitive ability tests.[8] Each of these three data sources is highly correlated with the scores that a child will earn on upcoming mandated state assessments. Using data from the previous year, it is possible create a prediction equation for the high-stakes tests (Creighton, 2007). This is done by using the assessment score actually earned by former students as one correlation variable (the criterion), and the other three factors can be combined by multiple correlation analysis into the predictor. The technology systems of all universities have excellent statistical software that can be employed for this purpose.

Once the multiple correlation has been calculated by the software, it is then possible to use the raw score weights associated with each predictor variable to create a prediction equation. The equation can then be used with all new student data: cognitive ability, previous assessment scores, and attendance. These scores when weighted by the equation from last year's students will predict how well each of the new students will do on this year's assessment test.

If all this seems like too much, the rule of thumb is that if a child has any two of the following three indicators of a potential problem, he or she should receive extra help preparing for the state assessment test.

Indicators

1. Scores on a test of cognitive ability more than one standard deviation below the mean (e.g., IQ is equal to or less than 85)

2. A score on the last assessment test that was below the proficient level, or more than one standard deviation below the mean on the standardized score report

3. More than 12 days absent from school during the previous 180-day academic year

The organization of school data for use in a multiple correlation equation for prediction can be easily managed by an experienced school technology consultant. The prediction system can be recalculated and used with the various subject areas and at all grade levels. A degree of error always exists in predictions based on correlational data; yet, this model makes it possible for a school administrator to prioritize students who will need extra services before they start school in the fall. Each summer, when the data from the previous year become available, new equations should be established and a new group of students who are at risk for being below proficient should be identified. An annually increasing database will also provide for a correlational prediction model that is ever more stable and useful.

Schedules

Having identified which students are most at risk for failure, it is then possible to initiate instructional efforts designed to improve assessment scores starting at the beginning of the school year.

For such programs to be successful, three things are required from the school's leadership. The first is good public relations. Every effort should be made to make this class a positive experience. It should never become the object of school humor. Second, only the best, most highly effective teacher(s) should be encouraged to teach these classes (Mindish, 2003). Reassignment of such teachers may also involve a trade-off such as extra preparation time or special consideration on the merit pay system. It takes a stellar teacher who is enthusiastic for the task to work with the at-risk students. Finally, the special class should be in addition to the child's regular load. These classes are best taught in a small group setting (N < 16), and they should be scheduled early in the school day.

Time on Task

One misconception about American education is that our children do not spend as much time in school as do the children of other nations. The truth is that our children are taught for about the same amount of time as the median of the world. The nations with the greatest school contact time are Austria and Mexico, each requiring about 1,100 hours, while the median for the various states in the United States is about 1,000 hours (Baker, Fabrega, Galindo, & Mishook, 2004).[9] Research into the relationship between the length of the school day and achievement outcomes has shown that the time factor can only account for about 2.2% of the variance in student achievement. Yet, even the small effect may be critical to schools that have been labeled "in need of improvement" on the basis of test scores. Massachusetts has estimated that it will cost the schools $1,300 per child to add an extra hour of instructional time for a school year (Schemo, 2007). The commonwealth added $6.5 million to the 2007–2008 budget to help pay for a lengthened school day. One plan for using the extra time is to provide the opportunity to reintroduce subjects and curriculum areas that were truncated, or even excised, because of the need for more time to teach high-stakes test skills.

There are two areas where time and achievement may interact significantly. One is the traditional 10-week summer vacation. All children lose ground over the long summer hiatus. The subject areas where this loss is most acute are mathematics and spelling. Perhaps because of summer library programs and free reading activities, the loss of learned reading ability is not as noticeable with middle-class children as for the children from impoverished communities (Alexander, Entwisle, & Olsen, 2007; Cooper, 2003). Children living in the inner cities experience very noticeable summer loss in reading as well as spelling and mathematics. This may reflect the lack of summer resources available to the families of these children. To combat this academic loss, an increasing number of schools are giving summer reading assignments and mathematics worksheets to complete before the fall term (Bennett & Kalish, 2006).

The best approach to combat the educational loss that occurs during the summer is to institute a program of summer instruction. This can be most effective with elementary and middle-school students, especially those who are at risk for not scoring well on the state-mandated assessments. Under the provisions of the No Child Left Behind Act, it is possible for school districts

Tell me, did you finish that book report yet?

Figure 16.1   Summer Vacation

SOURCE: Cartoon by Merv Magus.

to use Title I funds to establish summer programs for children at risk. These summer programs have even been initiated in the rural farming communities where the children of migrant workers are provided with a stable school environment while their parents are at work (Associated Press, 2005). Control group research conducted with children from the inner city of Baltimore who attended a multiyear summer program revealed that they achieved test scores that were half of a standard deviation higher than those who did not (Borman, 2007). This is a very large gain and may be one way to make a real difference for low-achieving children.

The traditional summer has been from mid-June to the start of September. Recently, a number of school systems have moved the date for the opening of the school year to the beginning of August. By making this move, schools have even more time to cram for the high-stakes tests in the spring. The truncated summer vacation is made up by providing several shorter vacations during the year. This trend has not been missed by either parents or state legislatures. A number of parent groups have sprung up, voicing opposition to the short summer vacations. These politically active groups include Texans for a Traditional School Year and Save Georgia Summers. State legislatures in 11 states have passed laws requiring that public school start classes near or following Labor Day (Bello, 2007).

The amount of time that can be spent teaching reading or mathematics could be increased if the school day were longer. While adding an additional hour each day to the time spent on a subject such as reading or mathematics could improve achievement, the cost would be beyond what our communities could tolerate. The problem is that the extra instructional expense would not be that cost-effective. This reflects the fact that an extra hour of reading instruction each day will only produce an average improvement of one-quarter of a standard deviation on assessment tests measuring reading achievement (Karweit, 1984). A better way to improve scores is to use time more efficiently. As an example, Illinois has a requirement that each elementary level school day include 300 minutes of instruction. An audit found that of the 7 hours each day that children in Chicago spend in elementary schools, only 4 hours are spent on instruction (Smith, 1998).

Time is lost at the start of the school year as well as at end of each school year. Instructional time is lost each day in "homeroom," more is lost at lunch and recess, and more yet for classroom transitions. Instructional days are lost for field trips, assembly programs, fire drills, and pep rallies. The amount of teaching time can be increased by a simple review of the school's schedule and a more efficient plan for the organization of each school day.

One way to change the culture of a school is to think in terms of instructional costs. Consider the cost per minute of any special program that interrupts the instructional process. If the cost of educating each child is $11,000 per year, and if a principal is planning a 30-minute assembly program for 500 students, the cost of the lost instructional time for that assembly is $2,750. This is found by dividing the cost per child for a year of education by the 1,000 instructional hours in the average school year. This means that each instructional hour costs $11 per child. An assembly of 30 minutes costs $5.50 per child in instructional time.

A large-scale study of the impact of increasing the instructional day for thousands of school children in Boston and Chelsea, Massachusetts, was started in 2006–2007. That study will increase the length of the school day by as much as 3 hours for public school children. It is hoped that the analysis of data from that research will provide a definitive model for the best instructional day for schools to follow (Maxwell, 2006).

CLASSROOM INSTRUCTION

Teachers are at point with the test-based accountability programs now in place in every state. In many ways it is our educators who are the people being left behind. The undergraduate programs they graduated from did not prepare them for the new standards-based accountability assessments, and their administrators have little to offer but encouragement. Yet, it is the classroom teacher who must bring every child up to a level of proficiency in all subjects being assessed. Failure in this task can lead to lower pay (no merit award), whole school penalties, and the loss of respect from all in the community. Parents of a community who have seen good report card grades come home with their children can quickly turn against the teachers, and become major critics of the school, if their children do not pass the state-mandated assessment (Shapira, 2006).

There is an obvious temptation to teach the test and prepare children to answer each of its questions before they must face the measurement. This is not only unethical, it is also illegal. The next obvious option is to "teach to the test." This involves a complete restructuring of the curriculum to stress specific skills assumed to be on the test. This approach to test preparation usually employs a drill-and-fill form of instruction. When a teacher teaches to the test, only those skills needed for the test are emphasized, and inquiry-oriented instruction is eschewed in favor of direct instruction (Firestone, Monfils, Schorr, et al., 2004).

Linda Crocker (2003), past president of the National Council on Measurement in Education, recommends another course. She suggests that teachers "**teach for the test**."[10] Teaching for the test involves knowing how cut scores are set, understanding how items are developed, and having an in-depth understanding of the content on which the children are to be tested (Boudett, Murnane, City, & Moody, 2005). Teaching for the test also involves the strategic introduction of instructional methodologies that have been shown to optimize the performance of children on the assessments. One aspect of this involves introducing children to the jargon-laden language and logic used on standardized tests. For example, all teachers teach children to find the "main idea" in a paragraph or story being read. Yet, test questions do not ask for this in those words. Tests ask children to "explain what the story is about" or "what is this passage about?" or "what was the author trying to tell you?" Children need to know that the word *passage* means "text" (Greene & Melton, 2007).

Reading

Starting in third grade, all public school children in the United States face a high-stakes test of their reading skill and ability. In 2000, the National Reading Panel (NRP) presented its review and summary of the research on reading, which has been completed and presented since the administration of Lyndon Johnson. From this review of over 100,000 dissertations, presentations, articles, and monographs, a series of conclusions and recommendations emerged (National Institute of Child Health and Human Development, 2000). It is important to note that the work of the NRP was completed before the passage of the No Child Left Behind Act in January of 2002. A number of studies have been published since that time that have examined the relationship between reading instruction and student outcome on state assessment test scores.

The NRP report focused on three levels: parent–child activities, instructional methods in school, and teacher preparation. The major focus for school instruction was on the primary-grade classroom. Here the report presented teachers of kindergarten and first grade with effective strategies for developing and building phonemic awareness. The NRP recommendations included a shift away from phonemic awareness instruction after about a year and the initiation of a full year of well-organized systematic phonics instruction in reading. This effort had the goal of forging the links between the letters of the written language with the sounds of the spoken language. By the end of a year (kindergarten) of phonics instruction, children should have significantly improved their word recognition and pre-spelling skills. During first grade, the teacher's efforts should focus on improving fluency and expanding the child's vocabulary. Before the start of third grade, the NRP recommended the teacher focus reading instruction on text comprehension. One reading program designed to meet the recommendations of the NRP is known as the "Success for All" program. This reading program is widely used to teach reading to primary-grade children in schools that receive Title I funding under the NCLB Act. For the most part these schools enroll many children from impoverished backgrounds. A well-controlled research study of this kindergarten to third grade reading program has shown that significant improvement in achievement test scores is possible when it is implemented (Borman et al., 2007).

To review the details of the report and the specific recommendations for instructional activities with examples, see www.nationalreadingpanel.org.

In addition to the instructional recommendations of the NRP, there are other steps that teachers of the primary grades can take to improve reading assessment scores for individual children before third grade. The first involves formative monitoring of the development of **prereading** and early reading strategies. This can be accomplished by the use of a reading assessment, which provides measures of basic **benchmark skills in reading**. Once a child's problem area is identified, extra instructional activities can be formulated and introduced to remediate and assist the child develop the missing reading strategy (Good, Simmons, & Kame'enui, 2001; Kame'enui, 2002).

Better assessment scores on state-mandated reading tests are found with the children who are in elementary classrooms that are filled with children's books. This type of environment encourages young readers and expands their reading interests. Classroom instructional strategies for teaching reading that have been shown to correlate with better scores on statewide assessment tests include both prereading and concurrent reading strategies. Prereading strategies are designed to activate the child's background knowledge and help him or her form a purpose for reading. These reading strategies are not intuitive but require direct and explicit teaching (Walkovic, 2003).

Starting at the elementary school level, reading comprehension may be correlated with the background of general knowledge held by the reader. Adults recognize this simple truth when they are asked to read a jargon-laden technical publication. It is easy to read any technical presentation if we have a background in the field. Children who are learning to read are much the same. The falloff in reading comprehension skills after third grade for children with limited experiences and backgrounds is to be expected (Hirsch, 2006). Currently, the normal school practice is to provide students at risk for reading problems with more instruction that is focused on basic skills. The time for this remedial instruction comes from other areas in the curriculum. The loss of field trips and special programs and the truncation of the curriculum are outcomes of the push for better test scores. The irony is that taking time away from general education designed to expand the backgrounds of young readers may be doing harm to their comprehension scores.

Pre-reading strategies that correlate with reading assessment scores among elementary school students include previewing and surveying

(Beserik, 2000). The strategy of self-questioning (forming one's own questions to guide reading) has been shown to improve the reading scores of fifth graders on a statewide assessment (Donnelly, 1999).

Concurrent strategies are those that a child should be taught to do while reading. These are strategies that have been demonstrated to improve reading comprehension scores on statewide assessments. The strategy of picturing what is being read, employing a deliberately slower rate of reading, rereading what was not understood, and outlining or taking notes on what is read are examples of successful concurrent reading strategies (Walkovic, 2003; Wells, 2002). Students who have been systematically taught to employ these reading strategies have significantly better reading comprehension scores on a statewide assessment than those who have not.

At the high school level similar findings were noted with students in the 11th grade (Rex, 2003). Those who took the time to reread sections of passages that they did not understand had significantly better reading comprehension scores compared with those who did not. The nonparametric correlation between self-reports of using this strategy and assessment test scores was quite significant ($r = 0.42$). It is interesting to note that at all three levels—elementary (Beserik, 2000; Donnelly, 1999; Wells, 2002), middle school (Walkovic, 2003), and high school (Rex, 2003)—none of the "post-reading strategies" correlated with assessment scores (Bukowiecki, 2007). Post-reading strategies involve expository writing in response to what has been read. It can also include scanning back over what was read to find the answers to content questions posed by the teacher.

A link has been identified between the writing requirements of high school English teachers and student reading achievement. The more time English teachers spend on analytical writing, and the more homework they assign and grade, the better are the reading test scores (Carbonaro & Gamoran, 2002, 2005). Paradoxically, the amount of time and effort spent in formal instruction of grammar is negatively correlated with reading achievement scores. It seems that the more effective secondary English teachers stress analytical writing, and less effective teachers stress syntax and grammar.

Writing

There are both general and specific strategies that can improve assessment scores that students earn on statewide writing tests. The general strategies that correlate to better writing scores include prewriting strategies such as brainstorming topic ideas with peers, planning the sequence and structure of what is to be written, and formulating a writing plan (Shields, 2000).

The assessment scores in writing are also positively influenced by teachers who provide practice with the writing format used by the state assessment. Teachers who wish to see better assessment scores should be trained in the state's writing test, including the approved rubric and anchors used to evaluate student writing samples (English, 2000). Classroom practice with timed writing assessments that are based on prompts can improve student scores. In such classroom exercises, the teacher should use the state-approved rubric to grade each student paper and explain why that score was assigned.

There is also evidence that the amount of time intermediate-grade elementary school teachers spend on improving student writing skills is directly related to writing assessment scores (Irvin, 2003). The recent addition of scoring software to the education marketplace will facilitate student practice and writing development without a concomitant time investment by classroom teachers. As the states move to the computerized scoring of student writing, there will be an inevitable spread of scoring software in the schools.

Technology provides another way to improve student writing. A few schools have begun to have children produce and write podcasts about their school and communities. These are subscribed to by both children and many of their parents. As this writing activity is very motivating, writing skills have been improving through practice.

A specific strategy that is being employed by teachers to improve student writing is the "five-paragraph essay." By this model, students are taught to read the writing test prompt and formulate their position on the premise that the prompt presents. Then they state their position in a short paragraph. Next, they are taught to write three short paragraphs, each providing an example in support of the position staked out in the first paragraph. The final paragraph is to provide a summation and conclusion. As most writing samples on state assessments only provide students with 20 minutes, students are taught to structure their answers quickly.

Mathematics

There is much less information on the relationship between scores on state-mandated assessments of mathematics and instructional programs than there is on the assessment and teaching of reading and writing. One thing that is well documented is that mathematics scores have changed only marginally over the past few decades (NAEP, 2004). Additionally, the achievement gap in mathematics between minority students and their Anglo-White peers has so far proven to be intractable. Between 5% and 6% of the population of school students have a significant learning problem with mathematics (see

Chapter 13). As with other learning problems, this one may also have a neurological basis (University College London, 2007).

In a review of the hundreds of published studies on mathematics instruction by the Institute of Education Sciences (IES) of the U.S. Department of Education, only a tiny handful were found to meet the criteria of a rigorous scientific basis. At the middle-school level, this review found only four programs with a solid scientific foundation, and of those four, only two could consistently demonstrate achievement gains.

To see the full report from the IES, see www.whatworks.ed.gov.

Both of these are computer-based programs. One, Cognitive Tutor Algebra I, provides a full year-long algebra program, including interactive computer-based tutoring, texts, and support material. The second is an online supported instructional program covering the 7th through the 10th grades. As an online program, it is self-paced and allows the student to work through instructional modules from home as well as from school. Further information on these two systems can be found at the following addresses:

www.bcps.org/offices/oit/CognitiveTutor.htm

www.icanlearn.com

Another computer package shown to assist students in passing the math section on a state high school graduation examination is Hotmath.com. This program offers students homework help in mathematics. This is done by providing complete, step-by-step solutions to all of the odd-numbered problems at the end of each chapter of standard texts of mathematics online. The theory behind this is that if a student who is working alone on homework reaches a problem that can't be solved, the computer will be able to provide tutoring in the solution to that one or the next one in the series. The help that this online program offers could also be provided by a classroom teacher willing to invest several hours each evening conducting online homework tutorials.

Information about this online approach is available at: www.hotmath.com.

The What Works Clearinghouse of the U.S. Department of Education identified the mathematics instructional program from the Wright Group/McGraw-Hill known as Everyday Mathematics as exhibiting "potentially positive" achievement effect (Viadero, 2007b). For more information, see http://ies.ed.gov/ncee/projects/wwc/elementary_math.asp.

One area of mathematics that is particularly difficult for many students involves word problems. These require students to read a problem statement and translate the written words into an equation and then solve for an unknown. Most teachers teach students to look for words in the problem that describe operations, such as *combined*, which translates to addition. Better results for students on word problem questions and higher scores on statewide assessments have been found when teachers instruct children using a single strategy for problems This method is described as schema-based instruction (SBI) (Jitendra et al., 2007).

In teaching algebra concepts, Amanda Ross (2007) has demonstrated that there is a latent factor in the instructional practices of the most successful teachers. That factor involves the use of constructivist approaches including inquiry, investigative work, and sharing ideas and explanations among students.

Mathematics is one subject that is more anxiety inducing for students than others (Cavanaugh, 2007). This anxiety has been shown to interfere with the ability of students to perform well on tests that require arithmetic as well as other more advanced forms of mathematics (Ashcraft, 1995). Evidence is also available that anxiety levels are greatest among children being taught by teachers who have only a sketchy background in mathematics. The confusion experienced by poorly prepared teachers is contagious and translates to heightened mathematics anxiety among the students.

One area of mathematics instruction that has caught public attention is the use of handheld calculators. The position taken by the National Council of Teachers of Mathematics (NCTM) (2003) is that students need to learn to use paper and pencils to solve problems. Also, NCTM posits that students must learn to estimate what answers should be and should develop the ability to make quick mental calculations. In addition to these core skills, though, handheld calculators should also be part of what goes on in a mathematics class. Tedious calculation of arithmetical expressions by students who know how to do the arithmetic is only a waste of time (Cavanaugh, 2005; NCTM, 1991, 2003, 2006). This is also true for advanced classes with high school students using books of mathematics tables to look up functions and transformations that are readily available in advanced calculators.

A statewide study of the relationship between the use of calculators in middle-school classrooms and mathematics achievement found a direct relationship (Smart Heilshorn, 2003). In this study of the self-reported level of calculator use by 140,000 eighth-grade students in 760 middle schools it was noted that the schools where students scored at the highest levels had students who reported moderate levels of calculator usage. In schools where calculators were used for almost every mathematics class and in those where calculators were rarely used, the mathematics assessment scores were lower.

Another concern of parents is that heterogeneous grouping has a corrosive effect on the learning of advanced mathematics by high-achieving children. In a study of 500 students in middle and senior high school it was demonstrated that heterogeneous grouping improves the learning of advanced mathematics for below-average and average students and has no effect on high-achieving students (Laitsch, 2006).

Test-Prep Curricula

Beginning with the standards-based assessments of the 1990s, there have been a number of educational publishers offering test preparation curricula for the schools. In a study of one such program, an elementary school mathematics curriculum package was found to be significantly less effective than a local curriculum initiative (Kristoback & Wright, 2001). The local curriculum was developed during a summer workshop by the district's elementary teachers working with the state standards and local curriculum experts. The findings suggest that teachers who feel ownership for a curriculum revision are more motivated in their teaching.

ARCHITECTURE AND SCHOOL DESIGN

School Buildings

Each school day one in five Americans spends some time in a school building. Yet, despite this high level of public awareness of schools, the buildings are among the most poorly maintained public buildings. Half of all schools have poor air-quality, containing molds, chemicals, chalk dust, and airborne bacteria. Poor air quality leads to absenteeism, lethargy, and a general malaise.

Our schools are also noisy places where the sound level in most common areas can approach that of a modern airline terminal. Most children do not develop the level of hearing acuity needed to separate a teacher's voice from background sounds until the middle-school years. Competing background noise comes into the classroom from outdoors, surrounding classrooms, mechanical system noises, hallway noises, as well as those generated by two dozen people together in a 12,000-cubic-foot box.

Many of the schools we use today are old enough to have earned historic site designations. The Francis Scott Key Elementary School in South Philadelphia, which serves over 400 children, was built in 1889.[11] Even the new wing on that school was completed 12 years before the First World War (Philadelphia Architects and Buildings Project, 2003). Temporary school facilities (portables) are no longer temporary, with some now approaching

50 years old. Most of the prisons in the United States are cleaner, newer, and in better physical condition than are our public schools. Throughout most of the middle latitudes of the continental United States, public schools are the only public places that are not air-conditioned.

Yet, the total impact of all these conditions adds up to only 2% of the variance among assessment scores. Much of that effect may reflect the fact that our oldest, noisiest buildings with the poorest air quality and the most deferred maintenance are where the children of our poor and minorities go to school.

Class Size

Public education is a labor-intensive task. The point at issue always hinges on the question of how many students a teacher will have in his or her class. The 20th-century addition of educational specialists to the schools has made education even less efficient. The requirement that schools provide special education programs for the children that 75 years ago would have been excluded from attending school has also worked to make schools seem less efficient.

School authorities have a vested interest in keeping classes as large as practicable, and teachers know from their personal experience that they are more effective with smaller classes. Research on this question of class size and educational outcomes has reached the consensus that small classes lead to better levels of achievement (see Figure 16.2). The effect of small class size is most pronounced for younger children (K–third grade) and for minority students. In large-scale research, the critical class size is between 15 and 18 students. Each increment over that parameter results in lower achievement. In reducing class size from the mid 20s to 15, the gain in achievement is around 6% (Krueger, 2002, 2003; Word et al., 1990). The statewide research from project STAR in Tennessee found that when African American children are assigned to smaller classes they experience a gain of about 8% on standardized achievement tests. White children assigned to smaller classes experienced only a 3% point gain (Krueger & Whitmore, 2001). This effect is even more pronounced if children are exposed to smaller classes from kindergarten onward (Nye, Hedges, & Konstantopoulos, 2000). It is likely that if African American children attend schools with smaller class sizes from kindergarten onward there would be a 60% reduction in the college admission score gap that now exists between the two groups (Krueger & Whitmore). Most of these positive effects would be greater if teachers were to be provided with specific training in how to work with small classes (Graue, Hatch, Rao, & Oen, 2007). In research involving class-size reduction and instructional practice, Graue et el. (2007) have shown that teachers typically continue teaching as though they were working with a large group.

A recent review of the literature has shed light on the mechanism by which this improved achievement occurs. Smaller classes actually change teacher instructional practices and improve student engagement. The point can be made that it is more difficult to "loaf" in a classroom if the class size is small than if it is large (N > 30) (Finn, Pannozzo, & Achilles, 2003).

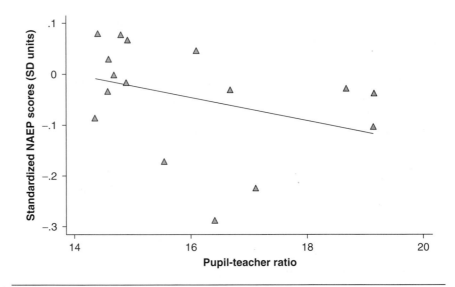

Figure 16.2   Relationship between math and reading NAEP scores and pupil-teacher ratio, 17-year-olds, 1970–96

SOURCE: From "A Response to Eric Hanushek's 'Evidence, Politics, and the Class Size Debate,'" in *The Class Size Debate*, by A. B. Krueger, 2002, Washington, DC: Economic Policy Institute'. Copyright by EPI Publications. Reprinted with permission.

School Size

There is evidence that smaller schools have a positive effect on student graduation rates. In a study of 306 schools systems of rural Arkansas, it was found that small school districts tend to have better graduation rates. There is evidence that small schools or districts have a very small advantage on mandated state achievement tests (Black, 2006). This phenomenon of small schools having better graduation rates is an example of what has been described as the "Hobbit effect." The effect reflects the higher engagement that small schools make possible for students. Co-curricular activities draw a great proportion of the student body into a school's activities, and classes tend to be smaller in size (Jimerson, 2006).

ADMINISTRATION

Leadership and Outcomes

School leadership at the building level has a clear relationship to the average achievement outcomes for students. The impact of the building's principal can be seen in all aspects of the school. To lead a school to optimal levels of achievement the principal must be a highly motivated and enthusiastic person (Renchler, 1992).

One administrative task linked to the achievement scores of a school is the hiring of new teachers. As was noted in Chapter 15, a new teacher can have an influence on a school over his or her 30-plus-year career. This makes the principal's role in hiring vital. Research by Bruce Baker and Bruce Cooper (2005) has shown that school principals who have strong undergraduate backgrounds tend to recruit, hire, and work to retain teachers from prestigious colleges who have solid academic credentials. This effect was found to be especially true in the schools of the inner cities.

Over the years, a number of studies have demonstrated the link between the leadership style of school administrators and school climate. From the teacher's point of view, school climate can range from a general feeling of malaise and a dread of going to work to a sense of being part of a close-knit community accompanied by feelings of professional fulfillment and pride. School climate can be viewed as the perceived total of all interactions between all the people (adults and children) the teacher deals with. For each teacher that perception of climate sets the tone for how they approach their work and how they view their careers (Goleman, 2006). A negative school climate and the concomitant poor faculty morale can undercut the success of an entire school community. This malaise can be intensified when a school's faculty is sanctioned under the NCLB mandates, thereby creating a cycle of failure and educational depression (Finnigan & Gross, 2007).

The development of a positive school climate takes years to achieve and the commitment of the principal to the goal of a positive school climate. Low morale and a negative climate are much easier to establish, and an ineffective principal can accomplish this in only a few months.

More than any other person, the principal sets the climate of a school. This climate does have a direct impact on the achievement outcome of children (Goleman, 2006). Middle-school research in Texas found successful school leadership was dynamic, communicative, and interactive (Brown, Claudet, & Olivarez, 2002). Research from California found that school climate as set by the principal was one of three core factors in the relationship between student achievement and leadership. Those things that work to produce good climate include communicating the school goals and the fair enforcement of school rules with students. Also, the principals of highly successful schools worked to open lines of communication both with teachers and between teachers. These school leaders worked to maintain high morale among faculty and were always enthusiastic and optimistic about the learning potential of students (Heck, Larson, & Marcoulides, 1990).

Leadership Style

A meta-analysis of over 60 studies from the United States originally reported during the 1980s and 1990s found that differences in elementary school leadership style could account for a shift of 0.11 standard deviations on measures of student achievement (Witziers, Bosker, & Kruger, 2003). Using data from Pennsylvania, James Cantwell (2007) found the important role that leadership style plays in determining achievement outcomes as measured on a mandated statewide assessment. He first identified elementary and middle-level schools that were in the top quartile in terms of average assessment scores for 3 consecutive years. Likewise, a group of schools in the lowest quartile for 3 years was also identified. The teachers in both groups completed climate questionnaires, and their principals responded to a questionnaire of their leadership styles. One finding from this research was that there is a lack of awareness on the part of the principals of low-performing schools as to what their leadership style really is. The principals of high-performing schools had a clear and accurate perception of their leadership styles. The principals of consistently successful schools are seen by their teaching faculty as more open and approachable, treating teachers as equals. They are seen as up front and easy to understand and are known to look after the welfare of the teachers and staff. These successful administrators required less busy work and routine chores from their teachers. Another difference is that the teachers in the successful schools were more collegial and had better communications with each other and were accepting of their colleagues and sensitive to the problems of other teachers. They were more willing to help new faculty, and they socialized with each other away from school. In a word, they were a community.

The special problem of leadership for inner-city schools was studied in a series of case studies of high-performing schools located in high-poverty communities. This **qualitative research** found that the principals of these anomalous schools had a missionary-like faith in their schools and the children who attended them. The principals and the faculty shared a team mentality. These administrators would "put it all on the line" by going into classrooms and modeling the teaching of a lesson when one of their teachers had difficulty in making a breakthrough. These highly successful leaders created environments of mutual respect and collaboration with the faculty. They were clever to the point of devious in bringing together a faculty that mirrored their own faith in children and the possibility of success for all children (Kannapel & Clements, 2005).

Summary

The pressure to have students succeed on high-stakes tests can be unbearable. The result is that there is a problem with cheating on the mandated assessments. Beyond out-and-out cheating, there are a number of strategies that parents and educators can employ to optimize both the achievement outcome for children and the apparent success of the school. In examining these strategies, the use of merit pay has not proven to be a method that will improve teacher effectiveness, and it may even trivialize the teaching profession.

Schools can employ statistical models that will prioritize students and identify which students will need extra help preparing for the high-stakes tests. By using the best teachers with the students that are identified, providing extra educational resources to these developmental classes, and maintaining a small class size, these students can have significantly better test scores. Careful planning of each school day to optimize the time-on-task for each student is another administrative activity related to better scores.

A successful school is one where stable leadership has created an atmosphere of trust among all parties. It is a collegial place where the principal and teachers believe in the potential of each child. Such a school is a place where teachers collaborate and share ideas with each other and have a cohesive and mutually supportive team spirit. The principal of such a school is a partner with each teacher in the effort to encourage student achievement.

Discussion Questions

1. Rent and watch one of the films about testing described in this chapter. Write a brief review of that movie. In your review discuss the reality or lack of reality regarding the reactions of adolescent children to the pressures they were experiencing as portrayed in the film.

2. Describe where the "line is drawn" dividing legal from illegal test preparation programs.

3. If you were given the task of developing and offering an inservice program for teams of middle-school teachers on the topic of optimizing student test scores on mandated statewide assessments, what would it include? Provide a content outline for an 18-hour-long inservice activity (3 hours a week for 6 consecutive weeks).

4. Explain and provide examples of the similarities and differences between the ideas of "teaching to the test" and "teaching for the test."

5. What are the characteristics of school leaders whose schools are consistently among the top scoring on high-stakes tests?

Student Study Site

Educational Assessment on the Web

Log on to the Web-based student study site at www.sagepub.com/wrightstudy for additional Web sources and study resources.

NOTES

1. A *juku* is a traditional (private) Japanese cram school attended by 60% of Japan's students after the regular school day. The jukus help students cram for placement examinations.

2. For example, Florida secretary of education John Winn suggested that the old tests be used for practice sessions (Mitchell, 2005).

3. The prize was won by a 15-year-old child who could not drive it or even pay the tax that was due on his winnings.

4. In 1960 more than 90% of the elementary school faculties were women while senior high school faculties were 70% male.

5. In 2004, the national median teacher pay was $47,750. A merit award of 5% would be about $200 per month before taxes. The after-tax net would be about $28 per week.

6. In 1998, Governor Jeb Bush of Florida signed into law a statute requiring school districts set aside 5% of their pay budget for professional teachers and use it to award up to 15% of the teaching staff performance merit pay bonuses. With the

tacit approval of most school systems and minimal cooperation by the teacher's associations, that law was stymied. The state provided no extra money for merit pay. The 5% for merit had to come out of the operating budgets of the school systems. That plan was revised and a new method for merit designed for 2008.

School districts can apply to the U.S. Department of Education for support for their merit pay plans under the Teacher Incentive Fund, which was written into the NCLB Act in 2006 (U.S. Department of Education, 2006)

7. A week after the awards were made the Houston School District realized that it made an error with 100 teachers and asked for the award checks back ("Houston Teachers," 2007).

8. These are variables that have been empirically demonstrated to have high correlations with assessment test scores. Other variables may prove to be more valuable in different school circumstances.

9. Forty-nine states and the District of Columbia require a specific number of teaching days or total hours of classroom instruction. The exception is Minnesota, where the state has no such requirement of the schools.

10. "Some object to regular testing because they believe schools will teach to the test, but if a test measures basic educational skills then teaching to the test means you're teaching a child the basic knowledge of reading and math." President George W. Bush, May 11, 2004.

11.   National Historical Register No. 86003296 (12/1/1986). There are several older "one room" schools that are still in use in the rural areas of northern Vermont. One of these was built in 1801 (during the first administration of Thomas Jefferson). In 2007, that school was still used to educate the children of the town of Hancock, Vermont.

Chapter 17

ACCOUNTABILITY AND EVALUATION

Seeing outstanding schools in action makes it clear why they succeed: local people, leadership, community commitment, and shared values, not federal tutelage.

—Robert Bennett

Issues and Themes

There is an old adage known by most golfers: "Drive for show, but putt for dough." This implies that in golf the large showy hit, the drive, isn't as important as the small detail shots of the game, exemplified by the putt. For educators this adage also carries an important implication. Schools have large obvious indicators of their success: the high-stakes test scores. However, the important indicators of a school's success are not as apparent and can only be highlighted by the systematic evaluation of the educational processes.

There are two major paradigms followed in the evaluation of schools and educational systems. One approach to evaluation assesses a school on the basis of both ongoing formative benchmarks of success and a summative measure of the educational outcomes. A second method for evaluation of schools and educational systems involves the assessment of the amount of growth that occurs within the learners themselves over time (Linn, 2007a).

The methodologies used in educational evaluations are drawn from both qualitative and quantitative research paradigms. By the 1980s the field of educational evaluation had grown and established a professional society and published standards for conducting evaluation research. The growth of educational evaluation was propelled by the requirements of the U.S. Department of Education for accountability with the grants schools received under the Elementary and Secondary Education Act. Systematic educational program evaluations can take many forms, including school accreditation evaluations and the long-range (strategic) plans some state departments of education require of local school districts.

The process of conducting a systematic evaluation of an educational program can be organized into a seven-step process, starting with goal setting. The instrument development involves the tasks of developing the objectives and an overall plan for the evaluation, data collection and analysis, report writing, and the implementation of recommendations. The various steps in this evaluation model involve a combination of both qualitative and quantitative tasks to be completed and analyzed.

More recently, another approach to program and school evaluation has been developed. This model is a pure example of a data-driven, quantitative approach to evaluation. This approach to evaluation has become the favored method used to measure school districts, teachers, and schools in a number of states. It is known as the value-added approach, which analyzes the achievement growth that takes place during the school year. This system provides an analysis of the effectiveness of individual teachers and schools. The advantage of the value-added model is that it is less contaminated by demographic factors and other extraneous variables. This model focuses on the individual achievement growth experienced by individual children. Average score changes for a classroom or whole school of children are less important as indicators of academic success than is a simple measure of individual growth for each child.

The system is limited by the quality of the test data that are used for the assessment. One advantage of the model is the identification of the most effective teachers, the true masters of the field.

Learning Objectives

By reading and studying this chapter you should develop the ability to do the following:

- Explain why school administrators should be skilled program evaluators.
- Describe the four areas included in the standards for conducting an evaluation.

- Explain the purpose of the EDGAR guidelines.
- Compare the value-added evaluation system with a systematic program evaluation.
- Describe the various sub-steps that need to be taken during the first (goal setting) phase of a systematic evaluation of an educational program.
- Explain how the objectives for the evaluation are developed.
- List and describe the seven steps to doing a systematic evaluation of an educational program.
- Discuss the planning process for a systematic program evaluation, and explain the use of a liner responsibility chart and Gantt chart in that plan.
- Describe the factors that can contaminate the evaluation of the effectiveness of schools and teachers.
- Explain the basics of the value-added approach to teacher and school evaluations.
- Describe the type of data contained in a teacher's report following a value-added evaluation.
- Discuss a method for using value-added assessment as a tool in a teacher inservice program.

EVALUATION OVERVIEW

During the 19th and much of the 20th century it was assumed that students were tested and assessed by their teachers. It was also assumed that some students "flunked," which was solely the child's fault. Today we have state-mandated assessments, and it is not just the students who can "flunk." Now there is a broader perspective on educational accountability, which goes beyond students and involves assessments of teachers, schools, and whole systems. The change in the focus for evaluation started in earnest during the 1960s when federal funding first reached the classroom.

Along with the infusion of new funding provided to our schools by the first Elementary and Secondary Education Act (ESEA) in 1965 came the requirement for accountability (P.L. 89-10, 1965).[1] In 2006, the amount of money for these funded programs had grown from the $1 billion of the Johnston administration to $38 billion. The early efforts of school administrators to provide a meaningful evaluation for the federally funded programs in their districts were spotty at best. To provide a more uniform model for the evaluation of Title I and other federally funded programs, the Department of Education published a set of evaluation guidelines known as the **Education General Administrative Regulations** (**EDGAR**). These guidelines are something all school administrators should be familiar with, and a current copy should be available in all school systems.

To learn more about the EDGAR guidelines, see www.ed.gov/print/policy/fund/reg/edgarReg/edgar.html.

This need for schools and school systems to be "held to account" spurred the development of the field of educational evaluation. Twenty years after Lyndon Johnson signed the first ESEA into law, a new professional society, the American Evaluation Association, was formed. This association of 4,000 educational evaluators publishes several journals and holds annual meetings during which new developments in the science of school and program evaluation are presented. This association has defined an evaluation as the activities required for "assessing the strengths and weaknesses of programs, policies, personnel, products, and organizations" (AEA, 2005).

Educational evaluation includes the knowledge base of educational measurement, which is used to design and select appropriate measures. It also draws from the educational research literature for the establishment of data collection methods and from educational statistics for data management and analysis. Finally, a systematic educational evaluation will also draw from the methods of qualitative research methods.

Evaluation Models

Numerous methods for doing an evaluation have been identified over the years. To carry out the evaluation activities, the evaluator must select the most appropriate strategy for collecting and analyzing data regarding the program being studied. These strategies range from those that are purely phenomenological (e.g., connoisseurship, anthropological/ethnographic, and hermeneutic analysis) to those that are highly rational and linear. The latter are models drawn from the empirical sciences (Fetterman, 1988). The linear model for evaluation stresses educational outcomes or products and studies the amount of change that occurred over the duration of the program. A qualitative approach to evaluation examines the ongoing ecology of the project and employs many qualitative data sources.

Perhaps the best evaluation for any educational program or activity is one that combines the elements of both the quantitatively focused, positivistic paradigm with naturalistic and more open-ended methodologies. This interaction of evaluation paradigms and methodologies has been condemned by the purists (Guba & Lincoln, 1988), but it provides a pragmatic answer to the incredibly complex task of conducting an educational evaluation. In the evaluation process, the combination of formative data collection using **ethnographic research** methods along with the statistical analysis of standardized test scores and other "hard" data make for a more complete picture of the school or program being studied.

Evaluation Standards

The great diversity in evaluation methodologies did not prevent a committee representing the academic disciplines involved with the evaluation process to develop a set of standards for conducting evaluations (Stufflebeam, 1981). These standards for evaluation were updated again in 1994. The standards are presented in four broad areas:

- Utility—describes the evaluator's credibility, the stakeholder identification, the clarity of the writing, and the evaluation's impact
- Feasibility—addresses questions of a practical nature, such as cost and local politics
- Propriety—concerns the human relations among those who are party to the evaluation, including subject rights and evaluator responsibility
- Accuracy—involves the quality of the data and analysis in the report and the justifiability of the conclusions

More is available on these standards for evaluations from www.ericdigests .org/1996-1/the.htm.

Accountability and Public Opinion

Knowledge of program evaluation is an important tool in the skill kit carried by successful school administrators and curriculum directors. Federal and state agencies as well as private foundations all require that applications for a subvention include a model for the evaluation of the project to be funded. Additionally, school boards and the public in general need to be apprised of the outcomes from a systematic assessment of new curriculums and revised educational approaches. From the perspective of school administrators, systematic program evaluations are empowering. Well-conceived and carefully executed program evaluations provide school administrators data-based answers to the most complex questions that can be raised by the public.

Educational accountability is something that is not going away anytime soon. This accountability concept is deeply ingrained in the political psyche. The 36th Gallup Poll of Public Attitudes Toward the Public Schools makes this very clear (Rose & Gallup, 2005). In this national sample, 49% of American adults felt that student performance on a single standardized test should be one of the bases for evaluating teachers, and almost as many felt that those scores should be part of any evaluation of the school principal. A number of the other features of the NCLB Act have lost support among adults, but the core appreciation of accountability is part of a bedrock set of beliefs.

BOX 17.1   Public Opinion 2005

In grading the nation's public schools on a scale of A to F, parents of public school children hold opinions very similar to those who do not have children in school.

How about the public schools in the nation as a whole? What grade would you give the public schools nationally?

	No Children in School %	Public School Parents %
A	2	3
B	22	23
C	47	42
D	14	8
Fail	3	6
Don't know	12	18

Five out of every nine members of the American public believe that teacher quality is something that is measured by student achievement tests.

In your opinion, should one of the measurements of a teacher's quality be based on how well his or her students perform on standardized tests or not?

	No Children in School %	Public School Parents %
Yes, should	53	52
No, should not	43	46
Don't know	4	2

Public opinion about the linkage between the quality of school principals and student outcomes is about evenly divided.

How about school principals? In your opinion, should one of the measurements of a principal's quality be based on how well the students in his or her school perform on standardized tests?

	No Children in School %	Public School Parents %
Yes, should	51	47
No, should not	44	51
Don't know	5	2

The emphasis on testing in the schools is viewed by the American public as a good thing.

In your opinion, is there too much emphasis on achievement testing in the public schools in your community, not enough emphasis on testing, or about the right amount?

	No Children in School %	Public School Parents %
Too much	35	39
Not enough	17	17
About the right amount	39	43
Don't know	9	1

SOURCE: From *The Phi Delta Kappan/Gallup Poll of the Public's Attitudes Toward the Public Schools,* by L. C. Rose and A. M. Gallup, 2005, Phi Delta Kappan, *87*(1), pp. 41–56. Copyright 2005 by Phi Delta Kappan International. Reprinted with permission.

SYSTEMATIC PROGRAM EVALUATION

The systematic evaluation of educational programs is a regular activity for educational leaders. These evaluations are carried out to make decisions on program quality, efficiency, and merit. Every federal grant, including all Title I programs, and most state funding applications require that a systematic evaluation be included. When funds are competitively awarded, the evaluation plan typically accounts for between 10% and 35% of the points awarded by the application reviewers.

All educational programs are highly complex enterprises. As such, a complete evaluation of an educational program is also a highly complex endeavor. Not only are the systematic evaluations of educational programs complex; they are also difficult to do well. The difficulty lies in the fact that organized curricula are designed to meet a multitude of student and community variables (e.g., socioeconomic level, cognitive ability, educational expectations, community resources, family's primary language, and parental academic motivation and interests). These and many more considerations moderate how the curriculum will address the content area to be taught.

BOX 17.2   Application Selection Criteria

Application for Funding Under the "Striving Readers Program" of the U. S. Department of Education for Fiscal Year 2005

Each of the selection criteria listed below is critical to the design and implementation of high-quality Striving Readers projects. This application must address both of the absolute priorities in addition to the seven selection criteria listed below.

Department program staff will review applications to ensure that applicants are eligible and that they meet the absolute priorities included in the Federal Register notice. The Department, through a peer review panel of experts, will evaluate each application based on the application selection criteria (worth up to 100 points).

The Department will select applicants for funding based on the quality of the applications, including their rank order based on the application selection criteria. Additionally, the Department may make awards so that Striving Readers funding is balanced between projects serving middle school and high school students. In making funding decisions, the Department will use the procedures in section 75.217 of EDGAR, 34 CFR 75.217.[2]

Selection Criteria	Maximum Points
1. Need for Project	5 points
2. Quality of the Project Design	40 points
3. Quality of Project Personnel	10 points
4. Adequacy of Resources	5 points
5. Quality of Management Plan	5 points
6. Quality of the Project Evaluation	30 points
7. Significance	5 points

SOURCE: U.S. Dept. of Education, Office of Elementary and Secondary Education, CFDA #84.371A.

Another source of complexity for educational evaluators is the fact that one teaching methodology shared by different teachers can produce significantly different outcomes. This reflects the fact that teaching is not a routinized production task but a very personal art form.

In addition to funding agencies, educational evaluations are routine in high schools that have regional accreditation. The process of earning accreditation includes writing a detailed self-study and having an external evaluation team provide in situ confirmation of how the school has met the standards of the accrediting body. All of the elements of the self-study, along with the on-site visit, are commonly used in systematic educational program evaluations.

STEPS IN A SYSTEMATIC EVALUATION

The first step in any evaluation is to determine what is being evaluated. During this step goals are identified and elaborated. The best time to begin this work is concurrently with the development of the initial plan for the funded program or evaluation project. Evaluations work best if they are conducted parallel to the operation of the program under evaluation study.

Stakeholder Identification and Goal Setting

The goal setting tasks should be conducted with the key players from the educational program being evaluated. This step is part of the "Utility" standard for quality evaluations. That standard requires that all persons involved in or by the evaluation should be identified and have their needs addressed (American National Standards Institute, 1995).

The goal-setting process also sets the focus of the evaluation and establishes the scope of the study. By prescribing the extent of the evaluation and setting limits for the effort, it becomes possible to identify the evaluation's stakeholders. These are people who perceive that they have a vital interest in both the evaluation process and its outcome. It is not only important to identify the various groups of stakeholders but it is also necessary to identify the concerns they may have with the program evaluation (Fleischman & Williams, 1996). If any group of stakeholders feels they were not considered in the development of the evaluation, they may sabotage the whole effort. For the most part, educators view themselves as being overworked, underpaid, burdened with great responsibility, and given no real authority. From this perspective it is easy to see why a systematic evaluation conducted by an

---

BOX 17.3   The Seven Steps in a Systematic Evaluation

Steps in Systematic Educational Program Evaluation

- **Goal Identification:** The core goals for the evaluation are the first items to be set. This makes it possible to determine the parameters within which the evaluation will work. This also makes it possible to identify stakeholders and to determine the audience for the evaluation.

- **Objective Writing:** Starting with the elaborated goals for the evaluation a series of objectives must be developed. This process should involve representatives of all stakeholder groups.

- **Management Plan:** The tasks that are required to meet each objective must be identified and the sequence for their completion needs to be determined. Also the people responsible for each of the tasks must be identified.

- **Data Collection:** This process follows the task sequence of the management plan. Data sources are typically both formative and summative in nature. During this process formative data can be used to inform the project manager and provide ongoing guidance to the project.

- **Data Analysis:** Both summative (statistical) and formative (qualitative) data are needed to develop a final project report.

- **Publication:** The various stakeholders and audiences should be informed of the evaluation conclusions and recommendations.

- **Dissemination:** Once the final report has been written it should be distributed according to the specifications of the management model.

---

outside agency may well be viewed with skepticism. Unless the educators "buy into it," the evaluation will be virtually impossible to carry out.

Evaluators must be mindful of the private agendas that some stakeholders will bring to the evaluation process. As each stakeholder or group of stakeholders is identified it becomes important for the evaluator to determine what, if any, special interest they may represent. One of the jobs of the evaluator is to keep all the hidden agendas in check or at least balanced.

For more information, see "Considerations on Point" at www.sagepub.com/wrightstudy

Case in Point (17a)

Many states require that local school systems develop a strategic or long-range plan on a cycle, usually 5 years. Much work goes into these plans, which often include conducting a self-study following an evaluation model. It is unfortunate that once completed and filed in the state education department office, they are never looked at again and are not examined until the next cycle of planning comes around.

In working with one school system in devising such a plan it became evident that one assistant superintendent of schools had an agenda of his own. He had volunteered to be the administrator who would supervise the development and writing of the strategic plan and the accompanying evaluation. In a sense he was the primary stakeholder. It seems that he was applying to replace that school district's retiring superintendent. He used the evaluation component of the strategic plan to provide evidence of the quality of his performance. Most of the evaluation became skewed toward his areas of responsibility and away from the areas of other administrators in the school system.

Audience

Along with the stakeholders, it is also necessary to identify others in the wider community who are likely to make up the audience for the evaluation results. These may include the local media outlets, parents of school children, taxpayers of the community, alumni, and members of booster groups. Beyond these, the audience will include other educational institutions that may consider adopting a similar program. Naturally, the most central of all audiences are the agents from the funding source sponsoring the program. This could be the board of school directors or a division of the Department of Education. The funding agency usually requires that it be kept informed of each step as the evaluation is developed and carried out.

Objectives

The next step after goal setting entails the task of developing evaluation objectives that are aligned with each of the goals. This step should include a representative sample of all groups of stakeholders working together as members of a "steering committee." This group may include school board members, teacher representatives, administrators, and the officials of parent organizations and interested community groups. A survey of the audience can help assure that all the stakeholder groups have been identified.

The steering committee has the task of providing the objectives for each goal of the evaluation. Inclusion of so many perspectives on the steering committee may well result in a surfeit of objectives, but this effort makes it possible for all parties to provide at least tacit, if not enthusiastic, support of the evaluation. Of special note is the fact that educational evaluations should always include teachers in the loop (Wolf, 1990). This effort to provide stake-holder representation should be reinforced by establishing a plan for ongoing communication with all parties throughout every phase of the evaluation. The systematic evaluation of an educational program is difficult enough to do without introducing the debilitating influence of hostile groups of stakeholders.

The last task involved with developing evaluation objectives is completed with a working subgroup of the steering committee. This group of stakeholder representatives has the task of winnowing the list of evaluation objectives down to a realistic number and crystallizing them by polishing the wording and clarifying the language. This group also has the responsibility of deciding on the priority of each of the goals and evaluation objectives.

Management Plan

Once the goals are set, and each of the objectives for the evaluation identified and assigned a priority, it is then possible to devise an evaluation management plan. The "Feasibility" standard of the standards for evaluations can be addressed by a comprehensive, practical, and frugal management plan. The plan should be politically prudent and realistic to the ecology of the system where it is being carried out.

A specific strategy needs to be devised for assessing each objective. This process starts by listing all of the evaluation tasks that will be designed and completed in the evaluation. Many of the evaluation tasks and activities will be formative in nature. In other words, they will be collected as the project is ongoing. Interim reports are usually specified for completion at several points in an evaluation. These formative reports provide tentative analyses along with other data in a format that is immediately useful to the project's leadership. These formative reports often result in a tweaking of the project while it is ongoing.

The two most critical questions to be asked when designing a management plan are, when should each part of the evaluation be conducted, and who should have the responsibility for doing the various tasks? (See Table 17.1.) This is best expressed graphically as two charts.[3] The first is a two-axis horizontal bar graph known as a **Gantt chart** (see Table 17.2). The abscissa of this type of chart is a timeline extending from the date when the project starts and running to the project's end. The ordinate of a Gantt chart presents a list of the tasks that are to be completed. The bars on the chart provide a visual reference for the timing and sequence of evaluation activities.

Another example is seen on the following Web page: www.hhmi.org/labmanagement.

On this Web page there is a **linear responsibility chart** from the Howard Hughes Medical Institute and the Burroughs Wellcome Fund. This full document describes the detail of a planning statement for alimenting new post-doctoral students and young faculty into a medical college. A liner responsibility chart assigns specific people with the various tasks listed on the Gantt chart. As the example demonstrates, the tasks that each person involved in the evaluation is responsible for are listed next to his or her name. When the evaluation is a small project involving only a few tasks and people, it is possible to combine the Gantt chart and linear responsibility chart by writing the name of the person who is responsible for each of the evaluation tasks next to the bar graph of the Gantt chart.

The problems of the logistics for the evaluation must also be addressed in the management plan. This includes the identification of office space and equipment and support personnel and establishing a financial management system. Finally, the **dissemination** of information and the publication of the evaluation outcome should be addressed.

Data Collection and Validity

The management plan should also specify the data-collection procedures that will be used with the evaluation. There is a need to collect data in legal and ethical ways that provide due care for the rights and welfare of individuals. This is part of the "Propriety" standard for educational evaluations.

There are numerous factors in any school environment that can cause changes of student test or evaluation scores. These factors provide alternative explanations for what is found during the evaluation and are referred to as sources of internal invalidity. The goal is to establish a data-collection plan that optimizes the likelihood that all measured outcomes are a function of the educational program and were not brought about by extraneous factors. These potential factors that can invalidate the findings of any educational research or evaluation project were first organized into a taxonomy by Donald T. Campbell and Julian C. Stanley (1963). This taxonomy was published in the first edition of the *Handbook of Research on Teaching*. Variations on this model for organizing the threats to the validity of educational research have appeared over the years in all educational research textbooks. The approach adopted here is a compilation of these efforts as they can change the outcome of evaluation efforts.[4]

Table 17.1   Linear Responsibility Chart

Example for a Project's Linear Responsibility Chart

Deliverable	Activity	Work Package	Project Manager	Conference Planner	Planning Committee	Speaker Coordinator	Registration Coordinator	Special Need Coordinator	Oil Site Coordinator	OEAM Sponsor	OEAM Service Line Manager
Invitation List	Determine Participants	1.1	x							x	x
	Prepare Contact List	1.2			x						
	Confirm Attendance	1.3	x								
Conference Workgroups	Determine Areas of Interest	2.1								x	x
	Contact Leaders	2.2				x					
	Confirm Workgroup	2.3		x							
Conference Schedule	Determine Date of Conference	3.1			x					x	
	Prepare Time Slot Schedule	3.2	x								
	Match Workgroup Leaders to Topics	3.3	x								

SOURCE: U.S. Dept. of Veterans Communication and Training Plan.

Table 17.2   Gantt Chart for Writing a Proposal for Federal Grant Support

Tasks	January Week 1	January Week 2	January Week 3	January Week 4	February Week 1	February Week 2	February Week 3	February Week 4	March Week 1	March Week 2	March Week 3	March Week 4
Meet With Superintendent	■											
Library Research	↑		→									
Internet Research		↑		→								
Develop Objectives			↑	→								
Review Objectives With Faculty Stakeholders					■							
Revise Objectives					↑	→						
Write Activities for Objectives					↑			→				
Meet with the Finance Director						■						
Plan a Budget						↑		→				
Meet the Superintendent								■				
Write Timelines for All Activities								↑	→			
Develop Staffing Plan									↑	→		
Complete Evaluation Model										↑		
Write Full Grant Application										↑	→	
Mail All Documents and Application to Washington, D.C.											■	

BOX 17.4   Factors Related to Internal Validity

Time-Related Factors

Each of these factors is linked to the length of time that the educational program being studied takes to complete. Most evaluations are longitudinal studies that run concurrently with the educational plan being assessed. There are ways to organize the data collection for systematic educational evaluations to avoid some of these validity problems (Suter, 2006).

- **Maturation:** As time passes subjects age and mature. This simple fact of life can produce differential outcomes at different ages/stages in human development. When an educational program for second- and third-grade children is being evaluated, the issue of maturation can have a powerful effect. This age (7–9 years) is one of rapid cognitive and conceptual development. Development will occur whether the child attends school or not. Throughout every lifetime are identifiable points when we are optimally sensitive and ready for growth and reorganization.
- **History:** The sobriquet given by Campbell and Stanley (1967) may be better expressed as "current events." This describes how ongoing ecology and human interactions can have a nonrandom effect on the outcome of an educational program. If an evaluator made the mistake of attempting to collect meaningful data on October 31 or November 1 of any school year he or she would quickly realize the powerful effect known as Halloween. There are a dozen or so days throughout the school year when the collection of meaningful data in a public school is impossible. Other issues can be more prosaic. For northern schools there are snow days. In southern states there are tropical storm days. The antics of the school custodian on a riding lawn mower outside the classroom of children being tested have also been shown to interfere with data collection.
- **Mortality:** In educational evaluation studies this term of Campbell and Stanley (1967) would be better expressed as mobility. Families move into and out of communities every day. This simple fact can play a major role in educational outcomes. The loss of even a single child can change the dynamic and *einstellung* of the entire class. The addition of children into an educational setting can also have a profound impact on the educational outcome. Once the school year or educational program is underway, an additional child will take extra time and effort by the teacher to help him or her catch up. That time can only come from that which would have been spent on the others in the classroom. Thus, any addition has the effect of diluting instructional effectiveness.

Measurement-Related Factors

Each of these factors is linked to the sequence and type of testing that is used by the evaluator. This issue works at several levels. For one, all stakeholders may not perceive measurements as having the same gravitas. Research involving the educators of three states has shown that teachers differ from administrators in how they view standardized measures. Administrators have much more faith in the value of standardized measures of all types than do classroom teachers. Thus, the selection of a measure is an important consideration in any evaluation study (Guskey, 2007). Once a measure is selected, the problem becomes one of how and when it/they are employed.

- **Instrumentation:** This term is used as a shorthand to represent those changes that will occur with the measuring technique and instruments over time. This can involve the subtle changes that occur with interviewers and raters. This change is a normal process reflecting the experience those people will gain over time. It also describes the changes that may occur with test materials that are reused. Any items handled by children will deteriorate with time and use. Even the practice that subjects receive in the use of computerized testing software can change the outcome of an evaluation.
- **Testing:** If a pretest is used with an evaluation, its presence may alert the participants to the issues in the program deemed to be important. There is also a normal tendency for most scores on large-scale tests to improve slightly on a second testing of a group of subjects. When a test or measure causes direct or indirect changes in subsequent measurement scores, that test is referred to as being a reactive measure. The closer together in time two sequential measures occur, the greater the potential for one test to react with the other. This effect has been demonstrated in studies of human cognition (Roediger & Karpicke, 2006).
- **Regression Toward the Mean:** What Sir Francis Galton referred to as regression toward mediocrity is now called regression toward the mean. Unusually high scores tend to move toward the test's mean on retesting. This is explainable by classical test theory. Assuming that any test score is made up of both a true score and some amount of error, a high score would have most of the measurement error on the positive side. On retesting, the statistical assumption is that the error would be more evenly distributed, and the extremely high score would shrink slightly. Likewise, low scores tend to improve on retesting to scores slightly closer to the mean score.

Design

The design features of the evaluation can have an impact on the outcome of the study. These design features can also be minimized by employing an appropriate methodology for data collection.

- **Selection:** The issue of selection is linked to the comparisons that may be made within the evaluation study. For example, if the state assessment scores for the school that received the enhanced program are compared (as part of the evaluation) with the scores from a neighboring school that did not participate, then selection may pose a problem. The problem is that the students in the two schools may be very different. This practice of comparing samples of convenience is very common in education and is fraught with the potential for error. Fortunately, systematic educational evaluations are usually self-contained. Most comparisons are made over time with the same subjects.
- **Interpersonal:** The nature of human beings poses significant problems for the evaluator. Within this category are the related problems of envy and the spread of effect. When some students or teachers are selected to take part in a "special program" it is natural for those not included to feel envious. This may result in subtle aggression against the program, which

(Continued)

BOX 17.4 (Continued)

was initiated and is being evaluated by an outside agency. To keep the peace, peer teachers are likely to share the "special programs equipment and methods" with their colleagues, making any comparison meaningless. Finally, there is another potential problem with non-selected teachers showing an unusual level of competitiveness. Some teachers in the "control group" will show their envy and resentment by working to assure that their instructional program produces a better outcome than the new program under study.

- **Novelty:** Most classroom teachers are familiar with the feature-length movie staring Robin Williams as an iconoclastic teacher, *Dead Poet's Society* (Haft, Witt, & Thomas, 1989). To break the mindset of a classroom of preparatory school students, the teacher (played by Robin Williams) does several absurd stunts, such as standing on his desk to teach. Naturally, such behaviors caught the attention of the otherwise uninspired and dry-as-dust students. While interesting and novel today, the logical question is, "What is the next act?" Students can be excited and interested in a novel approach or technique, but when the luster of this dernier cri has worn off, so will the motivation and interest in the program. Educational evaluators must be mindful of this tendency for the novelty of a new program to bring about a temporary change of its own accord.

Record Keeping

The "Accuracy" standard for educational evaluations requires careful program documentation. For that reason, one critical role that must be assigned to someone on the evaluation team is that of librarian. There will be an incredible amount of paperwork generated during an evaluation. These raw documents must be collected, organized, and stored. Also, the evaluator should keep a detailed journal documenting every step in the process, including any departure from the protocol provided in the management plan. The fact that the systematic evaluation is a part of an accountability demonstration and is subject to accounting oversight makes these steps mandatory.

Collection of Data

The fourth step in conducting a systematic evaluation of an educational program is data collection. As the evaluation is likely to be conducted concurrently with the project itself, it may include observational data, meeting notes, test grades, and various products of student learning. Other data sources may require the development of questionnaires and survey research. The careful selection of published assessment instruments and their appropriate and ethical use may also be sources of evaluation data.

Analysis

Accurate and careful data collection and analysis is also part of the "Accuracy" standard for educational evaluations. Analysis follows data collection and is the fifth set of tasks in the evaluation. Data analyses require the qualitative assessment of observational data as well as the statistical analysis of test scores and other quantitative data.

The summative data analysis is followed by the writing of the final evaluation report. This sixth activity is also one of the utility issues addressed in the standards for program evaluations. That standard requires that the program report provide a clear description of the program and the context in which the study was conducted. It should provide an accurate statement of the findings and a clear and unbiased interpretation of the data. Once again, the steering committee should be invited to offer suggestions for the specific

"Figure 1 shows our school's scores on this year's N.C.L.B. test. Figure 2 is the statistical clarification of those scores which the superintendent just sent to me."

Figure 17.1   Accurate and Careful Data Analysis

SOURCE: Cartoon by Merv Magus.

data analyses they would like included in the final project report. The final evaluation report will summarize the findings. To do this, each of the objectives will be explained and the data and analysis for each presented.

At its core, the summative report reflects the considered judgment of the evaluator. For that reason, it is best if the evaluator is not also a stakeholder. For example, it would be inappropriate for a school administrator to evaluate a project in a school in which he or she works. The person who does provide the lead role in a systematic evaluation for an educational program should have a solid knowledge base in quantitative and qualitative data analysis, research design, and psychometrics. Beyond that, the senior evaluator must have excellent people skills and the ability to communicate well.

For more information, see "Considerations on Point" at www.sagepub.com/wrightstudy

---

Case in Point (17b)

One of the most common uses of the systematic evaluations of educational programs is in the application for accreditation or in strategic planning. There are few tasks for public school administrators or college leaders that are less enjoyed than strategic planning. The development of an effective and cogent plan requires thousands of hours of time from the teaching and other professional staff. Most college faculties demand a tradeoff for their committed participation. Such quid pro quos may include a reduced load of classes to teach and/or a fully funded graduate assistant. Public schools cannot offer such perquisites and must rely on the personal loyalty of teachers to the principal. This does not come easily and must be won over the years by the quality of school leadership on a day-by-day basis. Teachers will also have requests for help couched in terms of professionalism and dedication. These words will likely fall on deaf ears if the principal has not built strong relations with the faculty.

Dissemination

The seventh and final step in an evaluation is the publication of the final report and the wider dissemination of the results. All too often the final report from a systematic evaluation ends up forgotten and filed in a school system's archives. The best result that can occur with the final evaluation report is that its analysis and recommendations become incorporated into the project as it becomes a regular feature of the curriculum. For this to occur, it is necessary to enlist the help of the various stakeholders. The evaluator should discuss the report with each stakeholder. One focus of these discussions should be the ways to carry out the recommendations and ideas from the evaluation.

The extent of the dissemination should have been decided on in advance of the project. The evaluator and the educational leadership should not find that they must discuss this question of dissemination after the fact. That initial negotiation for a dissemination model should include such issues as how to involve the local press, creating a Web page, and meeting with various groups of educators and members of the community.

VALUE-ADDED EVALUATION

The general public and the members of state legislatures support the use of scores from student assessment tests as the best approach to determining how well a teacher is doing his or her job. These same people also favor the use of student test scores as a way to evaluate the quality of public schools (Trotter, 2007). In opposition to this are the educators who see the use of student test scores as not being an appropriate way to assess the quality of instruction delivered in the classroom. As a group, educators favor using quality indicators such as the level of the teacher's education and his or her base of knowledge (Millman & Schalock, 1997).

A core concern of educators who are opposed to having student test scores serve as the basis for teacher evaluations is that some classes and schools enroll students who are more difficult to teach than are the children in other schools. The proof of this fact was provided again in 2006 in a statewide study of 5-year-old children in Ohio. That study demonstrated that the readiness scores for children entering kindergarten in 2005–2006 reflect the same well-documented ethnic and socioeconomic gap that exists throughout the other grades on achievement tests (Ohio State Board of Education, 2006). There is no debating the fact that an educator working with otherwise normal children from upper socioeconomic backgrounds will see high assessment test scores. Likewise, children from the lowest strata of the socioeconomic scale will not do as well on assessment measures. Thus, from the outset the idea of evaluating schools and teachers on the basis of assessment test scores is inherently flawed and unfair (Popham, 2000).

There are statistical procedures that can control for some of the preexisting differences among the children enrolled in different schools. In reality it is incredibly difficult to design educational research that controls all significant extraneous variables from the test data.[5] In most school based research it is possible to see a myriad of possible explanations for testing outcomes. One reason for this is that it is not ethically possible to create a true control group.[6] Another is that it is not possible to build statistical corrections (**covariance analysis**) that would remove all extraneous influences from the data. Variables such as family income, parental education levels, the amount of time children spend playing computer games and watching TV, race and ethnicity, the number of books and magazines read by the parents at home, the numerous dimensions that make up the child's health status, the number and ages of siblings at home, and the child's motivation for learning can all have an impact on educational outcomes. It would never be possible to collect and organize data on all of these variables for all children enrolled in the public schools of a state. This makes it impossible to use the average assessment test score from a classroom of children as a measure of a teacher's success.

The same principle can play havoc with school-to-school comparisons. An effective school enrolling children from impoverished backgrounds can be doing an excellent job but not have high average scores on assessment tests. Likewise, a suburban school located in a wealthy community can have very high average scores on the mandated assessments even though it is not doing a very good job improving the level of learning for its students. Even within a school, one cohort year of third-grade children may be very different from the next cohort year of students in the same grade. This can easily lead to a school failing to meet the target of adequate yearly progress. It is evident that what is needed is to move the focus of school accountability from the comparisons conducted between different schools to a careful analysis of what is going on within the schools (Hu, 2007).

Yet, we do use mean test scores to evaluate teachers and schools. In 2006, there were almost 1,800 public schools that had to be restructured for consistently failing to reach the target level for adequate yearly progress. At the same time, over 2 million minority children and children with disabilities were never tested on the mandated state assessments (Dizon, Feller, & Bass, 2006). These children had their scores hidden by their schools. This was done by employing one or another loophole in the NCLB reporting requirements.[7] It is very likely that the number of schools in need of restructuring will climb dramatically in 2007–2008. One reason for this is that Secretary of Education Spellings began a campaign for complete reporting of all scores in 2007.

Thus, there are two measurement dimensions required to understand how effective a school may be. The first one is the main focus of the NCLB Act: the average achievement or performance level. The second dimension is one that the NCLB Act does not adequately address: the rate of growth in achievement of children. The adequate yearly progress requirement of the law only provides predetermined annual proficiency targets for a school to meet. It does not take a longitudinal look at how much progress individual children are making as they progress through the grades. The graphic below depicts these two dimensions as achievement and growth.

ACHIEVEMENT

	(Low)	(High)
G	Low Achievement	High Achievement
R	High Growth	High Growth
O		
W	Low Achievement	High Achievement
T	Low Growth	Low Growth
H		

Some schools can provide high-achieving students with an instructional program that enhances their achievement levels even more each year, while other schools with similar students are not as effective. The worst-case scenario is the school that has low-performing students who are also not learning much each year. Finally, there are some very effective schools that are working with low-performing children but producing significant annual improvements in the achievement scores of their students.

The question then becomes, do good students make schools look good, or do good schools make students into high-performing young scholars? A method is needed that can separate academic achievement into two components: one that is attributable to the student and one that is the product of the instructional program (Hershberg, Simon, & Lea-Kruger, 2004).

Statistical Solution

At the present time, the statewide, high-stakes testing program of the vast majority of states involves a "**cross-sectional**" **model of evaluation**. This describes the fact that tests are given to third-graders this year, and based on those test scores, decisions are made about the third-grade teachers and curriculum. When the impact is felt, those tested children have moved on to the next grade (Kelly & Monczunski, 2007). Thus, the testing does not directly affect them. Any impact will be felt by the children entering third grade the next year. Naturally, the exceptions are the eight states that will not promote low-scoring third-graders.

When high-stakes test data from states like Texas, where up to 15,000 third graders score low enough to be retained in third grade, and Florida, where 25,000 third-graders are held back each year, the whole database for school and teacher evaluation becomes contaminated (McGill-Franzen & Allington, 2006). Consider the Florida teachers of the fourth grade. When the lowest-scoring 12.5% of the population are held back in third grade, their state assessment average scores are based [on a] smaller, more academically able cohort. Meanwhile, the third-grade teachers have an additional 12.5% of students who are older, and more developmentally advanced, added to the regular mix of new third-graders. This can also cause a shift in the average test scores. After one more year, only 60% of the third-graders who were retained the previous year will be promoted to fourth grade. Yet, still the mix of students in fourth grade is more academically able than the third grade, where so many children languish in the "do-loop"[8] of grade repetition and failure. The other 40% (N = 9,500) of third-graders will fail to reach the proficient criterion on the third-grade test for a second time. At that point, the third-grade teachers will be able (after two failures) to have the child referred for assessment as a potential candidate for special education. All of this grade retention produces a contamination of the test data used to assess schools and teachers.

Children were tested every year, but until the last 15 years, no one did a systematic analysis of the mass of data developed for each individual child. What became evident was that a system for the longitudinal assessment of the effectiveness of instruction was needed. The longitudinal analysis could not be a simple subtraction of last year's standard score on the high-stakes test from this year's score. That solution produces growth data that have a very low level of statistical reliability.[9]

The solution to the problem of data analysis was developed by a biostatistician at the University of Tennessee, William Sanders. Using public school test data he and his colleagues applied a mixed-model regression analysis to the task of identifying and measuring the effectiveness of classroom teachers, schools, and school districts. Sanders's method involved using the longitudinal data collection to determine the amount of achievement growth that each child experienced. As each child in Tennessee is tested annually under the NCLB mandates in both mathematics and reading (between grades 3 and 8) there is a large database with which to work. Sanders's (n.d.) system, known as value-added assessment, works by assuming each child's test transcript represents repeated measurements in the two core achievement areas. The method has typically been described in the media as a "growth model" (Hu, 2007). This analysis of growth, or value being added, makes the child his or her own statistical control. In this way the question of background and demographics and other confounding variables are all removed from consideration (Rivers-Sanders, 1999). The only focus is on the child and his or her repeated measurements.

William Sanders has described the value-added assessment system as being similar to the way parents track the physical growth of their children. He notes that it is common for parents to record the height of a growing child by making annual pencil marks on a door frame. This series of height marks can be thought of as one type of repeated measurement of the child. In that way, the marks on the door frame are similar to the annual school assessment tests, which are also repeated measurements. A glance at the door frame will show the parents which years saw the child grow the most and which years saw little growth. Sander's statistical model uses this same principle (Sanders, 1998).

The statistical model that is central to the analysis of test data in the value-added approach to evaluation is the **Henderson mixed-model equation** (HMME). William Sanders has a background in biostatistics, in which the use of HMMEs is common.[10] The HMME system is based on a multiple-correlation equation in which the predictors include both random and fixed variables.[11] To account for the repeated measurement of the criterion variable (all annual high-stakes test scores), those scores are entered as a variance matrix. The predictors are also entered as matrices. One matrix includes the **best linear unbiased estimators** (BLUE) of the fixed effects and the other as a matrix of the **best linear unbiased predictors** (BLUP) for the random variables. In these equations, the estimators (random effects) include the influence of the teachers and the schools attended.

Weights are determined from the data to account for the number of years that have passed since that teacher taught the student. In this way, every teacher that the student has been taught by over the years can be simultaneously included in the correlational relationship. The value-added model also can account for team teaching and departmentalization, in which a child will have a number of teachers in one year. The "teacher effect" has been demonstrated to be sensitive to the assessment test used to measure achievement (Lockwood et al., 2007). Thus a consistent and highly reliable achievement measure is needed to assess the effect of the teacher on each child's achievement.

Naturally, the influence of a teacher on assessment test scores wanes as time moves on. This value-added system also makes it possible to see how any change in a teacher's philosophy and practice influences his or her effectiveness in the classroom. The model also makes it possible to design student academic growth charts that can reflect the effectiveness of the instruction provided to the students (Betebenner & Sang, 2007).

The matrix of predictors included in Sanders's model includes student-related variance. When providing an analysis of the effectiveness of teachers, the system is not hindered if a few children missed taking the test or even if some of the children are repeating the grade. It is a truly robust statistical method (Ceperley & Reel, 1997).

Value-Added Outcome

From the teacher's perspective, the outcome from a value-added assessment includes a report based on data indicating how much change has occurred with the children that he or she taught. In the case of elementary teachers who teach several of the areas that are tested, value-added reports will be generated for each. An elementary school teacher who teaches all the subject areas included on the state's assessment will have a report that presents the amount of change he or she produced in children over all of the assessed areas of the curriculum. A middle-school teacher who only teaches one area, such as mathematics, would receive a report only on his or her effectiveness as a mathematics teacher. In some states, such as Tennessee, North Carolina, Ohio, and Pennsylvania, the report that teachers receive is based on 3 years of data on their teaching. This 3-year requirement provides enough time for the equations to stabilize and provide a reliable assessment. Naturally, the most recent year is weighted more heavily in determining the average **effectiveness score**. That effectiveness score is calculated as a linear combination of estimates and is itself an estimate of how a teacher compares to the "average teacher" in terms of student achievement growth (Baum, 2005).

Along with the effectiveness scores, the teacher also receives information on the reliability and standard error of measurement for those scores. To determine if he or she is a significantly effective teacher, the student improvement score should exceed a value that is equal to the standard error multiplied by approximately two (Score ≥ 1.96 x SE_M). The value-added evaluation makes it possible to provide reports that classify teachers into one of three effectiveness levels:

- **Highly effective** teachers who stretch students to provide achievement levels significantly above their past levels of performance
- **Effective** teachers who help students attain a year's worth of academic achievement growth during the school year
- **Ineffective** teachers for whom the student performance levels are significantly below their achievement growth levels in the past

Just as the value-added system can determine the growth being experienced by individual students, it can also see differential patterns of growth for identifiable groups. For example, the value-added analysis can identify which teachers are most effective in facilitating learning among low-achieving students. Beyond student growth and teacher effectiveness, value-added evaluations can also determine the effectiveness of an entire school or even a school system. In states such as Tennessee that are totally committed to the value-added model, the state department of education has access to value-added assessment scores at all three levels: teacher, school, and district (see Table 17.3). In other states, such as Pennsylvania, the professional associations of teachers have limited access to teacher data.

Table 17.3

Value Added Assessments in Education

Reverse Shed Pattern: This occurs when the highest performing students experience more than a year's achievement growth in a year, while low performing students make less than a year's growth in achievement.

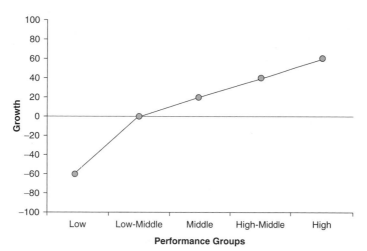

Tent Pattern: This occurs when average performing students make more than a year's achievement growth while both high performing and low performing students make less than a year's growth.

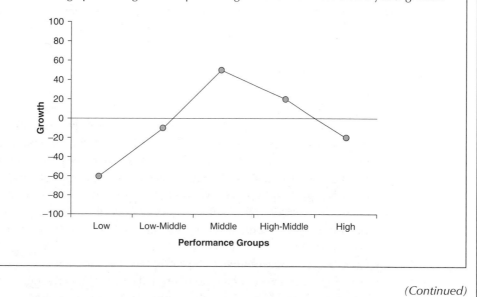

(Continued)

Table 17.3 (Continued)

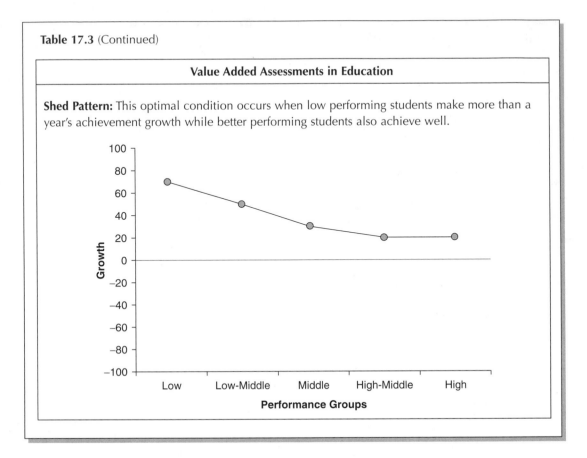

Value Added Assessments in Education

Shed Pattern: This optimal condition occurs when low performing students make more than a year's achievement growth while better performing students also achieve well.

Limitations of Value-Added Assessment

All educational applications of value-added assessments are "test bound." This describes the condition in which the entire data source is based on test scores. In the case of most statewide value-added assessment models, this comes down to a single test score per child each year. Thus, the quality of the test determines the quality of the assessment that is conducted of the teachers and schools (Lockwood et al., 2007; Resnick, 2004). Related to this is the very large statistical range (confidence interval size) associated with making causal statements about educational efficacy of teachers or schools (Braun & Wainer, 2007). For these reasons, Braun and Wainer suggest that value-added assessments are best employed as an initial screening system.

It should always be remembered that the "effectiveness score" that a teacher receives under a value-added system is only an estimated score (Braun, 2005). To make personnel decisions, such as tenure and merit pay, more data should be part of the evaluation (Popham, 1973). These data can include teacher portfolios and the results of traditional teacher observations.

Statewide Application of Value-Added Assessments

The first state to adopt the value-added model was Tennessee, in 1992. Following that lead, other states that have also adopted this model, including Arkansas, Colorado, Iowa, Minnesota, Pennsylvania, Ohio, North Carolina, and Washington. Both Florida and North Carolina have created a merit pay system that rewards teachers who are highly effective.[12] Florida's merit system is not a true value-added assessment and only involves the average of student scores for the previous year.

William Sanders is opposed to making the teacher reports from the value-added assessments public. His belief is that when teachers see the need to improve, they will take the necessary steps and modify their instructional practices. It is another unfortunate shortcoming of the value-added assessment model that it only examines student outcomes and provides no data on what teaching practices are linked to good student achievement.

The value-added system does appeal to many school board members who want to pay the highly effective teachers more than others. This is an idea that Sanders believes should not be imposed quickly. If merit pay is to be based on a value-added model, it should happen only after several years of experience with that evaluation system.

The data from Tennessee have shown that in the schools of many upper-income communities, teachers concentrate their efforts on teaching the high-achieving students. In these schools, the best and brightest children are the ones with the greatest achievement growth levels, while the few low-performing students experience little growth and improvement in achievement.

The opposite is often found in the schools located in the poorest communities. In many of these schools the primary effort of the teachers is for the development of the skill level of the lowest performing students, while the few precocious learners make only modest achievement progress. These patterns can be easily seen from the school report from a value-added assessment. Once these patterns are determined, the school working as a community of educators must chart a course of action.

Local Applications of Value-Added Data Management

Another application of a value-added statistical approach is the management of school district data. Even though the states have been slow to embrace the large-scale use of educational assessments based on a value-added model, local school systems have begun to use this type of approach in the management of their local achievement data. This approach makes it possible to track individual students and carefully monitor their progress. This involves a large initial expenditure of funds for the purchase of the statistical tools for the required analyses and the continuing cost of consultants to organize and interpret annual test data. One outcome of this has been improved scores on the statewide assessments (Higgins, 2007).

Staff Development and Value-Added Assessment

Value-added assessments can identify those teachers who are most effective in optimizing measured student growth. These teachers are a significant asset for school administrators. They can serve as the leaders of truly meaningful inservice staff development efforts. Thus, while not providing direct evidence of optimal instructional practice, the value-added model can provide for an identification of the most effective practitioners (Linn, 2003). In medical centers and teaching hospitals, the best physicians become the "attending physicians," and they have the responsibility to educate resident physicians and practitioner fellows. Value-added assessment provides the information that could be used to create a class of "attending" teachers who have inservice responsibilities. Such teachers could be used in the classrooms of less successful teachers, where they could model the best practice for a day or two each month with the developing teachers on a school's staff.

Summary

This chapter presented two views on the task of evaluating educational programs. The first is the standard model used by schools to provide evidence for external funding agencies, state education departments, and accrediting agencies. This model involves the development of a systematic evaluation plan by first involving all the applicable stakeholders. Once the goals and objectives for the evaluation have been agreed to, the tasks of data collection and analysis begin. This type of evaluation is both formative (process oriented) and summative (product oriented) and can strengthen and document successful educational endeavors as well as point out areas where projects or programs can be improved.

The second model is one that determines how efficacious the instructional program and the teachers actually are. William Sanders and his colleagues have been able to show that teachers do make a difference. At every grade level, the pupils having effective teachers make significant progress toward meeting the state learning standards. When children experience a sequence of highly effective teachers over several years, they are able to reach their true academic potential. In terms of student achievement outcomes, the influence of highly effective teachers is more than that of socioeconomic class, family education, class size, and the full range of other demographic variables. In addition to being able to determine teacher and school effectiveness, the value-added approach also provides a way to track children over time. Thus, it becomes possible to see which children are making the most progress with which teacher and in which school.

By making it possible to identify the most effective classroom teachers, school administrators have been given a magnificent new tool for use in the improvement of all students in all classrooms. These highly effective teachers can serve the role of the true master professional mentoring and modeling teaching in ongoing inservice efforts.

Discussion Questions

1. Visit the government Web page for the Education General Administrative Regulations (EDGAR): http://www.ed.gov/policy/fund/reg/edgarReg/edgar.html. Then review several sections, including part 98 and part 99. Make a brief list of new issues related to student records that you learned from this experience.

2. Visit a local school system's administrative center and ask for the opportunity to review a recent federal or state grant program, such as Title I. After reading this material, note the evaluation model with the application. Make note of any items that you were surprised to find and/or found lacking.

3. Build a Gantt chart that could be used to solve the task assignment and timeline for a project in your life. For example, the project could be the end-of-year faculty party or how to set up and host the family Thanksgiving dinner.

4. Visit the library of a local college or university and ask to read the most recent document that was used to gain accreditation for the institution. Or, as an alternative, visit a local high school (only if accredited) and ask to read the high school's accreditation report. Take notes on

the self-study portion and note any unusual sections. Also, note any sections or items you are surprised to find were not included.

5. Contact a private charitable funding agency and acquire an application that could be used to make an unsolicited application for support. Read the application and briefly outline a 2-year project that you could use to support a school with which you are familiar. Next write a one-page outline for an evaluation plan that could be used for the application. To learn about funding sources, see www.internet-prospector .org/found-us.html. In addition to this source there are thousands of other foundations, agencies, and institutions that offer financial support for educational programs. These can be found by conducting a standard Internet search using key words such as "Education funding support, foundation grants," "education grants," etc.

6. Assume that your school board has asked you to structure arguments that could be used to convince the local teachers association or union to accept a value-added assessment model as part of the teacher evaluation program during the next contract cycle. What arguments will you make to convince the teachers to join in and support this evaluation?

Student Study Site

Educational Assessment on the Web

Log on to the Web-based student study site at www.sagepub.com/ wrightstudy for additional Web sources and study resources.

NOTES

1. In a formal sense, *accountability* is defined as "to be held to account." In American education, the term has its roots in the business community and the process of cost accounting. The implication is that schools (like factories) should have learning standards (production goals) and the unit cost for achievement (product unit produced) can be determined. Once the unit cost has been determined, it is then possible to maximize efficiency and lower unit costs.

2. To review this application for funding, see www.ed.gov/programs/strivingreaders/ applicant.html. The next round of grants under this program is not due until the fall of 2008.

3. Management plans for large-scale assessments often include a "Program Evaluation and Review Technique," or PERT, chart. This graphic depicts all the evaluation activities in their required sequence. Some tasks occur concurrently, and others require that prerequisite activities to be completed first. The complex interlocking nature of the evaluation activities are easily identified on the PERT chart.

4. The taxonomy by Donald Campbell and Julian Stanley in 1963 was originally designed to demonstrate how different educational experiment designs were fraught with different types of potential problems. The taxonomy divided these problems into those related to the "external validity" of the research design and the "**internal validity**" of the design. The former refers to generalizability of findings to other settings and the latter to the fidelity of the treatment (independent variable) to outcome (dependent variable) link.

5. For example, if all high socioeconomic students enrolled in the class of one truly superior teacher, and the socioeconomic level of the children were statistically removed from the relationship, the effectiveness of the teacher would appear to be lower than it really is. This is because the student socioeconomic level is also correlated with the effectiveness of the teacher (Braun & Wainer, 2007).

6. A true control group would receive no educational treatment of any kind during the study.

7. These loopholes were described in Chapter 16. They include NCLB test reporting category shifting for the child.

8. In a number of computer languages (FORTRAN, BASIC, JAVA) a Do-Loop is a point where a repeated operation will continue constantly because a conditional expression is unfulfilled.

9. See Chapter 4 for a discussion of reliability and the problem of subtraction residuals.

10. Charles Roy Henderson (1911–1989) was born and educated in Iowa and taught at Cornell University. He developed equations to optimize the quality of dairy herds. His statistical models are used throughout the world in agriculture and microbiology.

11. For more information on multiple correlation, see Chapter 3.

12. California recognizes and rewards schools that have made above average progress toward meeting the state's learning standards. As this is a fixed-goal system, and not based on measured growth, it is not included with the states employing a value-added model.

GLOSSARY

a priori test assessment Conducted prior to using a new test. It provides a method of assuring quality and the validity of the measure.

ability grouping Placement of children into groups based on results from standardized tests of mental ability, aptitudes, and achievement.

academic redshirting Describes when parents of a young child elect not to enroll that child in school until he or she is a year older than the normal cohort of kindergarten children. This is done to provide the child with a developmental advantage over his or her peers.

accommodations Modifications in the testing or evaluation environment that are made to compensate for a child's disabling condition, which make the test more fair and inferences made on the basis of its scores more accurate.

accomplishment ratio A quantitative system for determining how efficacious the learning process is for a child. It is a statement combining the child's cognitive ability and achievement level into a single score. High scores show efficient learning, and low scores are indicative of underachievement.

accountability Being held to account for both the expenditure of educational funds and for the achievement outcomes for students.

achievement test A test measuring an individual's knowledge of specific facts and his or her proficiency in completing cognitive processes such as problem solving.

adequate yearly progress (AYP) AYP specifies the proportion of a school's students who achieve at a proficient or better level each year, as well as the attendance rates for the mandated tests, and the eventual graduation rates for the schools.

advanced placement A special advanced high school curriculum for as many as 27 different subject areas and a testing program that makes it possible for colleges to award collegiate credit for completing the AP course and passing the examination.

affirmative action A plan designed to increase the representation of traditionally underrepresented minorities in a program or activity.

alternate form reliability The correlation that can be obtained when two different but well-matched versions of a measure are administered to the same subjects.

alternative answers Alternatives are the possible answers to multiple choice questions and are composed of one correct answer (keyed response) and several wrong choices (distracters).

alternative assessments All extended-answer supply-type test items including a wide variety of assessment approaches that do not involve having the student select or choose between answer options (e.g., performance tasks, demonstrations, projects, and exhibitions).

alternative tracks Alternative routes for people to become teachers; initiated by the states to help meet the need for certified teachers.

American College Testing program (ACT) The American College Testing program is an alternative college admissions and guidance instrument used by one million students a year.

analytical assessment An approach to evaluation that uses a multifaceted rubric to examine a number of different aspects of the student product being assessed.

analytical intelligence One of the three types of intelligence that are part of Sternberg's proposed triarchic model of mental ability.

analytical rubric When a rubric assesses multiple aspects or dimensions of a performance by employing several ordinal scales elaborated as separate scoring rubrics. These can also be summed into a total overall score.

anchor items Test items used every year that serve to set the difficulty level of newly developed test items for subsequent editions of the assessment. Most high-stakes tests consist of up to 33% anchor items.

anecdotal observation Factual reporting of detailed behavior(s) as witnessed.

anecdotal record Ongoing linear report of an occurrence or incident. A written description of observations, devoid of judgments or evaluation.

answer The response made by a student to a query posed by the teacher.

Apgar In 1952, Dr. Virginia Apgar used her name as an acronym for the five subtests of her new measure of the status of newborn babies. It represented: A = appearance, P = pulse, G = grimace, A = activity, R = respiration. Today, the name Apgar is applied to an observational scale regarding the following factors: heart rate, respiratory effort, muscle tone, reflex response, and color.

appropriateness Component of validity referring to the application that the test is given. A particular test may be valid in one arena but inappropriate when used for another measurement task.

aptitude measures Assessment of the capacity for learning.

Army Alpha & Army Beta The first group-administered, paper-and-pencil tests of general intelligence administered to Army recruits beginning in 1917.

artificial intelligence The ability of a computer to perform those activities normally thought to require human intelligence.

assembly-line grading A name applied to the large-scale grading approach adopted by several universities to evaluate thousands of undergraduate essays by using graduate assistants and distributing the grading task over the Internet.

assessment The measurement of one or more variables related to the current condition, ability, status, or knowledge of an individual.

attention deficit disorder (ADD) Developmentally inappropriate lack of attention and focus on tasks and activities.

attention deficit/hyperactivity disorder (AD/HD) Disorder of a child's ability to attend to and focus on learning that may appear prior to school age and be manifested by impulsivity; high, randomly directed activity; and inattention to tasks and directions.

authentic assessment Performance assessment task based on a "real world" problem or task that is based on issues encountered in the world beyond the school.

basic interpersonal communication skill (BICS) The everyday level of language used in social settings. The language used by children on the playground and in the lunchroom or in sports.

bell curve Also known as the Gaussian normal curve. This symmetric curve represents the distribution of error around the average of a large set of independent observations.

benchmark skills in reading Operational descriptions and examples that highlight qualitative differences between achievement levels and serve as marker points on a rubric.

benchmarks A point of reference based on a standard for learning, including illustrative examples of successful completion or achievement.

best linear unbiased estimators (BLUE) Regression analysis that weights variables so as to create the best linear unbiased estimators for minimizing the error variance of prediction. The analysis assumes the core regression assumptions (Gauss-Markov) are met.

best linear unbiased predictors (BLUP) Random variables (those without fixed properties) used in regression analysis to estimate the outcome for another random variable. The matrix of predictors (i.e., estimators) is referred to as the BLUP.

binomial distribution A distribution of a large number of independent outcomes from a series of binomial occurrences.

Bloom's taxonomy Taxonomy for categorizing the level of abstraction required to answer questions that commonly occur in educational settings. A useful structure for categorizing test questions according to the cognitive skill level required to answer them correctly.

bluffing Guessing an answer for an extended supply-type question on an essay test, made in the hope that the person grading the question will be lenient.

Buckley Amendment The Family Education Rights and Privacy Act is often known by the name of the senator who was instrumental in its passage, James L. Buckley. This law provides rules for educational record keeping, psychological testing, and parental rights.

CAVD The four factors of E. L. Thorndike's model for mental ability: completion, arithmetic, vocabulary, and directions.

Carnegie Unit A unit of instruction that requires 120 clock hours to present. This time may occur in units of 45 minutes for 180 school days. Block schedules can provide a Carnegie unit of instruction in time blocks of 90 minutes for 90 days.

centered A term used by the Educational Testing Service to describe the process of establishing a new normative reference group of subjects for use when scoring individuals' tests. The process is sometimes referred to as "norming the test."

central tendency A measure of the "average" performance of individuals, determined as the arithmetical center of the data.

chance level The likelihood that a test taker will be able to guess the correct answer to a select-type question (e.g., multiple choice question). This is linked to the number of answer alternatives.

child study movement This era began in the 19th century when the methods associated with modern science were applied to the systematic study of human infancy and childhood.

class rank The absolute position, or rank, of a student compared to his or her peers in terms of total grade point average.

classical measurement theory The theoretical model explaining the relationship between the obtained score of a subject on a test and the amounts of measurement error and true score (a pure score, free of any error).

coefficient Kappa The coefficient of reliability used with criterion-referenced tests. Scores range from a minimum of 0.00 to a maximum value of 1.00.

cognitive ability A synonym for traditionally defined mental ability that emphasizes verbal, spatial, and mathematical reasoning ability.

cognitive academic language proficiency (CALP) The level of language that is required for formal academic learning in content-based subject fields.

cohort A group of individuals having a statistical factor (age or background) in common.

College Board A not-for-profit corporation originally chartered as the College Entrance Examination Board in 1901 to create and score examinations for students applying for college admission.

Committee on Secondary School Studies A committee of the National Education Association existing from 1892 to 1893 that established the high school as a four-year experience involving 24 year-long classes. It is also known as the Committee of 10.

common school Name given to what are now known as public schools by Horace Mann. Supplanted in the American lexicon by *public school* around 1900.

commonality The proportion of a variable's variance that is shared with a factor. The amount of common variance between the two.

composite score A combined score from several subtests into a single score.

computer adaptive testing Testing that employs software that can estimate the ability and background knowledge of each test taker and guide the appropriate selection of test items from a computerized item bank.

computer grading of essays An application of artificial intelligence whereby computer software is used to evaluate and even grade the answers of students on extended supply-type (essay) questions.

concurrent strategies Metacognitive processes used to create understanding of written language (e.g., reading, using context clues, personal identification, and imagery).

concurrent validity The correlation between a known test, outcome, or measure and the scores on another measure of the same dimension.

confidence interval A parameter linked to a normal curve of probability. It provides two points representing the limits of what obtained scores would have been randomly drawn from a normal population.

connectionism A principle of learning holding that the acquisition of new behaviors is a function of their outcomes and that more efficient connections between learned behaviors occur as a function of the satisfaction achieved by their performance and repetition.

construct validity A validation technique used with variables of hypothetical traits or abilities lacking an operational (observable) definition. This involves demonstrating both the legitimacy of the variable and the measure of it.

constructed items Synonym for supply-type items, including questions requiring extended answers such as those in essay format.

constructed-response formats Testing formats that include completion, short answer items, essays, and compositions.

content validity The fidelity of the test items to the topic that was taught and/or the goals of the curriculum area being measured.

convergent production The mental process of bringing together diverse and sundry material needed to find the solution for a problem.

core curriculum The high school curriculum recommended by the Committee of 10, including a distribution of courses that involve both classical and modern languages, mathematics, sciences, geography, government, and history.

correction for guessing Deducting points from students' scores equal to the number of items answered wrong divided by the number of distracters. Any item omitted by the test taker is not included in the process.

correlation A measure of the degree to which two variables are related.

correlation coefficient Any of a series of mathematical ratios (e.g., Pearson Product Moment Correlation Coefficient) that demonstrate the amount of variance shared by two variables. The numerical value is on a range of ±1.00 as the maximum and 0.00 as the minimum.

covariance The amount of common variance shared by two different measures. It is reported as a coefficient of correlation.

covariance analysis A statistical analysis of the difference between groups after a statistical correction for a priori group differences.

creative intelligence One of the three types of intelligence that make up the triarchic model for intelligence proposed by Robert Sternberg.

creativity The ability to use the imagination to organize ideas and make, design, or write unusual and highly productive products.

criterion-referenced test Tests designed to measure how well an individual has learned a specific skill or acquired specified knowledge. The reference is absolute and not dependent on a comparison to other test takers.

criterion variable A variable that is to be predicted in a multiple-correlation (multiple-regression) equation by two or more predictor variables.

critical thinking The skillful and disciplined use of the intellect in problem solving and/or creative production by going beyond the given and what is previously known and mentally exploring new dimensions or aspects of the task or problem.

Cronbach coefficient alpha A statistical estimation of test reliability or consistency that can be used with scaled and/or binary measures of a single dimension. This reliability is equivalent to the average of all possible permutations of split halves that can be made with a set of test item data from a sample of subjects.

cross-sectional model of evaluation The collection and analysis of data from different age groups to evaluate multiple levels of an educational system.

cross-validation An expression of both the statistical method and the outcome from that method. It is employed to determine the level of precision that a test or measure has when used to predict a future outcome. See *predictive validity*.

crystallized factor of ability That part of mental ability that is the product of what is learned, experienced, or absorbed from the culture.

curriculum-based assessment The combination of curriculum-based measurements with standardized achievement tests into a single assessment.

curriculum-based measurements Assessments conducted to identify problematic areas for the child by probing elements of the curriculum. These brief probes are conducted over time to provide a picture of the trend in the child's learning.

curriculum map A publicly available document that captures the scope and sequence (the school's master plan) of the learning objectives, activities, and assessments in each subject and in each grade.

curriculum probe Brief tests (5 to 10 min.) that are administered on a regular basis and are part of a curriculum-based measurement.

cut scores The raw score on a standards-based test that denotes a break between two ordinal levels of success (e.g., proficient vs. highly proficient).

DANTES Program A program that awards college credit to former soldiers on the basis of military training and experience.

decontextualized Assessment that does not involve tasks related to the perceived needs and/or interests of the individual. Most select-type questions are of this type, while authentic assessments are not.

deviation IQ scores A standard score used to express intelligence-test performance, usually with a mean of 100 and a standard deviation of 15.

diagnostic tests Tests with the goal of identifying the learning problems experienced by an individual. The differentiation among learning problems occurs by using measures exhibiting a high degree of negative skew.

differential item functioning This analytical method is used to test the appropriateness of individual test items for identified subgroups of the population taking the test (e.g., ethnic minorities).

disaggregated scores Descriptive statistics from mandated testing programs reported by population subgroups.

disaggregated subgroup mean The mean score for an identified subgroup of those people who were tested.

discrepancy The difference between a child's tested level of ability and his or her achievement. Used to assess for a learning disability.

discrimination level Statistic that describes how well individual items can identify test takers who do well on the test and those who perform badly. The range of possible discrimination levels is from a perfect +1.0 to the minimum of –1.0.

dissemination The distribution of results from an evaluation to all audiences and stakeholders. The parameters of the dissemination should be agreed upon prior to initiating the evaluation.

distracter analysis A step in item analysis involving an examination of the pattern of student selection of the various distracters from a multiple choice question.

distracters The wrong choice alternatives for multiple choice and other select-format test questions.

distribution An array of scores from the measurement of a variable aligned from low to high that can depict the frequency of occurrence for each of the possible scores.

divergent thinking Mental process of creating numerous productive and useful ideas and products starting from a single stimulus.

Dynamic Indicators of Basic Literacy Skills, 6th ed. (DIBELS) Test of mastery of early reading skills designed for use with children between kindergarten and third grade. Best employed as a classroom measure that monitors the progress of early readers rather than for identification of disabled readers.

EDGAR Acronym for the Education Department General Administrative Regulations.

educational standards Specified levels of accomplishment to be achieved by learners.

Educational Testing Service (ETS) The not-for-profit corporation that was chartered in 1948 to develop, score, and transcribe examinations used by educational programs, including the College Entrance Examination Board.

effectiveness score Score from a value-added assessment of a teacher that provides an expression of his or her efficaciousness.

Elementary and Secondary Education Act (ESEA) The Elementary and Secondary Education Act, passed in 1965 as (P.L. 89-10 [1965]). The law became the central education initiative of the administration of President Lyndon Johnson.

English-language learners (ELL) Children for whom English is not the native language and who are in the process of learning to achieve English at a cognitive academic level of proficiency.

entitlement decision Decision involving the provision of services or other assistance needed to "level the playing field" for children who have special needs.

equal protection Statement included in the 14th Amendment to the U. S. Constitution that has been used to argue for the inclusion of special education students in all aspects of public school programs.

error of prediction The difference between the predicted outcome and what was actually observed.

essay item A test question requiring the student to supply an answer of a paragraph or more.

essay item discrimination level Statistic that describes how well an extended-answer supply-type question (essay) differentiates between students who do well on the measure from those who do poorly. The range of values is from a perfect +1.0 to a minimum of –1.0.

ethnographic research Research that collects data by the direct, real-time observation of subjects in their natural setting. The researcher may or may not participate as a member of the group being observed.

eugenics movement Eugenicists believed the theoretical assumption that child growth and development was genetically driven and could be improved by preventing the mentally defective from being parents. The American Eugenics Society flourished during the first third of the 20th century.

evaluation Designed and facilitated to assess the strengths and weaknesses of programs, policies, personnel, products, and organizations.

evaluation standards Guidelines and appropriate procedures for educational evaluations first delineated by Daniel Stufflebeam in 1981.

executive function Cognitive process that controls and manages other mental processes and operations.

factor analysis Analytical procedure involved in estimating a common factor(s) that links the correlations among measured variables.

fair test A measure that is not affected by a priori differences between identifiable groups of test takers. Therefore, background and socioeconomic advantage have little impact on the scores from a fair test.

fairness Fairness implies that all children who are being tested have had an equal opportunity to have learned the material.

fidelity The accuracy of a test or measure for assessing a curriculum area, characteristic, or psychological trait. This is one of the primary components of test validity.

First International Mathematics Study (FIMS) The First International Mathematics Study was begun in 1964. One of the first of the international educational-outcomes-comparison studies.

First International Science Study (FISS) First International Mathematics Study compared the mathematics skills for students of 10 nations at the 4th-, 8th-, and 11th-grade levels.

fixed intelligence (g factor) model Based on the assumption that each individual's parameter for cognitive ability is set at conception and is composed of a central single factor of mental ability.

fluid intelligence An inherited type of intelligence that is needed to solve nonverbal problems that is independent of what is learned and isn't linked to experiences.

Flynn trend Assumption that cognitively demanding experiences serve as multipliers of the environmental effect on human ability. The increasing complexities of the Western world require different types of cognitive skills, a requirement that enhances the average cognitive ability with each generation. This effect is sometimes described as the generational effect.

formative evaluations Ongoing monitoring of the learners (e.g., integrating questions) during the teaching process. Measures or assessments that inform the ongoing instructional process.

free or reduced-cost lunch Subsidized and free lunches for children of families that are too poor to pay for them. In 2006–2007, a child of a single parent earning less than $24,421 per year would qualify.

Gantt chart Two-axis chart simultaneously depicting the timeline for a project and the tasks to be completed along the timeline. This chart can also identify the key personnel responsible for each of the tasks. Named for an American engineer, Henry Lawrence Gantt.

Gaussian normal curve Also known as the bell curve. The distribution of error around the average of a large set of independent observations.

general factor Factor analysis may identify a latent factor that accounts for almost all of the variance across the measures being analyzed. See *single-factor models of intelligence*.

gifted Educators consider gifted children to have special talents and high levels of academic aptitude (e.g., IQ ≥ 130).

grade equivalent score An ordinal scoring system that is purported to indicate the average grade level of students who have achieved at a particular level on an achievement test that is equal to what one particular test taker scored.

grade inflation A longitudinal trend for an upward shift in the average grades awarded.

grade point An ordinal number replacing a letter grade, usually from 4 = A to 0 = F. The points awarded can also be weighted to account for the level of difficulty of the course.

grade point average (GPA) The average obtained by dividing the total number of ordinal grade points earned by the total number of credits taken.

grade retention Grade retention occurs when a child is required to remain in the same grade for another school year while his or her peers move ahead to the next grade level.

grades The assignment of a value that is indicative of the quality and completeness of a student's work by the teacher.

grading by local norms Classroom teachers can convert scores from an achievement test into letter grades by assuming the distribution has the properties of a normal curve. This is known as "curving" the grades.

Gratz et al. v. Bollinger et al. Case for affirmative action involving admission decision involving the awarding of 20 bonus points to members of targeted minority groups. This case struck down this approach to affirmative admissions for minorities.

Great Society Part of a goal statement made by President Johnson during the State of the Union on January 4, 1965, which outlined a war on poverty.

Grutter v. Bollinger et al. Case involving law school admission policy that considered "soft variables" when accepting candidates for admission. This case made "holistic" admissions a possible approach to improving the diversity of membership in organizations.

guessing level The possibility of randomly guessing the correct answer for a select-type question.

halo effect The tendency for test graders to have their scoring influenced by prior knowledge of the students taking the test.

Harvard scholarships In 1933 the new president of Harvard University, James Bryant Conant, had his admissions dean, Henry Chauncey, develop a national scholarship program for Harvard. To do this, Chauncey selected the SAT, first developed at Princeton University, as the required measure for all students applying for the Harvard scholarships.

Head Start Program started by President Johnson in 1965, it was originally a summer program for children of poverty. It is now part of the Department of Health and Human Services, providing educational, nutritional, and developmental assistance to 925,000 preschool children from impoverished families a year.

Henderson mixed-model equation (HMME) Regression equation containing predictor variables, some of which have fixed levels while others have random variables. The equation contains both main effects (fixed and random) and interaction estimates of a random outcome effect.

hereditarian Belief that heredity plays a central role in all aspects of human nature and growth, including character traits, personality, and mental ability.

heteroscedastic Mathematical term for the condition that results when there is an inconsistent correlational relationship between two variables at the various levels of one of the variables. The result can be a pear-shaped scatterplot distribution between the two measures.

high-consensus items Test items designed to assess an area of knowledge where experts are in consensus agreement with the conceptual base being measured (e.g., language arts, basic arithmetic, and elementary reading).

high-stakes assessments Tests whose scores have significant consequences in the life of an individual.

Highly Objective Uniform State Standard of Evaluation (HOUSSE) Part of the No Child Left Behind Act designed to assure that all teachers are highly qualified.

highly qualified Description of teachers who have met exacting preparation standards as set by their state. The certification standards of the states must be first approved by the U.S. Department of Education.

histogram A representation of a frequency distribution having rectangular bars of different lengths. The height of each bar represents the score frequency on an ordinal variable.

history Alternate explanation for findings linked to the background environment and any ongoing unrelated activities that could cause changes.

holistic approach to admissions An admissions system approved at the outcome of *Grutter v. Bollinger et al.*, whereby the entire application file of a prospective student must be read and a multidimensional decision made as to admissions.

holistic assessment A "big picture" approach to evaluation that provides one ordinal score for the whole performance.

holistic rubric Scoring rubric that provides one "big picture" score for a performance assessment. It is used for evaluation by testing companies and with state assessments involving essay-writing tasks.

holistic scoring Scores reported as a single, comprehensive ordinal that represents multiple dimensions of a performance task, such as an essay. Holistic scores are assigned based on performance standards presented on a scoring rubric.

honor roll List of top achieving students based on grade point average.

honor society Academic organization open to the best achieving students in secondary schools and colleges.

honors track Sequence of advanced courses reserved for top achieving students in middle schools and high schools.

Hopwood et al. v. The State of Texas The result of a federal lawsuit in 1996 that struck down an affirmative admissions system that had been used with the Law School of the University of Texas.

Improving America's Schools Act President Clinton's legislative centerpiece for education, signed into law in 1994 as P.L. 103-382. This was the first step toward a federal requirement for standards-based testing programs.

Individual Family Service Plan (IFSP) Family-oriented plan that addresses the abilities and limitations of the child and provides a plan of action to remediate those areas of developmental delay.

Individualized Educational Plan (IEP) Plan required by law (IDEIA) for all disabled children that includes goals, services, accommodations, and description of how progress toward the goals will be measured. Required for every disabled child attending public school.

Individuals With Disabilities Educational Improvement Act (IDEIA) The 2004 reauthorization of the Education for All Handicapped Children Act (P.L. 94-142 [1974]), written to be more compatible with the mandates of the No Child Left Behind Act.

informal screening First step in the process of special education identification, usually carried out by teachers and counselors, involving observation, a review of records, collection of work samples, and parent conferencing.

Instructional Support Team (IST) A committee made up of the child's parents and all school personnel responsible for the child being referred for intervention. Formed to share information and address educational problems the child is having to map out strategies for the teacher and parent.

instrumentation Changes that will occur with the measuring technique and/or measuring instruments over time and by so doing pose an alternative explanation for the outcome.

intelligence test A test that provides a score estimating an individual's general mental ability by sampling performance on cognitive tasks.

internal consistency A reliability estimation based on one administration of a measure involving the intercorrelations of the individual items of the measure.

internal validity The linkage of the research question being asked and the research methods employed to answer the question. High internal validity implies that there are no viable alternative explanations for the outcome when the research methods are used.

International Adult Literacy Survey (IALS) Survey sponsored by the National Institute for Literacy of the U.S. Department of Education involving adults between the ages of 16 and 65 from 22 nations. First results were presented in 1998.

interpersonal An alternative explanation to the findings of an evaluation study that is caused by the personal needs and personality of participants (e.g., competition, need for approval, anxiety).

inter-rater reliability Statistical statement of the degree to which two or more raters (evaluators) agree when rating the same items.

interval data An ordered data set with each unit of measurement for the variable being equal and the distribution of scores scaled by reference to a standard score system.

IQ score Abbreviation for intelligence quotient. A score representing mental ability reported in a standardized form where the average is 100. Subscores of verbal IQ and mathematical IQ may be provided.

item analysis An analytical study of item quality before or after the test has been administered. Relates to test reliability as it makes it possible to build a bank of high-quality test items for use in future years.

item characteristic curve (ICC) This curve presents data from a cumulative distribution depicting the performance of test takers on a test item, showing the relationship between a latent characteristic (e.g., cognitive ability of the test takers) and success in answering the item.

item difficulty index The proportion of test takers who answered a test question correctly.

item discrimination index A value (max. = +1.00, min. = –1.00) describing the degree to which student success on an item matches the student level of success on the whole test. See *discrimination level*.

item response theory Both a theory and a statistical method used to link one or more latent traits of test takers (e.g., cognitive ability) to the probability that a test item will be answered correctly. It can be depicted using an item characteristic curve (ICC).

keyed answer The correct choice among the various alternative answers provided on a multiple choice question.

Kuder–Richardson–20 The statistical measure of reliability for tests scored using a binary (right–wrong) system. It is equivalent to a compilation of all possible permutations of split-half consistency (reliability) calculations.

Lake Woebegon effect Observation that most of the nation's school districts reported being "above average" on nationally normed achievement tests. Name taken from Garrison Keillor's mythical town of Lake Woebegon, where "all the children are above average."

latent component Hidden factors or elements that are necessary to fully conceptualize the meaning of what is evident from an evaluation. These can be derived by logic, clinical analysis, and/or by empirical statistical methods (e.g., the NFL believes that IQ is a latent component of being a good pro football player and tests the IQ of all rookies).

latent semantic analysis (LSA) Software written using a sophisticated form of artificial intelligence to grade essays and even recommend an overall letter grade.

level of precision The exactness of data. There are four broad categories used to designate the precision of data: Nominal, Ordinal, Interval, and Ratio.

level of proficiency An ordinal score describing the degree of a learner's achievement of the educational standards.

Likert scales Opinion-measuring scales composed of one or several simple declarative sentences about the topic being measured and statements (usually 5 or 7 in number) expressing a degree of agreement with the statements.

Limited English Proficient (LEP) Description used to identify children who have insufficient skill with the English language to succeed in an English-only classroom. Synonym is English Language Learner (ELL).

linear responsibility chart Graphic display connecting the tasks to be performed with the personnel responsible for their completion.

longitudinal data Data that are collected from a group of subjects over a long timeframe. Multiple tests or observations are made on the same group of subjects and analyzed for trends.

magic pencil A variation on "curving" where a histogram is created of all the students in terms of either average score or total points. The teacher then subjectively decides where to draw lines through the distribution to define the various letter grades.

magnet schools Open-enrollment schools offering students from a wide geographic area various advanced education opportunities. Originally their goal was to voluntarily reduce de facto racial segregation in urban communities.

mandated assessments Tests required by state regulation or law.

matching questions Select-type question that requires test takers to match a short list of stimulus words or terms with the words or terms on a second list.

matrix sampling Technique used to reduce testing time, involving the development of a complete set of test items to cover a topic and then sampling from that total collection to create several smaller tests. These are then given to different students. No student-to-student comparisons can be made.

maturation Normal ontogenetic processes that can produce changes in subjects over time, and by so doing be misread as an effect or outcome of the program being evaluated.

mean A measure of central tendency referred to as an arithmetic average of a set of scores.

measurement Procedure used to determine and document student's current status on a variable.

median The score equal to the center of a rank ordered data set. The 50th percentile.

mental age A measure of the difficulty level of problems that a person can solve expressed as a comparison to a reference sample of subjects of a particular age.

merit pay Extra compensation above and beyond the common pay scale in the form of a bonus awarded to teachers viewed as being highly effective.

merit scholars A scoring category from the PSAT indicating very high scores across the three tests of the battery (math, verbal, and writing). Awards for top scoring students are made by the National Merit Scholarship Corporation each year to over 10,000 students.

meritocracy The organization of a system in which rewards are provided to those shown through competition to be deserving of merit. Meritocracies are designed to reward talent, competence, and effort, not connections and social standing.

millennial generation Cohort including the 75 million Americans who were born between 1977 and 1998.

minimum competency test Assessment model in wide use during the 1970s and 1980s designed to assure that high school graduates could demonstrate a defined minimum level of knowledge and/or skills.

miracle of Texas A term used to describe the apparent improvement in the graduation rate and achievement scores for the children of Texas following state educational reforms, which later became part of the No Child Left Behind Act. Investigative reporters have expressed doubt about the reality of the "miracle."

mobility Extent to which children and their families move to different homes. The average American family moves once every five years.

mode The most frequently occurring score or outcome in a distribution of scores.

modified standards-based approach A method of grading by which the teacher starts with a grading scale that is fixed and divided into ordinal marks, which are presented as letters.

mortality Term used by Campbell and Stanley (1963) better expressed as mobility, to describe families moving into and out of communities.

multiple choice questions One of several select-type of questions that provides a stimulus question or statement and several alternative answers to select between.

multiple correlation The correlation between a variable and a weighted linear combination of predictor variables. This mathematical method is frequently referred to as multiple regression.

multiple-factor models of intelligence These mathematical models for human intelligence assume that there

exists a finite number of intellectual abilities of factors that can be independently identified and measured.

multiple-intelligences model (MI) Howard Gardner's model that focuses on eight unique human intelligences or evolutionary products that make interaction with the environment possible.

National Assessment of Educational Progress (NAEP) The NAEP is the only nationally representative test given continually since 1969.

National Association for the Education of Young Children (NAEYC) The professional association of teachers, professors, and researchers involved with the welfare and education of young children.

national certification The National Board for Professional Teaching Standards was conceived by Albert Shanker of the AFT and funded by the Carnegie Corporation in 1986. It provides an independent source of teacher-quality evaluations.

Nation's Report Card The National Assessment of Educational Progress is designed to provide a national picture of public schools and to present data on the status of American education. State-by-state comparisons were first published in 1994.

naturalistic methodology Evaluation method employing ethnographic data collection and analysis in an effort to capture the culture of the program or school being scrutinized.

No Child Left Behind A revamping of the Elementary and Secondary Education Act in 2002 (P.L. 107-100). The goal of the law was to "close the achievement gap with accountability, flexibility, and choice, so that no child is left behind."

nominal data Data from a variable that are expressed as a series of names or descriptors that are devoid of a mathematical measurement scale.

non-content factor Report card grade factors that go beyond the achievement of academic content and may include student motivation, effort level, cooperation, neatness, and self-control.

norm-based scoring system The assumption of a Gaussian normal curve underlies this grading technique, commonly referred to as "curving."

norm referenced The interpretation of the meaning of a test score is based on how a sample of other people performs on the same measure. An individual's score is then expressed in terms of a relative standing as compared with others.

norm-referenced test Test that reports scores to test takers in terms of their relative performance compared to a reference sample of subjects who took the test previously.

normal curve equivalent (NCE) A standardized transformation of normally distributed raw score data having a distribution with a mean of 50 and a standard deviation of 21.06.

normative group A distribution of measurement scores from a group of subjects with known characteristics (age, sex, grade in school, etc.) to whom a person's performance may be compared.

norms Tables or other devices used to convert an individual's test score to a norm-referenced test score.

novelty The likelihood that changes in the environment per se, not the treatment effect, produce what appears to be an effect or outcome with the variable being measured.

objective test A test that is designed to minimize all subjective aspects to scoring. Usually a select format test such as a multiple choice test.

ogive A graph of a frequency distribution curve in which the frequencies are cumulative.

on-line report cards Internet-based system for reporting student academic progress interfaced with a comprehensive system for teacher– parent online communication.

out of level testing Testing in which all of the items are very difficult to differentiate among the best students. Used when identifying those with the highest level of academic ability.

parameter A constant linked to a statistical value that is determined by an arbitrarily selected position on a statistical probability curve.

pearson Correlation Coefficient A statistical expression of the degree to which two variables co-vary. The minimum correlation is 0 and the maximum is ±1.

percentile Part out of 100. A 100th part of any group or set of data or objects.

performance-based assessments Assessments that measure both the skills and knowledge acquired by students and require students to demonstrate critical-thinking and complex problem-solving skills.

performance level Student outcomes presented on a four- or five-point scale ranging from the performance level "below proficient" to the highest performance level, "advanced proficiency."

performance test A measure involving the learner in creative tasks or problems requiring the application of learned skills and acquired knowledge.

personological factors Variables that are part of the psychological state of the individual and as such are considered attributes that resist experimental modification (e.g., mental ability, hand dominance, and reaction time).

pervasive developmental disability Psychiatric diagnostic classification for children involving stereotyped behavior, interests, and activities. Often paired with low IQ and poor communication skills.

phenomenological strategies Methodology in which data are derived from the eidetic recollections and mental reflection by subjects.

phonemic awareness Having knowledge of the link between small units of speech and the corresponding sounds represented by the letters of the alphabet.

phonics The connection between the sounds that result from the blending of phonemes (letters) together into word units. Also called the sound–spelling correspondence.

physical disability Loss of the ability to move and/or locomote owing to paralysis, tonic spasms, or severe pain.

placement decision A data-based decision for placing a student into the appropriate level for instruction by assessing the learner's level of previous achievement.

point–biserial correlation Correlation coefficient that can be used to express the relationship between how well students perform on a single test item (correct vs. wrong) and scores on the entire test. A method for determining the quality of an individual test item.

point system A variation on the modified-standards approach for grading in which everything (e.g., homework, tests, projects) that goes on in the classroom is assigned a point value (including possible "extra credit points").

polytomous model The expansion of the Rasch model for studying the response pattern of subjects on test items in which there are several possible answers to each question, and the ability of the subject is used as a defining variable.

portfolios A compendium of data sources documenting the growth of a student's skills and knowledge over time in an area.

positivistic paradigm Evaluation data derived by use of objective instruments and structured questioning. All data collected are verifiable and assumed to be real.

practical intelligence One of three mental abilities that make up Sternberg's proposed triarchic model of mental ability.

prediction equation A correlational equation used to predict future outcomes based on the careful examination of previous relationships.

predictive validity The ability of a test or measure to estimate how well a person will perform a task. High predictive validity implies excellent predictions while low predictive validity indicates there is much error in the predictions.

prereading strategies Strategies that support reading comprehension and include asking pre-questions about the title of the passage to be read, thinking about the meaning of cues and prompts, doing an overview of the passage, and examining the passage's graphics.

Primary Mental Abilities (PMA) L. L. Thurstone's Primary Mental Abilities model of intelligence, which is composed of seven unique factors: word fluency, verbal comprehension, spatial visualization, number facility, associative memory, reasoning, and perceptual speed.

principle component A form of statistical analysis that builds a core structure or factor from a series of measures that subjects have taken. The first statistical model of mental ability proposed by Charles Spearman (g factor) used principle component analysis.

process portfolio A portfolio of student work that includes periodic statements by the student that are self-reflections on the learning process as perceived by the student.

Programme for International Student Assessment (PISA) Comparison program sponsored by the Organization for Economic Co-operation and Development that is administered to 10th grade students every 3 years.

progress reports Term for teacher–parent communication replaced in education jargon by the term *report card*.

prompt The target statement about which students must write essays on a writing test.

psychoeducational assessment A multifaceted assessment that involves clinical observations of the child, interviews with parents, and a full range of specialized tests designed to give a full picture of the child.

pull-out program The removal of special students from the regular class schedule to provide them with a specialized educational offering. Commonly done with children enrolled in a school's program for the gifted.

qualitative research Research method assuming multiple, dynamic realities that can only be understood in context.

quantitative research paradigm Philosophy of research assuming the existence of a stable reality that is scientifically measurable and in which findings are generalizable.

randomly selected Selection of the members or elements to be included in a sample in such a way that each element of the original population has an equal chance of inclusion.

range The distance (as measured in score points) between the highest and lowest scores on a distribution. Found by simple subtraction of the lowest score from the highest.

Rasch model One of several statistical models developed by Goerg Rasch (1901–1980) for the analysis of test item functioning yields outcomes similar to those from the item response theory (IRT). In many presentations the two terms are used together.

rater drift The tendency for the evaluation scores assigned by a rater to become higher after evaluating many performance assessments.

ratio data A mathematical method for scaling data that employs real numbers of equal unit size. It includes the value 0 and can also include negative numbers.

raw score The number of questions answered correctly on a test or assessment. This number may be corrected for guessing, but no other statistical transformation will have occurred with raw score data.

readiness Mentally and/or physically prepared for a learning experience. Usually refers to readiness to enter school.

recentered A new normative group was employed in 1996 to provide the scoring basis for the SAT I. This revision was the first since the test was standardized in 1941 and reflected the greater diversity of the population of students applying to college in the 1990s.

receptive language The comprehension of spoken language.

referral The process of initiating a request for the further evaluation of a child in school. Can be initiated by teachers, administrators, and educational specialists.

regression toward the mean Effect describing the statistical tendency for extremely low and extremely high scores to become closer to the group mean when the subjects are retested.

reliability A statement of the stability and/or consistency of the test scores from the administration of a measure.

residual scores With test data, residual scores are the product of a subtraction of one score from a second test score from the same subjects. Residual scores have very low reliability.

responses The reaction of the student to a question or structured stimuli presented by the teacher as part of an assessment. See *answer*.

restructuring Four years of low student scores on the NCLB-mandated tests triggers a series of changes including transferring members of the teaching staff and possible firing of school administrators, or even the closing of the school.

rubric An ordinal sequence of qualitative ranks with definitions and examples for each level that can be used to evaluate performance assessments.

sample of convenience Nonrandom sample of subjects chosen because the researcher had easy assess for collecting data from them.

sampling inadequacy Sampling inadequacy occurs when the items of a measure do not represent an appropriate collection of what is being measured. It can also used to refer to a violation of a statistical assumption needed to create subsets within a large set of data.

SAT II Newest edition of the test published by the College Entrance Examination Board and developed, scored, and transcribed by the Educational Testing Service.

scatterplots Two-dimensional (linear coordinate) presentation of the simultaneous outcome for two variables measured on one group of subjects.

scholastic aptitude Indicates how much a child can be expected to learn. This is usually measured using a test of cognitive ability.

school psychologist Educational professional who is certified by a state education department to provide for the mental health of school students.

school report card One mandate of the No Child Left Behind Act requires that each school create and publish a report card showing the average achievement levels, attendance, and graduation rate for students.

score gap Significant mean differences found between groups when scores are disaggregated.

scoring guide Used to improve the scoring reliability of an essay test. It consists of the points that must be covered and the relative value assigned for each of them on the answers to an essay question. See *analytical rubric*.

scoring rubric Written criteria, organized as an ordinal scale, used for evaluating the quality of extended-response (essay) questions and performance tasks.

section 504 Section of the Rehabilitation Act of 1973 requiring that public schools provide the support services needed to make public education available to all children with disabilities.

select-type questions Objective test questions that require the test taker to respond to a prompt (question or stem) by selecting which of several answers is correct (e.g., true–false format, multiple choice, and matching).

selected-response format Testing formats that include true–false, matching, and various permutations of the multiple choice question.

selection Average score differences between groups that may occur when the subjects selected and assigned to each group are not equivalent prior to the study.

selection ratio The ratio between the number of applicants and the available admissions positions. This ratio can be used to set the difficulty level for a measure that will be employed to select those to be admitted.

sensitivity review An ethical step taken by test publishers prior to the publication of a new measure or evaluation. The step involves using a panel of experts representing various identifiable groups and subdivisions within the general population to evaluate individual test items for possible item fairness or bias problems.

showcase portfolio A portfolio of only the very best products produced by the student.

single-factor models of intelligence A mathematical model of human intelligence based on a central core factor of ability known as the "g," or general, factor. Charles Spearman used mathematical analysis on the scores from many measures of mental ability to identify one unitary factor of ability.

skew Asymmetry in a distribution of scores. Distribution is said to be negatively skewed when most scores fall on the high end of the distribution and positively skewed when most scores fall on the low end of the distribution.

Spearman Correlation Coefficient A method for expressing the amount of concordance shared by two ordinal measures on a group of subjects.

special education Educational programs designed to meet the specific learning needs of children with disabilities. Programs are mandated under the Individuals With Disabilities Educational Improvement Act of 2004 (P.L. 108-446).

special-needs children Children who have been identified as having a specific disability in one or more of the following areas: cognitive, physical, and sensory.

stability The reliability that demonstrates that the scores obtained on a measure by a group of subjects will be correlated with a retest using the same measure and subjects at a later time.

stakeholders People within an organization who perceive themselves as possibly being affected by a study or evaluation of that organization.

standard deviation The square root of variance. The square root of the squared individual variations of scores from the mean score.

standard error of measurement A statistic used to estimate the probable range within which a person's true score on a test falls. The standard deviation of scores obtained around an individual's true score.

standard score A derived test score expressed in deviation units indicating how far the score is from the mean score of the group.

standardized scoring Scoring method involving turning every test and other measure into a standard deviation score (z-score). Each z-score is then multiplied by the appropriate weighting factor before it is added to develop a grade for each student.

standardized test Factor analysis may identify a latent factor that accounts for almost all of the variance across the measures being analyzed. See *single factor models of intelligence*.

standards-based assessments High-stakes tests with close links to both the curriculum and the approved standards for learning. These tests are scored showing the extent to which the student reached the standard for achievement.

standards-based grades An evaluation of student performance based on a measure of an approved standard for learning.

standards gap The different rigor required by the achievement standards set for the children of different schools.

Stanford–Binet Scales Highly reliable test constructed as a measure of the human intellect as defined by the Cattell–Horn–Carroll (CHC) model of mental ability.

stanine A score system that divides the area under the Gaussian normal curve into nine parts. Each of the seven center parts is one-half of a standard deviation in width. From *sta*ndard *nine* (*stanine*).

STARS Nebraska's School-based, Teacher-led Assessment and Reporting System, which combines local assessments with commercially available instruments.

statistical bias This is evident when there is a systematic under- or overestimation of a select group of subjects on a test or other measurement.

stem The stimulus statement or question that frames the task on select-type questions, including multiple choice questions.

stereotype threat The extra stress felt by minority students facing high-states standardized tests. This stress is related to dominant stereotypical expectation held for those students.

structure of intellect model (SI) J. P. Guilford's model based on the identification of three universal dimensions for all mental abilities: operations, contents, and products. On each of these dimensions are a number of

subcategories that, when taken together, make it possible to identify 180 unique mental abilities.

student response pads A new approach to formative assessment using an interactive computer system, "classroom clickers," to give teachers real-time formative assessment data during instruction.

summary assessment (test) A test or examination taken by students following instruction used to provide a statement of how much was achieved by individual students after they were taught.

summative data analysis The statistical analysis and summary of evaluation outcome data. This analysis focuses on the outcomes of the project being evaluated.

supply-type questions Test questions requiring the test taker provide the answer to a question (e.g., completion questions, fill-in questions, and essay [extended-response format] questions).

table of specifications Two-dimensional blueprint for a test. Dimensions are the content and level of cognition the test items will require. This approach assures the measure will have content validity.

tacit knowledge The link between triarchic intelligence and real-world success as proposed by Robert Sternberg.

Teach for America program Liberal arts graduates from highly selective colleges and universities attend five weeks of summer classes in preparation for having their own classroom in the fall. They must contract to work a minimum of two years in the rural or inner-city school to which they are assigned.

teaching "for the test" Teaching the knowledge base and cognitive skills that make up the state's learning standards.

teaching "to the test" The direct instruction of students in preparation for a high-stakes test by teaching specific items from released test files.

test battery Test battery refers to a series of subtests that make up a larger measurement device. For example, the Armed Service Test Battery is composed of five separate subtests: Math Skills Test, Reading Skills Test, Mechanical Comprehension Test, Spatial Apperception Test, and Aviation and Nautical Information Test.

test bias This occurs when the test scores from an individual or identifiable group consistently under- or overestimate the capability or knowledge of that group or individual.

test–retest reliability The correlation between the scores from two sequential administrations of a test to one group of subjects, providing an estimation of test stability.

Third International Mathematics and Science Study (TIMSS) A parallel set of science and mathematics achievement surveys published beginning in 1995.

three-factor model of intelligence Robert Sternberg and E. L. Thorndike's model based on the identification of the three factors: practical intelligence, analytical intelligence, and creative intelligence.

triarchic model of intelligence Sternberg's conceptualization of mental ability as being composed of three elements: analytical, creative, and practical intelligences.

Troops to Teacher program (TTT) Fast-track program for providing teacher certification to returning military personnel. The TTT program was begun under the Clinton administration and expanded by President Bush under the NCLB Act in 2002.

true–false question Select-type item that provides a stimulus consisting of a statement and asks whether that statement is true or false.

true score An observed score plus or minus some amount of error.

University of California Regents v. Bakke The first challenge to affirmative action in admissions. This case struck down the use of racial set-asides in the admission process for a medical school.

upward drift The tendency for the anchor items of a test to appear to be less difficult on the subsequent annual test administrations. This results in ever-higher levels being set for the cut scores.

validity A statement of both the appropriateness of the test and its components and of the veracity of the test scores and their interpretations.

validity threat of testing When the subjects of an evaluation are tested sequentially, one after another, the test materials and/or test administrator may change over time and practice, thus influencing the outcome.

value added An assessment approach that focuses on the change that has occurred for each individual over a period of time. Seen as a method of evaluating growth and change within individuals.

value-added evaluation A data-driven longitudinal evaluation of schools, educators, and students by charting the growth of individuals in the educational context of the school.

variable A factor, conceptual entity, characteristic, or attribute that is likely to vary between individuals and/or within individuals over time.

variance The average of the sum of the squared deviations of individual scores from the mean.

war on poverty Sobriquet used by the administration of President Johnson to describe his domestic policy initiatives. One of these initiatives was the ESEA (1965).

Wechsler Intelligence Scale for Children (WISC) The most widely used intelligence tests in schools, having 11 subtests to measure ability along two major factors: verbal IQ and performance IQ.

Wechsler Preschool and Primary Scales of Intelligence, 3rd ed. (WPPSI) Highly reliable intelligence test battery used to assess the developing cognition of young children.

weighted combinations Combining marks and test grades by multiplying each by a weight that is representative of each evaluation's relative importance. This combination can then be used to produce a progress report grade.

weighted grades The number of grade points awarded for each course is differentiated according to the difficulty level of the course. Thus, Advanced Placement courses earn more grade points than do basic courses.

wrap-around assessments Assessments designed by local school systems in Nebraska to assess the standards not measured by the commercial achievement tests selected under the STARS system.

REFERENCES

Abedi, J., Hofstetter, C. H., & Lord, C. (2004). Assessment accommodations for English language learners: Implications for policy-based empirical research. *Review of Educational Research, 74*(1), 1–28.

Accountability Division. (2004). *Arizona's instrument to measure standards* [Special Education Report]. Phoenix, AZ: Arizona Department of Education. Retrieved on January 19, 2005, from http://www.ade.state.az.us/researchpolicy/sat9sped/aims

Achieve, Inc. (2005, February). *Rising to the challenge: Are high school graduates prepared for college and work?* Washington, DC: Peter D. Hart Research Associates. Retrieved February 7, 2005, from http://www.achieve.org/node/548

ACT (1997). *ACT assessment: Technical manual*. Iowa City: Author.

ACT (2004). Are high school grades inflated? *College Readiness: Issues in College Readiness.* Retrieved April 13, 2005, from http://www.act.org/path/policy/pdf/issues.pdf

Adams, G. R., & Ryan, B. A. (2000, June). *A longitudinal analysis of family relationships and children's school achievement in one and two parent families.* Quebec: Human Resources Development.

Ainsworth, L., & Viegut, D. (2006). *Common formative assessments: How to connect standards-based instruction and assessment.* Thousand Oaks, CA: Corwin Press.

Alexander, K. L., Entwisle, D. R., & Olsen, L. S. (2007). Lasting consequences of the summer learning gap. *American Sociological Review, 72*(2), 167–180.

Algozzine, B., Eaves, R. C., Mann, L., & Vance, H. R. (1988). Slosson Full-Range Intelligence Test: Normative/Technical Manual. Los Angeles: Western Psychological Corporation.

Alvarado, M. (2006, December 10). Swimming upstream in the mainstream. *Record* [North Jersey]. Retrieved February 27, 2007, from http://www.northjersey.com/

American Association for Colleges of Teacher Education. (1999). *Teacher education pipeline IV: Schools, colleges, and departments of education.* Washington, DC: Author.

American Educational Research Association (AERA) (2004a). Closing the gap: High achievement for students of color. *Research Points: Essential Information for Educational Policy, 2*(3). Author.

American Educational Research Association (AERA) (2004b). English language learners: Boosting academic achievement. *Research Points: Essential Information for Educational Policy, 2*(1). Author.

American Evaluation Association. (2005). *About us.* Retrieved August 22, 2005, from http://www.eval.org/News/news.htm

American National Standards Institute. (1995). *The program evaluation standards*. Washington, DC: Author.

American Psychiatric Association (APA). (1994). *Diagnostic and statistical manual of mental disorders* (4th ed.). Washington, DC: Author.

Americans With Disabilities Act of 1990 (P.L.101-576, 1990), 42 U.S.C.A. § 12101 *et seq.*

Amrein, A. L., & Berliner, D. C. (2002). *The impact of high-stakes tests on student academic performance: An analysis on NAEP results in states with high-stakes tests and ACT, SAT and AP test results in states with high school graduation exams.* Tempe, AZ: Educational Policy Studies Laboratory. Retrieved January 14, 2004, from http://edpolicylab.org

Anderson, L. W., & Krathwohl, D. R. (2001). *A taxonomy for learning, teaching, and assessing: A revision of Bloom's taxonomy of educational objectives.* New York: Longman.

Anton, H., Kolman, B., & Averbach, B. (1988). *Mathematics with applications for the management, life, and social sciences.* New York: Harcourt Brace Jovanovich.

Apgar, V. (1953). A proposal of a new method of evaluation of the newborn infant. *Current Researches in Anesthesia & Analgesia, 32,* 261–267.

Aratani, L. (2005, August 25). Group seeks to end gifted education. *Washington Post.* Retrieved August 27, 2005, from http://www.washingtonpost.com

Archer, J. (2005, April 13). R.I. downplays tests as route to diploma. *Education Week*. Retrieved April 13, 2005, from http://www.edweek.org/ew/articles/2005/04/13/

Arenson, K. W. (2004, April 18). Is it grade inflation, or are students just smarter? *New York Times*, p. WK2.

Arenson, K. W. (2005, March 22). Faculty panel at Cal faults way to pick Merit scholars. *New York Times*, p. A14.

Armbruster, B. B., Lehr, F., & Osborn, J. (2003). *Put reading first: The research building blocks for teaching children to read*. Washington, DC: National Reading Panel, Office of Educational Research and Improvement. Retrieved July 2, 2005, from http://www.nationalreadingpanel.org

Aronauer, R. (2005, September 30). Princeton's war on grade inflation drops the number of A's. *Chronicle of Higher Education, 52*(6), p. 47.

Ashcraft, M. H. (1995). Cognitive psychology and simple arithmetic: A review and summary of new directions. *Mathematical Cognition, 1*(1), 3–34.

Aspey, S., & Colby, C. (2005, May 10). Spellings announces new special education guidelines, details workable, "common-sense" policy to help states implement No Child Left Behind [Press release]. Washington, DC: U.S. Department of Education. Retrieved November 28, 2006, from http://www.ed.gov/print/news/pressreleases/2005/05/05/05102005.html

Associated Press (2005, July 25). *Migrant workers, children savor summer school*. cnn.com. Retrieved July 26, 2005, from http://www.cnn.com/2005/EDUCATION/ 07/25/school.on.the.move.ap/index.html

Atherton, J. S. (2005). *Learning and teaching: Bloom's taxonomy* [Electronic version]. Retrieved November 26, 2006, from http://www.learningandteaching.info/learning/bloomtax.htm

Ayers, K. (2005, December 14). Foreign classes leave their mark: Districts face hard issue of how to translate immigrants' transcripts. *Dallas Morning News*. Retrieved November 26, 2006, from http://www.dallasnews.com/sharedcontent/dws/dn/education/stories/121405dnccoforeigngrades.121a1297.html

Babu, S., & Mendro, R. (2003, April). *Teacher accountability: HLM-based teacher effectiveness indices in the investigation of teacher effects on student achievement in a state assessment program*. Paper presented at the annual meeting of the American Educational Research Association, Chicago, IL.

Bailey, P. (2007). Students get prizes for taking science test. *Miami Herald*. Retrieved January 29, 2007, from http://www.miami.com/mld/miamiherald/

Baker, B. D., & Cooper, B. S. (2005). Do principals with stronger academic backgrounds hire better teachers? Policy implications for improving high-poverty schools. *Educational Administration Quarterly, 41*(3), 449–479.

Baker, D. P., Fabrega, R., Galindo, C., & Mishook, J. (2004). Instructional time and national achievement: Cross-national evidence. *Prospects, 34*(3), 311–334.

Baldi, S., Perie, M., Skidmore, D., Greenberg, E., Hahn, C., & Nelson, D. (2001). *What democracy means to ninth graders: U.S. results from the international IEA Civic Education Study*. (Statistical Analysis Report, NCES 2001-096). Washington, DC: National Center for Educational Statistics.

Baldwin, D., & Wylie, E. (2004). Comprehensive testing program, 4th ed. New York: Educational Records Bureau.

Ballantyne, P. F. (2002). *Psychology, society, and ability testing (1859–2002): Transformative alternatives to mental Darwinism and interactionism*. Toronto, Canada: York University. Retrieved January 25, 2005, from http://www.comnet.ca/pballan/Index.html

Barkley, R. A. (1998). *Attention-deficit hyperactivity disorder: A handbook for diagnosis and treatment* (2nd ed.). New York: Guilford.

Barton, P. E. (2004). Why does the gap persist? *Educational Leadership, 62*(3), 9–13.

Basken, P. (2006, March 29). States have more schools falling behind. *Washington Post*. Retrieved March 29, 2006, from http://www.washingtonpost.com

Baum, H. I. (2005). *Using student progress to evaluate teachers: A primmer on value-added models* (Policy Information Perspective, Document 6463). Princeton, NJ: ETS.

Bello, M. (2007, August 28). Later school starts gain popularity. *USA Today*. Retrieved September 1, 2007, from http://www.usatoday.com/news/education/2007-08-28-school_N.htm

Belluck, P. (2006, February 5). And for perfect attendance, Johnny gets . . . a car. *New York Times*. Retrieved September 15, 2007, from http://www.nytimes.com

Ben-Shakhar, G., & Sinai, Y. (1991). Gender differences in multiple-choice tests: The role of differential guessing tendencies. *Journal of Educational Measurement, 28*(1), 23–35.

Bennett, C. I., McWhorter, L. M., & Kukendall, J. A. (2006). Will I ever teach? Latino and African American students' perspectives on PRAXIS I. *American Educational Research Journal, 43*(3), 531–575.

Bennett, G. K., Seashore, H. G., & Wesman, A. G. (1992). Differential Aptitude Tests, Fifth Edition. San Antonio, TX: Psychological Corporation, Harcourt Assessment.

Bennett, S., & Kalish, N. (2006, June 19). No more teachers, lots of books. *New York Times.* Retrieved June 20, 2006, from http://www.nytimes.com/2006/06/19/opinion/19bennett.html

Bennett, W. L. (1992). *The devaluing of America: The fight for our culture and our children.* New York: Summit.

Benton, J. (2006, September 2). Cheating: It's in the numbers. *Dallas Morning News.* Retrieved September 7, 2006, from http://www.dallasnews.com/cgi-bin/bi/gold_print.cgi

Berger, J. (2007, February 7). More help for the struggling, less for the gifted. *New York Times,* p. A17.

Bergstrom, B. (1998). [Review of the *Revised PSB health occupations aptitude examination*]. In J. C. Impara & B. S. Plake (Eds.), *The thirteenth mental measurements yearbook* (pp. 845–847). Lincoln, NE: Buros Institute on Mental Measurements.

Berliner, D. C. (1997, February). Manufacturing a crisis in education [Keynote address]. Eastern Educational Research Association, Hilton Head Island, SC.

Berliner, D. C. (2004, March/April). If the underlying premise for No Child Left Behind is false, how can that act solve our problems? (Occasional Research Paper # 6). The Iowa Academy of Education. Retrieved June 23, 2005, from http://www.finefoundation.org/Welcome.html

Berliner, D. C. (2005). The near impossibility of testing for teacher quality. *Journal of Teacher Education, 56*(3), 205–213.

Berliner, D. C., & Biddle, B. J. (1995). *The manufactured crisis: Myths, fraud, and the attack on America's public schools.* Cambridge, MA: Perseus Books.

Berliner, D. C., & Nichols, S. L. (2007, March 14). High-stakes testing is putting the nation at risk. *Education Week, 26*(27), pp. 48, 36.

Beserik, D. L. (2000). *Teacher beliefs and practices as they relate to the implementation of the Pennsylvania System of School Assessment.* Unpublished doctoral dissertation, University of Pittsburgh.

Betebenner, D. W., & Sang, Y. (2007, April). *Reference growth charts for educational outcomes.* Paper presented during the annual meeting of the American Educational Research Association, Chicago, IL.

Bhatt, S. (2005, January 3). Schools struggle to reduce high teacher turnover. *Seattle Times.* Retrieved January 29, 2006, from http://seattletimes.com

Bhola, D. S., Impara, J. C., & Buckendahl, C. W. (2003). Aligning tests with state's content standards: Methods and issues. *Educational Measurement Issues and Practices, 22*(3), 21–29.

Birk, L. (2005, May/June). Grade inflation: What's really behind all those A's? *Harvard Education Letter.* Retrieved June 5, 2005, from http://www.edletter.org/past/issues/2000-jf/grades.shtml

Birnbaum, R. (Producer), & Robbins, B. (Director). (2004). *Perfect score* [Motion picture]. United States: Paramount Pictures.

Black, S. (2006). The right size school [Electronic version]. *American School Board Journal, 193*(4). Retrieved March 23, 2007, from http://www.asbj.com/2006/04/0406research.html

Blackwell, J. (1996). *On brave old Army team: The cheating scandal that rocked the nation: West Point, 1951.* New York: Reed Business Information.

Bloom, B. S., et al. (Eds.) (1956). *Taxonomy of educational objectives: The classification of educational goals: Handbook I, cognitive domain.* New York: David McKay & Co.

Bloor, E. (2004). *Story time.* Orlando, FL: Harcourt Children's Books.

Bluebello, L. (2003). *Prediction of student performance on the Pennsylvania System of School Assessment at the fifth grade.* Unpublished doctoral dissertation, Widener University.

Boe, E. E., & Shin, S. (2005). Is the United States really losing the international horse race in academic achievement? *Phi Delta Kappan, 86*(9), 688–695.

Boeree, C. G. (1999–2000). *Wilhelm Wundt and William James.* Unpublished manuscript, Shippensburg University of Pennsylvania. Retrieved January 26, 2005, from http://www.ship.edu/~cgboeree/wundtjames.html

Booher-Jennings, J. (2005). "Below the bubble": Educational triage and the Texas accountability system. *American Educational Research Journal, 42*(2), 231–268.

Borja, R. R. (2007, February, 21). Nebraska tangles with U.S. over testing. *Education Week, 26*(24), p. 34.

Borman, G. (2007, May). *Multiyear summer school.* [Research summary]. Madison, WI: Wisconsin Center for Educational Research. Retrieved May 7, 2007, from http://www.wcer.wisc.edu/news/coverStories/multiyear_summer_school.php

Borman, G. D., Slavin, R. E., Cheung, A. C. K., Chamberlain, A. M., Madden, N. A., & Chambers, B. (2007). Final reading outcomes of the national randomized field trial of Success for All. *American Educational Research Association, 44*(3), 701–731.

Borsuk, A. J. (2006, June 1). State getting off easy on No Child law, report says [Electronic version]. *Milwaukee Journal Sentinel.* Retrieved June 2, 2006, from http://www.jsonline.com/story/index .aspx?id=430666&format=print

Borzekowski, D. L. G., & Robinson, T. N. (2005). The remote, the mouse, and the No. 2 pencil. *Archives of Pediatrics and Adolescent Medicine, 159*(7), 607–613.

Boudett, K. P., Murnane, R. J., City, E., & Moody, L. (2005). Teaching educators how to use student assessment data to improve instruction. *Phi Delta Kappan, 86*(9), 700–706.

Bowler, M. (2004, July 22). Special-education students struggle to pass state exams. *Baltimore Sun* [Electronic version]. Retrieved July 29, 2004, from http://www.baltimoresun.com/news/education/ balmd.msa22ju122,0,7929776.story?c

Boyd, B. (2007, April). *NCLB: A business perspective.* Paper presented during the annual meeting of the National Council on Measurement in Education, Chicago, IL.

Bradley, R. H. (1985). [Test review of the *Gesell school readiness test*]. From J. V. Mitchell Jr. (Ed.), *The ninth mental measurements yearbook* [Electronic version]. Retrieved January 29, 2005, from the Buros Institute's Test Reviews Online Web site: http://www.unl.edu/buros

Braun, H., & Wainer, H. (2007). Value-added modeling. *Handbook of statistics, 26* (pp. 867–892). Amsterdam, Netherlands: Elsevier.

Braun, H. I. (2005) Using student progress to evaluate teachers: A primer on value-added models [Policy information perspective]. Princeton, NJ: ETS. Retrieved August 24, 2007, from http://www.ets.org/ valueaddedmodels.html

Bridgeman, B. (1980). Generality of a "fast" or "slow" test-taking style across a variety of cognitive tasks. *Journal of Educational Measurement, 17*(3), 211–217.

Bridgeman, B., & Wendler, C. (2004). Characteristics of minority students who excel on the SAT and in the classroom (Policy Information Report). Princeton, NJ: Educational Testing Service.

Brock, K. C. (2006, March 16). Are they ready to go? Some experts believe starting school late can give kids an edge. *Southern Illinoisan.* Retrieved March 24, 2006, from http://www.southernillinoisan.com/

Brookhart, S. M. (1991). Grading practices and validity. *Educational Measurement: Issues and Practice, 10*(1), 35–36.

Brookhart, S. M. (1994). Teacher's grading: Practice and theory. *Applied Measurement, 7,* 279–301.

Brookhart, S. M. (2004). *Grading.* New York: Pearson Education.

Brookhart, S. M. (2005). The quality of local district assessments used in Nebraska's School-based, Teacher-led Assessment and Reporting System (STARS). *Educational Measurement: Issues and Practice, 24*(2),14–21.

Brown v. Board of Education, 347 U.S. 483 (1954).

Brown, D., & Resseger, J. (2005, November 28). *Ten moral concerns in the implementation of the No Child Left Behind Act* [A statement of the National Council of Churches Committee on Public Education and Literacy]. New York: National Council of Churches USA. Retrieved March 30, 2006, from http://www.NCCCUSA.org/pdfs/LeftBehind.pdf

Brown, S. R., Claudet, J. G., & Olivarez, A. (2002). Investigating organizational dimensions of middle school curricular leadership: Linkages to school effectiveness. *Research in Middle Level Education* [Electronic version]. Retrieved July 22, 2005, from http://www.nmsa.org

Brown, T. E. (2001). *Brown attention-deficit disorder scales for children and adolescents.* San Antonio, TX: Harcourt Assessment Division, Psychological Corporation.

Brown, W. (1910). Some experiment results in the correlation of mental abilities. *British Journal of Psychology, 3,* 296–322.

Brunsman, B. A. (2005). [Test review of the *DIBELS: Dynamic indicators of early literacy skills, sixth edition*]. From R. A. Spies & B. S. Plake (Eds.), *The sixteenth mental measurements yearbook* [Electronic version]. Retrieved July 2, 2005, from the Buros Institute's Test Reviews Online Web site: http://www.unl.edu/buros

Buchanan, J. (2002). Ignoble motivation: Arguments of opponents to the grading system. Unpublished manuscript, SUNY New Paltz. Retrieved June 26, 2005, from http://aboutime.strongverb.net/papers.html

Buhs, E. S., Ladd, G. W., & Herald, S. L. (2006). Peer exclusion and victimization: Processes that mediate the relation between peer group rejection and children's classroom engagement and achievement. *Journal of Educational Psychology, 98*(1), 1–13.

Bukowiecki, E. M. (2007). Teaching children how to read. *Kappa Delta Pi Record, 43*(2), 58–65.

Bunium-Murray Productions (Producer). (2005). *The Scholar* [Television series]. New York: NBC-Universal.

Buoye, A. J. (2004). *Capitalizing on the extra curriculum: Participation, peer influence, and academic achievement.* Unpublished doctoral dissertation, Notre Dame University.

Burke, K. (2005). *How to assess authentic learning.* Thousand Oaks, CA: Corwin Press.

Burney, M. (2006, December 20). New Jersey flags 40 schools for test scores. *Philadelphia Inquirer.* Retrieved December 20, 2006, from http://www.philly.com/mld/philly/news/

Burns, M. K., MacQuarrie, L. L., & Campbell, D. T. (1998). The difference between curriculum-based assessment and curriculum-based measurement: A focus on purpose and result [Electronic version]. *NASP Communiqué, 27*(6). Retrieved June 28, 2004, from http://www.nasponline.org/publications/cq276cba.html

Burson, K. C., & Wright, R. J. (2003, February). *What do state assessments really measure?* Paper presented at the annual meeting of the Eastern Educational Research Association, Hilton Head, SC.

Burt, C. (1955). The evidence for the concept of intelligence. *British Journal of Educational Psychology, 25,* 159–177.

Burt, C. (1958). The inheritance of ability. *American Psychologist, 13*(3), 1–15.

Bush, G. W. (2003, September 9). *President Bush discusses the "No Child Left Behind Act" in Florida* [Press release]. Retrieved June 5, 2005, from http://www.whitehouse.gov/news/releases/2003/09/print/20030909-3html

Camilli, G., & Monfils, L. F. (2004). Test scores and equity. In W. A. Firestone, R. Y. Schorr, & L. F. Monfils (Eds.), *The ambiguity of teaching to the test: Standards, assessment, and educational reform* (pp. 143–157). Mahwah, NJ: Lawrence Erlbaum Associates.

Campbell, D. T., & Stanley, J. C. (1963). Experimental and quasi-experimental designs for research on teaching. In N. L. Gage (Ed.), *Handbook of research on teaching* (pp. 171–246). Chicago: Rand McNally.

Canivez, G. L., & Konold, T. R. (2001). Assessing differential prediction bias in the developing cognitive abilities test across gender, race/ethnicity, and socioeconomic groups. *Educational and Psychological Measurement, 61*(1), 159–171.

Cantwell, J. G. (2007, February). *The principal's role in statewide testing: A national, state, and local school district perspective.* Paper presented at the annual meeting of the Eastern Educational Research Association, Clearwater, FL.

Carbonaro, W. J., & Gamoran, A. (2002). The production of achievement inequality in high school English. *American Educational Research Journal, 39*(4), 801–827.

Carbonaro, W. J., & Gamoran, A. (2005). The effect of high-quality instruction on reading outcomes [Electronic version]. *Research Brief, Association for Supervision and Curriculum Development, 3*(4). Retrieved July 20, 2005, from http://www.ascd.org

Carlson, J. E. (1998). [Review of the *Accounting-aptitude test*], In J. C. Impara & B. S. Plake (Eds.), *Thirteenth mental measurements yearbook* (pp. 14–17). Lincoln, NE: Buros Institute of Mental Measurements.

Carlson, J. E. (2007, April). *Vertical scaling issues.* Paper presented during the annual meeting of the American Educational Research Association, Chicago, IL.

Carnegie Forum on Education and the Economy's Task Force on Teaching as a Profession. *A nation prepared: Teachers for the 21st century.* New York: Carnegie Corporation of New York, 1986. (ERIC Document Number ED268120)

Carpenter, D. C., & Malcolm, K. K. (2001). [Review of the *Oral and written language scales written expression*]. In B. S. Plake & J. C. Impara (Eds.), *The fourteenth mental measurements yearbook* (pp. 864–868). Lincoln, NE: Buros Institute of Mental Measurements.

Carroll, J. B. (1963). A model for school learning. *Teacher's College Record, 64,* 723–733.

Cary, K. (2004).*The funding gap 2004: Many states still shortchange low-income and minority students.* Washington, DC: Education Trust. Retrieved October 16, 2006, from http://www.edtrust.org

Case, B. J. (2004, January). It's about time: Stanford Achievement Test Series, Tenth Edition [Assessment Report]. San Antonio, TX: Harcourt Assessment. (Originally published April 2003)

Cassady, J. C. (2001). The stability of undergraduate student's cognitive test anxiety levels [Electronic version]. *Practical Assessment, Research & Evaluation, 7*(20). Retrieved October 24, 2006, from http://PAREonline.net/getvn.asp?v=7&n=20

Casserly, M. (2004, March). *Beating the odds IV: A city-by-city analysis of student performance and achievement gap on state assessments, results from 2002–2003 school year.* Council of the Great City Schools. Retrieved May 30, 2005, from http://www.cgcs.org/

Castelli, R. A. (1994). *Critical thinking instruction in liberal arts curricula.* Unpublished doctoral dissertation, Widener University.

Catania, C. A. (1999). Thorndike's legacy: Learning, selection, and the law of effect. *Journal of the Experimental Analysis of Behavior, 72*(3), 425–428.

Cattell, R. (1963). Theory of fluid and crystallized intelligence: A critical experiment. *Journal of Educational Psychology, 1*(54), 1–22.

Cavanagh, A., & Robelen, E. W. (2004) Bush backs requiring NAEP in 12th grade. *Education Week 23*(31), pp. 32, 34.

Cavanaugh, S. (2005, June 8). NCTM elaborates on position on the use of calculators in classrooms. *Education Week, 24*(9), p. 9.

Cavanaugh, S. (2006, November 15). Technology helps teachers home in on student needs. *Education Week, 26*(12), pp. 10–11.

Cavanaugh, S. (2007, February 21). "Math anxiety" confuses the equation for students. *Education Week, 26*(24), p. 12.

Cawthon, S. W. (2007). Hidden benefits and unintended consequences of the No Child Left Behind policies for students who are deaf or hard of hearing. *American Educational Research Journal, 44*(3), 460–492.

Cech, S. J. (2007, August 15). 10-state pilot preparing teachers to develop tests. *Education Week, 26*(45), p. 10.

Ceperley, P. E., & Reel, K. (1997). The impetus for the Tennessee value-added accountability system. In J. Millman (Ed.), *Grading teachers, grading schools* (pp. 133–136). Thousand Oaks, CA: Corwin Press.

Chan, J. C. K., McDermott, K. B., & Roediger III, H. L. (2006). Retrieval-induced facilitation: Initially non-tested material can benefit from prior testing of related material. *Journal of Psychology/General, 135*(4), 553–571.

Chang, K. D. (2005, June 20). Attention-deficit/hyperactivity disorder. *E-Medicine.* Retrieved June 30, 2005, from http://www.emedicine.com/med/topic3103.htm

Cheng, Y., & Chang, H. (2007, April). *Two item selection routes for cognitive diagnostic CAT.* Paper presented during the annual meeting of the National Council on Measurement in Education, Chicago, IL.

Chiles, N. (1997, September 7). Wealth helps: A wealth of expectations. [Electronic version]. *Newark Star Ledger.* Retrieved August 21, 2004, from http://www.nj.com/news/ledger/schoolwealth.html

Christensen, D. D. (2001, December). Building state assessment from the classroom up. *School Administrator* [Electronic version]. Retrieved August 4, 2005, from http://www.aasa.org/publications

Chubb, J. E., & Moe, T. M. (1992). Educational choice: Why it is needed and how it will work. In C. E. Finn, Jr. & T. Rebarer (Eds.), *Education reform in the 90s* (pp. 36–52). New York: Macmillan.

Civil Rights Act (P.L. 88-352, § Sec. 402, 1964).

Cizek, G. J. (2003). [Test review of the *Woodcock–Johnson (r) III*]. From B. S. Plake & J. C. Impara (Eds.), *The fifteenth mental measurements yearbook* [Electronic version]. Retrieved March 1, 2005, from the Buros Institute's Test Reviews Online Web site: http://www.unl.edu/buros

Cizek, G. J., Bunch, M. B., & Koons, H. (2004). Setting performance standards: Contemporary methods. *Educational Measurement: Issues and Practice, 23*(4), 31–50.

Cizek, G. J., Johnson, R. L., & Mazzie, D. (2005). [Review of the *Terra nova* test] In *The sixteenth mental measurement yearbook* [Electronic version]. Retrieved November 8, 2006, from the Buros Institute's Test Reviews Online Web site: http://www.unl.edu/buros

Clabaugh, G. K., & Rozycki, E. G. (1990). *Understanding schools: The foundations of education.* New York: Harper & Row.

Clark, L. (2005). Gifted and growing. *Educational Leadership, 63*(3), 56–60.

Clarridge, P. B., & Whitaker, E. M. (1997). *Rolling the elephant over: How to effect large-scale change in the reporting process.* Portsmouth, NH: Heinemann.

Clements, A. (2004). *The report card.* New York: Books for Young Readers, Simon & Schuster.

Cloud/Thornburg, J. (2004, September 20). Saving the smart kids. *Time.* Retrieved September 23, 2004, from http://www.time.com/time/magazine/printout/0,8816,1101040927-699423,00.html

Clymer, J. B., & Wiliam, D. (2006/2007). Improving the way we grade science. *Educational Leadership, 64*(4), 36–42.

Coelen, S., & Berger, J. (2006). *First steps: An evaluation of the success of Connecticut students beyond high school* [Fact sheet]. Nellie Mae Education Foundation, Quincy, MA. Retrieved March 29, 2006, from http://www.nmefdn.org/research/

Cohen, J. (1960). A coefficient of agreement for nominal scales. *Educational and Psychological Measurement, 20,* 37–46.

Cohen, J. (1988). *Statistical power analysis for the behavioral sciences* (2nd ed.). Hillsdale, NJ: Lawrence Erlbaum Associates.

Cohen, K. (2006, July 7). Why colleges should thank private admissions counselors. *Chronicle of Higher Education, 52*(44), p. B20.

Cohen, M. (2007, April). *Aligned expectations? A closer look at college admissions and placement tests* [Project Report]. Washington, DC: Achieve.

Cohen-Vogel, L., & Smith, T. M. (2007). Qualifications and assignments of alternatively certified teachers: Testing the core assumptions. *American Educational Research Journal, 44*(3), 732–753.

Cohn, D., & Bahrampour, T. (2006, May 10). Of U.S. children under 5, nearly half are minorities. *Washington Post.* Retrieved May 11, 2006, from http://www.washington post.com

Colangelo, N., & Davis, G. A. (1997). *Handbook of gifted education* (2nd ed.). Needham Heights, MA: Allyn and Bacon.

Colby, S. A., & Smith, T. W. (2007, April). *Quality teaching and student learning: A validation study of national Board Certified teachers.* A paper presented during the annual meeting of the American Educational Research Association, Chicago, IL.

Cole, N. S., & Moss, P. A. (1989). Bias in test use. In R. L. Linn (Ed.), *Educational measurement* (3rd ed.) (pp. 201–219). New York: Macmillan Publishing Co.

Coleman, J. S. (1972). The evaluation of equality of educational opportunity. In F. Mosteller & D. P. Moynihan (Eds.), *On equality of educational opportunity* (pp. 146–167). New York: Random House.

College Board. (2005). *Advanced Placement report to the nation, 2005.* New York: Author. Retrieved March 19, 2006, from http://www.collegeboard.com

Collins, A., & Dana, T. M. (1993). Using portfolios with middle grade students. *Middle School Journal, 25*(2), 14–19.

Colom, R., Lluis-Font, J. M., & Andrés-Pueyo, A. (2005). The generational intelligence gains are caused by decreasing variance in the lower half of the distribution: Supporting evidence for the nutritional hypothesis. *Intelligence, 33*(1), 83–91.

Committee on Quality Improvement, Subcommittee on Attention-Deficit/ Hyperactivity Disorder (2000). Clinical practice guidelines: Diagnosis and evaluation of the child with attention-deficit/hyperactivity disorder. *Pediatrics, 105*(5), 1158–1170.

Committee on Quality Improvement and Subcommittee on Attention-Deficit/ Hyperactivity Disorder. (2001). Clinical practice guideline: Treatment of the school-aged child with attention-deficit/hyperactivity disorder. *Pediatrics, 108*(4), 1033–1044.

Communications Technology Amendment. (P.L. 105-220 [Title 29, U.S.C.], 794d § Sec. 508, 1998).

Conners, K. (1997/2000). *Conners' rating scales–revised.* Toronto, Canada: Multi-Health Systems.

Connolly, A. J. (1998). *Key math–revised.* Circle Pines, MN: American Guidance Service Inc.

Cooper, H. (2001). *The battle over homework: An administrator's guide to setting sound and effective policies* (2nd ed.). Thousand Oaks, CA: Corwin Press

Cooper, H. (2003, May). *Summer learning loss: The problem and some solutions.* Champaign, IL: University of Illinois, ERIC Clearinghouse on Elementary and Early Childhood Education. Retrieved July 18, 2003, from http://ceep.crc.uiuc.edu/eecearchive/digests/2003/cooper03.html

Cortese, A., & von Zastrow, C. (2006, January 18). Closing the staffing gap. *Education Week, 25*(19), p. 34.

Creamer, B. (2007, March 1). Teacher's workday averages 15.5 hours. *Honolulu Advertiser.* Retrieved March 17, 2007, from http://the.honoluluadvertiser.com/article/ 2007/Mar/01/In/FP703010362.html

Creighton, T. B. (2007). *Schools and data: The educators guide for using data to improve decision making* (2nd ed.). Thousand Oaks, CA: Corwin Press.

Crocker, L. (2003). Teaching for the test: Validity, fairness, and moral action [2003 NCME Presidential Address]. *Educational Measurement: Issues and Practice, 22*(3), 5–11.

Cronbach, L. J. (1951). Coefficient alpha and the internal structure of tests. *Psychometrika, 16,* 297–334.

Cronbach, L. J., & Meehl, P. E. (1955). Construct validity in psychological tests. *Psychological Bulletin, 52,* 281–302.

Cronin, J., Kingsbury, G. G., McCall, M., & Bowe, B. (2005, April). The impact of the No Child Left Behind Act on student achievement and growth, 2005 Edition. Northwest Evaluation Association. Retrieved June 23, 2005, from http://www.nwea.org/research/nclb/index.php

Crouse, J. (2006, March 27). Students rewarded for sacrificing Saturdays for FCAT training. *Lakeland Ledger.* Retrieved April 2, 2006, from http://www.theledger.com

Currie, R. A. (1994). *Predicting public school student achievement in a five county region in Ohio: The development of a prediction equation.* Doctoral dissertation, The University of Akron. (ProQuest document ID 747020331)

Damarin, F., (1985). [Test review of Creativity Assessment Packet]. From J. V. Mitchell Jr. (Ed.), *The ninth measurements yearbook* [Electronic version]. Retrieved February 14, 2005, from the Buros Institute's Test Reviews Online Web site: http://www.unl.edu/buros

Darling-Hammond, L. (2000). Teacher quality and student achievement: A review of state policy evidence [Electronic version]. *Education Policy Analysis Archives, 8*(1). Retrieved July 17, 2005, from http://epaa.asu.edu/epaa/v8n1/

Darling-Hammond, L. (2004). From "separate but equal" to "No Child Left Behind": The collision of new standards and old inequalities. In D. Meier and G. Wood (Eds.), *Many children left behind: How the No Child Left Behind Act is damaging our children and our schools* (pp. 3–32). Boston: Beacon Press.

Darling-Hammond, L. (2005, April). *Teacher characteristics and student achievement in the Houston Independent School District.* Paper presented at the annual meeting of the American Educational Research Association. Montreal, Canada.

Darling-Hammond, L., Holtzman, D. J., Gatlin, S. J., & Heilig, J. V. (2005, April). *Does teacher preparation matter? Evidence about teacher certification, Teach for America, and teacher effectiveness* (Working Paper). Palo Alto, CA: School of Education, Stanford University.

Darwin, C. R. (1859). *Origin of species by means of natural selection.* London: J. Murray. Reprinted (1976) New York: Random House.

Darwin, C. R. (1877). A biographical sketch of an infant. *Mind: A Quarterly Review of Psychology and Philosophy, 2*(7), 285–294.

Datar, A. (2003). *The impact of changes in kindergarten entrance age policies on children's academic achievement and the child care needs of families* (Report RGSD-177, 2003). Santa Monica, CA: Pardee Rand Graduate School, Rand Corporation.

Davis, G. (2004, July 2). Today, even B students getting squeezed out. *Chronicle of Higher Education: Chronicle Review.* Retrieved April 21, 2005, from http://chronicle.com/weekly/v50/i43b02001.htm

Dawson, D. A. (1991). Family structure and children's health and well-being: Data from the National Health Interview Survey on Child Health. *Journal of Marriage and the Family, 53,* 573–584.

de Vise, D. (2007, March 4). A concentrated approach to exams. *Washington Post.* Retrieved March 8, 2007, from http://www.washingtonpost.com/

Debra P. v. Turlington, 644 F. 2d 397, 402-403 (5th Cir. 1981).

Decker, P. T., Mayer, D. P., & Glazerman, S. (2004, June 9). The *effects of Teach for America on students: Findings from a national evaluation* [Technical report]. Princeton, NJ: Mathematica Policy Research Co. Retrieved July 8, 2005, from http://www.teachforAmerica.org/studies.html

Dee, T. S. (2005). A teacher like me: Does race, ethnicity, or gender matter? *American Economic Review, 95* (2), 158–165.

deFur, S. H. (2003). [Test review of the *Test of early reading ability, third edition*]. From B. S. Plake & J. C. Impara (Eds.), *The fifteenth mental measurements yearbook* [Electronic version]. Retrieved July 2, 2005, from the Buros Institute's Test Reviews Online Web site: http://www.unl.edu/buros/

DeGregory, L. (2005, February 10). For sick kids, FCAT's just one more exam. *St. Petersburg Times.* Retrieved March 20, 2006, from http://www.sptimes.com

DeLacy, M. (2004, June 23). The "no child" law's biggest victims? *Education Week,* p. 40.

DeMars, C. E. (2000). Test stakes and item format interactions. *Applied Measurement in Education, 13*(1), 55–77.

Dessoff, A. (2007). Certifying AP courses. *District Administration, 43*(4), 54–59.

DeStefano, L. (2001). Test review of the *Otis–Lennon school ability test, seventh edition.* From B. S. Plake & J. C. Impara (Eds.), *The fourteenth mental measurements yearbook* [Electronic version]. Retrieved March 3, 2005, from the Buros Institute's Test Reviews Online Web site http://www.unl.edu/buros

Dickens, W. T., & Flynn, J. (2006, October). Black Americans reduce the racial IQ gap: Evidence from standardized samples [Electronic version]. *Psychological Science.* Retrieved December 7, 2006, from http://www.econ.brown.edu/staff/Angelica_ Spertini/Dickens_IQ.pdf

Dillon, N. (2007). Crossing the line: School districts are getting tough with parents who hop boundaries to enroll students. *American School Board Journal.* Retrieved January 14, 2007, from http://www.asbj.com/current/coverstory.html

Dillon, S. (2006, March 26). Schools cut back subjects to push reading and math. *New York Times,* pp. 1, 22.

Dillon, S. (2007, February 7). Advanced Placement Tests are leaving some behind. *New York Times,* p. A17.

Dillon, S. (2007, June 18). Long reviled, merit pay gains among teachers. *New York Times, 156*(53979), pp. A1, 14.

DiMartino, J. (2007, April 25). Accountability or mastery? The assessment trade-off that could change the landscape of reform. *Education Week, 26*(34), pp. 44, 36.

DiMartino, J., & Castaneda, A. (2007, April). Assessing applied skills. *Educational Leadership, 64*(7), 38–42.

Dizon, N. Z., Feller, B., & Bass, F. (2006, April 18). States omitting minorities' test scores. *[Associated Press].* Retrieved April 21, 2006, from http://news.yahoo.com/

Dodd, A., & Morris, M. (2005, May 6). Gwinnett teacher who refuses to alter grade is fired. *Atlanta Journal-Constitution.* Retrieved November 5, 2006, from http://www.hannity.com/forum/printthread .php?t=5646

Doherty, K. M. (2004, August 11). Assessment [Education Issues A–Z]. *Education Week.* Retrieved August 22, 2004, from http://www.edweek.org/context/topics/issuespage.cfm?id=41

Doll, B. J. (2003). [Test review of the *Wechsler individual achievement test, second edition*]. From B. S. Plake & J. C. Impara (Eds.), *The fifteenth mental measurement yearbook* [Electronic version]. Retrieved July 6, 2005, from the Buros Institute's Test Reviews Online Web site: http://www.unl.edu/buros

Donnelly, A. M. (1999). *Self-questioning: A comparative analysis of what teachers and students report about the use of this reading comprehension strategy.* Unpublished doctoral dissertation, Widener University.

Donsky, P. (2005, May 15). When teachers cheat. *Atlanta Journal Constitution.* Retrieved May 17, 2005, from http://www.newslibrary.com/sites/ajc/

Dorans, N. J. (2002). The recentering of SAT scales and its effects on score distributions and score interpretations (College Board Research Report No. 2002-11, ETS RR-02-04). New York: College Examination Board.

Dorans, N. J., & Zeller, K. (2004). Using score equity assessment to evaluate the equatability of the hardest half of a test to the total test. Retrieved March 14, 2005, from Educational Testing Service Web site: http://ftp.ets.org/pub/res/researcher/RR-04-43.pdf

Dorr-Bremme, D. W., & Herman, J. L. (1986). *Assessing student achievement: A profile of classroom practices* (CSE Monograph in Evaluation No. 11). Los Angeles: University of California, Center for Evaluation. (ERIC Document Reproduction Service No. ED 338 691)

Dougherty, C., Mellor, L., & Shuling, J. (2006). *The relationship between advanced placement and college graduation.* Austin, TX: The National Center for Educational Accountability, University of Texas.

Duckworth, A. L., & Seligman, M. E. P. (2006). Self-discipline gives girls the edge: Gender in self-discipline, grades, and achievement test scores. *Journal of Educational Psychology, 98*(1), 198–208.

Duff, W. (1767, 1964). *An essay on original genius and its various modes of exertion in philosophy and the fine arts, particularly in poetry.* Gainesville, FL: Scholar's Facsimiles and Reprints.

Duncan, D. (2005). *Clickers in the classroom: How to enhance science teaching using classroom response systems.* San Francisco: Addison Wesley/Pearson.

Easley, M. (2003, March). *Governor Mike Easley's teacher working conditions initiative: Preliminary report of findings from a statewide survey of educators.* Retrieved July 11, 2005, from http://www .governor.state.nc.us/Office/Education/TeacherWorkingConditionsSurvey.asp

Easterbrook, G. (2004, October). College admissions 2004, Who needs Harvard? *Atlantic.* Retrieved March, 23, 2006, from http://www.theatlantic.com/doc/print/200410/easterbrook

Edmonston, B., Lee, S. M., & Passel, J. S. (2001). Intermariage, immigration, et statistques raciales aux Etats-Unis. *Critique Internationale, 12,* 30–38.

Educate America Act (P.L. 103-227, 1994).

Education for All Handicapped Children's Act (P.L. 94-142, 1975 [S. 6]).

Education of the Handicapped Act Amendments (P.L. 99-457, 1986), 20 U.S.C.A. § 1400 *et seq.*

Education Trust–West. (2005). *California's hidden teacher spending gap: How state and district budgeting practices shortchange poor and minority students and their schools* (A Special Report). Oakland, CA: Education Trust-West, the James Irving Foundation, and the Bill and Melinda Gates Foundation. Retrieved October 16, 2006, from http://www.HiddenGap.org

Eklöf, H. (2007, April). *Gender differences in test-taking motivation on low-stakes tests: A Swedish TIMSS 2003 example.* Paper presented during the annual meeting of the American Educational Research Association, Chicago, IL.

Elementary and Secondary Education Act [ESEA] of 1965 (P.L. No. 89-10, § Sec. 201, 1965).

Elementary and Secondary Education Act [ESEA] of 1994, Improving America's Schools Act (P.L. No. 103-382, 1994).

Elementary and Secondary Education Act [ESEA], Title I Program Directive (1998). retrieved June 20, 2005, from http://www.ed.gov/offices/OESE/archives/CEP/pdfm26.html

Elias, M. J., & Schwab, Y. (2004, October 20). What about parental involvement in parenting? *Education Week, 24*(8), p. 39.

Elliott, E. J. (1995, March 15, 16). *Professional benchmarks on PRAXIS tests: An application to NCATE accreditation* [Workshop Material]. Washington, DC: National Council for the Accreditation of Teacher Education.

Elvin, C. (2003). *Test item analysis using Microsoft Excel spreadsheet program*. Unpublished manuscript, Tokyo Women's Medical University. Retrieved March 16, 2007, from http://www.eflclub.com/elvin/ publications/2003/itemanalysis.html

Engle, S. (2002, January 28). *College freshmen more politically liberal than in the past, UCLA survey reveals* [Press release]. Los Angeles: Higher Education Research Institute. Retrieved June 25, 2005, from http://gseis.ucla.edu/ heri/norms_pr_00 .html

Engle, T. L. (1945). *Psychology: Principles and applications.* Yonkers-on-Hudson, NY: World Book.

English, F. W. (2000). *Deciding what to teach and test: Developing, aligning, and auditing the curriculum, Millennium Edition*. Thousand Oaks, CA: Corwin Press.

Erikson, E. H. (1968). *Identity youth and crisis.* New York: W. W. Norton.

Eshel, N. (2004, April 29). Effects of grade proposal debated. *Daily Princetonian.* Retrieved July 16, 2004, from http://www.dailyprincetonian.com/archives/2004/04/29/ news/10475.shtml

Espenshade, T. J., & Chung, C. Y. (2005). The opportunity cost of admission preferences at elite universities. *Social Science Quarterly, 86*(2), 293–305.

Eurydice. (2004). *Integrating immigrant children into schools in Europe.* Brussels, Belgium: Author. Retrieved November 18, 2006, from http://www.eurydice.org

Evans, L. D. (1990). A conceptual overview of the regression discrepancy model for evaluating severe discrepancy between IQ and achievement scores. *Journal of Learning Disabilities, 23,* 406–412.

Evers, W. M., & Walberg, H. J. (Eds.). (2004). *Testing student learning: Evaluating teaching effectiveness.* Palto Alto, CA: Hoover Institution Press.

Ewing, M. (2006). The AP program and student outcomes: A summary of research. *Research Notes, November.* New York: College Board.

Fager, J. (Producer). (2004, January 7). *60 Minutes* [Television broadcast]. New York: CBS.

Fair Test. (2007). *No Child Left Behind* [Web page]. Cambridge, MA: Fair Test. Retrieved March 19, 2007, from http://www.fairtest.org/

Fallone, G., Acebo, C., Seifer, R., & Carskadon, M. A. (2005). Experimental restriction of sleep opportunity in children: Effects on teacher ratings. *Sleep, 28*(12), 1279–1285.

Family Educational Right to Privacy Act (Buckley Amendment) [20 USC § 1232g; 34 CFR Part 99 (1974)].

Feistritzer, E. C. (1999, May 13). *Teacher quality and alternative certification programs.* Testimony of Emily C. Feistritzer before the U.S. House of Representatives Committee on Education and the Workforce. Retrieved February 9, 2005, from http://www .ncei.com/Testimony051399.htm

Feldt, L. S., & Brennan, R. L. (1989). Reliability. In R. L. Linn (Ed.), *Educational Measurement* (3rd ed.), (pp. 105–146). New York: American Council on Education and Macmillan Publishing.

Feller, B. (2006, May 9). Rising number of schools face penalties. *Boston Globe.* Retrieved May 11, 2006, from http://www.boston.com

Ferguson, R. F. (2002). *What doesn't meet the eye: Understanding and addressing racial disparities in high-achieving suburban schools.* Cambridge, MA: John F. Kennedy School of Government. Retrieved February 8, 2005, from http://iume.tc.columbia.edu/reports/ferguson_eye.pdf

Fetterman, D. M. (1988, November). Qualitative approaches to evaluating education. *Educational Researcher,* 17–23.

Figlio, D. N. (2003, November). Testing, crime, and punishment. Gainesville: University of Florida. Retrieved November 20, 2006, from http://bear.cba.ufl.edu/figlio/crime.pdf

Finchler, J. (2000). *Testing Miss Malarkey.* New York: Walker & Co.

Finder, A. (2006, March 5). Schools avoid class ranking, vexing colleges. *New York Times.* Retrieved March 5, 2006, from http://www.nytimes.com

Finley, M. T. (1995). *Critical thinking skills as articulated in the instructional practices, objectives, and examination items of higher level secondary school courses.* Unpublished doctoral dissertation, Widener University.

Finn, C. E., Jr. (1991). *We must take charge: Our schools and our future.* New York: The Free Press.

Finn, J. D., Pannozzo, G. M., & Achilles, C. M. (2003). The "whys" of class size: Student behavior in small classes. *Review of Educational Research, 73*(3), 321–368.

Finnigan, K. S., & Gross, B. (2007). Do accountability policy sanctions influence teacher motivation? Lessons from Chicago's low-performing schools. *American Educational Research Journal, 44*(3), 594–629.

Firestone, W. A., Monflis, L. F., Hayes, M., Polovsky, T., Martinez, M. C., & Hicks, J. E. (2004). The principal, test preparation, and educational reform. In W. A. Firestone, R. Y. Schorr, & L. F. Monfils (Eds.).

The Ambiguity of Teaching to the Test; Standards, Assessment, and Educational Reform (pp. 91–112). Mahwah, NJ: Lawrence Erlbaum Associates, Publishers.

Firestone, W. A., Monfils, L. F., Schorr, R. Y., Hicks, J. E., & Martinez, M. C. (2004). Pressure and support. In W. A Firestone, R. Y. Schorr, & L. F. Monfils (Eds.), *The ambiguity of teaching to the test: Standards, assessment, and educational reform* (pp. 63–69). Mahwah, NJ: Lawrence Erlbaum Associates.

Fisk, E. B. (1988, February 17). Standardized test scores: Voodoo statistics? *New York Times,* p. B9.

Flanagan, J. D., Shaycroft, J., Gorham, M., Orr, W., Goldberg, D., & Goldberg, I. (1962). *Design for a study of American youth.* Boston: Houghton Mifflin.

Fleischman, H. L., & Williams, L. (1996). *An introduction to program evaluation for classroom teachers.* Arlington, VA: Development Associates. Retrieved August 22, 2005, from http://teacherpathfinder.org/School/Assess?assess.html

Flood, P. H. (2004). *It's test day, Tiger Turcotte.* Minneapolis: Carolrhoda.

Flores, B. B., & Clark, E. R. (2005). The centurion: Standards and high-states testing as gatekeepers for bilingual teacher candidates in the new century. In A. Valenzuela (Ed.), *Leaving children behind: How "Texas-style" accountability fails Latino youth* (pp. 225–248). Albany, NY: State University of New York Press.

Flynn, J. R. (1987). Massive IQ gains in 14 nations: What IQ tests really measure. *Psychological Bulletin, 101,* 171–191.

Fortier, J. (1993). The Wisconsin Road Test as an empirical example of a large-scale, high-stakes, authentic performance assessment [Electronic version]. *OnWEAC, Newsletter of the Wisconsin Education Association Council.* Madison, WI: Wisconsin Department of Public Instruction. Retrieved September 21, 2007, from http://www.weac.org/resource/may96/perform.htm

Fouratt, S., & Owen, C. (2004). *CTP 4, Comprehensive testing program 4* [Technical Report]. Princeton, NJ: Educational Testing Service.

Frahm, R. A. (2006, April). Who's really fit to teach? *Hartford Courant.* Retrieved April 5, 2006, from http://www.courant.com

Frahm, R. A. (2006, November). Classroom discrepancy: Districts that face toughest challenges often hire least experienced teachers. *Hartford Courant.* Retrieved November 3, 2006, from http://www.courant.com

Frankenberg, E. (2006). *The segregation of American teachers.* Cambridge, MA: The Civil Rights Project, Harvard University.

Frary, R. B., Ross, L. H., & Weber, L. J. (1993, Fall). Testing and grading practices and options of secondary teachers of academic subjects: Implications for instruction in measurement. *Educational Measurement: Issues and Practice. 12,* 23–26.

Freedle, R. O. (2002). Correcting the SAT's ethnic and social-class bias: A method for reestimating SAT scores [Electronic version]. *Harvard Educational Review, 72* (3), 1–43. Retrieved June 21, 2005, from http://gseweb.harvard.edu/hepg/freedle.html

Freedle, R. O., & Kostin, I. (1997). Predicting black and white differential functioning in verbal analogy performance. *Intelligence, 24,* 417–444.

Fuchs, L. S., & Fuchs, D. (2002). Mathematical problem-solving profiles of students with mathematics disabilities with and without comorbid reading disabilities. *Journal of Learning Disabilities, 35*(6), 563–573.

Futernick, K. (2007). *A possible dream: Retaining California teachers so all students learn.* Sacramento: The Center for the Future of Teaching and Learning, California State University, Office of the Chancellor.

Gadbury-Amyot, C. C., Kin, J., Mills, G. E., Noble, E., & Overman, P. R. (2003). Validity and reliability of portfolio assessments of competency in a baccalaureate dental hygiene program. *Journal of Dental Education, 67*(9), 991–1002.

Gaetano, C. (2006, August 31). General education teachers face special education realities. *East Brunswick Sentinel.* Retrieved February 27, 2007, from http://ebs.gmnews.com/news/2006/0831/Schools/043.html%20

Gaffney, J. S., & Zaimi, E. (2003, November 14). *Grade retention and special education: A call for a transparent system of accountability.* Paper presented at the Conference of the Teacher Education Division, Biloxi, MS.

Gage, N. L. (Ed.). (1967). *Handbook of research on teaching. A project of the American Educational Research Association.* Chicago: Rand McNally.

Galton, F. (1883/1919). *Inquiries in human faculty and its development.* London: J. M. Dent & Sons.

Galton, F. (2001). *Hereditary genius: An inquiry into its laws and consequences.* Honolulu, HI: University of Hawaii Press. (Original work published 1869)

Gardner, D. (2007). Confronting the achievement gap. *Phi Delta Kappan, 88*(7), 542–546.

Gardner, H. (1999). *Intelligence reframed: Multiple intelligence for the 21st century.* New York: Basic Books.

Gardner, H. (2005, September 14). Beyond the herd mentality: The minds that we truly need in the future. *Education Week, 25*(3), p. 44.

Garnaut, J. (2007, May 21). Best teachers get top marks from study. *Sydney Morning Herald* (Australia). Retrieved May, 21, 2007, from http://www.smh.com.au/news/national/best-teachers-get-top-marks-from-study/2007/05/201179601244 341.html#

Gayler, K., & Kober, N. (2004). *Pay now or pay later: The hidden costs of high school exit exams.* Washington, DC: Center on Educational Policy.

Georgia Association of School Psychologists (2003). *The use of high-stakes testing* [Position statement]. Stone Mountain, GA: Author. Retrieved July 7, 2005, from http://www.gaspnet.org

Gershberg, A. I., & Hamilton, D. (2007, February 5). Bush's double standard on race in schools. *Christian Science Monitor.* Retrieved February 5, 2007, from http://www.csmonitor.com/2007/0205/p09s01-coop.htm

Gesell, A. L., & Thompson, H. (1929). Learning and growth in identical infant twins: An experimental study by the methodology of co-twin control. *Journal of Genetic Psychology, Monographs, 6,* 1–124.

Gewertz, C. (2007, January 10). Remediation for exit-exam failure proves daunting. *Education Week, 26*(18), p. 10.

Gilbert, A. (2005). *Teachers leave grading up to the computer.* CNET Networks. Retrieved May 1, 2005, from http://news.com.com/2102-1032_3-5659366.html?tag=st.util.print

Gill, B., Zimmer, R., Christman, J., & Blanc, S. (2007). *Student achievement in privately managed and district-managed schools in Philadelphia since the state takeover* (Research Brief RB-9239-ANF/WPF/SDP). Santa Monica, CA: Rand Corporation. Retrieved February 2, 2007, from http://www.rand.org/pubs/research_briefs/ RB9239/index1.html

Glaser, R. (1963). Instructional technology and the measurement of learning outcomes: Some questions. *American Psychologist, 18,* 519–521.

Glickman, J., & Babyak, S. (2006). The toolbox revisited: Paths to degree completion from high school through college. Retrieved March 1, 2006, from http://www.ed.gov/rschstat/research/pubs/toolboxrevisit/index.html

Glod, M. (2006, October 27). Closing the gap, child by child. *Washington Post.* Retrieved March 10, 2007, from http://www.washingtonpost.com/wp-dyn/content/article/2006/10/26/AR2006102601600_pf.html

Glod, M. (2007, February 1). Virginia is urged to obey "No Child" on reading test. *Washington Post.* Retrieved February 2, 2007, from http://www.washingtonpost.com/wp-dyn/content/article/2007/01/31/AR2007013102120_pf.html

Goddard, T. (2005, February, 9). *AIMS testing and special education* [Opinion paper]. Office of the Attorney General, State of Arizona, 105-002 (R04-037).Retrieved September 21, 2007, from http://www.azag.gov/opinions/2005/I05-002.pdf

Goldhaber, D. D. (2006, April). *Everyone's doing it, but what does teacher testing tell us about teacher effectiveness?* Paper presented at the annual meeting of the American Educational Research Association, San Francisco, CA.

Goldhaber, D. D., & Anthony, E. (2004, March). *Teacher quality: Can it be assessed?* Paper presented during the annual meeting of the American Education Finance Association, Salt Lake City, UT.

Goleman, D. (2006, September). The socially intelligent leader. *Educational Leadership, 64*(1), 76–81.

Gonzalez, E. J., & Kennedy, A. (2007, April). *Comparing three models to obtain scores for PIRLS.* Paper presented during the annual meeting of the American Educational Research Association, Chicago, IL.

Good, R. H., Kaminski, R. A., Moats, L. C., Laimon, D., Smith, S., & Dill, S. (2002/2003). *DIBELS: Dynamic indicators of basic early literacy skills, sixth edition.* Longmont, CO: Sopris West.

Good, R. H., Simmons, D. C., & Kame'enui, E. J. (2001). The importance of decision-making utility of a continuum of fluency-based indicators of foundational reading skills for third-grade high-stakes outcomes. *Scientific Studies of Reading, 5*(3), 257–288.

Good, T. L., & Brophy, J. (1995). *Contemporary educational psychology* (5th ed.). New York: Longman.

Goode, E. (2002, March 12). The uneasy fit of the precocious and the average child. *New York Times*, pp. 1, 2.

Goodkin, S., & Gold, D. G. (2007, August 27). The gifted children left behind. *Washington Post*. Retrieved August 27, 2007, from http://www.washingtonpost.com

Goodnough, A. (2002, September 21). Teachers dig deeper to fill gap in supplies. *New York Times.* Retrieved November 19, 2006, from http://www.learningexperts.com/McQuillan/teachers%20Spend%20Money%20092102.pdf

Gootman, E. (2006, October 19). Those preschoolers are looking older. *New York Times,* p. A 24.

Gordon E. E. (1995). *Musical aptitude profile* [1995 Revision]. Chicago: GIA Publications.

Gould, S. J. (1996). *The mismeasure of man.* New York: W. W. Norton.

Graham, S., & Malcolm, K. K. (2001). [Review of the *Oral and written language scales listening comprehension and oral expression*] In B. S. Plake & J. C. Impara (Eds.), *The fourteenth mental measurements yearbook* (pp. 860–864). Lincoln, NE: Buros Institute of Mental Measurements.

Graham, T. (2003). [Test review of the *STAR early literacy (r)*]. From B. S. Plake & J. C. Impara (Eds.), *The fifteenth mental measurements yearbook* [Electronic version]. Retrieved July 2, 2005, from the Buros Institute's Test Reviews Online Web site: http://www.unl.edu/buros

Graue, E., Hatch, K., Rao, K., & Oen, D. (2007). The wisdom of class-size reduction. *American Educational Research Journal, 44*(3), 670–700.

Grazer, B. (Producer), & McCulloch, B. (Director). (2003). *Stealing Harvard.* [Motion picture] United States: Imagine Entertainment.

Green, E. (2007, August 16). Student backlash brews against untimed tests. *New York Sun.* Retrieved August 18, 2007, from http://www.nysun.com/pf.php?id=60619&v= 3786837811

Greene, A. H., & Melton, G. D. (2007, August 16). Teaching with the test, not to the test. *Education Week, 26*(45), p. 30.

Gronlund, N. E. (1974). *Determining accountability for classroom* instruction [A title in the Current Topics in Classroom Instruction series]. New York: Macmillan.

Grossman, K. N. (2005, April 26). No early dismissals for underperforming CPS tutors. *Chicago Sun Times.* Retrieved June 23, 2005, from http://interversity.org/lists/arn-1/archives/Apr2005/msg00283.html

Guba, E. G., & Lincoln, Y. S. (1988). Do inquiry paradigms imply inquiry methodologies? In D. M. Fetterman (Ed.), *Qualitative approaches to evaluation in education: The silent scientific revolution.* New York: Praeger.

Guernsey, L. (2005). None of the above: The real world adds ambiguity to math and science questions. *New York Times,* pp. 4A, A18–19.

Guilford, J. P. (1946). New standards for test evaluation. *Educational and Psychological Measurement, 6,* 427–439.

Guilford, J. P. (1975). *Characteristics of creativity* (Report No. 1370.152). Springfield, IL: State of Illinois, Office of the Superintendent of Public Instruction, Department for Exceptional Children.

Guilford, J. P. (1988). Some changes in the structure-of-intellect model. *Educational and Psychological Measurement, 48*(1), 1–4.

Gulliksen, H. (1950). *Theory of mental tests.* New York: John Wiley & Sons.

Gupta, R. (2005, December 27). Music teachers' group pitches test to balance scales. *Palm Beach Post.* Retrieved January 3, 2006, from http://www.palmbeachpost.com

Guskey, T. R. (2002). *How's my kid doing? A parent's guide to grades, marks, and report cards.* San Francisco: Jossey-Bass.

Guskey, T. R. (2005, November). Mapping the road to proficiency. *Educational Leadership, 63*(3), 32–38.

Guskey, T. R. (2007). Multiple sources of evidence: An analysis of stakeholders' perceptions of various indicators of student learning. *Educational Measurement: Issues and Practice, 26*(1), 19–27.

Guy, S. (2007, February 28). Sometimes a bright idea just clicks. *Chicago Sun Times.* Retrieved February 28, 2007, from http://www.suntimes.com/technology/guy/275456,CST-FIN-ec0128.articleprint

Hacker, H. K., & Parks, S. (2005, February 16). Some states getting tough on cheating. *Dallas Morning News.* Retrieved February 16, 2005, from http://www.dallasnews.com

Hacker, H. K., & Stutz, T. (2006, June 12). Incentive pay enters classroom. *Dallas Morning News.* Retrieved, June 13, 2006, from http://www.dalasnews.com/cgi-bin/bi/gold_print.cgi

Haft, S., Witt, P. J., & Thomas, T. (Producers), & Weir, P. (Director) (1989). *Dead poets society* [Motion picture]. United States: Buena Vista.

Hall, D. (2005, June). *Getting honest about grad rates: How states play the numbers and students lose.* The Educational Trust. Retrieved June 24, 2005, from http:// www2.EdTrust.org

Ham, B. D. (2003). The effects of divorce on the academic achievement of high school seniors. *Journal of Divorce & Remarriage, 38*(3), 167–185.

Hambleton, R. K. (1989). Principles and selected applications of item response theory. In R. L. Linn (Ed.), *Educational measurement* (pp. 147–200). New York: Macmillan.

Hambleton, R. K. (2000). Emergence of item analysis modeling in instrument development and data analysis. *Medical Care, 38*(9) (Supplement II), 60–65.

Hambleton, R. K. (2004, June 24–25). *Traditional and modern approaches to outcomes measurement.* Paper presented at the 2004 conference of the National Institute of Cancer and the Drug Information Association. Bethesda, MD.

Hammill, D. D. (1998). Detroit test of learning aptitude, 4th Ed. Austin, TX: Pro-Ed, Pearson Measurement.

Hamre, B. K., & Pianta, R. C. (2005). Can instructional and emotional support in the first-grade classroom make a difference for children at risk for school failure? *Child Development, 76*(5), 949–967.

Hancox, R. J., Milne, B. J., & Poulton, R. (2005). Association of television viewing during childhood with poor educational achievement. *Archives of Pediatrics and Adolescent Medicine, 159*(7), 614–618.

Haney, W. (2000). The myth of the Texas miracle in education [Electronic version]. *Education Policy Analysis Archives, 8*(41). Retrieved January 24, 2005, from http://epaa.asu.edu/eppa/v8n41/

Haney, W. M. (2006, September). *Evidence on education under NCLB (and how Florida boosted NAEP scores and reduced the race gap).* Paper presented at the Hechinger Institute's "Broad Seminar for K–12 Reporters." Teachers College, Columbia University, New York.

Hanushek, E. A., & Rivkin, S. G. (2006, October). *School quality and the Black–White achievement gap* (NBER Working Paper No. W12651). Palo Alto, CA: Hoover Institution, Stanford University. Retrieved February 24, 2007, from http://ssrn.com/abstract=940600

Harcourt Assessment (2001). *Metropolitan achievement test, eighth edition.* San Antonio, TX: Author.

Harcourt Assessment (2003). *Stanford achievement test, tenth edition.* San Antonio, TX: Author.

Harcourt Brace Educational Measurement. (1996). *Stanford diagnostic mathematics test, fourth edition.* San Antonio, TX: Author.

Harman, A. E. (2001). *National board for professional teaching standards' national teacher certification.* Washington, DC: Eric Clearinghouse on Teaching and Teacher Education. (ERIC Document No. ED460126)

Harris, D. N., & Sass, T. R. (2007, April). *Teacher training, teacher quality and student achievement.* Paper presented during the annual meeting of the American Educational Research Association, Chicago, IL.

Harrison, S. (2005, June 28). Midyear promotions: Half flunk FCAT again. *Miami Herald.* Retrieved June 29, 2005, from http://www.miami.com/mld/miamiherald/news/local/

Hart, B., & Risley, T. R. (1995). *Meaningful differences in the everyday experience of young American children.* Baltimore: Paul H. Brooks.

Hart, B., & Risley, T. R. (1999). *The social world of children learning to talk.* Baltimore: Paul H. Brooks.

Haynes, W. O., & Shapiro, D. A. (1995). [Review of the *Communications abilities diagnostic test*]. In J. C. Conoley & J. C. Impara (Eds.), *The twelfth mental measurements yearbook* (pp. 214–219). Lincoln, NE: Buros Institute of Mental Measurements.

Heck, R. H., Larson, T. J., & Marcoulides, G. A. (1990). Instructional leadership and school achievement: Validation of a causal model. *Education Administration Quarterly, 26*(2), 94–125.

Hehir, T. (2007). Confronting ableism. *Educational Leadership, 64*(5), 9–14.

Herman, E. (2002, Winter). The paradoxical rationalization of modern adoption: Social and economic aspects of adoption. *Journal of Social History.* Retrieved January 29, 2005, from http://www.findarticles.com/p/articles/mi_m2005/ is_2_36/ai_95829286/

Herman, E. (2005, June 22). The adoption history project: Arnold Gesell. Department of History, University of Oregon. Retrieved August 13, 2005, from http://darkwing.uoregon.edu/~adoption/people/gesell.html

Herman, J. L., & Baker, E. L. (2005, November). Making benchmark testing work. *Educational Leadership, 63*(3), 48–54.

Herrnstein, R. J., & Murray, C. (1994). *The bell curve: Intelligence and class structure in American life.* New York: Simon & Schuster.

Hershberg, T., & Lea-Kruger, B. (2007, April 11). Not performance pay alone: Teacher incentives must be matched by systemwide change. *Education Week, 26*(32), pp. 48, 35.

Hershberg, T., Simon, V. A., & Lea-Kruger, B. (2004, February). Measuring what matters: How value-added assessment can be used to drive learning gains [Electronic version]. *American School Board Journal, 191*(2). Retrieved August 24, 2005, from http://www.asbj.com

Hess, A. K. (2001). [Review of the *Conners' rating scales-revised*]. In B. S. Plake & J. C. Impara (Eds.), *The fourteenth mental measurement yearbook* (pp. 331–337). Lincoln, NE: Buros Institute of Mental Measurements.

Higgins L. (2007, April 29). Schools hope data can boost scores: It can also help spot flaws in curriculum. *Detroit Free Press.* Retrieved May 2, 2007, from http://www.freep.com/apps/pbcs.dll/article?AID=/20070429/NEWS05/704290614/1007&template=printart

Higgins, L. T., & Zheng, M. (2002). An introduction to Chinese psychology: Its historical roots until the present day. *Journal of Psychology, 136*(2), 225–239.

Hill, R. K., & DePascale, C. A. (2003). *Reliability of No Child Left Behind accountability designs.* Portsmouth, NH: National Center for the Improvement of Educational Assessments.

Hinds, D. A., Stuve, L. L., Nilsen, G. B., Halperin, E., Eskin, E., Ballinger, et al. (2005). Whole-genome patterns of common DNA variation in three human populations. *Science, 307,* 1072–1079.

Hirsch, Jr., E. D. (2006, April 26). Reading-comprehension skills? What are they really? *Education Week, 25*(33), p. 52.

Hoff, D. J. (2007, June 8). State tests show gains since NCLB. *Education Week, 26*(39), pp. 1, 20.

Hoff, D. J., & Manzo, K. K. (2007, March 14). Bush claims about NCLB questioned. *Education Week, 26*(27), pp. 1, 26, 27.

Holbrook, R. G. (2003). *Impact of selected noncurricular variables on regular education student achievement as measured by the 2001–2002 reading and mathematics PSSA scores.* Unpublished doctoral dissertation, Widener University.

Holbrook, R. G., & Wright, R. J. (2004, February). *Non-curricular factors related to success on high-stakes tests.* Paper presented at the annual meeting of the Eastern Educational Research Association, Clearwater, FL.

Honawar, V. (2007, April). Alternative-certification programs multiply. *Education Week, 26*(33), p. 16.

Honawar, V. (2007, January). Bonuses for NBPTS-certified teachers at risk in South Carolina. *Education Week, 28*(20), pp. 5, 20.

Hopkins, K. D. (1998). *Educational and psychological measurement and evaluation* (8th ed.). Boston: Allyn & Bacon.

Houston teachers asked to give back bonuses. (2007, March 10). *Dallas Morning News.* Retrieved March 12, 2007, from http://www.dallasnews.com/sharedcontent/dws/news/texassouthwest/stories/DN-teacher_10tex.ART.State.Edition1.44bc740.html

Hresko, W. P., Reid, K. D., & Hammill, D. D. (1999). *Test of early language development, third edition.* Austin, TX: Pro-Ed.

Hu, W. (2007, July 6). Schools move toward following students' yearly progress on tests. *New York Times,* p. C10.

Huntsinger, C. (1999, April). Does K-5 homework mean higher test scores? *American Teacher.* Retrieved October 16, 2005, from http://www.aft.org/parents/k5homework.htm

IDEA (1986). Individuals With Disabilities Education Act Amendment: Preschool and Infant/Toddler Programs, (P.L. 99-457, 1986, now part c).

IDEA (1997). Individuals With Disabilities Education Act (P.L. 105-17, 1997 [20 U.S.C. 1401 et seq.]).

IDEIA (2004). Individuals With Disabilities Educational Improvement Act of 2004 (118 Stat. 2647, H.R. 1350, 108th Congress, No. 446).

IDEIA 2004 resources (2004). *Ed. gov. technical assistance and dissemination network.* Office of Special Education Programs. Retrieved June 16, 2005, from http://www.ed.gov/print/policy/speced/guid/idea/idea2004.html

Illinois Association of Directors of Title I. (2006). *2006 accountability workbook changes.* Springfield: Author. Retrieved March 20, 2007, from http://www.isbe.state.IL.us/nclb/powerpoint/accountability_work06.PPT#302,31

Impara, J. C. (1996). Assessment skills of counselors, principals, and teachers. *ERIC Digest.* Retrieved July 15, 2005, from http://www.ericdigests.org/1996-2/skills.html

Improving America's Schools Act (P.L. 103-382, 1994).

Institute for Education Sciences (2006, October 18). *State profiles: The Nation's Report Card.* Washington, DC: Institute for Education Sciences, National Center for Educational Statistics, U.S. Department of Education. Retrieved November 22, 2006, from http://nces.ed.gov/nationsreportcard/states/

Irvin A. (2003). *The influence of selected educational and teacher demographic variables on fifth grade reading and writing scores for the 2000 and 2001 Delaware Student Testing Program.* Unpublished doctoral dissertation, Widener University.

Jacobson, L. (2006, September 27). Teacher-pay incentives popular but unproven. *Education Week, 26*(5), pp. 1, 20.

Jacobson, L. (2007, April 4). Study casts doubt on value of "highly qualified" status. *Education Week, 26*(31), p. 13.

James, F. (2004, December 5). *Response to intervention in Individuals With Disabilities Education Act (IDEA), 2004.* Newark, DE: International Reading Association. Retrieved November 28, 2006, from http://www.Reading.ordownloads/resources/IDEA_RTI_report.pdf

Jehlen, A. (2007, April). Testing: How the sausage is made. *NEA Today*. Retrieved April 15, 2007, from http://www.nea.org/neatoday/0704/coverstory1.html

Jennings, J., & Rentner, D. S. (2006). *Ten big effects of the No Child Left Behind Act on public schools.* Washington, DC: Center on Educational Policy. Retrieved November 9, 2006, from http://www.cep-dc.org

Jennings, K. E. (2003). Test review of the *Brown attention-deficit disorder scales for children and adolescents*. From B. S. Plake & J. C. Impara (Eds.), *The fifteenth mental measurements yearbook* [Electronic version]. Retrieved June 29, 2005, from the Buros Institute's Test Reviews Online Web site: http://www.unl.edu/buros

Jensen, A. R. (1999). The g factor: The science of mental ability [Electronic edition]. *Psycoloquy, 10*(2). Retrieved February 15, 2005, from http://psycprints.ecs.soton.ac.uk/archive/00000658/

Jimerson, L. (2006, September 5). *The Hobbit effect: Why small works in public schools*. Arlington, VA: The Rural School and Community Trust. Retrieved November 20, 2006, from http://www.ruraledu.org/hobbiteffect

Jimerson, S. R. (2001a). Meta-analysis of grade retention research: Implications for practice in the 21st century. *School Psychology Review, 30*, 313–330.

Jimerson, S. R. (2001b). Synthesis of grade retention research: Looking backward and moving forward. *California School Psychologist, 6*, 47–59.

Jitendra, A. K., Griffin, C. C., Haria, P., Leh, J., Adams, A., & Kaduvettoor, A. (2007). A comparison of single and multiple strategy instruction on third-grade students' mathematical problem solving. *Journal of Educational Psychology, 99*(1), 115–127.

Johnson, D. J., Thurlow, M., Cosio, A., & Bremer, C. (2005). Diploma options for students with disabilities [Electronic version]. *Information Brief, 4*(1). Retrieved June 26, 2005, from http://www.ncset.org/publications/viewdesc.asp?id=1928

Johnson, D. R., & Thurlow, M. L. (2003). *A national study on graduation requirements and diploma options for youth with disabilities* (NCEO Technical Report No. 36). Minneapolis: University of Minnesota, National Center on Educational Outcomes. Retrieved June 26, 2005, from http://education.umn.edu/nceo/OnlinePubs/Technical36.htm

Johnson, E. B., & Johnson, A. V. (1990). *Communications abilities diagnostic test.* Chicago: Riverside.

Johnson, K. A. (2000). *Merit pay for teachers: A meritorious concept or not?* Unpublished manuscript, Center for Education, Widener University.

Johnson, L. B. (1966). *Public papers of the presidents of the United States, Book 1, 1965*. Washington, DC: U.S. Government Printing Office.

Johnson, S. M., Birkeland, S. E., & Peske, H. G. (2005, September). *A difficult balance: Incentives & quality control in alternative certification programs.* Cambridge, MA: Project on the Next Generation of Teachers, Harvard Graduate School of Education.

Joint Committee on Testing Practices. (2005). Code of fair testing practices in education. *Educational Measurement: Issues and Practice. 24*(1), 23–27.

Joireman, J., & Abbott, M. (2004). Structural equation models assessing relationships among student activities, ethnicity, poverty, parent's education, and academic achievement (Technical Report # 6). Seattle, WA: Washington School Research Center. Retrieved August 21, 2005, from http://www.spu.edu/wsrc/Ethnicity,%20parents%foreward.htm

Joseph, R. (2000). *Neuropsychiatry, neuropsychology, and clinical neuroscience.* San Diego, CA: Academic Press. Retrieved March 27, 2007, from http://72.14.209.104/search?q=cache:fep3Rw7EzJAJ:brainmind.com/RightParietallobe.html

Kaase, K., & Dulaney, C. (2005, May). The impact of mobility on educational achievement: A review of the literature (E & R Report No. 4.39). *Research Watch,* Wake County Public Schools, NC. Retrieved November 29, 2006, from http://www.wcpss.net/evaluation-research/reports/2005/0439mobility_review.pdf

Kalish, R. A. (1958). An experimental evaluation of the open book examination. *Journal of Educational Psychology, 49*(4), 200–204.

Kame'enui, E. J. (2002, March 5). *The teaching of reading: Beyond vulgar dichotomies to the science of causality.* The White House Conference on Preparing Tomorrow's Teachers. Retrieved April 3, 2006, from http://www.ed.gov/admins/tchrqual/learn/ preparingteachersconference/kameenui.html

Kamphaus, R. W., & Frick, P. J. (2002). *Clinical assessment of child and adolescent personality and behavior.* Boston: Allyn and Bacon.

Kanada, M., Kreiman, C., & Nichols, P. D. (2007, April). *Effects of scoring environment on rater reliability, score validity and generalizability: A comparison of standup local scoring, online distributed scoring, and online local scoring.* Paper presented during the annual meeting of the American Educational Research Association, Chicago, IL.

Kane, T. J., Rockoff, J. E., & Staiger, D. O. (2006, April). *What does certification tell us about teacher effectiveness? Evidence from New York City* (Working Paper 12155). Cambridge, MA: National Bureau of Economic Research.

Kane, T. J., & Staiger, D. O. (2002). Volatility in school test scores: Implications for test-based accountability systems. In Diane Ravitch (Ed.), *Brookings papers on Education Policy 2002* [Based on BEEP Conference on Accountability and Its Consequences for Students: Are Children Hurt or Helped by Standards-Based Reforms? May 15–16, 2001]. Washington, DC: The Brookings Institution.

Kannapel, P. J., & Clements, S. K. (2005, February). *Inside the black box of high-performing high-poverty schools.* Lexington, KY: Prichard Committee for Academic Excellence. Retrieved July 19, 2005, from http://www.prichardcommittee.org

Kaplan, J. (Ed.) (1992). *Familiar quotations* [John Bartlett] (17th ed.) (p. 772). Boston: Little, Brown and Company.

Karantonis, A., & Sireci, S. C. (2006). The bookmark standard-setting method: A literature review. *Educational Measurement: Issues and Practice, 25*(1), 4–12.

Karweit, N. (1984). *Extending the school year and day.* Eugene, OR: Eric Clearinghouse on Educational Management. Retrieved July 18, 2005, from http://www.ericdigests.org/pre-922/year.htm

Kasindorf, M., & El Nasser, H. (2001, March 12). Impact of census's race data debated. *USA Today.* Retrieved February 18, 2005, from http://www.usatoday.com/news/census/2001-03-12-censusimpact.htm

Kaznowski, K. (2004). Slow learners: Are educators leaving them behind? *NASSP Bulletin, 88.* Retrieved March 26, 2007, from http://www.sagepub.com

Keiger, D. (2000, April). What brilliant kids are hungering for. *Johns Hopkins.* Retrieved May 10, 2005, from http://www.jhu.edu/~jhumag/0400web/16.html

Keller, B. (2004, May 19). Schools employing online tests to screen prospects. *Education Week,* pp. 1, 22.

Keller, B. (2004, November 17). Pennsylvania outlines teacher-test alternatives. *Education Week, 24*(12), p. 18.

Keller, B. (2007, August 15). The National Board: Challenged by success? *Education Week, 26*(45), 1, 16.

Keller, H. R. (2001). [Review of the *Early childhood attention-deficit disorders evaluation scale*]. In B. S. Plake & J. C. Impara (Eds), *The fourteenth mental measurements yearbook* (pp. 442–446). Lincoln, NE: Buros Institute of Mental Measurements.

Kellow, J. T., & Willson, V. L. (2001). Consequences of (mis)use of the Texas Assessment of Academic Skills (TAAS) for high-stakes decisions: Comment on Haney and the Texas miracle in education [Electronic version]. *Practical Assessment, Research & Evaluation, 7*(24). Retrieved January 24, 2005, from http://PAREonline.net/getvn.asp?v=7&n=24

Kelly, C., & Finnigan, K. (2003). Organizational context colors teacher expectancy. *Educational Administration Quarterly, 39*(5), 603–634.

Kelly, T. (1939). The selection of upper and lower groups for the validation of test items. *Journal of Educational Psychology, 30*(1), 17–24.

Kelly, T. L. (1947). *Fundamentals of statistics.* Cambridge, MA: Harvard University Press.

Kelly, S., & Monczunski, L. (2007). Overcoming the volatility in school-level gain scores: A new approach to identifying value added with cross-sectional data. *Educational Researcher, 36*(5), 279–287.

Kingsbury, G. G., & Wollack, J. A. (2001). [Review of the *Key math–revised*] In B. S. Plake & J. C. Impara (Eds.), *The fourteenth mental measurements yearbook* (pp. 637–641). Lincoln, NE: Buros Institute of Mental Measurements.

Kinzie, S. (2007, May 1). At first they flirt, then colleges crush: Rejection rough on students and schools. *Washington Post.* Retrieved May 3, 2007, from http://www.washingtonpost.com/wp-dyn/content/article/2007/04/30/AR20070430001678_pf.html

Klein, A. (2007, February 5). Researchers see college benefits for students who took AP courses. *Education Week, 26*(22), p. 7.

Knight, H. (2005, December 12). Offering incentives boosts attendance and test scores. *San Francisco Chronicle.* Retrieved December 15, 2005, from http://www.sfgate.com

Kobrin, J. L., Deng, H., & Shaw, E. J. (2007). Does quality count? The relationship between length of response and scores on the SAT Essay. *Journal of Applied Testing Technology, 8*(1), 1–15. Retrieved March 2, 2007, from http://www.testpublishers.org/jattmain.htm

Kohn, A. (2002, November 8). The dangerous myth of grade inflation. *Chronicle of Higher Education: Chronicle Review.* Retrieved July 16, 2004, from http://www.alfiekohn.org/teaching/gi.htm

Kohn, A. (2006). *The homework myth. Why our kids get too much of a bad thing.* Cambridge, MA: Da Capo Press.

Koretz, D., Stecher, B., Klein, S., & McCaffrey, D. (1994). The Vermont portfolio assessment program: Findings and implications. *Educational Measurement: Issues and Practice, 13*(3), 5–16.

Krathwohl, D. R., Bloom, B. S., & Masia, B. B. (1964). *Taxonomy of educational objectives: Handbook II: Affective domain.* New York: David McKay Co.

Kristoback, J., & Wright, R. J. (2001, February). *The success of test preparation on the scores from the fifth grade level Pennsylvania System of School Assessment (PSSA).* Paper presented at the annual meeting of the Eastern Educational Research Association, Hilton Head, SC.

Kroeze, D. J. (2007, April). *Is a high-performing district's performance high enough for NCLB?* Paper presented at the annual meeting of the National Council on Measurement in Education, Chicago, IL.

Krueger, A. B. (2002). Understanding the magnitude and effect of class size on student achievement. In L. Mishel and R. Rothstein (Eds.), *The class size debate* (pp. 7–35). Washington, DC: Economic Policy Institute.

Krueger, A. B. (2003). Economic considerations and class size. *Economic Journal, 113,* F34–F63.

Krueger, A. B., & Whitmore, D. M. (2001). *Would smaller classes help close the Black–White gap?* (Working Paper #451). Princeton, NJ: Princeton University Industrial Relations Section.

Kuder, G. F., & Richardson, M. W. (1937). The theory of the estimation of test reliability. *Psychometrika, 2*(3), 151–161.

Kulik, J. A., & Kulik, C. L. C. (1992). Meta-analysis findings on grouping programs. *Gifted Child Quarterly, 36*(2), 73–77.

Kusimo, P. A. (1999). Rural African Americans and education: The legacy of the Brown decision. Clearing House on Rural Education and Small Schools (ERIC Document Reproduction Service No. ED425050). Retrieved October 17, 2006, from http://www.ericdigests.org/1999-3/brown.htm

Laczko-Kerr, I., & Berliner, D. C. (2002).The effectiveness of "Teach for America" and other under-certified teachers on student academic achievement: A case of harmful public policy [Electronic version]. *Education Policy Archives, 10*(37). Retrieved July 9, 2005, from http://epaa.asu.edu/epaa/v10n37/

Laitsch, D. (2006). Heterogeneous grouping in advanced mathematics classes. *American Educational Research Journal, 43*(1), 105–136.

Laitsch, D. (2007). *Educator community and elementary student performance* [Research brief]. Association for Supervision and Curriculum Development. Retrieved February 27, 2007, from http://www.ascd.org/portal/site/ascd/menuitem.6a9dfddd720040bf989ad324d3108a0c/?printerFriendly=true

Landgraf, K. M. (2005). *Testing: Snapshots should not lead to snap judgments* [Issue paper]. Retrieved July 15, 2005, from http://www.ets.org/aboutets/issues1.html

Lane, S. (2004). Validity of high-stakes assessment: Are students engaged in complex thinking? *Educational Measurement: Issues and Practice, 23*(3), 6–14.

Lankford, H. S., Loeb, S., & Wyckoff, J. (2002). Teacher sorting and the plight of urban schools: A descriptive analysis. *Educational Evaluation and Policy Analysis, 24*(1), 37–62.

Law, J. G., Jr. (2001). [Test review of the *Scales for diagnosing attention-deficit–hyperactivity disorder*]. From B. S. Plake & J. C. Impara (Eds.), *The fifteenth mental measurements yearbook* [Electronic version]. Retrieved June 29, 2005, from the Buros Institute's Test Reviews Online Web site: http://www.unl.edu/buros

Law, L. (Producer), & Méndez, R. (Director). (1988). *Stand and deliver* [Motion picture]. United States: Warner Studios.

Lawler, P. (1993). *A longitudinal study of women's career choices: Twenty-five years later.* Pre-convention workshop from the annual meeting of the American Association of University Women. Reprinted later in *Gender issues in the classroom and on campus: Focus on the twenty-first century* (pp. 187–192). Washington, D.C.: American Association of University Women.

Leach, J. M., Scarborough, H. S., & Rescorla, L. (2003). Late-emerging reading disabilities. *Journal of Educational Psychology, 95*(2), 211–234.

Leahy, S., Lyon, C., Thompson, M., & Wiliam, D. (2005, November). Assessment minute, day by day. *Educational Leadership, 63*(3), 19–24.

Lederman, D. (2006). Krist views efforts to clamp down on senioritis with skepticism. *Faculty in the news.* Stanford, CA: School of Education, Stanford University. Retrieved November 18, 2006, from http://ed.stanford.edu/suse/faculty/displayFacultyNews.php?tablename=notify1&id=587

Lee, J. (2006). *Tracking achievement gaps and assessing the impact of NCLB on the gaps: An in-depth look into national and state reading and math outcome trends.* Cambridge, MA: The Civil Rights Project at Harvard University.

Lee, J., & Fox, J. (2007, April). *Minority students at risk for low and high performance: A comparison of NAEP achievement gaps to special and gifted education placement gaps.* A paper presented during the annual meeting of the American Educational Research Association, Chicago, IL.

Lehmann, I. J., Nagy, P., & Poteat, M. G. (1998). [Review of the *Stanford diagnostic mathematics test, fourth edition*]. In J. C. Impara & B. S. Plake (Eds.), *The thirteenth mental measurements yearbook* (pp. 930–938). Lincoln, NE: Buros Institute of Mental Measurements.

Leischer, J. (2005, January 5). *State standards fail to meet NCLB challenge* [Research report]. Thomas B. Fordham Foundation. Retrieved January 6, 2005, from http://www.edexcellence.net/foundation/about/press_release.cfm?id=14

Lemann, N. (1999). *The big test.* New York: Farrar, Straus and Giroux.

Leslie, M. (2000, July/August). The vexing legacy of Lewis Terman. *Stanford.* Retrieved January 30, 2005, from http://www.stanfordalumni.org/news/magazine/2000/julaug/articles/terman.html

Levitt, S. D., & Dubner, S. J. (2005). *Freakonomics.* New York: HarperCollins.

Lewin, T. (2007, June 8). States found to vary widely on education. *New York Times,* p. A20.

Lichtenstein, R. (2002). Learning disabilities criteria: Recommendations for change in IDEA reauthorization [Electronic version]. *NASP Communiqué, 30*(6). Retrieved July 15, 2004, from http://www.nasponline.org/publications/cq3061dinsert.html

Lieberman, M. (2000). *Merit pay can't provide the incentives for improvement* [Weekly column]. Washington, DC: Education Policy Institute. Retrieved July 15, 2005, from http://www.educationpolicy.org

Lieberman, N. (2004). *Admissions.* New York: Time Warner Bookmark.

Lin, W. V. (2001). *Parenting beliefs regarding young children perceived as having or not having inattention and/or hyperactivity–impulsivity behaviors.* Unpublished doctoral dissertation, University of South Dakota, 2001. *ProQuest* publication number AAT 3007070.

Linn, R. (2003). *Accountability: Responsibility and reasonable expectations* [AERA presidential address]. *Educational Researcher, 31*(7), 3–13.

Linn, R. L. (2007, April-a). *Approaches to educational accountability.* Paper presented during the annual meeting of the National Council on Measurement in Education, Chicago, IL.

Linn, R. L. (2007, April-b). *Needed modifications of NCLB.* Paper presented during the annual meeting of the National Council on Measurement in Education, Chicago, IL.

Linn, R., & Gronlund, N. (2000). *Measurement and assessment in teaching.* San Francisco: Prentice Hall.

Linn, R. L., & Haug, C. (2002, April). *Stability of school building accountability scores and gains* [Center for the Study of Evaluation Report 561]. Los Angeles, CA: Center for the Study of Evaluation, Graduate School of Education & Information Sciences, University of California, Los Angeles.

Linn, R. L., & Miller, M. D. (2005). *Measurement and assessment in teaching* (9th ed.). Upper Saddle River, NJ: Pearson, Merrill, Prentice Hall.

Lipka, S. (2007, June 12). Elite company. *Chronicle of Higher Education, 53*(42), pp. A31–35.

Liu, J., Allspach, J. R., Feigenbaum, M., Oh, H., & Burton, N. (2004). *A study of fatigue effects from the New SAT* [College Board Research Report No. ETS RR-04-46]. New York: College Entrance Examination Board.

Lizama, J. A. (2004, October 5). Is the tide turning on class rank? *Richmond Times Dispatch.* Retrieved October 7, 2004, from http://www.timesdispatch.com/servlet/satellite?pagename=RTD%2FMGArticle%2FRTD_BasicArticle&cid=1031778339252&path=%21news&s=1045855934842

Lloyd, C. (2005, March 27). How much is a school worth? Parents add test scores into home-purchase equations. *San Francisco Chronicle.* Retrieved July 15, 2005, from http://sfgate.com

Lockwood, J. R., McCaffrey, D. F., Hamilton, L. S., Stecher, B., Vi-Nhuan, L., & Martinez, J. F. (2007). The sensitivity of value-added teacher effect estimates to different mathematics achievement tests. *Journal of Educational Measurement, 44*(1), 47–67.

Logerfo, L. (2006). Climb every mountain. *Education Next.* Stanford, CA: Hoover Institution, Leland Stanford Junior University.

Lonergan, D. (2006, March 27). *Dover–Sherborn High School student handbook.* Dover, MA. Retrieved April 13, 2006, from http://www.doversherborn.org/highschool/index.htm

Long, J. S. (1997). Regression models for categorical and limited dependent variables. *Advanced Quantitative Techniques: Volume 7 of the social science series.* Thousand Oaks, CA: Sage.

Longstaffe, J. A., & Bradfield, J. W. B. (2005, May). *A review of factors influencing the dissemination of the London Agreed Protocol for Teaching (LAPT): A confidence based marketing system* [Unpublished policy statement]. University College, London. Retrieved November 26, 2006, from http://www.ucl.ac.uk/LAPT/CBM_review.doc

Lord, F. M. (1952). The relationship of the reliability of multiple-choice to the distribution of item difficulties. *Psychometrika, 17*(2), 181–194.

Lord, F. M., & Novick, M. R. (1968). *Statistical theories of mental test scores.* Reading, MA: Addison-Wesley.

Lou, L. (2007, March 28). District considers "grade bump" incentives for students who do well on state tests. *San Diego Union Tribune.* Retrieved June 26, 2007, from http://www.signonsandiego.com/uniontrib/20070328/news_1mi28smgrade.html

Lubienski, C., & Lubienski, S. T. (2006, January). *Charter, private, public schools and academic achievement: New evidence from NAEP mathematics data.* New York: National Center for the Study of Privatization in Education, Teachers College, Columbia University. Retrieved April 6, 2006, from http://www.ncspe.org/publications_files/OP111.pdf

Lunz, M. E., & Bashook, P. G. (2007, April). *The impact of examiner communication ability on oral examination outcomes.* Paper presented during the annual meeting of the National Council on Measurement in Education, Chicago, IL.

Lyon, R. L. (1998, April 28). *Overview of reading and literacy initiatives of the Child Development and Behavior branch of the National Institute of Child Health and Human Development, National Institutes of Health* [Report to the House of Representatives, Committee on Labor and Human Resources]. Washington, DC. Retrieved July 1, 2005, from http://www.readbygrade3.com/lyon.htm

Maeroff, G. I. (1992). Reform comes home: Policies to encourage parental involvement in children's education. In C. E. Finn & T. Rebarber (Eds.), *Education reform in the 90s* (pp. 175–194). New York: Macmillan.

Malcolm, K. K., & Schafer, W. D. (2005). [Review of the *Comprehensive testing program 4*]. In R. A. Spies & B. S. Plake (Eds.), *The sixteenth mental measurements yearbook* [Electronic version]. Retrieved November 8, 2006, from the Buros Institute's Test Reviews Online Web site: http://unl.edu/buros

Manning, M. L. (2000). Child-centered middle schools. A position paper: Association for Childhood Education International. *Childhood Education, 76*(3), 154–159. (ERIC Journal No. EJ602130)

Manzo, K. K. (2005, March 16). Social studies losing out to reading, math. *Education Week, 24*(27), pp. 1, 16.

Marchant, G. J., & Paulson, S. E. (2005, January 21). The relationship of high school graduation exams to graduation rates and SAT scores [Electronic version]. *Education Policy Analysis Archives, 13*(6). Retrieved February 10, 2005, from http://epaa.asu.edu/epaa/v13n6/

Margolis, H., & Free, J. (2001). The consultant's corner: Computerized IEP programs: A guide for educational consultants. *Journal of Educational and Psychological Consultation, 12*(2), 171–178.

Marion, S. F., & Pellegrino, J. W. (2006). A validity framework for evaluating the technical quality of alternative assessments. *Educational Measurement: Issues and Practice, 25*(4), 47–57.

Marion, S. F., & Sheinker, A. (1999). *Issues and consequences for state-level minimum competency testing programs* (Wyoming Report 1). Minneapolis, MN: University of Minnesota, National Center on Educational Outcomes. Retrieved February 5, 2005, from http://education.unm.edu/NCE/OnlinePubs/WyReport1.html

Markow, D., & Martin, S. (2005). *The MetLife survey of the American teacher: Transitions and the role of supportive relationships.* New York: Harris Interactive.

Marrs, J. (2001). *Rule by secrecy.* New York: HarperCollins.

Marsh, H. W., Trautwein, U., Lüdke, O., & Baumert, J. (2007). The big-fish-little-pond effect: Persistent negative effects of selective high schools on self-concept after graduation. *American Educational Research Journal, 44*(3), 631–669.

Martin, M. O., Mullis, I. V. S., & Chrostowski, S. J. (2004). *TIMSS 2003 technical report.* Chestnut Hill, MA: TIMSS & PIRLS International Study Center, Boston College. Retrieved September 6, 2005, from http://timss.bc.edu

Maruti, S. S., Feskanich, D., Colditz, G. A., Frazier, A. L., Sampson, L. A., Michels, K. B., et al. (2005). Adult recall of adolescent diet: Reproducibility and comparison with maternal reporting. *American Journal of Epidemiology, 161*(1), 89–97.

Marvel, J., Lyter, D. M., Peltola, P., Strizek, G. A., & Morton, B. A. (2007, January). *Teacher attrition and mobility: Results from the 2004–2005 teacher follow-up survey* [NCES 2007-307]. Washington, DC: National Center for Educational Statistics, U. S. Department of Education.

Marzano, R. J. (2000). *Transforming classroom grading.* Alexandria, VA: Association for Supervision and Curriculum Development.

Marzano, R. J., Pickering, D. J., & Pollock, J. E. (2001). *Classroom instruction that works: Research-based strategies for increasing student achievement.* Alexandria, VA: Association for Supervision and Curriculum Development.

Massachusetts Department of Education. (2005, April). *Grade retention in Massachusetts public schools: 2003–2004.* Malden, MA: Author.

Mathews, J. (1988). *Escalante: The best teacher in America.* New York: Holt.

Mathews, J. (2005, June 14). Where some give credit, others say it's not due. *Washington Post,* p. A14.

Maxwell, L. (2006, September 6). Massachusetts schools experiment with extra time. *Education Week, 26*(2), pp. 30, 33.

Maxwell, L. A. (2007, February, 14). The other gap. *Education Week, 26*(23), pp. 25, 27–29.

Mayer, R. E. (1999). Fifty years of creativity research. In R. J. Sternberg (Ed.), *Handbook of creativity* (pp. 449–460). Cambridge, UK: Cambridge University Press.

McCarney, S. B., & Johnson, N. (1995). *Early childhood attention-deficit disorder evaluation scale (ECADDES).* Columbia, MO: Hawthorne Educational Services.

McClure, C. T. (2007, August). Ability grouping and acceleration in gifted education. *District Administration, 43*(8), 24–25.

McGill-Franzen, A., & Allington, R. (2006, June). Contamination of current accountability systems. *Phi Delta Kappan, 87*(10), 762–766.

McGrew, K. S. (2003, November 28). *Cattell–Horn–Carroll definition project.* Institute of Applied Psychometrics. Retrieved March 7, 2005, from http://www.iapsych.com/chcdef.htm

McNeil, S. (2004). *The 1970s: Influences on this period. A hypertext history of instructional design.* Retrieved January 8, 2005, from http://www.coe.uh.edu/courses/cuin6373/idhistory/1970.html

McTighe, J., & O'Connor, K. (2005, November). Seven practices for effective learning. *Educational Leadership, 63*(3), 10–17.

Mednick, S. A. (1962). The associative basis of the creative process. *Psychological Review, 69,* 220–232.

Meek, C. (2006). From the inside out: A look at the testing of special education students. *Phi Delta Kappan, 88*(4), p. 293–297.

Meeker, R. J., & Weile, D. M. (1971). A school for the cities. *Education and Urban Society, 3,* 129–243.

Mehring, T. (1995). Report card options for students with disabilities in general education. In T. Azwell & E. Schmar (Eds.), *Report card on report cards: Alternatives to consider.* Portsmouth, NH: Heinemann.

Méndez, T. (2005, February 15). Changing school with the season. *Christian Science Monitor.* Retrieved February 16, 2005, from http://www.csmonitor.com/2005/ 0215/p11s01-legn.html

Messick, S. (1989). Validity. In R. L. Linn (Ed.), *Educational measurement* (3rd ed.), (pp. 13–103). New York: American Council on Education and Macmillan.

Meyer, C. A. (1992, May). What's the difference between authentic and performance assessment? *Educational Leadership, 49*(8), 39–42.

Meyer, J. P. (2006, August 31). *ItemQual 0.9.2* [Free software]. Harrisonburg, VA: Center for Assessment and Research Studies, James Madison University. Retrieved March 16, 2007, from http://people.jmu.edu/meyerjp/ItemQual.asp

Miller, B. J., Sundre, D. L., Setzer, C., & Zeng, X. (2007, April). *Content validity: A comparison of two methods.* Paper presented during the annual meeting of the national Council on Measurement in Education, Chicago, IL.

Miller, D. (1995). [Review of the *Kaufman brief intelligence test*]. In J. C. Conoley & J. C. Impara (Eds.), *The twelfth mental measurements yearbook* (pp. 533–536). Lincoln, NE: Buros Institute of Mental Measurements.

Miller, G. E. (2004). Analyzing the minority gap in achievement scores: Issues for states and federal government. *Educational Measurement Issues and Practices, 22*(3), 30–36.

Miller, T. (2003). Essay assessment with latent semantic analysis. *Journal of Educational Computing Research, 29*(4), 495–512.

Millman, J., & Greene, J. (1989). The specification and development of tests of achievement and ability. In R. L. Linn (Ed.), *Educational measurement* (3rd ed.) (pp. 335–366). New York: Macmillan.

Millman, J., & Schalock, H. D. (1997). Beginnings and introduction. In J. Millman (Ed.), *Grading teachers, grading schools.* Thousand Oaks, CA: Corwin Press.

Mindish, J. M. (2003). *Predictions of grade 11 PSSA mathematics and reading scores.* Unpublished doctoral dissertation, Widener University.

Mitchell, T. (2005, August 19). Realistic FCAT practice is about to become available. *Florida Times-Union.* Retrieved August 22, 2005, from http://cgi.jacksonville.com/

Moore, A. S. (2004, August 1). Trouble in the ranks: The dog-eat-dog race of elite colleges has high schools reconsidering class rank. *New York Times,* pp. 10–11.

Morreale, S. P., & Suen, H. K. (2001). [Review of the *Test of early language development, third edition*]. In B. S. Plake & J. C. Impara (Eds.), *The fourteenth mental measurements yearbook* (pp. 1239–1242). Lincoln, NE: Buros Institute of Mental Measurements.

Moskal, B. M. (2007). Scoring rubrics: What when and how? [Electronic version]. *Practical Assessment, Research & Evaluation, 7*(3). Retrieved April 23, 2007, from http://PAREonline.net/getvn.asp?v=7&n=3

Murphy, G., & Likert, R. (1938). *Public opinion and the individual: A psychological study of student attitudes on public questions with a retest five years later.* New York: Harper Books.

National Assessment of Educational Progress. (2004). *The nation's report card.* Washington, DC: National Center for Education Statistics. Retrieved July 7, 2005, from http://nces.ed.gov/nationsreportcard

National Assessment of Educational Progress Authorization Act (P.L. 103-33, 1993).

National Association for Gifted Children. (2005). *Why we should advocate for gifted and talented children* [Position statement]. Washington, DC: Author. Retrieved November 5, 2006, from http://www .nagc.org/index.aspx?id=538

National Association for the Assessment of Young Children. (1987). *Standardized testing of young children 3 through 8 years of age* [Position statement]. Washington, DC: Author.

National Association for the Education of Young Children. (2004). *Where we stand, NAEYC and NAECS/SDE on curriculum, assessment, and program evaluation.* Retrieved March 23, 2007, from http://www .naeyc.org/about/positions/pdf/StandlCurrAss.pdf

National Association of Early Childhood Specialists in State Departments of Education. (2000). Assessment of young children. Retrieved June 20, 2005, from http://www.state.ia.us/educate/ecese/is/ecn/ primaryse/tppse05j.htm

National Association of School Psychologists. (2003). *Position statement on student grade retention and social promotion.* Retrieved January 13, 2005, from http://www .nasponline.org/information/pospaper/ graderetent.html

National Association of School Psychologists. (2005). Position statement on ability grouping and tracking. Retrieved October 16, 2006, from http://www.nasponline.org/information/pospaper_ag.html

National Board for Professional Teaching Standards. (1988) [First published in 1986]. *National board for professional teaching standards.* Washington, DC: ERIC Clearinghouse on Teacher Education. (ERIC Document No. ED304444, ERIC Digest # 88-6)

National Center for Educational Statistics. (2004). *Trends in international mathematics and science study.* Washington, DC: Author. Retrieved on November 2, 2006, from http://nces.ed.gov/pubs2005/timss03

National Center for Educational Statistics. (2007). *America's high school graduates: Results from the 2005 NAEP High School Transcript Study* [Commissioner's remarks]. Retrieved February 23, 2007, from http://nces.ed.gov/whatsnew/commissioner/remarks2007/2_22_2007.asp

National Commission on Excellence in Education. (1983). *A nation at risk: The imperative for educational reform.* Washington, DC: Superintendent of Documents, U.S. Government Printing Office.

National Council of Teachers of Mathematics. (1991). *Professional standards for teaching mathematics.* Reston, VA: Author.

National Council of Teachers of Mathematics. (2003, October). *The use of technology in the learning of mathematics* [NCTM position paper]. Reston, VA: Author. Retrieved July 21, 2005, from http://www.nctm.org/about/position_statements/position_statement_ 13.htm

National Council of Teachers of Mathematics. (2006). *Computation, calculators, and common sense* [Position statement]. Reston, VA: Author. Retrieved April, 3, 2006, from http://www.nctm.org/about/ position_statements/computation.htm

National Education Association. (2003). *Status of the American public school teacher 2000–2001.* Washington, DC: Author.

National Education Association. (2004, February). *Does the NCLB provide good choices for students in low-performing schools?* Cambridge, MA: Harvard Civil Rights Project. Retrieved June 25, 2007, from http://www.nea.org/esea/harvardcrpchoicesexesum.html?mode=print

National Education Association. (2007). *Professional pay.* Washington, D.C.: National Education Association, Author. Retrieved September 7, 2007, from http://www.nea.org/pay/maps/teachermap.html

National Institute of Child Health and Human Development. (2000). *Report of the National Reading Panel. Teaching children to read: An evidence-based assessment of the scientific literature on reading and its implications for reading instruction: Reports of the subgroups* (NIH Publication No. 00-4754). Washington, DC: U.S. Government Printing Office.

National Merit Scholarship Program. (2004). Retrieved February 3, 2005, from http://www.natioinalmerit .org/nmsp.html

National Partnership for Teaching At-Risk Schools. (2005). *Qualified teachers for at-risk schools: A national imperative* [Initial report]. Washington, DC: Author.

National Reading Panel. (2000, April). *Teaching children to read: An evidence-based assessment of the scientific research literature on reading and its implications for reading instruction* (National Institute of Health Publication No. 00-4769). Rockville, MD: National Institute of Health, National Institute of Child Health and Human Development.

National Register of Historic Places. (n.d.). *Welcome to the National Register of Historic Places.* Retrieved April 3, 2006, from http://www.nationalregisterofhistoricplaces.com/

New Jersey School Boards Association. (2003). Grading students. *School Leader* (Policy update). Trenton, NJ: Author. Retrieved May 31, 2005, from http://www.njsba.org

New York State Education Department. (1987). History of Regents Examinations 1865 to 1987. Retrieved March 16, 2007, from http://www.emsc.nysed.gov/osa/hsinfogen/hsinfogenarch/rehistory.htm

New York United Federation of Teachers (2004, July 13). "New" new report card lauded. *Education World: The Educators Best Friend.* Retrieved July 13, 2004, from http://www.education-world.com/a_admin/admin068.shtml

Nichols, S. L., Glass, G. V., & Berliner, D. C. (2005, September). *High-stakes testing and student achievement: Problems for the No Child Left Behind Act* (Report EPSL-0509-105-EPRU). Tempe, AZ: Educational Policy Studies Laboratory, Arizona State University.

Niguidula, D. (2005, November). Documenting learning with digital portfolios. *Educational Leadership, 63*(3), 44–47.

Nitko, A. J. (1996). *Educational assessment of students.* Englewood Cliffs, NJ: Merrill, Prentice Hall.

No Child Left Behind Act (ESEA) (P.L. 107-110, 2002).

Noble, J. P., Davenport, M., & Sawyer, R. (2001, April). *Relationships between noncognitive characteristics, high school course work and grades, and performance on a college admission test.* Paper presented during the annual meeting of the American Educational Research Association, Seattle, WA.

Noble, J. P., Roberts, W. L., & Sawyer, R. L. (2006, April). *Student achievement, behavior, perceptions, and other factors affecting ACT scores* [ACT Research Report Series, October 2006]. Paper presented during the annual meeting of the American Educational Research Association, Chicago, IL.

Noguera, P. A. (2003). *How race identity affects school performance.* Cambridge, MA: Harvard Education Letter.

North Central Regional Educational Laboratory (1993). *Integrating community services for young children and their families.* Retrieved June 5, 2005, from http://www.ncrel.org/sdrs/areas/issues/envrnmnt/go/93-3read.htm

Northwest Regional Educational Laboratory. (1989). *North Carolina end of grade testing program booklet.* Retrieved April 29, 2005, from http://www.ceap.wcu.edu/Houghton/Learner/think/thinkhigher order.html

Nye, B., Hedges, L. V., & Konstantopoulos, S. (2000). The effects of small classes on academic achievement: The results of the Tennessee class size experiment. *American Educational Research Journal, 37*(1), 123–151.

Obey-Porter Act (Elementary and Secondary Education Act [ESEA]), P.L. 105-78, 1998 § Title X, Sec. C.

O'Connor, J. J., & Robertson, E. F. (2003). Karl Pearson. Archive document, School of Mathematics and Statistics, University of St. Andrews, Scotland. Retrieved April 16, 2005, from http://www-groups.dcs.st-and.ac.uk/history/Mathematicians/Pearson.htm

O'Donovan, E. (2007). Making individualized education programs manageable for parents. *District Administration, 43*(7), 69.

Oh, H., & Sathy, V. (2007, April). *Construct comparability and continuity in the SAT.* Paper presented during the annual meeting of the national Council on Measurement in Education, Chicago, IL.

Ohio State Board of Education. (2006, April 10). *Report on the first year assessment of kindergarten readiness, literacy.* Retrieved May 10, 2006, from http://www.omea-ohio.org/advocacy/ArtsOnLine .04.10.06.html

Olson, L. (2003). Standards and tests: Keeping them aligned. *Research Points, 1*(1), 1–4.

Olson, L. (2004, December 1). NCLB law bestows bounty on test industry. *Education Week,* pp. 1, 18, 19.

Olson, L. (2006, August 30). Number of graduation exams required by states levels off. *Education Week, 28*(1), p. 28.

Olson, L. (2006, December 6). U.S. urged to rethink NCLB "tools." *Education Week, 26*(14), pp. 1, 19.

Organization for Economic Co-Operation and Development. (2005, June). *Teachers matter: Attracting, developing and retaining effective teachers.* Paris, France: Author. Retrieved July 16, 2005, from http://www.oecdbookshop.org

Organization for Economic Co-Operation and Development (2006, May 15). *OECD education systems leave many immigrant children floundering, report shows.* Brussels, Belgium: Directorate of Education, OECD. Retrieved November 18, 2006, from http://www.oecd.org/documentprint/0,2744,en_2649_201185_36701777_1_1_1_1,00.html

Ornstein, A. C., & Levine, D. U. (1989). *Foundations of education* (4th ed.). Boston: Houghton Mifflin.

Otis, A. (1925). *Statistical method in educational measurement.* New York: World Book.

Owens, A., & Sunderman, G. L. (2006, October). *School accountability under NCLB: Aid or obstacle for measuring racial equity?* [Policy Brief]. Cambridge, MA: The Civil Rights Project, Harvard University. Retrieved November 28, 2006, from http://www.civilrightsproject.harvard.edu/research/esea/NCLB_Policy_Brief_Final.pdf

Packer, J. (2006, January 19). More schools are failing NCLB law's "adequate yearly progress" requirements: Emerging trends under the law's annual rating system. Washington, DC: National Education Association. Retrieved April 5, 2007, from http://www.nea.org?esea/ayptrends0106html

Pakkala, T. (2006, May 31). Does it pay to reward students for success? *Gainsville Sun.* Retrieved June 5, 2006, from http://www.gainsville.com

Partin, R. L. (2005). *Classroom teacher's survival guide: Practical strategies, management techniques, and reproducibles for new and experienced teachers* (2nd ed.). San Francisco: Jossey-Bass.

Pascopella, A. (2007). Inside the law: Cheating on NCLB tests? Maybe. *District Administration, 43*(1), 20.

Pascopella, A. (2007). The dropout crisis. *District Administration, 43*(1), 30–36, 38.

PASE v. Hannon, 506 F. Supp. 831 (Northern District of Illinois, 1980).

Patrick, K., & Eichel, L. (2006, June 25). Education tests: Who's minding the scores? *Philadelphia Inquirer.* Retrieved June 26, 2006, from http://philly.com/mld/inquirer/living/education/14898076.htm

Paulson, A. (2005, May 23). Need a tutor? Call India. *Christian Science Monitor.* Retrieved March 30, 2006, from http://www.csmonitor.com/2005/0523/p01s01-legn.htm

Pellegrino, J. (2007). Should NAEP performance standards be used for setting standards for state assessments? *Phi Delta Kappan, 88*(7), 539–541.

Perez, M., & Ines, Y. (2004). *Validation of the Spanish version of the Behavior assessment system for children: Parent rating scale for children (6–11) in Puerto Rico.* Unpublished doctoral dissertation, Temple University.

Peske, H. G., & Haycock, K. (2006, June). *Teaching inequality: How poor and minority students are short-changed on teacher quality* [A Report and Recommendation by the Education Trust]. Washington, DC: The Education Trust. Retrieved June 18, 2006, from http://www2.edtrust.org/EdTrust/Press+Room/teacherquality2006.htm

Phelps, R. (2005) The source of Lake Wobegon. *Third Education Group Review, 1*(2). Retrieved October 13, 2006, from http://www.thirdeducationgroup.org/Review/Articles/v1n2.htm

Philadelphia Architects and Buildings Project. (2003). David Foy Combined Secondary and Primary School. Philadelphia: Author. Retrieved July 21, 2005, from http://www.philadelphiabuildings.org

Phillips, G. W. (2007). *Expressing international educational achievement in terms of U.S. performance standards: Linking NAEP achievement levels to TIMSS.* Washington, DC: American Institutes for Research.

Phillips, S. E. (2005, June). Legal corner: Reconciling IDEA and NCLB. *NCME Newsletter, 13*(2), 2–3.

Piaget, J. (1930). *The child's conception of physical causality* (M. Gabian, Trans.). New York: Harcourt Brace.

Piaget, J. (1964). *The child's conception of number* (C. Gattegno & F. M. Hodgson, Trans.). London: Routledge & Paul. (Original work published in Switzerland in 1941; first English translation in 1952)

Pianta, R. C. (2007, March). Opportunities to learn in America's elementary classrooms. *Science, 315,* 1795–1796.

Picard, C. J. (2004, August 18). [Press release]. Office of the State Secretary of Education. Baton Rouge, LA. Retrieved August 21, 2005, from http://www.doe.state.la.us

Plessen, K. J., Bansal, R., Zhu, R., Amat, J., Quackenbush, G. A., Martin, L., et al. (2006, July). Hippocampus and amygdale morphology in attention-deficit/hyperactivity disorder. *Archives of General Psychiatry, 63*(7), 795–807.

Pope, J. (2006, May 12). Student fatigue may explain drop in SATs [Associated Press]. *Boston Globe.* Retrieved May 13, 2006, from http://www.boston.com/

Popham, W. J. (1973). Found: A practical procedure to appraise teacher achievement in the classroom. In A. C. Ornstein (Ed.), *Accountability for teachers and school administrator* (pp. 25–27). Belmont, CA: Fearon.

Popham, W. J. (1990). *Modern educational measurement: A practitioner's perspective* (2nd ed.). Englewood Cliffs, NJ: Prentice Hall.

Popham, W. J. (1999). *Classroom assessment: What teachers need to know* (2nd ed.). Boston: Allyn and Bacon.

Popham, W. J. (2000, December). The mismeasurement of educational quality. *School Administrator* [Electronic version]. Retrieved September 21, 2004, from http://www.aasa.org/publications/sa/2000_12/popham_mismeasurement.htm

Popham, W. J. (2005, May). All about accountability/NAEP: Gold standard or fool's gold? *Educational Leadership, 62*(8), 79–81.

Popham, W. J. (2006, April). Branded by a test. *Educational Leadership, 63*(7), 86–87.

Popielarski, J. (1998). *Characteristics, background, and teaching methodologies of advanced placement U.S. history teachers.* Unpublished doctoral dissertation, Widener University.

Posner, D. (2004, June). What's wrong with teaching to the test? *Phi Delta Kappan, 85*(10), 749–751.

Powers, D. E., Burstein, J. C., Chodorow, M., Fowles, M. E., & Kukich, K. (2001, March). *Stumping E-Rater: Challenging the validity of automated essay scoring* (Report No. 98-08bP). Princeton, NJ: Educational Testing Service.

Pressey, S. L., & Pressey, L. C. (1923). *Introduction to the use of standard tests: A brief manual in the use of tests of both ability and achievement in the school subjects.* Yonkers, NY: World Book.

Psychological Corporation. (2001). *Wechsler individual achievement test–second edition.* San Antonio, TX: Author.

Public Education Network. (2005). *Open to the public: Speaking out on "No Child Left Behind."* Retrieved June 23, 2005, from http://www.publiceducation.org/nclb_NationalReport.asp

Rabb, T. K. (2005). *Crisis in history: A statement.* National Council for History Education. Retrieved June 22, 2005, from http://www.history.org/nche/

Rachmil, M. (Producer), & Rosman, M. (Director). (2004). *A Cinderella story* [Motion picture]. United States: Warner Bros.

Rado, D., & Dell'Angela, T. (2005, June 14). Reading test may get easier to pass. *Chicago Tribune* [Electronic version]. Retrieved June 16, 2005, from http://www.chicagotribune.com/news/local/chi-0506140233 jun14,1,7163850.story?

Rahman, T. (2007). *Mapping 2005 state proficiency standards onto the NAEP scales* [Research and development report]. Washington, DC: National Center for Educational Statistics, U.S. Department of Education.

Rakes, G. C. (2005–2006). *The effect of open book testing on student performance in online learning environments* [Research by Project RITE grant]. Martin, TN: University of Tennessee. Retrieved October 28, 2006, from http://edtech.ten nessee.edu/rite/rite2006/rakes_rite_06pdf

Ramos, I. (1996, April). Gender differences in risk-taking behavior and their relationship to SAT-mathematics performance. *Find Articles, Look Smart.* Retrieved October 26, 2006, from http://www.findarticles.com/p/articles/mi_qa3667

Rasch, G. (1960/1980). An individualistic approach to item analysis. In P. F. Lazarsfeld and N. W. Henry (Eds.), *Readings in mathematical social science* (pp. 89–107). Chicago: Science Research Associates.

Ravitch, D. (1995). *National standards in American education: A citizen's guide.* Washington, DC: The Brookings Institution Press.

Ravitch, D. (2000). *Left back: A century of battles over school reform.* New York: Touchstone Books of Simon & Schuster.

Raymond, M., & Fletcher, S. H. (2002, August). *Teach for America* [Research report]. Palo Alto, CA: CREDO Group, the Hoover Institution. Retrieved July 10, 2005, from http://www.educationnext.org

Reardon, S. F., & Galindo, C. (2002). Do high-states tests affect students' decisions to drop out of school? Evidence from NELS (Working Paper 03-01). State College, PA: Population Research Institute, The Pennsylvania State University.

Reckase, M. D. (1995). Portfolio assessment: A theoretical estimate of score reliability. *Educational Measurement: Issues and Practice, 14*(1), 12–14, 21.

Reed, J. B. (2004, October, 29). Smart kids may be the ones left behind. *News Press,* pp. B1–B2.

Rees, N. S. (2003, October 20). *No Child Left Behind's education choice provisions: Are states and school districts giving parents the information they need?* Testimony of Nina S. Rees before the U.S. House of Representatives. Retrieved June 24, 2005, from http://edworkforce.house.gov/hearings/108th/edr/nclbchoice102003/rees.htm

Reeves, P. (2005, February 12). *Internet tutors from India aid U.S. kids with math.* NPR [Radio broadcast]. Retrieved June 23, 2005, from http://www.npr.org/templates/story/story.php?storyId=4497026

Rehabilitation Act, 1973 (P.L. 93-112 [87 Stat.355] § 504).

Reid, K. (2006, October 30). Parents, teachers confused over new report cards. *Stockton Record.* Retrieved November 5, 2006, from http://www.recordnet.com/apps/pbcs.dll/article?AID=/20061030/NEWS01/610300317/1001

Reid, K. D., Hersko, W. P., & Hamill, D. D. (1981/2001). *Test of early reading ability, third edition (TERA-3).* Austin, TX: Pro-Ed.

Renchler, R. (1992). Student motivation, school culture, and academic achievement: What school leaders can do. *ERIC/CEM Trends and Issues Series, Number 7* (ERIC Document No. EA 023 593).

Renzulli, J. S., & Park, S. (2002). *Giftedness and high school dropouts: Personal, family, and school-related factors* (RM02168). Storrs, CT: The National Research Center on the Gifted and Talented, University of Connecticut. Retrieved November 5, 2006, from http://www.gifted.uconn.edu/nrcgt/renzpark.html

Resnick, L. B. (Ed.) (2004). Teachers matter; Evidence from value-added assessments. *Research Points: Essential Information for Educational Policy, 2*(4), 1–4.

Rex, S. L. (2003). *Reading strategies as a predictor of student scores on the Pennsylvania System of School Assessment Reading Exam at the eleventh-grade level.* Unpublished doctoral dissertation, Widener University.

Reynolds, C., & Kamphaus, R. (2004). *Behavior assessment system for children, third edition.* Circle Pines, MN: American Guidance Service, Pearson Education.

Richman, S. (2001, April). *Parent power: Why national standards won't improve education* (Policy Analysis No. 396). Washington, DC: The Cato Institute. Retrieved June 26, 2005, from http://www.cato.org

Ritchie, S. (2004). Horace Mann. *Dictionary of Unitarian & Universalist Biography.* Retrieved June 21, 2005, from http://www.uua.org/uuhs/duub/articles/horacemann.html

Rivers-Sanders, J. C. (1999). *The impact of teacher effect on student math competency achievement.* Doctoral dissertation, University of Tennessee. ProQuest document ID 730840811.

Rodriguez, M. C. (2005). Three options are optimal for multiple-choice items: A meta-analysis of 80 years of research. *Educational Measurement: Issues and Practice, 24*(2), 3–13.

Roediger, III, H. L., & Karpicke, J. D. (2006). The power of testing memory: Basic research and implications for educational practice. *Perspectives on Psychological Science, 1*(3), 181–208.

Rogers, J., Holme, J. J., & Silver, D. (2005). *More questions than answers: CAHSEE results, opportunity to learn, and the class of 2006.* Los Angeles: UCLA Institute for Democracy, Education, and Access. Retrieved August 25, 2005, from http:// www.idea.gseis.ucla.edu/resources/exitexam/index.html

Roid, G. H. (2003). *Stanford–Binet intelligence scales, fifth edition.* Itasca, IL: Riverside.

Rojstaczer, S. (2003). *Grade inflation at American colleges and universities.* Retrieved June 5, 2005, from http://gradeinflation.com/

Romanowski, M. K. (2004). Student obsession with grades and achievement. *Kappa Delta Pi Record, 40*(4), 149–151.

Roschewski, P., Isernhagen, J., & Dappen, L. (2006). Nebraska STARS: Achieving results. *Phi Delta Kappan, 87*(6), 433–437.

Rose, L. C., & Gallup, A. C. (2005, September). Pie Delta Kappa/Gallup Poll of the public's attitudes toward the public schools. *Phi Delta Kappan, 87*(1), 41–57.

Roseberry-McKibbin, C., & Brice, A. (2005). *Acquiring English as a second language: What's normal, what's not.* Rockville, MD: American Speech-Language-Hearing Association. Retrieved March 30, 2006, from http://www.asha.org/public/speech/development/easl.htm

Rosen, C. L. (1985). [Test review of the *Creativity assessment packet*]. From J. V. Mitchell Jr. (Ed.), *The ninth mental measurements yearbook* [Electronic version]. Retrieved February 14, 2005, from the Buros Institute's Test Reviews Online Web site: http://www.unl.edu/buros

Rosenberg, S. (2005, November 5). Teachers chip in as budgets shrink. *Boston Globe.* Retrieved September 16, 2006, from http://www.boston.com/news/local/articles/2005/11/06/teachers_chip_in_as_budgets_shrink

Ross, A. (2007, April). *The effects of constructivist teaching approaches on middle school student's algebraic procedural and conceptual understanding.* Paper presented during the annual meeting of the American Educational Research Association, Chicago, IL.

Ross, R. P. (1992). Accuracy in analysis of discrepancy scores: A nationwide study of school psychologists. *School Psychology Review, 21*(3), 480–493.

Rotherham, A. J. (2006). *Making the cut: How states set passing scores on standardized tests.* Washington, DC: Education Sector. Retrieved October 25, 2005, from http://www.educationsector.org/usr_doc/EXPCutScores.pdf

Rothstein, R., & Jacobsen, R. (2006). The goals of education. *Phi Delta Kappan, 88*(4), 264–272.

Rothstein, R., Jacobsen, R., & Wilder, T. (2006, November 29). "Proficiency for all" is an oxymoron. *Education Week, 26*(13), pp. 44, 32.

Rowlings, J. K. (2003). *Harry Potter and the order of the phoenix.* New York: Arthur A. Levine Books of Scholastic Press.

Rudin, S., & Gale, D. (Producers), & Kasdan, J. (Director). (2002). *Orange County* [Motion picture]. United States: Paramount Pictures.

Rumberger, R. W., Gándara, P., & Merino, B. (2006, Winter). Where California's English learners attend school and why it matters. *University of California Linguistic Minority Research Institute Newsletter, 15*(2), 1–3.

Rumberger, R. W., Larson, K. A., Ream, R. K., & Palardy, G. J. (1999). *The educational consequences of mobility for California students and schools* (PACE Research Series 99-2). Berkeley, CA: Policy Analysis for California Education, University of California, and Stanford University.

Rural School and Community Trust. (2007, March). Nebraska STARS provides assessment can inspire loyalty [Electronic version]. *Rural Policy Matters, 9*(3). Retrieved March 21, 2007, from http://www.ruraledu .org/site/apps/nl/content.asp?content_id= {F777430F-87F2-4186-B6A9-9FD3AE73191F}&notc=1&c=t

Russell, J., & LaCoste-Caputo, J. (2006, December 4). More kids repeating kindergarten. *San-Antonio News Express.* Retrieved December 6, 2006, from http://www.mysanantonio.com/

Ryman, A. (2005, January 6). Parents can check children's grades, homework online. *Arizona Republic.* Retrieved January 7, 2005, from http://www.azcentral.com

Ryser, G., & McConnell, K. (2002). *Scales for diagnosing attention-deficit/hyperactivity disorder.* Austin, TX: Pro-Ed.

Sacchetti, M. (2004, December 9). Report cards remake the grade. *Boston Globe.* Retrieved November 5, 2006, from http://www.boston.com/news/education/k_12/articles/2004/12/09/report_cards_remake_the_grade

Sacchetti, M. (2005, December 19). Advanced classes see dip in diversity Program prepares for exam schools. *Boston Globe.* Retrieved December 21, 2005, from http://www.boston.com/news

Sadker, D., & Zittleman, K. (2004). Test anxiety: Are students failing tests or are tests failing students? *Phi Delta Kappan, 85*(10), 740–744, 751.

Salvia, J., Ysseldyke, J. E., & Bolt, S. (2007). *Assessment in special and inclusive education* (10th ed.). New York: Houghton Mifflin.

Samuels, C. A. (2007, April 11). States seen renewing focus on education of gifted. *Education Week, 26*(32), pp. 20, 23.

Sanbonmatsu, L., Kling, J. R., Duncan, G. J., & Brooks-Gunn, J. (2005). *Neighborhoods and academic achievement: Results from the moving to opportunity experiment.* Cambridge, MA: National Bureau of Economic Research. Retrieved March 31, 2006, from http://nber15.nber.org/papers/w11909

Sanders, L. (n. d.). *Accountability mechanisms and processes: "Value added": Telling the truth about schools' performance.* London: National Foundation for Educational Research in England and Wales. Retrieved April 22, 2006, from http://www1.worldbank.org/education/est/resources/topic%20papers/ Valueadded.doc

Sanders, W. L. (1998). Value-added assessment. *School Administrator* [Electronic version]. Retrieved August 21, 2005, from http://www.aasa.org/publications/sa/1998_12/ sanders.htm

Sanders, W. L., Ashton, J. J., & Wright, S. P. (2005). *Comparison of the effects of NBPTS certified teachers with other teachers on the rate of student academic progress* (Final Report). Washington, DC: National Board for Professional Teaching Standards.

Sanders, W. L., & Horn, S. P. (1998). Research findings from the Tennessee value-added assessment system (TVASS) database: Implications for educational evaluation and research. *Journal of Personnel Evaluation in Education, 12*(3), 247–256.

Sanders, W. L., & Rivers, J. C. (1996). *Cumulative and residual effects of teachers on future student academic achievement* [Research progress report]. Knoxville, TN: Value Added Assessment Center, University of Tennessee.

Sanders, W. L., Saxton, A. M., & Horn, S. P. (1997). The Tennessee value-added assessment system, a quantitative, outcomes-based approach to educational measurement. In Jason Millman (Ed.), *Grading teachers, grading schools: Is student achievement a valid evaluation measure?* (pp. 137–162). Thousand Oaks, CA: Corwin Press.

Sandholtz, J. H., Ogawa, R. T., & Scribner, S. P. (2004). Standards gaps: Unintended consequences of local standards-based reform. *Teachers College Record, 106*(6), 1177–1202.

Sattler, J. M., & Dumont, R. (2004). *Assessment of children: WISC-IV and WPPSI-III supplement.* La Mesa, CA: Jerome M. Sattler.

Saulny, S. (2005, December 27-b). In middle class, signs of anxiety on school efforts. *New York Times.* Retrieved December 28, 2005, from http://www.nytimes.com/2005/12/27/nyregion/27middle.html

Saunders, D. L. (2007, March 4). Higher grades, lower scores. *San Francisco Chronicle.* Retrieved March 8, 2007, from http://sfgate.com/

Sax, G. (1989). *Principles of educational and psychological measurement and evaluation* (3rd ed.). Belmont, CA: Wadsworth.

Sax, G. (1997). *Principles of educational and psychological measurement and evaluation* (4th ed.). Belmont, CA: Wadsworth.

Scarborough, A. A., Spiker, D., Mallik, S., Hebbeler, K. M., Bailey, D. B., & Simeonsson, R. J. (2004). A national look at children and families entering early intervention. *Exceptional Children, 70*(4), 469–483.

Schafer, W. D., Gangé, P., & Lissitz, R. W. (2005). Resistance to confounding style and content in scoring constructed-response items. *Educational Measurement: Issues and Practice, 24*(2), 22–28.

Schemo, D. J. (2007, March 26). Failing schools see a solution in longer day. *New York Times,* pp. 1, 18.

Schmidt, P. (2007, February 23-b). Regent's diversity vote means trouble for U. of Wisconsin. *Chronicle of Higher Education, 53*(25), pp. A17–A18.

Schooler, C., Mesfin, S. M., & Oates, G. (1999). The continuing effects of substantively complex work on the intellectual functioning of older workers. *Psychology and Aging, 14*(3), 483–506.

Schultz, E. M. (2006). Commentary: A response to Reckase's conceptual framework and examples for evaluating standard setting methods. *Educational Measurement: Issues and practice, 25*(3), 4–13.

Schworm, P. (2004, July 12). MCAS detour proves tough. *Boston Globe.* Retrieved August 13, 2004, from http://www.boston.com/news/education/k_12/mcas/articles/2004/07/12/

Schworm, P. (2005, April 3). War on words: In class, grammar rears its ugly head. *Boston Globe.* Retrieved April 5, 2005, from http://www.boston.com/news/local/articles/2005/04/03/war_of_the_words_in_class_grammar_rears_its_ugly_head/

Scott, C. (2007). *Now what? Lessons from Michigan about restructuring schools and next steps under NCLB.* Washington, DC: Center on Education Policy. Retrieved March 28, 2007, from http://www.cep-dc.org/index.cfm?fuseaction=contentsearch.verity search&nodeid=1

Scriven, M. (1997). Student ratings offer useful input to teacher evaluations, *ERIC Digest.* Retrieved April 4, 2006, from http://www.ericdigests.org

Semrud-Clickeman, M. (2003). *Phonological processing, automaticity, auditory processing and memory in slow learners and children with reading disabilities.* Unpublished doctoral dissertation, University of Texas. ProQuest document identification number 765200031.

Shamberg, M., & Cantillon, E. (Producers), & Holland, S. S. (Director). (1989). *How I got into college* [Motion picture]. United States: Twentieth Century Fox.

Shanahan, T. (2005). [Test review of the *DIBELS: Dynamic indicators of early literacy skills, sixth edition*]. From R. A. Spies & B. S. Plake (Eds.), *The sixteenth mental measurements yearbook* [Electronic version]. Retrieved July 2, 2005, from the Buros Institute's Test Reviews Online Web site: http://www.unl.edu/buros/

Shankar, J. (2005, August 29). Tutoring U.S. math students adds new twist to Indian outsourcing saga. *Middle East Times.* Retrieved September 1, 2005, from http://www.metimes.com

Shapira, I. (2006, November 21). Those who pass classes but fail tests cry foul. *Washington Post.* Retrieved November 21, 2006, from http://www.washingtonpost.com/

Shaw, P., Lerch, J., Greenstein, D., Sharp, W., Clasen, L., Evans, A., et al. (2006, May). Longitudinal mapping of cortical thickness and clinical outcome in children and adolescents with attention-deficit/hyperactivity disorder. *Archives of General Psychiatry, 63*(5), 540–509.

Shaw, S. R., & Gouwens, D. A. (2002). Chasing and catching slow learners in changing times [Electronic version]. *NASP Communiqué, 31*(4). Retrieved January 13, 2005, from http://www.nasponline.org/publications/cq314slowlearner.html

Shaywitz, B. A., Shaywitz, S. E., Pugh, K. R., Mencl, W. E., Fulbright, R. K., Skudlarski, P., et al. (2002). Disruption of posterior brain systems for reading in children with developmental dyslexia. *Biological Psychiatry, 52*(2), 101–110.

Shaywitz, S. E., & Shaywitz, B. A. (2005). Dyslexia (specific reading disability). *Biological Psychiatry, 57,* 1301–1309.

Shaywitz, S. E., & Shaywitz, B. A. (2007). What neuroscience really tells us about reading instruction. *Educational leadership, 64*(5), 74–76.

Shedd, J. (2003). *The history of the student credit hour.* Unpublished manuscript, Office of Institutional Research and Planning, University of Maryland. Retrieved March 19, 2007, from http://virtual.parkland.edu/todtreat/presentations/cet103/shedd2003% 20history%200f%20credit%20hour.pdf

Shepard, L. (2000). The role of assessment in a learning culture. *Educational Researcher, 29*(7), 1–14.

Shields, R. N. (2000). *Writing strategies as predictors of student scores on the Pennsylvania System of School Assessment Writing Test.* Unpublished dissertation, Widener University.

Shurkin, J. N. (1992). *Terman's kids: The groundbreaking study of how the gifted grow up.* Boston: Little, Brown.

Siegel, S., & Castellan, N. J. (1988). *Nonparametric statistics for the behavioral sciences* (2nd ed.). New York: McGraw-Hill.

Silverlake, A. C. (1999). *Comprehending test manuals: A guide and workbook.* Los Angeles: Pyrczak.

Simon, R. (2004, May 19). Nebraska Assessment Letter #3. [Letter to Commissioner From the U.S. Department of Education]. Retrieved September 22, 2007, from http://www.ed.gov/admins/lead/account/finalassess/ne3.html

Sireci, S. G. (2004, April). *How psychometricians can help reduce the achievement gap: Or can they?* Paper presented at a symposium, The Achievement Gap: Test Bias or School Structures? During the annual meeting of the National Association of Test Directors, San Diego, CA. Retrieved July 3, 2005, from http://www.natd.org

Sireci, S. G., & Parker, P. (2007). Validity on trial: Psychometric and legal conceptualizations of validity. *Educational Measurement: Issues and Practice, 25*(3), 27–34.

Sizer, T. R. (2004). Preamble: A reminder for Americans. In D. Meier & G. Wood (Eds.), *Many children left behind: How the No Child Left Behind Act is damaging our children and our schools* (pp. xvii–xxii). Boston: Beacon Press.

Skinner, R. A. (2005, January 6). State of the states. *Education Week.* Retrieved June 18, 2005, from http://www.edweek.org/ew/articles/2005/01/06/17sos.h24.html

Slavin, R. E. (1994). *Educational psychology: Theory and practice.* Boston: Allyn & Bacon.

Smallwood, S. (2005, January 14). Faculty group censures Benedict College again. This time over "A for effort" policy. *Chronicle of Higher Education.* Retrieved January 14, 2005, from http://chronicle.com/daily/2005/01/20050114n.htm

Smart Heilshorn, K. (2003). *Calculator usage as a predictor of student success on the Pennsylvania System of School Assessment grade eight mathematics test.* Unpublished doctoral dissertation, Widener University.

Smith, B. (1998). *It's about time: Opportunities to learn.* Chicago: Consortium on Chicago School Research at the University of Chicago. Retrieved July 19, 2004, from http://www.consortium-chicago.org/publications/p0f03.html

Smith, D. (2004, November 28). Homework disparity points to education gap. *Kansas City Star.* Retrieved November 30, 2004, from http://www.kansascity.com/mld/kansascity/living/education/10285688.htm

Smith, J. K. (2001). [Review of the *Detroit tests of learning aptitude, fourth edition*]. In B. S. Plake & J. C. Impara (Eds.), *The fourteenth mental measurements yearbook* (pp. 382–386). Lincoln, NE: Buros Institute on Mental Measurements.

Snipes, J., Williams, A., Horwitz, A., Soga, K., & Casserly, M. (2007). *Beating the odds: A city-by-city analysis of student performance and achievement gaps on state assessments.* Washington, DC: Council of the Great City Schools. Retrieved September 21, 2007, from http://www.cgcslists.org/reports/beat_the_oddsIV.html

Solochek, J. (2006, October 20). A test beyond the norm. *St. Petersburg Times.* Retrieved October 24, 2006, from http://www.sptimes.com/2006/10/20/Citytimes/A_test_beyond_the_norm.shtml

Spearman, C. (1904). General intelligence, objectively determined and measured. *American Journal of Psychology, 15,* 201–293.

Spearman, C. (1939). Determination of factors. *British Journal of Psychology, 30,* 78–83.

Spellings, M. (2006, April 6). Secretary Spellings' prepared testimony before the House Committee on Education and the Workforce [Press release]. U. S. Department of Education. Retrieved April 27, 2006, from http://www.ed.gov/print/news/speeches/2006/04/04062006.html

Spellings, M. (2006, July 27). *Building partnerships to help English language learners.* Washington, DC: U.S. Department of Education. Retrieved November 13, 2006, from http://www.ed.gov/nclb/methods/english/lepfactsheet.pdf

Steadman, S. C., & Simmons, J. S. (2007). The cost of mentoring non-university-certified teachers who pays the price. *Phi Delta Kappan, 88*(5), 364–367.

Steele, C. M. (1997). A threat in the air: How stereotypes shape intellectual identity and performance. *American Psychologist, 52,* 613–629.

Steele, C. M. (1999, August). Thin ice: "Stereotype threat" and black college students. *Atlantic, XX,* 44–54.

Steinberg, J. (2002). *The gatekeepers: Inside the admissions process of a premier college.* New York: Penguin.

Steinberg, L. (1996). *Beyond the classroom: Why school reform has failed and what parents need to do.* New York: Touchstone.

Stephens, S. (2006, May 7). Exam proves what teachers know. *Cleveland Plain Dealer,* p. B1

Stern, W. L. (1928). *Intelligenz der kinder und jugendlichen und die methoden ihrer untersuchung.* Leipzig, Germany: Verlag von Johann Ambrosius Barth.

Sternberg, R. J. (1999). Intelligence as developing expertise. *Contemporary Educational Psychology, 24,* 359–375.

Sternberg, R. J. (2007, July). Finding students who are wise, practical, and creative. *Chronicle of Higher Education*, 53 (44), pp. B11–12.

Sternberg, R. J., Grigorenko, E. L., & Kidd, K. K. (2005). Intelligence, race, and genetics. *American Psychologist, 60*(1), 46–59.

Sternberg, R. J., Wagner, R. K., Williams, W. M., & Horvath, J. A. (1995). Testing common sense. *American Psychologist, 50*(11), 912–927.

Stevens, N. (1993). *Perceived mentor outcomes from the mentoring experience in a formal teacher induction program.* Unpublished doctoral dissertation, Widener University.

Stevenson, J., et al. (2007, September 6). Food additives and hyperactive behaviour in 3-year-old and 8/9 year-old children in the community: A randomized, double-blinded, placebo-controlled trial. *Lancet.* Retrieved September 8, 2007, from http://www.thelancet.com/journals/lancet/article/PIIS0140673607613063/fulltext

Stiggins, R. J. (2002). Assessment crisis: The absence of assessment for learning. *Phi Delta Kappan, 83*(10), 758–765.

Stiggins, R. J. (2004). New assessment beliefs for a new school mission. *Phi Delta Kappan, 86*(1), 22–27.

Stiggins, R. J., & Bridgeford, N. J. (1985). The ecology of classroom assessment. *Journal of Educational Measurement, 22*(4), 271–286.

Stiggins, R. J., Frisbie, D. A., & Griswold, P. A. (1989). Inside high school grading practices: Building a research agenda. *Educational Measurement: Issues and Practice, 8*(2), 5–14.

Stoneberg, Jr., B. D. (2004, March). *A study of gender-based and ethnic-based differential item functioning (DIF) in the spring 2003 Idaho Standards Achievement Tests applying the simultaneous bias test (SIBTEST) and the Mantel–Haenszel Chi Square Test.* Unpublished manuscript, University of Maryland, Measurement, Statistics, and Evaluation Department. Retrieved November 8, 2006, from http://www.sde.state.id.us/admin/docs/ayp/ISATDIFStudy.pdf

Stoskepf, A. (1999). The forgotten history of eugenics [Electronic version]. *Rethinking Schools, 13*(3). Retrieved March 22, 2007, from http://www.rethinkingschools.org/ archive/13_03/eugenic.shtml

Strauss, V. (2006, March 21). Putting parents in their place: Outside class. *Washington Post.* Retrieved March 22, 2006, from http://www.washingtonpost.com

Stufflebeam, D. L. (1981). A brief introduction to standards for evaluations of educational programs, projects, and materials. *Evaluation News, 2*(2), 141–145.

Summa cum lawsuit (2004, September/October). *Legal Affairs.* Retrieved November 5, 2006, from http://www.legalaffairs.org/printerfriendly.msp?id=622

Sunderman, G. L., & Kim, J. (2005, May 5). *Teacher quality: Equalizing educational opportunities and outcomes.* Cambridge, MA: The Civil Rights Project, Harvard University. Retrieved July 12, 2005, from http://www.civilrightsproject.harvard.edu/research/archive.php

Sunderman, G. L., Kim, J. S., & Orfield, G. (2005). *NCLB meets school realities: Lessons from the field.* Thousand Oaks, CA: Corwin Press.

Suter, W. N. (2006). *Introduction to educational research: A critical thinking approach.* Thousand Oaks, CA: Sage.

Suzuki, T., Swuz, D. (Producers), & Sheetz, C. (Director). (2001). *Recess: School's out* [Motion picture]. United States: The Walt Disney Company.

Talbot, M. (2005, June 6). Best in class. *New Yorker, 81*(16), 38–43.

Tatsuoka, M. M., & Lohnes, P. R. (1988). *Multivariate analysis: Techniques for educational and psychological research.* New York: Macmillan.

Tellez, K., & Waxman, H. (n.d.). *Effective community programs for English language learners* (Draft report). Santa Cruz, CA: University of Santa Cruz. Retrieved November 26, 2006, from http://education.ucsc.edu/faculty/ktellez/effective-com-ell.pdf

Terman, L. M. (1916). *Stanford revision and extension of the Binet–Simon scale.* Retrieved February 1, 2005, from http://www.riverpub.com/products/clinical/sbis/home.html

Testing, assessment, and evaluation to improve learning in our schools (1990). Oversight hearing before the Subcommittee on Elementary, Secondary, and Vocational Education of the Committee on Education and Labor, U.S. House of Representatives, 101st Congress, Second Session.

Texas Assessment of Skills and Knowledge (n.d.). Student Assessment Division. Retrieved April 5, 2006, from http://www.tea.state.tx.us/student.assessment/resources/release

Thernstrom, A., & Thernstrom, S. (2003). *No excuses: Closing the racial gap in learning.* New York: Simon and Schuster.

Thiers, N. (2005). Supporting new teachers [Electronic version]. *Educational leadership, 62*(8). Retrieved December 11, 2005, from http://www.ascd.org

Thomas, D., & Bainbridge, W. (1997, January). Grade inflation: The current fraud. *Effective School Research.* Retrieved July 16, 2004, from http://schoolmatch.com/articles/ESRJAN97.htm

Thorndike, E. L., Cobb, M. V., & Bergman, E. O. (1927). *The measurement of intelligence.* New York: Teachers College Press.

Thurlow, M. L., & Bolt, S. (2001). *Empirical support for accommodations most often allowed in state policy* (Synthesis Report 41). Minneapolis, MN: University of Minnesota, National Center for Educational Outcomes. Retrieved November 17, 2006, from http://www.tourettesyndrome.net/Thurlow_Bolt.htm

Thurlow, M. L., Lazarus, S., Thompson, S., & Robey, J. (2002). *2001 state policies on assessment participation and accommodations* (Synthesis Report 43). Minneapolis: National Center of Educational Outcomes, University of Minnesota.

Thurstone, L. L. (1927). A law of comparative judgment. *Psychological Review, 3,* 273–286.

Thurstone, L. L. (1938). *Primary mental abilities* (Psychometric Monograph No.1). Chicago: University of Chicago Press.

Thurstone, L. L. (1947). *Multiple-factor analysis: A development and expansion of the vectors of the mind.* Chicago: University of Chicago Press.

Tierney, J. (2004, November 21). When every child is good enough. *New York Times.* Retrieved November 22, 2004, from http://www.nytimes.com/2004/11/21/weekinreview/21tier

Toch, T. (2006). *Margins of error: The education testing industry in the No Child Left Behind era* (Education Sector Report). Washington, DC: Education Sector.

Tonn, J. L. (2007, February 7). Houston in uproar over teacher's bonuses. *Education Week, 26*(22), pp. 5, 13.

Torrance, E. P. (1966) *Torrance tests of creativity.* Princeton, NJ: Personnel Press.

Torrance, E. P., Goff, K., & Satterfield, N. B. (1998). *Multicultural mentoring of the gifted and talented.* Waco, TX: Prafrock Press.

Torrance, E. P., & Myers, R. E. (1970). *Creative learning and teaching.* New York: Harper Collins.

Torrance, E. P., Safter, T. H., & Ball, O. E. (1992). *Torrance tests of creative thinking streamlined scoring guide: Figural A and B.* Bensenville, IL: Scholastic Testing Service.

Torres, S., Santos, J., Peck, L., & Cortes, L. (2004). *Minority teacher recruitment, development, and retention.* Providence, RI: The Education Alliance at Brown University.

Tracey, C. A., Sunderman, G. L., & Orfield, G. (2005, June). *Changing NCLB district accountability standards: Implications for racial equality.* Cambridge, MA: The Civil Rights Project, Harvard University. Retrieved July 14, 2005, from http://www.civilrightsproject.harvard.edu

Trauwein, I. W., Lüdke, U. O., & Baumert, J. (2007). The big-fish-little-pond effect: persistent negative effects of selective high schools on self-concept after graduation. *American Educational Research Journal, 44*(3), 631–669.

Treffinger, D. J. (1985). Test review of the *Torrance tests of creative thinking*]. From J. V. Mitchell Jr. (Ed.), *The ninth mental measurements yearbook* [Electronic version]. Retrieved February 14, 2005, from the Buros Institute's Test Reviews Online Web site: http://www.unl.edu/buros

Trotter, A. (2007, August 29). Poll finds rise in unfavorable views of NCLB. *Education Week, 27*(1), p. 10.

Tucker, A, (2004). *The New York Regents math test problems* [Report of the New York Regents Math Panel]. State University of New York, Stony Brook. Retrieved April 5, 2005, from http://www.ams.sunysb.edu/~tucker/MathAPaper.pdf

Tuckman, B. W. (2003). The effect of learning and motivation strategies training on college students' achievement. *Journal of College Student Development, 4,* 430–437.

Twarog, M. A. (1999). *Experimental study of individual versus blanket-type homework assignments in elementary school mathematics with a computerized component.* Unpublished doctoral dissertation, Widener University.

University College London. (2007, March 23). Finding math hard? Blame your right parietal lobe. *Science Daily*. London: Author. Retrieved March 29, 2007, from http://www.sciencedaily.com/releases/2007/03/070322132931.htm

U.S. Department of Education. (2005). Assistance to states for the education of children with disabilities. *Federal Register, 70*(118), 35782.

U.S. Department of Education, Office of Elementary and Secondary Education (2006). Teacher incentive fund. *Federal Register, 71*(83), 25580–25581.

U.S. Department of Education, National Center for Education Statistics. (2004). *Third International Mathematics and Science Study (TIMSS)*. Washington, DC: U.S. Government Printing Office.

U.S. Department of Education, Office of the Secretary of Education (2007). Decision letters on each state's final assessment system under No Child Left Behind (NCLB). Retrieved March 16, 2007, from http://www.ed.gov/print/admins/lead/account/nclbfinalassess/index.html

U.S. Military Entrance Processing Command. (1968, 1992). *Armed service vocational aptitude battery* [Forms 18/19]. North Chicago, IL: Author.

Vait, A. (Producer), & Painter, M. (Director). (2004). *Admissions* [Motion picture]. United States: Hart Sharp Video.

Van Moorlehem, T. (1998). Home sales, custody fights hinge on exam. *Detroit Free Press*. Retrieved July 15, 2005, from http://www.freep.com/news/meap/qaffect19.htm

Vasluski, T., McKenzie, S., & Mulvenon, S. W. (2005). *Examining predictors of college remediation: The effects of high school grade inflation*. Fayetteville, AK: University of Arkansas. Retrieved April 13, 2005, from http://normes.uark.edu/current_research/ AERA04%20Paper%205%20Predictors.pdf

Vedder, R. K. (2000). *Can teachers own their own schools? New strategies for educational excellence*. Oakland, CA: The Independent Institute.

Vernon, P. E. (1961). *The structure of human abilities* (revised ed.). London: Methuen & Co.

Viadero, D. (2006, November 29). Potential of global tests seen as unrealized. *Education Week, 26*(13), pp. 1, 14, 15.

Viadero, D. (2007, January 10). Study links merit pay to slightly higher student scores [Electronic version]. *Education Week, 26*(20). Retrieved January 26, 2007, from http://www.edweek.org//ew/articles/2007/01/10/18merit.h26.html?print=1

Viadero, D. (2007, January 24). "What Works" reviewers find no learning edge for leading math texts. *Education Week, 28*(20), pp. 1, 21.

Viadero, D. (2007, June 13). Evidence thin on student gains from NCLB tutoring. *Education Week, 26*(41), p. 7

Voltaire (1947). *Candide, or optimism*. (J. Butt, Trans). New York: Penguin Books. (Original work published in French in 1759)

Vu, P. (2006, June 23). *States do not narrow teacher equity gap*. Philadelphia: Stateline.org, Pew Charitable Trusts. Retrieved June 24, 2006, from http://www.stateline.org/live/issues/Education

Walkovic, C. E. (2003). *Reading strategies as predictors of school scores on the Pennsylvania System of School Assessment Reading Test*. Unpublished doctoral dissertation, Widener University.

Wallach, M. A., & Kogan, N. (1965). *Modes of thinking in young children: A study of the creativity–intelligence distinction*. New York: Holt, Reinhart, & Winston.

Wallis, C. (2007, January 12). Is the Autism epidemic a myth? *Time*. Retrieved January 16, 2007, from http://www.time.com/time/printout/0,8816,1576829,00.html

Wang, J. & Lin, E. (2005). Comparative studies on U.S. and Chinese mathematics learning and the implications for standards-based mathematics teaching reform. *Educational Researcher, 34*(5), 3–13.

Wang, S., Young, M. J., Brooks, T. E., & Jiao, H. (2007, April). *A comparison of computer-automated and human scoring methods for a statewide writing assessment*. Paper presented during the annual meeting of the American Educational Research Association, Chicago, IL.

Wang, X. B. (2007). *Investigating the effects of increased SAT Reasoning Test length and time on performance of regular SAT examinees* [College Board Research Report No. 2006-9]. New York: The College Board.

Wasley, P. (2006, March 10). A new way to grade. *Chronicle of Higher Education, 52*(27), pp. A6, A8–9.

Wasley, P. (2007, February 23). College Board reports more takers, and higher scores, for Advanced Placement tests. *Education Week, 53*(25), p. 18.

Wasta, M. J. (2006). No Child Left Behind: The death of special education. *Phi Delta Kappan, 88*(4), 98–299.

Watch for curves (2007, March 16). *Chronicle for Higher Education, 53*(28), p. A6.

Way, W. D. (2006, September). *Precision and volatility in school accountability systems* (Research Report RR-06-26). Princeton, NJ: Educational Testing Service. Retrieved November 10, 2006, from http://www.ets.org/portal/site/ets/menuitem

Webb, N. L. (2002, April). *An analysis of the alignment between mathematics standards and assessments for three states.* Paper presented at the annual meeting of the American Educational Research Association, New Orleans, LA.

Webb, N. L. (2005, April). *Issues related to judging the alignment of curriculum standards and assessments.* Paper presented at the annual meeting of the American Educational Research Association, Montreal, Canada.

Webb, N. L. (2007, September). Aligning assessments and standards. *Newsletter of the Wisconsin Center for Education Research.* Retrieved September 5, 2007, from http://www.wcer.wisc.edu/news/coverStories/aligning_assessments_and_standards.php

Weber, C. (Producer), & Rosman, M. (Director). (2004). *A Cinderella Story* [Motion picture]. United States: Warner Bros.

Wells, F. (2001). Zip codes shouldn't determine our students' future [Electronic version]. *California Educator, 5*(8). Retrieved July 8, 2005, from http://www.cta.org/

Wells, J. A. (2002). *A correlational study of grade five studies and PSSA testing of reading in Pennsylvania.* Unpublished doctoral dissertation, Widener University.

Wessmann v. Gittens, 160 F. 3d. 790 (1st Cir. 1998).

Wheelan, S. A., & Kesselring, J. (2005). Link between faculty group development and elementary student performance on standardized tests. *Journal of Educational Research, 98*(6), 323–330.

Williams, F. E. (1986). The cognitive–affective intervention model for enriching gifted programs. In J. S. Renzulli (Ed.), *Systems and models for developing programs for the gifted and talented.* Mansfield Center, CT: Creative Learning Press.

Williams, J. (2007, May 10). State board approves mandatory exit examination for special education. *San Francisco Chronicle.* Retrieved May 12, 2007, from http://sfgate.com/cgi-in/article.cgi?f=/n/a/2007/05/10/state/n161700D89.DTL

Williams, R. (2006). The power of normalized word vectors for automatically grading essays. *Issues in Informing Science and Information Technology, 3,* 721–728.

Wilms W. W., & Chapleau, R. R. (1999, November 3). The illusion of paying teachers for student performance. *Education Week, 19*(10), pp. 34, 48.

Winerip, M. (2003, September 24). On front lines, casualties are tied to new U.S. law. *New York Times,* p. B9.

Winerip, M. (2004, May 28). On education: The changes unwelcome, a model teacher moves on. *New York Times,* p. B7.

Witziers, B., Bosker, R. J., & Kruger, M. L. (2003). Educational leadership and student achievement: The elusive search for an association. *Education Administration Quarterly, 39*(3), 398–425.

Wolf, R. M. (1990). *Evaluation in education. Foundations of competency assessment and program review* (3rd ed.). New York: Praeger.

Wolverton, B. (2006, February 16). NCAA panel proposes changes in eligibility requirements to combat academic fraud at unregulated high schools. *Chronicle of Higher Education.* Retrieved February 16, 2006, from http://chronicle.com/daily/2006/02/2006021601n.htm

Woodcock, R., McGrew, K. S., & Mather, N. (2001). *Woodcock–Johnson III—Tests of achievement.* Itasca, IN: Riverside.

Woodruff, D. J., & Ziomek, R. L. (2004). *High school grade inflation from 1991 to 2003* (ACT Research Report Series, 2004-4). Iowa City, IA: American College Testing Program. Retrieved June 5, 2005, from http://www.act.org/path/policy/education/k12.html

Woods, M. (2007, March 4). Hey kids, lets make an FCAT deal. *Florida Times-Union.* Retrieved March 21, 2007, from http://cgi.jacksonville.com/tuonline/stories/030407/woo_8371517.shtml

Word, E., Johnston, J., Bain, H., Fulton, D. B., Boyd-Zaharias, J., Lintz, N., et al. (1990). *Student/teacher achievement ratio (STAR): Tennessee's K-3 class size study.* Nashville: Tennessee Department of Education.

Wright, R. J. (1975). The affective and cognitive consequences of open education on middle-class elementary school students. *American Educational Research Journal, 12*(4), 449–468.

Wright, R. J. (2006, February). *Teachability and proficiency on the National Assessment of Educational Progress.* Paper presented at the annual meeting of the Eastern Educational Research Association, Hilton Head Island, SC.

Wright, R. J., & Lesisko, L. J. (2007, February). *The preparation of technology leadership for the schools.* Paper presented at the annual meeting of the Eastern Educational Research Association, Clearwater, FL.

Wybranski, N. A. M. (1996). An efficacy study: The influence of early intervention on the subsequent school placements of children with Down syndrome. Doctoral dissertation, Widener University. ProQuest number AAT9701172.

Yell, M. L., Drasgow, E., & Lowrey, E. (2003). *No Child Left Behind: Analysis and implications for special education* [PowerPoint presentation]. Columbia, SC: Center for Autism, University of South Carolina. Retrieved March 19, 2007, from http://www.scautism.org/misc/NCLB-SAS.pdf

Yi, Q., Zhang, J., & Chang, H. (2006). Assessing CAT test security severity. *Applied Psychological Measurement, 30*(1), 62–63.

Zabala, D., & Minnici, A. (2007). *It's different now. How exit exams are affecting teaching and learning in Jackson and Austin*. Washington DC: Center on Education Policy. Retrieved March 15, 2007, from http://www.cep-dc.org/highschoolexit/JacksonAustin/Jackson&Austin.pdf

Zackon, J. F. (1999). *A study of the Pennsylvania System of School Assessment: The predictive value of selected characteristics of Pennsylvania school districts for student performance on the PSSA.* Unpublished doctoral dissertation, Widener University.

Zehr, M. A. (2007a). Missouri seeks to aid ELLs now overlooked: Those with disabilities. *Education Week, 26*(34), p. 7.

Zehr, M. A. (2007b). States adopt new tests for English-learners. *Education Week, 28*(20), pp. 26, 31.

Zimmerman, B. J. (1989). A social cognitive view of self-regulated academic learning. *Journal of Educational Psychology, 8*(3), 329–339.

Zirkel, P. (2004, April, 28). No child left average? We should drop the gamesmanship of eliminating class rank. *Education Week, 23*(33), p. 36.

Zirkel, P. (2007, March 28). Grade inflation: High school's skeleton in the closet. *Education Week, 26*(29), pp. 40, 32.

Zweigenhaft, R. L. (1993). Prep schools and public school graduates of Harvard: A longitudinal study of the accumulated social and cultural capital. *Journal of Higher Education, 64*(2), 21–225.

Zwick, R., & Schlemer, L. (2004). SAT validity for linguistic minorities at the University of California Santa Barbara. *Educational Measurement: Issues and Practice, 25*, 6–16.

INDEX

Ability grouping, 48, 565
Academic redshirting,
    11, 308, 565
Accommodations, 415–418, 565
Accomplishment ratio, 565
    standardized tests and,
        320–321, 323
Accountability:
assessment and, 4–6
    definition, 562n1, 565
    and evaluation overview,
        533–537
    and funding, 72, 75, 426
    and grading, 272
    issues/themes of, 531–532
    learning objectives, 532–533
    NCLB Act and, 8
    public opinion and, 535–537
    and schools' test
        preparation, 497–502
    special education 417
    variables in school-based
        educational research
        and, 94
Accounting Aptitude Test, 358
Achievement tests. *See also*
    Standardized tests
    accomplishment ratio and,
        320–321
    Case in Point, 326, 339
    characteristics 324
    Comprehensive Testing
        Program (CTP),
        330–333
    classroom use 173, 221
    definition, 12, 13, 565
    and explaining test scores to
        parents, 316–318
    growth and, 553
    historical aspects of
        achievement batteries,
        322–324

Iowa Tests of Basic Skills
    (ITBS), 329–330
mental ability and, 468
Metropolitan Achievement
    Tests, 326–328
NCLB Act and, 8, 552–553
NCLB and, 325–326
sources/types of, 12–16
Stanford Achievement
    Tests, 327
and state-mandated
    assessments, 333–340
as summative evaluations,
    173–174
Terra Nova test, 327
test publishers and, 321–322
validity of, 151
Adequacy of the coverage of
    tests, 16
Adequate Yearly Progress (AYP):
    and cost of failure, 498–499
    definition, 566
    ELL students and, 492n2
    high-stakes tests and, 13
    NCLB Act and, 8, 13, 75
    NCLB and, 463n17
    sanctions and, 446
    special education and, 457
Administration:
    data management and,
        510–511
    scheduling and, 512
    and schools' test
        preparation, 525–527
    time on task and, 512–515
Admissions:
    early case law on, 26–27
    educational ethics and, 35
    predictors of college
        potential for, 31
    weighted combinations
        and, 33

Advanced placement,
    148, 289–290, 565
Advanced program admission,
    25–26
Affirmative action, 566
    measurement practices in
        schools and, 31–32
Air Force Officer Qualifying
    Test (AFOQT), 66
Alternate form reliability,
    566, 124–125
Alternative answers, 184–185,
    191, 566
Alternative assessments,
    152, 259, 412–413, 566
Alternative tracks, 485, 566
Alternatives as answers in
    questions, 185, 191
American Association of
    University Professors
    (AAUP), 301
American College Tests (ACT):
    aptitude testing and, 376–377
    definition, 566
    description, 104
    Lindquist, E. F. and, 329, 376
    as published test, 14
    score gap and, 27–29
American Counseling
    Association (ACA), 34
American Educational Research
    Association (AERA), 34
American Eugenics Society
    (AES), 45
American Evaluation
    Association, 534
American Guidance Service, 410
American Psychological
    Association (APA), 34
American Speech-Language-
    Hearing Association
    (ASHA), 34

Analytical assessments, 566
Analytical intelligence, 566
Analytical rubrics, 254–256, 566
Anchor items, 137, 566
Anderson, Lorin, 179
Anderson's taxonomy, 179
Anecdotal observation, 419, 566
Anecdotal record, 386, 566
Angoff model, 135–136
Annual yearly progress
    (AYP), 130
Answer and qualitative
    assessments, 19, 566
Apgar test, 6, 565
Appropriateness of test:
    definition, 567
    description, 22
    validity and, 155–156
Aptitude measures, 567
Aptitude testing:
    administered to groups,
        354–360
    aptitude definition, 345
    and assessment of
        talented/gifted
        children, 360, 363
    Case in Point, 376–377
    connectionism and, 368–369
    creativity and, 366–368
    Educational Testing Service
        and, 374
    first college boards and, 373
    Harvard scholarships and,
        373–374
    IQ scores and, 346–347
    issues/themes of, 343–344
    learning objectives, 344
    measures, 567
    merit scholars and, 365–366
    scholastic aptitude and
        intelligence, 345–347
    and tests of intelligence
        administered one-on-
        one, 348–354
    and training of test
        administrators,
        347–348
Architecture/school design,
    522–525
Armed Services Vocational
    Aptitude Battery (ASVAB),
    360–362
Army Alpha/Beta tests, 53–60,
    349, 567

Army–Navy Qualifying Test, 374
Artificial intelligence,
    215–217, 567
Assembly-line grading, 214, 567
Assessment. See specific type,
    i.e., Performance
    assessments
    accountability and, 4–5
    published assessments,
        13–15
    definition, 567
Assumptions for tests, 16–17
Attention deficit disorder
    (ADD), 394, 567
Attention deficit/hyperactivity
    disorder (AD/HD)
    Case in Point, 351
    definition, 567
    description, 383
    and formal assessments of
        attention/focus, 394–395
    measurement scales for,
        396–400
Authentic assessments, 163, 567
Authentic-type performance
    assessments, 258–259

Bakke, University of
    California Regents v.,
    32, 592
Basic interpersonal
    communication skill
    (BICS), 458, 567
Behavior Assessment System
    for Children, 2nd Edition
    (BASC-2), 396–397
Bell curve, 81, 84, 91–92,
    95, 567
Benchmark skills in reading,
    284, 517, 567
Benchmarks, 8, 171, 213,
    247, 567
Benedict College (SC), 301
Best linear unbiased estimators
    (BLUE), 555, 567
Best linear unbiased predictors
    (BLUP), 555, 568
Binomial distribution, 92, 568
Birth order, 466
Bloom's taxonomy, 178–179,
    206, 568
Bluffing, 209–210, 568
Board of Education, Brown v.,
    26–27, 62

Bollinger et al., Gratz et al., 33
Bollinger et al., Grutter v.,
    33–34, 39–40n13
Brookhart v. Illinois State
    Board of Education, 23
Brown ADD Scales for
    Children/Adolescents,
    397–398
Brown v. Board of Education,
    26–27, 62
Buckley Amendment, 20, 568
Burt, Cyril, 51, 53
Bush, George W., 22, 74–75,
    299, 445, 529n10
Bush, Jeb, 529n6

California Achievement Test.
    See Terra Nova test
California Diagnostic Reading
    Test (CDRT), 406
Campbell, Donald T.,
    543, 563n4
Cannell, John J., 5, 42, 71, 103
Carnegie Corporation, 438, 488
Carnegie Unit, 274, 568
Carrow-Woolfolk,
    Elizabeth, 407
Case in Point:
    ACT/SAT and, 377
    aptitude testing of young
        children and, 351–352
    and assessment of
        talented/gifted
        children, 363–364
    authentic-type assessment
        and, 259
    cheating and, 211
    class rank and, 292
    computers for disabled
        students, 171
    ethics and, 506
    eugenics, 62
    grade retention and, 13–14,
        304–305
    hiring qualified teachers
        and, 482
    historical aspects of
        achievement batteries
        and, 323–324
    history of testing, 43–44
    homework and, 200
    international comparisons
        and, 437
    item difficulty index and, 229

learning problems identified and, 388–389
literacy as testing problem, 339
magnet schools and, 459
mandated assessments and, 8
Mantel-Haenszel Test of Differential Item Functioning, 326
minority teachers, 484–485
NCLB and, 446–448, 451
ordinal scales and, 86
parental involvement and, 474–475
percentiles and, 102
performance assessment and, 245–248
and planning of tests, 172
planning of tests and, 169, 190
predictors of college potential, 31
ratio scales and, 89
reliability and, 124–126, 135, 142
SAT and, 216
SAT II, 376
school strategies and, 9–11
and schools' test preparation, 499
scoring guide and, 212
skew and, 95–96
standard deviation and, 98–99
standard error of measurement and, 131
statewide testing programs and, 443
strategic planning and, 540–541
summative evaluations and, 173–174
teacher empowerment and, 490
technology in parental access, 18
Texas reforms, 22
validity and, 147, 156
Cattell, James McKeen, 44–45
Cattell, Raymond B., 64
Cattell-Horn-Carroll model of human cognitive ability, 65, 346
CAVD, 568

Centered, 568
Central tendency, 90–91, 568
Certification of teachers, 76, 423, 466, 486–491
Chance level, 189, 568
Charter schools, 341n2
Chauncey, Henry, 373–374
Cheating, 211, 500–502
Child study movement, 46–47, 568
Civics Education Study, 433
Civil Rights Act of 1964, 32, 72
Class rank, 31, 292–293, 568
Class size, 523–524
Classical measurement theory, 130, 569
Classroom development and extended answer tests:
bluffing and, 209–210
Case in Point, 200, 211–212, 216
completion/short answer questions and, 202–205
essay tests and, 207–209
essay tests format and, 210–211
and grading homework, 199–200
and grading of essay writing, 211–215
and historical aspects of homework, 198–199
and impact of homework, 201–202
issues/themes of, 197–198
learning objectives, 198
parents and homework, 200–201
short answer/mini-essay questions and, 205–207
and size of assignments, 201
Code of Fair Testing Practices in Education, 502
Coefficient Kappa, 569
Coefficient Kappa (κ), reliability and, 141–142, 569
Cognitive Abilities Test (CogAT), 355
Cognitive ability, 367, 465–466, 468, 569
Cognitive Academic Language Proficiency (CALP), 458–459, 569

Cognitive academic language proficiency (CALP), 569
Cognitive level:
essay tests and, 208–209
and planning of tests, 177–178
school strategies and, 11–12
short answer/mini-essay questions and, 206
Cognitive Tutor Algebra I, 520
Cohort, age, 143, 157, 569
College Board or College Entrance Examination Board:
aptitude testing and, 373
as published test, 14
SAT, 104, 215–216, 374–375
College Entrance Examination Board, 215–216
Committee on Secondary School Studies, 274, 569
Common schools, 5, 569
Commonality, 154, 569
validity of test and, 82
Communication Abilities Diagnostic Test (CoADT), 407
Communication, educational ethics and, 34–35
Composite score, 569
Comprehensive Testing Program, 324–325
Comprehensive Testing Program (CTP), 324–325, 330–333
Computer Adaptive Graduate Admissions Testing, 105
Computer Adaptive Testing, 12, 221, 234–235, 569
Computer adaptive testing, 221, 234–235, 569
Computer essay grading, 214–215, 569
Computerized grading, 19
Conant, James Bryant, 373
Concurrent strategies, 518, 569
Concurrent validity, 148, 162n1, 569
Conferences, portfolio, 263–264
Confidence interval of standard errors, 131, 570
Confidentiality, 35
Connectionism, 368–369, 570

Conners' Rating Scales-Revised
(CRS-R), 398
Consistency, retesting and, 81
Construct validity,
149, 152–153, 162n2, 570
Constructed items, 230, 570
Constructed response, 570
Constructed response format,
178, 180–181, 570
Content fidelity, 151–152
Content validity, 149–150, 570
Convergent production,
368–369, 570
Core curriculum, 130, 570
Correction for guessing, 30, 570
Correlation, 570
Correlation coefficient, 570
Country school, 529n11
Covariance, 107–108, 570
Covariance analysis,
551–552, 570
Creative intelligence, 570
Creativity, 571
    aptitude testing and,
        366–368
    school strategies and, 11
    Torrance tests of, 371
Criterion referenced tests,
    published tests as, 14
Criterion variable, 82, 571
Criterion-oriented validity, 162n1
Criterion-referenced tasks,
    140, 571
Critical thinking, 443, 571
Critical Writing Test, 216, 219n3
Cronbach α, 144n4, 571
Cronbach coefficient α, 129,
    144n4, 231, 571
Cross-sectional model of
    evaluation, 553, 571
Cross-validation, 159, 571
Crystallized factor of ability,
    64–65, 345, 571
CTB McGraw-Hill, 13
Curriculum:
    mandated assessments
        and, 7
    and schools' test
        preparation, 516–522
Curriculum maps, 174–175, 571
Curriculum probes, 571
    and administration of
        published tests, 15

Curriculum-based assessment
    (CBA), 394, 571
Curriculum-based
    measurements, 393, 571
Curriculum-based
    measurements (CBM), 393
Cut scores, 15, 135–139, 571

DANTES program, 487,
    493n6, 572
Darwin, Charles, 43
Debra P. v. Turlington,
    23, 463n11
Decontextualized, 572
Descrepancy, 572
Detroit Tests of Learning
    Aptitude, 359
Deviation IQ scores,
    103–104, 572
Diagnostic and Statistical
    Manual, 4th ed., 395
Diagnostic tests:
    and administration of
        published tests, 15
    definition, 572
    item selection/analysis
        and, 227
Differential Aptitude Test
    (DAT), 360
Differential item
    functioning, 572
Differential item functioning
    (DIF), 143, 160,
    236, 572
Difficulty index, 225–229
Disabled students, NCLB and,
    75. *See also* Special
    education
Disaggregated scores, 459–460,
    572
Disaggregated subgroup
    mean, 572
Discrimination level of item,
    230–234, 572
Dissemination, 550–551, 572
Distracter, 185, 572
Distracter analysis,
    229–230, 572
Distracter of item in
    questions, 185
Distracters, 572
Distribution, 91, 572
Divergent thinking, 368, 573

Dropouts, 304–305. *See also*
    Grading/progress
    reports/report cards.
Dynamic Indicators of Basic
    Literacy Skills, 6th ed.
    (DIBELS), 404, 573

Early Childhood ADD
    Evaluation Scale
    (ECADDES), 398–399
EDGAR, 573
Education for All Handicapped
    Children Act of 1975,
    381–383
Education General
    Administrative Regulations
    (EDGAR), 533–534
Educational Assessment: Tests
    and Measurements in the
    Age of Accountability,
    118, 143
Educational standards, 74, 573
Educational Testing Service (ETS)
    aptitude testing and, 374
    definition, 573
    as information source, 16
Effectiveness score,
    480, 556, 573
Elementary and Secondary
    Education Act (ESEA),
    6–7, 438, 573
English-language learners,
    75, 468, 573
Entitlement decision, 573
    school strategies and, 10
Environment of testing:
    architecture/school design
        and, 522–525
    one-room schools, 529n11
    student preparedness
        for, 171–172
Equal protection:
    and affirmative action in
        admissions, 32
    definition, 573
Error of prediction, 573
Essay item discrimination level,
    233, 573
Essay items, 208, 573
Essay, grading:
    assembly-line grading of, 214
    computer grading of,
        214–215

grading of, 211–215
mini essays and short
    answer 205–207
SAT and, 215–216
score gap and, 31
testing formats and,
    207–215
Ethics:
    Case in Point, 506
    merit pay and, 507–509
    private school transfers
        and, 502–503
    rewards, 506
    school strategies and,
        505–506
    testing and, 34–35
    West Virginia Code of
        Ethics, 503–504
Ethnicity:
    and affirmative action in
        admissions, 31–32
    class size and, 523–524
    first IQ tests and, 54–55
    minority teachers and,
        484–485
    NCLB Act and, 8
    NCLB and, 39n11
    score gap and, 27–29
Ethnographic research,
    535, 574
Eugenics movement/
    organizations, 44–45,
    62, 574
Eugenics organizations,
    44–45
Evaluation. *See also*
    Systematic program
    evaluation
    commercially published
        tests and, 5
    definition, 38n2, 574
    naturalistic methodology 583
    overview, 533–537
    standards, 535, 574
    value-added, 551–560
Evaluation standards, 574
Evaluative portfolio, 260–261
Executive function, 574
Exit exams, percentages of
    students passing, 24–25

Factor analysis, 51, 574
Fair test, 333, 574

Fairness of tests:
    and accommodations for
        children with
        disabilities, 415–418,
        420n2
    definition, 574
    description, 143
    performance assessment
        and, 250
    validity and, 158–160
Family Educational Rights and
    Privacy Act, 20, 317.
    (*See also* Buckley
    Amendment)
Family factors in test scores:
    Case in Point, 474–475
    home environment, 473–474
    home-school
        communication,
        474–475
    issues/themes of, 465–466
    learning objectives, 467
    mobility, 475–476
    parental education, 472–473
    parenting, 476, 478
Ferguson, Plessy v., 39n7
Fidelity of tests, 142, 150–153, 574
First and Second International
    Math Study (FIMS &
    SIMS), 20
First International Math Study
    (FIMS), 20, 427–428, 574
First International Science
    Study (FISS), 428, 574
Fixed intelligence (g factor)
    model, 50–53, 574
Fluid intelligence, 64, 349, 574
Flynn trend, 62, 575
Formative evaluations. *See also*
    Systematic program
    evaluation
    Case in Point, 172
    definition, 575
    and planning of tests,
        167–172
    school strategies and, 10
Freedle, Roy O., 159
Free/reduced-cost lunch,
    130, 413, 575
Funding:
    for achievement tests, 325
    application under "Striving
        Readers Program," 538

cost of educating/child,
    514–515
NCLB and, 460
school districts and teacher
    pay, 529n6
Funding for Goals 2000, 73–74

Galton, Francis, 43–44, 133
Gantt chart, 542, 575
Gardner, Howard,
    66, 68–69, 437
Gaussian normal distribution.
    See also Bell curve
    definition, 575
    elaborated, 93
    ogives and, 241n5
    test scores and, 81
Gender:
    and motivation of
        students, 195n1
    score gap and, 27–29
General factor, 44, 51, 575
Gesell, Arnold L., 46–48
Gifted students:
    aptitude testing and,
        363–364
    definition, 575
    grading and, 287–290
    school strategies and, 11
Goddard, Henry, 54–55, 62
Grade equivalent score, 106, 575
Grade inflation, 296–300, 575
Grade point average (GPA), 575
Grade point average/class rank,
    292–293
Grade point, prediction of,
    114–115, 575
Grade retention, 13–14, 576
Grades:
    definition, 576
    published tests and, 15
    school strategies and, 10
Grading by local norms,
    278, 575
Grading/progress
    reports/report cards:
    best application of, 282
    Case in Point, 294, 304–305
    for the gifted, 287–289
    grade inflation and,
        296–300
    grade point average/class
        rank and, 292–293

historical aspects of, 273–276
Internet comments regarding, 286–288
issues/themes of, 271–272
learning objectives, 272
local norms and, 280
magic pencil/histogram and, 281–282
modified standards-based approach to, 278–279
online report cards, 286–287
point system and, 279–280
problems and, 280–281
promotion/graduation and, 301–306
purposes of, 276–278
for special needs students, 290, 310n7, 310n9
standardized scores and, 282–283
standards-based grades and, 283–285
teacher-parent conference and, 295–296
transfer students and, 292
weighted combinations and, 279
Graduate Admissions Testing, 105
Graduate Management Admissions Test (GMAT), 214
Graduate Record Examination (GRE), 105
Gratz et al. v. Bollinger et al., 32–33, 576
Great Britain and testing (historical), 38n1
Great Society, 438, 576
Grey Oral Reading Test, 4th ed. (GORT-4), 406
Grigham, Carl, 215
Group testing, 354–360
Grutter v. Bollinger et al., 33–34, 39–40n13, 576
Guessing correction, 30
Guessing level, 132, 144n6, 226, 576
Guilford, J. P., 64, 66–67, 103, 368

Hall, G. Stanley, 46, 73
Halo effect, 213, 576

Handbook of Research on Teaching (Campbell and Stanley), 543, 563n4
Harcourt Assessment, 13
Harvard scholarships, 373, 576
Head Start programs, 6, 451, 576
Henderson mixed-model equation (HMME), 555, 576
Hereditarian, 43, 49, 576
Hereditary Genius: An Inquiry Into Its Laws and Consequences (Galton), 43
Heteroscedastic, 366–367, 577
High consensus, 151, 577
High Objective Uniform State Standard of Evaluation (HOUSSE), 487
High-consensus, 577
Higher education, measurement practices in schools and, 26
Highly Objective Uniform State Standard of Evaluation (HOUSSE), 466, 577
Highly qualified, 447, 466, 481, 577
High-stakes assessment, 4
High-stakes test:
   definition, 577
   fidelity and, 151
   and learning problems identified, 382
   measurement practices in schools and, 23–25
   NCLB achievement test problems, 334, 336–340
   NCLB and, 451, 455
   portfolio evaluation and, 261–262
   private school transfers and, 502–503
   as published achievement test, 13
Histogram, 281–282, 577
History, 546, 577
History of testing:
   Burt, Cyril on single-factor model, 51, 53
   Case in Point, 43–44, 62

Cattell, Raymond B. on multiple-factor models, 64
child study movement and, 46–47
contemporary public schools and, 70
and empirical foundation of measurement science, 313–314
European connection, 42–44
first IQ tests, 52–55
Funding for Goals 2000 and, 73–74
Gardner, Howard on multiple-factor models, 66, 68–69
grade 8 graduation test (1895), 444
grading and, 273–276
Great Britain and, 38n1
Guilford, J. P. on multiple-factor models, 64, 66–67
issues/themes of, 41–42
learning objectives, 42
mental ability and, 48–49
meritocracy in America and, 49–50
Nation's Report Card and, 71
NCLB and, 74–77
readiness and, 47–48
score gap and, 72
Spearman, Charles on single-factor model, 50–52
Sternberg, Robert on multiple-factor models, 69–70
and study of gifted, 49
Thorndike, E. L. on multiple-factor models, 63–64
Thurstone, L. L. on multiple-factor models, 63
between WWI and WWII, 55–62
Holistic approach to admissions, 33, 577
Holistic approach to scoring, 252–254, 261
Holistic assessment, 577
Holistic rubric, 218, 577
Holistic scoring, 19–20, 577

Homework:
  completion/short answer
    questions and, 202–205
  grading of, 199–200
  historical aspects of, 198–199
  impact of, 201–202
  importance of, 217
  parents and, 200–201
  and size of assignments, 201
  as student factor in test
    scores, 470–471
Honor roll, 294, 577
Honor society, 273, 577
Honors track, 289, 578
*Hopwood et al. v. The State of
  Texas*, 32–33, 578
Human cognitive ability model
  of Cattell-Horn-Carroll, 65

Illinois State Board of
  Education, v.
  Brookhart, 23
Immigration:
  European schools
    and, 462n5
  first IQ tests and, 54–55
  impact on Europe (1924), 61
Improving America's Schools
  Act of 1994, 21,
  76–77, 578
Individual Educational Plan
  Format, 415–416
Individual Educational Program
  (IEP) committee, 388–393
Individual Family Service Plans
  (IFSP), 124, 578
Individualized Educational Plan
  (IEP), 382, 411–415, 578
  Individual Educational Plan
    Format, 415–416
  Individual Educational
    Program Committee,
    388–393
Individuals With Disabilities
  Educational Improvement
  Act (IDEIA), 384, 400, 578
Informal screening,
  384–385, 578
Institute of Education Sciences
  (IES), 520
Instructional Support Team
  (IST), 382, 386–388, 578
Instrumentation, 547, 578

Intelligence test,
  48, 346–354, 578
Internal consistency, 578
Internal consistency, reliability
  (as measure of test
  quality) and, 81, 122,
  126–129, 578
Internal validity, 546–548,
  563n4, 578
International Adult Literacy
  Survey (IALS),
  432–433, 579
International Baccalaureate
  Diploma, 310n5
International testing programs.
  See Testing programs,
  international/national/
  statewide
Interpersonal validity threat,
  547–548, 579
Interpersonal Communication
  Skill (BICS), 458
Interpretation of tests,
  educational ethics and, 35
Inter-rater reliability,
  140, 257, 579
Interval data, 86, 579
Interval scales, 86
Iowa Every-Pupil Testing
  Program, 329
Iowa Test of Educational
  Development (ITED), 330
Iowa Tests of Basic Skills
  (ITBS), 329–330, 376
IQ scores, 579
IQ tests:
  and group-administered
    aptitude tests, 356–360
  historical aspects of, 52–55
  hypotheses for improvement
    in, 62
  scores, 346–347, 579
  Wechsler Intelligence Scale
    for Children (WISC)
    and, 103
Item analysis, 223, 230–231, 579
Item characteristic curves
  (ICCs), 137–138, 222,
  236–238, 579
Item difficulty index, 221,
  225–229, 579
Item discrimination,
  230–234, 579

Item response theory, 579
Item Response Theory (IRT),
  136, 221, 235–239, 579
Item selection/analysis:
  Case in Point, 229
  classroom testing and,
    222–223
  computer adaptive testing
    and, 234–235
  with constructed/supply-type
    items, 230
  discrimination and,
    230–234
  distracter analysis and,
    229–230
  issues/themes of,
    221–222
  item difficulty index and,
    225–229
  item response theory (IRT)
    and, 235–239
  learning objectives, 222
  priori qualitative assessment
    and, 224–225
Item stem, 185–186, 191

Johnson, Reynold, 374
Juku, 505, 528n1

Kaufman tests, 353
Keillor, Garrison, 71
Kelly, Truman, 231
Kennedy, Robert F., 26
Keppel, Frederick R., 438
Key Math-Revised, 409–410
Keyed response of item in
  questions, 185, 187, 579
Kuder-Richardson approach to
  reliability, 128–129, 579
Kuhlmann-Anderson Tests
  (KA), 355

Lake Woebegon effect,
  71, 580
Language/speech problems
  identified, 406–408
Larry P. v. Riles, 23
Latent component, 51, 580
Latent semantic analysis, 216
Latent semantic analysis
  (LSA), 580
Law School Admission Test
  (LSAT), 105–106

Leadership, school
administration:
data management and,
510–511
description, 526–527
scheduling and, 512
time on task and, 512–515
Learning problems
identification:
and accommodations for
children with
disabilities,
415–418, 420n2
and assessment of
language/speech
problems, 406–408
and assessment of
mathematical learning
problems, 408–410
assessment process, 393–394
and assessments of reading
problems, 400–401
and early reading
tests, 402–406
formal assessments of
attention/focus,
394–396
incidence and, 384
Individualized Educational
Plan (IEP) and, 410
informal screening and,
384–385
instructional support team
and, 386–388
issues/themes of, 381
referral/assessment/IEP
committee and, 388–393
Legal/ethical testing
requirements, 502
Level of precision,
85, 88–89, 580
Level of proficiency, 8, 136, 580
Likert scales, 580
Likert type of scale, 234,
240n2, 580
Limited English Proficient
(LEP):
definition, 580
NAEP and, 462–463n7
NCLB, 458
Lindquist, E. F., 329, 376
Linear responsibility chart,
543–545, 580

Linguistic aspects of tests and
score gap, 30
Local norms and grading, 280
Longitudinal chart/data:
definition, 580
evaluation, 554
NAEP, 440,
Lunch, free or reduced-
cost, 130

Magic pencil/histogram and
grading,
281–282, 580
Magnet schools, 459, 580
Magnetic resonance imagery
(MRI), AD/HD
and, 394–395
Mandated assessments,
5, 7–8, 580
Mann, Horace, 5, 463n8
Mantel-Haenszel Test of
Differential Item
Functioning, 326
Matching questions,
183–185, 581
Mathematics:
problems identified, 408–410
and schools' test
preparation, 519–522
Matrix sampling, 429, 581
Maturation, 546, 581
Mean, 90, 133, 581
Mean as variable in research, 90
Measurement, 6, 581
Measurement practices in
schools. See also Variables
in school-based
educational research.
and administration of
published tests, 15
advanced program
admission and, 25–26
affirmative action and, 31–32
and assumptions made by
test developers, 16–17
Case in Point, 8–11, 18, 22
computerized grading, 19
court challenges and, 32–34
definition, 38n2
and early case law on
admissions, 26–27
and early use of computers
in testing, 17–18

educational ethics and,
34–35
higher education and, 26
high-stakes tests and, 23–25
issues/themes of, 3–4
learning objectives, 3–6
legislation and, 20–21
and new technology, 18
online report cards, 18–19
parental factors and, 29–31
qualitative assessments,
19–20
reasons for testing, 6–12
school strategies and, 9–12
score gap and, 27–29
scoring criteria, 14–15
special education and, 22–23
Texas and, 21–22
types/varieties of tests,
12–16
web-based student
study site, 38
Media and test preparation,
23, 500
Median as variable in
research, 90–91
Mental age, 48, 581
Merit pay, 8, 507–509,
529n5, 581
Merit scholars, 365–366, 581
Meritocracy, 49–54, 581
Metropolitan Achievement
Tests, 323, 326–328
Military:
Air Force Officer Qualifying
Test (AFOQT), 66
Armed Services Vocational
Aptitude Battery
(ASVAB), 360–362
Army Alpha/Beta tests and,
53–60
Army–Navy Qualifying
Test, 374
first IQ tests and, 53–55
WWI testing, 1, 45, 84
Millennial generation,
475–476, 581
Minimum competency tests,
72–73, 581
Miracle of Texas, 21, 581–582
Mobility, 466, 475, 582
Mode as variable in research,
91, 582

Modified standards-based approach to grading, 278–279, 582

Mohonasen Central School District (New York), 174–175

Moment in time, and assumptions made by test developers, 16

Mortality, 546, 582

Motivation of students, 195n1, 273, 469

Multiple choice questions: definition, 582

as dominant state-mandated test method, 5

formula for correction for guessing on, 30

and planning of tests, 185–193

Multiple correlation/regression, 84, 115, 119n9, 582

Multiple intelligences (Gardner), 68, 582

Multiple-factor models, 63–70, 582

Multiple-intelligences model (MI), 582

Musical Aptitude Profile, 359

Nation at Risk, A: The Imperative for Educational Reform, 20, 72, 443, 488

Nation Prepared, A: Teachers for the 21st Century, 488

National Assessment of Educational Progress (NAEP)

accountability and, 425–427

and criterion-referenced tests, 140

definition, 438, 582

description, 6

ESEA and, 438–442

homework and, 470–471

National Association for the Education of Young Children:

definition, 582

position, 451

readiness testing and, 80n6

National Association of School Psychologists (NASP), 34

National Association of Test Directors (NATD), 34

National Board for Professional Teaching Standards, 466

National Center for Learning Disabilities, 389

National certification, 488–489. *See also* Teacher factors in test scores

National Collegiate Athletic Association (NCAA), grade inflation and, 299

National Commission on Excellence in Education, 72, 462n1

National Counsel on Measurement in Education (NCME), 34

National Merit Scholarship Program, 365–366

National Reading Panel, 76

National Reading Panel (NRP), 76, 516

National Science Foundation (NSF), 363

Nation's Report Card, 71, 438, 582

Naturalistic methodology, 583

No Child Left Behind Act (NCLB):

and accommodations for children with disabilities, 416–417, 420n2

and achievement test positive outcomes, 336–340

and achievement test problems, 334, 336

achievement tests and, 325–326

annual yearly progress (AYP) and, 130

and assistance for children, 447–449

beginning in third grade, 13

Case in Point, 446–448, 451, 459

concerns/problems of, 451, 455

definition, 583

and Education for All Handicapped Children Act of 1975, 382

emergence of, 6–7, 445–446

and Individual Educational Plan Format, 415–416

interim outcome and, 449–451

justification for, 423–424

legislation of, 74–77

measurement dimensions of, 552–553

parents of gifted, 12, 102

percentiles and, 102

performance assessment and, 244–245

promotion/graduation and, 301–304

public reaction to, 455–456

reading and, 516–517

requirements/sanctions of, 446–447

score gap and, 159

special education conflict and, 411–415

state concerns of, 456–460

and state-mandated assessments, 333–340

statewide portfolio assessment programs and, 266–267

test examples and, 452–454

testing children with disabilities, 102

Texas Educational Assessment of Minimal Skills (TEAMS) and, 21

Nominal data, 583

Nominal scales, 88

Non-content factor, 277, 583

Norm referenced, 14, 583

Normal curve equivalent (NCE), 319, 583

Normative group, 583

Norm-based scoring system, 280, 583

Norm-referenced tests, 14, 583

Norms, 583

Novelty, 548, 583

Obey-Porter Act, 77

Objective tests, 5–6, 583

Ogive, 236–237, 241n5, 583

Ogives, 241n5
One-room schools, 274, 529n11
Online report cards, 287–288
On-line report cards, 287–288, 584
Oral and Written Language Scales tests (OWLS), 407–408
Ordinal scales, 86–88
Ordinary least squares regression (OLS), 115, 119n9
Origin of the Species by Means of Natural Selection (Darwin), 43
Otis-Lennon test, 355–356
Out of level testing, 584
Out-of-level testing, 227–229, 236

Parameters of scores, 131, 584
Parametric vs. nonparametric, variables in school-based educational research, 88–89
Parent strategies, 502–503
Parental factors, measurement practices in schools and, 29–31
Parental Involvement Report Card, 477
Parental reports:
  explaining test scores to, 316–318
  and planning for conferences, 172
Parents in Action on Special Education (PASE), 23
Pearson Assessments, 13
Pearson, Carl, 44
Pearson Correlation Coefficient, 108–110, 584
Pearson, Karl, 44, 79n2
Percentile, 584
Percentiles, variance and, 99–102, 584
Performance assessments:
  authentic-type, 258–259
  Case in Point, 245–246, 259
  description, 246–251
  instruction and, 245–246

issues/themes of, 243–244
learning objectives, 244
portfolios and, 259–267
reliability and, 257
scoring and, 252–259
validity and, 257–258
Performance level, 283–284, 584
Performance test items, 139–140, 584
Performance-based assessments, 163–164, 246–247, 584
Personological factors and measurement error, 131, 584
Pervasive developmental disabilities, 417, 584
Phenomenological strategies, 534, 584
Phonemic awareness, 401, 584
Phonics, 516, 584
Physical disability, 381, 584
Placement decision, 23, 585
Planning/construction of tests:
  Case in Point, 169, 171, 173–174, 190
  formative tests, 167–172
  issues/themes of, 165–166
  learning objectives, 166
  matching questions, 183–185
  multiple choice questions, 185–193
  selected/constructed response formats and, 180–181
  summative evaluations, 173–179
  teaching and, 166–167
  true-false questions, 181–183
PLATO (Programmed Logic for Automatic Teaching Operations), as early learning system, 17
Plessy v. Ferguson, 39n7
Point system and grading, 279–280, 585
Point-biserial correlation, 230–234, 585
Polytomous items, 234, 585
Popham, James, 493n5, 501
Popular culture and test preparation, 499–500

Portfolios:
  advantages/disadvantages of, 264–265
  conferences, 263–264
  contents of, 265–266
  definition, 585
  evaluative, 260–261
  high-stakes evaluation, 261–262
  initiation of, 262–263
  statewide assessment programs and, 266–267
Positivistic paradigm, 534, 585
Practical intelligence, 69, 585
Prediction equation, 113–114, 585
Prediction of grade point, 112, 114–115
Predictive functions, validity and, 154–155
Predictive validity, 148–149, 162n1, 585
Preliminary Scholastic Aptitude Test (PSAT), 366–367
Prereading strategies, 517, 585
Primary Mental Abilities (PMA), 63, 585
Principal component, 51, 585–586
Priori qualitative assessment, 224–225, 565
Process portfolio, 262–263, 586
Pro-Ed AD/HD identifier, 399–400
Professional schools admission testing, 105–106
Programme for International Student Assessment (PISA), 429, 432, 586
Progress in International Reading Literacy Study (PIRLS), 433–435
Progress reports, 274, 586. See also Grading/progress reports/report cards
Prompt of essay, 215, 586
Psycho-educational assessment, 393, 586
Psycho-educational diagnostic assessments, 142
Public schools, standardized tests and
Published achievement tests, 12–16, 322–332
Pull-out program, 288, 586

Qualitative assessments, 19–20
Qualitative research, 527–528, 586
Quantitative research paradigm, 531, 534, 586

Randomly selected, 439, 586
Range, 98, 586
Rasch model, 137, 236, 586
Rater drift, 586
Ratio data, 587
Ratio scales, variables in school-based educational research and data, 85, 91, 587
Raw scores, 14–15, 587
Readiness:
    definition, 587
    and Gesell School Readiness Test, 47–48
    school strategies and, 10
Reading:
    assessment of problems, 400–401
    early tests of, 402–406
    extra time to complete tests in, 417–418
    and schools' test preparation, 516–518
    "Striving Readers Program," 538
Recentered, 587
Recentering (SAT), 374, 587
Receptive language, 406, 587
Referral, 382, 587
Regression toward the mean, 133, 547, 587
Rehabilitation Act of 1973, 381
Reliability:
    performance assessments and, 257
    retesting and, 81
Reliability (as measure of test quality):
    alternate form, 124–125
    and alternate forms over time, 125
    Case in Point, 124–126, 131, 135, 142
    coefficient Kappa (κ), 141–142

of cut scores, 135–139
    definition, 587
    gains/losses and, 129–130
    impacting factors of, 132–135
    internal consistency and, 126–129
    Iowa Tests of Basic Skills (ITBS) and, 330
    issues/themes of, 121–122
    learning objectives, 122
    of performance tasks/ criterion tasks, 139–142
    and standard error of measurement, 130–131
    test-retest reliability, 124
    validity and, 160
Report cards, 18–19, 287–288. *See also* Grading/progress reports/report cards
Residual scores, 133–135, 587
Resources:
    companion web site, xxix
    instructor's CD, 79
Responses in essay tests, 207, 587
Restructuring, 334, 587
Reverse shed patterns and value-added assessments, 557
Revised PSB Health Occupations Aptitude Examination, 358–359
Riles, Larry P. v., 23
Riverside Publishing, 13
Rubrics, 253–256, 587

Sample of convenience, 547, 587
Sampling inadequacy, 427–428, 587–588
Sanders, William, 554, 559
Scatterplots, 112–113, 367, 588
Scholastic aptitude, 588
Scholastic Aptitude Test (SAT):
    definition, 380, 588
    description, 104
    essay tests and, 215–216
    by family income, 29–31
    II, 375–376
    precursor of, 374
    recentering, 374
    Stanley, Julian and, 365

School assessments, 442–445
School psychologists, 13, 588
School report card, 15, 588. *See also* Grading/progress reports/report cards
School size, 524–525
School-based, Teacher-led Assessment and Reporting System (STARS), 19
Score gap:
    definition, 30, 588
    historical aspects of, 72
    validity and, 159
Score gap of ACT, 27–29
Scoring guide, 212, 252–259, 588
Scoring rubric, 139–140, 253, 588
Second International Math Study (SIMS), 20, 428
Section 504 of Rehabilitation Act of 1973, 420n2, 588
Security and confidentiality of test, 35
Selected response format:
    definition, 588
    description, 180–181
    matching questions, 183–185
    multiple choice questions, 185–193
    true-false questions, 181–183
Selection, 547, 588
Selection ratio, 229, 588
Select-type questions, 194, 588
Sensitivity review of major tests, 143, 160, 589
Shed patterns and value-added assessments, 560
Showcase portfolio, 263, 589
Signing bonus, 507–508
Single-factor models, 50–62, 588
Skew as variable in research, 92–95, 589
Slosson Full-Range Intelligence Test (S-FRIT), 155, 354
Spearman, Charles, 44, 50–52
Spearman Correlation Coefficient, 110–112, 589
Spearman-Brown approach to reliability, 127–128

Special education. *See also*
   Learning problems
   identified
   cut scores and, 135
   definition, 384, 589
   designated talented/gifted
      schools, 39n9
   formative evaluation and,
      170–171
   grading and, 290–292
   and history of the study of
      gifted, 49
   measurement practices in
      schools and, 22–23
   NAEP and, 462–463n7
   NCLB Act and, 8
   school strategies and,
      11–12
Special-needs education, 589
Split-half reliability, internal
   consistency and, 126–127
Stability, 121, 589
Stakeholders, 539, 589
Standard deviation, 97–99, 589
Standard error of
   measurement,
   130–131, 589
Standard scores, 103–106, 589
Standardized scores, 282–283
Standardized scoring, 589–590
Standardized tests:
   accomplishment ratio and,
      320–321
   Case in Point, 323–324
   Comprehensive Testing
      Program (CTP),
      330–333
   definition, 590
   and explaining test scores to
      parents, 316–318
   historical aspects of, 70
   historical aspects of
      achievement batteries,
      322–324
   Iowa Tests of Basic Skills
      (ITBS), 329–330
   Metropolitan Achievement
      Tests, 326–328
   Stanford Achievement
      Tests, 327
   Terra Nova test, 327
   test publishers and, 321–322
Standards gap, 455, 590

Standards-based assessments:
   definition, 590
   description, 158
   evaluations and, 535
   and planning of tests, 171
Standards-based grades,
   283–285, 590
Stanford Achievement Tests,
   323, 327
Stanford Diagnostic
   Mathematics Test, 4th ed.
   (SDMT-4), 410
Stanford Diagnostic Reading
   Test, 4th ed. (SCRT-4), 406
Stanford-Binet Scales, 155, 346,
   348–349, 590
Stanine, 103, 590
Stanley, Julian, 364–365, 563n4
Stanley, Julian C., 543
STAR Early Literacy test, 405, 590
The State of Texas, Hopwood
   et al. v., 32–33
State rights, NCLB and, 460
State-mandated assessments
   and achievement tests,
   333–340
Statistical bias, 159, 590
Statistical Package for the Social
   Sciences (SPSS), 234
Status of American
   Education, 433
Steele, Claude, 30
Stem of item in question, 590
Stem of item in questions, 185
Stereotype threat, 30, 590
Sternberg, Robert, 69–70
Structure of the Intellect model
   (Guilford), 67, 590
Student factors in test scores:
   ability, 468
   attendance, 472
   English-language learners,
      468–469
   homework, 470–471
   motivation, 469
   peers, 471–472
   work habits, 469–470
Student response pads,
   169–170, 590
Summative assessments,
   165, 591. *See also*
   Systematic program
   evaluation

Summative data analysis,
   549, 591
Summative evaluations, 173
Supply-type questions, 591
Systematic assessment,
   442, 535
Systematic program evaluation:
   audience for, 541
   data analysis and,
      540, 549–550
   data collection/validity and,
      540, 546–549
   definition, 543
   dissemination and,
      540, 543, 550–551
   linear responsibility chart
      and, 543–545
   management plan and,
      540, 542–545
   objectives of, 540–542
   record keeping and, 548
   stakeholder
      identification/goal
      setting for, 539–541

Table of specifications,
   174–177, 591
Tacit knowledge, 591
Take-home tests, 195n3, 198
Taxonomies, comparison of
   Bloom/Anderson, 178–179
Teach for America program,
   466, 487–488,
   493n7, 591
Teacher factors in test scores:
   alternative tracks, 485–488
   Case in Point, 482,
      484–485, 490
   empowerment, 489–490
   experienced teachers,
      482–483
   hiring of effective teachers,
      480–481
   hiring of qualified teachers,
      481–482
   impact of teacher, 479–480
   minority teachers, 484–485
   national certification,
      488–489
   teacher examinations,
      483–484
Teacher-parent conference,
   172, 295–296

Teaching "for the test,"
515–516, 591
Teaching "to the test," 437, 591
Terman, Lewis M., 48–49,
363–364
Terman's Stanford Revision of
the Binet Scale, 346
Terra Nova test, 327, 355
Test batteries, 6, 15, 325, 591
Test bias, 158–160, 591
Test length, 132–133
Test of Being Artistic
(TOBA), 153
Test of Cognitive Skills, 356
Test of Early Language
Development
(TELD-3), 408
Test of Early Reading Ability,
3rd Edition (TERA-3),
404–405
Test patterns and value-added
assessments, 557
Test preparation for successful
schools:
administration and, 525–527
architecture/school design
and, 522–525
classroom instruction and,
515–522
data management and, 558
legal/ethical requirements
and, 502
merit pay and, 507–509
private school transfers and,
502–503
Test retest reliability, 591
Testing programs,
international/national/
statewide:
Case in Point, 437, 443
international comparisons,
427–433
national comparisons,
437–445
NCLB and, 445–460
and status of American
education, 433–437
Texas Assessment of
Knowledge and Skills
(TAKS), 21
Texas Educational Assessment
of Minimal Skills
(TEAMS), 21

Third International Math and
Science Study (TIMSS),
429–432, 591
Third International Math Study
(TIMSS), 20
Thorndike, E. L., 63–64, 568
Three-factor model of
intelligence, 69, 592
Thurstone, L. L., 63
TICCIT (Time-Shared
Interactive Computer
Controlled Information
Television), 17
Torrance tests, 369–372
Transfer students and
grading, 292
Trends in International
Mathematics and
Science, 429
Triarchic model of intelligence,
69, 592
Troops to Teacher program
(TTT), 466, 487, 592
True score, 122, 131, 592
True-false questions,
181–183, 592
True-false questions, and
planning of tests, 181–183
Turlington, Debra P., 23
Turlington, Debra P. v., 23, 463n11
Tutoring and NCLB, 447–449

Unit cost, 562n1
*University of California
Regents v. Bakke*, 32, 592
Upward drift, 137, 139, 592
U.S. House Oversight
Committee on Testing
Assessment and
Evaluation, 71–72

Validity:
case in Point and, 147
data collection and, 546–549
internal, 563n4
performance assessments
and, 257–258
Validity of test (as measure of
quality), 22, 592
approaches to, 82
Case in Point, 156
classroom measurements
and, 174–175

comparison groups and,
157–158
in contemporary context,
150–156
fidelity and, 150–151
problems and, 157
test bias/fairness and,
158–160
and threat of testing, 592
in traditional context,
146–150
Value added, 592
Value-added evaluation:
assessments, 554, 558–559
limitations of, 558
local applications of, 569
national certification
and, 489
staff development and, 560
statewide application
of, 559
statistical solutions and,
554–562
and teacher outcome,
555–556
Variables in school-based
educational research:
Case in Point, 89, 95–96,
98–99, 102
correlation and, 108–116
interval scales, 86
mean/median/mode
and, 90–91
multiple correlation
and, 115–116
nominal scales and, 88
normal distribution (Bell
curve), 91–92, 95
ordinal scales, 86–88
parametric vs.
nonparametric, 88–89
percentiles, 99–102
precision and, 89
ratio scales and, 85
skew and, 92–95
standard deviation, 97–99
standard scores and,
103–106
validity and, 155
variation and, 107–108
Variables of score gaps, 30
Variance, 84, 96–98, 592
Variation in scores, 107–108

War on Poverty, 438, 593
Wechsler Individual
    Achievement Test
    (WIAT-II), 403
Wechsler Intelligence Scale for
    Children (WISC),
    103–104, 155,
    349–352, 593
Wechsler Preschool and
    Primary Scales of
    Intelligence, 351–352, 593

Weighted combination and
    admission, 33, 593
Weighted combinations and
    grading, 280
Weighted grades, 290, 593
What Works Clearinghouse
    of U.S. Department of
    Education, 520
Woodcock-Johnson
    tests, 353, 402–403,
    421n8

Word utilization patterns and
    score gap, 30
World Book Company,
    322–323
Wrap-around assessments,
    267, 593
Writing, and schools' test
    preparation, 518–519
Wundt, Wilhelm, 43

Yerkes, Robert M., 62

ABOUT THE AUTHOR

Robert J. Wright. After five years in public education, first as a science teacher (chemistry certification), then as a secondary school guidance counselor, I returned to graduate school (Temple University) and completed my Ph.D. in educational psychology. Later, I completed postdoctoral work in clinical assessment and school psychology at Lehigh University. Through these studies and practice, I have achieved state certification as a teacher of general science and chemistry. I am also a licensed guidance counselor and a licensed psychologist in Pennsylvania.

During my 34 years in higher education I have taught educational measurement, statistics and research, counselor education, and educational psychology. I spent 14 years serving as associate dean and director of teacher education within Widener University's School of Human Service Professions. I have also been a consultant for the Pennsylvania Department of Education in the development of a teacher certification examination and a reader for the SAT II writing test.

As a faculty member I have chaired 112 doctoral dissertations in education, presented scores of research-oriented papers at national meetings, and published numerous articles and several monographs. I have also consulted with several learned and professional societies in medicine as a psychometric specialist with their resident-in-training examination programs.

eduplace.com